POLITICS AND THE ORDER OF LOVE

Politics and the Order of Love

AN AUGUSTINIAN ETHIC
OF DEMOCRATIC CITIZENSHIP

⧾

Eric Gregory

THE UNIVERSITY OF CHICAGO PRESS ‡ CHICAGO AND LONDON

The University of Chicago Press, Chicago 60637
The University of Chicago Press, Ltd., London
© 2008 by The University of Chicago
All rights reserved. Published 2008
Paperback edition 2010

Printed in the United States of America

19 18 17 16 15 14 13 12 11 10   2 3 4 5 6

ISBN-13: 978-0-226-30751-0 (cloth)
ISBN-13: 978-0-226-30752-7 (paper)
ISBN-10: 0-226-30751-4 (cloth)
ISBN-10: 0-226-30752-2 (paper)

The University of Chicago Press gratefully acknowledges the generous support of Princeton University toward the publication of this book.

Grateful acknowledgment is given for permission to use materials from the following essays: "Augustine and Arendt on Love: New Dimensions in the Religion and Liberalism Debates," *Annual of the Society of Christian Ethics* 21 (2001): 155–72. "Before the Original Position: The Neo-Orthodox Theology of the Young John Rawls," *Journal of Religious Ethics* 35, no. 2 (June 2007): 179–206. "Love and Citizenship after Augustine," *Polygraph: An International Journal of Politics & Culture* 19/20 (2008).

Library of Congress Cataloging-in-Publication Data

Gregory, Eric.
  Politics and the order of love : an Augustinian ethic of democratic citizenship / Eric Gregory.
    p. cm.
  Includes biographical references (p.) and index.
  ISBN-13: 978-0-226-30751-0 (cloth : alk. paper)
  ISBN-10: 0-226-30751-4 (cloth : alk. paper)   1. Augustine, Saint, Bishop of Hippo. 2. Love—Religious aspects—Christianity. 3. Political science—Philosophy. 4. Liberalism.   I. Title.
  BR65.A9G76 2008
  241'.62092—dc22

2008006951

In Memory of

Carlton Herbert Gregory
(1918–1985)

*And when they find inwardly
that what they have been told is true,
they praise their teachers.*

AUGUSTINE, *The Teacher* 14.45

*But when a man has grown older, then his life usually remains
what it already has become, a dull repetition and re-writing of the
same; no possibility rouses one to wakefulness and no possibility
exhilarates the renewal of youth. Hope becomes something which
nowhere has a home, and possibility a rarity like greenness in winter.
Without the eternal one lives by the help of habit, prudence, conformity, experience, custom, and usage. In fact, take them all, put them
all together, prepare the mixture over the smouldering or merely
earthly ignited fire of passions, and you will discover that you can
get all kinds of things out of it: variously concocted tough slime which
men call a realistic view of life—but one never gets possibility out
of this, possibility, the miracle which is so infinitely fragile (the most
tender shoot in springtime is not so fragile), so infinitely delicate (the
finest woven linen is not so delicate), and yet, brought into being,
shaped, by the very help of the eternal, it is nevertheless stronger than
anything else, if it is the possibility of the good!*

SØREN KIERKEGAARD, *Works of Love*

╫

*But there remains also the truth that every end in history
necessarily contains a new beginning; this beginning is the promise,
the only 'message' which the end can ever produce. Beginning,
before it becomes a historical event, is the supreme capacity of man;
politically it is identical with man's freedom. Initium ut esset
homo creatus est—'that a beginning be made, man was created,'
said Augustine. This beginning is guaranteed by each
new birth; it is indeed every man.*

HANNAH ARENDT, *Origins of Totalitarianism*

╫

It is winter, but within there is freshness and vigor at the root.

AUGUSTINE, *Tractatus in epistolam Iohannis*

CONTENTS

᛭

ACKNOWLEDGMENTS

✢

This manuscript benefited from the generous financial, intellectual, and moral support of many people and institutions. Its origins date back to undergraduate courses in religion and politics with Harvey Cox, William Hutchison, Harvey Mansfield, Richard Niebuhr, and Michael Sandel. Three years at Oxford University (1992–95), under the patient and wise direction of Oliver O'Donovan and Nigel Biggar, initiated me into classical and modern traditions of theological ethics. In particular, as I hope this book suggests, Oliver O'Donovan transformed my understanding of theology and political theory by allowing me to think beyond the terms set by dominant approaches. During this time, I also spent an important period in pre-democratic South Africa, working with religious communities involved in voter education while reading Charles Taylor and various liberation theologians. This experience greatly expanded my horizons for thinking about Christianity and democracy. I am grateful to Harvard College, the Rhodes Trust, and the fellows of Trinity College, Oxford, for these educational opportunities. I also thank Yale University and the Princeton University Committee on Research in the Humanities and Social Sciences for their financial support.

Parts of this project began as a dissertation in the Department of Religious Studies at Yale University, submitted in 2002. I especially would like to thank my principal advisor, Gene Outka, for his generous and careful supervision. He modeled for me the vocation of both scholar and teacher, always providing an encouraging yet critical voice which allowed me to try out my own. My effort to extend interpretations of both *agape* and Augustinianism is a tribute to his influence. Margaret Farley also demonstrated the art of charitable interpretation, notably by introducing me to discussions of feminist theory and Catholic social thought. David Kelsey and Nicholas Wolterstorff were gracious readers and conversation partners, adding their considerable theological and philosophical acumen to a dream dissertation committee. Other New Haven discussions, formal and informal, with Bruce

Ackerman, Robert Adams, Louis Dupré, Richard Fern, George Lindbeck, Thomas Ogletree, Cyril O'Regan, Harry Stout, and Miroslav Volf all influenced the arguments of this book.

Since 2001, it has been my good fortune to teach in the stimulating and congenial environment of Princeton University's Department of Religion. This book owes much to discussions with excellent students and colleagues, especially Leora Batnitzky, Eddie Glaude, Jeff Stout, and Cornel West. Most of all, I thank Jeff Stout for his close reading of previous drafts, astute observations, and for many leisurely conversations in the lounge of 1879 Hall. Beyond the Department of Religion, Peter Brown, John Cooper, Robert George, Steve Macedo, George Kateb, Paul Sigmund, and Robert Wuthnow generously exchanged ideas in ways that helped me advance my arguments. Princeton has also been home to a learned group of visiting faculty, including James Wetzel, Sarah Coakley, and Eugene Rogers. Each of them, both directly and indirectly, influenced this project.

I thank Charles Mathewes for inviting me to join his interdisciplinary manuscript workshop at the University of Virginia's Center on Religion and Democracy in the summer of 2002. Alongside Brett Wilmot, Ann Mongoven, Paul Lichterman, and Pamela Hass Cochran, he offered valuable guidance in the early transition from dissertation to book. In 2004–2005, a large part of that transition took place during a sabbatical sponsored by the Erasmus Institute of the University of Notre Dame, which is directed with care and erudition by Robert Sullivan and Dianne Phillips. I also benefited from responsive audiences at various universities and conferences, including the American Academy of Religion, the Society of Christian Ethics, the University of Chicago Divinity School, Indiana University, the University of Notre Dame, the Catholic University of America, and Columbia University. I thank Lewis Ayres, David Decosimo, William Schweiker, Aaron Stalnaker, Richard Miller, Nancy Levene, Gerald McKenny, Tobias Hoffman, Kurt Pritzl, Peter Casarella, Wayne Proudfoot, and Jonathan Kahn for profitable discussion on these occasions.

I also extend my sincere appreciation to many friends and scholars who shaped my thinking along the way, notably Alasdair MacIntyre, Jennifer Herdt, David Novak, Patrick Deneen, Jonathan Chaplin, John Finnis, Phillip Cary, Thomas Lewis, Jesse Couenhoven, Howard Rhodes, Amy Laura Hall, William Danaher, David Clough, Rufus Black, Jean Bethke Elshtain, Robin Lovin, Travis Kroeker, Gilbert Meilaender, Andrew Chignell, George Hunsinger, Scott Davis, Doug Hicks, Michael Horton, Martin Kavka, Chris Eberle, Chad Pecknold, Christopher Steck, Brian Stiltner, Todd Breyfogle, Robert Markus, Thomas Martin, John von Heyking, Jean Porter, John Carlson, Todd Cioffi, Raluca Eddon, John Bowlin, Paul Weithman, Daniel Morehead, James O'Donnell, and Thomas Breidenthal. In particular, John Cavadini and James Wetzel frequently shared their profound Augustinian wisdom and helped me clarify my thinking.

Stanley Hauerwas and Timothy Jackson served as external reviewers for the manuscript. I am very grateful for their extensive comments and suggestions. With Jeff Stout, they helped me think about the implications of this project and to say what I wanted to say with greater concision. I am indebted to Alan Thomas, my editor at the University of Chicago Press, for efficiently shepherding the manuscript through the publication process and also to the perceptive and careful copyediting skills of Richard Allen.

My family has been a source of constant support. My mother, Diane Gregory, always encouraged a balance of contemplation and action. Her love, alongside that of Donna, Scott, Jazz, and Scotty, was invaluable to completing this task. My father and stepmother, Bruce Gregory and Paula Causey, always encouraged my academic pursuits and offered discerning comments about religion and politics at the kitchen table. My father supported me, financially and intellectually, through a longer period of education than either a father or son should expect.

Finally, this book is dedicated to my grandfather, the late Rev. Dr. Carlton Gregory. He was not only a good philosopher but a great Scrabble player. I have imagined him as reader and critic, inspired by his devotion to Christian traditions of learning and social justice. I wish he were here to argue with me about the loves we share in common.

ABBREVIATIONS

⧾

The following abbreviations are used for frequently cited works in the text. In cases of multiple English translations, references to Augustine's works also note the translation used. However, unless otherwise noted, references indicate *City of God,* R. W. Dyson (1998); *Confessions,* M. Boulding (1998), *Eighty-Three Different Questions,* D. Mosher (1982), *On Christian Teaching,* R. P. H. Green (1997), *Homilies on 1 John,* J. Burnaby (1980), and *The Trinity,* E. Hill (1991). References to Augustine's sermons and letters include pagination from E. M. Atkins and R. J. Dodaro, eds., *Augustine: Political Writings* (Cambridge: Cambridge University Press, 2001). For example, *Ep.* 91, 5 refers to Letter 91, page 5. For modern authors, citations refer to page numbers in the cited text. Full bibliographical information for all references is given in the bibliography.

AUGUSTINE

Conf	*Confessiones*
	Confessions
CA	*Contra academicos*
	Against the Skeptics
CFaust	*Contra Faustum Manichaeum*
	Against Faustus the Manichee
CD	*De civitate Dei*
	City of God
DDC	*De doctrina Christiana*
	On Christian Teaching
DT	*De Trinitate*
	On the Trinity
DVR	*De vera religione*
	Of True Religion

DBV   *De beata vita*
On the Happy Life

DeDiv.   *De Diversis Quaestonibus Octoginta Tribus*
Eighty-Three Different Questions

EnPs.   *Enarrationes in Psalmos*
Expositions on the Psalms

Ep.   *Epistulae*
Letters

GL   *De Genesi ad Litteram*
Literal Commentary on Genesis

IoEp.   *Tractatus in epistolam Iohannis ad Parthos*
Tractates on the First Epistle of John

IoEv.   *In evangelium Ioannis Tractatus*
Tractates on the Gospel of John

Mor.   *De moribus ecclesiae catholicae et de moribus manichaeorum*
On the Catholic and Manichean Ways of Life

Retr.   *Retractationes*
Retractions

S.   *Sermones*
Sermons

Solil.   *Soliloquiorum*
The Soliloquies

THOMAS AQUINAS

ST   *Summa Theologica*

MODERN AUTHORS

AE   Anders Nygren, *Agape and Eros* (Philadelphia, 1953)

ATB   John Rist, *Augustine: Ancient Thought Baptized* (Cambridge, 1997)

BCE   Paul Ramsey, *Basic Christian Ethics* (New York, 1950)

BR   John Milbank, *Being Reconciled* (New York, 2003)

CS   Robert Markus, *Christianity and the Secular* (Notre Dame, 2006)

DN   Oliver O'Donovan, *The Desire of the Nations* (Cambridge, 1996)

HC   Hannah Arendt, *The Human Condition* (1958; repr., Chicago, 1989)

LPJ   Paul Tillich, *Love, Power, and Justice* (Oxford, 1954)

LP   Jean Bethke Elshtain, *Augustine and the Limits of Politics* (Notre Dame, 1995)

LV   James Wetzel, *Augustine and the Limits of Virtue* (Cambridge, 1992)

TST   John Milbank, *Theology and Social Theory* (Oxford, 1990)

PL   Timothy P. Jackson, *The Priority of Love* (Princeton, 2003)

PSL   Oliver O'Donovan, *The Problem of Self-Love in St. Augustine* (Yale, 1980)

SAE   Robert Markus, *Saeculum* (Cambridge, 1970)

UT   Martha Nussbaum, *Upheavals of Thought* (Cambridge, 2001)

Augustine and Modern Liberalism

Augustine was not a liberal. He was not even a proto-liberal. Like his fellow denizens of antiquity, Plato and Aristotle, he never had a thought about the political arrangements or the cultural conditions of modern societies. No one knows how to determine what he would have thought about such societies had he been transplanted into one of them. Yet the continuing debate over modern liberalism has to a large extent consisted in variations on Augustinian themes and antiphonal responses to them. It would not be a great exaggeration to see these debates as a series of footnotes to Augustine.

Christian thinkers often appeal directly to Augustine's authority, as if the authentically Augustinian view, once established, were binding. But they do not all interpret Augustine in the same way. Thinkers standing outside the church have often paid tribute to Augustine indirectly by recasting his ideas in secular form. Many other thinkers, whether inspired by non-Augustinian strands of Christianity or by non-Christian ideas, have made the case for their political theories by arguing against a received conception of Augustine's vision.

This book has two related objectives. The first is to analyze the debate over modern liberalism as a debate over the political implications of the Augustinian legacy. I show that many distinct types of political Augustinianism are still alive and kicking even as each comes with its own detractors. Some Augustinians reject liberalism wholesale, just as some liberals are thought to reject Augustinianism. But I identify three prevailing types which reflect modern appropriations of Augustine for liberal purposes: Augustinian realism (as in Reinhold Niebuhr and his followers), Augustinian proceduralism (as in John Rawls and his followers), and Augustinian civic liberalism (as in Martin Luther King Jr and his followers). These types are fluid because of a common affirmation of secularity and a keynote accent on the limits and corruptibility of politics. At the same time, each proposal stresses a distinct virtue: realists emphasize hope, proceduralists emphasize justice, and civic liberals emphasize love. Descriptively, this task is to make clear how, in each of the types, the interpretation of Augustine interacts with a normative proposal concerning how politics should be conceived and conducted.

The second objective is to offer my own rational reconstruction of Augustinian liberalism. Richard Rorty describes this approach as a way of doing philosophy, without historical anachronism, by engaging in conversation with the "re-educated dead."[1] Reeducating the dead means updating or restating aspects of their thinking in light of more recent philosophical work and our own cultural situation. Here the question is: What is the best available version of Augustinian liberalism? Or, to put it a bit differently: Which variations on which themes from the Augustinian tradition, when combined in the right way, would give the most adequate normative account of the responsibilities and virtues of citizens, leaders, and institutions in a liberal democracy? My answer to these questions, which involves appeal to the ancient concepts of love and sin, will yield both a distinctive version of Augustinian liberalism and a more complex understanding of both traditions.

Augustinian realists offer a limited conception of politics as restraining evil, a conception that often travels with a troubling form of moral consequentialism. Augustinian proceduralists allow more positive political ideals, but themselves offer a minimalist conception of justice which privatizes important virtues such as friendship and compassion. I defend and extend Augustinian civic liberalism as a corrective to these more dominant types. I do so by highlighting the central role that love (of God and neighbor) can and should play in an Augustinian social vision. My defense of this tradition constitutes a response both to *critics* of Augustine who *defend* liberal democracy (such as Hannah Arendt, Paul Ramsey, Martha Nussbaum, Robert M. Adams, and Timothy P. Jackson) and to *fans* of Augustine who *attack* liberal democracy (such as Alasdair MacIntyre, Stanley Hauerwas, Robert Kraynak, and John Milbank).

By adopting these objectives, I attempt to settle neither the historical question of what, if any, political theory Augustine actually subscribed to, nor the counterfactual questions of what Augustine would have wanted to say about liberal politics had he lived to experience it. My primary interests are systematic and conceptual. The history that most concerns me is that of

1. Rorty, "Historiography," 52.

the modern West rather than fifth-century North Africa. I do occasionally commend a view about how Augustine, within the context of his own time and place, can most plausibly be read. Some of these exegetical comments track traditional debates about the meaning of secularity, freedom and grace, unity and diversity, and the status of politics in Augustine's theology. I also consider other issues that I take to be just as relevant for political Augustinianism. For example, I express my opinion on how the crucial theme of "using and enjoying" should be read in its original textual settings. Augustine's distinction was included in Peter Lombard's *Book of Sentences*, making it central for a diverse range of medieval and early modern commentary (for example, it is important for both Ockham and Calvin).[2] This contested topic, now dislodged from its scholastic context, has become the subject of considerable interest in modern theology and religious ethics. It is taken to be a paradigmatic instance of Augustine's Platonism, something which modern philosophers deny, lament, or celebrate.

Consider the case of Anders Nygren's classic text, *Agape and Eros*. Augustine's supposedly stark contrast between *uti* and *frui* was Nygren's smoking gun in his indictment of Augustinian *caritas* on behalf of Lutheran theology (*AE*, 503–12). Nygren charged that Augustine corrupted the purity of Christian love (gratuitous *agape*) by lodging it within a Platonic structure of acquisitive and egocentric desire to possess the Good *(eros)*. In short, he turned Augustine's inventive argument about the prideful character of Platonic willing and loving against Augustine himself. Nygren held that Augustine's view of love reveals "the same idea as Plato had in urging us not to be captivated by the beautiful things in this world, but to use them as a ladder on which to ascend to the higher world" (*AE*, 512). Jerusalem, as it were, remained merely the ornamental suburb of philosophical Athens, which is the real downtown of Augustinian theology despite its formal protests. Nygren, by contrast, pit the charity of Jerusalem (decidedly a Christian Jerusalem) against the erotics of self-interested Athens. His text set off a firestorm of scholarly debate that preoccupied much of twentieth century

2. For medieval discussions, see A. S. McGrade, "Enjoyment at Oxford after Ockham," in *From Ockham to Wyclif*, ed. Anne Hudson and Michael Wilks (Oxford: Oxford University Press, 1987), 63–88, and Thomas Osborne Jr, *Love of Self and Love of God in Thirteenth Century Ethics* (Notre Dame, Ind.: University of Notre Dame Press, 2005). For Calvin's appropriation, see *Institutes*, 3.10. Charles Taylor hints at the distinction's influence on Puritan ideas of vocation and sanctification (Taylor, *Sources of the Self*, 221–27).

Protestant and Roman Catholic thought. It also led to a welcome renewal of philosophical and theological analysis of Christian love and eudaimonism.[3] My book contributes to these debates, especially by adopting a radically Incarnational and social reading of Augustinianism. But I revive "use and enjoyment" as part of my political reconstruction—the very modes of loving that an Augustinian like Reinhold Niebuhr (following Nygren) rejected as "grave errors in Augustine's account of love."[4] For Niebuhr, Augustine finally "bids us to flee mortality, including the neighbor in favor of the immutable good."[5] The power of Nygren's antitheses as a route into the philosophical history of religions is not to be denied. His construction of an issue, like Augustine's, powerfully determined the dynamics of a debate that often lost its theological focus partly as a result of Nygren's stated aim of bringing "*out a difference in type, not a difference of value*" (*AE*, 210). The "Nygren debate" in many ways parallels secular discussions of love given the influence of Kant's analogous concept of disinterestedness within a kingdom of ends. I want to loosen Nygren's (and Kant's) dichotomous hold—even on my fellow Augustinian liberals—in order to show that an Augustinian theology of love can offer more than mystical absorption into the One and unjust obliteration of the neighbor. Indeed, I argue that quite the opposite is the case. These remarks on Augustinian love, however, are made in the service of bringing these debates more explicitly to bear in social and political ethics.

The distinction between *uti* and *frui* raises important yet neglected issues for Augustinian moral psychology which are relevant for politics. An ethic of *caritas* and a psychology of enjoyment—usually subordinated by conventional readings of Book 19, *City of God*—should be important themes for any Augustinian political theology. The distinction allows me to raise aspects of Augustine's understanding of God and creation which are neglected in modern political Augustinianism because of its tendency to collapse all theology into a never-ending story about politics as a response to sin. I think

3. The most influential analysis in Christian ethics remains Outka, *Agape*. For a recent review of Nygren's work and its reception, see Werpehowski, "Anders Nygren's *Agape and Eros*." Critical responses to Nygren include Burnaby, *Amor Dei*; Canning, *Unity of Love for God and Neighbor in St. Augustine*; O'Donovan, *Problem of Self-Love in St. Augustine*; Vacek, *Love, Human and Divine*; Vlastos, "The Individual as Object of Love in Plato"; and Osborne, *Eros Unveiled*.

4. Niebuhr, "Augustine's Political Realism," 130.

5. Ibid., 140.

this neglect is a mistake. It has truncated the theological and the political resources of Augustinian liberalism. "Using the world" and "enjoying God" may be infelicitous phrases to modern ears who hear in them only manipulation (following Kant) and alienation (following Feuerbach). No doubt they have been historically employed for these purposes, and it is important for Augustinians to recognize the tradition's complicity in them. The language of "use and enjoyment" can be abused, especially when terms are reduced to a deistic world of subjects and objects. It need not be mobilized in this way. This language provides helpful categories for thinking about the significant asymmetries between *moral* perfectionism and *political* perfectionism as well as between *political* pluralism and *value* pluralism. Suitably reconstructed, they provide a different conceptual and linguistic starting point for Augustinian reflections on politics that neither denies nor valorizes the importance of sin. Nevertheless, neither of my principal objectives in writing this book would be jeopardized if I turned out to be wrong about what Augustine meant by "use and enjoyment," or some other disputed texts and themes.

The historian's task is to make considered judgments on these questions. They attempt to offer the best reading of the historical Augustine. I have benefited from exegetes who, in the hope of telling us what Augustine actually meant, adhere to the rules of what philosopher Robert Brandom calls *de dicto* interpretation.[6] I have also benefited from the remarkable developments in the study of late antiquity. Modern social-historical scholarship on Augustine and his age has flourished—now to the point of carefully deconstructing and resisting Augustine's self-presentation and the familiar terms through which he and his opponents have been read.[7] It is a field that scru-

6. Brandom, *Tales of the Mighty Dead*, 1–17 and 94–99. In *de dicto* textual interpretation, "one seeks to know so thoroughly what an author actually said, how his thought developed over his lifetime, what the rhetorical strategy of each work is and how it was understood by its author as fitting into the oeuvre, what his extraphilosophical concerns, attitudes, and experiences were that one can answer questions on his behalf in something like his own voice" (98–99). My hermeneutical strategy of reading Augustine in the context of contemporary beliefs and concerns adheres more to Brandom's account of *de re* interpretation. Brandom's distinction, which does not separate the two, fine-tunes the hermeneutics of both Richard Rorty and Hans-Georg Gadamer in mediating ideas we ascribe to ourselves and those of the dead.

7. See, for example, O'Donnell, *Augustine: A New Biography*. For an overview of modern historical scholarship, see Brown, "Introducing Markus"; Markus, "Disciplinary Contexts"; and O'Donnell, "Strangeness."

pulously aspires to abandon innocence in its reception of Augustine's master narratives of Christian orthodoxy and pagan philosophy. At the same time, this freedom from Augustine's spell might also free us from his conventional critics. Whether or not Augustine meant the things he is thought to have said about abandoning the self to God, hating the world, taking flight from the temporal and the particular, rejecting pagan virtue as splendid vice, and privileging "inner" piety against "outer" morality, it is tempting to construct this alternative as something to oppose. Opponents in his day tried to push him into such positions, and Augustine's legacy bears the marks of his efforts to refute them.

Augustine himself was a master of this strategy. He was a culture warrior and a trained rhetorician, bringing with him all the anxieties and polarizations of identity politics that we see in our pluralistic societies. It is telling, for example, that Augustine wrote as if Platonism was an *alternative* pagan religion to his Christian faith. Does he protest too much? If his rhetoric sometimes exceeds his theology, it is because he does not want to give an inch to his opponents in an agonistic age when all sorts of ideals were in flux. So he sometimes did go to places where his opponents pushed him. No doubt Augustine's texts, in all of their unsystematic glory, can be pressed into service by all sorts of projects, including my own. Part of Augustine's genius lies in the fact that by reading him we often come to read ourselves and wish for another Augustine. There have been many interpretive efforts to save Augustine from his followers, his critics, and, at times, from himself. We are confronted with a burdened history of making and unmaking, reading and misreading. Given the weight of this history and our dependence on it, James J. O'Donnell muses that "Augustine was lucky that he never had to read anything like Augustine."[8] Augustine, like other canonical figures, invites such heated disputes. His influence on certain topics (i.e., sex and politics), his polemical style, his internal inconsistencies, and the significance of the era in which he lived for the development of Western culture only add fuel to the fire.

My work will poach from historical discussions, especially as they relate to recent work in ethics. Rational reconstruction is not opposed to historical reconstruction. Exegesis and normative theorizing are distinct, albeit related, tasks. Conflating them has a strong tendency to produce misreading in the

8. O'Donnell, *New Biography*, 125.

guise of scholarship. I aim to be clear about what should be attributed to Augustine and what should be attributed to me or to others. On my reading, Augustine has much to say to our own questions. It is an important and demanding task to distinguish the received Augustine from the "real" Augustine. But, for my purposes, what Augustine actually meant is less central than the ways in which the relevant passages from his works have been interpreted (and applied to politics) in the modern period. I will selectively appropriate readings and *mis*readings alike. Words do not work the same way in normative theorizing as they do in historical inquiry. It is enough that "Donatist," "Pelagian," and "Manichean" exist as live options in moral, political, and religious discourse—even if Augustine or later storytellers invented them in order to coordinate doctrine with their experience of God in Christian faith and practice.[9] These words, and the narrative scripts they signify, provide broad classifications for a range of commitments. They do a lot of conceptual work in practices that organize self-understanding and locate commitments in relation to others. The same could be said about "Stoic," "Platonic," and, for that matter, "Augustinian," "Modern," and "Liberal." Historical and philological scholarship certainly helps dislodge settled grooves of thought and make us skeptical of the stories we tell. They can show the normative consequences of how we construct intellectual histories. They can also challenge us with an Augustine we thought we already knew by helping us understand the world behind the texts. But concern for subtext also has its limits, agendas, impositions, biases, and uncertain judgments. Historians, Augustine would remind us, often have their own stories. In any case, my conceptual analysis of modern Augustinianism can swing free from the quest for the historical Augustine.

What is needed, if we are going to understand the history of Augustinianism in modern political thought, is a reception history, not a definitive account of the historical Augustine plus a list of the many mistakes people have made in interpreting him. I do affirm the humanist conviction that allows for meaningful conversations with dead philosophers about shared concerns. The dead can reeducate us, if we let them. Of course, we might be amused, troubled, or simply confused by their concerns that we do not share. We also

---

9. See, for example, Peter Brown's discussion of Pelagianism as both a "body of ideas" and a Roman "movement" (Brown, *Augustine of Hippo*, 346). Brown, however, questions whether "the Pelagian teachings can be related to a precise movement" (ibid., 346n2).

can be surprised by how many of our concerns, for good or for ill, stem from theirs. That is part of the ongoing conversation, particularly when concerns that preoccupied a dead philosopher seem to be back on our agenda. It is one of the reasons why someone like Augustine crops up in so many disciplines. Augustine can disrupt the myopia of our parochial ways of thinking even as we might continue to hear his voice within modern thought.

Stephen Menn has argued that Augustinianism differs from traditions like Aristotelianism because it is not characterized by "a series of thinkers reading Augustine through their predecessors, and distinguished by some common doctrine from thinkers outside the school" (*Descartes and Augustine*, ix). Rather, the history of Augustinianism is a history of punctuated revivals by individuals who discover "some new aspect of Augustine's thought which seemed to offer a way out of the impasses of their contemporaries, and to suggest a new philosophical or theological project" (69). This reading accounts for the plurality of Augustinianism and its eclecticism as a tradition. Menn's book, for example, shows the diversity of seventeenth-century Augustinianisms: "Descartes' was a *De Libero Arbitrio* Augustinianism. . . . It is very different from the anti-Pelagian Augustinianisms such as that of Jansen, although Arnauld tried his best to reconcile the two" (70). My book is an effort to find "a way out" of the impasses of my contemporaries.

Augustinian liberalism typically has been a *De Civitate Dei* 19 Augustinianism, though in a very different way than its medieval readers could imagine. I affirm aspects of this modern tradition, notably what is today called the separation of church and state supporting a constitutional regime of check and balances. I also affirm its capacity to deflate moral and political pretension. Augustinians, with all of their eschatological longings, are right to expose lazy claims to have satisfied the demands of justice even as they search for a just ordering of society. They also are right to recognize tensions and fault lines between the goals of the good citizen and the good person. For theological reasons, they neither expect nor want the state to become a confessing religious community. But I want to push this tradition in a new direction in order to reconstruct a kind of *Augustinian civic virtue* that might in turn encourage a more ambitious political practice. By more "ambitious" political practice, I mean the promotion of an actual society that is more just, more egalitarian, and more charitable. This practice need not be statist, though the state is necessary given the practical challenges of securing the shared goods of actual "peoples." The depressing realities of liberal democracies marked by dramatic political and economic inequalities do not inspire confidence in such a vision. Augustinianism, with both cosmopolitan aspiration and attention to virtue's origins in local communities, should avoid the reduction of politics to state-centered government activity. Like Arnauld, then, I am trying to reconcile different kinds of Augustinianisms. Augustinian Christians, according to their own theological lights, should establish political friendships necessary to sustain liberal democracy threatened by entrenched elite interests. They should offer more than their conventional contribution to liberal politics: a demythologized notion of original sin as a basis for anti-utopian foreign and domestic policy. They should offer a vision of citizenship open to social transformation by attending to virtue. More philosophically, I argue that an Augustinian ethics of citizenship can be *perfectionist* without trading in sentimentalism, Pelagian notions of achieved *perfectibility,* or elitist conceptions of undemocratic politics.

My Augustinian civic virtue generally corresponds to moderate forms of liberal perfectionism that offer ethical accounts of human flourishing believed to be intrinsically valuable. Politically, these theories are interested in meliorist practices that promote human flourishing and discourage practices that diminish it. They are not governed by procedural appeals to seemingly neutral principles that are sociologically indifferent to their consequences for social welfare. They also want more from liberal politics than the creation of a space where we do not kill each other and we do not interfere with conditions of economic exchange. Liberal perfectionists are *liberal* because they recognize the limited authority of the state and the instrumental quality of political goods for individuals in their multiple communities and various loyalties. They also are attentive to goods like autonomy and self-respect precisely because these goods are valuable and necessary components of human flourishing.[10] Liberal citizens, as both self-aware and interdependent political agents, should not understand themselves as unrecognized objects

---

10. Liberal perfectionists and their accounts of autonomy admit tremendous variety in contemporary political philosophy. In chapter 3, I discuss a number of feminist theorists and Christian social ethicists that I consider "moderate liberal perfectionists." In political theory, liberal perfectionists include Joseph Raz, Vinit Haksar, Thomas Hurka, George Sher, and John Finnis. For helpful reviews as well as independent proposals, see Steven Wall, *Liberalism, Perfectionism, and Restraint* (Cambridge: Cambridge University Press, 1998), and Kimberly A. Yurako, *Perfectionism and Contemporary Feminist Values* (Bloomington: Indiana University Press, 2003).

of another person's unintelligible desires. The liberalism I wish to defend is that of a political practice grounded in moral appeal to the equal dignity of persons and shared goods protected by a constitutional government in which liberty and equality are respected.

In addition to liberal perfectionism, this kind of liberalism (which indirectly enables perfectionist aspirations through political cooperation) corresponds to what some scholars now term "civic liberalism." Civic liberalism is a virtue-oriented liberalism that aims to avoid individualistic and rationalistic assumptions about human nature as well as romantic or totalitarian conceptions of political community. It critically appropriates selective features of both procedural liberalism and civic republicanism. But it is its own emerging tradition that allows for substantial recognition of the rights, the interests, and the actual needs of a diverse citizenry. To cite one proponent, it is dedicated to "individual rights and civil liberties together with an insistence upon the parallel importance of a strong public sphere inhabited by social equals and directed toward perpetually evolving and dialogically contested common purposes."[11] Civic liberals and liberal perfectionists allow ideal conceptions of human flourishing into the full light of the public square, conceptions that already shape practical deliberations of public decision-making and normatively evaluate the effects of liberal justice.

This strategy may be too radical for some, especially those wary of interloping ethicists doing violence to historical texts and canonical figures. I remind them, however, that what Augustine actually meant does not settle the normative question of what a modern Augustinian thinker, let alone a secular one, ought to believe about liberal democracy. On any point where Augustine's statements prove unacceptable, incomplete, or ambiguous, his intellectual descendents are free to amend them; and the improved theory need not take the form of a revisionist account of what Augustine really meant or would have meant.

I begin with the dominant strand of Augustinian liberalism in the twentieth century: Augustinian realism. This type reconstructed Augustine's controversial doctrine of original sin and his dramatic narrative about "two cities" in order to temper the enthusiasm of democratic optimism and to support something like the "secular" order of liberalism. The term secular here trades upon Augustine's own theological meaning—"in this passing

11. Spragens, *Civic Liberalism*, xv.

age" (*CD* 1.Pref.)—rather than the modern sense of secular as nonreligious or atheistic. Augustinianism tends to contrast "secular" with "eternal" rather than with "sacred."[12] On this view, Augustine's two cities do not exist in different worlds, but "in this present world mixed together and, in a certain sense, entangled with one another" (*CD* 11.1). Between World War I and the end of the Cold War, Augustinian realism was closely allied with another kind of realism indebted to Machiavelli and Weber. Its principal spokesperson in American politics was the Protestant theologian Reinhold Niebuhr. Many theorists, activists, and statesmen cited Niebuhr as a formative intellectual influence. George Kennan, for example, called Niebuhr "the father of us all" and Morton White famously dubbed a group of Niebuhr's readers as "atheists for Niebuhr."[13] In Niebuhr's version of politics, the central fact of human nature this side of the Eschaton is sin, and it is the purpose of government, not to eliminate sin, but to constrain or ameliorate its bad effects by passing laws and using armed force prudently (albeit tragically). Sentimental attempts to derive a social ethic from the gospel commandment of love are dangerous. Love is best conceived as a utopian ideal that discloses what life will be like when God brings human history to a close by establishing his kingdom. Niebuhr sought to avoid cynicism even as he tended to assume that utopian striving within historical time is the seed of totalitarian oppression. Liberal democracy is the least bad form of government because it recognizes government's limited, sin-constraining role. In defending it, we need a realistic understanding of human nature and a willingness to use force and the threat of force in the interest of maintaining order and approximating justice.

12. Robert Markus argues that "the sacred and the profane were both familiar in antiquity; but until it was imported by Christianity, there was no notion of the 'secular' in the ancient world" (*CS*, 4). For Markus, "from the Christian point of view, the secular is roughly equivalent to what can be shared with non-Christians" (6). He argues that "some notion of a secular realm is an essential constituent of Christian belief but that its content is variable, contingent upon the historical circumstances" (13). I consider Markus's influence in chapter 2 and adopt a version of his theological notion of the "secular." Occasionally, I adopt the more familiar modern usage in ways that should be clear from context.

13. Fox, *Niebuhr*, 238 and 246. Niebuhr's obituary in *The New York Times* cites Niebuhr's influence on Arthur Schlesinger Jr, Paul Nitze, Dean Acheson, McGeorge Bundy, Louis Halle, Hans Morgenthau, and James Reston (Whitman, "Reinhold Niebuhr is Dead").

Modern Augustinian liberalism begins with Niebuhr's realism, and its scholarly counterparts, in ascendancy. This reading of Augustine, in large part, was governed by pressing questions about secular rationalism, the relation of Christianity to liberal democracy, the use of force in a rough and tumble world threatened by fascism and Marxism, and the failure of responses to these ideologies. Another variety of Augustinian politics emerges in positive response to the massive influence of John Rawls's theory of "justice as fairness" in the 1970s and 1980s. This variety builds on the Niebuhrian emphasis on sin, but in a distinctive way by emphasizing the significance of fairness as a political virtue for a liberal society marked by conditions of pluralism. Still another type, represented by figures like Jean Bethke Elshtain, Timothy P. Jackson, and Oliver O'Donovan, emerges in the 1990s, when suspicions about realism and Rawlsianism led to a revival of conceptions of civic virtue. I trace the roots of this third type to important elements of four influential Christian theologians, Paul Tillich, Martin Luther King Jr, Paul Ramsey, and Gustavo Gutierrez. I highlight this type's interest in recovering the Augustinian notion that human beings and the societies they form are best understood in terms of the loves they embody and express (*CD* 19.24). Each of these types, to varying degrees, understands itself to be a form of liberalism. A fourth type of modern Augustinianism, however, is antiliberal. It is to be found in the recently influential movement known as Radical Orthodoxy.

All four types of political Augustinianism represented in debates over liberalism—three varieties of liberalism and one antiliberal—take familiar themes and passages from Augustine's writings as their points of departure. What makes this fourth type different from the others is not its degree of commitment to Augustine's authority, but its distaste for liberal political arrangements. It imagines liberal democracy as morally and spiritually bankrupt, a social expression of theological heresies. On the other hand, Augustine also figures prominently in the same debates as a villain. Hannah Arendt and numerous feminist theorists have had much to say about Augustine's deficiencies as a political thinker. It is incumbent upon modern Augustinians to meet these objections. I also consider them noteworthy because their political visions are remarkably similar to my preferred third type of Augustinian civic liberalism. Important differences remain, but there are unnoticed parallels between their critical accounts of political liberalism and an Augustinian ambivalence about both liberal theory and practice. One ironic conclusion of my descriptive analysis is that the third type of

Augustinian liberals and the feminist critics of Augustinianism are much closer than one might have thought.

In setting out the structure of, and motivations behind, each of these positions, I also assess their criticisms of each other. I am aware that such a "narrative task itself generally involves participation in conflict,"[14] and I cast my lot with a version of Augustinian liberalism. The third type of Augustinian civic liberalism, with its emphasis on love and civic responsibility, succeeds in exposing weaknesses in Niebuhrianism, in Rawlsianism, and in Radical Orthodoxy. It is the only extant version of Augustinianism that has any real chance of meeting the Arendtian and feminist objections. It can incorporate the best of the other liberal types as well as the attractive features of the antiliberal one. Of the leading varieties of political Augustinianism, it is therefore the best candidate for theoretical elaboration and defense. In the final chapters of the book, I show what a maximally acceptable form of Augustinian liberalism, modeled on this third type, would look like. In the end, my defense of this tradition significantly alters its practical relevance for non-Augustinian liberals and leaves my fellow Augustinian liberals less vulnerable to their political and theological critics. Put more positively, I here propose *an Augustinian ethic of citizenship for the morally ambivalent conditions of liberal democracy*. It joins three clusters of ideas and practices usually held to be incompatible: Augustinian moral psychology, perfectionist ethics, and liberal politics. I use this approach to help the political traditions of Augustinianism and liberalism correct the weaknesses of the other.

LOVE, SIN, AND POLITICS: MODERN VARIATIONS ON AUGUSTINIAN THEMES

For a pluralist society in search of political wisdom, Augustine, unlike Socrates, does not immediately come to mind as a great exponent of the dialogical life. Among modern thinkers, he is more feared than loved. Rumors about Augustine and Augustinianism abound. Some of them are true. But they are spread for different reasons. The very name "Augustine" can conjure diverse images: dour apocalyptic, hopeless romantic, cosmopolitan intellectual, court theologian, provincial bishop, narcissistic existentialist, austere authoritarian, defender of mediocrity, angst-ridden sexist patriarch,

---

14. MacIntyre, *Whose Justice? Which Rationality?*, 11.

and spiritual psychologist of the inner life. Tenacious rumors damn him, resurrecting his ghost for the sake of burying the cultural baggage of his legacy once and for all. Others praise him, finding in his writings a telling diagnosis of the human condition that might deliver us from the thin gruel of modern, and now postmodern, alternatives. By reputation, and sufficient historical example, Augustinians are pessimistic, dogmatic, coercive, and intoxicated by desire for God. They favor the bounded structures of the ecclesial rather than the wild plurality of a world where individuals freely revise their own plans for life. They long for the transcendent with authoritarian abandon and puritanical anxiety, tending either toward theocratic efforts to hasten its arrival or sectarian withdrawal that radically subordinates the social role of citizenship to that of Christian discipleship. No doubt those unfamiliar with the tradition of Augustinian liberalism, given their rival stereotypes, already may resist this pairing as a category mistake. Liberalism, whether by way of Kant or Hume or Locke, is about leaving dreary Augustinianism behind and celebrating individual autonomy as the basis of liberal democracy. Augustinian liberals, like Oliver O'Donovan, try to overcome these stereotypes by presenting an Augustinian theology that supports "a *normative political culture* broadly in continuity with the Western liberal tradition" (*DN*, 230). In particular, they defend religious liberty not by separating law and morality but by affirming a "sphere of individual responsibility before God in which the public good is not immediately at stake" (*DN*, 255).[15] In chapter 2, I describe the strange alliance of these contested traditions, clarifying what I take to be the defining characteristics of this "nonstandard version of liberalism."[16] My defense of this nonstandard version is doubly nonstandard because it relies on a virtue-oriented rather than merely sin-oriented Augustinian politics. Before I give this account, however, it is necessary to introduce the Augustinian theme that organizes both my descriptive and normative objectives: the dynamic relation between love and sin. I elevate this relationship as a central Augustinian problematic—one that preoccupied Augustine himself—as a new route into thinking about the political

15. O'Donovan argues that political authority is constrained by its task of defending against wrong because no one can "declare comprehensively what is right to do—for what is right to do lies in the sphere of freedom, and is the subject of an infinite number of decisions by an infinite number of people" (O'Donovan, *Ways of Judgment*, 58).

16. Stout, *Ethics after Babel*, 6.

implications of Augustinianism. As I make clear in the next chapter, the conceptual relation between love and sin also offers an alternative approach for thinking about religion, liberalism, and civic virtue.

I consider two basic paradigms for how love and sin function in political morality. These paradigms can be found in both Augustinian and non-Augustinian traditions. One places too much confidence in love; the other casts too much suspicion. The error of both views is a failure to relate love and sin to each other in ways that constrain both appeals. Left unconstrained by sin, a first paradigm of politics appeals to love (and related notions of friendship, fraternity, care, community, solidarity, and sympathy) in ways that have justified antiliberal perfectionist politics—indeed, a theocratic one, if possible. Left unconstrained by love, a second paradigm of politics relies on realist appeals to sin (and related notions of cruelty, evil, and narrow self-interest) in ways that have justified essentially negative forms of political liberalism. Both outcomes, arrogant perfectionism and negative liberalism, are normatively inadequate.

In my treatment of Hannah Arendt, I discuss her historical examples of the first paradigm in terms of the violent and totalitarian possibilities of politicizing love. Augustine's troubled, if ostensibly reluctant, defense of imperial coercion of the majority of Christians in North Africa ("schismatic Donatists") provides another example. It is often used as a paradigmatic example for Hume's observation that monotheism upset the easygoing tolerance of polytheism. Augustine couched his political appeal in terms of the need for the harsh discipline of pastoral love, often relying on medical metaphors of healing through bitter pain. It marks an important instance where Augustinian theology, attentive to the self-deceptions of claims to virtue, can be better than Augustine's practice of paternalistic compassion. Augustine knew the "tricks that paternalism can play, not only on its victims but on its perpetrators."[17] But he gave into these tricks when he thought they met with empirical success—the reform of vicious sinners to their true end of shared fellowship in God. Augustine did hold that Christians should not zealously try to rush in the Eschaton by fully enacting the good in secular politics. If it is a matter of God's grace, he argued against Donatist perfectionists, Christians should not desire a pure community of the holy "before the time is right" (*Ep*. 189, 217). Nevertheless, he lost his own emphasis on

17. TeSelle, "Augustinian Politics," 91.

forbearance in order to "do whatever seems likely to benefit those we should wish well" (*Ep.* 138, 37). It is a sad fact that Augustine's willingness to use political might to lovingly "correct" religious opponents has frequently been pressed into the service of paternalist politics and love crusades of different kinds.[18] It would not be hard to expand this list, especially if one were to draw from a long history of religious appeals to love that fund various theocratic experiments in living. Here, perhaps controversially, I am thinking of figures as diverse as the French Augustinian Jacques-Benigne Bossuet (1627–1704), the radical Anabaptist Thomas Münzer (1489–1525), the Puritan statesman John Winthrop (1588–1649), and the utopian socialist Charles Fourier (1772–1837). These cases, of course, admit tremendous historical and theoretical complexity. They reveal the volatile difficulty of reconciling accounts of love and sin in the realm of political power.

Consider, for example, Bishop Bossuet. His classic defense of divine-right absolute monarchy, *Politics Drawn From the Very Words of Holy Scripture*, opens with an extended discussion of the unity of the love commandments and the "fraternity of men."[19] Yet Bossuet, unlike his contemporary Leibniz, quickly abandons a project of Christian political theory that institutionalizes justice as a rational form of charity (the *vinculum substantiale*).[20] Bossuet's personal ode to the universality of Christian love evaporates into a relentlessly realist defense of political necessity. Patrick Riley notes: "Bossuet seems (as it were) to push charity back, before the Fall: it has little present weight in politics."[21] This capacity for an idealist appeal to love to deteriorate, as if in a mimetic rivalry, into an excessively realist appeal to sin continues throughout the Augustinian tradition.

Reinhold Niebuhr, unlike Bossuet, will not push charity back to the Fall as much as he will push it forward to the Eschaton. Niebuhr's account of love offers a taunting impossibility that lies "beyond history" and has only a shadowy social existence in politics. Sin, finitude, paradox, and political

18. For textual evidence of how an Augustinian ethic of love was used to motivate religious crusades in the eleventh-century, see Jonathan Riley-Smith, "Crusading as an Act of Love," *History* 65 (1980): 177–92.

19. Bossuet, *Politics,* 2d and 3d Propositions.

20. For Leibniz's notion of justice as *caritas sapientis* ("charity of the wise"), see Riley, *Leibniz' Universal Jurisprudence: Justice as the Charity of the Wise* (Cambridge, Mass.: Harvard University Press, 1996).

21. Riley, introduction to Bossuet, *Politics,* xxxii.

prudence dominate. Religious love, at times, is simply contrasted to rational justice—a contrast particularly evident in one of his most popular works, *Moral Man and Immoral Society*.[22] The purity of his Christian *agape*, demonstrated in the suffering love of the cross, can not provide a social ethic even as it mercifully judges any social ethic. The impossible possibilities of love simply "hover over every system of justice."[23] According to Niebuhr's liberalism, "love, which depends upon emotion, whether it expresses itself in transient sentiment or constant goodwill, is baffled by the more intricate social relations in which the highest ethical attitudes are achieved only by careful calculation."[24] Niebuhr has other things to say about love and justice, especially in terms of a disinterested love born of grace and contrition, "without which all moral striving generates a stinking sweat of self-righteousness and an alternation of fanatic illusions and fretful disillusionments."[25] These more nuanced statements, which still admit interpretive difficulty, soften the rhetorical blow of his apparent dualisms and close the distance of love from justice. Two of the most energetic and provocative programs in theological ethics today, laying claim to the Augustinian tradition, have declared Niebuhrianism a theological and political failure. These movements associate *any* defense of political liberalism with the failures of theological liberalism and secular nihilism.

Against John Milbank and Stanley Hauerwas, I do not share this view. Theological orthodoxy and political liberalism are not alternative answers to the same question. Niebuhr's dramatic anthropology of human beings as free yet bound offered a useful corrective in his day to those liberal optimists enchanted by democratic freedom and those pessimists enchanted by the

22. Niebuhr writes: "A rational ethic aims at justice, and a religious ethic makes love the ideal. A rational ethic seeks to bring the needs of others into equal consideration with those of the self. The religious ethic ... insists that the needs of the neighbor shall be met without a careful computation of relative needs" (Niebuhr, *Moral Man*, 57; see also 263).

23. Niebuhr, *Nature and Destiny of Man*, 1:302. Niebuhr allows justice could be a mutual love that still falls short of the sacrificial love of agape, but love's dialectical relation to justice remains the counterpart of "the general relation of super-history to history" (*Nature and Destiny*, 2:69).

24. Niebuhr, *Moral Man*, 74.

25. Niebuhr, *Reflections on the End of an Era*, 296.

disappointments of the moral life.[26] He consistently tried to relate the *agape* of the cross to responsible moral living in ways that would frustrate both liberals and fundamentalists. His dialectical vision was not without problems, including his failure to recognize the Augustinian claim that church (not state) is itself a historical, sacramental reality. In the end, despite his rhetorical blasts against naïve liberalism, Niebuhr was too much a part of the liberal theology he was trying to describe to be able to offer an alternative Christian ethic. His lack of interest in systematic theology verged on the edge of equating the Christian Gospel with a liberal democratic creed or, at least, implying that Christianity was primarily to be the custodian of a creed that made a pragmatic virtue out of tragic necessity. Despite his accent on gratitude and contrition, he was devoted to giving American civilization just enough religion he thought it needed without giving it too much theology.[27] I will argue that his critics swing too far in an opposite direction by allowing ecclesiology to overwhelm Augustinian political theology (especially an ecclesiology that subsumes both Christology and pneumatology).

The narrative of accommodation or capitulation, familiar to Augustine, often is told by those who self-identify with orthodoxy. I want to undermine the seductive power of this narrative, especially its work in critical accounts of modern society that elide what I take to be a necessary distinction between political liberalism and theological liberalism. Drawing from the insights of these authors, however, I will challenge the common belief that liberal Protestant Niebuhrianism *simply is* Augustinian liberalism. Indeed, one conclusion of this book is that Martin Luther King Jr, not Reinhold

26. Robin Lovin calls for a shift among contemporary Niebuhrians that is consistent with the goals of my book: "Today, it may be that Christian Realism best serves the children of the light, especially political liberals among them, by reintroducing the motive power of moral and religious ideals to those who learned too well the earlier lessons against sentimentality" (Lovin, *Reinhold Niebuhr*, 232). According to Lovin, the role of Christian Realism today "is not to talk about realistic limits, but to expand political imagination" (246).

27. Niebuhr shunned the label of theologian, preferring to be known as an ethicist and social philosopher. Well before Hauerwas and Milbank, Wilson Carey McWilliams challenged the "bankruptcy" of Niebuhr's liberalism and vague theology. McWilliams argued: "The Heavenly City of Reinhold Niebuhr retains a distinctly modern form in which to cast its eternal perfections. In fact, the best state in the world—as opposed to the heavenly ultimate—seems strikingly to resemble the United States" (McWilliams, "Reinhold Niebuhr," 881).

Niebuhr, is the great Augustinian liberal of modernity.[28] This effort to free Augustine from Nieburhian realism does not altogether abandon Niebuhr, and it still remains at odds with Hauerwas and Milbank. But my development of Augustinian Christology complements their effort to recast political theology in terms of the perfections of Christian virtue, although it is not built on the back of antiliberalism. Niebuhr's continuing popularity in both liberal and conservative political circles helps us see the attraction of his sober appeals to sin.[29] Here we find my second paradigm for love and sin in political morality. This version of liberalism, usually fortified with Augustine's anti-Pelagian texts exposing the dangers of perfectionism, has proved attractive to many Augustinian liberals.

In secular political thought, analogous appeals that rely on a blunt opposition of sin and love have justified essentially negative forms of political liberalism. This antipathy to love in the public square was exacerbated in the twentieth century by a liberalism largely motivated by anti-totalitarianism.[30] It led to a devaluing of love by a more impartialist, justice-focused understanding of political morality and a concern for political stability that typifies post-World War II liberal ethics of citizenship. Historical antecedents of this kind of suspicious liberalism, evident in figures like Thomas Hobbes and David Hume, lie in the reactions to the religious violence of post-Reformation Europe. The memory of these wars of religion and the enthusiasms that inflamed them play a formative role in Rawlsian liberalism.[31] Another example of this paradigm of politics can be found in Judith Shklar's influential "liberalism of fear." Shklar's liberalism, reacting against the emphasis on the *summum bonum* in communitarian politics, is grounded in fears

---

28. I thank Stanley Hauerwas for helping me to see this point more clearly.

29. See, for example, Beinart, *Good Fight*, 196–97; Peretz, "Losing our Delusions," 17–19; Dionne, "Faith Full," 12–15; and Brooks, "Man on a Gray Horse," 24–25. Ironically, many invocations of Niebuhrian liberalism (or laments about its demise) resemble the nostalgic invocations of medieval sacramentalism or the purity of the early church of the martyrs that sometimes characterize followers of Milbank and Hauerwas.

30. For a compelling account of the formative impact of World War II on Anglo-American legal and political thought, see Richard A. Primus, *American Language of Rights* (Cambridge: Cambridge University Press, 1999).

31. Rawls, *Political Liberalism*, xxiv–xxxiv. Rawls's liberal theory is motivated by his reaction against utilitarianism, but a diagnosis of the religious dimensions of totalitarianism also is evident.

about a *summum malum*: the evil of cruelty. For Shklar, as for many Augustinians, liberalism is "more a recipe for survival than a project for the perfectibility of mankind."[32] The liberal desire for freedom from fear, as critics of American foreign policy point out, has its own way of justifying antiliberal politics in the name of survival rather than perfectibility. Suppressing fear is a dangerous game that can invite forms of cruelty in the name of liberalism. For Augustine, freedom from fear was an eschatological hope rather than an earthly possibility. But the key point to be illustrated is Shklar's liberal tendency to associate love with the instability of political sentimentalism. She argues that liberals should be "suspicious of ideologies of solidarity, precisely because they are so attractive to those who find liberalism emotionally unsatisfying, and who have gone on in our century to create oppressive and cruel regimes of unparalleled horror."[33] Augustinian liberals share these concerns about *ideologies* of solidarity as much as they do Shklar's refusal to identify politics with emotional satisfaction and extensive bonds of natural affection. Yet, I will argue, they should resist the negativity of a liberal politics grounded in fear even as they should resist theocratic politics grounded in prideful paternalism. Recognition of sin and the ubiquity of cruelty might itself motivate (even if it also can chasten) a liberal politics of solidarity.

We can now, at least in preliminary fashion, identify two flawed possibilities for the political implications of an Augustinianism: one primarily oriented to love, the other primarily oriented to sin. The challenge for Augustinian liberalism is to work out a version of this relationship that avoids both arrogant forms of perfectionism and essentially negative forms of liberalism. Here is one possible way to begin. From an Augustinian point of view, love and sin in fact constrain each other. This recognition opens a space for something other than the two alternatives sketched above. Sin, for Augustinians, is a species within an internally diverse conception of love. Sin always plays a role in human loving. As such, the fragile relationship between love and sin must always be held in full view. The promise of love certainly interrupts or disturbs the resigned complacency of premature appeals to sin. Augustinians may derive their account of sin from a prior account of love, but they should not collapse forgetfully into one-sided appeal to either. A naïve appeal to love as a panacea for the discontents of liberalism

32. Shklar, *Ordinary Vices*, 4.
33. Shklar, "Liberalism of Fear," 36.

would be as unwarranted as a fixation with sin and the tragic hypocrisy of all politics. The danger of this collapse, I think, is one of the reasons critics of Augustine charge that his ethics is too preoccupied with goodness or too preoccupied with evil to be of use for liberal democracy.

Caught not beyond but between good and evil, an unbalanced Augustinianism yields a schizophrenic political morality—one otherworldly or sectarian, the other zealously persecutorial, and yet another that possibly swings between the two. For his critics, Augustine's ambivalent attitude toward any temporal project at best renders political action radically indeterminate and sponsors indifference and ascetic inwardness (in the deceptive guise of love of God). At worst, it promotes the violent legitimation of coercion and undermines a core liberal value of autonomy (in the manipulative guise of love of neighbor). By emphasizing the dialectical relation between sin and love, I want to avoid this schizophrenia and point to the surprising possibilities of Augustinian civic virtue. How robustly can Augustinians appeal to love or appeal to sin without throwing this relationship out of kilter? In order to pursue this question, I return to Augustine's own formulations of human beings as bundles of loves.

Here is the Augustinian story. In contrast to standard liberal anthropology, Augustinians think human beings are best understood as bundles of loves. Mortal creatures are lovers constituted by loving, and being loved by, others and God. These primordial relations are neither essentially conflictual nor simply aggregate, foreclosing any possibility of a peaceful intersubjective social ontology. They also do not immediately pit autonomous action or feeling over against publicly shared action or feeling. This Augustinian story expresses much of classical Greek and Christian philosophy that allows analogy between the personal and the social. A self always stands in relation to the world, including the political world, in terms of her loves. These loves are oriented by what Charles Taylor has termed a "moral ontology."[34] But all is not well with our relation to this ontology. Human loves are various and in conflict. In a fallen world, they are disordered, misdirected, and disproportionate. Their operations are diverse and often self-defeating. Love has multiple directions and is beset by many potentially pathological

34. Taylor, *Sources of the Self*, 8. Whatever problems attach to his account of the inwardness of the Augustinian self, Taylor's account of the self as inescapably in relation to the good (understood in terms of love) is decidedly Augustinian.

corruptions that disrupt an original justice: the order of the soul that opens up to relations with others. Pride, typically identified by love of self and an overweening confidence in one's own reason or moral achievement, distorts love even as it too remains a kind of excessive love. It is a love that refers virtue to oneself and "hates a fellowship of equality under God" (*CD* 19.12). There is a fundamental continuity between all loves and desires, whether or not they are distinguished as "natural" or "supernatural." Sin is predicated on bad love, not desire as such. Humility, typically identified with love of God and God's own humility in Christ, corrects disordered love *(dilectio inordinata)* and moral presumption without abandoning the needs of the self to love and be loved. It serves as the ground of piety because it admits the resources of God's infinitely compassionate love. Different loves differentiate human agency and action. Virtues and values critically depend on the manner in which the self exercises virtue and responds to value. True virtue is a matter of loving well and loving freely. Justice is about getting our loves arranged in the appropriate manner, giving and receiving love in the right sorts of ways. The greatest failure of love is when love itself is not receptive to the reality of another lover; that is, when the lover is pridefully unwilling to be beloved. Through a kind of *askesis,* the self must learn to love rightly, transferring the "weights" of bad loving to good loving. The life of charity is only progressively realized, always in danger of being corrupted by prideful self-possession. This account will serve as the crucial hinge between Augustinian liberalism and my normative account of the ethics of democratic citizenship. What is left for me to do in this introduction is outline the progression of the individual chapters.

THE PROJECT

In chapter 1, I expand this initial discussion of love and sin as a route into contrasting my approach with other ways of thinking about religion, virtue, and liberal politics. Modern scholars, often engaging in Protestant or post-Protestant polemic, have repaid their debts to Augustine's influential account of love's complicit relation to sin by emphasizing the dangers of following Augustine on love. By pursuing an alternative reconstruction, I argue that these themes offer a more promising direction for debates about religion and liberalism than the current preoccupation with religious speech and epistemic justification. As proponents of the language of virtue have argued, accounts of moral and political life are conditioned by the categories employed to interpret these phenomena. Is there another way for liberals to think and to talk about religion and civic virtue? The ethics of speech remain important concerns for liberal democracies. But the terms of these debates have become too narrow and the arguments too predictable. They fail to address the severe challenges facing liberal political culture, including those challenges of stability that are thought to require increasingly thin descriptions of civic virtue. The concepts of love and sin can help us in this regard. They move discussion beyond the ethics of justification. In short, they allow more focused attention to motivations, affections, and desires.

In chapter 2, I provide a guide to contemporary Augustinian liberalism and its critics. The story of Augustinian liberalism, once coterminous with the story of realist rejections of liberal Protestant social ethics or Catholic liberation theology, has been dramatically complicated. The incongruity of the term "Augustinian liberalism" equally appeals to those who wish to defend liberalism against Augustinianism, those who wish to defend Augustinianism against liberalism, and those who want to undermine both traditions. In order to gain some clarity on these debates and set the stage for my own account, I distinguish my three different types and associate each with the particular virtue it promotes for a liberal citizen.

The first type—Augustinian realism—represents the dominant strand of Augustinian liberalism and most clearly reflects the interests of twentieth-century readers. This type links Augustinianism with realist schools in political theory, highlighting "Augustine's pessimistic realism and lack of sentimentality about politics."[35] The dominant virtue for this Augustinian liberal citizen is *hope*, particularly eschatological hope that transcends the tragedies and tensions of politics. A second type, evident in the writings of Paul Weithman and Edmund Santurri, updates this more traditional reading by linking Augustinianism with Rawlsian liberalism. It highlights "an Augustinian vision of political life" that "supports, at least in modern contexts, the kind of philosophically and religiously neutral political arrangements typically commended by liberal political theory."[36] The dominant virtue for this Augustinian liberal citizen is *justice*, particularly justice conceived as basic fairness mediated by the virtue of respect. My third type, Augustinian

---

35. Deane, *Political and Social Ideas of St. Augustine*, xiii.
36. Santurri, "Rawlsian Liberalism," 1.

civic liberalism, distinguishes Augustine's desacralization of politics from the bifurcation of politics and the aspirations of virtue. The dominant virtue of this Augustinian liberal citizen is *love,* though only Timothy P. Jackson has explicitly advanced a version of this thesis (even as he explicitly rejects Augustine's doctrine of love). This third type is the best Augustinian candidate for a political ethic that recognizes the extent to which human beings are vulnerable and dependent by attending to the emotions of solidarity which make a liberal politics of freedom and equality possible. I aid and abet this third type of Augustinian liberalism by re-reading Augustine's account of love and sin and by connecting it to recent work in feminist political theory. Throughout this chapter, I show how Augustinian civic liberalism evades its theological critics, especially those who claim that it merely places theology in the service of liberal politics.

Chapter 3 builds on the second chapter by bringing together two sets of literature that rarely intersect: the political implications of a feminist "ethics of care" and a Christian "ethics of love." In rethinking love as a virtue of liberal citizens in need of political affirmation, my project parallels various efforts in feminist theory. While initially provoked by Carol Gilligan's distinction between care and justice in her seminal work, *In A Different Voice: Psychological Theory and Women's Development,* these efforts have moved beyond this classic formulation. I argue that Augustinianism shares much in common with feminist political theory, especially as advanced by Joan C. Tronto, Eve Fedder Kittay, and Martha Nussbaum. Two features of modern liberalism come under feminist attack that resonate with communitarian tropes but are used by these authors for liberal purposes: a concept of autonomy that erases the sense in which human beings are relational creatures, and a concept of rationality that imagines emotions as disruptions of practical moral reason, unworthy of being attributed cognitive or moral status. Building from these positions, these feminist liberals are critical of the alleged "privacy" of the private sphere and the exclusion of care from public life. They offer promising models for a liberal politics that is attentive to human flourishing without pitting virtues like compassion against more dominant liberal virtues like respect. Analogous to critics of Rawls's "idea of public reason," they argue that the privatization of love as a moral orientation is motivated by a desire to exclude women and women's experience from public life. Unlike much of analytic moral philosophy, they also provide accounts of caring that are not reducible to individualistic, altruistic, and sentimental conceptions of love.

In order to connect these developments with Augustinian liberalism, I read them alongside some of the most significant figures in modern Christian so-cial ethics. My focus will be restricted to the issue of love's relation to justice and power, and how this relationship informs the attitudes and dispositions of citizens. This convergence allows me to address how the virtue of love is concretized in action and not rendered dumb when confronted with the challenges of principled political judgment.

Chapter 4 marks a shift from Augustinianism to Augustine. With these more general frameworks at hand, I can reconstruct Augustinian liberalism in light of responses to Augustine's moral psychology of love and sin. To crys-tallize challenges to my reading, I turn to Hannah Arendt's 1929 Heidelberg dissertation on Augustine's idea of love and her broader analysis of the danger-ous relation of love to liberal politics. Written under the influence of Martin Heidegger, Rudolph Bultmann, and Karl Jaspers, Arendt's text has been ne-glected in both Augustine and Arendt studies. I outline Arendt's rejection of love as a relevant political virtue under the heading "the problem of passion." More systematically, I present Arendt's specific critique of Augustine's theol-ogy of love under the heading "the problem of God." This critique focuses on the Augustinian structure of love as desire and the multiple ways it jeop-ardizes genuine love for neighbor. Conveniently, Arendt's thesis powerfully confirms my claim that the relation between love for God (that supposedly points beyond the world) and love for neighbor (who manifestly is in the world) is a promising but troubled site for Augustinian political theology. In fact, contrary to most existentialist readers, Arendt recognizes that Augustine's greatest question may not be that he became a question to himself. Rather, the "magna quaestio" he asks is "whether humans should enjoy one another or use one another, or both"—or put differently, "whether one person should be loved by another on his own account or for some other reason" (*DDC* 1.22.20). Her criticisms of Augustine predate Nygren's more influential reading and are particularly problematic for my account because of her distinctively political concerns. Yet I argue Arendt's concerns about self-absorption and the demise of the public realm amidst a plurality of human loves are deeply Augustinian. Arendt imagines a common political world that "gathers us together and yet prevents our falling over each other" (*HC*, 52). Her antipathy to love is moti-vated by a moral concern to release politics from the exhausting demands of goodness. It is as if, for Arendt, the temptations of goodness inevitably lead to a premature intimacy that pridefully obliterates the diversity of public appearances and so shatters the common world. Like Augustinian liberals, I argue, Arendt is attracted to a grander style of politics, but she both embraces and reluctantly tolerates liberalism.

Despite its neglect, Arendt's dissertation prefigures much of today's revived philosophical interest in Augustine's notions of "inwardness," "subjectivity," and "otherness." Arendt's reading is more theological than most political interpretations of Augustine, but she pays a high analytic price for abstracting Augustine's account of love from his mature Christology. I offer a close reading of her three efforts to help Augustine find a place for genuine neighbor-love given his doctrine of God (God as "absolute future," God as "absolute past," and God "in Community"). In order to see more clearly how my Augustinian liberalism differs from Arendt and the vast majority of theologians and political theorists, I conclude the book with two chapters on potential resources within Augustine's writings that can help civic liberals respond to these challenges.

Chapter 5, on the "problem of passion" for liberal citizens, considers Augustine's criticism of the Stoics. Augustine assumes that love is an anthropological fact, and so it is ordinary to the human condition. Love is ordinary (not pathological), but it is hard and troubled on many sides. To use an analogy frequently repeated in his writings, our loves are like weights that guide us—or enchain us—through life. His moral psychology, grounded in his account of "rightly ordered loving," highlights human *agency* in terms of internal problems of habit, affection, motivation, and perception. The problem of loving is not simply a problem of knowing facts about the good, or of being free from external constraint. These problems, Augustine might think, are liberal (and Pelagian) fictions that miss the real mark: the *mala voluntas*, the "iron of my own will" that "hardens into compulsion" (*Conf.* 8.5.10). The problem of agency is learning how to love in the right way at the right time with the right will. Augustine does have a notion of love as benevolence, but it is not reducible to any familiar definition because of his complex account of the relation between loving, understanding, and willing. The structure of Augustinian love (like Platonism) is couched less in terms of "the will" and primarily in terms of vision and attention—the dynamic perception of the reality of other persons and the obligations this given reality commands. Augustinian love is primarily a willed mode of loving perception that involves both taking responsibility for oneself and solidarity with others and concern for their flourishing.

The mature Augustine holds that affections are necessary for this life of attention. They morally shape how we understand and see the world. How does this famous critic of his passions arrive at this position? I trace the development of Augustine's discussions of reason and emotion, relying heavily on a distinction he makes between passion *(pertubationes)* and emotion *(affectus)*. Augustine can depict the capricious and unstable character of the experience of the passions with the best of ancient Stoic and modern liberal accounts. He paints a dim picture of the "irrational passions of the soul" that toss a person "like a stormy sea" (*CD* 9.3). This is the Augustine who seeks in the changeless God the "rest and tranquil life" that will "fear nothing" (*Conf.* 2.10.18). But, I argue that his criticism of the Stoic ideal of freedom from emotion (*CD* 9 and 14) offers a radical break with significant political implications. Moreover, I offer a revisionist reading of the two most famous examples of Augustine's supposed attraction both to Stoic invulnerability and the neo-Platonic ascent of love: his regret at weeping over the death of Dido and his grief after the death of his unnamed friend. I argue their common use in criticism of Augustinian love is misguided given their dramatic and theological function. Through appeal to Iris Murdoch, I show that Augustine's concern is with escapism, a projection or retreat into simulacra that is actually a failure of emotion and love rather than an instance of their affirmation. The problem, he discovers, is that his emotions and loves were illusions and phantoms—enchantments of a lover refusing to love. In both cases, this is the pain that he confesses: not that he loved too much, but he did not really love (either the world or God) at all. It is only when he sees the compassion of God, the God who would become human, that Augustine would break from the hold of Stoic philosophy.

Breaking from Stoicism, however, generates its own set of problems. Thinking about love and politics at the same time is risky and liable to pathology. One contemporary theorist laments: "It is difficult to write of generosity today without conjuring up images of terror wrought by a religion that at once placed the movement of *caritas* and *agape*, giving and love, at the foundation of being and swept across the Americas during the conquest with a holocaust of 'generosity'."[37] My final chapter takes up the most contested texts in Augustine's account of the *ordo amoris* in response to this kind of problem.

37. Coles, *Rethinking Generosity*, 1.

Chapter 6 responds to the second of Arendt's challenges by refuting the claim that love for God either eclipses or instrumentalizes love for neighbor so as to render Augustinian love inconsistent with liberal politics. My argument again turns this criticism on its head: where Arendt finds antiliberal otherworldliness and others find pathological authoritarianism, I find an Augustinian ethics of democratic citizenship that both celebrates love and respects difference. Synthesizing the vast literature on Augustine's theological eudaimonism, I argue against readings of Augustine's "use" and "enjoyment" that rely on a preconceived subordinationist teleology (one that subordinates proximate goods as means to an ultimate good). These readings employ metaphysical categories of "hyper-transcendence" or "hyper-immanence" that need not be Augustinian (nor, for that matter, Platonic). My argument focuses on the moral dimensions of Augustine's discussions of the radical unity of the love of God and the love of neighbor. I connect these texts with some modern theological proposals. By way of conclusion, I discuss the power of traditional images in political theory and themes of nostalgia and the sacred.

Such is the structure of my book. Political theory and theology are contextual enterprises, and my interest in retrieving an Augustinian account of political motivation based on the relational virtue of love has its own motivations. One of the earliest motivations behind this book was a concern that an overly familiar characterization of political Augustinianism threatened the tradition (like Augustine's own restless self) with premature rest. On the one hand, a prideful Augustinianism is content to repeat its mantras about sin and the realistic limits of politics and virtue. This appeal to the limits of politics often travels with a stern appeal to a politics of necessity that can justify all manner of injustice in the name of two kingdoms, regretful responsibility, and "dirty hands." Lutheran streams of Augustinian politics are particularly vulnerable to this temptation, evident most recently in theological justifications of the use of torture to combat terrorism. On the other hand, an equally prideful Augustinianism celebrates its retreat into a postliberal withdrawal from political life altogether. In either case, I worried that a vital tradition of inquiry is in danger of becoming simply an entrenched cultural mood rather than a living argument that might still matter for our politics. This concern joined a frustration that sophisticated treatments of love in both Augustine studies and Christian ethics were disconnected from renewed efforts to relate virtues to liberal politics. This neglect has been enforced by theoretical preoccupation with epistemological issues related to democratic justification. At the same time, I also came to think that liberal theorists had become overly suspicious of love and that Augustinian liberals only rarely connect Augustine's account of love to their own proposals. This book is my effort to address these concerns and frustrations.

I

＋＋

Beyond Public Reason
Love, Sin, and Augustinian Civic Virtue

*Ethics should not be merely an analysis of ordinary mediocre
conduct, it should be a hypothesis about good conduct and
about how this can be achieved. How can we make ourselves better?
is a question moral philosophers should attempt to answer.*

IRIS MURDOCH, *The Sovereignty of Good*

*For it is one thing to inquire into the source of
evil and another to inquire how one can return to his
original good or reach one that is greater.*

AUGUSTINE, *Retractions*

＋＋

Augustinian liberalism is a modern tradition of theological inquiry and
social criticism. Though less dominant than during its heyday in the
twentieth century, this tradition's luminaries once included established Augustine scholars, influential Christian ethicists, social activists, and prominent public intellectuals. But that is no longer the case.

This kind of liberalism traditionally has been associated with wise counsels to observe the limits of politics and virtue, restrain evil through the constitutional rule of law, and remain alert to the self-defeating frustrations and real harms that haunt even our best moral efforts in a fragile and uncertain world. These counsels, especially in the West, are often held up as bulwarks against the excesses of democratic optimism and the dangers of theocratic authoritarianism. My project does not reject these counsels.

The realism of limits and the unmasking of vice, however, do not exhaust an Augustinian repertoire. The purpose of this study is to provide a "rational reconstruction" of Augustinianism that responds to recent developments in theology, political theory, and moral philosophy. Some of these developments offer strong challenges to Augustinian liberalism and have made it less attractive to religious and secular citizens alike. Other developments, especially in feminist and neo-Aristotelian ethics, offer positive resources that have not been sufficiently recognized by Augustinian liberals. Any reconstruction of Augustinian liberalism should not give comfort to a civil religion, however mild or subtle. My proposal does not offer another politics of meaning or a science of techniques that delivers us from the disappointing realities of human relations. And it certainly does not suggest we can "go back" to Augustine, clean up his theology, and enter a golden age of civic friendship, transparent intimacy, and moral progress. True to their origins, contemporary Augustinians are skilled in the arts of suspicion, poking holes in dreams and ideologies. Augustine would have none of the self-congratulation of the Romans or the noble lies of the Greeks: "Away, then, with concealments and deceitful whitewashings! Let these things be examined openly" (*CD* 3.14). He wanted to unmask illusion, to "strip off the deceptive veils," and "subject the facts to a strict inspection" (*CD* 3.14). Even a reconstructed Augustinian liberalism is bound by this Augustinian suspicion. There can be no truck with the "spin doctors" of empire—whether democratic, liberal, American, or Roman.[1]

Augustinians are usually identified as leading critics of Enlightenment ideas of progress that are guided by secular principles of rationality. They look to the happy end of the world, not the ruthless clamor of this grim, dying age of sadness. Like Augustine, they are impressed by a pirate's response to Alexander the Great: "Because I do it with a little ship I am called a robber, and because you do with a great fleet, you are an emperor"

1. Robert Dodaro notes that "we are not accustomed to reading Augustine in politically progressive tones" ("Eloquent Lies, Just Wars and the Politics of Persuasion," 79). In this essay, however, Dodaro aligns Augustine's critique of pagan rhetoric with Noam Chomsky's adoption of Augustine as his "patron saint" in his critique of the role of mass media in debates about the first Gulf War (ibid., 78). I borrow the metaphor of "spin doctor" from Dodaro: "For Augustine, Satan was the original 'spin doctor'; the archetypal political speech writer, campaign director and press secretary all rolled into one" (90).

(*CD* 4.4). Civic virtue, on this view, is a pagan sham. Textbook treatments of Augustinianism tend to stop here with an exclamation point. Yet the time has come to put Augustinian liberalism more explicitly within its proper context of critical admiration of liberal virtues and the aspirations of perfection rather than one of relentless negation. Here I follow Robert Markus's argument about the pirate story: "The point Augustine is making is not that societies are morally equally bad, or neutral, or all equally deficient, but that none can claim the only true justice, which is to be found only in the heavenly City" (*CS,* 63). Recent developments in revisionist liberal theory that take account of the moral life of citizens help my cause. But my approach is more novel, and more focused, than simply a restatement of an Augustinian liberalism responsive to these developments. Augustine's moral psychology of love—often taken to be his most antiliberal feature—can help Augustinians develop a more positive account of the social virtues proper to good citizenship in a liberal polity. This constructive approach is premised on a belief that Augustinian suspicions about the prideful elements of both politics and virtue, like Adam's Fall, do not go all the way down.

Augustinian liberals have emphasized the deeply fractured and broken features of the fallen human condition marked by sin and death, including their distinctive expressions in late modernity. They also have chastened the mythical hold that the ideal of political citizenship can have on accounts of those many excellences that constitute a life well lived, including the corporate worship of God. This "anti-politics" of rebellious spiritual liberation has been politically transformative, often inspiring social and political change despite itself. Augustine praised martyrs holding fast to their faith in ways that "shamed the laws by which it was forbidden, and caused them to be changed" (*CD* 8.19). But the tradition has not successfully contextualized these emphases within broader explorations of the plurality of human loving. It has been even less successful in finding a place for political engagement within a coherent (but always compromised) life of graced participation in the beauty and goodness of God radically expressed in the incarnate gifts of God.[2] These issues relate to a basic question from the introduction: how

2. For an elegant proposal regarding transcendence and immanence in contemporary theology, see Tanner, *Jesus, Humanity, and Trinity,* especially 1–33. Tanner draws from various patristic sources, but not Augustine. In modern theology, Augustine often is as-

robustly can Augustinians appeal to love or appeal to sin without throwing this relationship out of kilter?

Responding to this question will require doing some theological reconstruction. Given the relative neglect of theology in academic political theory, I take this to be a virtue of necessity in writing about Augustinianism. One does not have to hold that "ideas drive history" to think that beliefs about God's relations to the world play a significant role in actual democratic politics. Modern political history suggests that "theological rhetoric, child of political experience, may also be mother of political change."[3] If the idea of secularization as a fixed law of historical progress continues to turn out to be a scholar's myth, more theological reflection rather than less may help mitigate some of the potentially corrosive influences of religion in concrete relations of power.

The relation of love and sin has not been adequately formulated and balanced by the Augustinian tradition because its own proponents (alongside its critics) skew the relation either by avoiding the theological context in which these concepts arise or by accepting distorted modern refractions of some of their crucial elements. Augustinian liberals give too much comfort to their more theologically confident critics when they abandon talk about God. Nevertheless, non-Christian theorists should be interested in this project of formulating love and sin within the context of Augustinian liberalism for at least two reasons. First, Augustine is no marginal figure in the history of political thought. He belongs in the canon of great political theorists. His influence is wide and varied. Indeed, "Augustinianism" continues to be a seductive trope in an intellectual world that has largely rejected many of its core beliefs. To understand Augustinian politics, it is not enough to relegate distinctively theological commitments as incidental to "religious"

---

sociated with "philosophical" views (namely, neo-Platonic monism, radical subjectivity, and the opposition of time to eternity) at odds both with the revival of Trinitarianism in modern theology and contemporary efforts to overcome stark dualities between nature and grace. The tide, however, has turned on this familiar reading. Throughout this book, I rely on authors most responsible for this turn, including Henri de Lubac, Eugene TeSelle, John Milbank, Jean-Luc Marion, Lewis Ayres, Denys Turner, David Burrell, and Rowan Williams. My reading of the political implications of Augustinian theology is consistent with Tanner's general principles regarding a "non-competitive relation between creatures and God, and secondly, a radical interpretation of divine transcendence" (ibid., 2).

3. Nicholls, *Deity and Domination*, 14.

or "philosophical" views. Second, non-Christian theorists have their own versions of love and sin (often justified on anthropological grounds) that parallel those of Augustinians. They also suffer from the oscillation between antiliberal perfectionism, grounded in appeal to a secular analogue of Christian love, and merely negative political liberalism, grounded in appeal to a secular analogue of Christian sin. In fact, in addition to Hannah Arendt, my own formulation of these themes emerged via two non-Christian political theorists, William Connolly and Romand Coles.

These authors have wrestled with a wide range of Augustine's texts in illuminating ways. They have demonstrated the political implications of theological ideas often thought to be distant from the world of both political theory and democratic politics. Rather than dismiss Augustine's religious ideas, they have recognized that their "daunting task is to *reoccupy* them with alternatives that touch chords of being to which they respond."[4] Or, as Coles puts it, "Augustine's critique of the Roman pagan self can—among other things—draw attention to some of the dangers we face as we attempt to 'go it alone' without God."[5] In the end, Coles and Connolly find Augustine's monotheistic therapy for the conceits of imperialism, nihilism, and egoism serves to exacerbate rather than heal the disease of unreceptive closure to otherness. For them, Augustinian theology is more poison than cure, more about self than others. Its confessions, heresies, and conversions conceal structures of power and secure "moral identity through de-moralization of the other."[6] But, these authors show the value of exploring love and sin for secular political theory, especially for theorists who feel cramped by the legacy of the liberalism-communitarian debates and its safe construction of "religion and politics."

As a response to communitarian critics, secular conceptions of friendship, care, community, and sympathy also assume a more prominent role in Anglo-American neo-liberal thinking. Moreover, in addition to the love

4. Connolly, "Realizing Agonistic Respect," 510.

5. Coles, *Self/Power/Other*, viii. For Coles, "Augustine's analysis of the pagan illuminates a dynamic of egoism in a manner very significant for political social philosophers today (in a world where both conceptually and practically an atomistic individualism has reached extremes exceeding even those Augustine depicted)" (ibid., 49).

6. Connolly, *Augustinian Imperative*, xviii.

commands themselves, the parable of the Good Samaritan (Luke 10:25–37), the claim that "God is love" (1 John 4:8), and Paul's discourse on love (1 Cor. 13:1–13) all remain inscribed within the rhetorical, symbolic, and moral consciousness of even the most secularist societies. As for sin, the case for the continuing relevance of its secular analogues is even clearer. Many liberals adopt a realistic understanding of human nature largely guided by selfish concerns and narrow sympathies. Given that both theology and political theory share an interest in properly formulating these themes, convergence on similar solutions has the additional advantage of helping religious and secular liberals join together against antiliberalism. Before suggesting the normative arena for such a convergence, I need to say a bit more about Augustinian theology.

ORDERING LOVE: A CONTESTED THEOLOGICAL LEGACY

Political Augustinians are rarely accused of sentimentalist naïveté. My introduction made clear that Augustine's doctrine of love is no quick and easy alternative to his doctrine of sin. Love is not to be confused with trivial recollections of Sunday school politeness or teenage melodies, and political solidarity will not be free of agonistic conflict. The promise of love, even a love experienced as a command that "does not insist on its own way" (1 Cor. 13:5), certainly interrupts premature appeals to sin. But, for Augustine, sin always plays a role in human loving. It finds its mysterious birth in the radical freedom of love itself. Put another way, sin is a species within his internally diverse conception of love.[7] Vice always lurks among the virtues. And love, like cholesterol, can be healthy or deadly. Augustine, in fact, is famous for his ascetic account of the dangers and deceptions of love gone wrong. His

---

7. Augustine uses three primary terms for love: *amor*, *dilectio*, and *caritas*. I note their distinctive nuances when relevant, but in general I follow Augustine's tendency to use the terms interchangeably. I adopt the generic and multivalent word "love" for my own proposal for an ethic of citizenship. At times, I appeal to other modern idioms ("compassion," "charity," or "personal care") in order to highlight the way in which "love" exceeds any definition. In general, I follow Ramsey's claim that "love is just love, the genuine article, for which perhaps one univocal word should be reserved" (Ramsey, *Nine Modern Moralists*, 170).

erotic tales were meant to urge his readers to persevere in the steep ascent of wisdom, even if they now travel with the grim Augustine of most political anthologies and liberal imaginations. This is the Augustine who speaks of disordered love: "have not these trials everywhere filled up human affairs?" (*CD* 19.5). Augustinian political realism continues to attract religious and secular proponents. Yet, the prior logic of Augustine's theological account of love's relation to sin has its share of critics. In particular, these critics attack it as the bad fruit of his ostensibly Platonic account of love for God and love for neighbor. Despite a long history of scholarship that rejects this characterization of Augustine's eudaimonism, it remains the site where critics identify an otherworldly and life-denying solipsism fueled by a tournament of loves, human and divine, that is most unwelcome in modern religious and philosophical ethics. Some theological traditions, notably Protestant ones, would become wary of Augustine's language of love, preferring instead the language of faith; other philosophical traditions, notably Kantian ones, would become wary of the language of love as fragile, preferring the distance and stability of respect. Love, then, remains one of those words we can use to play out the history of massive theological and philosophical debates. My effort to rehabilitate an Augustinian conception of love in defense of a liberal politics may appear doomed from the start by turning to the most contested and antiliberal feature of Augustinianism.

Moral philosopher Annette Baier, for example, places Augustine against Hume alongside her other misamorists, Plato, Descartes, Spinoza, and Kant. She does so not because of Augustine's refusal to love, but because of his flight from the creaturely temporality of loving. For Augustine, she writes, "love of God will be a sort of live vaccine that will block any riskier loving."[8] Paul Ramsey, the Christian ethicist most responsible for restoring a concept of love to modern political ethics, shares the view that "something has gone wrong in Augustine's analysis" (*BCE,* 123). According to Ramsey, the religiosity of Augustine's Neoplatonism ensures that "the neighbor too often seems lost in God, love for neighbor in love for God" (123). Most political liberals, we shall see, worry about the political consequences of both Baier's risky loves and Ramsey's Christian neighbor-love. They would just as soon jettison love from our political vocabulary. Some associate love with the weakness of self-sacrifice or the confusions of benevolence faced with

8. Baier, *Moral Prejudices,* 36.

complex circumstances of scarcity and narrow sympathy. Both associations make it a poor cousin to justice. More worrisome for many liberals, however, is love's connection to Homeric *thumos,* Platonic *eros,* organicist *Gemeinschaft,* or a Rousseauian compassion that seeks to "make men free." As Paul Tillich noted more than fifty years ago, love has been "rejected in the name of a formal concept of justice, and under the assumption that community is an emotional principle adding nothing essential to the rational concept of justice—on the contrary, endangering its strictness" (*LPJ,* 62). At best, love must wait until liberty and equality have their say. These associations perpetuate liberal assumptions about an opposition between love and respect. The experience of love may be one of the summit experiences of a human life, but it is dangerous for a politics that is tempted to enforce moral goodness.

Given the demoralizing historical connection between love and religious violence, adverting to a love that has a divine referent only exacerbates liberal concerns. As one defender of liberalism puts it, "what makes for poetry in the soul begets fascism in the city."[9] Paraphrasing Richard Rorty's account of the need to separate public and private morality, Gary Gutting here captures the classically liberal claim that, though religious love may sometimes be beautiful, it is publicly terrifying. Martha Nussbaum, by contrast, commends Augustine for reopening the significance of human emotions and for refusing a Platonic "wish to depart from our human condition" (*UT,* 547).[10] She concludes that his achievements are not compatible with liberal politics for a different reason: "The aim of slipping off into beatitude distracts moral attention from the goal of making this world a good world, and encourages a focus on one's own moral safety that does not bode well for earthly justice" (553).

9. Gutting, *Pragmatic Liberalism,* 59. For a similar diagnosis, see Stephen Holmes, "The Permanent Structure of Antiliberal Thought," in Nancy L. Rosenblum, ed., *Liberalism and the Moral Life* (Cambridge, Mass.: Harvard University Press, 1989), 227–53.

10. Nussbaum offers a more positive portrait of Augustine in this work than in her other writings that tend to cast his ideas in terms of a dehumanizing escapism. Nussbaum's commendations, however, remain qualified by her adoption of Hannah Arendt's reading of Augustine's account of love, the subject of my third chapter. She endorses Arendt's claims "with some tentativeness" (*UT,* 552), a tentativeness expressed in Nussbaum's remarks that "it is a little unclear what role is left in *The Confessions* for loving real-life individual people" (549) and "there is some question as to how this confessing lover can be said to have a neighbor at all" (550). But Nussbaum's final negative verdict of Augustine is decisive: "Augustine assails as the origin of evil the very root of liberal politics" (556).

For Nussbaum, the austerity of Augustinian love ultimately yields this advice: "Instead of taking action as best we can, we had better cover ourselves, mourn, and wait" (556). Augustinian love furnishes a spiritual eroticism unsuitable for this historical world that demands material action against injustice and "an ongoing compassion for human life" (590).[11] In Christian theology, Rosemary Radford Ruether similarly argues that Augustine fails to provide "a sufficiently hopeful basis for conducting a moral struggle toward the political order."[12] In effect, Augustine's defeatism makes history a waiting game. The political dramas of the world are to be endured until the Christian self inwardly related to the eternal is delivered from this tragedy. Enthusiastic triumphalism or passive quietism is the dialectic of Augustinianism. My rehabilitation of the political implications of an Augustinian theological ethics of love will dramatically depart from these varied judgments.

Under the pressure of his reading of the Christian Scriptures and his identification of God with the compassion of the crucified Jesus, Augustine sought not to bury but to redeem the moral and emotional dimensions of life "in this time." In particular, by highlighting the summary and the fulfillment of the law in terms of the twofold love commands (Matt. 22:37–40), he would try to *open the cultural space for emotional investment with those who suffer injustice* and to accentuate the practical responsibility this entails. The figure of Jesus presented Augustine with the flesh and blood of compassion. Emotions, then, are not simply sentiments. In moving us to action, they become instruments of justice in accord with right reason. In chapter 5, I discuss the relation of these emotions to a justification for making a civic appeal that public officials ought to be held accountable for ordering a shared life responsive to injustice and ordered as much as possible toward human flourishing. Here I want to highlight the way in which Augustinianism provides a complex geography of love.

Augustine's original account of Christian love can be seen as navigating between the cultural and philosophical assumptions of "ethically respon-

---

11. Nussbaum contrasts Augustinian Christianity with her own understanding of Judaism that "gives the moral sphere considerable autonomy and centrality, seeing the concern of God for man as essentially moral and political, focused on this-worldly concerns and actions, and intelligible from the point of view of a this-worldly use of intelligence" (*UT*, 549). For a critical interpretation of Nussbaum's understanding of religious ethics, see Kavka, "Judaism and Theology in Martha Nussbaum's Ethics."

12. Ruether, "Christian Political Theology," 263.

sible" Stoicism and "spiritual" Platonism. My Augustinian account of love that follows Augustine's innovations on these classical traditions is both affective and cognitive, and oriented both to the world and God. To briefly preview this argument, Augustinianism motivates and sustains love for the neighbor (even the neighbor as fellow citizen), but it also recognizes the need to discipline our incontinent loves in a world constrained by sin. In fact, to put it crudely, the problem of political morality for an Augustinian is not so much that we love others too little. This is the familiar problem of motivation in contemporary ethical theory that tries to generate other-regard in the face of self-interest. But the deeper problem is that we love too much in the wrong ways. Our motivations and desires are out of whack, not simply lacking. Our affections are distracted and crowded by their very excess not their scarcity. They need ordering, not the pruning or repression of desire. To reverse traditional readings, Augustinian lovers suffer from plenitude, not poverty. We are overwhelmed by the good things of the world and, in moments of speculative excess, we are tempted to grasp the Good as our own rather than to be in relation with it. This recognition does not "instrumentalize" the world; rather, it releases political communities from pressures they cannot bear even as it addresses the self-enclosed anxieties about otherness that often generate antiliberalism and religious persecution.

Augustine's critics, both secular and religious, have become too enamored by his formative rhetorical contrasts between *amor Dei* ("love of God") and *amor mundi* ("love of the world") as well as his more technical distinction between *uti* love of neighbor ("using" love) and *frui* love of God ("enjoying" love). It is difficult to read him without reading into him the future of both Christian spirituality and metaphysics, or at least the dualistic future that now dominates modern memory of his legacy.[13] The difficulty of maintaining the unity yet duality of these double loves is not a uniquely modern one. Hyper-Augustinianism—with its visions of a totalitarian God and worthless humanity or a false "public body" and a true "inner soul" safely locked up and protected from the world—has been the besetting temptation of the

---

13. For the mistaken reception history of Augustinian metaphors (especially "interiority," "ascent," "light and darkness," and "oneness with God"), see Turner, *Darkness of God*, 50–101. Turner argues that "modern interpretation has invented 'mysticism' and that we persist in reading back the terms of that conception upon a stock of mediaeval authorities who knew of no such thing—or, when they knew of it, decisively rejected it" (7).

Augustinian legacy for some time. It lies deep in the history of Western intellectual and artistic culture.[14] It provided the context for much of early modern moral and political philosophy intent on carving out a space for human autonomy and self-governance within the world. And, in a variety of ways, it continues to shape contemporary discussions of religion, politics, and virtue.

Is there another way to interpret Augustine's account of love different from those described above? I think there is a defensible and attractive alternative that does not competitively abandon God for the sake of the human. It involves a shift in perspective from the prevalence of static metaphysical categories to a more dynamic theological account of moral psychology. Augustine does not separate moral psychology from what we now call ontology. That refusal is part of what makes Augustine a challenging, though interesting, figure for contemporary thought bent on overcoming metaphysics. Augustine does not, like many religious thinkers (including some Augustinians), reduce theology to anthropology. In fact, the ontological character of love—predicated on a difference between God and creation—is an important feature of Augustinian thought that diverges from a modern focus on the ethical character of love as fellow-feeling or benevolence. Nonetheless, Augustine's intellectual energies are devoted to an exploration of how one is to love without desperately trying to possess and consume any good (finite or infinite). It is tempting to claim that Augustinian political theology is moral, not metaphysical. We might just turn nouns into verbs: the order of love (the "what") into the ordering of love (the "how"). But that is a misleading formulation at this point. It pushes the apophatic moments in Augustinian theology over the edge, and it fails to account for the way in which the radical transcendence of God is a way of making room for that which is not God. Ontology still matters. To love an eternal and incomprehensible God, for Augustine, stretches the soul to allow for a qualitatively different kind of love which can now include all that is not God. God is not an exhaustible or scarce resource, subject to competing claims. In his God, "our love will know no check" (*CD* 11.28; see also *De Libero Arbitrio* 2.37).

14. See, for example, R. Freyhan, "The Evolution of the Caritas Figure in the Thirteenth and Fourteenth Centuries," *Journal of the Warburg and Courtauld Institutes* 11 (1948): 68–86. Freyhan traces artistic representations of *amor Dei* and *amor proximi* in terms of an emerging division between religious and moral life.

Sin does find its ground in the excessive attachment to finite goods—a claim that worries many of his modern readers who see a flight from the natural world. But Augustine's worry is neither the status of these objects qua finite objects nor the finitude of human nature as such. His account of creation, incarnation, and resurrection precludes such a view, particularly if this worry is understood as devaluing the goodness of created objects or putting them in conflictual relation with one another. "Everything that exists is good," he famously declares, and "all exist because they are severally good but collectively very good, for our God has made all things exceedingly good" (*Conf.* 7.12.18). This conviction underlies his privation theory of evil as perversion of good: "There cannot exist a nature in which there is no good . . . in so far as it is a nature, not even the nature of the devil himself is evil" (*CD* 19.13). To be sure, Augustine does highlight what he takes to be the foundational ontology of a person: a creature of God that is not God but participates in the divine life. But his ethical analysis allows us to concentrate on the narcissism that characterizes the quality of our attachments and desires themselves: "In all such matters what is reprehensible is not the use made of things but the user's desire" (*DDC* 3.12.18).

Augustine focuses like a laser on the way in which human loving compensates for contingency and mortality by projecting onto these goods our own little self-referential worlds of fixed meaning. Possessiveness and corruptibility, marked by the failure to acknowledge vulnerability and dependence, are the key terms of his moral psychology. *Affectus* and *intentio* lie at the crossroad of "psychology" and "ontology." The intersection of this crossroad is the Augustinian concept of an *ordo amoris*. Recent discussions of this concept invariably focus on the "what" of loving, but I want to move to the related category of the "how" of loving. Augustine is not engaged in an abstract metaphysical speculation on *what* one can safely consider to be appropriate objects of love. Augustine's God does not compete with the neighbor for the self's attention, as if God were simply the biggest of those rival objects considered worthy of love. In short, his God is not a *particular* thing.[15]

---

15. For similar claims about Aquinas's God, see Denys Turner, "On Denying the Right God: Aquinas on Atheism and Idolatry," in Jim Fodor and Frederick Christian Bauerschmidt, eds., *Aquinas in Dialogue: Thomas for the Twenty-First Century* (Oxford: Blackwell Publishing, 2004), 137–56.

For Augustine, "That Which Is" (*Conf.* 7.17.23) is the very source of love and existence. All things have existence "through Him Who simply is" (*CD* 8.6). Augustine's God transcends any metaphysical frame of reference that might measure the reality of God in relation to other realities in some hierarchy of ascending goods. His God is not a collection of the maximal set of possible attributes—having qualities like goodness or beauty. For Augustine's God, "it is not one thing to exist and another to live, as if he could exist without living; nor, to Him, is it one thing to live and another to understand, as though he might live but not understand" (*CD* 8.6). This God is "improperly called substance, in order to signify being by a more usual word" (*DT* 7.3.10). To love this God, according to Augustine, is not to love "this or that good but good itself" (*DT* 8.2.4). As such, rather than being morally paralyzed by the infinite claims of the neighbor or spiritually distracted by the infinite claims of God, the Augustinian self loves the neighbor in God. To love the neighbor "in God," Augustine's mature formulation, aims to morally protect the neighbor from the self's prideful distortion that the neighbor exists only in terms of one's own ends, or that the neighbor is a threat to the self's relation to this infinite God. Disordered loving *(cupiditas)* grasps at carnal images of divinity and the neighbor, refusing to recognize them as really and inexhaustibly other. It makes them our own and places them under our control *(libido dominandi)*. This is the Platonic and Pelagian lust—to grasp what can only be given—that is humbled by grace in order to share in the social life of a "plurality of persons" (*CD* 15.16, Bettenson). Augustine values individuality and the separateness of plurality, but this kind of atomistic individualism, to borrow from one of his favorite metaphors for sin, would be a kind of theft—robbing the fellow neighbor and the transcendent God of their separate identity beyond our absorbing self-conceptions. *On Christian Doctrine, On the Trinity,* and Augustine's many homilies and letters can best be read as reflections on the dangers of a "thieving" adolescent love that dominates both neighbor and God. This imagery provides political Augustinianism with resources that can overcome the unhelpful tendency to read the *Confessions* merely as spiritual autobiography and the *City of God* merely as depressing political theory.

Augustinians do not love their neighbor "for their own sake," as if any person actually exists independently of a relation to others participating in the goodness of God.[16] To be sure, Augustinians claim to love *them*, as creatures: "Not that the creature is not to be loved, but if that love is related to the creator it will no longer be covetousness but charity" (*DT* 9.2.3). Our love is "one and the same love," but we "love God because He is God; we love ourselves and the neighbor, however, as orientated to God" (*DT* 8.9.12). Human nature is not a wicked, false reality to be abandoned and passed over. Even the "enemy," a highly unstable category for Augustine, is to be loved and respected as a creature of God. Augustinians can provide reasons for this love and respect. But these justificatory reasons rely on a belief that human beings, in a strict theological sense, are not autonomous. They are not unconditioned ends in themselves simpliciter. Anthropology and morality, then, are not separate from theology just as grace is not only a response to human sin (*DT* 13.4.15). God and creation are radically distinct, but there are not two orders of reality, one spiritual and the other natural. It is logically possible to imagine such a self-sufficient being, but an Augustinian world always already suspended in God resists such a possible metaphysical reality. Human nature "refers to human nature in its concrete, divinely dependent reality."[17] To admit this much is to raise the contested question of the independence of the natural from the supernatural, a prominent debate in twentieth century Thomism that now spills over into Protestant theology and ethics.[18] On the Augustinian view, the dignity of a particular human person is grounded in participation with something other than what that person privately possesses or determines. The person is a creature of God and to be loved as such. Augustine uses the Latin word *dignitas* over forty times in his corpus, but it is clearly a transformation of heroic Roman "dignity." The dualistic idea of a human nature with a self-generating natural end and an eschatological supernatural end is denied in order to fend off an implicit naturalism

16. Aquinas maintains Augustine's position: "It would be wrong if a man loved his neighbor as though he were his last end, but not, if he loved him for God's sake" (*ST*, II-II.23.1; cf. *ST*, I-II.1.6, and I.II.99.1). For commentary, see Milbank, *TST*, 231.

17. Louis Dupré, introduction to Henri De Lubac, *Augustinianism*, x.

18. See, for example, Milbank, *TST*, 206–55, and Milbank, *The Suspended Middle: Henri de Lubac and the Debates Concerning the Supernatural* (London: SCM, 2005). I take issue with Milbank's "post-political theology," but he is right to highlight the political implications of this theological revolution and the limits of Christian social ethics detached from theological doctrine.

that turns both grace and God merely into an addendum to what is already present "naturally." Kierkegaard would accent this Augustinian claim in his presentation of God as the "middle term" in all relationships.[19] Theocentric reference, as it were, goes all the way down without conflating the grace of incarnation and the grace of creation. This is a striking and potentially scandalous claim for post-Kantian liberals (and some Christian proponents of *agape* who fear a love always looking over the neighbor's shoulder to God). They fear moral obligation and rational agency are somehow threatened by this appeal to love. I argue it need not be a pernicious love that vitiates the moral integrity of the neighbor by treating her as a mere means to an end or loving only what she might yet become.

Christian love is more than either liberal respect or utilitarian benevolence. But that "more" neither denigrates respect for persons nor elevates altruism above self-regard. To love the neighbor "for the sake of something else" (*propter aliud,* Augustine's early phrase) is to love the neighbor "in virtue of" and "in the way that" a loving God also loves any neighbor. To love someone in virtue of another loving that person, even in human relationships, does not eclipse the value of the beloved or deny the importance of mutual recognition. In fact, I will argue that it protects the neighbor from a human tendency to consume one another, to exhaust others with our enjoyment of them rather than participate with them in the enjoyment of God. Neighbors can really be my neighbors when they are not just my neighbors in my world. Love overcomes any absolute bifurcation of utility and delight. It attends to the individual person as a wonderful creature participating in the luminous beauty of God. The neighbor is concretely loved in her own particular identity as a "rational soul," and not simply as a general instance of a common humanity or derivative of a love for God.[20] But a neighbor's sui generis identity participates in the differentiated reality of God's creation. For Augustinians, then, the internal and coincident relation between love

19. Kierkegaard, *Works of Love,* 113. Thus, Gene Outka emphasizes love for God may "throw up certain limits around the character and intensity of neighbor-love" (Outka, *Agape,* 52).

20. The modern English word "self" does not have an exact Latin equivalent, but Augustine scholars tend to read *animus* ("soul") and *mens* ("mind") as the closest equivalents to what English-speaking philosophy calls the "self" or the "personal subject." A credible case, however, can also be made for *cor* ("heart") as the self—see Edgardo de la Peza, *El Significado de 'Cor' in San Augustin* (Paris: Etudes Augustiniennes, 1962).

of God and love of neighbor provides an integrated motivational ideal for human action *(caritas)* that does not place these two loves in principled competition with one another.[21] In fact, Augustine makes a bracing move that has played an important role in modern Christian social ethics: "The two commandments cannot exist without each other" (*DT* 8.5.12). Indeed, for Augustine, "if you do not love the brother whom you see, how can you love God whom you do not see?" (*IoEp.* 9.10). On this view, self-reliance is a kind of slavery, not Emersonian nirvana.

At a sociological level, this conception of loving another as a fellow creature in God ("one for whom Christ has died") has fostered compelling commitments to the equal dignity of persons and the creation of civic institutions that manifest this commitment. It is also likely, though I do not pursue this claim, that this conception of equality before a loving God has encouraged a fearless independence of mind and spirit that is necessary for the self-respect a democratic society requires—especially among those most threatened by cultural constructs that demean them. To know oneself as a beloved "child of God"—"born of the Spirit," "raised with Christ," and called to a distinct vocation of one's own—is perhaps the ultimate form of mutual recognition. It may encourage false consciousness, but it can also encourage a certain distance from the assigned social roles of the dominant culture. Augustine makes this very argument against the vanity of the classical citizens beholden to the opinion of others (*CD* 1.28). He also claims that "turning the other cheek" is an allegorical form of confident assertion of identity rather than passive submission (*EnPs.* 120.10 and *Ep.* 138, 34–39). His church was meant to be a site of real equality. Regardless of how pagan society operated, everyone shared fully and equally in its sacramental life. Martha Nussbaum, no fan of Augustine's theology, credits Augustine's

---

21. Robert M. Adams has highlighted the need to develop the ethics of motivational structures within contemporary moral philosophy and theological ethics (Adams, *Finite and Infinite Goods*, 177–98). My Augustinian formulation of the love commands is consistent with Adams's proposal to organize "the ethics of motives around an ideal of love for the good as such" (179), particularly in terms of his theistic proposal of the good and his own solution to the problem of "accommodating genuine love for finite objects within an ideal devotion to God" (192). Adams, however, explicitly rejects Augustine's motivational account of love because of what he takes to be its subordinationist teleological structure. In chapter 6, I reject this reading and suggest that Augustine's Trinitarian account is responsive to Adams-like concerns.

Christianity "in moving society toward equal concern for the deprived, the poor, and the different" (*UT,* 548). To be sure, Augustinians should not ignore ideological abuses of claims about eschatological identity before God in order to subjugate and to pacify the marginalized. Criticism of slave morality is not to be dismissed out of hand. It may well be the case that some Christians believe, as one critic argues, that "the lesson Christians are supposed to learn from Jesus' humiliating journey is to consider humiliating behavior as a trial rather than a sound reason for feeling humiliated."[22] Augustinian Christianity, as we shall see, can valorize humiliation (even violent humiliation) as a lesson against pride. But radical deconstructions of the historical reality of Christian resistance to humiliation, to my mind, often adopt the perspective of the comfortable rather than the afflicted in rejecting any role for an eschatological vision.

Reinhold Niebuhr argued that "the paradox of man as creature and man as child of God is a necessary presupposition of a concept of individuality, strong enough to maintain itself against the pressures of history, and realistic enough to do justice to the organic cohesions of social life."[23] My argument remains agnostic as to whether or not alternative justifications of equal dignity (for example, secular conceptions of rational capacity) can motivate and sustain this commitment.[24] I highlight Augustine's participationist anthropology not only to challenge his critics but to make this emphasis more explicit among political Augustinians. Rather than undermining liberalism, this Augustinian notion of love can support some perhaps surprising commitments. To refer love and virtue to God releases self-righteous possession of moral goodness and introduces a vigilant skepticism toward the prideful motives lurking behind the promotion of virtue in others.[25] This way of conceiving, or better yet, practicing love addresses the dangers of those appeals to love that have fostered oppressive and paternalistic violations of the dignity of human persons. As such, a reconstructed Augustine provides

22. Margalit, *Decent Society,* 12. Margalit offers a compelling argument that "a civilized society is one whose members do not humiliate one another, while a decent society is one in which the institutions do not humiliate people" (1).

23. Niebuhr, *Nature and Destiny,* 1: 24.

24. For arguments that these formulations do not generate this commitment, see O'Donovan, *Resurrection,* 237–44, and *Ways of Judgment,* 40–51.

25. I owe this accent on the significance of "reference" and "dispossession" for Augustine's account of virtue to conversations with James Wetzel and John Cavadini.

a model for correlating autonomy and compassion through a this-worldly love based on a "nonpossessive eros."[26] By refusing the antithetical opposition of autonomy and compassion, an Augustinian conception of a social self might also refuse both a liberal politics of self-interest and a communitarian politics of benevolence. It provides an Augustinian liberalism that is both more theological and able to enrich contemporary secular discussions of the virtues and emotions of liberal citizens.

EXPANDING AUGUSTINIAN LIBERALISM BEYOND BOOK 19

The reader might still wonder what is actually new in this approach. Have not love and sin always been fundamental categories, at least for political Augustinianism if not modern political philosophy?[27] Isn't political Augustinianism all about interpreting the relevance of Augustine's pregnant claim that "two cities, then, have been created by two loves" (*CD* 14.28)? Love and sin have been fundamental themes, but their relation to ethics and politics has been obscured for two related reasons. The first reason has been a narrow concentration on the locus classicus of political Augustinianism: Book 19 of the *City of God*. There are good reasons for the authority of this particular text. I do not intend to undermine its canonical status for Augustinian liberalism. It is "a microcosm of Augustine's social thought."[28] Augustinian liberals, however,

---

26. I appropriate this term from H. Richard Niebuhr, *Christ and Culture*, 18. Niebuhr, however, uses the term to describe divine rather than human love. Some scholars argue that Platonism also offers something like a "non-appetitive *eros*." See John P. Rist, *Eros and Psyche: Studies in Plato, Plotinus and Origen* (Toronto: University of Toronto Press, 1964), especially 30–34 and 204–207, and Osborne, *Eros Unveiled*, especially 52–85.

27. I use the term "political Augustinianism" in a broader sense than its meaning given prominence by H.-X. Arquilliere, *L'augustinisme politique: Essai sure la formation des theories politique du moyen age* (Paris: Vrin, 1934). Arquilliere's expression refers to medieval appropriations of Augustine (i.e., Gregory the Great and Isidore of Seville) that are thought to identify the "supernatural" church and the "natural" state. In fact, Arquillere's thesis generally implies the theocratic absorption of nature by supernature. My use refers to the political implications of Augustinianism, whatever these implications are taken to be. Significantly, Arquilliere did not ascribe political Augustinianism to Augustine himself, but suggests Augustine's rhetoric left the medieval West open to this development (especially during the Carolingian period).

28. O'Donovan, "*City of God* 19," 72.

too often claim this book either as a vague endorsement of the modern separation of church and state or as license to contrast ancient concepts of virtue with a proto-modern Augustinian politics of liberty.[29] The second reason for the eclipse of love in political Augustinianism emerges when a narrow focus on sin coincides with such misleading generalizations, especially with regard to Augustine's moral hostility to classical conceptions of virtue and political community. This methodology has left Augustinian liberals particularly vulnerable to more theologically ambitious Augustinian critics.

Augustine's complex and contested relation to ancient philosophy—beginning with his enthusiasm for philosophy after reading Cicero's *Hortensius*—has been an enduring subject in modern Augustine studies. These studies offer discrete accounts of Augustine's eclectic relation to pagan philosophy and culture, but they each propose a more subtle relationship than mere discontinuity and negative judgment. Augustine belongs to both philosophy and theology. I here take a side in the long debate about "philosophy" and "theology," agreeing with James Wetzel that Augustine's "invective against philosophy should be set in the context of his family quarrel with past philosophers and not dramatized into his rejection of philosophy per se" (*LV*, 10).[30] This does not mean I read Augustine as a philosopher of the virtues, bracketing all that theology. With Wetzel, I worry about those commentators who do Augustine the "dubious favor of saving his philosophy from his theology" (*LV*, 9). This strategy has been particularly attractive for political Augustinians who like to talk about religion but are not sure what to do with the particularity of Christian God talk.

In addition to these developments in Augustine studies, scholars of Greco-Roman philosophy have recast our image of ancient philosophical texts by emphasizing their therapeutic function and setting. Ancient texts, these scholars argue, should be not be read as technical doctrinal theses on metaphysical and epistemological topics. Rather, they serve as practical meditations for moral and spiritual formation *(askesis)*. In fact, Pierre Hadot

29. O'Donovan points out that the "separation of Church and state," is by itself an "uncommunicative formula, to be sure, since those words assert nothing that could have perturbed the most traditional apologist for dual jurisdiction in Christendom" (*DN*, 244).

30. Carol Harrison points out that "in contrast to his positive attitude to much of pagan philosophy, and in particular Platonism, Augustine's attitude to pagan religious practice is unreservedly negative" (*Augustine*, 21).

bracingly has described ancient philosophy as "spiritual exercises."[31] To put this in Augustinian terms, the point of all inquiry is eminently practical: the living wisdom that is the love of God and neighbor. The cool rationality of the seminar room is not the right context for understanding this approach that joins prayer to philosophy in order to change lives, not just "philosophical" opinions. Classical philosophy was not consumed with the security of holding proper beliefs. As John Rist puts it, it was not even "a mere ethic of good training inducing good habits"; it was "an ethics of inspiration" (*ATB*, 153). It was Augustine's reading of *Hortensius* that provoked his quest for wisdom rather than cleverness or eloquence. He claims this book "changed my way of feeling" (*Conf.* 3.4.7). The change of *feeling* is notable. As with his reading of the Platonist books, emotion could release him "*intellectually* from the prison of his materialist philosophy."[32] It is important to note that it changes *his* way of feeling, not just any wise person's. This is the "inwardness of radical reflexivity" that Charles Taylor claims is one of Augustine's signal contributions to Western thought.[33] Of course, as Taylor argues, it is an inwardness that opens the self to God. Augustine engages his reader so that she might also love and feel rightly just as much as he desperately wants to be known. His confession is a narration for others, and it is "this intersubjective quality that makes Augustine's *Confessions* unique in ancient literature of the soul."[34] Augustine's loving is neither gentle nor mild; ascent to this wisdom is always being "swept back" and "dragged away" by habits and passions (*Conf.* 7.17.23). Philosophy is as much a struggle as the moral life. This language of being "swept" or "beaten" back is pervasive. His demanding response is not without danger.

Augustine thought confession and repentance play a central role in a life that always presses forward in the struggle for moral excellence and self-discovery. *Askesis* and *disciplina* have their dark sides, even when embarked upon in the name of removing obstacles for the sake of self-realization and freedom before a holy God. Augustine, as much as Foucault, knew the pathological dangers as well as the social inevitability of practices that work

31. Hadot, *Philosophy as a Way of Life*, especially 81–144.
32. Turner, *Darkness of God*, 67.
33. Taylor, *Sources of the Self*, 130.
34. Stock, *Augustine the Reader*, 16.

on the body and the soul.[35] Power has its negative and positive expressions in shaping and reorganizing our moral dispositions. Peter Brown notes that Augustine was "obsessed by the difficulties of thought, and by the long, coercive processes, reaching back to the horror of his schooldays that had made this intellectual activity possible."[36] Unlike many moderns, Augustine held it was a plain fact that the beliefs and desires of fragile creatures like us can be changed by external pressure. To think otherwise, for Augustine, was the illusion of an autonomous self. Obsession, coercion, prayer, and charity make a potent combination when allied to authoritarian practices of manipulative examination and legal punishment. Therapy and confession can construct their own prisons of surveillance, especially when wedded to a demand to make every virtue and vice a public concern. Religious ethicists, especially those interested in the ethics of virtue, have begun to make effective use of this different genre of philosophy as both theory and practice.[37]

How might this turn relate to political Augustinianism? The intensity of Augustine's psychological drama continues to preoccupy readers concerned with the art of living. But one of the great achievements of Augustine's *City of God* was its capacity to frame moral anthropology as social philosophy: "Two cities, then, have been created by two loves: that is, the earthly city by love of self extending even to contempt of God, and the heavenly city by love of God extending to contempt of self" (*CD* 14.28). Indeed, for Augustine, "the source of blessedness is not one thing for a human being and another for a city" (*Ep.* 155, 92). It was this reading of politics that led to his transformation of Cicero's definition of a "people" as a multitude "united in fellowship by common agreement as to what is right and by a community

---

35. Joyce Schuld argues that "for Augustine as well as for Foucault, the inescapable hazards of our social environment are rooted in the fragility of human relationships and the formative dynamism of relational desires" (*Foucault and Augustine*, 8). In recommending Foucault's "theology of Church history," John Milbank also highlights the dangers of discipline and order becoming ends in themselves, "concentrating on the minute regulation of bodies in time and space" (*TST*, 433).

36. Brown, *Augustine of Hippo*, 232.

37. See, for example, Aaron Stalnaker, "Spiritual Exercises and the Grace of God: Paradoxes of Personal Formation in Augustine," *Journal of the Society of Christian Ethics* 24, no. 2 (Fall/Winter 2004): 137–70, and E. Jane Doering and Eric O. Springsted, eds., *The Christian Platonism of Simone Weil* (Notre Dame, Ind.: University of Notre Dame Press, 2004).

of interest" (*CD* 19.21). Rejecting this idealist claim to justice, Augustine apparently proposed a more empirical definition focused on acts of willing and loving:

> Let us say that a 'people' is an assembled multitude of rational creatures bound together by a common agreement as to the objects of their love. In this case, if we are to discover the character of any people, we have only to examine what it loves. If it is an assembled multitude, not of animals but of rational creatures, and is united by a common agreement as to what it loves, then it is not absurd to call it a 'people,' no matter what the objects of its love may be. Clearly, however, the better the objects of this agreement, the better the people; and the worse the objects, the worse the people. (*CD* 19.24)

Interpretations of this passage focus on the implicit relation between Augustine's political ontology and the possibility of a "relative" justice for earthly communities. These issues remain hotly contested in Augustine studies. Some defend a "neutral" or "empirical" reading, others defend an "idealist" reading, and still others bring them together.[38] For my purposes, what is striking is the way in which this text functions in contemporary Augustinian social criticism.

Taking up Augustine's invitation to view a "people" in terms of their objects of love, Augustinian liberals have engaged in immanent criticism of a variety of social practices and institutions that jeopardize the dignity of the human person and the goals of justice and peace. At their best, these Augustinians offer positive alternatives to these social practices. One might think

---

38. The "neutral, positivistic" reading can be found in Markus, *SAE*, 65. Rowan Williams rejects Markus and argues that Augustine's redefinition is ironic, serving to further expose the injustice and atomistic individualism of a political society that is not ordered by the love of God (Williams, "Politics and the Soul"). Oliver O'Donovan considers Markus under the rubric of the "realist" reading, and Williams under the rubric of "idealist" reading. He offers a reading on which the two might converge: "In denying 'justice' to religiously defective societies, Augustine meant what he said; yet the 'justice' which the heavenly city embodies is not merely supramundane: it answers to 'the right' as it is generally recognized and universally desired" (O'Donovan, "*City of God* 19," 61). Robert Dodaro argues that Augustine's primary interest is not the "respective merits of a Christian or secular state," but a Christological focus on the person of Christ "as both the only completely just human being ever to have lived and the only exponent of virtue whose teaching effectively establishes justice in other human beings" (Dodaro, *Just Society*, 17 and 26).

that Augustine himself would have engaged in this style of criticism. It was certainly available to him. His unmasking of the consoling illusions of Roman imperialism is considered an ur-text for all social criticism. In fact, for John Milbank, we discover in Augustine's writings "the *original* possibility of critique that marks the western tradition, of which later Enlightenment versions are, in certain respects, abridgements and foundationalist parodies" (*TST,* 389). With the moral seriousness of a satirist, Augustine ridiculed Rome's impotent yet violent efforts to secure virtue, charging that they were based on an excessive love of glory and a perverse culture of shame and honor. Peter Brown likens Augustine's sarcastic unmasking of Roman civic mythology to a "nineteenth-century free-thinker demolishing a religious belief."[39] This is the Augustinian deconstruction.

Augustine's account of the need to discipline the desires of citizens (beyond concern for social recognition and material goods) implies, however, that the city itself might positively encourage what is noble and discourage what is base. Augustine does distinguish between better and worse practices of his society, especially by highlighting the tremendous power of culture to shape and create moral emotions. He condemns Rome as a society where it is "all right if the poor serve the rich, so as to get enough to eat and to enjoy a lazy life under their patronage; while the rich make use of the poor to ensure a crowd of hangers-on to minister to their pride" (*CD* 2.20, Bettenson) and where "actors live in luxury at the expense of the very rich—while the poor can scarcely find what they need to live" (*Ep.* 138, 38). The harsh diagnosis of Rome serves to "denaturalize" civic virtue, exposing its artificial dimensions and thus rendering it open to improvement or distortion as a learned cultural practice. I here disagree with John Rist's claims that Augustine holds "all earthly societies would seem to be equally bad in practice, not merely in potentiality" (*ATB,* 305) and "*no change in the present social structures would be an improvement*" (230). These claims, at least, do not follow from a prior belief that the earthly city (as opposed to earthly societies) might not be capable of promoting goods that are "seriously educative, but only perverse" (*ATB,* 305). Against John Milbank as well, I think this "denaturalizing" of the Roman mythos does not simply subvert the value of a secular political order. Augustine, in his less polemical moments, grants the value of "that imperfect kind of virtue" (*CD* 5.19) displayed by the Romans in the service

39. Brown, *Augustine of Hippo,* 308.

of temporal peace. He admits, "it is not rightly said that the goods which this city desires are not goods; for in its own human fashion, even that city is better when it possesses them than when it does not" (*CD* 15.4). Even the heavenly city, Augustine famously declares, "makes use of the earthly peace during her pilgrimage, and desires and maintains the co-operation of men's wills in attaining those things which belong to the mortal nature of man, in so far as this may be allowed without prejudice to true godliness and religion" (*CD* 19.17). This is the Augustine sometimes read as an ambivalent social critic trying to arouse a nobler vision for the relative peace of the civil community itself. It is an Augustine for whom "being imperfectly just is not the same thing as being unjust" (Markus, *CS,* 44).[40]

Might Augustinians then critically support a liberal democracy that will never have true and perfect justice? Might they even support a liberal democracy that is destined to an end when "it will no longer be a city" (*CD* 15.4)? Might they work for a liberal democracy that is less unjust? Or—as Augustine characterizes some empires—not "yet holy; they are less vile" (*CD* 5.13)? Perhaps "civic virtues even without true religion" (*Ep.* 138, 41)?

Augustine's experience with the intractable yet eroding authority of Roman law and the failures of its political economy placed severe constraints on his imagination for politics as anything other than a perpetual response to disorder. Rist points out that Augustine's "view of human society was as much coloured by his life in the declining Roman Empire as the view of Plato and Aristotle had been coloured by the exuberant and pagan city-state" (*ATB,* 305). Augustine knew little about the distributive capacities of government and the possibilities of structural reform—even within a politics in some eschatological sense always on the precipice of disintegration and ultimately to be eclipsed by the truly just society of the followers of Christ. With the notable exceptions of monasticism and marriage, institutional and legal designs are noticeably lacking. This may be an intentional snub of classical politics in the service of the "citizens of the redeemed city" (*CD* 15,3). But, as Markus notes, Augustine prefers to "speak of emperors rather than of empire, of kings and magistrates rather

---

40. Markus notes, "Augustine's polemic against the virtues of the pagans should not induce us to believe that all acts of virtue, to be virtuous, need to be perfectly virtuous, that justice can be real only when perfect" (*CS,* 43).

than of state or government" (*SAE*, 149).[41] He focuses on the theme of citizenship and its many forms, but he does not imagine the role an individual citizen or a group of citizens (rather than magistrates) might play within the life of a political society—even if only symbolically. It would be ironically prideful to blame Augustine or any other premodern author for limited historical horizons of social and economic reform, most especially in relation to his often neglected moral criticisms of slavery. Augustine was no abolitionist. But he rejected natural slavery, calling the expanding slave trade a "wicked form of commerce" (*Ep.* 250, 46). He argued that Roman authorities need to enforce the laws so that more Africans do not "lose their personal freedom to a fate worse than Babylonian captivity" (*Ep.* 250, 45; see also *Ep.* 10, 43–45). Augustine and his church, at least on these points, cannot be singled out as somehow responsible for the denigration of civic participation or the demise of politics in the Christian West. No doubt Augustine can issue rather negative conclusions for those seeking earthly liberation. At the very least, however, his lack of institutional analysis may have less to do with his theology of love and more to do with his limited experience of political reform.[42]

The renaissance of the social history of late antiquity, especially in terms of the cultural function of Christian rhetoric, does provide us with a new portrait that challenges the folk image of Augustine the pessimistic naysayer longing for that otherworldly heavenly city. He did not merely endure the tragic experience of politics as just desert for human sins.[43] Augustine's

41. Markus now emphasizes a less personalist Augustine, one attuned to "the cumulative effect of long consequences of human action, shaped by collective behavior over many generations, routinised and institutionalized over time" (*CS*, 44). But he also notes that "Augustine, of course, could scarcely be expected to have had the concepts and the language available to him to speak of practices and institutions" (*CS*, 45).

42. John Rist claims that "Augustine's unwillingness to attack the *institution* of slavery seems connected with his limited (though, as we have seen, gradually expanding) notion of love of neighbour" (*ATB*, 238). Rist, however, rightly notes that Augustine "has not considered whether one's neighbour can be 'hated' systematically" (239).

43. Peter Brown had already upset this negative image by his description of Augustine's movement beyond Plotinus and beyond mere pilgrimage: "For the *peregrinus* is also a temporary resident. He must accept an intimate dependence on the life around him: he must realize that it was created by men like himself, to achieve some 'good' that he is glad to share with them, to improve some situation, to avoid some greater evil; he must be genuinely grateful for the favourable conditions that it provides.... So the *City of God*,

service on the "bishop's tribunal" (a fifth-century version of small claims court), his repeated interventions for clemency on behalf of those facing the death penalty, his opposition to the use of torture, his use of church funds to free slaves, his provision of temporary sanctuary for those facing crushing debt, and his defense of citizen's rights before the Roman courts might well be considered political activism without "anachronism."[44] In this light, Augustine's civic engagement, rather than being an anomalous departure from a strict antithesis of the institutional injustice of the earthly city to the personal charity of the heavenly city, appears as one forum where he exercised his love of God and love of neighbor. Modern Augustinians might develop an account of neighbor-love that analogically mediates ecclesial identity to the social role of citizenship without conflating the two. In the words of Paul Ricoeur, neighbor-love "passes *through*" our collective sociopolitical existence and, at other times, "rises up *against*" it.[45] As such, Ricoeur argues, a theological opposition between the direct charity of the personal neighbor and the more abstract charity of the public citizen is a false alternative. Revisionist scholars like Peter Burnell and John von Heyking have even begun to challenge the long held consensus that politics for Augustine is a postlapsarian remedy for sin—a providential stopgap to limit the worst cruelties—rather than a natural good. For these scholars, Augustine's antipolitical rhetoric serves the polemical function of taming the priority of civic life, not eradicating its value for a life of Christian virtue.[46]

These developments offer suggestive avenues for Augustinian liberalism. They are consistent with my elevation of the moral psychology of love and sin, but I do not rely on their claims in order to provide a complete Augustinian description of political authority. It is unimaginable to offer

---

far from being a book about flight from the world, is a book whose recurrent theme is 'our business within this common mortal life'; it is a book about being otherworldly in the world" (*Augustine of Hippo*, 323–24). For a review of the recent literature, see Sabine MacCormack, "Sin, Citizenship, and the Salvation of Souls: The Impact of Christian Priorities on Late-Roman and Post-Roman Society," *Comparative Studies in Society and History* 39, no. 4 (October 1997): 644–73.

44. Dodaro, "Between Two Cities," 99.

45. Ricoeur, "The *Socius* and the Neighbor," 105.

46. For historical criticism of these revisionist claims, see Peter Kaufman, "Patience and/or Politics: Augustine and the Crisis at Calama, 408–409," *Vigiliae Christiana* 57, no. 1 (2003): 22–35.

an Augustinian account of *coercive* political authority as a created good, though there might be a sense in which even "shepherds of flocks" constitute a form of political rule (*CD* 19.15). I am not interested, however, in the nature of political authority. My interests are in its condition. Politics does not have to be "natural" for it to warrant moral status within Christian experience; and we need not anachronistically turn Augustine into a radical political reformer in order to rehabilitate an Augustinian ethic of democratic citizenship.

For my project, here following Augustine more than most conventional Augustinian liberals, I will focus less on the "objects of love" or the "status of politics" and more on the character of the lovers themselves—the citizens of this multitude in a fallen world. Public policy and institutional arrangements are not neglected, as they play an important role in the cultural formation of civic virtues. My focus, however, will be on citizenship rather than a general theory of statecraft. Peter Brown suggests that Augustine's redefinition of a commonwealth "focuses attention upon that 'middle distance' of human habits, values, and instincts, which, far more than its structure remains the greatest mystery of political society."[47] I want to reconstruct an Augustinian account of the "habits, values, and instincts" of liberal citizens. I pursue normative questions: What should be the virtues of these citizens? Can a 'loving' citizen be liberal, or are the dangers of paternalism too great? Can liberal citizens be motivated by religious love? What emotionally motivates a liberal citizen in the first place? Can a loving citizen be a just citizen? Is love a necessary, though not sufficient, virtue for a better ethic of citizenship? These questions push current models for thinking about religion, politics, and the ethics of citizenship in a different direction. Exposing the limits of these current models will show the value of my joining debates about Augustinian liberalism with debates about love and civic virtue.

AFTER RAWLS: RELIGION, POLITICS, AND VIRTUE

The ambiguous relationship between the ethical experience of democratic citizenship and modern religious practices was a dominant theme of twentieth century social and political reflection. The trials of our new century suggest these concerns will continue. Some citizens think liberal democracy is at

47. Brown, *Religion and Society in the Age of Saint Augustine,* 42–43.

odds with their deepest religious convictions. Prominent neo-Augustinians have voiced this opinion, arguing that Christians "have learned to police their convictions in the name of sustaining such social orders."[48] One neo-Augustinian, from a quite opposite direction, has recommended a return to "constitutional monarchy under God."[49] Others, perhaps more numerous, think religious convictions are the greatest threat to democracy. Given the interpenetration of Christianity and democracy, especially in American public life, either position might strike a historian as untenable. Western democracy, it is claimed, can trace its origins to developments in European and American Christianity, especially by way of Locke, Calvin, and Madison.[50] Today, outside of the West, Christianity and liberal democracy often are twinned as indistinguishable menace. A vast majority of Americans still associate faith with morality and view religion as an antidote to perceived declines in civic morality. Yet continuing political controversies and polarizing trends in the professional education of elites suggest that those who believe democracy is bad for religion or religion is bad for democracy will continue to wield influence.[51] These positions represent more than historical remarks. They express normative judgments about the moral poverty of democracy and the moral dangers of religion.

48. Hauweras, *Dispatches from the Front*, 92. Hauerwas argues that Christians need to abandon their concerns about the form of secular rule and, by recapturing "the posture of the peasant," the church might become less fascinated by "democratic ideology" and more capable of sustaining its distinctive virtues (105).

49. Kraynak, *Christian Faith*, 232.

50. Some scholars, adapting Perry Miller's famous description of the "Augustinian strain of piety" in colonial New England, have argued that Augustinian theology was a formative background for the emergence of American liberal democracy; see Barry Alan Shain, *The Myth of American Individualism: The Protestant Origins of American Political Thought* (Princeton: Princeton University Press, 1994), and Graham Walker, "Virtue and the Constitution." For a fascinating (and compelling) account of an American rejection of Augustine from the colonial period through the nineteenth century, see Peter Theusen, "The 'African Enslavement of Anglo-Saxon Minds': The Beechers as Critics of Augustine," *Church History* 72, no. 3 (September 2003): 569–92.

51. Jeffrey Stout worries that "we are about to reap the social consequences of a traditionalist backlash against contractarian liberalism" (*Democracy and Tradition*, 75). In response, he advances the position that democracy, contrary to most of its Christian critics and liberal defenders, is "a culture, a tradition in its own right. It has an ethical life of its own, which philosophers would do well to articulate" (13).

These are religious citizens who believe democracy undermines the integrity of faith, and democratic citizens who believe that religious convictions invariably undermine the viability of democratic ways of living. True religion survives, on the former account, only by resisting a democratic culture. On the latter account, democracy survives by taming the divisiveness of religion. In such general terms, it is not always clear that either position means to reject a particular expression of a historical religion or a particular story about how democracy is justified. Clarity can be gained by these distinctions, but I hope the point is sufficiently ordinary. Contested debates about religion and politics are nothing new. The ways in which such debates are constructed, however, does admit novelty.

The categories of religion and politics are themselves historically contingent, a commonplace thought in academic departments of anthropology, postcolonialist studies, and religion.[52] To speak of "religion and politics" as universal phenomena provides a loaded template for inquiry, usually one already shaped by modern categories and Christian presuppositions (notably, Augustine's own *De vera religione*). Contemporary Augustinians, especially those styled as modernity-critics, often adopt this language even when trying to undermine it. My reading a particular aspect of Augustinianism overcomes the abstractions that can limit genealogical approaches to "religion and politics" which engage in a metaphysical "clash of civilizations" or a general thesis about religion and the "legitimacy of the modern age."[53] These debates fail to register the promising avenue of discrete attention to the kinds of questions about civic virtue that I ask in this book. My admittedly more low-flying project focuses on the motivational structure of an ethics of citizenship. But it does not retreat from conflicting stories about human nature, the world, and God that characterizes some of these disputes. This

52. John Milbank's restatement of political Augustinianism extends such claims to theological inquiry as well: "Theology has rightly become aware of the (absolute) degree to which it is a contingent historical construct emerging from, and reacting back upon, particular social practices conjoined with particular semiotic and figural codings. It is important realize that my entire case is constructed from a complete *concession* to this state of affairs" (*TST*, 2).

53. I here allude to Samuel Huntington's controversial thesis in *The Clash of Civilizations and the Remaking of World Order* (New York: Simon and Schuster, 1998), and the debates over Hans Blumenberg, *The Legitimacy of the Modern Age*, trans. Robert Wallace (Cambridge, Mass.: MIT Press, 1983).

inquiry, which finds Augustinianism both within and against modernity, may be less dramatic than grand narratives of declension or progress. Such narratives, however, are inconsistent with an Augustinian sensibility about the mixed moral qualities of any age and the need to always remain open to the gifts that others might bear. Augustinian social criticism can succumb to what Robert Markus has called the "besetting temptation" of prophetic Christianity: "to allow the biblical imagery to develop on a grand historical or cosmic scale, and thus to compromise the unique completeness of the sacred history as concluded in the biblical canon" (*SAE*, 159–60).[54] I do not abandon the distinctiveness of Christian beliefs and practices for understanding Augustinian liberalism. I am not making Augustine safe for democracy. It seems helpful, however, at this point in the debates over politics and theology, to couch these inquiries in dialogue with one another about shared interests rather than in exclusively conflictual terms.

Focusing on the ethics of citizenship does not introduce a foreign vocabulary into political theology. It seems to me that the earliest Christian traditions were offering moral or pastoral accounts of civic life in a way that did not simply display their virtues over against the defeated powers of the world. However one reads the controversial status of the governing authorities in Romans 13, it is clear that the Pauline letters admonish their readers to "live as citizens in a manner that is worthy of the gospel of Christ" (Phil. 1:27; see also Phil. 4, Gal. 6, and Rom. 12). In fact, Augustine was consumed with the task of responding to the allegation that "Christ's teaching and preaching must be incompatible with the ethics of citizenship [*rei publicae moribus*]" (*Ep.* 136, 29). His persistent efforts to make love the form of the

---

54. Markus here cites Joachim of Floris and Teilhard de Chardin. On a much less grand scale, some contemporary Augustinians place their interpretations within a narrative that dangerously employs theological metaphors as descriptions of intellectual history. Consider, for example, the opening lines of a recent book on Augustine and modernity: "This book is about a fall from grace. It charts the transition from a conception of self-hood rooted in the Body of Christ and the love of the Trinity to a notion of self as a graceless autonomy of the will" (Hanby, *Augustine and Modernity*, 1). Hanby offers insight into both Augustine and modernity, and I applaud his method that does not "treat the philosophical Augustine separately from the doctrinal Augustine" (ibid., 1). In particular, I have learned from his effort to distinguish Augustinian volition in its doxological context from Cartesian willing. But I fear the larger narrative framework ironically can adopt the sort of "possessiveness" about the sacred that both Hanby and I reject.

virtues led to a cultural revolution. A recent introduction to Augustine's thought notes:

> Christianity's distinctive emphasis upon the practice and rhetoric of love in its Scriptures and preaching enabled it to create a linguistic community in which the central message of the faith could both be understood and communicated in such a way that it was then practiced and lived. In other words, the central message of love of God and neighbour was interpreted and preached in such a way that it inspired and moved the hearer to love. We cannot therefore underestimate the social and cultural function of exegesis of Scripture, and preaching upon it, in the formation of Christian culture and society.[55]

What is this ethics of citizenship today? A pronounced feature of political and religious discourse is renewed invocation of the social role of citizen and its relevant moral dimensions. As one scholar puts it, "like the corpse in a classic ghost story, the body of the citizen keeps reappearing from the grave, revived ... as the figure of new political projects (whether postmodern, populist, social-democratic, neoconservative, or other)."[56] While some associate this interest with nostalgic longing for a golden age of public life marked by strong bonds of affection, the diversity of these invocations suggests more than nostalgia at work.

Critics of various stripes express concern that modern democracies corrode civic virtues that foster shared political identity and motivate constructive political reform. At the same time, many religious and secular critics remain alert to the dangers of shared political identity and the promotion of what Robert Putnam has termed "social capital." The carnage of the twentieth century testifies to the validity of both anxieties. It was a history of totalitarian terror and humanitarian neglect. Today, the rise of religious fundamentalisms, the challenges of large-scale transitions in a global market economy, the continuing patterns of racial, class, and gender discrimination,

---

55. Harrison, *Augustine*, 67.

56. Scobey, "Specter of Citizenship," 13. Scobey detects this pattern: "heightened attention to citizenship as a fundamental social category; heightened fear for its robustness in the face of various threats; heightened hopes for its renovation as a means of overcoming those threats" (12). See also, Will Kymlicka and Wayne Norman, "Return of the Citizen: A Survey of Recent Work on Citizenship Theory," in *Theorizing Citizenship*, ed. Ronald Beiner (Albany: State University of New York Press, 1995), 283–322.

and the sociological facts of pluralism continue to generate interest in the ethics of citizenship.

One aspect of these debates, especially prominent among religious ethicists, legal scholars, and political theorists, has been the appropriate role of religious speech in political argument. The widely influential work of John Rawls has set the terms of this debate. In *Political Liberalism,* Rawls made one overarching feature basic to a liberal account of civic virtue: the aspiration for an "idea of public reason" that placed moral restrictions on reasoning from religious convictions to political commitments.

According to Rawls, "the ideal of citizenship imposes a moral, not a legal, duty—the duty of civility—to be able to explain to one another . . . how the principles and policies they advocate and vote for can be supported by the political values of public reason."[57] When Christians, for example, argue in certain political forums they should appeal only to public reasons that are accessible to all human beings regardless of their philosophical or religious backgrounds. Importantly, to his mind, Rawls limits these restrictions to deliberation on constitutional essentials and question of basic justice. To make appeals based on private religious opinion in these fundamental contexts is somehow unbecoming of a democratic citizen.

These restrictions, for many religious citizens, raise doubts about the legitimacy of democratic practices and institutions. Despite repeated claims to the contrary by those who propose such restrictions, religious citizens wonder whether committed liberals must be skeptical about religious faith or believe that religious convictions are incapable of rational justification. They further wonder whether being reasonable, on Rawls's view, simply means accepting his story about contractarian politics and its epistemic justification. Given the considerable attention to this issue, one gets the impression that it constitutes the most morally relevant feature of the role of religion in democratic public life. My book, in part, represents an effort to move beyond these debates.

To put my cards on the table, I agree with those who find these restrictions on religious speech in public life troubling, whatever praiseworthy moral concerns they try to address in establishing a political conception of justice. The restrictions are troubling for the following reasons. They are (1) impractical (our rational justifications are always relative to epistemic

57. Rawls, *Political Liberalism,* 217.

or cognitive context), (2) historically naïve (religious convictions have inspired some of the most democratic episodes in public life), (3) strategically
self-defeating (sterilizing public speech will not alleviate, and may fuel, the
very real political dangers of religious convictions), and (4) antidemocratic
(these restrictions impose an unjust political burden on many religious citizens that often betrays an excessive fear of democratic politics and stifles
the capacity for dissent). It would take some time to justify these assertions
and respond to potential objections. I merely invoke them to indicate how
my project will differ from now standard routes into debates about religion
and democratic citizenship.

A number of philosophers, religious and secular, have mounted compelling attacks on restrictive views associated with an "idea of public reason." The most successful focus on the unwarranted and often unexamined
epistemologies that ground liberal notions of rational discourse and inform
subsequent accounts of the obligations of mutual respect.[58] For critics of
Rawlsian public reason, citizens should not be held morally accountable
to an idealized standard of rationality that (falsely) imagines a capacity to
justify oneself according to the confident canons of some neutral or uniform
political language. In the development of his writings, Rawls consistently
moved to a less and less restrictive view. His mature statements, with all of
their qualifications, might relieve some of his critics. In his discussions of
"witnessing" and "conjecture," Rawls is clear that citizens are free to argue
as they wish in what he calls the "background culture." He is clear that he
intends no favor for "secular" reasons over against "religious" reasons. He
even opens for the door for religious reasons in the political domain when,

---

58. Nicholas Wolterstorff comments: "It would take a good deal of exegetic industry
to figure out what Rawls means by 'reasonable,' and even more to figure out what he
means by 'rational.' In spite of the fact that epistemological concepts and claims are
at the very center of his theory, his inarticulateness on matters of epistemology, when
contrasted with Locke, for example, is striking" (Wolterstorff and Audi, *Religion in the
Public Square*, 98). Rawls, however, claims that the idea of being reasonable is "not an
epistemological idea" but rather "part of a political ideal of democratic citizenship that
includes the idea of public reason" (*Political Liberalism*, 62). Reasonableness is a virtue
concept, not an evidentialist theory of knowledge. But this move does not relieve the
idea of public reason itself from epistemological claims. For an effort to read Rawls as a
virtue thinker, see Bonnie Honig, *Political Theory and the Displacement of Politics* (Ithaca:
Cornell University Press, 1993).

in due course, proper political reasons are provided. But, substantively, even this late introduction of "the proviso" holds out a rather restricted standard of rationality. Rawlsianism can be pushed in different directions on justification, but Rawls himself never abandons the search for a "shareable public basis of justification for all citizens."[59] Practically, the theory appears quite optimistic in its epistemic demands.

Notable "restrictionists," such as Richard Rorty and Robert Audi, show evidence of expansive moves under the philosophical pressure of recent work in epistemology.[60] Similar trends can be identified in related debates about "deliberative democracy" that emerge from the influential work of the German philosopher Jürgen Habermas and his theory of "communicative action." "Communicative action" differs from "public reason" in many respects, but for my purposes both unnecessarily rely on strategies of exclusion because of their overly ambitious ideals of linguistic and rational agreement—a point eloquently put by Danielle Allen in *Talking to Strangers*.[61] It is not my aim to get into the details of these discussions about the ethics of democratic discourse, let alone legal debates about free speech or the distinctive obligations of judges and elected officials. My project does not depend on this issue in any formal sense.

A more freewheeling ethic of citizenship can be dangerous. But that is democratic politics in all of its rhetorical and emotional imperfections. Democratic deliberation means we should let a thousand flowers bloom in the garden of political discourse. I do think that any ethics of citizenship should offer *moral* constraints on political discourse, but these constraints need not take account of whether or not such speech is "religious" or not. Examples of negative constraints might include prohibitions against fraud and coercion. Examples of a more positive kind, what might be called edifying constraints, include admonitions to "cultivate the virtues of democratic

59. Rawls, "Public Reason Revisited," 608.

60. For Rorty's revised position, see Richard Rorty, "Religion in the Public Square: A Reconsideration," *Journal of Religious Ethics* 31, no. 1 (2003): 141–49. For Audi's revised position, see Robert Audi, *Religious Commitment and Secular Reason* (Cambridge: Cambridge University Press, 2000).

61. For Allen, "the real project of democracy is neither to perfect agreement nor to find some proxy for it, but to maximize agreement while also attending to its dissonant remainders: disagreement, disappointment, resentment, and all the other byproducts of political loss. A full democratic politics should seek not only agreements but also the democratic treatment of continued disagreement" (*Talking to Strangers*, 63).

speech, love justice, and say what you please."[62] Citizens certainly have rights that allow them to act at odds with norms of responsible citizenship, but this does not render them immune from moral criticism. Ideals of civic virtue, including edifying constraints, operate at a different level from strict juridical appeals to legal and moral rights. These more positive duties may lead us, in any given case, to question the virtue of explicit appeals to religious convictions alone.

In fact, to speak about just one religious tradition, Christian citizens have internal theological (and moral) reasons for trying their rhetorical best to communicate about human goods with those who do not share their religious convictions. Appealing to the central virtue analyzed in this book, Robin Lovin, a leading Christian ethicist, argues "the best evidence that I have achieved some understanding of what love requires is that I can talk about the good of others in terms they recognize."[63] To fellow theists, the Christian might make one sort of appeal; and, to those who find this appeal simply absurd, she might make some other sort of appeal without contradiction or duplicity. Some Christians may find this task onerous or impossible. They protest, "We can not translate!" I am sympathetic to this argument and do not require translation. But there are sufficient conceptual resources

---

62. Stout, *Democracy and Tradition*, 85. For Stout, the virtues of democratic speech include "the ability to listen with an open mind," "the temperance to avoid taking and causing offense needlessly," "the practical wisdom to discern the subtleties of a discursive situation," "the courage to speak candidly," "the tact to avoid sanctimonious cant," "the poise to respond to unexpected arguments," and "the humility to ask forgiveness from those who have been wronged" (85). Stout's rich description appears consistent with Christopher Eberle's "*ideal of conscientious engagement*" (*Liberal Politics*, 19). Given his criticism of classical foundationalist epistemologies, however, I am unsure of Eberle's qualification that a citizen has an obligation to pursue a "*widely convincing secular rationale for her favored coercive laws*" (10). Stout offers a helpful distinction between a secularized discourse that relies on commitment to secularism and a secularized discourse that simply does not privilege, or take for granted, any particular religious authority (*Democracy and Tradition*, 93–100). Eberle's defense of pluralism seems to entail such a view or, at least, a view not inconsistent with Stout's. Rawls, no doubt, would agree that political liberalism can not be committed to a comprehensive doctrine like secularism.

63. Lovin, *Reinhold Niebuhr*, 200. Ralph Waldo Emerson makes a similar claim about "a believing love" that democratic citizens adopt in trying to communicate with their fellow citizens. Hans Von Rautenfeld likens Emerson's account of mutual understanding to Augustine's belief in *Conf.* 10.3, that he "shall be believed by those whose ears are opened to me by charity" (von Rautenfeld, "Charitable Interpretations," 83n24).

within democratic cultures that can be drawn upon, most of the time, to facilitate Christian political advocacy. I will return to this particular argument and its potential domestication of prophetic witness. Here it raises a more general aspect of the relationship between rhetoric and morality.

Lovin's remark signals how communication requires rhetorical skills that are morally significant. This recognition holds true even for those who share basic religious convictions. Consider, for example, Augustine's homiletic practice in a society that placed a high premium on speech.[64] In an account of what we might call the theological ethics of rhetoric, John Cavadini examines the complementary relationship between Augustine's doctrinal treatises and sermons. Cavadini is interested in the ecclesial ramifications of Augustine's plain style of preaching, but the context of his investigation is clearly moral. In late antiquity, language was a marker of prestige, elite privilege, and "a means of expressing social distance."[65] Augustine rejects these antidemocratic pretensions and offers a theology for the masses: "The Law of God should be given not to one man or to a few wise men, but to a whole nation and a great people, by the awesome proclamation of angels, the great things which were done on Mount Sinai were done before the whole people" (*CD* 10.13). As Cavadini puts it, "Augustine rhetorically positions himself and his audience as embarked upon a joint venture of inquiry."[66] This inquiry for the people is governed by a morality but not a technical grammar. A number of scholars have creatively begun to apply Augustine's discussions of rhetoric to current debates about deliberative democracy.[67]

---

64. Scholars estimate Augustine delivered eight thousand sermons (O'Donnell, *New Biography*, 133). They "were delivered to a broad audience, the faithful as well as the hangers-on and the curious, the 'pagans' and Jews for that matter, any of whom might, though more likely not, eventually be baptized" (148).

65. Brown, *Power and Persuasion*, 39.

66. Cavadini, "Simplifying Augustine," 75. See also Michael C. McCarthy, "'We Are Your Books': Augustine, the Bible, and the Practice of Authority," *Journal of the American Academy of Religion* 75, no. 2 (June 2007): 324–52.

67. See John von Heyking, "Disarming, Simple, and Sweet: Augustine's Republican Rhetoric," in *Talking Democracy: Historical Perspective on Rhetoric and Democracy*, ed. Benedetto Fontana, Cary J. Nederman, and Gary Remer (University Park: Pennsylvania State University Press, 2004), 163–86; Joshua Mitchell, "The Use of Augustine, After 1989," *Political Theory* 27, no. 5 (1999): 694–705; Gary Remer, "Political Oratory and Conversation: Cicero versus Deliberative Democracy," *Political Theory* 27, no. 1 (February 1999): 39–64; and Catherine Pickstock, "Ascending Numbers: Augustine's *De Musica* and

My position on Rawlsian public reason remains strongly contested, and it may remain in the minority for some time. I am not waiting for universal consensus, a curious hope for someone with my views. I predict the debate will become increasingly stale if it continues to focus narrowly on the question of the epistemological status of public speech. This staleness will be acute for societies with established histories of religious tolerance, checkered as they are, like the United States and Europe. I hope it will strike theorists and their fellow citizens that this issue is not as central a problem as they now think. Sometimes philosophical and moral progress can be achieved by deciding not to answer certain questions. Given the centrality of speech for democratic politics, we will continue to talk about the ethics of political talking. Liberals should remain attuned to those voices that do not speak and those silences that are not heard. But an emphasis on epistemology, whether implicit or explicit, tempts theorists to say too much about other people's rationality or irrationality (just as Augustinians are often tempted to say too much other people's morality or immorality). There are other ways to think about the intersection of religion and democratic civic virtue, especially given the need to replenish the moral energies that sustain liberalism.

These debates mask and distort fundamental matters. Debates about restricted speech can sideline discussion of social needs and cut short the welcome possibility of unlikely democratic coalitions. They also, ironically, restrict inquiry into underlying issues of the motivational aspects of intellectual and moral virtues. We are left with an impoverished ethical terrain for thinking about liberal politics. Motives, in general, are a neglected feature of contemporary moral and political philosophy. The debates about public reason do raise important issues related to civic virtue, especially given the demands of virtue in the context of the coercive use of political power. These issues partially arise in discussions about religious reasons and political argument. Discussions of public reason, at their best, focus on what it means to trust and to show respect for fellow citizens. My worry, however, is that they focus only on those aspects of virtue directly related to public (epistemic) justification. Augustinian liberals should affirm Rawls's thoughtful account of what he calls "burdens of judgment," those epistemic sources of political disagreement that generate his commitment to public reason as an expres-

the Western Tradition," in *Christian Origins: Theology, Rhetoric and Community,* ed. Lewis Ayres and Gareth Jones (New York: Routledge, 1998), 185–215.

sion of democratic toleration.[68] I think it is an open question whether or not Rawls's purportedly agnostic position implies a more radical skepticism than he intends.[69] An Augustinian liberal, however, will first want to place these "burdens" within the broader context of those moral sources, motivations, affections, and desires that extend beyond formal accounts of moral psychology bound up with epistemology.[70]

Some proponents of epistemological constraints recognize a distinction between an ethics of justifying reasons and an ethics of motivation. Robert Audi, for example, distinguishes between an epistemological "principle of secular rationale" and a virtue "principle of secular motivation."[71] In addition to clarifying a difference between epistemic responsibility and other virtue concepts, Audi's distinction suggests something like a distinction between acting merely in conformity with civic virtue and acting from it. Rational agents have motives for action, and much of what makes virtuous behavior interesting lies in the characterization of these motives (even if one holds a Kantian position that the fulfillment of moral duties is not dependent on an agent's motives). These distinctions open the door for a richer discussion beyond epistemic justification of particular speech-acts to include more general attention to the overall character of citizens.

68. Rawls, *Political Liberalism*, 55–58. Rawls lists six sources of these burdens, ranging from empirical concerns about evidence to the indeterminacy of hard cases and conflicting value judgments about the lexical ordering of goods. These burdens are distinct from the "prejudice and bias, self- and group interest, blindness and willfulness [that] play their all too familiar part in political life" (58).

69. Rawls encourages this skeptical reading when claims that "political liberalism applies the principle of toleration to philosophy itself" and that it "does without the concept of truth" (*Political Liberalism*, 10 and 94). For discussion of Rawls and liberal skepticism, see Kymlicka, *Liberalism, Community and Culture*, 11–13 and 21–43. I follow Kymlicka's advice to "drop the misleading language of the priority of the right or the good" (22).

70. In addition to his more discussed claim that his liberalism is "political, not metaphysical," Rawls argues that his account of moral psychology is "philosophical not psychological" (*Political Liberalism*, 86). Elsewhere, Rawls writes, "accounts of human nature we put aside and rely on a political conception of persons as citizens instead" ("Public Reason Revisited," 609).

71. Audi, in Wolterstorff and Audi, *Religion in the Public Square*, 33. Audi argues that the epistemological justification principle is more important than the virtue principle but here does not provide an argument for this position. For criticism of Audi's principle of secular motivation, see Weithman, *Obligations of Citizenship*, 152–55.

Advocates of "virtue theory" or "virtue ethics" argue that ethical theory has not sufficiently recognized the role of virtue or the virtues in the moral life. They want to expand the moral domain beyond questions about what we ought to do and include questions about what is good to be or what is good to love. Stated in this way, attention to virtues need not be formulated as an independent moral theory that might rival other theories (i.e., deontology or consequentialism). Some philosophers, notably Linda Zabzegbski, have tried to build explicit attention to virtue into epistemology itself. In fact, she claims intellectual virtues are forms of moral virtue. To be reliably virtuous, a moral agent must be "disposed to have characteristic emotions, desires, motives, and attitudes."[72] I do not know of any explicit attempt to employ Zabzegbski's account of "virtue epistemology" in debates about religion and the idea of public reason. For my purposes, Zabzegbski's proposal dovetails with my more discrete effort to enrich liberal political ethics by attending to the emotionally involved motivational qualities of those dispositions and traits of character that are necessary to be a good citizen. She helpfully joins resurgent interest in the virtues in moral philosophy with the more recent interest in the emotions. Adapting Alasdair MacIntyre's influential definition of virtue, Zabzegbski defines a virtue as "a deep and enduring acquired excellence of a person involving a characteristic motivation to produce a certain desired end and reliable success in bringing about that end."[73] Augustinians are usually nervous with the language of habituation given their strong doctrine of grace (there is no ascent without the prior descent) and their strong doctrine of sin (the perpetual ruptures of the will in obeying moral demands placed upon us in any given moment). Indeed, for Augustine, habit *(consuetedo)* tends to solidify vice rather than promote virtue.[74]

Too much trust in virtue can lead one to take credit for what does not be-

---

72. Zagzebski, *Virtues of Mind*, 15.

73. Ibid, 137. MacIntyre defines a virtue as "an acquired quality the possession and exercise of which tends to enable us to achieve those goods which are internal to practices and the lack of which effectively presents us from achieving any such goods" (*After Virtue*, 178). He elsewhere describes virtues as "those qualities of mind and character that enable someone both to recognize the relevant goods and to use the relevant skills in achieving them" (*Dependent Rational Animals*, 92).

74. Augustine, however, did praise the cultivation of discipline in resisting bad habits. See, for example, his account of Monica's maidservant who trained children to prevent drunkenness (*Conf.* 9.8).

long to you and also to imagine that a life of virtue becomes easier with time. Felicity in virtue, for Augustine, is not something we "achieve rather than receive" (*Ep.* 155, 90). Virtues in themselves are neither the sole criterion of morality nor its object—the persevering task of virtue is simply to "wage perpetual war against the vices" (*CD* 19.4). But Augustinians need not make virtue an enemy of confession. His protest against false virtue affirms the life of virtue in response to God.[75] Indeed, it is grace that is meant to allow us to become virtuous. Augustinians are also usually nervous about the language of success given their attention to proper intention rather than the maximization of utility. In later chapters, I relieve these anxieties by finding analogies to virtue ethics in Augustine's writings without jeopardizing his strong doctrines of sin, grace, and eschatology. I conclude that habituation and concern for moral success are not antithetical to an Augustinian account. Augustinian liberalism has suffered from its allergic neglect of virtue language in both its readings of Augustine and its own proposals. A reconstructed political Augustinianism needs to emphasize ways in which the practice of love is a virtue. The faithfulness of other-regarding love includes consideration of consequences in a world of complex injustices, especially in terms of practical knowledge of nonmoral facts about empirical economic, social, and political conditions. Love should not be blind to effectiveness in meeting needs. Augustinians, however, should remain wary of the moral dangers associated with certain kinds of habituation and the possibility of loving maximal outcomes more than human persons. In a later chapter, I address the difficult question as to whether love is a virtue or an emotion, or something more than either term allows. But here I note that virtues involve desires and feelings as well as dispositions to act in accord with norms of virtuous conduct.

Some "virtue ethicists," frustrated by ethical theories that focus exclusively on rules or consequences, argue for a strong claim that these virtue concepts are more basic than the concepts of right and wrong. For these theorists, considerations of virtue are prior to any specification of the rightness of an action or desirability of a state of affairs. They contrast an "act-

---

75. It is clear that Augustine did not *want* to pit grace over and against virtue. James Wetzel offers a subtle reading of Augustine that does not exonerate his views but helpfully contrasts his doctrines of redemption and reprobation. He argues that "Augustine's negation of the Pelagian ideal of initiative and effort is not the negation of initiative and effort, but a reclaiming of virtue under a new wisdom" ("Snares of Truth," 127).

centered morality" to an "agent-centered morality." The ethics of motives tends to be associated with these agent-centered accounts of morality. Despite Augustine's attention to agential virtue in his analysis of moral action (especially in terms of affection and intention), Augustinian moral theology has not been a prominent voice in the current philosophical resurgence of this kind of virtue ethics. One reason for this neglect is the association of "virtue ethics" with neo-Aristotelian and neo-Thomist moral theory that often contrasts itself with the unsystematic theological baggage of Augustinian ethics. For example, while MacIntyre's other works include significant attention to Augustine and Augustinianism, *After Virtue* includes only one reference to Augustine.[76] My project does not depend on a strong version of virtue ethics. I think it is misleading to set moral evaluation of persons over against judgments about actions, and so will argue against those proposals of Christian love that rely exclusively on deontological or consequentialist accounts of act-specification. But for my purposes, any inquiry into the virtues of a citizen is an important part of the ethics of citizenship, whatever brand of ethical theory one happens to accept.

Rawls himself remained insistent that political liberalism "may still affirm the superiority of certain forms of moral character and encourage certain moral virtues—the virtues of fair social cooperation such as the virtues of civility and tolerance, of reasonableness and the sense of fairness."[77] Liberal society, he empirically recognized, relies on these political virtues. In fact, he saw the idea of public reason as part of a kind of "civic friendship."[78] With Rawls, I agree that these are demanding virtues of great value. They protect society from the moral egoism that often lies behind appeals to lofty ideals, particularly when these appeals press the state into service as the institution of moral purification.[79] They appeal to a liberal concern for political stability,

76. For two studies in moral philosophy that challenge a sharp contrast between Augustine and Aquinas, see Thomas Osborne Jr, "The Augustinianism of Thomas Aquinas' Moral Theory," *The Thomist* 67 (2003): 279–305, and T. H. Irwin, "Splendid Vices? Augustine For and Against Pagan Virtues," *Medieval Philosophy and Theology* 8 (1999): 105–27.

77. Rawls, *Political Liberalism*, 179–80.

78. Rawls, "Public Reason Revisited," 579.

79. I take this to be a central element of Friedrich Nietzsche's effort to "abolish the word 'ideal,'" in *The Will to Power*, ed. and trans. Walter Kauffman (New York: Vintage, 1968), 180. From a quite different perspective, Rawls argues that the "spiritual ideals of saints and heroes can be as irreconcilably opposed as any other interests. Conflicts in

civic equality, and justice that should not be dismissed by religious citizens. In fact, the most influential treatment of Christian love in contemporary theological ethics has defined Christian love as an "equal regard" for others that has deep "material overlap" with equalitarian and impartialist notions of justice.[80] Principles like equal respect and impartiality serve as analogues of divine love. Awareness of the multiple and insidious ways that human beings can be cruel to each other under the pretense of moral concern or appeal to community membership is a prominent feature of both modern Augustinianism and liberalism. Nonetheless, it seems to me that the liberal emphasis on respect, civility, and reciprocity, for all their value, have their limits when forced to do all the work for an ethics of citizenship. They are not sufficiently rich enough concepts to sustain a liberal order and political practice. These limits are only exacerbated when the "ideal of citizenship" narrowly focuses on a moral duty to endorse public policy based on "principles and ideals acceptable to their common human reason."[81] This strategy demands too much of epistemic virtue, particularly when detached from the affections and dispositions that shape the moral habits of actual citizens. It also demands too little of moral virtues that are undermined by making them private or only implicitly endorsed rather than affirmed. Rawls himself paid considerable attention to moral psychology and virtue in the third part

---

the pursuit of these ideals are the most tragic of all. Thus justice is the virtue of practices where there are competing interests and where persons feel entitled to press their rights on each other" (Rawls, *Theory of Justice*, 129).

80. Outka, *Agape*, 9 and 309. For Outka, Christian love "enjoins man not to let his basic attitudes toward others be determined by disparities in talent and achievement and the inequalities in attractiveness and social rank which differentiate men. . . . He is enjoined to identify with the neighbor's point of view, to try to imagine what it is for him to live the life he does, to occupy the position he holds" (262–63). This view plays a large role in his liberal emphasis on rights and equality and his aversion to certain principled forms of altruism. Outka, however, argues that the strong convergence of Christian *agape* and liberal justice does not mean the terms are "interchangeable" (309; see also Outka, "Universality and Impartiality," 62–63). For Outka, "equal consideration is not identical treatment" (*Agape*, 268). My earlier account of an Augustinian understanding of the love commands is consonant with Outka's "theocentric" case for the universal scope of Christian love: "Love for God—as the most basic and comprehensive human love of all—includes fidelity to God in loving whom God loves" (Outka, "Universal Love and Impartiality," 2).

81. Rawls, *Political Liberalism*, 137.

of *A Theory of Justice*.[82] With the turn to political liberalism, however, liberal theory has tended to neglect this dimension of his work. I would connect this neglect of moral psychology with the eclipse of the "difference principle" among Rawlsian liberals as forms of democratic solidarity and social obligation come under increasing attack in market societies governed by rational choice theories. One of my hopes is that Rawlsians drop "public reason" and restore the "difference principle" as a practical form of political solidarity.[83] In religious ethics, preoccupation with epistemological issues related to justification also has marginalized the full relevance of virtues for supporting religious practices and democratic citizenship.

The terms of the debate—rationality, religion, politics—bracket moral and theological analysis that virtue concepts like faith, hope, and charity tend to generate. They also make it difficult to learn from premodern figures such as Augustine who was alert to the coded discourses of power, emotions, and virtue but also saw them as inseparable political goods. Political ethics limited to ever more technical accounts of the appropriate role of religious speech fail to address the severe challenges facing democratic political culture, including those challenges of stability that are thought to require thin descriptions of civic virtue. These approaches restrict "thicker" discussion of those moral virtues that make democratic life attractive to its citizens as well the cultivation of those motivations and qualities of emotion necessary to sustain a liberal democracy.[84] Augustinian liberals share the Rawlsian rejec-

82. For an interesting account of these early themes, see Susan Mendus, "The Importance of Love in Rawls's Theory of Justice," *British Journal of Political Science* 29 (1999): 57–75.

83. Rawls's "difference principle" held that "social and economic inequalities are to be arranged so that they are . . . to the greatest benefit of the least advantaged" (*Theory of Justice*, 302). He considers it a democratic "ideal of fraternity" (106). Rational choice theorists have argued that Rawls's egalitarianism is not compatible with situations of rational choice; see, for example, David Gauthier, *Morals by Agreement* (Oxford: Oxford University Press, 1986), 245–67. For a Christian defense of this early Rawls, see Harlan Beckley, "A Christian Affirmation of Rawls's Idea of Justice as Fairness," *Journal of Religious Ethics* 13 (1986): 210–41. For an effort to apply the "difference principle" (even across national borders), see Charles Beitz, *Political Theory and International Relations* (Princeton: Princeton University Press, 1989).

84. On the notion of thick and thin in moral philosophy, see Alan Gibbard, *Wise Choices, Apt Feelings* (Cambridge: Harvard University Press, 1990).

tion of a political perfectionism that tries to maximize "the achievement of human excellence in art, science, and culture."[85] For their own theological reasons, they also reject the actual possibility of moral perfection in this life. These two rejections, however, do not require rejecting a perfectionist ethics that calls citizens to aspire to a better quality of political loving in relation to a transcendent good. Perfectionism, in this sense, need not be limited to consequentialist registers of maximizing excellence, as Rawls appears to assume.[86] Augustinian liberals endorse the liberal distinction between legality and morality. But they should not scale down their ethics of citizenship in ways that simply deny what might be morally possible. Definitions of the domain of the political are distinct from the kinds of moral considerations appropriate for an ethics of citizenship. Any ethics should always be realistic (that is, adequate to human creatures) but also encourage transformation of actual practices and characters of citizens. Ethical perfectionists need not be romantic about the challenges to the moral life nor intolerantly purist about the communities that allow human beings to seek their perfection. If ethics is just about lamenting what we fail to do, justifying mediocrity, and telling us what it will be like when there is no need for ethics, it does not seem worth the effort. Indeed, it may actually never allow us to be or do otherwise.

I have argued for the relevance of my project and demonstrated how it tries to push both Augustinian liberalism and the ethics of citizenship in new directions. I have signaled how my reading of Augustine's moral psychology of love and sin reorients more conventional interpretations that

85. Rawls, *Theory of Justice*, 325. Rawls argues: "The government can no more act to maximize the fulfillment of citizens' rational preferences, or wants (as in utilitarianism), or to advance human excellence, or the values of perfection (as in perfectionism), than it can act to advance Catholicism or Protestantism, or any other religion" (*Political Liberalism*, 179–80).

86. Jeffrey Stout helpfully distinguishes this restricted understanding of perfectionism from other kinds of perfectionism (*Democracy and Tradition*, 310n9). Stout draws attention to the close connection (and relevant differences) between Augustinian Christianity and "Emersonian perfectionism." For Stout, Emersonians are committed to an "ethics of virtue or self-cultivation that is *always* in the process of projecting a higher conception of self to be achieved and leaving one's achieved self (but not its accumulated responsibilities) behind" (29).

have become a stumbling block for Augustine's political critics and his theological defenders. I can now tell my story about the modern development of Augustinian liberalism in order to offer a nontraditional account of the tradition. In order to see how my Augustinian civic liberalism works, I need first to distinguish it from these more standard versions. To these I now turn.

2

+++

From Vice to Virtue
The Development of Augustinian Liberalism

*The term "Augustinian liberalism" will strike those familiar with
Augustine's politics—as he developed them during the Donatist
controversy, for example—as oxymoronic. The political theories
historically associated with Augustine and Augustinianism have not,
after all, been notably tolerant. Finally, the qualities of character
liberalism fosters—among them tolerance and self-assertion—
might be thought antithetical to Augustinian Christianity.*

PAUL WEITHMAN, "Toward an Augustinian Liberalism"

+++

Paul Weithman's description of the oxymoronic character of Augustinian
liberalism provides an apt introduction for this chapter. The term itself
does strike many as oxymoronic; though, for many, it is simply moronic. This
is not the Augustinianism commonly known to historians of late antiquity
and medieval society. It is not the Augustinianism one finds in standard anthologies of political thought. Perhaps even more surprising given its many
strengths, the recently published *Augustine Through the Ages: An Encyclopedia*,
failed to include discussion of Augustinian liberalism.[1] In these places, one

---

1. See Oliver O'Donovan's otherwise positive review of the encyclopedia in *International Journal of Systematic Theology* 2, no. 3 (November 2000): 353–55. O'Donovan is
right to point out the neglect of a comprehensive treatment of Augustine's political ideas,
either through the concept of *civitas* or Augustine's relation to liberal society. One can
discern, however, elements of Augustinian liberalism in the short entry by Joanna Scott,
"Political Thought, Contemporary Influences of Augustine's," in Alan Fitzgerald, ed.,
Augustine Through the Ages, 658–60.

is more likely to find extended discussion of religious coercion, the social realities of Augustine's world, or some treatment of Christianity's antipolitical (or, more cautiously, transpolitical) otherworldliness. Numerous dissents from the liberal reading suggest more than initial puzzlement. They demonstrate a sustained refusal of any theoretical alliance (even strategic or provisional) between Augustinianism and liberalism. Such dissents, often connected to larger debates about religion and modernity, can be motivated on behalf of either liberalism or Augustinianism.[2]

There are textual warrants for resisting the idea that Augustine was a liberal. No liberal could claim, as Augustine does, that "security . . . lies in the happy condition of living rightly rather than in being safe to act wrongly" (*Ep.* 91, 5). Liberals rightly worry about the implications of Augustine's praise of the citizen who considers the "interests rather than preferences" of his fellow citizens (*Ep.* 138, 38). But liberal readings dominated the renaissance of Augustinianism in the twentieth century. These readings can be viewed in terms of the century's social and political context. Coming to terms with the experiences of war and totalitarianism—as well as secularization and pluralism—motivated liberal reconstructions of Augustinianism. This Augustinianism relied on a particular Augustine: one that spoke to the hopes and the anxieties of American and European scholars in the period. Some interpreters would dismiss such readings as necessarily illegitimate. Much depends, of course, on the genre in which one is writing, and how one understands what it means to do ethics through appeal to historical figures and traditions.

Most of the authors discussed in this chapter are philosophers and ethicists who implicitly adopt my method of rational reconstruction. It is noteworthy that one of the most distinguished historians of late antiquity, Robert Markus,

---

2. The literature on political Augustinianism (even in the modern period) is immense. For a collection of classic essays, see Dorothy F. Donnelly, ed., *The City of God* (New York: Peter Lang, 1995). Apart the authors discussed in this chapter, the following works are generally representative of the *liberal case against Augustinianism* (though their own accounts of liberalism differ): M. J. Wilks, "St. Augustine and the General Will," *Studia Patristica* 9 (1966): 487–522; Rosemary Radford Ruether, "Augustine and Christian Political Theology"; Elaine Pagels, *Adam, Eve, and the Serpent;* and Peter Kaufman, *Redeeming Politics* (Princeton: Princeton University Press, 1990). Elements of the *Augustinian case against liberalism* can be found in Michael J. White, "Pluralism and Secularism in the Political Order: St. Augustine and Theoretical Liberalism," *The University of Dayton Review* 22, no. 3 (Summer 1994): 137–54.

also adopts this approach when he speaks to the political implications of Augustine's thought. His now classic study, *Saeculum: History and Society in the Theology of St. Augustine*, is the scholarly lodestar for Augustinian liberalism. In *Saeculum*, Markus took inspiration from Augustine's invocation of Cyprian's call to return to the apostolic tradition and "carve a channel from them to our own times" (*SAE*, ix). Markus argued that "to find oneself, willing or unwilling, involved in a dialogue with [Augustine] on questions agitating theology today, cannot be condemned as unsound, either in historical or in theological procedure" (*SAE*, ix). In his most recent study, Markus explicitly pursues an "*Augustinus redivivus*" (*CS*, 52). With Markus and Weithman, my project supports the claim that there are "arguments to support political liberalism that can be described as Augustinian."[3] But just as there are different kinds of liberalism, so too are there different kinds of Augustinian liberalism.

For most of this chapter, I set aside objections to Augustinian liberalism. It is helpful to locate my liberal reading within the recent history of this tradition before advancing my account. I do so in order to identify a version of Augustinian liberalism that will prove receptive to those "thick" moral concepts I discussed in the previous chapter, especially the motivational components of intellectual and moral virtues. By situating the project in this way, I rely on some established literature as a way into the more focused questions that arise for an ethics of citizenship.

The purpose of this chapter is not to adjudicate which type most accurately reflects Augustine's writings. It has a separate goal. The chapter highlights the use to which the Augustinian tradition was put in the latter half of the twentieth century. To paraphrase James O'Donnell's challenge to traditional Augustine studies, my interest in Augustine here lies very much "in what he has become" rather than "what he was."[4] More specifically, I illustrate how certain kinds of Augustinianism proceed from different characterizations of a citizen's attitudes and dispositions in political life. These attitudes and dispositions, in turn, shape accounts of the virtues of liberal citizens in Augustinian terms. These accounts have not been developed with adequate clarity or explicitness. This lack of development can be attributed partially to the priority of questions related to the origin and status of political authority in Augustine's theology. Most Augustinian liberals also have focused on the

---

3. Weithman, "Augustinian Liberalism," 304.
4. O'Donnell, "Next Life of Augustine," 231.

category of vice as an alternative to virtue—a move that limits the conceptual power of an Augustinian moral psychology that pictures vice as a perpetual danger internal to the practices of virtue. As James Wetzel puts it, "the genealogy of human vice is everywhere bound and tied to the genealogy of human virtue."[5] My version of Augustinian liberalism takes account of this complexity and so contributes to contemporary readings of Augustinianism as a virtue-oriented tradition. Hence my chapter title. Recent developments in political and moral philosophy that highlight the role of virtue and emotion encourage more direct attention to these issues within Augustinian liberalism. In order to advance an Augustinian voice in these conversations, I need first to provide this more general account of Augustinian liberalism.

I identify three ideal types of Augustinian liberalism. Each type remains a kind of liberalism. Every Augustinian liberal affirms secularity as a shared time afforded all humanity by the common grace of God. This affirmation, following Augustine's overcoming an initial attraction to imperial theology of the Constantinian establishment, rejects the sacralization of earthly political communities as vehicles of salvation. This move serves as the crucial element that opens the door for a separation of the political and the ecclesial without separating morality from politics or condemning the religious to private subjectivity. Augustinian liberals find their inspiration in Augustine's mature response to the anxieties of both pagans and Christians after the fall of what both thought to be the eternal Roman order. Augustine wrote, as Garry Wills puts it, "to dethrone the *idea* of Rome."[6] To the pagans, he satirized their prideful claims to have built an empire through humility and justice, reminding them of the violence on which the empire was built and sustained. He accused them of making empire their religion. To the Christians, he tempered their enthusiasm for the empire's conversion. He warned them not to make empire their religion as well. Christians were to be pilgrims on earth, resident aliens, leaving this world's political struggles opaque to the kingdom of charity—yet, and this is an important yet, always trying to discern (the often surprising) Christ-like events of humanization in the world. The contingent fortunes or misfortunes of any particular historical political community were no longer tied immediately to the economy of salvation. The moral of this Augustinian story: beware communitarianism and the overbearing reach of the coercive state.

5. Wetzel, "Splendid Vices," 276.
6. Wills, *Augustine*, 114.

In their dual commitment to limited government and an ultimate loyalty to a community beyond the state, Augustinian liberals recognize earthly politics cannot fulfill the deepest longings of a human person or community. Serious constraints are placed upon political life by the treachery of human action, the ambiguous deliverances of human judgment, the elusiveness of stability, the structural intransigence of injustice, and the incommensurability of proximate ends to be pursued. There is no unity of ethics and politics for Augustine; at least no unity short of the heavenly, eternal city. Augustinian liberals lower the stakes involved in politics. All is broken and incomplete, and politics can not heal the rupture. This imagination vexed medieval Christendom, tempting it to close in on itself in false unanimity, but it can also encourage a principled stance of patient attention to the plurality of creation that views liberal society as a providential gift to be constructively sustained. In this sense, a Christian affirmation of the term "secular" is not to be understood as a synonym for a politics marked by religious or moral neutrality—either in the so-called public or private realm. The drama of the secular lies precisely in human capacity for good or evil, rather than in some autonomous *tertium quid* that is delivered from moral or religious significance. The "secular" refers simply to that mixed time when no single religious vision can presume to command comprehensive, confessional, and visible authority. Secularity, then, is interdefined by its relation to eschatology. This definition does not deny the Christian claim that the state remains under the lordship of Christ, providentially secured in its identity "in Christ." But it does claim that the secular is the "not yet" dimension of an eschatological point of view.

Despite this common agreement among Augustinian liberals, proponents offer discrete accounts of political life that are revealed by the controlling virtues and emotions which shape their moral psychologies. These different kinds of Augustinian liberalisms are like religious cultures themselves—each offering symbols and metaphors that induce in their adherent "a certain set of dispositions (tendencies, capacities, propensities, skills, habits, liabilities, pronenesses) which lend a chronic character to the flow of his activity and the quality of his experience."[7] They are cultures with strong family resemblance, but the different idioms they employ constitute distinguishable descriptions of political realities. They shape the experiences of these

7. Geertz, *Interpretation of Cultures*, 95.

realities and reflect the different social contexts in which they arise. They are like cultural-linguistic systems of symbols and actions that have their own conceptual grammar.[8] Put more colloquially, they evoke different moods. They employ distinct rhetoric. They motivate different kinds of citizens.

There are aspects of each type that would require detailed discussion to pursue distinctions within each type. These distinctions, for example, might emerge in fuller discussions of the legitimacy of political authority, the nature of the church, or familiar soteriological disputes between Protestants and Roman Catholics. Moreover, the types are not mutually exclusive. Features of each type can support one another, and there are fluid elements in each type's paradigmatic virtue. These relationships raise difficult questions about the unity of the virtues that I address later in the book. It may be the case that any given moment in political history requires preference for one type over another. The task of this chapter is to demonstrate how different kinds of Augustinian liberalism highlight different aspects of Augustinianism in ways that promote discrete moral visions of liberal citizenship. My preference for the third type of Augustinian liberalism—civic liberalism—does not constitute a wholesale rejection of the other types. Rather, to return to my two paradigms from the introduction, I recommend the third type because it best captures the significance of love (constrained by sin) as a central virtue of political morality. This political morality is other-regarding yet does not denigrate the importance of justice for a society of free and equal citizens. Love proves to be a concept rich enough to include both hope and justice.

The first type, associated with thinkers such as A. J. Carlyle, H. D. Friberg, F. Edward Cranz, W. Kamlah, J. N. Figgis, Herbert Deane, Reinhold Niebuhr, and Robert Markus, represents the dominant strand of Augustin-

---

8. I here borrow from George Lindbeck's influential proposal for a rule theory of Christian doctrine. My point is only to suggest an analogy between Lindbeck's cultural-linguistic approach to Christian doctrine and my approach to Augustinian liberalisms. Lindbeck follows Geertz (following Gilbert Ryle) by emphasizing religions as cultures that require "thick description" (*Nature of Doctrine*, 115). Augustine, I think, suggests something like this approach in his discussion of Christology and divine rhetoric in *DT* 2.1. C. C. Pecknold provides a more comprehensive effort to read Augustine and Lindbeck together: "Augustine is the prototypical semiotician for postliberalism.... His semiotics are a kind of Trinitarian understanding of the incarnation of the Word of God" (Pecknold, *Transforming Postliberal Theology*, 37).

ian liberalism.[9] It most clearly reflects the interests of twentieth-century readers of Augustine. This type links Augustinianism with realist schools in political theory. In political rhetoric and popular belief, this association remains dominant when the figure of Augustine is invoked. Drawing primarily from Augustine's eschatology and doctrine of sin (particularly through the lens of Books 5 and 19 of the *City of God*), it highlights the "darkness that attends to the life of human society" (*CD* 19.6, Bettenson). Politics is a "realm in which fallible, sinful men work out imperfect, precarious solutions to recurring difficulties and tensions."[10] The dominant virtue of this type is *hope*. A second type, associated with Paul Weithman and Edmund Santurri, updates this more traditional reading by linking Augustinianism with Rawlsian liberalism. The dominant virtue of the Augustinian liberal of this type is *justice*. For a third type, I introduce the notion of a "morally robust" Augustinian civic liberalism. I appeal to the work of Timothy P. Jackson and Jean Bethke Elshtain in order to contrast their interpretations with the realist and Rawlsian types. Their work on broader issues in political theory and theology illuminate my more explicit case for Augustinian civic virtue. The dominant virtue of the Augustinian liberal of this type is *love*.[11] I want to extend this third type of Augustinian liberalism, both by making its account more explicitly Augustinian and by connecting it to recent work in feminist political theory. This third type is the best Augustinian candidate for meeting the challenges facing Augustinian liberalism.

9. The importance of British and German scholarship for modern Augustinianism is helpfully outlined by Miikka Ruokanen, *Theology of Social Life in Augustine's De civitate Dei* (Gottingen: Vandenhoeck & Ruprecht, 1993), 9–18.

10. Deane, *Political and Social Ideas of St. Augustine*, 222. Deane argues that Augustine's thought encourages a "politics of imperfection" (233).

11. Eugene TeSelle, Robin Lovin, Rowan Williams, David Hollenbach, Michael J. Perry, Oliver O'Donovan, and the more recent Robert Markus could also be positioned in my third type of Augustinian civic liberalism. Like Lovin, TeSelle seeks an Augustinian "corrective to premature forms of 'Christian realism'" (TeSelle, "Augustinian Politics," 88). He points out that Augustine attacked the realists of his own day by advocating an ethic of love which involves "appreciating and acting toward each in a way appropriate to its being" (89). TeSelle also emphasizes "the importance of motivation in political life—motivation not only on the part of the political decision-maker and actor . . . but also on the part of ordinary citizens" (94). TeSelle's politics makes moves quite compatible with my own effort; see Eugene TeSelle, *Living in Two Cities: Augustinian Trajectories in Political Thought* (Scranton: University of Scranton Press, 1998).

AUGUSTINIANISM AS REALIST LIBERALISM

"Augustine was, by general consent, the first great 'realist' in Western history."[12] So wrote Reinhold Niebuhr in 1953, in one of his many testimonies to Augustine as the fount of Christian Realism and "a more reliable guide than any known thinker."[13] Niebuhr's influence in associating Augustine with political realism should not be underestimated. For many citizens, at least in American churches and universities, Niebuhr is the standard route into political Augustinianism. In fact, given the relative neglect of Augustinianism in twentieth-century Catholic social thought, it is not too much to claim that Niebuhr's Augustine has become the Augustine of both Protestant and Catholic political imagination. The authority of Niebuhr's Augustine continues to be invoked whenever policies appear to indulge in the illusions of utopianism or sentimentalism—an anti-perfectionist invocation that tends mistakenly to identify Christian Realism as inherently conservative given its preoccupation with order and stability.[14] Niebuhr has a recessive voice that might qualify, or at least clarify, his received pronouncements. He argued that Augustinian realism "should be made the servant of an ethic of progressive justice and should not be made into a bastion of conservatism, particularly a conservatism of unjust privileges."[15] When he focused on equality rather than the failures of liberal anthropology, Niebuhr could argue that the "highest social obligation is to guide the social struggle in such a way that the most stable and balanced equilibrium of social forces will be achieved and all life will thereby be given equal opportunities of development."[16] In fact, this recessive voice emerges in his criticisms of Augustine's "excessive emphasis upon the factors of power and interest."[17] This aspect of Augustinianism, he claims, feeds "the Reformation's basic mistake of finding no standard

12. Niebuhr, "Augustine's Political Realism," 121.

13. Ibid., 146.

14. For a compelling challenge to Niebuhr's association with establishment conservatism, see McCann, *Christian Realism*, 6–22, and West, *American Evasion of Philosophy*, 150–64. For a review of recent interpretations of Niebuhr and his legacy, see Robin Lovin, "Reinhold Niebuhr in Contemporary Scholarship," *Journal of Religious Ethics* 31, no. 3 (Winter 2003): 489–505.

15. Niebuhr, *Man's Nature and His Communities*, 16.

16. Niebuhr, *Interpretation of Christian Ethics*, 175–76.

17. Niebuhr, "Augustine's Political Realism," 127.

of justice between the pinnacle of love and the base of order."[18] Niebuhr insisted that politics involves "not only contests of interest and power, but the rational engagement and enlargement of native sympathy, a sense of justice, and residual moral integrity, and a sense of the common good in all classes of society."[19] He saw his own work as mediating between optimism without sentimentality, irony without tragedy, and realism without cynicism. It offered a middle ground, he thought, between the apolitical elements of Kierkegaard's existentialism and Barth's transcendentalism. As he famously remarked, "man's capacity for justice makes democracy possible; but man's inclination to injustice makes democracy necessary."[20] The aims of this chapter, however, are better served by turning to another reader of Augustine who captures the scholarly mode of Augustine studies in the twentieth century.

Robert Markus's extrapolation of the Augustinian tradition is representative of the liberal-realist type, though his recent book signals movement towards my own preferred third type. In *Christianity and the Secular*, Markus clarifies, and at times revises, his initial portrait of an Augustinian model for present society. Markus's Augustine remains the leading Christian critic of the ideology of empire and a crucial figure for a theological affirmation of secularity. But, a new Augustine emerges. Under the influence of Michael Walzer and Charles Taylor, Markus offers an Augustine more attentive to the importance of shared moral vocabularies that bind a society together.[21] In particular, through analysis of the liberal-communitarian debates of the 1980s and criticism of the emergent Augustinian antiliberalism of the 1990s, Markus distances his proposal from those kinds of liberalism associated with atomistic individualism, liberal proceduralism, and the state neutrality of the social contract tradition. He maintains his provocative suggestion that Augustine's critique of Rome is really a critique of any politics of

---

18. Niebuhr, "Order of Creation," 268.

19. Niebuhr, *Man's Nature and His Communities,* 51.

20. Niebuhr, *Children of Light*, xiii.

21. This theme was present in *Saeculum* but muted by the realist reading (especially, Markus, *SAE*, 62 and 102). It can also be found in his other writings. For example, he found that Augustine encourages this duality: "government as domination and government seen as guardian of the common good" (Markus, "Common Good," 253). See also, Markus, *Signs and Meanings*, especially 125–46, in the context of magic, semiotics, and the bonds of community.

"possessive individualism."[22] He does not, however, abandon the case for a kind of Augustinian liberalism. Before further identifying this shift in his position, it is important, given its continued widespread influence, to characterize the relevant theses from *Saeculum*.

Markus's landmark book is a historical study. It does not address traditional topics of political theory. There is, for example, no commentary on various forms of government or the nature of law. Though implicit in his discussion of empire, he does not pursue Augustine's more explicitly political discussions of property, justice, or war. Rather, Markus asks: "How did Augustine conceive the purpose of human society, in relation to his conception of man's ultimate destiny?" (*SAE*, vii–viii). This question elicits a work that is primarily historical and exegetical.

At this level, Markus does much to clarify Augustine's thinking on a range of issues (especially those changes in Augustine's ecclesiology and eschatology that follow the intense period of rereading St. Paul in the 390s). The power of Markus's study for political and social ethics lies in the way he generalizes from this detailed historical study. Peter Brown recently noted:

> *Saeculum* has always struck me as a book written with a passionate concern to reconstruct those aspects of the thought of Augustine, and those changes of his mind over the decades, that served to protect the merciful opacity of human affairs. In declaring the *saeculum* to be largely opaque to human scrutiny, Augustine protected the richness of human culture from the hubris of those who wanted to relate every aspect of the world around them directly to the sacred.... *Saeculum* was a book written against the future of Catholic Western Europe.[23]

Markus's later scholarship, especially on Gregory the Great, shows that he certainly was writing against the future of European Christendom. He also was retrieving Augustine for his own era. In the preface to *Saeculum*, Markus admits: "To read Augustine for fifteen years or more would have been intolerably tedious had it not in some way given insight into the problems such as that of a 'Christian society' or a 'secular city'" (*SAE*, xiii–ix). Markus postpones explicit treatment of these insights for the last chapter

22. Markus, "Common Good," 254. The term refers to C. B. MacPherson, *The Political Theory of Possessive Individualism* (Oxford: Clarendon Press, 1962).

23. Brown, "Introducing Markus," 184.

of the book, the chapter where the theological climate of the 1960s is most evident.[24] But the two recurring themes that structure the entire book confirm the emphases I here associate with Augustinian realism. They are Augustine's doctrine of sin and a homogenization of secular history between the first and second comings of Christ. For Markus, both themes are interpreted in terms of their "realist" breaks from classical traditions of "creative politics."[25]

For Markus, the great achievement of this realism is Augustine's *civitas peregrina:* a strange pilgrim city that humbles the ultimate significance of extrabiblical history and extra-ecclesial politics but also creates a this-worldly space for a shared public culture. The *civitas peregrina* is content to allow a politics (literally) restricted to mundane tasks: "those things which are necessary to this mortal life" (*CD* 19.17). Emphases on the pretensions of earthly politics and the radical ambiguity of historical progress open space for an autonomous and (at times in this early Markus) a positivistic conception of political society. This is the Augustine that Markus finds attractive for liberal society.

Two passages characterize this achievement and show the allure of this realist point of view for a liberal, pluralist society. They merit extended quotation:

24. The intellectual climate of Christian theology in the 1960s, particularly the theological status of secularism, is evident throughout *Saeculum*: notably, Dietrich Bonhoeffer's "adulthood" of the world and "religionless Christianity," Harvey Cox's "secular city," and Jürgen Moltmann's "theology of hope." Markus's references to the poetry of T. S. Eliot and the novels of William Golding also give some indication of his literary milieu. In *Christianity and the Secular*, Markus discusses the relation of these influences on his early reading of Augustine to the current theological climate that is hostile to "secular theology" (i.e., the diverse influences of John Howard Yoder, John Milbank, Stanley Hauerwas, and Oliver O'Donovan). He writes, "this was the intellectual climate in which I wrote my book *Saeculum*, and it would be dishonest to pretend that I was immune to its influence" (*CS*, 3).

25. Markus argues that Augustine's "break with the classical idea of 'creative politics' appears at its clearest in his rejection of the 288 actual and possible philosophical statements concerning the ultimate good of man" (*SAE*, 83). The phrase, "creative politics," refers to Cochrane, *Classical Culture*, 249 and 510. Cochrane highlights Augustine's rejection of the "pretensions of creative politics," but he also helpfully points out that Augustine's rejection is "not with a view to setting up a new heresy, comparable with any of the anti-political heresies current in the classical and post-classical world" (Cochrane, *Classical Culture*, 510).

In Augustine's mature thought there is no trace of a theory of the state as concerned with man's self-fulfillment, perfection, the good life, felicity, or with 'educating' man towards such purposes. Its function is more restricted: it is to cancel out at least some of the effects of sin. Political authority exists to resolve at least some of the tensions inevitable in human society.... Political authority serves to remedy the conflict, disorder, and tensions of society. In a world of radical insecurity—'this hell on earth' [*City of God*, 22.4]—the state exists *propter securitatem et sufficientatiam vitae*. All the institutions of political and judicial authority, with their coercive machinery, serve this purpose: 'while they are feared, the wicked are held in check, and the good are enabled to live less disturbed among the wicked' [*Ep.* 153.6.16].... to secure the space for the free exercise of virtue in a society racked by the insecurity which is woven into the very texture of human existence. (*SAE*, 94–95)

Augustine's attack on the 'sacral' conception of the Empire liberated the Roman state, and by implication, all politics, from the direct hegemony of the sacred. Society became intrinsically 'secular' in the sense that it is not committed to any particular ultimate loyalty. It is the sphere in which different individuals with different beliefs and loyalties pursue their common objectives in so far as they coincide. His 'secularisation' of the realm of politics implies a pluralistic, religiously neutral civil community. Historically, of course, such a society lay entirely beyond the horizons of Augustine's world. After centuries of development it has begun to grow from the soil of what has been Western Christendom: but it is still far from securely established in the modern world. It is assailed from many sides. Even Christians have not generally learned to welcome the disintegration of a 'Christian society' as a profound liberation for the Gospel. Augustinian theology should at least undermine Christian opposition to an open, pluralist, secular society. (*SAE*, 173)

These passages provide insight to Markus's own commitments as well as the two themes central to Augustinian realism: sin and eschatology. This first passage captures the way in which the liberal-realist reading of political Augustinianism employs Augustine's doctrine of sin. Let's first think about sin and realism.

Using a standard realist trope, Markus contrasts Augustine's affirmation of the naturalness of human sociality with an equally emphatic insistence on the fallenness of political community. Markus repeats this claim throughout his book: "If social life is natural, it is nevertheless, in the actual conditions of a politically organized community of sinful men, a burden, like a disease"

(99; see also 84, 173, and 206). Political life is marked primarily by "tension, strife, and disorder" (83) and "the inescapable dilemmas, the uncertainties surrounding human justice even at its best" (99). Without explicitly citing Niebuhr, Markus gestures that Augustine knew "the endemic insecurity, the painful exigencies of trying to be moral man in immoral society" (99). This view, often contrasted with Aristotle's influence on Aquinas, is repeated throughout realist readings of Augustine. Herbert Deane, for example, supports his realist reading by sharply contrasting Augustine's emphasis on the sinfulness of human nature to classical political thought. According to Deane, Augustine's anthropology funds a view that the state exists to punish the wicked rather than being "the vehicle by which men could attain true justice, true virtue, or true happiness" (*Political and Social Ideas of St. Augustine*, 222). Because politics is remedial, Augustine "is at the opposite pole from the classical, and especially Greek, conception that the purpose of the state is to promote the good life and educate its citizens so that they become good and virtuous citizens" (7). The political and legal system rests on the assumption of sin: " The motives upon which it relies when it makes laws and imposes penalties must be the drives that impel men to such action, and its expectations should never outrun the characteristics that they can be presumed to possess" (116–17). For Deane's Augustine, "politics is a realm in which paradox, irony, and dark shadows abound" (222). Markus agrees: " The Augustinian vision springs from a sense of the conflicting purposes, of uncertainties of direction and of tensions unresolvable in society" (*SAE*, 177). Markus relies heavily on the contrast with Aristotle. He writes: "In place of the Aristotelian confidence in the established order, the Augustinian tradition is inspired rather by a sense of its precariousness, and by an awareness of the perpetual proximity to disintegration" (*SAE*, 177; see also 73 and 75). Given this repeated invocation of Aristotle by Augustinian realists (and my own effort to abandon stereotypes of Augustine), it is important to pause for a moment and at least note that current scholarship on Aristotle challenges this reading of Aristotle's claim that the earthly political community "aims at the most authoritative good of all" (*Politics* 1252a5).

Aristotle, it seems, knew something about the tensions, conflicts, and limits of virtue in any actual political community. Bernard Yack, for example, describes an "Aristotelian communitarian account of political conflict and competition" that is similar to my version of civic liberalism (*Problems of a Political Animal*, 2). According to Yack, Aristotle's account of political community "signifies a conflict-ridden reality rather than a vision of lost or future harmony" (2) Aristotle knew that no actual political community is well-ordered: "All actual political regimes fall short of unqualified justice, and Aristotle's recommendations for improvement would still leave them short of the mark" (6–7). Indeed, on Yack's reading of Aristotle, "the end of the polis is thus not to develop itself into a complete and perfect form but rather to contribute to the development and perfection of human beings" (16). This reading would challenge the familiar role that Aristotelianism plays in Augustinian liberalism, especially by those who take their cue from Luther's radicalization of Augustine. Lutheran theologian Gilbert Meilaender, for example, finds this theological rationale for the contrast: "A Christian ethic ought to recognize the ideal of civic friendship as essentially pagan, an example of inordinate and idolatrous love" (*Friendship*, 75). Meilaender issues a sharp distinction between a politics that leaves "the individual free for his or her private concerns" with the classical ideal of "a participatory-communal polity" (71). Meilaender rejects any concept of civic friendship and supports an impersonal rule of law rather than a politics that claims to "extend the boundaries of *love*" (77). I do not want to adjudicate between Yack and Meilaender on Aristotle. I do find Meilaender's rhetoric, at least in this essay, confusing. He claims he does not wish to denigrate citizenship but only to chasten those who "seek from it more than it can give" (77). Fair enough. That sounds like Augustinian liberalism. But does this position require the extreme contrast (rather than justifiable distinction) between friendship and citizenship?

Good ethics and good politics surely will not necessarily coincide for an Augustinian, but Meilaender's account of love and law here strikes me, to trade on some stereotypes, as more Lutheran than Augustinian.[26] Augustinians should endorse Meilaender's concerns about the reduction of Christian love merely to a civic virtue. On my view, however, they should resist any radical separation of Christian love from civic virtue. Civic virtue does not satisfy the aspirations of the Augustinian heart, but civic expressions of love remain intelligible. Indeed, there are analogies between private bonds of friendship and the political bond of citizenship. Anthropologically,

---

26. As with Augustine studies, there is a lively ongoing debate about Luther's own view of politics that challenges traditional notions that politics is a remedy for sin (proposing instead that politics is "supralapsarian"). See, for example, Wannenwetsch, *Christian Citizens*, especially 61–55 and 185–88.

Meilaender's criticism of Aristotle comes across as surprisingly atomistic given his other writings. Is he really willing to cede the ground of politics to impersonal justice? Despite my affinities with his Augustinian liberalism, our differences may simply be a function of my rejection of his empirical claim that "in our society the private bond of friendship is usually regarded as far less important than the public bond of citizenship" (*Friendship*, 68). I see no evidence for this statement, especially within Christian communities that today are profoundly shaped by therapeutic and romantic idioms. Regardless, if something like Yack's story is closer to the truth, this might lend further credence to recent studies of Aquinas which have challenged the similarly sharp contrast between Augustinian and Thomistic political theory.[27] For my purposes, I want to pursue how these rhetorical positions shape realist accounts of the ethics of citizenship and their image of the Augustinian citizen.

By accentuating the sinful and tension-ridden dimensions of politics, the liberal-realist reading of Augustine encourages citizens to focus continually on what Markus calls the "radically 'tragic' character of existence" (*SAE*, 83). The realist's Augustine is the one who claims that righteousness in this life "consists only in the remission of sin rather than in the perfection of virtue" (*CD* 19.27). The disposition of the citizen is shaped by this perpetual awareness of the tragic limits of politics and the instability of civic life—the "precariousness of human order secured and maintained in the teeth of chaos and perpetually threatened by deep human forces poised delicately between civilisation and savagery" (*SAE*, 174). For Markus, the Augustinian citizen thinks of politics with a "pragmatic posture" (172). Politics offers a necessary

27. See Finnis, *Aquinas*, 245–52. Finnis's Thomistic account of the state's "specific common good" as public and limited also bears a strong relationship with the "secularity" of Augustinian liberalism. Suggestively, Finnis includes extended discussion of neighbor-love as the first precept of natural law in ways that recall Timothy Jackson's case for love as a metavalue (especially, 111–38 and 312–19). Finnis reconstructs Aquinas's most primary moral norm as: "one should love one's neighbor as oneself *by reason of* the divine goodness as it is participated, reflected, and imaged in that neighbour as in every human being—a goodness that can be both respected and nurtured in those in and for whom one can do good. In short, one is to love one's neighbour as oneself on account of, and (so to speak) for the sake of God {propter Deum}, the God whom we all should seek (and help each other to seek) to resemble and adhere to, and whose glory all human beings have the capacity to share" (314).

way to minimize disorder and foster a "lowly form of 'peace'" (174). Politics is simply a "human contrivance" that "secures a living space for society in the midst of strife and conflict" (174). Its task is "to prevent men from devouring each other like fish, as Irenaeus put it in a graphic image" (84). This image of politics on the brink of disintegration and the subsequent dispositions it motivates are consistent with the second long passage from Markus quoted above. Here we find the source of what Markus terms "the originality of Augustine's mature attitude to the Roman Empire" (55). This move involves eschatology and realism.

Markus shows an Augustine who for a brief period during the 390s "joined the chorus of his contemporaries in their triumphant jubilation over the victory of Christianity" (*SAE*, 31). But Augustine's mind changes. There can be no identification of the Roman order with a Christian one—no *imperium Christianum* and no *Reichstheologie*. Augustine's Eusebian-like enthusiasm for, or wonder at, the success of the once persecuted church and the apparent demise of paganism gives way to profound ambivalence.[28] Persecutions may return. The church is filled with pagans. Some who are pagans today may yet be Christians tomorrow. The bishop does not have much power anyway.[29] Christian princes will come and go, and they may not be very good. Roman virtues would ultimately stumble, turning in upon themselves under their own counterfeit weight. For all the worthy qualities of Rome that Augustine praises without irony, the Christian must remain ambivalent.[30] Why? Au-

---

28. For a helpful discussion of "ambivalence" in Augustine's early social imagination, see Frederick H. Russell, "'Only Something Good Can Be Evil': The Genesis of Augustine's Secular Ambvialence," *Theological Studies* 51 (1990): 698–716.

29. New historical scholarship challenges more traditional accounts of Augustine's influence over the Roman authorities. For discussion of this point in relation to newly discovered sermons and letters, see Brown, *Augustine of Hippo*, 482–513, and Neil McLynn, "Augustine's Roman Empire," *Augustinian Studies* 30 (1999): 29–44.

30. Markus claims that Augustine's polemic against Roman virtue reveals "the presence of a reverse side to Augustine's real feelings" (*SAE*, 57). His "tone is often unmistakably and authentically Roman, and full of legitimate pride in the stock *exempla* of Roman virtue" (57). For Augustine's more positive evaluations of Roman virtues, see *CD* 1.24, 5.19, 9.5, 10.13, 19.17, and especially his praise of Virgil who had a "shudder of compassion" when recounting the brutality of the empire (*CD* 3.16). Peter Brown captures the point well: "Augustine regarded the Ancient Romans with the same intense ambivalence as we [modern English] regard our Eminent Victorians" (*Augustine of Hippo*, 307).

gustine answers: "They do not have reference to God" (*CD* 19.25). Augustine thinks bad theology makes for bad morals: "What justice can we suppose there to be in a man who does not serve God?" (*CD* 19.21). The self-sufficient virtues of the pagans can never escape the closed and totalizing economy of virtue that has no capacity to refer beyond itself (and, thus, unable to imagine virtue as a shared gift rather than an individual possession). The bad theology of the pagans reflects their pride. In fact, it seems that bad morals actually make for bad theology. According to Markus, Augustine thought "what was wrong was not what the Romans did, but that they took credit for it."[31] He attacked "their self-conscious boasting of the Roman 'white man's burden'; not their concern for the *res publica*."[32] I return to Augustine's complicated discussion of "pagan virtue" and the common good.

Markus elevates the category of *ambivalence* for the Augustinian citizen. Ambivalence delivers Augustine from both apocalyptic hostility to Rome as an apostate demonic order and sacral identification of Rome as a sacramental vehicle of grace:

> In Augustine's hands the Roman Empire has lost its religious significance. Rome has been removed from the *Heilsgeschichte*, the Empire is no longer seen as God's chosen instrument for the salvation of men. It is no longer indispensable for the unfolding of [God's] providential plan in history. Nor is it, on the other hand, a Satanic obstacle to its realization. . . . The Empire has become no more than a historical, empirical society with a chequered career, whose vicissitudes are not to be directly correlated with the favour of the gods, pagan or Christian, given in return for services rendered. It is theologically neutral. (*SAE*, 55)

This move from ambivalence to an ascription of theological neutrality, Markus now admits, was fraught and mistaken. In Augustine's theological world, nothing is neutral. The primary point remains: the real moral division of Augustine's two cities "lies in the dimensions of men's will, in their inner response to their world and their experience" (*SAE*, 63). The state is simply "the sphere in which the concerns of individuals with divergent ultimate loyalties coincide" (69). As such, for Markus, the Augustinian distinction between human destinies is finally "eschatological, rather than sociological or

31. Markus, "Common Good," 253.
32. Ibid.

historical" (123). Markus's realism, though always attuned to the limits of politics, encourages the Augustinian citizen neither to formally embrace nor to
anathematize the political community itself. Augustine's eschatology means
that the state simply exists suspended between two ages. The Augustinian
citizen does not invest ultimate concern in its virtues and vices, its failures
and successes. Petty dramas will pass away; in fact, with the arrival of Christ
they have already been put in their place. This relativization need not solicit
passivity or quietism. But the focus of the human drama shifts elsewhere: the
"inner response to the world and their experience" (63). The homogeneity of
history between the first and second coming of Christ promotes an "Augustinian agnosticism about secular history" (159). Markus structures his book
according to the secularization of history (chapters 1 and 2), the secularization
of the Roman Empire or any social institution (chapters 2, 3, and 4), and even
the secularization of the church (chapter 5).[33] This strategy of "secularization"
that pervades Markus's early reading of Augustine trades upon Augustine's
"acute sense of being a wanderer . . . a *peregrinus*—a foreigner—in land where
it behooves him to travel light, with ardent love for distant country" (83). Between Incarnation and consummation, history is an "interim" that is "dark in
its ambivalence" (23). The citizen relates to the political community without
illusion about its pretensions or dangerous realities. Augustine encourages a
"dispassionate estimate of political life" (64). Since Christ founds a new Israel,
why get exercised about the foolish and futile dying gasps of Rome, the United
States, and the European Union?

Many scholars have challenged Markus's interpretation of the supposed
neutrality of the political order.[34] Markus himself has changed his mind
on this aspect of his earlier work. He tried hard to avoid a sectarian Augustine. It is clear that "the social order does not constitute an irrelevance

33. For Markus, "the Church is no more 'sacred' than the world is 'profane': they are
both 'secular'" (*SAE*, 179). Markus appears to disagree with Niebuhr's Protestant claim
that the "prophetic insight of Augustine's was partially obscured by his identification,
however qualified, of the city of God with the historic church, an identification which was
later to be stripped of all its Augustinian reservations to become the instrument of the
spiritual pride of a universal church in its conflict with the political pride of an empire"
(Niebuhr, *Nature and Destiny*, 1:230).

34. See, for example, Michael J. Hollerich, "John Milbank, Augustine and the 'Secular,'" in *History, Apocalypse and the Secular Imagination*, ed. M. Vessey, K. Pollmann, and A.
D. Fitzgerald (Bowling Green, Ohio: Philosophy Documenation Center, 1999), 311–26.

to the Christian life and that political engagement and commitment are inescapable duties laid upon the Christian by the exigencies of his social existence" (*SAE*, 167). Moreover, despite the rhetorical accent on the dark, tragic, and fleeting character of political life, Markus tries to deliver his reader from a gloomy pessimism. By highlighting "eschatology as politics" (166), he imagines a "politically radical" Augustinianism that "is bound to be unremittingly critical of all and any human arrangements, any actual and even any imaginable forms of social order" (168). But it is also the "negation of ideology" (171). The Augustinian citizen "seeks out opportunities for protest" and is encouraged continually to put "awkward questions" to the ruling powers of the world (169). Like Niebuhr, Markus distinguishes his Augustinian realism from both optimism and pessimism: "Historical optimism and pessimism are equally alien to its eschatological transcendence, and to the historical agnosticism which is its correlative" (166). For my part, I am generally skeptical about the usefulness of the categories of optimism and pessimism. I prefer not to use them at all. I think the language of the virtues offers a richer and more concrete mode of description. It does seem clear that they are not subtle enough terms to describe Markus, Niebuhr, or, for that matter, Augustine.

What then is the dominant virtue that characterizes Augustinian liberalism in the liberal-realist type? Markus identifies *hope* as "the characteristic virtue of the wayfarer: by this he is anchored to his real home" (*SAE*, 83). Christian political commitment itself is "no less and no more than the operation of this eschatological hope in present society" (166). It is this marked attention to hope that is typically presented by Augustinian realists as the proper virtue of the citizen. Eschatological hope is both consoling balm and provocative incitement to action. Hope counters the potential defeatism that can follow from the relentless focus on sin and the agnosticism about history and politics. Hope consoles, but it is not a cheap deliverance. Consistent with realism more generally, the hope of the Augustinian realist still means "political discernment and action must become fragmentary, *ad hoc*, piecemeal" (171). This feature of the first type of Augustinian liberalism is found in the closing passage of Niebuhr's influential *Nature and Destiny of Man*:

> Thus wisdom about our destiny is dependent upon a humble recognition of the limits of our knowledge and our power. Our most reliable understanding is the fruit of 'grace' in which faith completes our ignorance without

pretending to possess its certainties as knowledge; and in which contrition mitigates our pride without destroying our hope.[35]

Both Markus and Niebuhr wrestle with the difficulties of joining the realism of their account of sin and the potential progressivism of their constructive account of hope. The relation between hope and sin may involve the same characteristics I described in terms of the dialectical relation between love and sin. Too much fascination with sin and ambivalence can render a rather fantastical moral psychology of hope. Realist hope often assumes a negative form: hoping worse things do not happen rather than a hope that aspires to a better moral or political future.[36] Nonetheless, Markus tries to give the positive sense of hope its due in the latter pages of his book.

"Hope," Markus writes, "is a permanently unsettling force, seeking to prevent social institutions from becoming rigid and fixed, always inclined to treat the *status quo* with suspicion" (*SAE*, 169). The attitude of the "eschatological restlessness" that grounds this hope of the realist is not "mere unshaped discontent or unrealistic perfectionism" (170). It provides a complex psychological location from which the Christian might still critically affirm liberal values. Here we might imagine the attitude of an Augustinian affirmation of contemporary liberal appeals to rights, equality, and freedom: yes, but! There is real affirmation of non-Christian values but not any "simple self-identification" (168). Markus, aware of the premature forms of realism, does not paint an unrelieved version of realism as cultural criticism or withdrawal. His emphasis on Augustinian homelessness does not signal a retreat into a Christian enclave. To the contrary, for Markus's Augustine, "what prevented the Christian from being at home in his world was not that he had an alternative home in the Church, but his faith in the transformation of the world through Christ's victory over sin and death and his hope in the final sharing of this victory in His kingdom" (167). The Augustinian "sense of identity in the world comes not from membership of a closed group, but from the eschatological posture of hope" (167–68).

35. Niebuhr, *Nature and Destiny*, 2:322.

36. For sociological analysis of this tendency in a politically significant group of American Christians, see Daniel Johnson, "Contrary Hopes: Evangelical Christianity and the Decline Narrative," in *The Future of Hope: Christian Tradition Amid Modernity and Postmodernity,* ed. Miroslav Volf and William Katerberg (Grand Rapids, Mich.: Eerdmans, 2004), 27–48.

What happens to love given Markus's attention to sin and eschatological hope? Markus does link hope to love. But it is not a strong link. Indeed, it is rather weak. There is no explicit treatment of love's relation to political engagement or hope. There is no explicit treatment of the dangers of love. Love comes into *Saeculum* only as a kind of *amor ex machina*. With passing reference and a realist's stern necessity, he claims that political responsibility is "a duty laid upon Christians as a demand of love" (*SAE*, 172). Though Markus does not draw the connection at this point, here we recall Augustine's ironic account of the wise man willing to take his seat on the judge's bench: "Clearly, he will take his seat; for the claims of human society, which he thinks it wicked to abandon, constrain and draw him to this duty" (*CD* 19.6). It is as if, for Markus, Augustine's portrait of the anxious, utilitarian judge who must torture innocents is the paradigm for all civic responsibility. The tone is one of reluctance, resignation, recalcitrance, and prudent moderation. Political engagement is an externally imposed duty for an exigent circumstance. It is an imposition. Christian love is *commanded*, but here one finds no inner dynamic that might lead one to see citizenship in relation to discipleship. In fact, there is little motivational role for love at all. Hope constrains a truly tragic account of sin, but as with Niebuhr, love seems forever deferred to the eschatological community. This community, "the fully human community of love promised by God," does disclose "injustice and inhumanity in the best of social structures" (*SAE*, 169). But one is left wondering how love relates to the Augustinian citizen here and now? How might the Augustinian pilgrim not only regret with hope but love responsibly? My third type, which draws heavily from Markus, provides an account that can at least approach such a question. Before turning to this type, however, my sketch of Markus's influential presentation prepares the way for a second type of Augustinian liberalism.

AUGUSTINIANISM AS RAWLSIAN LIBERALISM

The second type of Augustinian liberalism shares many characteristics with the first type. But it offers more explicit discussion of moral psychology and the ethics of liberal citizenship because it tracks arguments advanced by John Rawls. In particular, these authors find a common Augustinian cause with Rawls in that "the zeal to embody the whole truth in politics is incompatible

with an idea of public reason that belongs to democratic citizenship."[37] Paul
Weithman and Edmund Santurri defend this second type.

While he differs from Markus as to the relevant differences between Augustine and Aquinas on the nature of political authority, Weithman shares
his characterization of the limited ambitions of Augustine's insistence that
politics is about "earthly peace" and "mortal life" ("Augustine and Aquinas,"
359–60).[38] Weithman repeats the realist claim that "Augustine locates the origins of political authority in the consequences of sin because he thinks that the
moral improvement to which political subjection conduces is either remedial
or illusory" (359). Augustinianism finds no room for a "common good" that
could function "as the definitive motive of the good citizen" (373). The accent
remains on the constraints of sin. There is no civic friendship. There is no political analogy to the "ties binding those who love one another with the love of
charity" (375). Again, we see an eschatological invocation that serves to chasten
any robust tribute to citizenship: for Augustine, the fragile bonds of political
society "pale beside the communion of fellow members of the City of God"
(375). Interestingly, however, Weithman's own version of Augustinian liberalism does not stress the importance of the state as necessary restraint that exists
primarily to minimize disorder. Given Augustine's providential view of history,
Weithman thinks interpretations maintaining that Augustine has a "negative"
or a "morally neutral" view of politics are overstated.[39] His Augustine does not
place politics "beyond ethical assessment" or "beyond theological critique."[40]
Weithman employs Augustine's understanding of sin for purposes different
from those of traditional realism. He capitalizes on Augustine's moral psychology in order to provide a liberal account of civic virtue.

Weithman repeats realist dispositions in his aversion to "perfectionist political projects, projects in which political power would be employed to eradicate sin or to impose on human beings political institutions that their fallen

37. Rawls, "Public Reason Revisited," 574.

38. Weithman argues that Markus's reading "obscures important differences between
the ways in which Augustine and Aquinas think political subjection morally improving.
For Augustine, political subjection improves by humbling and disciplining; other qualities that pursuit of the common good requires are not true virtues. For Aquinas, on the
other hand, political authority genuinely improves those subject to it by fostering in them
a concern for the common good of political society" ("Augustine and Aquinas," 360).

39. Weithman, "Augustine's Political Philosophy," 244.

40. Ibid., 248.

nature makes it impossible to sustain."[41] In fact, according to Weithman, "no one was more pessimistic than Augustine about the reliance on political authority to do more than hold pride in check or to foster genuine moral improvement" (318–19). But, on Weithman's view, Augustine's analysis of pride supports rather than undermines a liberalism.

Augustinian theology supports liberal principles of political legitimacy, especially in terms of "principles that restrict reasons and values that can be appealed to when justifying the exercise of public power" (305). As with Rawls, Weithman's account of Augustinian civic virtue focuses primarily on the epistemic responsibilities of a liberal citizen. He does not *equate* Augustinian liberalism with Rawlsian liberalism. His modest goal is to show that modern Augustinian Christians "have reason to accept some form of political liberalism" (307). The focus of Weithman's account turns to the ethics of justifying reasons.

Like Rawls and other liberals, Weithman is wary of "the use of political power to coerce belief, to purify society, or make it more Christian" (317). He considers such efforts to be "acts of pride" (317). This Augustinian concern "with the vice of pride and with the consequent need for humility provide reasons for accepting political liberalism" (307). Given the temptations of politics as an arena of prideful activity, the restraints of political liberalism offer an effective check on human pride that should be attractive to Augustinians. Christians who are sympathetic with Augustine's account of sin should be "sensitive to their own undue attraction to the prospect of dominating others and aware of their need to curb it" (313). The epistemic constraints of liberal conceptions of civic virtue "foster habitual restraint on the desire to dominate others" (313). Using Rawlsian arguments, Weithman argues "pride could be effectively contained by coming to respect other citizens as reasonable: as capable of deliberating well about what conception of a good life to pursue and as capable of participating in political argument and honoring the demands of justice" (317). Of course, one could imagine an Augustinian view of sin and pride moving in the opposite direction.

Historically, this sort of argument has been put to lamentable effect: given that one's fellow citizens will *not be reasonable*, it is necessary to check their disordered wills through political coercion. Weithman cites Judith Shklar's

---

41. Weithman, "Augustinian Liberalism," 314–15. Parenthetical references in this section of the text refer to this essay.

argument that "those who hate pride and not cruelty most of all often resort to 'pious cruelty' to restrain offense to God" (312).[42] But Weithman's account of respect turns this argument on its head. For Weithman, liberal respect can find its ground in Augustinian counsels against pride, especially the concern for pride that motivates "an undue desire for *preeminence* or *superiority*" (308). Vigilant Augustinians should endorse liberal concerns about the potential arrogance of religious speech, especially when this speech establishes itself as the true interpreter of the divine will on any given concrete political or legal matter. Weithman theologically rejects such advocacy as "motivated by the presumptuous supposition of nearer proximity to God than one's fellows" (317). Respect for justice as fairness promotes civility and consensus-building by recognizing the equal moral capacities of fellow citizens.

A liberalized Augustinian respect, characterized by humility and tolerance, need not imply abject submission. Liberalism "is incompatible with habits of servility or excessive acquiescence toward other human beings" (317). Like Markus, Weithman argues for an Augustinian liberalism that is capable of criticizing immoral features of society, such as racial discrimination and the unjust distribution of wealth. However, rather than drawing from religious arguments, he thinks the liberal democratic tradition is developed enough to criticize "extant regimes that purport to realize liberal and democratic ideals" (316).[43] Weithman admits that this restriction of prophetic appeals to religious convictions may not provide Christians with adequate arguments. For example, he claims, "perhaps arguments for the ille-

42. Shklar, *Ordinary Vices*, 240. Weithman notes Shklar's discomfort with an Augustinian moral psychology that follows from an emphasis on the remedial state (Weithman, "Augustinian Liberalism," 307 and 311). Shklar's liberalism, Weithman argues, essentially ignores "the deadly sins identified by patristic and medieval Christianity" and instead deplores "the vices that she, following Montaigne, dubs 'ordinary'" (311). Weithman effectively counters that the picture of pride that Augustine (and Aquinas) paint is quite compatible with the emphasis on the ordinariness of sin.

43. Weithman's shares Rawls's notion that the public culture of democracy provides a "shared fund of implicitly recognized basic ideas and principles" (Rawls, *Political Liberalism*, 8). Given the commitment to public reason, however, Rawlsians are vulnerable to sociological claims that this "shared fund" will atrophy because of the unintended consequences of its restrictiveness. Robert Song helpfully points out that the stability of Rawls's overlapping consensus is threatened by the possibility that "in the long term the content of the public conceptions of justice will be determined by the content of various elements of the background culture" (Song, *Christianity and Liberal Society*, 113).

gality of all abortions ... will not be forthcoming" (317). But "given Christian abhorrence of pride," he thinks, "Christians would do better to look for and employ such arguments than to run the risk of pride that religiously based political argument poses" (317). This admission will trouble those Christians who think that democracy requires their abandoning fundamental aspects of their moral identity. My primary objection lies elsewhere, however.

As with Markus, it is unclear what role love plays in this vision of Augustinian civic virtue. Weithman's high doctrine of "respect of others as reasonable" (317) does check unconstrained appeals to sin that could yield an arrogant antiliberal perfectionism. Yet there seems no conceptual role for the virtue of love in his account, at least in terms of his Augustinian liberalism. I could imagine Weithman linking the virtue of respect to the virtue of love in a way that supports his claims about equal moral worth. Respect might be the condition for the possibility of love, or respect might be the form of love in political life. Or, as we see in a later chapter, love itself might be a particular kind of emotionally invested respect. In fact, the relation between respect and love has become so established in Christian social ethics that they are often identified without comment: "One cannot live in a truly human way without respect for others and respect for oneself, that is, without love."[44] But Weithman does not advance this argument. Elsewhere, he does recognize the centrality of love for political Augustinianism and discusses Augustine's claim that "human beings are moved by what he calls their 'loves.'"[45] He offers an eloquent and nuanced statement of love and Augustine's two cities. But like most Augustinian liberals, there is no further account of love, or its motivations, in relation to the life of the liberal citizen. There seems to be a missing step in his account, an omission connected with his Rawlsian preoccupation with epistemic virtue. What motivates the Augustinian citizen to find herself in the situation of political advocacy in the first place? How do theological virtues function for a believing Augustinian in the public square? Weithman's Augustinian liberalism has well-defined narrow ambitions and these questions fall outside its scope. His account could provide a compelling answer to these questions, but the limits of this second type fall prey to my argument about the limits of the preoccupation with epistemology for accounts of civic virtue influenced by John Rawls (Weithman's dissertation

44. Tinder, *Against Fate*, 5.
45. Weithman, "Augustine's Political Philosophy," 235.

advisor). Consider another Augustinian case for Rawlsian liberalism. This case identifies Augustinian and Rawlsian liberalism even more closely than does Weithman. This move raises a set of issues that divides them.

Like Markus and Weithman, Edmund Santurri highlights Augustine's theology of *saeculum* and the political priority of earthly peace to eschatological perfection. Santurri writes:

> Since the ultimate success of God's redemptive economy does not depend on the character or the course of particular political regimes, Christianity's political establishment is unnecessary for all eschatological intents and purposes. Thus the state may be neutral religiously without detriment to salvation history. Indeed, for the Augustinian political goals *qua* political are provisional and worldly, only indirectly eschatological; that is, the central function of political arrangements is to promote and preserve temporal peace and not to advance salvation, even if such peace might play an instrumental role in God's eschatological economy, e.g., by contributing to the temporal welfare of the church, whose mission is essentially salvific. . . . Given the radically diverse views of the good life held by citizens of modern complex societies and given the regrettable yet pervasive human desire to dominate others both physically and spiritually (what Augustine called the *libido dominandi*), temporal peace is served best by political institutions assuming allegiance to no particular all-encompassing world view.[46]

Without reading too much into Santurri's notion of religious neutrality, this passage reflects the general view I ascribe to any Augustinian liberal. But Santurri makes a distinctive move that deserves some comment before turning to his vision of citizenship. Unlike Weithman, Santurri casts his version of Augustinian liberalism in contrast to the meta-ethical presuppositions of Rawlsian liberalism. He agrees with Weithman that Augustinian liberalism should incline citizens toward "a Rawlsian conception of liberally neutral arrangements as *politically* or *pragmatically* grounded in the sense that their normative justification abstracts from 'comprehensive' visions of the good as well as from *certain* 'metaphysical' commitments" (2). This move appears to coincide with Weithman's arguments for the neutrality of public justification, but Santurri's italics and scare quotes signal his neutrality will be distinctive, if not peculiar.

46. Santurri, "Rawlsian Liberalism," 1. Parenthetical references in this section of the text refer to this essay.

His account provides not only a liberal story about epistemic civic virtues but also a particular story about *both* metaphysics and moral realism. The stress that Santurri places on metaphysics and moral realism shows that his defense of liberalism aims to criticize the overly "pragmatic" posture he identifies with Richard Rorty and, at times, Rawls himself (2). The appeal of liberal neutrality is a moral one. Rawls defends liberal neutrality through moral appeal rather than (as Rawls would put it) an exigent political defense of liberal arrangements "merely as a *modus vivendi.*"[47] Rorty, and his fellow pragmatists, also think of their defense of liberal neutrality as a moral one. But Santurri puts a significant twist on the philosophical requirements for the moral appeal of neutrality: "Moral appeals require, *pace* Rorty and Rawls, certain metaphysical commitments affirming the existence of a transcendent moral order" (2). At this point, the respect in which this liberalism is *neutral* becomes unclear because it presupposes a controversial metaphysics that some citizens might reject. Indeed, many religious and secular citizens now identify metaphysics precisely with the morally pernicious consequences that liberalism tries to overcome. Why does Santurri disturb the philosophical reticence of liberal neutrality with this foundational requirement? Why does he think liberals need to say more about their theories of truth or transcendent order? Why does his contextual notion of epistemic justification also demand a metaphysics?

The underlying motivation lies in his aversion to historicist and constructivist defenses of liberalism. These theoretical justifications jeopardize the "*moral* concern for peace that best explains the Rawlsian affirmation of *principled* commitment to liberal structures and institutions" (15). If liberalism is as contingent and metaphysically austere as Rorty and Rawls make it out to be, Santurri argues, then it cannot sustain its own commitments. It cannot generate liberal practices necessary to ward off the many attractions of antiliberalism, especially when democratic arrangements afford those in political power the opportunity to adopt illiberal policies. Santurri may believe this kind of liberalism cannot *sociologically* or *psychologically* sustain these moral practices over the long haul. I take this empirical concern seriously. But commitment to liberal democracy has endured, even flourished, at the same time as the metaethical positions that Santurri rejects have extended their reach beyond a few

47. Rawls, *Political Liberalism*, xxxix.

intellectuals.[48] Bad ethical theory, including relativism or "Enlightenment" autonomy, rank rather low on my list of threats to both liberal democracy and Christian orthodoxy. Faced with extreme poverty, militarism, recurrent nationalisms, disease, scarce water, excessive consumption in rich societies, and the distorting role of money and the media in the democratic process, excessive preoccupation with problems in ethical theory seems misguided. Augustinians should agree with Gary Gutting's recognition that human beings "have never had any problem finding rationalizations for our sins, and this highly intellectualized addition adds a quite small weight to an already heavy pan."[49] But social criticism is not the direction of Santurri's argument.

Rather, he thinks that liberalism conceptually needs a more solid metaphysical allegiance to a fairly specific account of moral realism. Presumably he also wants some political expression of public support for this account. Santurri's anxieties rely on frequently cited passages from Rorty's antimetaphysical rhetoric of "postmodernist bourgeois liberalism." In a revealing passage, Santurri defends his version of moral realism against an imagined Rortyian interlocutor. Santurri ascribes moral value to liberal political society by way of a metaphysical picture that transcends social convention:

> Appeals to this transcendent order are necessary precisely to render intelligible claims that liberally neutral political institutions, because they foster social peace, are *morally* preferable to political domination and social strife. If we judge that the "enemies of liberal democracy" are morally misguided because they are willing to sacrifice freedom, equality, political neutrality and social peace to advance some other normative goals, we mean to say more than simply, "This is 'the sort of thing we don't do' given the way things have just happened to turn out—though things might have turned out differently, in which case there would be nothing wrong with political domination, hierarchy, and

48. There is a surreal dimension to many Christian criticisms of liberalism. Consider, for example, the opening lines of a recent book: "The liberal political tradition, despite its innumerable philosophical deficiencies, has been able to beat the oddsmakers to become the most authoritatively durable modern political form" (Walsh, *Liberal Soul*, 6). This durability, it seems to me, should not be attributed simply (as Walsh does) to its "impressive moral hegemony that limits even our capacity to visualize an alternative that is not itself a development of the liberal impulse" (ibid., 7). Given the history of alternatives and the fertile soil that Christianity provided for the emergence of the liberal tradition, it strikes me as odd to be so preoccupied by misguided justifications of liberal society.

49. Gutting, *Pragmatic Liberalism*, 158.

social strife." On the contrary, in taking *moral* issue with liberalism's adversaries, we imply that a society which *has* turned out to value neutral, peaceable political arrangements under pluralistic conditions has turned out *better*, morally speaking, than one which has not turned out this way, and this claim makes sense only if one assumes the existence of an independent moral standard or reality that can be tracked, more or less, by a society's conventions and practices, a reality transcending and judging the "contingent," linguistic-moral constructions of particular historical communities. (9)

A contemporary pragmatist would be justified in thinking that this rhetorical characterization should not be taken as the best representative of a "pragmatic" posture toward "truth."[50] Santurri himself distinguishes between what he calls the "metaphysical modesty" of Augustinian and Rawlsian liberalism from the "radically antimetaphysical constructivism" of Richard Rorty (19). But he seems to think that Rawlsians, given their inadequate evasion of a theory of truth, are vulnerable to Rorty's effort to push them in a constructivist direction. At the same time, however, Santurri believes that the neutrality of political liberalism only requires some version of moral realism.[51] Given the plurality of moral realisms, including nonmetaphysical ones, I remain confused about both the neutrality of—and even the need for—Santurri's appeal to a transcendent moral order. What further justificatory or explanatory role does his account of the transcendent moral order provide for a liberal democracy?

It should go without saying that any Augustinian—liberal or not—will be a moral realist. If the God that Augustine worships really exists, then the source of moral values cannot be merely a function of human social discourse and practice: "True inward righteousness takes as its criterion not custom but the most righteous law of almighty God" (*Conf.* 3.7.13). As created and historical beings, however, social practices and biological conditions will play

50. For a subtle discussion of truth, metaphysics, and social practice by a contemporary pragmatist, see Stout, *Democracy and Tradition*, chapter 11. Stout describes his position as "modest pragmatism" (ibid., 251). Gutting also offers a "humdrum realism" that avoids Rorty's rhetorical excess and tries to respond to the sorts of objectivist concerns that motivate Santurri (Gutting, *Pragmatic Liberalism*, 128).

51. In a telling footnote, Santurri allows his proposal "abstracts from the question of the precise sort of moral realism required by Rawlsian liberalism" (Santurri, "Rawlsian Liberalism," 33n46). He alludes, for example, to Hilary Putnam's "internal realism" as a viable (though, to his mind, unsatisfactory) theoretical candidate that would "preserve the full force of liberalism's moral commendations" (ibid., 33n46).

a decisive role in mediating our access to this source: "Does this mean that justice is fickle and changeable? No, but the epochs over which she rules doe not all unfold in the same way" (*Conf.* 3.7.13). Social practices are neither infallible nor exhaustive. Given the noetic effects of sin, an Augustinian will believe that epistemic access to this moral reality faces severe challenges—not the least of which includes our capacity adequately to theorize about moral reality. Augustine himself, for theological reasons, resists the urge to provide a complete "metaphysics."[52] If there is a transcendent moral order, then providing a comprehensive theoretical description of this order escapes our epistemic capacity and may not offer much help in sorting out practical moral judgments in specific circumstances. In fact, many Augustinians want to resist this way of thinking altogether. John Milbank, for example, argues that "Augustine is basically right: truth, for Christianity, is not correspondence, but rather *participation* of the beautiful in the beauty of God" (*TST*, 427). Philosophers will continue to debate these topics with merit, even in terms of the transcendental conditions that make normative discourse possible. In fact, I find Santurri's work on meta-ethical issues deeply illuminating for both theoretical and practical concerns. Theory often helps us with our practical decisions. But should commitment to a meta-ethical view be held as a requirement for continued moral conversations about how to order society? Does the moral health of democracy depend upon the adequacy of meta-ethical positions or upon reaching agreement on them? I hope not. I agree with Robert Adams's claim that "the moral agreement democracy needs, however, is not to be found in a common ethical theory or even in a common theory of justice, but in the unsystematic plurality of agreements that constitute common morality."[53] In the next chapter, I discuss love's relation to moral realism more explicitly in the context of a liberal politics that has features of a modest perfectionism. I suspect most democratic citizens

52. According to Rist, "While Augustine offers us a moral account of what human nature must be like, with a phenomenological 'psychology' to go with it, the 'metaphysics' is incomplete and inadequate. That is because, for Augustine, we do not *know* what a man, that is, a perfect man, is like" (*ATB*, 147).

53. Adams, "Religious Ethics," 107. Elsewhere, Adams argues (against Rawls) that "those who take a more Niebuhrian view of human sinfulness . . . might expect more guidance from a theory that devoted less attention to ideal conditions of rational agreement, and more to acceptance and limitation of conflict" (Adams, *Finite and Infinite Goods*, 222).

implicitly adopt Santurri's position, but why make contested positions on metaphysics so central to the well-being of liberal society?

Santurri clearly affirms epistemic humility by his appeal to the "gap between moral language and moral reality" (10). Recognition of the limits of human knowledge, however, does not yield radical skepticism or the reduction of truth to utility. He admits: "Anything Rawls says about the historically conditioned character of political justification is entirely compatible with a construal of liberal values in realistic terms" (19). But who claims they are incompatible for *political purposes?* This is not my argument, and it is not one made by pragmatists like Jeffrey Stout. Santurri worries that this gap between language and reality becomes a nihilistic chasm when fallibility migrates into metaphysical relativism or indifference.[54] Santurri thinks political *philosophy* cannot abide this evasion. It must explain "metaphilosphically the normative values lying behind commitments to liberal political arrangements" (18). My point has been that liberal society can abide this evasion (as it already has), even if I am open to the sociological concern that theoretical description can jeopardize moral practice. Perhaps Santurri only intends to justify his appeal to make political theory an intelligible discipline, but I suspect there is more to his argument. He thinks we need metaphysics to make sense of liberal moral commitments. Given my primary focus on the portrait of an Augustinian citizen, the adequacy of Santurri's move to transcendental argumentation and something like a cosmic support for liberalism ultimately lies beyond the interests of this chapter. I can take refuge here in Santurri's own claim that "liberal politics may be practiced while leaving certain *theoretical* questions unexamined" (18). A liberal citizen can be a good citizen without having to settle theoretical accounts about the practice of good citizenship, let alone a vocabulary for a theory of moral realism. Maybe a liberal philosopher cannot abide this evasion, but a good citizen can. What does the good Augustinian liberal citizen look like for Santurri? Here I find a compelling set of images, ones that for political purposes do not rely on Santurri's controversial metaphysics.

Notwithstanding his differences with Rawls, Santurri furthers the image of liberal citizens as valuing the goods of "peace, order, and consensus" (22). Given

---

54. I take this to be the anxiety behind his careful reviews of Stout's earlier work: Edmund Santurri, "Nihilism Revisited," *Journal of Religion* 71, no. 1 (January 1991): 67–78, and "The Flight from Pragmatism," *Religious Studies Review* 9 (October 1983): 330–38.

the pluralism of contemporary society and the dangers of political coercion among a society of free and equal citizens, he encourages commitment to liberal institutions and practices. Augustinian concern for peace is consistent with a liberal understanding of autonomy since "infringements on human freedom, after all, typically disturb the peace of individuals and groups" (23). Given this fact, he reasons, "normative concerns of peace and autonomy will converge in a commendation of neutral political structures under pluralistic conditions" (23). His defense of autonomy is derivative of his concern for peace rather than "a Kantian respect for persons as free or autonomous in some metaphysical sense" (29). But it is not merely an instrumental defense. It is driven by moral concerns that he takes to be constitutive of the Augustinian tradition.

According to Santurri, Augustine believes that the temporal peace afforded by political life is not simply an instrumental good but also "an *intrinsic* good that informs the created order and can be possessed *qua* good by unbeliever (citizen of the *earthly* city) and believer (citizen of the *heavenly* city) alike" (25). Of course, Santurri quickly points out, this temporal peace is "unfinished and relatively impoverished" (25). The real problem is not the status of the politics that secures temporal peace for Santurri's Augustine. It is how citizens put it to "bad use" (25). Like Markus, Santurri focuses on the direction of the wills that engage political life. Here Santurri offers a suggestive and intriguing line of thought: "Given the command to love the neighbor as well as the determinations of natural law, Augustinian Christians will have decisive *moral* reasons to *seek* this good of temporal peace for all human beings, whether Christian or not" (25). He later suggests that love of neighbor—when exercised by responsible authorities—justifies political coercion "in defense of peaceable citizens" (28). Against John Milbank, Santurri argues that a rejection of a non-tragic use of force privileges the "pedagogic" justification of coercion to the neglect of another normative justification that views coercion as legitimate when "utilized by officials charged to keep the peace" (35n61).[55] I return to this important argument in the next chapter

---

55. Milbank acknowledges this aspect of Augustine's writing but argues that it is inconsistent with an Augustinian rejection of "any ontological purchase to *dominium*, or power for its own sake" (*TST*, 419). It violates Augustine's own commitment to the "ontological priority of peace over conflict" (363). On this view, punishment can never be positive; it is only by way of the forgiveness of sins that we can "unthink the necessity of violence" (411).

when I consider the writings of Paul Ramsey, a prominent social ethicist who linked the just war tradition with Augustinian neighbor-love. Like Markus and Weithman, however, Santurri does not systematically explore what it means to love the neighbor in Augustinian terms. Love, precisely as a "moral reason," gets the short end of the stick compared to Santurri's extended discussion of metaphysics as the condition for the possibility of liberal society. Santurri, no doubt, has considered views on the relevance of love for political Augustinianism. They are signaled by his brief remarks I cite above. I want to make these moments in Augustinian liberalism—of the realist and Rawlsian type—more explicit. Santurri might think that appeal to love is tied up with his appeal to a "transcendent moral order," but that is a separable question from the relation between love of neighbor and love of God (who is more than a "transcendent moral order"). I want to encourage Santurri's succinct claim that the "essential disposition of the Augustinian Christian toward the peaceable political order is one of critical appreciation rather than critical opposition" (27). In this respect, Santurri's version of Augustinian liberalism anticipates my third type.

AUGUSTINIANISM AS CIVIC LIBERALISM

I introduce Augustinian civic liberalism by noting two short responses to Santurri's essay. These two responses help introduce the larger patterns of understanding that shape this emerging type.

Timothy P. Jackson's response to Santurri identifies differences among Augustinian liberalisms and, combined with his other writings, is a primary source for morally perfectionist yet politically liberal Augustinianism. In *"Prima Caritas, Inde Jus:* Why Augustinians Shouldn't Baptize John Rawls," Jackson takes issue not with Santurri's defense of the liberal state but the equation of liberalism with Rawlsian neutrality. He questions the preoccupation with stability that he thinks lies behind the attraction of neutrality. This attraction undermines the possibility of the prophetic in public discourse, a voice that can challenge the presumptions of liberal discourse. Santurri, according to Jackson, misplaces the justification of Augustinian liberalism. The virtues of political restraint that Santurri (and Weithman) credit with Rawlsian neutrality are not Augustinian. Rather, for Augustinians, *"the state is constrained out of love itself, not some 'neutral' public rationality.*"[56] Jackson denies what he considers the anemic Rawlsian notion that citizens *qua* citizens should "prescind as much as possible from judgments about truth, goodness, the meaning of life, and the proper object of love" (49). To endorse the procedural language of consensus and the thin conception of the good is "to leave Augustine's social reflection behind" (50). Augustinian liberals, according to Jackson, should adopt "proper love" rather than "neutral justice" as "the defining metaphor of liberal society" (57). For an Augustinian, "goods such as respect for individual conscience are the *fruit* of basic theological convictions, not the *seed*, and these fruits require rich nutrients" (51). Jackson writes: "The question is one of priority. What Rawls would guarantee *a priori* by distancing comprehensive doctrines and largely privatizing theological virtues, the Augustinian promotes as the *a fortiori* upshot of true doctrines and right loves. In short, Augustinian liberalism is morally robust, not morally empty or even morally minimalist" (51). On this view, Rawlsian liberalism offers an unrealistic political sociology and weak moral justifications of its own professed commitment to freedom and equality.

Jackson locates these failures in the liberal unwillingness to speak conceptually to issues of moral motivation. He does not question Rawls's own "good intentions." He questions how any moral motivation can find its place in a Rawlsian account. Jackson's Rawls effectively denies any role for love in the political life of religious believers in a liberal society. In this short essay, Jackson's reveals that his larger project is motivated by a desire to *"recapture the distinctively religious and philosophical foundations of Western liberalism"* (57). For Augustinians, he identifies these foundations as "common sinfulness" and "common dignity" as well as a common "inequality with God" and "equality with one another" (57). These foundations are familiar to the first and second types of Augustinian liberalisms. It is in the conclusion to his essay that Jackson distinguishes his account and moves toward the third type of Augustinian liberalism.

"If Augustinian Christians believe in anything, it is in the priority of love" (59). In this passing line that he elsewhere develops at length, Jackson opens the door for a distinctive kind of Augustinian civic liberalism. He concludes:

---

56. Timothy P. Jackson, *"Prima Caritas, Inde Jus,"* 49. Parenthetical references in this section of the text refer to this essay.

Rational self-interest and social reciprocity are genuine goods in proportion, but when they are the central political motivation, justice itself atrophies. The surest way to secure peace may be to work for justice, but the surest way to promote justice is not to value it too highly or to aim at it to the neglect of other virtues, such as love. . . . Otherwise we forget those human ties that bind—compassion, mercy, forgiveness—and reduce our life together to contractual obligation or historical convention. . . . Augustinians consider themselves indebted to God and called to serve one another politically and legally beyond anything that reciprocity or self-interest can express or enjoin. . . . If citizens are merely just—whether defined negatively as not harming others or positively as giving others their distributive due—they are less than human. To affirm *"Prima caritas"* is to aver that we all live by the grace of God and the kindness of strangers, whether we acknowledge this or not. In leaving so little room for the fallible (yet public) expression of these truths, Rawls parts company with anything I can square with specifically Augustinian political thought or even broadly Christian moral motivation. (*"Prima caritas,"* 59)

I quote this passage at length because it presents Jackson's broader claims about love and liberalism. Alongside feminist theory, Jackson's writings have decisively influenced my effort to advance a revised Augustinian defense of liberal citizenship that emerges from basic convictions about love's relation to justice.[57] However, I do not adopt all of his positions or interpretations. These differences will emerge more fully in later chapters, but it is helpful to introduce some of them at this point.

Jackson's account of the early Rawls on motivation, for example, is misleading. He does not take sufficient account of the circumscribed role of the original position as an artificial device of justification that tries to imagine the circumstances of impartial justice rather than offer a complete anthropological description. Rawls is clear that "the motivation of persons in the original position must not be confused with the motivation of persons in everyday life who accept the principles of justice."[58] Ethical egoism is not assumed at the level of motivation. In fact, according to Rawls, the original

57. Jackson also expresses his debts to feminist thought, particularly Carol Gilligan, Susan Moller Okin, and Eve Fedder Kittay, in developing his emphasis on interpersonal care and a relational view of the self (see *PL*, 3–11 and 54–61, and *Love Disconsoled*, 100n20).

58. Rawls, *Theory of Justice*, 128.

position "involves no particular theory of human motivation."[59] In *Political Liberalism*, Rawls even more clearly states that "rational agents approach being psychopathic when their interests are solely in benefits to themselves."[60] Some Rawlsians might be faulted for allowing the discourse of justification to migrate into their accounts of motivations. But Rawls does not.

More importantly, I distance myself from Jackson's insistence on the (chronological and moral) priority of love as a metavalue that is self-generating and uniquely stands apart from other virtues and values. Jackson's move forces *agapic* love to do too much work without correlate appeal to other values (such as righteousness and even Christian *eros*). Despite his repeated insistence that love never does less than justice, for example, the above negative account of the "merely just" citizen slights the Augustinian insight that love always already plays a role in justice (even as *suum cuique*).[61] Jackson seems so intent on contrasting biblical love with modern theories of justice that he neglects other possibilities for love's relation to justice itself. At times, he appears only to want to contrast the love of "biblical theology" with the contractual or reciprocal justice of secular "modern philosophy" (*PL*, 33). But that way of relating love and justice stacks the deck and does not support his general claims about love and justice. 1 Cor-

59. Ibid., 130. Rawls here does not reduce self-interest to selfishness as the basic feature of the human condition. The interests are not "in the self" but "interests of a self that regards its conception of the good as worthy of recognition and that advances claims in its behalf as deserving satisfaction" (127). In fact, he allows that "although justice as fairness begins by taking persons in the original position as individuals, or more accurately as continuing strands, this is no obstacle to explicating higher-order moral sentiments that serve to bind a community of persons together" (192). Rawls explicitly rejects the notion of a "private society" in his defense of a "well-ordered" society where human beings "need one another as partners in ways of life that are engaged in for their own sake" (522–23). Christian ethicists often mistakenly identify Rawls with ethical (and metaphysical) egoism. In addition to Jackson, see Vacek, *Love, Human and Divine*, 219–23. If anything, I think Rawls's description of the original position can be seen as an analogy for original sin. Jackson, then, is wrong to contrast the original position with the creation narrative rather than the Fall (Jackson, "To Bedlam and Part Way Back," 429).

60. Rawls, *Political Liberalism,* 51; see also "Reply to Hegel's Criticism," in *Political Liberalism,* 285–88.

61. Despite his criticisms of modern justice as *suum cuique*, Jackson can claim that "*agape* may be seen as something like a marriage of classical *eros* and modern justice" (*PL*, 68) and "the most distinctive biblical contribution to social ethics is that we owe one another love" (67).

inthians 13:13 does announce that love is the "greatest," but only here in relation to faith and hope which do not abide. Indeed, Jackson admits that "it seems best to say that love is not independent of justice" (8n23). In fact, jeopardizing his account of love as metavalue, he claims both that "if justice is understood as biblical righteousness, it is virtuously synonymous with *agape*" (33) and that "biblical 'justice' effectively equals what I call 'charity'" (35n20). At other times, he holds that love is "*supra justitiam*" (105). Which is it? Jackson rejects a competition between love and justice. But justice, if it truly involves giving each his or her due in all respects, already involves loving what merits love and giving due acknowledgement of all that we depend on. For an Augustinian, the recognition of love's sinful promiscuity requires a sense of justice to reign in its tendency to spend or direct itself idolatrously. Or, put a better way, *proper* love includes a notion of justice that resists any straightforward hierarchical ranking of virtues or meta-ethical division between love and justice. For Augustinians, "justice is not an external constraint on love, it is the critical corrective love imposes upon itself in order to ensure that it does not overwhelm its object."[62] Despite himself, Jackson's insistent and repeated endorsement of the "priority of love" misleadingly perpetuates a value conflict between love and justice, like the disciples arguing about which "of them was to be regarded as the greatest" (Luke 22:24).[63]

More fundamental moral and theological differences emerge. Because I adopt a version of Augustine's theological eudaimonism, I resist Jackson's Stoic uncoupling of Christian charity from traditional Christian beliefs about the Eschaton. I share Jackson's moral concerns about the role of rewards and economies of exchange in an account of Christian virtue. Eudaimonism can denigrate earthly life and instrumentalize charity as a base incentive for getting into heaven. Jackson's effort to provide a more "incarnational" model of Christian love does fend off the excesses of those who would

62. Mathewes, *Augustinian Tradition*, 140.

63. Does Jackson hope, for example, that justice might perdure in the Eschaton? It is not clear. David Hume and John Rawls both claim that justice would not be necessary in a paradise, but Augustine held otherwise: "Justice however is immortal, and will rather then be perfected in us than cease to be" (*DT* 14.3.12). Aquinas held a similar view (*ST* I.II Q.67). For an interesting meditation on justice under utopian conditions of extensive benevolence with (implicit) significance for eschatology, see John P. Reeder, "Assenting to Agape," *Journal of Religion* 60 (January 1980): 17–31.

reduce love to a motivation contingent on contractual understandings of getting something "above and beyond." Standing within a medieval tradition of disinterested love, he wants Christians to have the purity of will to love God only for the sake of God. But to borrow from the title of his other major work, *Love Disconsoled*, what needs to be disconsoled is not love but the sort of future-oriented eschatology that divides God's gracious work in creation from incarnation and redemption. The beatific vision—as medieval Augustinians would come to speak about the vision of God that makes us eternally happy—is constituted by participation in the fellowship of virtue. Unlike Augustine who momentarily catches a glimpse of this communal vision *in dialogue* with another (Monica), Jackson seems to imagine a private heaven that "is full of people who are not particularly concerned with being there."[64] Augustine's account of love, by contrast, always sees love as a relation: "For love is not loved unless it is already loving something, because where nothing is being loved there is no love" (*DT* 9.1.2). Indeed, Augustine famously claims, in love "there are three, lover and what is being loved, and love" (*DT* 8.10.14). Jackson's Christian love is disconsoled too much. He offers an inspiring ethic of perseverance and commitment "without lapsing into either despair or delusion."[65] Bereft of the connection between other-regard as "internal" to the end of *eudaimonia*, however, Jackson himself departs

---

64. O'Donovan, *PSL*, 155. It is theologically significant that Augustine's vision at Ostia occurs in *shared conversation* rather than in *solitary delight*: "And as we talked and panted for it, we just touched the edge of it by the utmost leap of our hearts; then, sighing and unsatisfied, we left the first-fruits of our spirit captive there, and returned to the noise of articulate speech, where a word has a beginning and an end" (*Conf.* 9.10.24). Garry Wills draws attention to this episode as "communal, not a private ascent" (Wills, *Augustine*, 62). He glosses: "The prayer at Ostia shows how the bond of company *(socialis necessitudo)* can lift one up to heaven—in contrast with the way it dragged Adam down when he joined Eve's motion away from God" (62). Rowan Williams also emphasizes that the episode at Ostia is a "powerful challenge to the 'Platonic' model of individual escape from words and matter, because of its conversational character" (Williams, "Language, Reality and Desire," 145). I later argue that the dialogic character of this episode should temper Romand Coles's contrast between the confessional Augustine and ways of living that entail "a continual dialogical encounter with *otherness* and *others*" (Coles, *Self/Power/Other*, 85).

65. Jackson, *Love Disconsoled*, 230.

from an Augustinian social philosophy.[66] My concerns are not predicated on Jackson's nuanced account of the role of self-sacrifice in the Christian moral life. They are more broadly theological: in hunting down Platonism, Jackson's disconsolation risks the very "coherence of the divine Personality" which he intends to recover (*PL*, 24). He embraces a hyper-ethical destiny that purifies even the resurrection hope that remains in him. On the one hand, his *agape* does not seem to care whether or not there is a social relation that involves *my* presence (admittedly transformed by the encounter with the concrete neighbor and the presence of God). On the other hand, this leads to his theological speculations of a God willing not to exist. This conception of God comes dangerously close to providing a Pelagian occasion for celebrating the anthropocentric purity of the agent's own motives.

Jackson's theological ethics is imaginative and challenging. However, to speak theologically, I fear it verges on a kind of Christomonism whereby the eternal processions of the Trinity are reduced to the temporal mission of the cruciform Son. In fact, it is not clear what role the Trinity plays, or can play, in his account. Epistemologically, it may be that God on the cross is the only God we can "know" by faith. Jackson, however, takes Kierkegaard's heuristic expression of neighbor love (the pure disinterested love of the dead) to its final ontological extreme: the only God to be loved is the dead God. Unlike Kierkegaard, Jackson offers a God whose resurrection is uncertain. To make divine self-extinction a possibility conflicts with his own confession that the Persons of the Trinity "eternally love" (*PL*, 24) one another and that the Cross is not "all we know of divinity" (23). If God's kenosis is so risky that the divine life is itself exhaustible, there can be no "worm hole" for the faithful, as Jackson maintains.[67] This *radicalized* kenoticism departs from Augustine and Augustinianism, and, to put it most polemically, appears to confirm Nietzsche's claim

---

66. I use "internal" here in the sense that Alasdair MacIntyre "calls a means internal to a given end when the end cannot be adequately characterized independently of a characterization of the means" (MacIntyre, *After Virtue*, 184). Jackson is vulnerable to John Milbank's concern that "other-regarding" Christian ethics is "more Christian than Christianity" (*BR*, 141). Referring to an earlier version of Milbank's argument, Jackson notes that Milbank's critique of "disinterested self-giving" is "powerful" (*PL*, 23n64). But Jackson faults Milbank for failing to distinguish between self-sacrifice as a means to various ends and an end in itself.

67. Jackson, *Love Disconsoled*, 128.

that "after Christian truthfulness has drawn one inference after another, it must end by drawing its *most striking inference*, its inference *against* itself."[68]

Augustine counsels otherwise: "No one is wrong to want immortality if human nature is capable of receiving it as God's gift" (*DT* 13.3.11). In fact, unlike aspects of Platonism, it is not the personal condition of immortality as such that is desired but the perfection of our nature in God. Indeed, for Augustine, "the reward of virtue will be God Himself, Who gives virtue, and Who has promised Himself to us" (*CD* 22.30). The happy life is "to rejoice in [God], about [God] and because of [God]" (*Conf.* 10.22.32). Here there is no "muscular grab for heaven."[69] The life of virtue that includes proper self-love is not predicated on getting anything; remember, for Augustine, God is not a thing. Augustine's notion of freedom explicitly rejects as pernicious servitude those who love "through fear of penalty and not through love of righteousness" (*De spiritu et littera* 14.26). Christ's compassion is not a forgery and God is good for us, but God's kenosis for us *(pro nobis)* is a gift that does not give God *(in se)* away because that is who an inexhaustible God is—eternally interpersonal even in incarnation and crucifixion, "like light flowing from light" (*DT* 4.5.27). To love and take delight in this good (which means to accept knowledge of God as gift) is not something Christians need abandon or find morally shameful. Jackson opens the door for such a reading when he admits that self-realization is "a consequence (a double effect) of discipleship" (*PL*, 8). But these concerns put me closer to Paul Ramsey's account of love in the opening chapter of *Basic Christian Ethics*, and to an even greater extent, Paul Tillich's account of love in *Love, Power, and Justice*. Tillich, for example, formulates the ecstatic element of *agape* as "love cutting into love" that does change the character of justice (*LPJ*, 33). But he does not conceive of love in terms of a priority that calls justice into question.[70] In this light, I am a weak agapist in Jackson's terms. The relations of love and justice, like those between Christ's humanity and divinity, are too complex to argue for love as a metavalue.

68. Nietzsche, *Genealogy of Morals*, 161.

69. Jackson, *Love Disconsoled*, 29.

70. Jackson worries that Tillich "virtually identifies love and justice" (*PL*, 38). Jackson's worry may be predicated on an unwarranted conflation either of the ethical and the ontological dimensions of love or of Tillich's notion of justice with modern liberal justice. But it is not clear what he means by "virtual identification"? Does Jackson mean to condemn any nonunivocal analogy between love and justice?

The direction which I push Augustinian civic liberalism, however, is generally consistent with Jackson's larger vision of the viability of love and liberalism. His original and powerful constructive interests lead him away from commenting extensively on particular Augustinian texts; and, he departs from Augustinianism on crucial issues related to a theology of love. Putting forward his claims, however, will help my effort to push Augustinian liberalism in a new direction.

Like many Christian modernity-critics, Jackson fears the success of political liberalism is parasitic on social structures and moral capacities that it undermines. He shares Alasdair MacIntyre's belief that modern "moral judgments are linguistic survivals from the practices of classical theism which have lost the context provided by these practices."[71] Political liberalism, on Jackson's account, is not as innocent as it claims to be. However one reads its formal analysis of neutrality, liberalism suggests a "preferred perspective on reality."[72] Rawls admits the *de facto* influence on comprehensive views that his version of political liberalism requires, but he considers this reality an inevitable feature of any political regime.[73] Jackson worries that political liberalism of this kind is more pernicious than Rawls's admission suggests. In particular, for Jackson, modern liberalism is self-defeating because it promotes a moral and political culture that undermines its own values.[74] His project aims to "protect charity against the corrosive effects of modern contract theory by insisting that love rises above the demands of secular

71. MacIntyre, *After Virtue*, 60.

72. Fern, "Religious Belief in a Rawlsian Society," 41.

73. Rawls, *Political Liberalism*, 196n31.

74. This criticism also can be found in much of the theological literature on love. For example, James E. Gilman argues that if "[liberals] insist, as Rawls does, that matters of virtue are not demanded by the basic structure of society, a society is likely to develop a culture of self-absorption and breed habits of insensitivity, indifference, and social neglect" (Gilman, *Fidelity of Heart*, 148). Gilman's constructive recommendations are also consistent with Jackson. Gilman claims that "neither liberalism's 'veil of ignorance' nor communitarian's 'virtue of character,' but compassion's 'vale of tears' should take priority in public life and policy. . . . For although differing, as do convex and concave, justice and virtue share a concrete, moral ground in compassion" (150). These arguments, may too easily contrast compassion and other-regard with a viable Christian account of autonomy, but Gilman does argue for "a liberal sense of compassionate justice" (150).

justice."[75] I have already indicated my disagreement with this strong reading of social contract liberalism as not other-regarding by its very foundations, at least in terms of Rawls. Liberal respect can itself be motivated by an affirmation of the other through a demanding form of intersubjective recognition. Nonetheless, unlike critics such as Stanley Hauerwas who advise Christians to abandon "the liberal project in its epistemological or political form,"[76] Jackson remains a "wary but willing champion of the liberal state."[77] Hauerwas's prolific attacks on the liberal project are grounded in what he takes to be Augustinian convictions regarding the alien status of Christian citizenship and the dangerous captivity of Christian social ethics since the conversion of Constantine. My book tries to move contemporary Augustinianism toward Jackson's liberal agapism and away from Hauerwas's antiliberalism.[78]

Jackson's basic claim against much of contemporary liberalism is the belief that liberal political culture requires "a prophetic value more basic than autonomy and still more meta than reciprocal justice: personal care, or what the Christian tradition calls 'charity'" (*PL*, 68). Jackson continues:

> Without the cultivation of care for and by individuals within a community, private choice and public cooperation become unimaginable. Without attention to objects worthy of desire and to people due solidarity, both personal happiness and equal regard for others (cornerstones of liberalism itself) vanish, or never emerge. . . . We must recognize human dependency as well as freedom, nurture love as well as fairness. (*PL*, 68)

75. Jackson, "Is God Just?," 395. Jackson also insists that "love can never fall below such justice into unfairness or arbitrariness and remain love" (395). As he later puts it, "love precedes justice and often rises above it, but love also sometimes stoops to embrace justice, thereby limiting itself" (400).

76. Hauerwas, *After Christendom?*, 35.

77. Jackson, "*Prima Caritas*," 49.

78. I do not take Hauerwas to advocate a sectarian withdrawal. But his dominant voice suggests that any search for alternative social and political practices within liberal democracy is doomed to remain a "Constantinian" search. At other times, Hauerwas's recessive voice seems to endorse a project that exploits the best of liberalism. He claims, for example, to have no objection to supporting liberalism's defense of respect for persons "as long as it does not underwrite a nationalism that legitimates an uncontrollable self-righteousness" (Hauerwas, *After Christendom?*, 35). Jackson cites similar ambiguities ("Christian Love and Political Violence," 184–85). These ambiguities, I suspect, derive from the competing influences on his thought (i.e., Aquinas, Barth, H. R. Niebuhr, Wittgenstein, Gustafson, MacIntyre, Yoder, and Milbank).

Such cultivation is an important feature of liberal education and an important part of moral development that should be affirmed in the public culture. Rawlsian liberals, on my view, need not deny these clams, but Jackson is right to highlight their insufficient attention in liberal theory. The priority of charity, which Jackson associates with Abraham Lincoln and Martin Luther King Jr, attempts to "*hold the prophetic values of need and desert in dynamic tension with the more modern goods of liberty and equality*" (*PL*, 56).[79] By attending to these values (if one can call need and desert "values"), Jackson tries to imagine a better liberalism by appeal to love. It is a prophetic liberalism "founded on a positive willing of the good for others as fellow creatures of God" (*PL*, 62). Jackson, however, is acutely aware of the objections to the priority of love for an ethics of liberal citizenship.

In addition to identifying traditional critics of Christian love such as Nietzsche and Freud, Jackson accurately identifies the dominant liberal concern. He writes:

> In general, the secular liberal argues, Christian love generates a self-righteousness that foments dogmatism and aggression. The theological virtues frequently move those who think they have them to extirpate those who supposedly do not. Although believers may feel commissioned to "save" others, the fact that this salvation may come in spite of others' actual preferences means that agapists often end up "loving" others to death (as in the Inquisition). Hence it is no surprise that "bourgeois liberals" like Richard Rorty want to distance all talk of "true virtue" as inclining us to "bash each

---

79. Jackson claims that public education should emphasize biography over theory and assign works "on Buddha, Krishna, Moses, Christ, and Mohammed—as well as Cicero, Napoleon, Marx, Freud, and Susan B. Anthony" (*PL*, 69). Interestingly, the aims of this sort of compassionate education are not dissimilar from Augustine's early education. Peter Brown writes that Augustine's classical education encouraged him "to weep, and to make other's weep" (*Augustine of Hippo*, 37). Edward Vacek also supports something similar to Jackson's curricular reforms: "Our culture invests enormous resources to the education of the intellect. Unfortunately our educational system does not devote as much energy to educating the emotions, and therefore does not sensitize us to the breadth and depth of the realm of values. In fact, traditional schooling probably stifles emotional growth as much as it helps" (*Love, Divine and Human*, 7–8). Gilman argues that "if compassion is to be successfully practiced as public policy, then it is a habit that must be taught and learned not only in the home but in the schools, both public and private" (*Fidelity of Heart*, 152). Since public schools are important sites of civic formation, it is not surprising that debates about values curriculum figure centrally in liberalism.

other's head in" for the sake of dominant goods (natural or supernatural) about which we can get no popular agreement. (*PL*, 41)

Jackson's response to this objection to the paternalist possibility of politicized love begins by undermining the "overly Platonic vision of love" that the liberal objection assumes (*PL*, 52). If love is primarily oriented toward an abstract ideal such as a *summum bonum* rather than to particular persons, Jackson argues, then the liberal objection takes hold. Repeating a familiar argument against a so-called Platonic view of love, Jackson fears that "respecting the particularity of finite people will matter far less than promoting the *summum bonum* (e.g., God's will) in which they participate. . . . Individuals will be, at best, interchangeable, and anyone may be sacrificed for the greater good which is the true source of value" (52). Indeed, despite his identification with much of the realist legacy of political Augustinianism, Jackson argues that Augustine's own account of love moves in this direction. Civic agapism, therefore, must reject Augustinian *caritas*. Rather than turn to Augustinianism as a resource for a more charitable liberalism (my position), he claims that this tradition supports a bad view of charity by "claiming that only God is to be 'enjoyed' for His own sake, thus that human beings are to be 'used' for the sake of something higher" (52). Revealing his debts to Anders Nygren, Jackson offers an account of *agape* and the relation between divine and human love that emphasizes concern for the concrete particularity of the good of other persons without ulterior motives or extrinsic rewards in view.[80] My account argues that Jackson, like his mentor Paul Ramsey, misreads Augustinianism. I reject his understanding of what he ominously terms "the Plotinian-Augustinian God" (90). On my view, faithful Augustinians can share Jackson's worry about a monistic love of the highest good that leads to idolatry or oppression. But, at this point, it is helpful first to consider Jackson's powerful response to the liberal objection.

80. While he does believe proper self-love as a kind of self-transcendence via interpersonal service is compatible with *agape*, Jackson admits that his "debt to Anders Nygren is considerable" (*PL*, 8n25). His rejection of Augustinian *caritas* involves other rejections of traditional Christianity that are not distinctively Augustinian: "A whole tradition of Christian consolers (from Augustine to Aquinas and beyond) goes wrong in deeming charity to be aimed primarily (if not exclusively) at God, fully guaranteed (if not necessitated) for some people by God, and exquisitely invulnerable (if not solitarily self-sufficient) in relation to other creatures. Or so I think" (Jackson, "Disconsolation of Theology," 28).

Jackson argues that for Christian *agape*, "love of neighbor is preceded by and grounded in, but not negated by, love of God" (*PL*, 53). This is not a chronological order but a testimony to the way in which divinity empowers humanity. Jackson rejects the conflation of the love commands even as he finds them normatively bound to one another through the person and work of Jesus Christ. Combining technical terms from both Ramsey and Outka with his own emphasis on passional commitment, Jackson argues that *agape* is characterized by three features: "(1) unconditional commitment to the good of others, (2) equal regard for the well-being of others, and (3) passionate service open to self-sacrifice for the sake of others."[81] Drawing on these features in response to the liberal objection, he argues, "the agapist notes that love honors the free consciences of others (within the widest possible limits) precisely because they are fellow creatures made in the Image of God, distinct beings worthy of respect yet marred by the same Fall that touches everyone."[82] This formulation appears at odds with Jackson's Nygren-like concerns not to ground the motivation to love in a set of attributes or in an appraisal of worthiness of respect (even as identified by the image of God). I take Jackson's point, however, to be that Christian love imitates Christ and follows Pauline counsels that the believer is to endure in patience, to suffer for others, to care for others' physical and psychological health, and to remain open to the stranger. Such love "undergirds and transcends but does not violate reciprocal justice."[83] *Agape*, he claims, resists arrogant paternalism.

Jackson's vision of *agape* "requires a self-emptying orientation toward the other, whose reality, need, and otherness count for everything."[84] Such an orientation promotes a strong civic agapism that relies on the charisms of love, compassion, and goodness. Jackson is aware that these emphases are thicker than most liberal theories. But, on his view, the price that liberalism has paid for tolerance and ethical formalism is too high and unnecessary. It has led to a vacuity in liberal discussions of moral identity and an ethics of citizenship that neglects love. Irony (Rorty) and fear of cruelty (Shklar), whatever their status as political virtues, are insufficient. His political elevation of love emerges from solidarity with the shared humanity of fellow citizens that remains open to

81. Jackson, *Love Disconsoled*, 15; see also *PL*, 10.
82. Jackson, "Political Violence," 212.
83. Ibid., 212.
84. Jackson, *Love Disconsoled*, xi.

the giftedness of the other. While Jackson rejects Augustine's account of love, he explicitly trades on realist Augustinian themes mediated through Niebuhr, Ramsey, and Outka. One detects Augustinian commitments in his account of the chastening of *agape* that emerges from a fallibist epistemology and a willingness to accept those fragile vulnerabilities of human life that cannot be overcome by assertion of autonomy.

Jackson offers an attractive vision of a citizen motivated not by "self-referential fear" but "other-regarding love."[85] But Augustinians, perhaps alongside the bourgeois liberals he criticizes, might still worry about potential arrogance in Jackson's civic agapism. Augustinian civic liberals should look critically at his proposal in both theory and practice. Jackson's agapism, motivated by self-sacrificial love of strangers and enemies, exceeds the kind of political love that can be normatively basic for the governance of earthly political community. To put it crudely, he allows too much of one interpretation of Kierkegaard and not enough of another interpretation of Augustine.

The liberal, not convinced that arrogance has been abandoned, might wonder who is being asked for openness to self-sacrifice. By what political means is it being enforced? Inquisitions are not the only political form of love gone wrong. Must we all, Christian and non-Christian, embrace Jackson's kenotic vision of political love to have a chance at a decent society? Is his model of *agape*, conceived so radically self-emptying that otherness counts for everything, a ready model for civic virtue? Christian love stands ready to meet the needs of others, but is his model psychologically appropriate even for familial or ecclesial relations, let alone civic relations? Does it try too hard to see "face to face"? Are there other ways to think about a political account of *agape*, like caring for the proximate one in need, accepting self-sacrifice as a sometime consequence of a care that should be distributed broadly among citizens? In the following chapters, I hope to answer these questions by rehabilitating Augustine's doctrine of love in response to the concerns about liberalism that I share with Jackson. I show how Augustinian love is balanced by an account of sin that nonetheless offers more than a minimalist set of civic virtues. If successful, perhaps Jackson's liberalism can be made even more Augustinian. I might also relieve a Christian love that goes political from some of the difficulties I have identified. For now, I conclude this section with a more promising example of Augustinian civic liberalism.

Jean Bethke Elshtain's response to Edmund Santurri also travels in the direction of my preferred third type. Again, the purposes of my book do not

85. Ibid.

require me to endorse or pursue many of Elshtain's broader claims, but I point to her work as a suggestive alternative to realist or Rawlsian types of Augustinian liberalism.

Like Jackson, Elshtain holds that "Santurri overassimilates Augustine's position to Rawls's."[86] Unlike Jackson, however, Elshtain offers a more positive evaluation of Augustine's doctrine of love. On her account, Augustinian love provides the sort of other-regarding affirmations that Jackson enjoins for liberal theory. For Elshtain, Rawls and Augustine have radically different anthropologies that force an Augustinian Rawlsian to neglect the fundamental role of love and the direction of desire in Augustine's account of social life. In the final lines of her response, Elshtain suggestively hints at the importance of this difference:

> For, finally, Augustine is about love—love of God and love of neighbor—and this is where justice enters as well. Augustine's definition of a people starts with love. A people is the association of a multitude of rational beings united by a common agreement on the objects of their love. It follows that to observe the character of a particular people we must examine the objects of its love. Between Augustinian love and Rawlsian neutrality there is an unbridgeable chasm.[87]

These themes are developed in her more extended treatment of political Augustinianism, *Augustine and the Limits of Politics*.

Early in this book, Elshtain seems to concur with those who judge Augustine an unsuitable source for liberalism. She writes: "[Augustine] was certainly no liberal democrat; he didn't talk about a social contract; rights are not part of his political vocabulary; his understanding of authority is pretty much opaque to us, believing, as we do, that even persuasion is a form of imposition" (*LP*, 5). And yet, like other Augustinian liberals, Elshtain moves beyond satire to argue that this initial rejection requires a reinterpretation.

As the title of her book suggests, she shares in the realist (and Rawlsian) affirmations of "the extent to which our control over the world is limited" and "the fact that human beings live indeterminate and incomplete lives" (*LP*, 67). Sin remains in Elshtain's vision of political Augustinianism: "the earthly city is 'marked' or 'stained' by sin" which provides a "rueful recognition of limits" (*LP*, 94). But rather than turn to Augustine's account of sin to ground her defense of Augustinian liberalism, she turns to his confessional

86. Elshtain, "Unbridgeable Chasm," 45.
87. Ibid., 47.

and affective account of the self. This complex layering of moral and political identity ensures "the filaments of affection must not stop at the portal of the *domus*" (*LP*, 102). In fact, Elshtain argues that it was this feature of Christianity that was particularly appealing to women. She writes:

> What I am clearer on now is the appeal of what I called "the language of Christianity" to women in the late antique world, because the things Christ held dear and cherished—forgiveness, succor, devotion—helped to forge the terms of their own lives, that and the fact that the Christian rhetoric Augustine at first found inelegant and even vulgar was simple and direct—told in the language of the people, cast in the forms of everyday speech, speech that communicated, speech with a liberatory moment that reached out to incorporate into a new community—the *koinonia*—those who were severed from the classical polis, women and the poor. (*LP*, 29)

From these moves, one discerns a different kind of Augustinian liberalism.

Love "provides the horizon" for Augustine's account of selfhood (*LP*, 59). This anthropology is very different from what Elshtain calls the "thin" selves of liberal political theory. In contrast to Augustine's self that is drawn out of "the vortex of immediacy," Elshtain argues that modern liberalism has "turned the loss of a confessing self who is drawn *out* of the self in order to be *for* others into an all-consuming self, an expressivist exhibition" (6; see also 59). This expressivist self leaves little room for a civic culture of solidarity and responsibility because of its tendency toward self-enclosure. It isolates the self from others and threatens the possibility of public life by a manipulative egoism that has no space for the claims of others. Here we see similarities with Jackson's diagnosis of liberal failures. But, for Elshtain, Augustine's fascination with lust and concupiscence (which she helpfully distinguishes from simply being the hang-ups of the sexually confused) demonstrates Augustinian awareness of the moral struggle with "narcissistic self-absorption" (11). For Elshtain,

> *contra* much of what has gone under the name Political Augustinianism, a closer look at Augustine on the nature and purpose of social forms and civic life shows us that these are not, crudely, what sin has brought into the world but what man, who is sinful, has wrought through the use of his God-given reason and his capacity for love, as well as his lust for dominance. (*LP*, 27)

Like John Milbank, Elshtain finds in Augustine a radical critique of the individualism she considers to be characteristic of the ethics of both antique and late modern liberal culture. The founding myths of liberal theory—with its notions of a freestanding individual who stands in relation to the state through a series of reciprocal rights and obligations—strike Elshtain as thoroughly foreign to the spirit of Augustinianism.

Elshtain thinks the persistent image of Augustine as "as a dour, late antique Hobbesian" is misleading because it fails to capture the Augustinian sense that "one's dependence on others is not a diminution but an enrichment of self" (*LP*, 36). Elsewhere, she puts it this way: "If we presume that we are the sole and only ground of our own being, we deny our dependence on others, beginning with that Other who made us in his image."[88] Elshtain wants to reimagine what the "old hat" distinction between *caritas* and *cupiditas* might mean for political Augustinianism. Linking Augustine's theology of love to political ethics, she argues that Augustinian *caritas* is not to be identified with "moralistic self-abnegation but an abundant overflowing of the fullness of life" (36). Like human beings themselves, political Augustinianism has been too captivated by "our enthrallment to *cupiditas* and our all-too-frequent abandonment of *caritas*" (37). Despite his famous descriptions of the miseries of life and false friendship, Elshtain's Augustine makes society central to the enjoyment of the supreme good and provides a countervailing image.[89] Her Augustine continues to dismiss utopianism and stress the difficult business of peace, but "he similarly torments cynics who disdain any project of human community, or justice, or possibility" (91). There is always the possibility of a community tempered by *caritas* that is "generative, not controlling" (94). Community "tempered" by *caritas* here rightly offers a more modest vision than Jackson's goal for political liberalism "grounded" in the priority of *agape*.

88. Elshtain, "Augustine and Diversity," 98.

89. Elshtain misleads, however, in her attribution to Augustine of the definition of friendship that extends to fellow-citizens (*LP*, 38). In the passage she cites (*CD* 19.3), she fails to include Augustine's opening words, "the Philosophers say...." Later in 19.5, Augustine does claim that "the philosophers also consider the life of the wise man is a social one; and this is a view of *which we much more readily approve*" (emphasis mine). The accent of Augustine's argument, however, falls on his more "pessimistic" immediate claim that "who, however, could manage to number and weigh the great ills which abound in human society and the woes of this mortal condition? The philosophers should listen to a character in one of their own comedies expressing a sentiment with which all men agree. 'I took a wife; what misery I found there! Children were born, and more cares came'" (19.5). Augustine's point seems to be that the "philosophers" do not adequately understand sociality. On the difficulties of interpreting these passages, see O'Donovan, "*City of God* 19," 51.

"Only someone caught up in a love affair with the world," Elshtain nicely points out, "would describe so deliciously its many delectations and articulate so artfully its temptations" (*LP*, 89). This alternative way of thinking and being provides a "complex moral map that offers space for loyalty and love and care, as well as for a *chastened form of civic virtue*" (91, emphasis mine). Again, we see that Elshtain positions a "chastened form of civic virtue" as a more moderate alternative to the ambitions of Jackson's agapic form of civic virtue. (Though, on my account, an Augustinian civic liberal might see love and care precisely *as* civic virtue, rather than "as well as" civic virtue.)

Augustine's moral ontology imagines a political world that both "beckons" and "enchains" (*LP*, 60). Despite the realist sounding title of her book, Elshtain's own Augustinian version of the *limits* of politics shifts the accent of political Augustinianism to the *possibilities* of a politics of limits. Augustinians are not to be morally or politically paralyzed by what they know about sin, either in the world or in themselves. An Augustinian ethics of citizenship remains that for a pilgrim. But it is the ethic of a pilgrim citizen "who is tethered to this earth and its arrangements through bonds of affection and necessity" even as it "recognizes at the same time that these arrangements are not absolute and not final" (96). As Peter Brown puts it, "the members of the *civitas peregrina* . . . maintain their identity not by withdrawal, but by something far more difficult: by maintaining a firm and balanced perspective on the whole of range of love of which men are capable in their present state."[90] Elshtain points to Augustine's doctrine of love as the source of this ethic: love of God and love of neighbor "underscore and animate the other" (96).[91] My remaining chapters provide more systematic

---

90. Brown, *Augustine of Hippo*, 325.

91. Elshtain, unlike Jackson, does not pursue the conceptual problems related to the Augustinian logic of the relation of the love commands. Interestingly, however, she cites the work of sociologist Robert Putnam as empirical evidence that those who are regular churchgoers "are more deeply involved in serving their neighbors and in being trustworthy and reliable than those who are not thus involved" (Elshtain, *Limits of Politics*, 130n21). Augustine himself often invokes this kind of argument: "Let them give us provincials, husbands and wives, parents and children, masters and servants, kings, judges, and finally even tax-payers and tax-collectors, of the sort that the teaching of Christ demands. Then let them dare to say that this teaching is opposed to the commonwealth!" (*Ep.* 138, 39). Edward Vacek cites psychological studies "that show believers are generally *less* loving than nonbelievers" (*Love, Human and Divine*, 144).

analysis of this vision of Augustinian political ethics. In so doing, I hope to confirm Elshtain's judgments and refigure the ways in which the Augustinian tradition can be interpreted for liberal politics.

REDUCING RELIGION TO ETHICS? THE TROUBLE WITH DISPOSITIONS AND THE CHALLENGE OF RADICAL ORTHODOXY

I end this chapter by considering a significant internal challenge to each of the Augustinian liberalisms I have identified. This challenge is not specific to the role of love as an appropriate virtue for Augustinian liberalism, or to my theological re-reading of Augustinian love as Incarnational and social. While justice and hope have been the dominant virtues of Christian social reflection in the past thirty years, some Christian ethicists have challenged recent liberal efforts to reintroduce love as a focal virtue for political theology (*PL*, 15–27). Here I want to address a larger issue that informs these challenges. I examine the criticism through the writings of John Milbank, a prominent antiliberal theologian who also places love at the center of his political Augustinianism. Milbank is the central figure associated with an influential movement called "Radical Orthodoxy" that emerged out of Anglican social thought (especially Christian socialism) in the late 1980s. It is an intellectual, cultural, and ecumenical movement that seeks to transcend liberal Protestant theology, conservative politics of free market capitalism, and liberal politics of welfare bureaucracy. Because I rely on Milbank for my own reconstruction of Augustine's theology of love and the significance of Christian charity for liberal society, it is important to clarify where my liberalism differs from his antiliberalism.

I consider one forceful and basic criticism. It is a criticism that aligns Milbank with Stanley Hauerwas and John Howard Yoder: the refusal to ally Christian social ethics with liberalism because of its hegemonic commitment to secularism. I highlight what I take to be the source of this criticism because I am deeply sympathetic with aspects of their visions for Christian ethics, their criticisms of liberal theory, and their desire to place checks on morally corrosive capitalist practices. The underlying source of their refusal is a shared concern with abstract appeals to dispositions, especially in contemporary Christian social ethics. I primarily focus on Milbank rather than Hauerwas or Yoder for two reasons. First, Milbank's antipathy toward liberalism is not governed by a pacifist stance against the coercive use of force in political life.[92] Second, he more explicitly identifies "Christ" with "Church." Milbank's ecclesiology makes "Christological and atonement doctrines . . . theoretically secondary to definitions of the character of the new universal community or Church."[93] Nevertheless, both Milbank and Hauerwas want to resist thinking of social action in terms of the dispositions and the attitudes that theological beliefs generate. Mediated by what Milbank calls the "poverty of Niebuhrianism," this criticism charges that to approach politics in this way yields an inadequate attitudinal (and individualistic) ethics separated from Christian theology and practice. A dispositional approach, despite its ostensible connection to a Christian worldview or ethos, does not account for the radical interruption Christianity makes for the interpretation of politics. For shorthand, it provides a distorted subjective *Moralitat* that focuses on the goodness of motives, but no truly Christian *Sittlichkeit* that is "a moral practice embedded in the historical emergence of a new, and unique community" (*TST*, 381). Here is Milbank's negative description of this sort of method: "The ethical, reduced to motivation, remains problematically empty of content, and the religious, reduced to the regulation of the ethical, still more so" (237). Christian ethics falls prey to the moralist's temptation: abandoning evangelical identity in order to prop up illegitimate and sinful social orders under the guise of being a "responsible" Christian. According to Milbank, modern political theologians (whether conservative or liberal) adopt this method even when they deny it because they are bored with God-talk yet feel compelled to "discover how to fulfill Christian precepts

92. Milbank argues that pacifism "seeks to have a kind of cheap and easy participation in the eternal; it tries to leap out of our finitude, embodiment, and fragility" (*BR*, 40).

93. Milbank, "Name of Jesus," 148. Hauerwas also explicitly wants to marginalize "Christology," but he does so by making the "Jesus we find portrayed in the Gospels . . . its starting point" (Hauerwas, *Peaceable Kingdom*, 72). For Milbank, the Gospels are to be read not as the story of Jesus but "as the story of the (re)foundation of a new city, a new kind of human community, Israel-become-the-Church. Jesus figures in this story simply as the founder, the beginning, the first of many" (Milbank, "Name of Jesus," 150). By contrast, Hauerwas argues that "Christologies which emphasize the cosmic and ontological Christ tend to make Jesus' life almost incidental to what is assumed to be a more profound theological point" (Hauerwas, *Peaceable Kingdom*, 73; O'Donovan expresses a similar concern in *DN*, 161).

about charity and freedom in contemporary society in an uncontroversial manner" (2). Hauerwas echoes this charge: "After Reinhold Niebuhr, liberal Protestants thought the way to be 'political responsible' was to leave talk of Jesus behind and instead talk about love and justice."[94] This kind of *dispositionalism* betrays an uncritical cultural Christianity governed by instinctive pragmatism and vague maxims.

It is true that much of twentieth-century Augustinianism relied on the promotion of dispositions and sentiments shaped by secularized virtues dislodged from their theological context. Social ethics, especially in the context of liberal Protestantism, often was practiced by abstracting principles of "biblical wisdom" or motivations from a pious Jesuology that were then applied to political realities through analysis of the given terms of public policy. Christian confessions about Incarnation and creation were abstracted and generalized into motivational or epistemological principles for a universal system of ethics. Augustinian approaches to ethics tended to emphasize interior motivations in ways that frustrate more comprehensive political theologies or normative judgments wedded to particular narratives and practices. In his review of Niebuhr, Milbank singles out an Augustinian realism that ontologically grounds a fascination with tragic ambiguity and lesser evils as a failure of normative political theology. For Milbank, much of what passes for Augustinian realism is a collection of clichés dressed up by religious sentiment or a pious mood borrowed from a secularized Christianity. In short, political Augustinianism has been neither politically nor theologically Christian. It likes religious language, but it is conceptually atheistic. I share Milbank's misgivings about the viability of strands of liberal Protestant realism and the "false humility" of modern theology (*TST*, 1). But his criticism of Niebuhr (and of liberation theology) might be extended to my project and to each of the authors I have discussed in this chapter.

My support of love as a motivational component of civic virtue consistent with liberal democracy might be seen as reducing Augustinianism to a secularized ethical humanism. It abandons theological description in favor of some phenomenology of the ethical in order to make Christianity less threatening to the liberal consensus of modern secularism. Augustinian civic liberalism is just another misguided project of tinkering with liberal

94. Hauerwas, *Performing the Faith*, 230.

democracy, rearranging the deck chairs on a sinking ship. Ironically, given Milbank's argument against liberation theology, it should be noted that this charge against dispositionalism was first made by liberation theologians *against* Christian Realism. But it is now associated with Milbank's "postmodern critical Augustinianism" and his "post-political theology." It is to be contrasted with liberal readings of political Augustinianism (like mine) which supposedly do not capture the radical opposition of Christian theology to liberal practices.[95] Liberal readings fail to recognize that liberalism is not theologically innocent precisely because it makes "ethics the mediating term between political commitment and theological interpretation" (*TST*, 236). Religion is reduced to ethics, and ethics is reduced to subjective motivation in a way that obscures critical attention to the demonic "counter-theology" of liberal society. In short, Augustinianism should deliver a more critical (rather than ambivalent) evaluation of liberal democracy. "More critical" is a mild way of characterizing Milbank's polemic.

On Milbank's view, liberal democracy is (a) "a continuous horror almost as grave as the Holocaust, and a more troublingly sustainable mode of nihilism, appropriately disguised by an unparalleled reign of *kitsch*" and (b) "a mere virtual circus designed to entertain the middle-classes of the privileged world" (*BR*, 5). In various passages, authors associated with Radical Orthodoxy identify liberal democracy with lots of "isms": totalitarianism, paganism, terrorism, materialism, fascism, absolutism, technologism, fetishism, and gnosticism.[96]

95. Stanley Hauerwas has expressed reservations about Milbank's triumphalism. Most recently, Hauerwas characterizes his difference this way: "Milbank wants Christians to win. . . . I think at best we should want as Christians to endure" (*Performing the Faith*, 217n4). Milbank has distanced his position from Hauerwas with perhaps a note of exasperation: "I am an Anglican, not an Anabaptist!" (Milbank, "Invocation," 38).

96. These associations rightly have elicited severe criticism. Hans Joas, for example, writes, "whoever calls Western democracies a more subtle form of totalitarianism, does not know what totalitarianism is" ("Social Theory and the Sacred," 240). Joas also points out that Milbank "does not even try to use social-scientific knowledge about the rather ambivalent consequences of globalization and about the social causes of poverty or environmental problems. His attacks on capitalism and bureaucracy at once sound like old style Critical Theory, and Milbank may be one of the last authors to speak of 'late capitalism' after the collapse of communism" (240).

A number of vexed issues are attached to these objections, particularly in Milbank's admission that Augustine himself neglects the dramatic implications of the "ontological" antagonism between the two cities. Milbank's objection moves beyond methodological concerns to reveal fundamental theological disagreements about the relation between ecclesiology and Christology. Unlike Milbank, for example, I agree with those Protestants who follow Barth in claiming that "pending the final disclosure of the Kingdom of God, the church and the society are in a dialectical relation, distant from each other as well as identified" (O'Donovan, *DN*, 251). The kingdom of God is much bigger than the church, and the church experiences the same sinful divisions and broken ruptures that characterize the world. God *belongs* to neither the church nor the world, though both offer differentiated witnesses to God. As Hauerwas once put it in surprisingly Barthian terms, the church is a "natural institution."[97] In this vein, Hauerwas held that "the church can learn from society more just ways of forming life."[98] I am tempted to escape these difficult issues, however, by emphasizing my project aspires neither to provide a *theory* of liberalism nor to *repristinate* Niebuhrian realism. I am not trying to provide a Christian theory of the state, whatever that ambiguous identity might mean in a world where we never encounter "the state" but rather its various agencies dispersed throughout local, national, and international civil communities. I am not putting forth an ethics for the world as a "totality, self-sufficiently closed in upon itself" (*TST*, 229).

I *am* interested, however, in the neglected motivational aspects of the ethics of citizenship. Motivation is an important part of ethics, Christian or otherwise. Attending to motivation should be an important part of an ethics that highlights the significance of virtue (refusing to separate act and agency) and of a theological ethics that takes "politics" seriously (refus-

---

97. Hauerwas, *Peaceable Kingdom*, 102; on Barth, see 166n5. Here, Hauerwas could claim that the church and the world are "companions on a journey that makes it impossible for one to survive without the other, though each constantly seeks to do so" (101).

98. Hauweras, *Truthfulness and Tragedy*, 142. More recently, as I note below, Hauerwas insists that the world is "necessarily lost without the church" (*Grain of the Universe*, 193).

ing to separate personal and social ethics). Discerning the implications of dogmatic theology need not always imply a subjectivist, rationalist, or emotivist theory of morality. In fact, appeal to "dispositions" can be seen as another way to talk about narratives and virtues as ways of living in the world. Robin Lovin, for example, claims that what Niebuhr calls a critical and responsible "attitude" is compatible with the recent turn to narrative and virtue. According to Lovin, Niebuhr's ethics is not governed by mediating principles cut loose from theology so that Christians can offer their non-Christian citizens advice on politics. Rather, Niebuhr calls for an attitude that is "a settled disposition to view situations in a certain way, and to choose and to act in ways appropriate to that view."[99] Holding criticism and responsibility together in single disposition is a difficult task, but the larger point is that Augustinians should stand with Thomists in holding that right dispositions are necessary for moral discernment. Such dispositions are revealed in both the rhetoric and content of theological evaluations of liberalism. My account does not appeal to theological beliefs as a "faint regulative gloss upon Kantian ethics" that is "simply another effort to reinterpret Christianity in terms of a dominant secular discourse of our day" (Milbank, *TST*, 208). Christian love is not reduced to motivation. However, political Augustinians should not abandon motivation, especially given the checkered career of Augustinian ontology in actual political history. For the sake of simplicity, and at the risk of moralism, I think Christian ethicists should worry about motivating works of love and cultivating the desire to do justice in this world (though always remembering to put "morality" in its place). At this level of vagueness, Milbank, Hauerwas, and Yoder no doubt share this conviction. Ironically, Niebuhr's effort to be responsible also pushed aside attention to motive, leaving a vacuum waiting to be filled by consequentialism.[100] Good motives are not good enough for either social justice or adequate theology. But a fear of the language of motives is debilitating. In the next chapter, I examine how Christian ethicists committed to liberal democracy try to connect motivation with political action in ways that avoid reducing love to subjective motivation. This interest

---

99. Lovin, *Reinhold Niebuhr*, 95.

100. Niebuhr writes: "Preoccupation with motive is an unvarying characteristic of the religious life, which has its own virtues, but is also perilous to the interests of society" (*Moral Man*, 74).

may be distinct from proposing a political theology that seeks to connect "political themes with the history of salvation as a whole" (O'Donovan, *DN*, 22). But it is not antithetical to it.

My Augustinian account of love is wedded to Trinitarian theology, a theology that makes a difference in relation to liberal ethical theories dependent upon Kantian, Stoic, or utilitarian assumptions. Theological specification matters for religious and moral experience. Moreover, I do not think intellectual reconstruction of "love" offers obvious or immediate answers to political problems. Milbank is right to question liberal beliefs that "the single imperative to 'love' others, which means to desire their liberation, is supposed to well automatically from the depths of the human heart" (*TST*, 230). Love is not the idle possession of a pure heart or pure will, hidden in a private experience. It requires public expression, or better yet, it is constituted by and known only as a social reality: "For love is not loved unless it is already loving something, because where nothing is being loved there is no love" (Augustine, *DT* 9.1.2). With Milbank, and many feminist thinkers, I agree that love is "a highly complex, learned practice" (*TST*, 236).[101] These emphases go a long way, I think, to relieve me of some the force of these criticisms. But not the whole way. Fundamental disagreements remain. Against Milbank, I do not think Augustinian theology rules out any coalition of Christianity and political liberalism. Political liberalism is not simply an alien imposition on Christian thought.

These issues emerge more concretely in the following chapters, where I highlight the interruptive character of the Augustinian Christ rather than Christianity, the church, or, as Milbank sometimes suggests, theology itself.[102] I do not separate Christology and ecclesiology, but I push a more

---

101. In an analogous vein, Danielle Allen argues that "friendship is not an emotion, but a practice, a set of hard-won, complicated habits that are used to bridge trouble, difficulty, and differences of personality, experience, and aspiration" (*Talking to Strangers*, xxi).

102. Milbank claims "*only Christian theology* now offers a discourse able to position and overcome nihilism itself" (*TST*, 6, emphasis mine). Elsewhere, he writes that "the theologian feels almost the entire ecclesial task falls on his own head . . . the theologian alone who must perpetuate the original making strange which was the divine assumption of human flesh" (*Word Made Strange*, 1). One critic argues that Radical

dialectical relation than Augustine, Hauerwas, and Milbank would allow.[103] I do not offer an individualistic, non-sacramental conception of the church (neither, to be sure, does the Catholic Augustine). Since Pentecost, God does work through the witness and proclamation of the visible church, but neither Christology nor Christian social ethics should be univocally *identified* with ecclesiology.

In this, I do not in any way disagree with the spirit of Stanley Hauerwas's influential thesis that "the church does not have a social ethic; the church is a social ethic."[104] I do worry, however, that this claim has taken on a self-

---

Orthodoxy is another modern theological project of ideal speculation: it substitutes "creative production of theological theory for the redemptive power of Christ" (Reno, "Radical Orthodoxy," 41) such that "authority shifts out of the particularity of word and sacrament into a supervening theory or concept" (42). For arguments that Milbank's project is modern from a different angle, see Leora Batnitzky, "Love and Law: John Milbank and Hermann Cohen on the Ethical Possibilities of Secular Society," in *Secular Theology: American Radical Theological Thought*, ed. Clayton Crockett (London: Routledge, 2001), 73–91.

103. Protestant scholastics frequently cited Augustine's anti-Pelagian and anti-Donatist writings in order to support their case against Roman Catholicism, especially in terms of doctrines of grace, church order, and sacraments. They were suspicious of Augustine's "Platonism" that shifted the ethical into the realm of the ontological and potentially left no room for a new economy of grace in Christ, and subsumed atonement and incarnation into creation and ecclesiology. The incarnation, to use their terms, was for Augustine only *conveniens* (a demonstration of God's beauty) rather than *necessaria* (a "once for all" response to an ethical breach). Niebuhr, for all his theological vagueness, stands with the scholastics in his claim that "the Atonement is the significant content of the Incarnation" (Niebuhr, *Nature and Destiny*, 2:57). Such distinctions, however, would be anachronistically applied to Augustine's theology which is not governed by questions about a separable order of salvation or distinctions between Christ as *exemplum* and *sacramentum*. These issues return in an impressive contemporary project inspired by classical Reformed orthodoxy that appropriates aspects of Augustine's theology but is critical of Milbank's Augustinianism for similar reasons (Horton, *Lord and Servant*, 203 and 230).

104. Hauerwas, *Peaceable Kingdom*, 99. I do remain confused about the force of his influential thesis in *The Peaceable Kingdom*. First, he qualifies the claim by noting "the *first* social ethical task of the church is to be the church" (99, emphasis mine). At least on these pages, he does not give an account of what a second, or third, social ethical task might be or look like. Second, his account of church and world is vitiated (at least rhetorically) by his claim that Christians believe "our true home is the church itself" (102)

referential life of its own and strips the world of its created goodness. To his credit, Hauerwas transformed Protestant ethics by a renewed emphasis on virtues and sanctification that was critical of Barth's actualism. He was right to highlight the modern avoidance of the Christian *qualifier* of ethics as temptation for a confused (often violent) universalism which abandoned the narrative of the Christian story. His more recent work, however, backtracks from his earlier affirmation of a Barthian ecclesiology under the pressure of his desire to identify a reliable site for the social practices of embodied Christian virtue. He still issues a prophetic concern against the cultural accommodation of the Gospel to the world. But it is couched less in terms of the witness *of the church* through the Spirit to Christ and more in terms of a witness *to the church* as the Spirit of Christ. Now, against Barth, Hauerwas holds that "the community called the church is constitutive of the gospel proclamation."[105] This move pushes him closer to Milbank and makes it harder to maintain the view that world stands under the gospel judgment of Christ, not an eternal church.

Hauerwas still emphasizes the performances of the church and Christians who "witness to the One who has made our lives possible."[106] Milbank's theological polemic, however, becomes especially problematic when "the church" (despite his formal protests) appears to stand above the real, creative, fragile, and historical diversity of Christ-like reconciling action in the world.

---

rather than "the foretaste of the kingdom" (97), or even "where we find those who, like us, have been formed by a savior who was necessarily always on the move" (102). And, third, I am still not clear what this thesis means for Christian social ethics that does more than just posit an alternative practice. For example, how should a Christian think about, or even advocate for, political proposals like the Family and Medical Leave Act or the Americans with Disabilities Act? Hauerwas claims that "we [Christians] must . . . in the interest of charity ask the state to live up to its own standards of justice—to feed the poor, clothe the naked, aid the weak—but we must never delude ourselves that the justice of the state is what is required of us as people formed by God" (Hauerwas, *Truthfulness and Tragedy*, 141). Can Christians, then, have a social ethic even if the church does not? Are these necessarily bad Constantinian questions that betray assumptions of power politics, a latent desire to rule, a capitulation to efficiency? Or, are they appropriate questions for Christian folks trying to muddle through life in a liberal society as best they can, using the opportunities it provides without delusion?

105. Hauerwas, *Grain of the Universe*, 145.
106. Ibid., 207.

At the same time, Milbank departs from an Augustinian perspective when he declares that secular institutions and practices should be *characterized* as "fundamentally sinful" (*TST*, 390). Or, as he later puts it, "the realm of the merely practical, cut off from the ecclesial, is quite simply the realm of sin" (406). I conclude this chapter by pointing out contradictions in Milbank's writings that allow him to adopt these positions. I also point to a theological alternative that issues a different assessment of liberalism.

I begin with a brief remark about Milbank's own method. It is not clear to me how Milbank's effort to privilege Christian theology—and subsequently depict all the traditions of modernity as Pelagian "anti-theologies" or some other ideological legacy of bad theology—relates to his effort to overcome the Enlightenment demands of universal ahistorical theorizing. For all his critical attention to orthopraxis and his postmodern desire to undermine theoretical essentialism, a lot of abstraction does a lot of work in his narrative. His totalizing narrative, albeit aesthetic rather than propositional, exhibits the same post-Kantian ambitions and linguistic closures that he rejects in secular theory. He claims to radicalize Alasdair MacIntyre's general philosophical argument about virtue and tradition by highlighting a more distinctive and committed Christian *mythos*: "a counter-ethics, embodying a social ontology" (*TST*, 422). But MacIntyre argues that "abstract changes in moral concepts are always embodied in real, particular events."[107] Milbank's intellectualist narrative implies that we can just think our way into virtue by "unthinking" the mistakes of nominalist and voluntarist theology since 1300. This approach takes liberal theory and secular reason—not to mention the practices of doctrinal or theological affirmation—much too seriously. If one is looking for a culprit in the emergence of secular modernity, might it not be better to look at eucharistic and clerical practices that initiate these theologies rather than embody or express them (or, at least, give a more dialectical story about their relation)?[108] Milbank writes as if two ontologies (peace or violence) float above history, waiting to be instantiated in practice or mistakenly employed by expert theologians. He is vulnerable to his own

107. MacIntyre, *After Virtue*, 61.
108. See, for example, Peter J. Leithart, "The Gospel, Gregory VII, and Modern Theology," *Modern Theology* 19, no. 1 (January 2003): 5–28. If Leithart is right, the "evil source" of modernity gets pushed back further and further to Gregorian reforms in the 11th century.

indictment of Anglo-American linguistic philosophy as excessively formal and smug. Or, even worse by his own lights, he perpetuates a metaphysical epistemology by privileging the category of "ontology" as the hermeneutical key to understanding social practice (whether ecclesial or secular). Ontology here assumes priority over practice.[109] In fact, the theory, like salvation itself, becomes the ecclesiology. Milbank's composition, his own *poesis*, offers an updated Augustinian narrative of the two cities that is bold and breathtaking. But let me step down from the heights of his prose in order to focus on the dispositions that his own theology might generate. I am not here foisting Milbank into my method. I take his own emphasis on the rhetoric of persuasion to invite something like imagining one's being-in-the-world. How would an Augustinian citizen see the world with this hermeneutic and this metaphysical vision?

Milbank's "outnarrating" of secular modernity and liberal democracy finds its energy in an Augustinian retrieval of the church as "an *altera civitas*, on pilgrimage through this temporary world" (*TST*, 380). I grant that Milbank (like Hauerwas and Yoder) is not advocating a sectarian withdrawal from the world or an idealized vision of the visible church. This is the popular face of all three authors, one that has launched a thousand ships of criticism. It is also the popular face that has persuaded many eager converts to see church as where "love" happens and the secular as where "sin" happens. Since Milbank rejects a stark duality between nature and grace that would close off the "natural" from the "supernatural," the Augustinian citizen is not hungering after some future space where the divine will finally arrive. Creation after the Fall is not stripped of its goodness. Even fallen creation really participates in transcendence. Milbank's Augustinian citizen does not huddle around the Eucharist fending off a profane world. The divine freely has arrived in Christ, which is a dramatic intensification of the grace of sensible creation. The Augustinian citizen remains an ecclesial pilgrim in a fallen world that awaits the Eschaton. But this citizen also knows that divine transcendence upholds the worth of this world; in fact, creatureliness and temporality are divine gifts to be celebrated rather than simply endured.

---

109. Bernd Wannenwetsch puts it this way: "Does not the assumption that something is existing prior to its embodiment, necessarily characterize a metaphysical epistemology which cannot but eventually violate the matter (material) from which it is first separated?" ("Political Worship of the Church," 275).

Finitude is rightly distinguished from sin. This affirmation leads to a diffuse conception of liturgical offering that includes *all* human being and making: "When we contingently but authentically make things and reshape ourselves through time, we are not estranged from the eternal, but enter further into its recesses by what for us is the only possible route" (*BR*, ix). As such, Radical Orthodoxy claims to offer an embodied Augustinian citizen a world-affirming vision that is "more incarnate, more participatory, more erotic, more socialized" than any liberal self-understanding that refuses to see materiality as analogical participation in God.[110]

That is the polemic. Milbank's writings are littered with references to "counter-narrative," "counter-ontology," "counter-history," counter-polity," and "counter-ethics." But Milbank's polemic starts to lose its edge, if not its coherence, the more Milbank says about the church, modernity, and the state. He announces that "all 'political' theory, in the antique sense, is relocated by Christianity as thought about the Church" (*TST,* 406). This seems to denigrate the social functions of non-ecclesial communities that aspire to justice. But then, two pages later, he qualifies the force of this claim by recommending that "the bounds between Church and state be extremely hazy, so that a 'social' existence of many complex and interlocking powers may emerge, and forestall either a sovereign state, or a hierarchical church" (408). Despite his assault on the excessive modernity of liberation theology, he praises "base communities where the lines between Church and world, spiritual and secular are blurred" (408). In fact, Milbank believes that "*all* human society in some degree foreshadows ecclesia and in this way always mediates some supernatural grace"[111] Revelation is "lodged in all the complex networks of human practices, and its boundaries are as messy as those of the Church itself" (*BR*, 122). Presumably this could include the civil rights movement as a story of the church and the world rather than an example of liberal Protestant decadence. So what happened to the rhetorical thunder of Christian ethics as ecclesiology?

Perhaps I misunderstand his emphasis on the real, historical "church" as the alternative to liberal, bourgeois nihilism. Milbank is quick to point out

---

110. John Milbank, Catherine Pickstock, and Graham Ward, "Introduction: Suspending the Material: The Turn to Radical Orthodoxy," in *Radical Orthodoxy: A New Theology* (New York: Routledge, 1999), 3.

111. Milbank, "Gift of Ruling," 231 (emphasis mine).

that he does not "imagine the Church as Utopia."[112] Indeed, the church can inspire "an anti-Church" and promote "a hellish society beyond any terrors known to antiquity" (*TST*, 433). This recognition, however, is not followed by a distinctive account of the pilgrim church and its particular virtues and characteristic vices in the *saeculum*. The church exceeds any spatial terms: "it exists, finitely, not in time, but as time."[113] Its redemptive promise remains "a vague rumour" (*BR*, 105). It is "like a fleeting passage of an aerial creature amongst the trees, which we are scarcely sure we have glimpsed at all" (105). This is not your familiar Church Dogmatics. It is certainly not what most Christians would take from his claim that the church stands against secular modernity. I remain unclear about Milbank's claim that his elevation (even identification) of church as Christ's body "restores concreteness to the notion of incarnation."[114] Milbank's church is "neither a programme, nor a 'real' society, but instead an enacted, serious fiction . . . the ritual distance of the Church from itself defines the Church, or rather deflects it from any definition of what it is."[115] Like MacIntyre's account of the good life, the church consists of those "perpetually questing for the Church itself . . . the passing of signs, of shadows that are foreshadowings" (105–106).[116] Indeed, "the Church, like grace, is everywhere" (138). The sacred is everywhere. And nowhere: "We are that body of Christ we can never yet see."[117] The terms now shift. Distance. Shadows. Complex spaces. Fuzzy boundaries. Nomadic exodus. Secrecy. Is Milbank a Montanist? Even these distances and shadows might suggest profound analogy—a generous plenitude that points even to the prospect of "the obliteration of boundaries" that remains open to the infinity of difference (196). The Augustinian citizen might continue to wonder about that stark polemic, the assertion of an identity against the other. At one point, Milbank seems to slip from his polemic against the counterfeit. He claims that Augustine thought the antique virtues were "ambiguously virtuous" (*TST*, 411). Maybe Christian love can indeed find expression in a liberal democracy, even in the ambiguity of liberal justice as one of those

112. Milbank, "Enclaves," 341.

113. Ibid., 142.

114. Milbank, "Name of Jesus," 153.

115. Milbank, "Enclaves," 342.

116. For MacIntyre, "the good life for man is the life spent in seeking for the good life for man" (*After Virtue*, 219).

117. Milbank, "Complex Space," 280.

networks of human practices where revelation is lodged? Maybe the Spirit (that testifies to the continuing work of Christ) is also at work in the aspirations of liberal society and secular modernity? Is that what it means to declare "the infallible presence of the Holy Spirit in the whole body of the Church and by extension humanity across all times and places"?[118]

Yes, it must. Sounding more like Charles Taylor than the author of *Theology and Social Theory*, Milbank can show ambivalence toward modernity: "not outright refusal, nor outright acceptance" (*BR*, 196). He can even recognize that "the Enlightenment has gained for us the formal principles of individual liberty and equality, which sometimes guard against the very *worst* tyrannies, but at the same time we have lost certain practices of free association for common purposes."[119] Defenders of Radical Orthodoxy might protest I am pushing them into some liberal model of Christ and culture that presumes a spatialized division of nature and grace like Niebuhr's vision of history as "a vast middle ground between the realm of grace and the realm of nature."[120] I am not. Stick to thinking about time: gains and losses. That is a different story, one that still has critical power. However, unlike Milbank, I do not think that "true political theology" must always be a "theological critique of society and politics" (*TST*, 208). Critique is one important mode of political theology, but it is not the only mode. My point is that *ambivalence* rather than *hostility* must be the disposition toward liberal democracy for someone who is willing to identify himself as "in some ways still a Marxist, albeit a heretical one."[121] This is the Milbank who encourages cooperation with "secular co-workers: socialists, communists and anarchists" (*BR*, 210).[122] Perhaps it is Milbank's own modernity that is really doing the work in his

---

118. Milbank, "Gift of Ruling," 231.

119. Milbank, "Complex Space," 279.

120. Niebuhr, "Providence of God," 39.

121. Milbank, "Invocation," 22.

122. Milbank insists, however, that these fellow co-workers "have little grasp of the counter-empire, since for them it is still a matter of simply unleashing more undifferentiated liberty, going yet further beyond the Law" (*BR*, 210). I think this may count as the answer to Jeffrey Stout's question: "The practical issue is whether Christians, for their own theological reasons, may join hands with others in the struggle for justice—and do so without holding their noses in the presence of their comrades" (Stout, *Democracy and Tradition*, 105). In an earlier version of this essay, Milbank refers to his "secular brethren"; see "The Gospel of Affinity," *Ethical Perspectives* 7, no. 4 (December 2000): 220–32, at 231.

criticism of liberal democracy (as he reluctantly accuses Gustavo Gutierrez)? In any case, it seems odd to embrace, albeit heretically, one heresy of modernity and condemn another. Critical rapprochement with Marxism, socialism, communism, and anarchism, but the modernity of political liberalism is off limits!

I take it that for Milbank the deepest Augustinian problem with liberal society is that it is not really a society at all. It has no interests in its citizens. Liberal political society is a grand illusion—incredibly powerful and destructive, but in the light of the "ontological peace" of the Kingdom, all smoke and mirrors. That is why he can believe "America is less an actual place with roots and history than it is a virtual microcosm of the globe."[123] I do not here aim to defend America or globalization, whatever that might mean. Nor do I aim to defend the potential dignity of evangelical *kitsch* that otherwise receives Milbank's extreme contempt (perhaps also his voyeuristic gaze?). However much I agree with his criticism of the fusion of market capitalism, jingoistic nationalism, and religious identity in the United States, I find it disturbing that Milbank is willing to indulge in familiar European tropes about the rootless America without history. Augustinians should be wary of bourgeois liberal claims to innocence, but better to heed the advice of Stanley Hauerwas: "It would be a mistake to make the church look good by making American society look bad."[124] It is certainly a strategic mistake if one wants social change. But Milbank's reader begins to wonder what happened to the celebration of cultural difference, the infinite blending of difference, and "a thousand kinds of community" (*BR*, 167). Is the Spirit not willing to find America, even the religion of working-class America, theologically interesting? Does Milbank wish to overturn Augustine's denial of the claim "that the Roman people was not really a people, or that Rome was not a commonwealth" (*CD* 19.24)? Perhaps. But this move would require him to deny the reality of any such "peoples" and affirm only "persons." That move would imply a kind of rootless cosmopolitanism that I think Milbank rejects. As it stands, Milbank's America—the new Rome, the latest subtle

123. Milbank, "Gift of Ruling," 233.

124. Hauerwas, *Against the Nations*, 19. Despite his charge that "liberalism is not simply a theory of government but a theory of society that is imperial in its demands," Hauerwas claims that "the issue is to help the church recover a sense of its own integrity that it might better be able to make discriminating judgments about the society which we happen to call America" (18–19).

expression of the old Babylon—is configured without the moral patience that attends even to the idolatrous reality of Augustine's robber bands (*CD* 4.4). It is just erased, narrated away into nihilistic oblivion under the gaze of the ecclesial pilgrim. One of Milbank's readers has noted that his "conception of 'counter' has no room for 'encounter.'"[125] I agree. Indeed, Milbank seems to embrace this criticism; he wants to "replace 'dialogue' with 'mutual suspicion.'"[126]

Milbank does not encourage nostalgia for some lost medieval gothic, or even the late nineteenth-century guild socialism of England. He rightly points out that his narrative identifies late medieval Catholicism as the source of our decadence. He claims to want to save modernity from itself, though it does seem always to be a future that just *might have been* if better theologians had been around. This must mean that liberal society is not fundamentally sinful—a curious description of anything for an Augustinian who should be more guarded about the language of "fundamentally *bad* ends" (*TST*, 406). Milbank often uses the language of "parody" and "heresy" to describe Enlightenment versions of liberty, equality, and fraternity. Secular discourses are constituted in their "secularity by 'heresy' in relation to orthodox Christianity, or else a rejection of Christianity that is more 'neo-pagan' than simply anti-religious" (3). But are secular modernity and liberal democracy, like the church, still on the way (liable to further decay, or, by the grace of God, possible reformation)? Isn't that an Augustinian point of locating politics within the realm of history rather than being or nature? Isn't that what Milbank implies by his claim to "envisage history as radically contingent and open-ended" and "ceaseless loss and gain."[127]

Here, I think, is the nub. Milbank identifies the "secular" with immanence and the denial of transcendence. On these terms, it is impossible to offer an ambivalent assessment of liberal democracy. It is pushed into a corner, just as Milbank feels cramped by its supposed immanence. In this sense, it may be that the Augustinian liberal and the Augustinian antiliberal are quarreling about words or speaking past one another. The "secular" that feeds Milbank's polemic is neither Markus's *saeculum* (stripped of its mistaken

---

125. Wannenwetsch, "Political Worship of the Church," 273.
126. Milbank, "End of Dialogue," 190.
127. Milbank, "Complex Space," 274 and 279.

relation to religious neutrality) nor Stout's "secularized discourse" (which denies commitment to secularism). No doubt many citizens committed to liberal democracy are committed to secularism. But why should Milbank take one version of the liberal story to be the whole story? He claims that his "point is not to question all formal mechanisms of democracy, but rather to insist on the priority of an educative culture which will sustain and extend them" (*BR*, 183). I return to the theme of an educative culture in a later chapter, picking up on Milbank's claim that the church "has far less definite ideas than the polis concerning the kinds of individuals it desires to produce."[128] But the more Milbank gives content to this theme it continues to take away the luster of his polemic. He boldly calls for the "Christianisation of the State and the subsumption within the ecclesia."[129] "The Church, to be the Church," he writes, "must seek to extend the sphere of the socially aesthetic harmony—'within' the state where this is possible" (*TST*, 422). Theocratic alarm bells go off. This sounds worse than anything the politically mobilized religious right in the United States might propose or has any chance of pulling off. Surely, this view can not create alliance with liberal democracy. But, what does this "subsumption" actually look like?

Milbank is critical of liberation theology for not offering more concrete alternatives to liberal economic and political practices. His own political prescriptions, however, are far from specific and not terribly radical. From his descriptions, they include state activism "with respect to pensions, care of children, job training, education, and public museums and trusts" and "public banks, price and wage regulating bodies, intertrade councils . . . [state] oversight in some areas (national transport, e.g) and a role in others (education)."[130] He rejects state socialism and encourages a blend of localism and transnational governing bodies, claiming that the key distinguishing mark of Christian social teaching is the emphasis on "intermediate associations" that "variegate the monotonous harmony of the sovereign state and sovereign individual."[131] His Christian socialism realizes "that one must marry checks and balances, and a democratic distribution of power . . . ensuring

128. Milbank, "Name of Jesus," 154.
129. Milbank, "Invocation," 38.
130. Ibid., 38.
131. Milbank, "Complex Space," 271. With a note of surprise and perhaps confusion given his account of the "secular," he is encouraged that "a somewhat similar advocacy seems to be now once more surfacing to view amongst secular radicals" (ibid.).

that market exchanges are also democratically or freely assented-to trans-actions—the outcomes of processes of free and equal negotiation—which repeatedly seek to preserve or extend a distribution of resources held to be 'just.'"[132] He also calls for the "eradication of poverty" through a "global liturgical polity."[133] Indeed, despite his polemic against liberal Protestant complicity with capitalism, his postmodern radicalism often sounds like progressive Christian rhetoric from the 1960s and reads like today's mainline Protestant social statements issued from denominational offices (and largely unread). Throughout his writings, he expresses concern that Christian social thought has been hijacked by ideological programs of the political right and the political left, fueling a "stand-off between an increasingly atheist social-ism, and an increasingly conservative Church."[134] His is trying to find an alternative. But if this is theocracy, it will disappoint secularists (and religious liberals) looking for an enemy of civil society and democratic deliberation.

Milbank sometimes sounds like his fellow Anglican reader of Augustine, Oliver O'Donovan. They share many of the same theological concerns and diagnoses of late modernity as a perverse parody of Christian social order. Both have reconstructed patristic and medieval habits of thinking in the hope of renewing a theology that is political simply by being adequately theological. For example, O'Donovan shares Milbank's worry that political theology has been reduced to "ethics, especially an ethics of interior motiva-tion" that "provides a safe mediation, insulated against theocratic misunder-standing, by which religion may make politics more honest without presum-ing to make it more divine" (DN, 2–3). Like Milbank, he rejects autonomous political order and tries to "push back the horizon of commonplace politics and open it up to the activity of God" (2). He too sounds harsh notes against "the social agnosticism of liberal pietist individualism" (121) and "concepts of politics as economic management" (271). He too rejects prideful projects of "civilisational legitimation" that fail to recognize the conflict between "true and false Messianism" (214–15). He too sees "in the meeting of liberal voluntarism and technological reasoning the nuclear fusion that energises the Leviathan of our age" (227). He too wants to re-imagine the contested legacy of Christendom as something more than an unrelieved struggle for

132. Ibid., 271.
133. Milbank, "Gift of Ruling," 238.
134. Milbank, "Complex Space," 273.

power, an ideology in search of a theology, a temptation yielded, an identity sacrificed, and a failed witness to excessively realized eschatology. He too urges political theology to attend to its "ecclesiological mode, which takes the church seriously as a society and show how the rule of God is realized there" (123). He too rejects "a neoorthodox interpretation of Augustine [that] can be so concerned with the self-love of the *civitas terrena* that it forgets that there is also a city of God to contrast with it, albeit a city on pilgrimage and far from its final peace" (*PSL*, 106). He too worries that "much Christian enthusiasm for 'pluralism' has less to do with a relation to the state than the church's yearning to sound in harmony with the commonplaces of the stock exchange, the law-courts and the public schools" (*DN*, 226). He too sees Rawlsian liberalism as a "deist answer to a Christian question."[135] But, unlike Milbank, O'Donovan does not perpetuate an ideological rivalry between the *antiliberal* Christian and *liberal* non-Christian. For O'Donovan, the church is neither apologist for nor antagonist of the liberal order. He opens a space for encounter because he is driven, not by a project of modernity criticism, but by one of discovering "Christian constitutionalism" (240) and "Christian liberalism" (278)—even "the triumph of Christ in liberal institutions" (228).

I believe his refusal of this rivalry emerges from his emphasis on Christ rather than church as the "desire of the nations." If Augustinian liberalism moves eschatology to the center of political theology, and Milbank moves ecclesiology to the center of eschatology, then O'Donovan corrects these moves by putting Christology at the center of both eschatology and ecclesiology. It is the Christ-event, displayed in narrative form and rooted in the economy of grace, which shapes his political theology. It is this same Christ-event which shapes the identity of the individual before God. As such, O'Donovan's evangelical rejection of liberal neutrality does not rely upon Milbank's ontological dualisms. O'Donovan, like Markus, highlights the importance of the "two cities" and the "two ages" for understanding how the eschatological imagination of early Christianity would influence Western political thought. O'Donovan renders this imagination in terms of his intentionally elastic phrase, a "doctrine of the Two" (*DN*, 211). Christian reflection on this theme takes up Israel's alienation in exile (which distinguished their immediate subjection to Babylon from their ultimate citizenship in Zion) and places it within the public climax of history in the life,

135. O'Donovan, *Ways of Judgment*, 185.

death, and resurrection of the Christ. In fact, the ministry of Jesus is concerned with the "reauthorising of Israel rather than with the deauthorising
of Rome" (117). Because Christ's triumph has already occurred but is not yet
fulfilled, there is both eschatological expectation (evidenced by mission)
and reservation (evidenced by a patient willingness to suffer the pretensions
of defeated powers and principalities). Set in this theological framework,
his intellectual and missiological history of liberalism provides room for
a complex appreciation of the liberal tradition as itself a viable Christian
political tradition—even if liberalism's "central Christian witness does not
always lie on its surface" (229). For O'Donovan, there is an "analogy—not
a rhetorical metaphor only, or a poetic image, but an analogy grounded in
reality—between acts of God and human acts" and, as such, "earthly events
of liberation, rule, and community foundation provide us partial indications
of what God is doing in human history" (2). The analogies and events allow
for political society to be more than just demonic. To put it most starkly,
Babylon sits nearer to Jerusalem for O'Donovan than Milbank: "The curious thing about the two cities in the Apocalypse, Babylon and Jerusalem, is
the continuity between them. . . . The reason why John of Patmos will not
allow the church a distinct social presence is that its witnesses claim back
the Great City to become the Holy City" (156). This theology is central to his
more positive account of liberal society: capable of surprising virtue, yet also
capable of demonic vice. O'Donovan shares Milbank's Augustinian posture
of going beneath the surface of liberal appearance. But he does so in order
to go beyond the suspicion of Milbank's polemic.

The novelty of O'Donovan's critical yet constructive approach arises
in contrast to the mutual suspicion between politics and theology that he
takes to be a debilitating feature of contemporary discourse. Suspicion is
not simply a post-Kantian sullenness; it claims early Christian origins in the
preaching of the kingdom of God. Augustine is now taken to be the original
master of suspicion. Nonetheless, O'Donovan fears that a persistent strategy
of "unmasking" has left both politics and theology unable to break free from
an empty "rhetoric of scepticism" (DN, 10). While Christian tradition has
consistently held that all political orders (and theology itself) stand under
the judgment of the God, it is also the case that Christian political thought
discriminates among various imperfect ideologies and institutions. In fact,
these ideologies and institutions have analogous relations with Christian
thought and practice. Milbank dismisses secular discourse as "the oracular

voice of some finite idol" (*TST*, 1). O'Donovan thinks the church's witness allows "saying yes as well as saying no" (*DN*, 215). He writes, "in the light of Christ's ascension it is no longer possible to think of political authorities as sovereign; but neither is it possible to regard them as mere exhibitions of pride and lust for power."[136] In fact, the judgments of political communities do not "lay outside the reach of redemption, walled off from the grace of God."[137] O'Donovan's impressive narrative of liberalism as both child and "prodigal son" of Christian social thought has influenced my own interpretation. But I should note an important difference.

At times, O'Donovan suggests that the secular political community is merely to be *tolerated* as a passing conquered reality which secures the social space necessary for the preaching of the Christian gospel and the gathering of God's kingdom. In light of Romans 13, O'Donovan argues that government bears only the desacralized "rump of political authority which cannot be dispensed with yet, the exercise of judgment" (*DN*, 151). His accounts of the practice of corrective judgment and the judicial tasks of the state are rather extensive. Against libertarian minimalism, he supports various activities of the welfare state and international legal institutions appropriate to the task of judgment as consistent with the authority of the state. At other times, however, O'Donovan seems to want even more from the state: not civil religion or imposed theocracy, but the promise of Christian government. In a mistaken move by my lights, he criticizes what he takes to be the "revolutionary" liberalism of the First Amendment because it "excluded Christology" and "freed the state from all responsibility to recognize God's self-disclosure in history" (245). In this, O'Donovan stands closer to Augustine than most Augustinian liberals. Other Augustinians (including myself and, I think, the later Markus) would reject this *epistemological* hope for a confessional Christian government that responds to the church's public witness to society. State neutrality may be a myth, but O'Donovan's sanguine confidence that religious questions are open to public arbitration *and* subsequent political favor seriously threatens his stated defense of pluralism. O'Donovan extends the early modern liberal belief that competitive discourses might yield a catholic vision of the common good because of his Christian conviction that "the authority of God is not incommunicable, interior and removed from public view" (141). It seems

---

136. O'Donovan, *Ways of Judgment*, 5.
137. Ibid., 5.

to me that one could agree in principle with these claims without making the connection to determinate political confessions. My view does not replace Christology with democracy, but it does not expect the state to *know* what the church *knows* about grace for precisely Christological reasons. The state is humbled by the presence of non-state communities (i.e., the church), but its activities only indirectly reflect Christian norms in its pursuit of justice.[138] It is ironic that my account refuses this hope but affirms the secularity of political communities in more positive terms as promoting moral identities responsive to the shared goods that the state can secure for particular cultures (even if other identities precede them). By contrast, O'Donovan worries about this identity-conferral and is emphatic that "membership in Christ replaced all other political identities by which communities knew themselves" (148). If this is the case, we might ask O'Donovan how these political communities know anything, let alone the grace of Christ?

Despite these differences, I side with O'Donovan's support for secularity against Milbank. Augustine's own polemical caricatures of the earthly city provide the space for O'Donovan's difference with Milbank. For O'Donovan, Augustine's radical characterization of earthly societies in terms of their moral disorder is itself "an explanation of their political *order*, since, in Augustine's decisively Platonic view, disorder is nothing but a failure of an underlying order."[139] Just as some societies have better or worse loves, so some societies suffer from greater or lesser forms of moral disorder. The vices of earthly politics are disordered virtues, aiming at some good (albeit not the supreme good). Liberalism is celebrated for its emphasis on freedom and equality within the context of a responsible and legitimate state under the rule of law and guided by constitutional principles. These are signs

138. I take this difference to lie at the heart of O'Donovan's criticism of Barth's political theology. According to O'Donovan, Barth's analogy of state and church to the Kingdom of Christ is a contradiction because it allows the state to be a witness to Christ's rule without knowing it. O'Donovan asks: "How is this constitutionally pagan state, by definition ignorant of its own righteousness, 'reminded' of what it never knew?" (*DN*, 214). But I take Barth's point to be that the state's epistemic relation to Christ *is* different than the church's epistemic relation to Christ. Moreover, I am not sure how O'Donovan's language of "deference to the transcendent" (*Ways of Judgment*, 76) or "cosmic aspirations of mankind" (*DN*, 122) does not itself exclude Christology. I thank Todd Cioffi for helpful conversation on these issues.

139. O'Donovan, "*City of God* 19," 63.

of aspiration not heresy. This perspective does not deprive Christian social criticism of its sting: Milbank's indictments of the "increasingly joyless and puritanical world" of liberal society that marginalizes and disciplines "the young, the old, the cultural misfits and the poor . . . for the psychopathological amusement of the successful" remain fair game (*BR*, 25). O'Donovan is no enthusiast for the stories contemporary liberals tell themselves about the rise of liberalism. Rawls and Locke take a back seat to figures like Wyclif and Grotius. He worries that we are continuing to move politically beyond post-Christendom Christian liberalism into a corrupt period of moral chaos and insecurity, one that "has lost its orientation to deliberation on the common good and has come to serve the assertion of competing interests" (*DN*, 282). But O'Donovan's rhetoric does not strip liberal society of its own (deficient) moral reality and the good public purposes its serves.

He recognizes that liberalism is not a fixed unchanging doctrine. Unlike Milbank's counter-everything, O'Donovan's "counter-narrative" is meant to "describe a crossroads, a moment of decision" for liberalism (*DN*, 284). For O'Donovan, we can not go back to some moment before the liberal tradition in order to move beyond it. Christendom is an even more distant Christian witness than liberalism itself:

> The liberal tradition . . . has right of possession. There is no other model available to us of a political order derived from a millennium of close engagement between state and church. It ought, therefore, to have the first word in any discussion of what Christians can approve, even if it ought not have the last word. . . . We cannot simply go behind it; it has the status of a church tradition, and demands to be treated with respect. (*DN*, 228)

The challenge of the present moment is "to think of other liberalisms, different possibilities of combination and development than those which have woven our contemporary bondage" (*DN*, 228). He does not identify some pure form of liberalism but tries to sketch ways in which other features of modern thought have distorted the Christian witness of liberalism itself.

The limited goals of my book do not require a general thesis about Christianity and liberalism; or, for that matter, a general theory of political theology. This chapter has provided a context for my more limited ambition by organizing three types of Augustinian liberalisms in a way that shows the importance of a focus on love that might help imagine a better liberalism. This setting will provide the background for a more systematic examination of two important challenges to this claim in my third chapter. These challenges are found in the writings of Hannah Arendt. In this chapter, I have given a typology that responds to what I take to be the development of Augustinian liberalism. Along the way, I also introduced two difficult questions that have yet to be fully resolved. The first involves the unity of the virtues, and the second involves the relation between Christ and the church for Christian political reasoning. I have shown that the two dominant forms of Augustinian liberalism (realism and Rawlsianism) fail to highlight the potential significance of Christian love for political practice here and now. I have argued that an emerging kind of Augustinian civic liberalism offers a promising extension of the best insights of these more dominant Augustinian liberalisms, even as it breaks new ground in raising questions that are not typically asked in liberal political theory. I have also challenged an influential alternative to each of these proposals by pointing to its internal contradictions and to its unfortunate rhetorical excess that leaves little room for the kind of moral conversation about politics that Augustinians should foster. To return to the theme of my introduction, each of these alternatives to Augustinian civic liberalism trade upon a contrastive account of love and sin. Realists and Rawlsians appeal to sin without an operative conception of love for political ethics. While Milbank offers a promising insertion of love back into political Augustinianism, his identification of liberal society with sin offers little possibility for political ethics itself (except as ecclesiology). In the next chapter, I continue my project of reconceiving Augustinian liberalism by turning to another nonstandard kind of liberalism that receives too little attention in contemporary political theology: feminist liberalism. This encounter, I believe, provides one avenue for responding to O'Donovan's characterization of the challenge of the present moment.

3

✠

A Liberal Ethic of Care
Feminist Political Theory and Christian Social Ethics

*Let him, or her, who would rather be the object of
benevolence than of love cast the first stone.*

ROBERT M. ADAMS, *Finite and Infinite Goods*

*You have enjoined upon us not only continence,
which means restraining our love from certain objects,
but also justice, which requires us to bestow it on
certain others; and you have willed that our charity should
be directed not to you alone but also to our neighbor.*

AUGUSTINE, *Confessions*, 10.4.5

✠

Augustine was not a feminist. His writings and their legacy rightly have
come under attack by those critical of a patriarchal church and society.
Most of these condemnations relate to Augustine's views on women, gender, sexuality, the body, marriage, and family life—views problematically expressed both in his doctrinal treatises and the anxious narrative of his own life.
The spectrum of responses to these charges in the scholarly literature is varied.[1]

---

1. For judicious assessments, see Lamberigts, "Critical Evaluation of Critiques of
Augustine's Views of Sexuality"; Harrison, *Augustine*, 169–77; and Rist, ATB, 112–21. The
best critical statement is now Kim Power, *Veiled Desire: Augustine on Women* (New York:
Continuum, 1996).

Like most topics in Augustine interpretation, these issues are vexed by the multiple settings in which they arise, their lack of systematic presentation, and the social distance that separates us from his epistemic world. Some scholars blame Augustine for misogyny in Western culture. Some scholars portray him as an original bright light relative to other patristic or classical authors. Still others, with qualification, find resources for an Augustinian feminism. In Augustine studies, these debates tend to focus on the tension between his formal affirmation of the embodied spiritual equality of women (as directly created in the image of God and redeemed in Christ) and a host of anthropological and theological assumptions that materially subordinate women to men and the feminine to the masculine.[2] These assumptions continue to play a pernicious role in debates about the role of women in the church, the interpretation of the Scriptures, the appropriateness of feminine imagery for the divine, and theological method. Augustine knew the power of signs and the images we attach to words, and it is remarkable how much feminine imagery one finds in Augustine.[3] Given the interaction between religious practices and the broader culture, the political relevance of these debates should not be underestimated. In this chapter, however, I pursue a different approach.

My purpose is neither to refuse the significance of these debates for Augustinian civic liberalism nor to redeem Augustine from his feminist critics. Recent scholarship provocatively aligns Augustine with dimensions of radical feminist thought consistent with my reading of Augustinian alternatives to certain liberal conceptions of the self as a disembodied, autonomous, ra-

2. Kari Elisabeth Borresen, for example, defends Augustine's "feminism" in that he "strove to include women in Godlike humanity, in spite of their femaleness" and that his writings "advocate women's human equivalence as strongly as possible within the limits of his patriarchal culture" (Borresen, "In Defence of Augustine," 411). She argues that he does not hold Eve (or sexual desire) responsible for original sin, and he affirms the goodness of male and female creation. Unlike his predecessors, he does not believe that women will become men at the resurrection or that there would have been no sex in Eden without a fall. But, to my mind, she provides compelling evidence that Augustine's soteriology, ecclesiology, and eschatology do privilege male gender hierarchies or androgynous categories that turn femaleness into something "deviant and/or alien" (424).

3. See Jennifer Hockenbery, "The He, She, and It of God: Translating Saint Augustine's Gendered Latin God-talk into English," *Augustinian Studies* 36, no. 2 (2005): 433–46.

tional agent.[4] Augustine, in fact, is an important cultural and intellectual figure who breaks—however haltingly and mistakenly—from conceptions of virtue tied up with individualistic conceptions of rational self-mastery. Peter Brown has helped us see that Augustine's fascination with "concupiscence" was not fundamentally concerned with the body as such but was directed primarily at "a dark drive to control, to appropriate, and to turn to one's private ends, all the good things that had been created by God to be accepted with gratitude and shared with others."[5] Even more explicitly, Catherine Conybeare has drawn attention to Augustine's noteworthy departures from classical conventions of (male) philosophizing. To her surprise, she finds a dialogical Augustine whose style and relational motifs can be helpfully juxtaposed with the work of Luce Irigaray.[6] To this extent, I do think there is room for a more pluralistic view of Augustinianism by feminist theorists. But my primary purpose is to demonstrate a convergence of themes in feminist theory with the sort of Augustinian liberalism I advance.

I do this by comparing and contrasting political appeals to an "ethic of care" with similar debates about love's relation to justice in Christian social ethics. In later chapters, I defend two theses that strike many as implausible. First, Augustinianism shares with feminist political theory of a perfectionist sort a common diagnosis of the failures of dominant liberal discourse: (a) conceptions of autonomy that find little room for dependency and vulnerability, and (b) conceptions of rationality and duty that find little room for affectivity and emotions except as natural energies to be constrained by reason. These claims coincide with attention to virtues of mutual recognition and solidarity in both feminist and Augustinian ethics that distinguish them

---

4. John C. Cavadini compares Augustine's dissatisfaction with sexual pleasure to feminist analyses of sexuality in a patriarchal society. He argues that Andrea Dworkin's "radical hermeneutic of suspicion vis à vis our own culture gets closer to the approach Augustine takes than the rest of us do, content as we are to isolate 'sexual pleasure' as though it were an unimpeachably fixed quantity innocent of political dynamics, far from being contoured or warped by ideologies of power and domination" (Cavadini, "Feeling Right," 198).

5. Brown, *Body and Society*, 418.

6. Conybeare, *Irrational Augustine*, especially 195–202. Conybeare argues that for all of the scholarly attention to gender and the role of women in Augustine's writings, there is a striking neglect of "*gendered* themes: issues raised, above all, by the embodied self and its characteristic activities" (65).

from most utilitarian and Kantian theories. It also distinguishes both feminist and Christian ethics from game-theoretic styles of analytic philosophy.
Both traditions resist the valorization of formal methods in ethics and promote the importance of moral attention that avoids the instrumentalism and
legalism of rationalist ethics. Both traditions offer a vision of earthly political community that aspires for more than just not killing each other and a
conception of liberal civic virtue beyond Mill's harm principle. Second, no
less bracing to conventional thought, I claim that Augustinianism provides a
neglected tradition of inquiry for a liberal political practice informed by the
virtues of Christian neighbor-love and a feminist "ethic of care." Both traditions resist the tendency of justice (narrowly conceived in terms of "public"
impartiality) to overwhelm attention to any other virtue within a liberal
ethics of citizenship. The primary challenges to this relationship that I will
consider are the appropriate liberal worries about the practical psychological
possibilities of rationalizing unjust coercion under the guise of love and the
claim that the particularity of love can not provide an adequate account of
the distinctive public obligations of civic virtue.

The resurgence of Augustinianism in the past fifteen years has not been
notable in its attention to feminist concerns.[7] The implicit relevance of this
revival for feminist thought, and the possibility of mutual engagement between feminism and neo-Augustinianism, has not gone without notice.[8]

---

7. By contrast, compare two works done in the 1980s. Elaine Pagels and Jean Bethke
Elshtain both set feminist concerns at the center of their influential accounts of the
political implications of Augustine's theology. Pagels held that "Augustine's pessimistic
views of sexuality, politics, and human nature" led to a betrayal of earlier Christian affirmations of human freedom and political liberty (Pagels, *Adam, Eve, and the Serpent*,
98–126). Elshtain held that Augustine's Christianity "ushered a moral revolution into the
world which dramatically, and for the better, transformed the prevailing images of male
and female, public and private" (Elshtain, *Public Man, Private Woman*, 56). She claimed
that "Augustine, taken all in all, is one of the great undoers of Greek misogyny which
dictated a separate and inferior female nature and consigned women to a 'lesser' realm of
'necessity'" (73). I point to these competing interpretations only to highlight the subject
matter, not resolve the dispute.

8. See, for example, the suggestive work of Debra Dean Murphy, "Community, Character, and Gender: Women and the Work of Stanley Hauerwas," *Scottish Journal of Theology* 55, no. 3 (2002): 338–55, and "Power, Politics, and Difference: A Feminist Response to
John Milbank," *Modern Theology* 10, no. 2 (April 1994): 131–42.

Both traditions offer critical accounts of liberal practices and the epistemological and metaphysical views that undergird them. One finds a similar spectrum of responses to this situation in both Augustinian and feminist camps, ranging from wholesale rejection of liberalism to amendment and reconstruction. Constructive work in feminist theory and political Augustinianism tend to operate in different worlds. Any effort to bring these worlds together, even under the rubric of conversation, risks eliding differences for ideological purposes. But such dangers are common to any project of rational reconstruction or interdisciplinary encounter.[9] Augustinian liberalism already risks such engagement with a tradition ("liberalism") and an academic discipline ("political theory") that today have radically different starting points. The reader might wonder if further alchemy would be needed to bring Augustinian liberalism alongside feminist theory.

Feminist theologians have developed sophisticated avenues of intersection between feminist philosophy, Christian ethics, and the wider context of cultural politics. An "ethic of care" has been an important element of feminist theological reflection often neglected by feminist philosophers.[10] With the exception of J. Joyce Schuld's study of Foucault and Augustine, even these efforts have not included sustained attention to Augustine. Occasional references can be found in somewhat surprising places.[11] Feminist philosophers have developed interpretations of various ancient philosophers, and some have begun to trace the roots of care theory "back deeply to some interesting strands" in Christian and Jewish theology.[12] Ruth E. Groenhout's

9. For an exemplary discussion of relevant moral traditions in dialogue ("liberal individualism," "neo-Aristotelianism," and "an ethics of caring or love"), see John Reeder Jr, "Three Moral Traditions," *Journal of Religious Ethics*, 22, no. 1 (Spring 1994): 75–92.

10. Carol Gilligan briefly hints at this connection: "The underlying epistemology correspondingly shifts from the Greek ideal of knowledge as a correspondence between mind and form to the Biblical conception of knowing as a process of human relationship" (Gilligan, *Different Voice*, 173). For theological discussion, see Kathryn Tanner, "The Care That Does Justice: Recent Writings on Feminist Ethics and Theology," *Journal of Religious Ethics* 24, no. 1 (Spring 1996): 171–91, and Serene Jones, *Feminist Theory and Christian Theology* (Minneapolis: Fortress Press, 2000).

11. One of the few positive appropriations of Augustine's theology of love in feminist philosophy can be found in Julia Kristeva, *Strangers to Ourselves*, 83–84.

12. Groenhout, "Theological Echoes in an Ethic of Care," 1.

recent work on care theory includes a chapter on Augustine.[13] But these connections are only beginning to be drawn, and they tend to highlight the more recent work of Jewish philosophers like Martin Buber, Franz Rosenzweig, and Emmanuel Levinas. Surprisingly, despite occasional references to theology, feminist political theory pays scant attention to the role (positive or negative) of religious communities in practices of care.[14]

A separate debate has emerged in religious ethics regarding the harmful effect on women of Augustinian theologies predicated on male experience. Critics argue these theologies give univocal priority to pride as the fundamental sin of humanity and subsequently endorse a self-sacrificial vision of *agape* (modeled on Christ's self-emptying Incarnation and the suffering love of the cross) as its antidote.[15] Feminist theologians claim this diagnosis *(superbia)* and its cure *(kenosis)* serve only to further patterns of oppression within religious communities and the larger political culture. They fail to name the sin of many men and women who suffer not from excessive self-interest but rather something more like a loss of self.[16] As such, they cannot

13. Groenhout, *Connected Lives*, 52–78. Groenhout argues for a "number of important connections between Augustine's account of human existence and that implicit in care theory" (52). In particular, she claims: "Augustine never assumes that all humans are adult, independent, fully rational beings, but rather assumes that humans exist as embodied beings, developing in ways that require constant contact with other people" (60).

14. This neglect is doubly surprising within the reception of these debates in religious studies. An otherwise helpful survey of the "ethics of care" debates for scholars of religion makes no mention of religion; see Cynthia S. W. Crysdale, "Gilligan and the Ethics of Care: An Update," *Religious Studies Review* 20, no. 1 (January 1994): 21–28.

15. Early statements of this criticism include Valerie Saiving, "The Human Situation: A Feminine View," in *Womanspirit Rising: A Feminist Reader in Religion,* ed. Judith Plaskow (New York: Harper and Row, 1979), 25–42; Judith Plaskow, *Sex, Sin and Grace: Women's Experience and the Theologies of Reinhold Niebuhr and Paul Tillich* (Washington, D.C.: University Press of America, 1980); and Susan Nelson Dunfee, "The Sin of Hiding: A Feminist Critique of Reinhold Niebuhr's Account of the Sin of Pride," *Soundings* 65, no. 3 (Fall 1982): 316–27. For a qualified feminist defense of Niebuhr, see Rebekah L. Miles, *The Bonds of Freedom: Feminist Theology and Christian Realism* (Oxford: Oxford University Press, 2001).

16. Harry Frankfurt argues that "coming to love oneself is the deepest and most essential—and by no means the most readily attainable—achievement of a serious and successful life" (*Reasons of Love*, 68). He offers a conception of self-love as a kind of

adequately speak to the particular grace that might set these persons free. Against dominant notions of *agape* as "other-regard" and "self-sacrifice," many feminists propose "mutuality" as a better way of conceiving Christian love for personal and social ethics because it does not presuppose an agonistic relation between the self and the other. Others suggest, often by appeal to Karl Barth, that overreaching pride and passive self-abnegation (or diffusiveness) are complementary temptations of faithlessness before a loving God. For some, false humility (denying one's worth before God) remains a paradoxical form of pride. But each sin warrants distinct responses, serving to "enlarge the canvass" of human sinfulness beyond any single vice.[17] These authors resist a polarization of "self-sacrifice" and "mutuality" as binary oppositions, especially following Gene Outka's development of love as "equal regard" that does not issue indiscriminate "blank checks" to others.[18] In Paul Tillich's terms, this unjust love is "chaotic self-surrender, destroying him who loves as well as him who accepts such love" (*LPJ*, 68). Or, as Niebuhr at times could say, "the ideal possibility is a loving relationship between the self and the other self in which alienation but not discrete identity is transcended."[19] Kathryn Tanner proposes the helpful concept of "nonidolatrous esteem" as a way of viewing self and others in light of God.[20] This view is compatible with Outka's emphasis on affirming theocentric identity and enjoining "persistence in the face of obstacles and continued concern for

---

"wholeheartedness" that is not at odds with "disinterested" love of others, and associates it with Augustine's struggle for volitional unity and Kierkegaard's "purity of heart" (94–95).

17. Outka, "Universal Love," 54. Robin Lovin argues that "sin is present not merely in the ambition that remakes the world to suit its own plans, but in the sensuality that loses itself in immediate possibilities, in the sloth that absorbs itself in petty concerns and excuses its mediocre performance, and even in the disciplined pursuit of excellences that have been carefully defined by someone else" (Lovin, *Reinhold Niebuhr*, 147).

18. Outka, *Agape*, 21. Outka writes: "However difficult to apply in practice, *for the sake of the neighbor*, one may have to resist his exploitation as well as attend to his needs" (21). Even though he rejects the kind of altruism that persistently subordinates the self to the neighbor, Outka does find in the Christian tradition "an ongoing practical *swerve* away from concentrating on what one owes oneself toward what one may do for others" ("Universal Love," 82).

19. Niebuhr, *Nature and Destiny*, 1:82.

20. Tanner, *Politics of God*, 228.

another's welfare despite lack of personal benefit."[21] The diverse examples of Christian saints, moreover, resist any singular (let alone exclusively moral) conception of the imitation of Christ as a model for Christian living.[22] These theological debates are rarely applied to political theory, but Robin Lovin (drawing from Niebuhr) has argued that contemporary political society exhibits both the sin of pride and the sin of sloth. Prideful assertions of group egoism remain relevant, but political institutions and practices of social criticism display increasingly passive "acceptance that our own community and culture provides the largest moral universe we can fathom."[23] An Augustinian theology of *caritas*, detached from Augustine's views on women, may provide a more appealing vision for feminist religious ethics. It does not privilege *agape* as self-sacrifice (though it affirms willing sacrifice for the sake of a greater good). It does not assume that human beings naturally love themselves well. And it challenges prevailing cultural assumptions in liberal political theory by always hoping for something better, and even something new.[24] My reconstruction of Augustine's account of love that correlates autonomy and care by remaining attentive to love's relation to sin tries to aid such efforts. Such an account does not assume that the basic problem of the moral life is a lack of motivation to be attentive to others; rather, as I have argued, it assumes that demands of morality arise under conditions of an excess of motivations and desires that are disordered. The primary interest of this chapter lies in the way feminist political theorists have extended debates about an "ethic of care" into ambivalent judgments about liberal democracy. How does this evaluation relate to Christian social ethics and Augustinian civic liberalism? In answering this question, I will continue to focus on my overarching goal of exploring the organizational structure of motivations that characterize a liberal citizen.

21. Outka, *Agape*, 11. Outka's affirmation of direct self-regard is not simply derived from other-regard itself. As we see, this view differs from both Ramsey and "pure" forms of altruism and impartiality.

22. See, for example, Adams, *Finite and Infinite Goods*, 52–56.

23. Lovin, *Reinhold Niebuhr*, 156.

24. Barbara Hilkert Andolsen suggests this possibility in relation to the work of Martin D'Arcy, but considers it a "minority opinion in twentieth-century American ethics" (Andolsen, "Agape in Feminist Ethics," 73). Catholic scholars responding to this debate have typically relied on Thomas Aquinas's account of charity. For a detailed account of Augustine's texts responsive to feminist concerns, see Schlabach, *For the Joy Set Before Us*, xv, xxi, 12, 21, 23, 143, 146, 148, and 217n28.

FEMINIST "CARE" AND MODERATE LIBERAL PERFECTIONISM

I indicated in my introduction that many liberals fear that to say too much about love in a political context raises the specter of dangerous sentimentalism and paternalist moralism. This fear motivates the common objection to political agapism. Liberalism is suspicious of an erotic politics of compassion because it is thought to raise the stakes of politics too high—jeopardizing the integrity of political actors by encouraging too thick a notion of political responsibility and moral obligation. Introducing love as a political virtue of democratic citizenship threatens the capacity of individuals to enjoy their liberty and equality and undermines the gains of liberal justice that overcome the ("private") partiality of love. Love is something for poets and caregivers in the private domestic sphere, but it is unfit for public virtue and political affirmation. Personal relations might need love, but politics requires hard-nosed principles of rational discrimination and judgment. Love is inappropriate for liberal moral or political analyses. Love undermines social justice when it goes political.

My Augustinian liberalism is sympathetic to these concerns and stresses a love appropriate to political citizenship in a liberal culture. Loving can be a dangerous thing, especially when wielded as a political trope. It is for this reason that fraternity has become a notorious poor cousin compared to liberty and equality, and love has been eclipsed by justice as the first virtue of political institutions. Augustinian conceptions of sin should make Augustinians alert to the fact that the best moral philosophy may not be the best political philosophy. But they should resist the liberal tendency to equate a morally ambitious ethics of citizenship with a necessarily antiliberal politics. In the next chapter, I argue that Hannah Arendt, like other modern liberals, misconstrues love by focusing on its political pathologies and construing love solely in terms of sentimental benevolence or fellow-feeling. She fails to discern the legitimacy and, at times, the necessity of love for healthy politics. If it truly involves giving each his or her due in all respects, justice must also involve loving what merits love and securing, as best possible, the conditions for persons to flourish. If love can be redeemed from its critics, we can better imagine how a just society is "simply *the loving society*."[25]

---

25. Slote, "Love and Justice," 160n14.

This neglect or mistrust of love as a political motive—not giving love its due—is limiting for both Augustinians and liberals in their evaluations of political society and in their civic proposals for citizens. It opens liberals to the familiar charges of radical individualism, bourgeois commercialism, and narrow rationalism that have haunted liberalism since the Enlightenment.[26] It also distorts liberal approaches to politics in ways that undermine both its descriptive capacity (what is going on in political life? what motivates social movements?) and its prescriptive capacity (what should motivate and sustain liberal politics?). Liberalism has achieved great moral and political gains, even in terms of its focus on the impartiality of procedural rules. By simply abandoning love as part of its political psychology, however, liberalism provides little by way of vocabulary or conceptuality that might organize the disordered loves it rightly fears and that are perpetually expressed in political societies.

In rethinking love as a motivation for political action, my own project parallels various efforts in feminist theory that critically evaluate liberalism in light of Carol Gilligan's seminal work, *In A Different Voice: Psychological Theory and Women's Development.* Emerging out of "second-wave" or "difference" feminism, Gilligan's work distinguished between a masculine *justice* approach to morality and a feminine *care* approach.[27] Like Augustine's explorations of love in the *Confessions,* Gilligan's study linked these approaches to personality formation in childhood and adolescence. She claimed that Lawrence Kohlberg's influential model of the stages of moral development excluded, and could not hear, the distinctive moral voice of adolescent girls. For Gilligan, each approach entails a distinctive set of sensibilities and underlying assumptions about the human condition. Initial responses to

26. I do not examine the contested relation between liberalism and the Enlightenment. For an interesting challenge to the equation of liberalism and the Enlightenment that focuses on questions of religious liberty, see James Schmidt, "Liberalism and Enlightenment in Eighteenth Century Germany," *Critical Review* 13 (1999): 31–53.

27. These themes are further developed in Carol Gilligan, "Moral Orientation and Moral Development," in *Women and Moral Theory,* ed. Eva Kittay and Diana Meyers (Totowa, N.J.: Rowman & Littlefield, 1987). For a helpful survey of the field since Gilligan, see Samantha Brennan, "Recent Work in Feminist Ethics," *Ethics* 109 (July 1999): 858–93. On a broad interpretation, other advocates of care would include a diverse array of male thinkers such as Hume, Shaftesbury, Hutcheson, Adam Smith, Schopenhauer, and Heidegger. I would add Augustine to this list.

Gilligan's work focused on the status of its apparent gender essentialism and the racial and class assumptions of a neo-romantic advocacy of a "women's morality."[28] Like Christian ethicists who challenge a dualistic conception of love and justice, feminist theorists have challenged the apparent dichotomy of justice and care in the work of both Gilligan and the author who first formulated "care" as a moral theory, Nel Noddings.[29] Some feminists have tried to shift from "psychological" to "economic" stories about the moral influence of capitalist exchange relations on patterns of socialization that privilege public justice over and against private care. This literature interestingly parallels John Milbank's account of the fate of Christian charity in the West (providing further confirmation that Milbank's analyses of the hegemony of contemporary social science relies on a caricature).[30] Still another development, associated with Seyla Benhabib, Martha Nussbaum, Joan C. Tronto, and Eva Feder Kittay, emphasizes the political relevance of a moral theory of care that is not blind to justice and power. These arguments are

28. On "care" promoting gender stereotypes, see Anne Phillips, ed., *Feminism and Politics* (Oxford: Oxford University Press, 1998), and Claudia Card, "Women's Voices and Ethical Ideals: Must We Mean What We Say?" *Ethics* 99 (1998): 125–36. In the preface to the new edition, Gilligan argues that her work should not be "cast in terms of whether women and men are really (essentially) different or who is better than whom" but in terms of questions "about our perceptions of reality and truth; how we know, how we hear, how we see, how we speak" (*Different Voice*, xiii.) While the perspective of care empirically may be more prominent among women because of contingent cultural conditions, there are many passages in the original edition that clearly state this feature of her argument: "The different voice I describe is characterized not by gender but theme . . . the contrasts between male and female voices are presented here to highlight a distinction between two modes of thought rather than to represent a generalization about either sex" (2).

29. Noddings rejects the claim that "care" is a gendered morality (Noddings, *Caring*, 2–6, and Noddings, *Starting at Home*, 45). Noddings also claims that there are "major and irreconcilable differences" between her account and "Christian ethics" (Noddings, *Caring*, 29). But, more than most feminist theorists, she includes significant attention to Jewish and Christian authors, especially Søren Kierkegaard and Martin Buber. For an exceptional treatment of Kierkegaard, Ricoeur, and Taylor, see Maria Pia Lara, *Moral Textures: Feminist Narratives in the Public Sphere* (Berkeley and Los Angeles: University of California Press, 1998).

30. See, for example, Gabrielle Meagher and Julie A. Nelson, "Survey Article: Feminism in the Dismal Science," *Journal of Political Philosophy* 12, no. 1 (March 2004): 102–26.

the most significant for my account of Augustinian civic liberalism. I begin, however, with Gilligan in order to show how feminist theory has developed her insights.

According to Gilligan, justice emphasizes equality, universal fairness, rights, impersonal procedural rules, formal obligations, and noninterference. Care emphasizes dependence, responsibility, contextual narrative, and empathetic attention to the concrete needs of particular persons. Gilligan claimed traditional psychological theories of moral development fail because they operate with male value assumptions that privilege separation, conflict, and autonomy over intimacy, attachment, and cooperation. These assumptions fit better with a "justice" approach and tend to marginalize the morality of "care." From a male perspective, "a morality of responsibility appears inconclusive and diffuse" and is characterized as morally immature (22). She suggested, with some ambiguity, that the two views of morality are "complementary rather than sequential or opposed" (33). Displaying her tendency to identify justice and care as independent features of morality, however, she spoke of the need for a "mutuality of respect and care" (104), even a "fusion of justice and love" (172).[31] As such, she did not deny the gains for women under the rubric of rights and justice. Indeed, of particular relevance to Christian discussions of *agape* as self-sacrifice, her attention to female voices was meant to liberate women from the self-abnegating confusions "inherent in the conventions of feminine goodness" (74).[32] But, for Gilligan, this does not require abandoning the language of care or its distinctive moral point of view. This different voice reveals "the importance throughout life of the connection between self and other" and the "universality of the need for compassion and care" (98). To deny the perspective of care was, according to Gilligan, "an adolescent ideal" (98) with strong links to masculine violence

31. On the independence of justice and care in Gilligan, see Reeder, "Three Moral Traditions," 84–85 (cf. note 9). Reeder elsewhere notes Gilligan's developed views accentuate justice and care as distinct "moral orientations" that "cannot be 'integrated' or employed 'simultaneously'" ("Analogues to Justice," 298).

32. For Gilligan, "once obligation extends to include the self as well as others, the disparity between selfishness and responsibility dissolves" (*Different Voice*, 94), and "responsibility for care then includes both self and other" (95; see also 173). This move is structurally similar to Gene Outka's *"theocentric case for valuing one's particular life"* in Outka, "Universal Love," 51.

and the nihilistic belief "that the strong need not be moral and that only the weak care about relationships" (124).

Gilligan argued moral maturity involves the convergence of both points of view. She writes:

> The morality of rights is predicated on equality and centered on the understanding of fairness, while the ethic of responsibility relies on the concept of equity, the recognition of differences in need. While the ethics of rights is a manifestation of equal respect, balancing the claims of other and self, the ethic of responsibility rests on an understanding that gives rise to compassion and care. Thus the counterpoint of identity and intimacy that marks the time between childhood and adulthood is articulated through two different moralities whose complementarity is the discovery of maturity. (165)

But modern moral theory has neglected care because of its professed interest in liberty and autonomy. Gilligan called for a move beyond "the paralyzing injunction not to hurt others to an injunction to act responsively toward self and others . . . joining the heart and the eye in an ethic that ties the activity of thought to the activity of care" (149). Care enjoins positive responsibilities to help as well as negative duties to not harm. But Gilligan and other feminists are wary of general or universal accounts of the human good that typically follow from such claims. As such, she saw her work as "an attempt to turn the tide of moral discussion from questions of how to achieve objectivity and detachment to how to engage responsively and with care" (xix). The post-Gilligan debates, once dominated by discussion of gender or meta-ethical discussion of care's relation to justice, have proved illuminating for debates about liberalism in political theory.[33]

Political proponents of an "ethic of care" typically begin their criticism of liberalism by pointing to historical conditions that subordinate women.

---

33. See Bat-Ami Bar On and Ann Ferguson, eds., *Daring to be Good: Essays in Feminist Ethico-Politics* (New York: Routledge, 1998); Diemut Bubeck, *Care, Gender, and Justice* (Oxford: Oxford University Press, 1995); Grace Clement, *Care, Autonomy, and Justice: Feminism and the Ethic of Care* (Boulder: Westview Press, 1998); Cass Sunstein, ed., *Feminism and Political Theory* (Chicago: University of Chicago Press, 1990); and Virginia Held, *Feminist Morality: Transforming Culture, Society, and Politics* (Chicago: University of Chicago Press, 1993).

Marilyn Friedman refers to these conditions as "a division of moral labor along the lines of gender."[34] According to Friedman:

> The tasks of governing, regulating social order, and managing other 'public' institutions have been monopolized by men as their privileged domain, and the task of sustaining privatized personal relationships have been imposed on, or left to, women. . . . Justice and rights have structured male norms, values, and virtues, while care and responsiveness have defined female moral norms, values, and virtues.[35]

Many feminists argue that the privatization of love as a moral orientation is motivated by a desire to exclude women and women's experience from public life.[36] As Seyla Benhabib puts it, "the definition of moral autonomy, as well as the ideal of moral autonomy . . . in universalistic, contractarian theories from Hobbes to Rawls, lead to a *privatization* of women's experience and to the exclusion of its consideration from a moral point of view."[37] Some theorists persuasively connect this privatization of women's experience with "the privatization of religion and notions of the good."[38] According to Leora Batnitzky, "this double privatization has the effect of placing concerns about the good and caring into the private realm while leaving only discussion of justice in the realm of public discourse."[39] The subordination of love as an aspect of moral reasoning in political debate (particularly among neo-Kantians) is part of an unwarranted larger pattern of circumscribing concrete discussion of goods in ways that repress expressive and agonistic modes of political activity. Of particular interest for Augustinian liberals, a compelling feature of feminist criticism is the belief that liberalism reflects a "deep prejudice . . . that we are so embarrassed by all talk of care in political contexts."[40] This embarrassment

34. Friedman, "Beyond Caring," 94.

35. Ibid, 94.

36. See Susan Miller Okin, "Thinking like a Woman," in *Theoretical Perspectives on Sexual Difference*, ed. D. Rhode (New Haven: Yale University Press, 1990), 145–59, and Carol Pateman, "'The Disorder of Women': Women, Love, and the Sense of Justice," *Ethics* (1991): 20–34.

37. Benhabib, *Situating the Self*, 152.

38. Leora Batnitzky, "Dependency and Vulnerability," 137.

39. Ibid.

40. Schwarzenbach, "On Civic Friendship," 123.

is exacerbated in the field of Christian social ethics under the influence of "realist" criticism of the sentimentality of liberal Protestantism. Realists, like Niebuhr, were adamant that a "sense of justice is a product of the mind and not of the heart."[41] Tough-minded rational justice is to guide political life.

While modern liberals have rejected the exclusion of women from public life, many liberals continue to endorse a division of virtue's labor as basic to the fundamental liberal distinction between public and private life. Liberal feminist theorists dissent from this aspect of modern liberalism. They argue that liberal cultural norms effectively privilege the public against the private because, in the words of Joan C. Tronto, they continue to value male "activities of production" more than female "activities of care."[42] Tronto argues that "because our society does not notice the importance of care and the moral quality of its practice, we devalue the work and contributions of women and other disempowered groups who care in this society" (157). This devaluing of care is exacerbated by traditional liberal distinctions between the public and the private, a distinction that raises "an opaque glass rendering women and their traditional spheres of activity invisible and inaudible."[43] Feminist liberals are critical of what they perceive as dubious liberal arguments about the apolitical character of the private sphere and the exclusion of care from public life.

Many feminists reject liberalism *tout court*, opting for a variety of anti-liberal or postliberal positions. These feminists tend to think care and justice are incompatible, and are highly suspicious of the public/private distinction itself.[44] Liberalism is simply irredeemable on this score. My own view is

41. Niebuhr, *Moral Man*, 29. Robert Markus is surely right to remind us that "'love,' in Augustine's vocabulary, represents much more than simple moral—let alone emotive—dispositions" (*SAE*, 66). Ernest Fortin shares Markus's anxious rejection: "[Augustine's] understanding of love has nothing of the sentimentality that attaches to this notion in the modern mind" ("Augustine and the Hermeneutics of Love," 48). Markus's and Fortin's tone, I fear, here unconsciously reflects the modern assessment of emotions rather than Augustine's. Paul Ramsey also can adopt this position: "Christian love depends on the direction of the will, the orientation of intention in an act, not on stirring emotion" (*BCE*, 100).

42. Tronto, *Moral Boundaries*, 166. Parenthetical references in this section of the text refer to this book.

43. Benhabib, *Situating the Self*, 12.

44. Nel Noddings' early work tended in this direction, and, in some respects, can be allied with that of Sara Ruddick, *Maternal Thinking: Toward a Politics of Peace* (Boston: Beacon Press, 1989). Noddings is usually taken as the most emphatic defender of care's

more sympathetic to those who believe that liberalism has proved a resilient tradition in the face of antiliberal threats of traditionalism, inherited authority, and religious dogma. Recent feminist thought has resisted a simple opposition between feminist care and liberal justice, or a wholesale rejection of the appropriate differences between public and private realms. An ethic of care, for these feminists, can be assimilated into a revised liberal justice perspective without rejecting the larger liberal framework. For example, according to Susan Moller Okin, "the best theorizing about justice . . . has integral to it the notions of care and empathy, of thinking of the interests and well-being of others who may be very different from ourselves."[45] Okin, once a critic of the ethics of care approach, claimed Rawls's theory of justice already includes rather demanding notions of mutual engagement and equal concern for others.[46] Against Kant and with her reconstructed Rawls, she argued that principles of respect and impartiality *presuppose* care rather than disinterestedness. At the center of Rawlsian liberalism is finally "a voice of responsibility, care and concern for others."[47] Other feminist philosophers

---

opposition to liberal justice. More recently, Noddings claims liberalism "contains serious defects," but "it would be foolish (and ungrateful, in a way) to brush aside the social progress that liberalism has promoted under the banner of rights" (*Starting at Home*, 2 and 35). In her terms, "caring-about (or, perhaps, a sense of justice) must be seen as instrumental in establishing the conditions under which caring-for can flourish. . . . Caring-about is empty if it does not culminate in caring relations" (23). She remains committed to the belief that "care theory takes a Humean position on motivation and inverts Kantian priorities" (24).

45. Okin, *Justice, Gender, and the Family*, 15.

46. According to Okin, "to think as a person in the original position is not to be a disembodied nobody. This, as critics have rightly pointed out, would be impossible. Rather, it is to think from the point of view of everybody, of every 'concrete other' whom one might turn out to be" ("Reason and Feeling," 248). Most feminist political theorists are less sanguine about this interpretive possibility. For recent criticisms, see Noddings, *Starting at Home*, 24–25, and Kittay, *Love's Labor*, 75–82.

47. Okin, "Reason and Feeling," 230. Okin is critical of Kant's claims that acts motivated by love or sympathetic inclination do not have moral worth, even if they do make us aware of moral obligation. I consider Kant's claims, and revisionist Kant scholarship that suggests a more complex view of empathy and benevolence, in chapters 4 and 5. Margaret Moore, while critical of Okin's reading of the original position, has also argued that Rawls's account of moral development "seems to *presuppose* the existence of a morality of care" (Moore, "The Ethics of Care and Justice," *Women & Politics* 20, no. 2 (1999): 1–16, at 8). Moore claims that Rawls's neglected account of the acquisition of a sense of justice shows that "it is not the *justice* of the institutions of moral development which

point out that that a Rawlsian just society requires a range of virtues and emotional dispositions:

> A deep respect and admiration for just institutions and those who uphold them; indignation with officials who act unjustly; solidarity with the victims of injustice; an absence of resentment when one's property is redistributed in accordance with the difference principle; an adequate sense of self-esteem; an absence of contempt or hatred for other groups within the polity whose conceptions of the good are different from one's own; and shame at feelings of covetousness or partiality which conflict with the demands of justice.[48]

Okin was critical of Rawls's neglect of gender and his failure to apply his principles of justice to the family as a basic institution of a liberal society. Her criticisms were foundational, but they were in the service of "improving" Rawlsian liberalism. She argued for a revised liberalism that takes feminist criticism into account without jeopardizing other liberal commitments. Rawlsians, she argues, need not choose between an ethic of justice and an ethic of care. Rather, it is "a tool for feminist criticism."[49]

While Okin helpfully offers a new direction for Rawlsian liberals, I have found Tronto's work to be the most illuminating and sustained account of care and political theory. Like Augustinian civic liberals, Tronto resists the separation of politics from morality. "When the world is rigidly divided between realms of power and of virtue," she writes, "we lose sight of the facts that power requires a moral base, and more importantly for our present purposes, that virtue exerts a kind of power" (93). In fact, like Augustine's reading of the cultural discourses of his own day, she recognizes that "moral theory" itself "conveys power and privilege" (93). Liberal theory often provides a way to evade the messiness of politics altogether. Tronto differs from many feminists, however, because she does not abandon meta-ethical interests in favor of political practice.[50] Tronto's theoretical interests in rejecting

---

socializes individuals into morality but the care and affection of particular individuals for other particular individuals" (10).

48. Susan James, "Passion and Politics," in *Philosophy and the Emotions,* ed. Anthony Hatzimoysis (Cambridge: Cambridge University Press, 2003), 231.

49. Susan Moller Okin, "'Forty Acres and a Mule' for Women: Rawls and Feminism," *Politics, Philosophy & Economics* 4, no. 2 (2005): 233–48, at 240.

50. For similar efforts, see Julie White, *Democracy, Justice and the Welfare State: Reconstructing Public Care* (University Park: Penn State University Press, 2000), and Selma

the opposition of care and justice are motivated by a concern that "the debate between advocates of rights and advocates of community does not offer a clear alternative to feminists who might advocate an ethic of care."[51] She provides such an alternative. Her political ethic of care is not advanced as a women's morality. Care is a "central concern of human life" (180). She offers this definition of "caring": "*a species activity that includes everything that we do to maintain, continue, and repair our 'world' so that we can live in it as well as possible.* That world includes our bodies, our selves, and our environment, all of which we seek to interweave in a complex, life-sustaining web" (103).

By refusing a "dyadic" or "individualistic" account of caring relationships, Tronto allows for a politically viable understanding of care as an ongoing pro-cess of joint action and feeling—as "both a practice and a disposition" (104). More traditional definitions of caring, she rightly notes, tend "to be sentimen-talized and romanticized" (118). They are easily privatized, leaving out moral and political analysis of care-receiving and care-giving. Tronto, and other feminist liberals, do not advocate an abolition of the distinction between the public and private. They also resist the communitarian turn that often marks advocates of care. Tronto does not envision the public realm as an "enlarged family" (169). She rejects feminist arguments that project imagery of "mother-ing" into political practices. As Neera Badhwar recognizes, "exchanging the oppression of husbands and fathers for that of the state is hardly an advance on the road of liberation."[52] How could care be a political idea without indulg-ing in the bad faith of transforming "the political realm into 'one big happy family'" (169)? Or, perhaps worse, another "slave-morality"?[53]

Tronto offers a compelling challenge to those accounts of care that reject liberalism. She argues that liberal moral premises should not be undermined but shown to be "incomplete" (157). She wants to redraw the boundaries of moral and political theory, not "destroy or undermine current moral prem-

---

Sevenhuijsen, *Citizenship and the Ethics of Care: Feminist Considerations on Justice, Moral-ity and Politics* (New York: Routledge, 1998).

51. Tronto, "Beyond Gender Difference," 651.

52. Badhwar, "Love, Politics, and Autonomy," 21.

53. For an interesting example of this charge, see John Paley, "Caring as a Slave Morality: Nietzschean Themes in Nursing Ethics," *Journal of Advanced Nursing* 40, no. 1 (2002): 25–35. Benhabib provides an illuminating challenge to those feminists who read "care theory" as another slave morality (*Situating the Self,* 194–96).

ises" (157). In fact, she claims that care is not a fully sufficient moral ideal for an ethics of citizenship, particularly when care is posited as a moral ideal or emotion that is then "imported wholesale into a principle for social and political order" (158).[54] Such applications are naïve and dangerous. They tend to assume the absence of social conflict and fail to recognize relations of power, especially given the role of race, class, and gender in the work of care. This insight is relevant for Augustinian civic liberals who draw upon Christian love and keep realist observations about power and sin in full view. For Tronto, these naïve applications invoke "communitarian forms of thinking" that undermine the importance of rights and political equality (161). They promote versions of care that "are apt to see the world only from their own perspective and to stifle diversity and otherness" (161). Tronto's liberalism does admit what usually are thought to be communitarian theses. She emphasizes the values of attachment, community, and social responsibility. She argues, for example, "the conception of rational, autonomous man has been a fiction constructed to fit with liberal theories" (162). Feminists condemn this fiction in terms of a hypermasculine understanding of autonomy linked to an abstract account of freedom as sheer power to initiate action. But, for Tronto, this fiction already is premised on a false choice between autonomy and dependence within the liberal imagination. The need for care does not fit into liberal models that see only autonomy or dependence. In reality, she claims, "since people are sometimes autonomous, sometimes dependent, sometimes providing care for those who are dependent, humans are best described as interdependent" (162). Failures of the liberal imagination result in false choices between individualist "projects" or "interests" and appropriate social responsibility for the needs of others. Needs, according to Tronto, are politically relevant because they arise within these conditions of social interdependence and inequality: conditions where "some must work so that others can achieve their autonomy and independence" (165). The importance of politically responding to needs is masked by dominant liberal discourses wedded to a separation of public and private and tied to "a commodity and

---

54. Tronto considers several "misdirections that proponents of care have taken in translating their concern for care into political views" (*Moral Boundaries*, 158). She is critical, for example, of Charlotte Gilman, Nel Noddings, Elizabeth Fox-Genovese, and Mary Anne Glendon (160–61).

exchange notion of justice" (140). Care is displaced as a political ideal by liberal social contract theorists committed to the notion that politics is only about interests. Liberal justice can actually perpetuate patterns of domination or, at least, inadequately frame pressing social and political issues that do not fit easily into the category of injustice; for example, the political challenges of famine and poverty relief, drug addiction, homelessness, unemployment, illiteracy, and environmental destruction.[55] These theories assume that "all citizens are equal," but a care perspective "would have us recognize the achievement of equality as a political goal" (164). To make this achievement a political goal, citizens should not simply think of themselves as fully autonomous creatures who enter the world ready to "truck and barter." Liberal political society should not assume a "strange world" where "individuals are grown up before they have been born."[56]

Eva Feder Kittay argues for what she calls the "dependency critique" of liberal theories of equality: "A conception of society viewed as an association of equals masks inequitable dependencies, those of infancy and childhood, old age, illness and disability."[57] Liberal theory tacitly relies on the work of care-givers to prop up its version of a just society, but it provides no way of giving an account of these practices on its terms (other than identifying care as a private choice).[58] For example, Rawls's account of the sense of justice "takes it for granted that there will be loving parents rearing the children in whom the sense of justice is to develop."[59] This charge of a *lack* of realism,

---

55. See Fiona Robinson, *Globalizing Care* (Boulder: Westview Press, 1999).

56. Benhabib, *Situating the Self*, 157. Timothy P. Jackson affirms this criticism of liberal theory when he claims that "right and duties are parasitic on charity as the uncalculating care that nurtures rights-bearers into existence" (*Love Disconsoled*, 28).

57. Kittay, *Love's Labor*, xi. See also Peter Alexander Meyers, "The 'Ethic of Care' and the Problem of Power," *Journal of Political Philosophy* 6, no. 2 (1998): 142–70.

58. Margaret Moore poses the problem forcefully: "Liberal society depends on an elaborate myth; and being grounded in myth runs counter to the traditional liberal emphasis on the transparency of reason" ("The Ethics of Care and Justice," 12). She cites the work of Nancy Fraser and Linda Gordon on American welfare debates, which show that "the tendency to conceive of care for others as a 'private choice,' as a self-interested act, locates the problem of welfare with the single mother herself, rather than with the economic and structural conditions in which welfare operates" (13).

59. Baier, *Moral Prejudices*, 6. Baier continues: "Rawls's theory, like so many other theories of obligation, in the end must take out a loan not only on the natural duty of parents to care for children (which he will have no trouble including) but on the natural *virtue* of parental love (or even a loan on the maternal instinct?)."

ironically, turns liberalism into another form of utopianism despite liberal claims to simply operate within a minimal set of moral commitments and presuppositions of extensive sentiment. Given realities of dependency and the need for care, Tronto argues, care should inform "the practices of democratic citizenship" (167). But how should a political community distinguish between the various needs that present themselves? What if those in need do not recognize their need or refuse the offer of care? What prevents "care" from slipping into what Alasdair MacIntyre identifies as the manipulative moralities of "bureaucratic and managerial expertise" of modern society?[60] What about the self-deception that characterizes our notions of what other people need? Or, to put this in Augustinian terms, how do we balance care for the well-being of others with the recognition of our sinful tendencies?

Because of the dangers of paternalism, Tronto argues, "care is only viable as a political ideal in the context of liberal, pluralistic, democratic institutions" (158). These political conditions offer the greatest hope that multiple perspectives and modes of attention will contribute to public decisions about needs and human capacities. But it is not institutions alone that warrant attention. There is a mutually reinforcing dynamic between the virtues that shape a caring person and the institutions that seek to ensure care is not abused. Care offers an account of civic virtue as practice and disposition that continually checks itself. Tronto's ambivalent assessment of liberalism does not make it any less radical than full-scale assaults on the philosophical shortcomings of liberalism. Such assaults often provide little by way of constructive alternatives. Tronto does not simply add "care" to liberalism, as if it were another regulative principle or commodity to be incorporated into a theory. Rather, as she puts its, "even conventional liberal thought will be transformed if we take caring seriously" (xi). Liberal thought, and, we might add, the practices of liberal democratic citizenship, will be transformed. Tronto's interests extend beyond theorizing a new ethics of citizenship

---

60. MacIntyre, *After Virtue*, 75. Criticizing the often denied moral assumptions that support the centrality of "effective" management in the modern world is a central part of MacIntyre's influential thesis. In fact, he calls it "the key to much of the modern age" (86). He argues that the concept of effectiveness is "inseparable from a mode of human existence in which the contrivance of means is in central part the manipulation of human beings into compliant patterns of behavior; and it is by appeal to his own effectiveness in this respect that the manager claims authority within the manipulative mode" (74).

because she applies an ethic of care to actual practices in liberal society. Two passages support this claim:

> The qualities of attentiveness, of responsibility, of competence, or responsiveness, need not be restricted to the immediate objects of our care, but can also inform our practices as citizens. They direct us to a politics in which there is, at the center, a public discussion of needs, and an honest appraisal of the intersection of needs and interests. If attentiveness is presumed to be a part of public values, then the absence of attentiveness to the plight of some group in the society (or the world) becomes a public issue, worthy of public debate. (167–68)

> In all, to include the value of caring in addition to commitments to other liberal values (such as commitment to people's rights, to due process, to obeying laws and following agreed upon political procedures) makes citizens more thoughtful, more attentive to the needs of others, and therefore better democratic citizens. (169)

Tronto suggests that this perspective would not only affect funding decisions but would transform debates about welfare, health care, political reform, and civic education.[61]

Tronto is aware that an ethic of care (like the liberal theory of justice) has characteristic internal problems. Much like Hannah Arendt's criticism of

---

61. Eva Feder Kittay's proposals regarding welfare reform and the Family and Medical Leave Act provide examples of how a public ethic of care, "cognizant of the indispensable role of dependency workers," might transform debates about these issues, in *Love's Labor*, 117–46 (146). Kittay proposes a principle of justice that includes the social responsibility of care: "*to each according to his or her need to care, from each according to his or capacity for care, and such support from social institutions as to make available resources and opportunities to those providing care, so that all will be adequately attended in relations that are sustaining*" (113). While John Milbank does not discuss feminist liberalism, he also tries to overcome the strict antimony between the *oikos* and the *polis*: "As for Plato, so for Augustine, and other Christian thinkers: the public ecclesial (and even ecclesio-political) rule becomes pastoral, immediate and direct (ideally without law, as in Plato's myth of the tutelary deities) and therefore 'economic' in character. Inversely, the domestic—child care, economic activity, artisanal production, medical care—becomes 'political,' a matter of real significance for law, education, religion, and government (although this has only been spasmodically realized in Christian history)" (*TST*, 368).

Augustine, Tronto points out that the ethic of care is tempted by *paternalism* and *parochialism*. Caregivers can infantilize those who receive care and "may well come to see themselves as more capable of assessing the needs of care-receivers than are the care-receivers themselves" (170). Moreover, the ethic of care promotes a partiality that can become parochial, particularly if the model for care is understood as "the metaphorical relationship of a mother and child" (170–71). Tronto's solution to both of these problems is to connect love with justice in a democratic way. Her theory of justice does not abandon commitments to familiar liberal values of universalizability. My own account of love and justice coheres with this claim. At times, however, I am not sure about Tronto's formulations. I find her langue of "connecting" care to a theory of justice to be at odds with her own insights about the practice of care. She goes to great lengths to resist the split between care and justice and the privileging of theory to practice. But she seems to abandon this insight by assuming that care can "go public" only by being plugged into an existing theory of justice. She perpetuates an implicit division between the two values without adequately insisting that love transforms (without simply colonizing) a theory of justice. My own account of love's relation to justice seeks resources internal to the perspective of care that deflect the temptation to paternalism and parochialism. Tronto's emphasis on democratic practices of deliberation about needs and justice, however, is a helpful safeguard against paternalism and parochialism.

In the end, Tronto offers some frank and wise admissions about the dangers that remain even for a democratic ethic of political care. She does think theory can help change the way we see the political world. Care admits a universal imperative: "one should care" (153). But it is not a new "first principle of social virtue" (154). A principle of care cannot be separated from the practices of care in a given situation. Tronto recognizes that "there is no universal principle that we can invoke that will automatically guarantee that, as people and society engage in care, that care will be free from parochialism, paternalism, and privilege" (153). Augustinians should share such sentiments. The political world is risky, fragile, and imperfect. Human beings will abuse the rhetoric of "care" just as much as they abuse the rhetoric of "justice." It will be employed to manipulate and exploit rather than address situations of manipulation and exploitation. This reality, however, should not mean that liberal democracies can proceed as if care is not necessary for a political practice responsive to injustice, persons in need, and the social conditions that frustrate human flourishing.

By challenging the strict liberal dichotomy between public and private, feminist liberals cast a different light on liberal goods and liberal virtues. Tronto's emphasis on the complexities of an ethic of care construes a different political world than the traditional distinction between public and private allows. This aspect of feminist political theory has shown how attention to civic love can be extended to structural evaluations of political institutions and the moral ethos of societies that rely upon the value and work of care.

Martha Nussbaum, perhaps more than any other liberal thinker, has argued persuasively for an approach to compassion in public life that operates at "both the level of individual psychology and the level of institutional design" (*UT*, 403). This twin individual and structural approach complements those approaches that one sometimes finds in religious ethics. These more individually oriented approaches to the ethics of citizenship focus on the moral character of individual citizens ("Good Samaritans") or the formulation of universal principles of action (follow the "Golden Rule"). Nussbaum, of course, does not deny the importance of emotions for individual moral decisions: "Some emotions are at least potential allies of, and indeed constituents in, rational deliberation" (454). But she extends her analysis to include the recognition that public institutions play a role in shaping possible emotions: "Compassionate individuals construct institutions that embody what they imagine; and institutions, in turn, influence the development of compassion in individuals" (405). Nussbaum argues that liberalism typically does not provide adequate theoretical warrant or recognition for caring relations. Like other social goods in liberal theory, works of love and sacrifice are taken for granted. But they are not affirmed, and they are often denied or hidden from view. Liberals assume such goods happen but they do not adequately recognize ways in which they are themselves "shaped by social and legal structures" (422). In fact, by strictly policing the division between public and private virtue, they make it difficult for these goods to be nurtured in public life. By introducing care—and its attention to situations of vulnerability and dependency—into the political vocabulary of liberal institutions and democratic practices, Tronto and Nussbaum have offered valuable contributions to the ethics of citizenship.

Within the context of my analysis of Augustine's conception of love for Augustinian civic liberalism, I align myself with these feminist critics of liberal neglect of care that do not reject liberalism. Feminist "care" and Augustinian *caritas* are not the same thing, but they are similar enough to warrant attention together. Is "care" an alternative to justice? Does "care" provide a synthesis of love and justice? Is "care" an alternative to love and justice? These questions track debates in religious ethics. The connection between a feminist "ethics of care" and Augustinian *caritas* has not been noted in the literature of moral or political philosophy. My thoughts on these connections were provoked by Jean Bethke Elshtain's aside that Augustine's "metaphors are fascinating and fascinatingly feminine, if I may dare say, having to do with collecting, emptying, receiving, rather than mastering, attacking, gaining" (*LP*, 56). Augustinians can learn from the important emphasis feminists place on the power dynamics of the structural dimensions of care-giving—an emphasis consistent with Augustine's attention to the power of Roman civic practices in shaping emotions. They should also learn from the emphasis that feminist theorists place upon the material conditions of human flourishing. Feminists, no doubt, might find Augustinian accounts of the persistence of evil, self-deception, and the whitewashing of injustice by a political society illuminating for their purposes. Augustinians can learn from feminist efforts to focus attention not only on the moral importance of being a "carer" as a part of a life of human excellence but also on "the effects on recipients of our care."[62] Feminist insights challenge Augustinians to think more about the consequences of love for the "cared-for," especially given that Augustinians tend to focus on the inner dispositions that organize the moral life. At the same time, as Tronto points out, feminist appeals to caring can ironically adopt those liberal accounts of love that equate care with an uncritical endorsement of benevolent concern and altruism. Advocates of care can perpetuate a narrow preoccupation with conative dimensions of love that enforce liberal notions that love is a sentimentalist, possessive feeling. Nel Noddings, for example, speaks of the "essentially nonrational nature of caring" and claims that principles of justice are "the language of the father" that "separate us from each other."[63] For Noddings, "a caring society must

---

62. Noddings, *Starting at Home*, 30.

63. Noddings, *Caring*, 61, 1, and 5. At times, however, Noddings also speaks about the "receptive rationality of caring" (1) or the "pre-act consciousness of the one-caring" (28). But her emphasis remains the "constitutive engrossment" that disrupts rational discrimination (25). Groenhout argues that Noddings does not "assume that rationality and affective response are two completely separate forces. Instead, her notion is that natural caring, the connection between agent and other, is not solely an intellectual grasping of the other's condition, but a holistic response, including, but not primarily distinguished

sometimes intervene in the lives of adults to prevent them from harming themselves."[64] This rhetoric gives rise to appropriate concerns that care is a dangerous proposal for a political or moral practice.

The rhetoric of care feeds into liberal suspicion and limits the extent to which love is a virtue analyzable within the terms of either morality or politics. Risking a univocal and idealized phenomenology of love as benevolence or mere emotion, the subsequent character of appeals to love or care jeopardize their applicability to the special relation of citizenship in a pluralist society. Feminists, when highly critical of liberalism, enforce liberal attitudes about the necessary conflict between compassion and reason, autonomy and interdependence, and between justice and care. Theorists of care, such as Tronto, are now beginning to distinguish the phenomenology of care in its diverse expressions in varied moral and political relationships. Nussbaum's work persistently recognizes that "compassion is a highly fallible motive" (*UT*, 447). An Augustinian account of reason and emotion set within the context of love's relation to sin can support these arguments. In fact, as I try to show throughout this book, feminism and Augustinianism offer similar correctives to liberalism. Securing this connection might elicit political alliances between feminist and religious organizations on a number of practical issues (for example, as is already the case, in efforts to combat sex trafficking and to expand educational opportunities for women in developing countries).

In unwitting ways, Augustine's influential formulations contributed to a characterization of love as "inner" emotion and to the personalization of politics on the model of intimate relations.[65] As we have seen, Augustine stood in the long classical tradition of identifying the virtues of political institutions with the virtues of its rulers (*CD* 4.3). Augustine's confessional

---

by, intellectual comprehension" ("Theological Echoes in the Ethics of Care," 10). Noddings distinguishes "natural caring" from "ethical caring"—the latter apparently involves more cognitive reflection than the former (*Caring*, 80). For a helpful comparative reading of Noddings and Levinas, see Batnitzky, "Dependency and Vulnerability," 130–32.

64. Noddings, *Starting at Home*, 2.

65. In the context of legal theory, John Noonan also suggests this reading of Augustine when he writes: "The central problem . . . of the legal enterprise is the relation of love to power. We can often apply force to those we do not see, but we cannot, I think, love them. Only in the response of person to person can Augustine's sublime fusion be achieved, in which justice is defined as 'love serving only the one love'" (Noonan, *Persons and Masks of the Law*, xii).

anthropology, while always rooted in a social network, overlaps with Gilligan's effort to find an "inner voice" (22) consistent with her claim that "the political has become psychological."[66] Moreover, Augustine often speaks of political activity with the imagery of domestic housekeeping that can lead to an idealized notion of politics as an extension of the *paterfamilias*. Augustine considered a "man's household" to be "the beginning, or rather a small component part of the city" (*CD* 19.16). The household is a microcosm of the larger *civitas*; it is to be ruled in such "a way that it is brought into harmony with the city's peace" (*CD* 19.16). These passages are ripe for feminist criticism. But, as Jean Bethke Elshtain points out, "Augustine's insistence on an *internal* relationship between *this* beginning and what we call civic life is not only compatible with, but [is] a strong buttress of, feminist claims that public and private are not hermetically sealed off one from the other" (*LP*, 35). Not hermetically sealed. Yes. But just as many liberal feminists do not collapse the distinction between public and private, Augustinian civic liberals should make space for love within the discourse of liberal politics without romanticizing the possibilities of politics.

By connecting Augustinianism with feminist theory, my aim is not to bring Augustine into an emancipatory feminist model. Nor do my interests include a theoretical evaluation of liberalism or Western rationality as whole. Rather, I appeal to feminist discussions as an illuminating resource for a more coherent and complex ethics of liberal citizenship that does not abandon justice but also does not privatize love. This constructive connection between Augustinianism and feminist political ethics can further extend discussions of religion and the ethics of citizenship beyond a limited focus on epistemology and the nature of "public reason." Before turning to Augustine more explicitly, I want to suggest ways in which feminist theory dovetails with modern Christian social ethics more generally.

LOVE AS POLITICAL PRACTICE IN CHRISTIAN SOCIAL ETHICS: A CHALCEDONIAN PROPOSAL

Political theologians often view love as something more than justice or they focus on justice as the form of love in political ethics. They say little, however, about the political implications of love itself or about love as a motivation for

---

66. Gilligan, *Different Voice*, xxvii.

liberal citizens in political life, particularly citizens who believe they are to "make love their aim" (1 Cor. 14:1). Like feminists who reject the opposition of love and justice, I believe love and justice are distinguishable concepts that need not compete for attention in an ethics of democratic citizenship. Love and justice elicit distinct political dispositions, as we saw in the previous chapter. But they need not be jealous of one another: they can serve together in the process of moral judgment even as they are distinct capacities of our moral personalities.[67] Love can play an important role as political practice and public value.

The twentieth century witnessed a tremendous explosion of philosophical and theological analysis of Christian love, especially in terms of the distinctive elements of Christian understandings of *agape*. These developments can be traced to the influence of a number of figures I have already mentioned: Anders Nygren, Paul Tillich, Reinhold Niebuhr, Paul Ramsey, Gene Outka, and Gilbert Meilaender. I have considered points of overlap between some of these authors and my Augustinian liberalism. These overlaps can be extended to feminist liberalism as well.

Given my distinctive interest in relating love for God and love for neighbor in politics, I need to highlight aspects of these debates that are most relevant for my purposes. They are underdeveloped in the literature. Discrete love for God has always been a component in Protestant discussions, most notably in Paul Tillich and Gene Outka. But the accent of many Protestant thinkers falls heavily on neighbor-love conceived as *agape* rather than as *philia* or *eros*. Catholic scholars, such as Edward Vacek, have criticized this aspect of the Protestant literature on love.[68] Contemporary discussions of

67. Margaret Farley offers a careful analysis of these themes in the context of medical ethics. According to Farley, compassion and respect are "mutually illuminating, and together they constitute a way of seeing the concrete reality of those who are in need" (*Compassionate Respect*, 42).

68. I affirm Vacek's emphasis on the emotional dimensions of Christian love, his focus on the explicit love for God, and his effort to limit love's work with counsels to do no harm. But I remain unsure about his characterization of love's opposition to respect that fuel his criticisms of Outka. At the level of interpretation, I think it is unfair to claim that Outka's account of love "conveys the cool indifference of a government worker issuing welfare checks" (161). More substantively, I have argued that love and respect should not be as strongly contrasted as Vacek assumes. Vacek admits that "we respect those we love" but he thinks "love's intimacy tends to dissolve respect's distance" (132). While the immediate context of this discussion is love for God, I worry about the dangers of

love in Christian ethics have also focused on the relation between rationality and affectivity.[69] Both Protestant and Catholic discussion of love's relation to justice draws deeply from these wells.

The developed work of theological ethics on love's relation to justice offers a largely unexamined resource for a *political* ethic of care—whether feminist or Augustinian. These developments offer meta-ethical analyses that problematize dominant liberal views that strictly oppose love/justice, universality/particularity, and selfhood/otherness. These analyses should be extended to help secure the political viability of love as a civic virtue. To return to my general theme from the introduction, they provide promising accounts of love and sin that avoid both hyper-individualism and hyper-communitarianism. In so doing, they avoid arrogant perfectionism and negative liberalism.

Before turning to how these discussions in Christian moral philosophy might be extended to political ethics, let me first suggest how my reading of Augustinianism will bear on these issues. A Christian understanding of love and justice takes its inspiration from a vision of God in Christ—a God of both love and justice. Reconciling God's love and God's justice, of course, is one of the most difficult exercises in systematic theology. It stands with the problem of reconciling the humanity and divinity of Jesus Christ as one of the great issues in theology. Both efforts typically generate massive debate, lead to schisms in the church, and can trade upon pernicious caricatures of Christianity's relation to Judaism. Learning how to say both claims at the same time without denying the other—God is just and God is love—God is human and God is divine—is part of what Christian theology is all about.

---

this understanding of love that may literally "dissolve" the self and the neighbor. Vacek's process Thomism (a kind of panentheism he calls "theanthropy") is much more comfortable with this language than Outka's more classically Lutheran commitments to the separateness of persons. But Vacek also proposes a "dialectical tension of self-affirmation and other-affirmation, each under the grace or vocation that we receive from God" (273). Vacek argues that much of Christian ethics (particularly Protestant ethics under the influence of a strong doctrine of grace) provides little room for proper self-love in the sense of taking responsibility for one's own moral development. At the level of political ethics, Vacek rejects policies of social or legal coercion that would force citizens to be loving. Like Outka, he offers a theological rationale for rejecting theocratic temptation: "We are not finally responsible for the neighbor's acceptance of God's love" (223).

69. Stephen J. Pope, "Love in Contemporary Christian Ethics," *Journal of Religious Ethics* 23, no. 1 (Spring 1995): 167–97.

Theologians craft grammatical rules to regulate how to affirm these claims. Building on this claim, I think a helpful analogy for thinking about love and justice might borrow from the conceptual grammar of Chalcedonian Christology.[70]

The migration of doctrinal formulations to ethical or metaphysical categories is not unproblematic. I suggest these analogies only tentatively, especially given that my interests will move more in political than in meta-ethical, ontological, or dogmatic directions. At a general level, I propose that Augustinians say that love and justice are "without confusion, without change, without division, without separation, the difference of the natures being by no means removed because of the union."[71] This proposal resists a dualistic approach to love and justice by insisting on a "hypostatic" union that denies substantial identity but inextricably allows love and justice to "communicate their attributes." There is a hypostatic union between love and justice such that a duality is affirmed that does not sacrifice unity. Unity, nevertheless, still admits an asymmetry between love and justice. The integrity of each should not be put at risk in some form of subordinationism. Nevertheless, love could be seen as the condition for the possibility of justice, like a center to periphery even as both witness to Christ. This logical condition of dependency, a differentiation-in-unity and unity-in-differentiation, does not break the indissoluble link between love and justice. Or, to borrow from Trinitarian formulations, Augustinians might also say that justice is a work sent of love but not less than love. On this view, love is never love without justice, just as the Father is never the Father without the Son. We might even speak of the work of justice returning to the love from which it is sent. Love and justice, like the Persons of the Trinity, are eternal in their mutual and dynamic relational coinherence. Justice, then, is not "accidental" to love. Like most classical authors, Augustine believes in the reciprocity of the virtues, "although they each mean something different from the others, they can in

70. In dogmatic theology, George Hunsinger proposes a structural pattern based on the Chalcedonian formula as a way of reading Martin Luther's and Karl Barth's coordination of grace and freedom (Hunsinger, *Disruptive Grace*, 302–303). I am proposing that this pattern is also a useful way of thinking about love's relation to justice within theological ethics.

71. J. N. D. Kelly, *Early Christian Doctrines*, 5th ed. (London: A & C Black, 1997), 340.

now way be separated from each other" (*DT* 6.1.6).[72] This distinction without division is characteristic of my general reading of Augustinianism. It is a reading consistent with John Burnaby's famous remark that Augustinian love is the "confounder of antitheses."[73]

I think these analogies help explain Augustine's account of the cardinal virtues and his efforts to non-univocally identify both love and justice as the form of virtue.[74] For feminist theologians, they might provide helpful ways of thinking about their calls for "compassionate respect," "just love," or "caring justice." These are the claims I pursue more fully in chapters 5 and 6, especially in response to Nygren's and Arendt's criticisms of Augustine.

The analogies with doctrinal formulations could be extended even further. One might characterize certain meta-ethical formulations as *docetic* if they radically oppose love and justice. They might be *arian* if they subordinate love to justice. The list could go on. But I want to explore how this way of thinking relates to the development of love's relation to justice in modern Christian social ethics. I have already gone a long way in identifying some of these points. But I need to establish more fully the relation between these meta-ethical considerations and political practice. In order to do so, I will first show how Paul Ramsey's Augustinian liberalism corrects Niebuhr's account of love and yet mistakenly condemns Augustinianism in the process. Second, I briefly will provide a reading of two authors not typically considered in terms of Augustinian liberalism: Martin Luther King Jr and Gustavo Gutierrez. Much has been written about each of these authors. I do not intend an exhaustive review. My focus will be on associating these thinkers with feminist ethics and my kind of Augustinian civic liberalism.

72. Augustine goes on in this passage to discuss the "simple multiplicity and multiple simplicity" of Trinitarian relations. The proximity of this discussion lends support to my proposal.

73. Burnaby, *Amor Dei*, 82. In this respect, my proposal also does not conflict with Paul Tillich's sketch of an analogy between love/justice and revelation/reason (*LPJ*, 83–84).

74. Consider, to cite one example, Augustine's description of the "four virtues of the soul" in *DeDiv.* 61.4. Prudence is "the knowledge of things to be sought after and things to be avoided," moderation is "the bridling of desire for temporal pleasures," courage is "the strength of mind in the face of temporal setbacks," and justice is "the love of God and neighbor, which is diffused through all the others." The association of love with justice by a classical author, as we shall see, is striking and innovative.

LOVE TRANSFORMING:
PAUL RAMSEY AND REINHOLD NIEBUHR

Given my effort to push political Augustinianism toward a virtue-oriented civic liberalism, the first thing to say about Paul Ramsey is that he read Augustine as a virtue thinker. To be sure, he did not endorse what he took to be Augustine's theory of virtue, but he read him as a virtue thinker nonetheless. Ramsey was ahead of his time in recognizing that "the enterprise of analyzing virtues of moral character constitutes a large part of general ethical theory" (*BCE*, 192). Ramsey highlights the extent to which Augustine admired Roman virtues and yet was able to maintain love as the principle of unity among the virtues. But all is not well with Augustinian *caritas*. Augustine fatefully introduced disunity into a Christian ethics of love by dividing love itself "into two sorts of love or love for two different objects" (208).[75] Augustine here succumbs to Platonism and what Ramsey called "general religiousness" (117). This problem of dividing religious and ethical duties, for Ramsey's Augustine, was laid in the foundational distinction between use and enjoyment. As we have seen, Ramsey is not alone in this diagnosis and criticism. The remaining chapters of my book will focus on this problem. For now, Ramsey's discussion of Augustine allows me to introduce a distinctive aspect of Ramsey's ethics of virtue: the emphasis on neighbor-love as the basis of political ethics.

Ramsey believed Augustine's theocentric account of love was misguided and authoritarian with regard to virtue. According to Ramsey, Augustine's diagnostic mistake was his primary focus on the bad metaphysics of paganism rather than the ethical issue at hand. This accent on virtue without reference to God missed the real problem; namely, the priority of reference to the neighbor. Ramsey sought to revise, but not abandon, Augustine's criticism of non-Christian virtues: "The statement that virtues are rather vices than virtues so long as there is no reference to the *neighbor* in the matter has definite ethical meaning and may be defended, without reference to

75. Ramsey writes: "One set of virtues will appear as forms of man's love for God, another as forms of his love for neighbor. Thus, Christian character, as we have seen of duties in general, would imitate Don Quixote dashing off at once in at least two directions" (*BCE*, 208). Ramsey believes Augustine is committed to this view because he logically "places God in the same class with other shareable goods even though he be also the highest good and the only inalienable good" (114n13).

metaphysics, as an entirely accurate account of moral experience" (*BCE*, 212). The author of *Basic Christian Ethics*—"an essay in the Christocentric ethics of the Reformation" (xiii)—was not here advocating a version of secular humanitarianism. Indeed, Ramsey refused any "coalition ethics" that permanently bound Christian love to any moral philosophy or social science. Concrete love for neighbor is obedience to the loving God of Jesus Christ: "Obedience to one's own virtue *with the neighbor's benefit in view* is always a present decision not far removed from obedience to God" (219). Obedient neighbor-love, rather than mystical God-love, was Ramsey's central category for Christian ethics. This love is the "ground-floor" of Christian ethics (344). It is fundamental to his effort to develop a prophetic justice transformed by *agape*.

Ramsey was not an Augustine scholar. But he is fairly called an Augustinian liberal. In Protestant social ethics, he is both successor and rival to Niebuhr's Augustinian realism.[76] Like Niebuhr, Ramsey held that "political democracy may be given compelling justification only if some reference be made to the problem of restraining and remedying sin" (*BCE*, 330).[77] Ramsey's defense of democracy, however, does not rest on the opposition of love and justice. His biblical ethics can distinguish love and justice, but it cannot separate them in Niebuhrian fashion as a way of charting a middle course between belief and overbelief. Love is not a kind of optional selfless charity that goes beyond the duty of justice only by way of negation or supercession. There is eschatology, but no rigid opposition of Christian love "within history" and "beyond history." Ramsey's ethics does not affirm only those actions which appear as irrational acts of sacrifice. Niebuhr, despite his rhetoric of paradox, could also recognize a love that is relevant for political morality. He insisted that "the prophetic

---

76. See G. Scott Davis, "'Et Quod Vis Fac': Paul Ramsey and Augustinian Ethics," *Journal of Religious Ethics* 19, no. 2 (Fall 1991): 31–69. Davis's essay is the best guide to Ramsey's relation to Augustine, Niebuhr, and Augustinian ethics.

77. Ramsey offers a conventional Protestant justification for democracy: "Because of the sinfulness of man, we must be democratic in technique, as well as in the principle that justice must be general in application and rights be accorded to all. . . . Out of the conflict of public pressures in which all participate, 'laws' may be forced to become more lawful" (*BCE*, 333–34). I leave aside the interesting question as to whether or not Ramsey betrayed his own convictions by implying a permanent coalition between Christianity and democracy.

tradition in Christianity must insist on the relevance of the ideal of love to the moral experience of mankind on every conceivable level."[78] The implicit relevance of love usually takes the political form of equal justice and the calculations of rights in a fallen world. This recurrent theme, to borrow from my Chalcedonian formula, tends toward a docetic account of love and justice—love "appears" as justice but it really can not have anything to do with social justice *unless* it is self-sacrifice. Niebuhr, however, equally insisted that "any justice which is only justice soon degenerates into something less than justice."[79] At times, he could even claim that love is a "source of discriminate judgment upon various systems of justice."[80] In particular, disproportionate access to power fuels injustice and requires an ethic that condemns inequality and does not give comfort to the powerful in the name of ultimate religious ideals. But, unlike Niebuhr, Ramsey does not speak about sacrificial love and powerlessness as ideals that find only ambivalent echo in the rational calculations of political morality. He does not speak in consistent refrains about love's transcendence that calls justice to be something other than justice. Ramsey's account of the diversity of love's work can be distinguished from Niebuhr's dualistic tendency to restrict love to interpersonal relations and give political

---

78. Niebuhr, *Interpretation of Christian Ethics,* 98.

79. Niebuhr, *Moral Man,* 258. For insightful defense of Niebuhr's ethic of "irresoluble tension between love and justice," see Flescher, "Love and Justice," 64. Flescher argues that the Hegelian aspect ("fulfills yet negates") of Niebuhr's account "has enormous pragmatic value to the extent that it serves as the transcendent measuring stick by which to judge our distance from the ethical utopia of full human fellowship" (68). Any Augustinian could cheer for this interpretation. But I remain confused as to why (biblical) justice and love might not both serve to expose the easy conscience of the "responsible" liberals who assume their moral tasks are fulfilled? At the same time, I worry about angelic conceptions of moral obligation that can conflate the conditions of finitude with the conditions of sin. Nevertheless, there is pragmatic value in Niebuhr's caution against "exceeding the bounds of creatureliness which God has set up on all human enterprises" and his recognition of "the essential goodness of the finiteness, dependence and insufficiency of the self" (*Nature and Destiny,* 1:150 and 143).

80. Niebuhr, "'Order of Creation,'" 270. Niebuhr criticizes Brunner: "I suspect that Luther's doctrine of the 'Two Realms' plus the influence of Martin Buber's great work, *I and Thou,* has persuaded Brunner to make this too radical distinction between the realm of the personal and the institutional and to reserve love only for the realm of the personal, indeed, individual relations" (271).

communities over to utilitarian calculations.[81] Like many feminist defenders of a political ethic of care, Ramsey challenges those who would condemn love to a private virtue consigned to the "interstitial spaces" (*BCE,* 3). He also does not denigrate justice in order to elevate love, a denigration that often blinds Niebuhrians to injustices in the private realm and permits injustice through the "dirty hands" of the public realm. As Jackson interprets Ramsey, *"love does not choose between justice and mercy, for these two goods are internally related to agape"* (*PL,* 110). Love, while not subject to a rule-morality, is itself a radical obligation to serve the neighbor in need rather than an impossible suffering selflessness that "may obscure the ultimate purposes of providential action."[82] "The commands of love," Ramsey writes, "are as stringent as the needs of the world are urgent: sensing this, let any man *then* do as he pleases" (*BCE,* 90). This ethic, for Ramsey, stems from the radicality of God's own love for the neighbor, a love that is not limited by eschatological expectation or restricted to powerlessness as the only way to admit divine activity in the history of the people of God.

The relation between obligation and an ethics of love is a fundamental subset of love's relation to justice. Ramsey thinks Christians owe people love. Feminists might see this move as yet another masculine morality of deontological obligation, even if it extends the range of considered virtues beyond liberal justice. Christian *agape,* on this reading, implicitly assumes a justice framework even while rejecting it. But it is an odd kind of morality of obligation that would focus on "traits of character, forms of action, and concrete social consequences."[83] Neighbor-love of this sort is neither rationalistic nor does it issue into a persistently self-sacrificial ethics of benevolence or radical altruism. Unlike Niebuhr, Ramsey allowed room for the self within an ethics of love and he did not reduce justice to contractual reciprocity. Neighbor-love remains central in terms of ethical justification, but it can cast up various possibilities. These include concern for one's own rights (albeit, *for the neighbor's sake*) and a concern to protect innocent others against harm (again,

81. For Jackson, "Ramsey's signal contribution is to retrieve Augustine's view of charity and in its light to elaborate the love/justice relation so as to avoid both Niebuhr's hard paradoxes and his tendency to soft consequentialism" (*PL,* 106).

82. Outka, *Agape,* 175.

83. Jackson, *Love Disconsoled,* 31.

for the neighbor's sake). The first move protects both the self and the neighbor: "Often an individual can more certainly and effectively care for himself than he can do anything of real, immediate worth for his neighbor" (*BCE*, 163). "Christianity," Ramsey writes, "does not advise that men brush one another's teeth" (163). The neighbor is the subject of love, not their improvement as such. The second move provides the logic for Ramsey's controversial thinking about doing justice in war as a work of love for the neighbor. Obedient love is not simply a kind of moral intuitionism waiting for every moment of political decision. Intuitionism affords too little content for the moral life of *agape*. But, at least in his early work, Ramsey also worried that traditional natural law approaches provide too much content and subordinate charity in their application of principles.[84] Obedient love is primarily attentive to concrete neighbors in need. It is an "indefinite, indeterminate, and liberating norm" (343). But it is a norm nonetheless. Ramsey's love ethic can issue moral rules. Against the exclusive act-agapism of Joseph Fletcher, Ramsey argued for exceptionless moral rules in the context of social practices directed against injustice. It also serves to direct positive content for a social policy beyond the realist recognition of negative constraint. Ramsey's ethic would both honor fellow human dignity and guide the ethos of a political culture by highlighting love's relation to justice. Importantly, Ramsey sees love not simply as a subjective motivation of the will but as a norm itself, embedded in the covenanted structures of human living. It does not float free of right reason, equity, natural justice, and the structures of public law. In his applied work in medical ethics and the ethics of war and peace, Ramsey more clearly exemplified his claim that a "Christian, impelled by love whose nature is to incarnate itself wherever there is need, cannot remain aloof but must enter fully into the problem of determining right action under the particular, concrete circumstances" (345–46). I return to the question of war below, but pause to identify an important conceptual point.

84. William Werpehowski argues that "the weakest discussions in *Basic Christian Ethics* treat the relationship between Christian love and natural morality or natural law" (*American Protestant Ethics*, 37). Werpehowski traces the development of Ramsey's account of natural morality, noting the significance of Ramsey's appropriation of Barth's "view that creation is the external basis of covenant, and covenant the internal basis of creation" (38). Even in his later work, however, Werpehowski judges that "little material attention is given to a view of creaturely well-being; ceaseless dialogue risks ceaselessly proceeding, in need of a theological signpost" (41).

Rather than holding love and sin apart, Ramsey affirmed what I have highlighted as a central Augustinian recognition: "the element of sin in all human love" (*BCE*, 330). Here we can turn to Ramsey's political morality that will help me connect Christian social ethics to feminist theory. Ramsey himself connected his thought to another form of liberal perfectionism that emphasizes human rights, the British idealism of T. H. Green (187).[85] I want to display his social ethics as a kind of Augustinian liberalism.

For Ramsey, "Christian love is always in search of a social policy" (*BCE*, 326).[86] It enters into alliances with the best of social science and philosophical insight. This search begins with the recognition that "sin must be checked in every one, ruler and ruled alike" (331). He applauded Reinhold Niebuhr's famous aphorism, "man's capacity for justice makes democracy possible; but man's inclination to injustice makes democracy necessary" (337).[87] But love itself does more political work for Ramsey than it does for Niebuhr. The divisiveness of self-interest is ever present in the struggle for rights and equality. It is because of this reality that political ethics demands a "radical remedy for a radical disease."[88] Love demands a "vigorous and ceaseless action on behalf of human rights in Christ's name and for his neighbor's sake."[89] In fact, Ramsey famously defines justice as "what Christian love does when confronted by two or more neighbors" (347). This principled commitment finds expression in Ramsey's claim that when ones "neighbor's need and the

85. Ramsey claims that his derivation of human rights as forms of neighbor-love is similar to Green's derivation of rights as socially recognized claims to exercise power or capacity for the common good. For Green's liberal perfectionism, see David Brink, *Perfectionism and the Common Good: Themes in the Philosophy of T. H. Green* (Oxford: Oxford University Press, 2003).

86. For Ramsey, "Christian love remains what it is, dominant and free. It does not transform itself into the coin of any realm, though it enters every realm and becomes debtor both to the Greek and to the barbarians" (*BCE*, 344).

87. In a review of Niebuhr's *The Children of Light and the Children of Darkness*, Ramsey endorses Niebuhr's view as conventional, an "old word, namely the simple, hard doctrine that Christians endorse the machinery and coercion of political institutions partly in order that sin be restrained in themselves and in others" (Ramsey, "Theory of Democracy," 251). But he argues that Niebuhr mistakenly neglects the role of this notion for modern secular democratic theory, especially idealistic social philosophy following Rousseau and Green.

88. Ramsey, "Theory of Democracy," 265.

89. Ibid., 265.

just order of society are at stake, the Christian still governs himself by love and suffers no injustice to be done nor the order necessary to earthly life to be injured."[90] We can see Ramsey's working out of this claim in his writings on just war.

Ramsey's defense of the just war tradition relies on a central justificatory connection between neighbor-love and the resort to force. He held the controversial view that "the western theory of the just war originated, not primarily from considerations of abstract or 'natural' justice, but from the interior of the ethics of Christian love, or what John XIII termed 'social charity.' "[91] Ramsey's judgment is contestable if it is only taken as a complete statement about intellectual history. Allowing love to justify armed force, moreover, is not the paradigmatic instance of Ramsey's notion of *agape* that equips a Christian conscience for political action. Love need not vindicate war as the most compelling arena of Christian vocational duties or as a normative human activity. War, however, is not to be condemned to a twilight beyond morality. Affirming the just war tradition is a clear expression of his political ethics that relates love to justice in a fallen world where innocents need protection: "It is the work of love and mercy to deliver as many as possible of God's children from tyranny, and to protect from oppression, if one can, as many of those for whom Christ died as it may be possible to save" (143). In fact, Ramsey connects resort to force with a reading of the parable of the Good Samaritan. The compassion of the Good Samaritan invites a further step that imagines it to be a "work of charity to resist, by force of arms, any external aggression against the social order that maintains the police patrol along the road to Jericho" (142).[92] People who commend the Good Samaritan should not only support their local police—and the political institutions that pay their salaries; they should also assist the police in combating the criminal gangs that make a business of assault and robbery. In yet another imaginative reading, Ramsey claims that "while Jesus taught that a disciple in his own case should turn the other cheek, he did not enjoin that his disciples should lift up the face of another oppressed man for *him*

---

90. Ramsey, *War and the Christian Conscience*, 178.

91. Ramsey, *Just War*, 142–43. Parenthetical references in this paragraph and the next are to this work.

92. Ramsey hypothetically asks: "What do you think Jesus would have made the Samaritan do if he had come upon the scene while the robbers were still at their fell work?" (142–43).

to be struck again on *his* other cheek" (143). Both of these novel scriptural interpretations yield Ramsey's basic point: "When choice must be made between the perpetrator of injustice and the many victims of it, the latter may and should be preferred—even if effectively to do so would require the use of armed force against some evil power" (143). It may be Luther's "strange work" of love to resort to force in cases of necessity, but love itself charges political authorities with the duty to protect the innocent and the vulnerable.[93] Ramsey's appeal to love in *jus ad bellum* finds further support in his discussions of *jus in bello*. Love justifies resort to force, but it also place severe limits on the conduct of war.

Christian love provides the ground for the legitimacy of resort to force. But neighbor-love simultaneously limits this force. Because "the sake of the innocent and the helpless of the earth" gives rise to a conscience that even considers force, Christian love can never "proceed to kill equally innocent people as a means of getting at the enemy's forces" (143). Love inspires a principled discrimination between combatants and noncombatants and a proportionate consideration of good and evil consequences. Love "can never approve of unlimited attack upon any human life not closely cooperating in or directly engaged in the force that ought to be repelled" (145). Jackson is correct to see Ramsey's defense of the just war tradition as "a corrective to Niebuhr's occasional readiness to embrace a too purely utilitarian approach to political means" (*PL*, 107). Ramsey drew upon Christian Realism, but he self-consciously distanced himself from Niebuhr: "There is more to be said about justice in war than was articulated in Niebuhr's sense of the ambiguities of politics and his greater/lesser evil doctrine on the use of force" (260). The principle of discrimination provides, in part, the content of this "more"

---

93. Tillich criticizes Luther for not seeing clearly enough that this strange work of love is "not only the strange but also the tragic aspect of love. It represents a price which must be paid for the reunion of the separated" (*LPJ*, 50–51). Tillich's reading of Luther parallels Werpehowksi's criticisms of Ramsey's language of just war and excessive deference to political authority that "may operate to mask or marginalize realities of killing, injury, and human suffering" (*American Protestant Ethics*, 59). Without this tragic recognition, Werpehowksi warns against a "sort of cultural Christianity that ironically leaves to the state the embodiment of 'Christ,' the highest ideal feasible among the options in political life" (62). Werpehowski allows that Ramsey's "analysis make a place for the 'shudder,'" but also sees that "if this was not Ramsey's view, it should have been" (101–102).

that avoids consequentialism. But we should also note that Ramsey's just war tradition was more than a checklist of principles and criteria. The tradition is more like a theory of just statecraft, motivated by love, which casts war in a legal and moral framework. This casting allows the use of force in promoting the common good but restricts the use force to specific authorities and seeks to limit the violence of these authorities. This framework is set within an even broader philosophy of history and moral anthropology that today often is attributed to Augustine. Ramsey thought an Augustinian conception of the just war tradition is "an excellent prism through which to see the several elements of a Christian theory of statecraft" (xiii). Whether or not Ramsey was right about Augustine, it is surely the case that Augustinian liberalism has held that just war thinking is one fruit of the Augustinian tradition.

Contractarian liberal traditions often focus on domestic justice and then try to extend outward to the international sphere. Modern Augustinianism primarily has exercised influence in foreign affairs because of its just war heritage. This logic of the just war tradition, however, can and should be applied "back" to domestic politics in a manner consistent with Joan Tronto's discussion of care as political practice. That is, love motivates a concern for the innocent and vulnerable that subsequently justifies (potentially extensive but not unlimited) state coercion on their behalf. This appeal to love, then, involves the exercise of communal power but not a full-fledged paternalist reorientation of desire. It also means developing political friendships in local communities that can transcend the barrenness of "culture war" politics. Notably, the Augustinian tradition has rarely been used in this way, and doing so will require reconstructing Augustine and Augustinian liberalism. Ramsey's emphasis on a neighbor-love that resists evil in the service of innocent others provides a link to another significant tradition within modern Christian social ethics.

LOVE ACTING: GUSTAVO GUTIERREZ AND MARTIN LUTHER KING JR

It is not surprising to find Gustavo Gutierrez and Martin Luther King Jr linked by those who desire a Christian spirituality that affirms the pursuit of earthly justice, especially for the weak and abused of history. Both took themselves to be challenging dualistic theologies that separated spirituality from attention to material existence. King and Gutierrez can also be surprising resources for my conversation between Augustinian liberalism and a feminist ethics of care. Passing references to King's political activity and his readings of Tillich, Ramsey, and Niebuhr can be found in the literature on Augustinian liberalism. Gutierrez, when invoked, tends simply to play the role of Marxist utopian foil for Augustinian realists. For Augustinian antiliberals, Gutierrez represents yet another "universal humanism, a *rapprochement* with the Enlightenment and an autonomous secular order" (Milbank, *TST*, 207). Critics of Augustinian political theology often celebrate Gutierrez and King as alternatives to establishment ideology, theocratic conservatism, or otherworldly pietism. As with my discussion of Ramsey, I do not aim to provide a thorough account of either of these authors. Many issues raised by their influence on Christian social ethics remain to be picked up in later chapters. This final section, albeit briefly, focuses on the relevance of love's relation to justice for these two figures.

Liberation theology is commonly identified with the virtues of justice and hope. However, Gutierrez's foundational text, *A Theology of Liberation*, explicitly explores the relationship between the love commands as a resource for political theology.[94] Gutierrez repeatedly appeals to 1 John 3:14 and Matthew 25:31–46 as central biblical resources for a theology that aims to be a new *City of God*, "a true analysis of signs of the times and the demands with which they challenge the Christian community" (5). He proclaims charity to be "the center of the Christian life" (6). Moreover, he also highlights the importance of a normative relation between love for neighbor and love for God that does not reduce the one to the other.[95] Critical attention to Gutierrez's appropriation of Marxism and socialism has obscured the centrality of his understanding of political love. Though a less studied aspect of his contextual theology, Gutierrez's extension of Christian love for political ethics is perhaps second only to Martin Luther King Jr in its practical impact on recent Christian political engagement.

94. Gutierrez claims that his definition of "the function of theology as critical reflection on praxis" has its roots in an Augustinian theology of history (*Theology of Liberation*, 5). Page references in this section of the text refer to this book.

95. Black and womanist theologians have appropriated Gutierrez's attention to Matthew 25. See, for example, James Cone, *A Black Theology of Liberation*, 2d ed. (Maryknoll, N.Y.: Orbis Books, 1988), and Ada Maria Isasi-Diaz, "Solidarity: Love of Neighbor in the 1980s," in *Feminist Theological Ethics*, ed. Lois Daly (Louisville: Westminster/John Knox Press, 1994), 77–87.

In his effort to problematize the legacy of Christian theologies that separate the vertical (eternal) and the horizontal (temporal), Gutierrez seeks to recover social notions of sin and salvation as historical reality. Sin is "a breach of the communion of persons with each other" (85). Sin is a refusal to love within personal and social realities. Neither sin nor love is reducible to existentialist and individualist categories. Salvation, as participation in the fullness of God's love, requires the public restoration of this breach of communion through concrete action. Theologically, it is the Incarnation which brings about this restoration and reveals how "the bond between the neighbor and God is changed, deepened, and universalized" (112). It is this joyful and gratuitous spirituality that sustains political action in the face of despair. Because of the Incarnation, Gutierrez famously announces, "to know God *is* to do justice" (118). It is revealing that within these crucial parts of *A Theology of Liberation*, Gutierrez easily moves between the language of justice and the language of charity. Charity, in fact, is "God's love in us and does not exist outside our human capabilities to love and to build a just and friendly world" (113). Like Ramsey, Gutierrez primarily focuses on loving the concrete *person* rather than the subjective intention, the charitable act, or whatever revisable social-scientific theory is thought to best enable effective love for persons. Indeed, for Gutierrez, the neighbor is a *sacrament of God*. Evangelical conversion is a conversion to the neighbor:

> It is not enough to say that love of God is inseparable from love of one's neighbor. It must be added that love for God is unavoidably expressed *through* love of one's neighbor. . . . It is in the temple that we find God, but in a temple of living stones, of closely related persons, who together make history and fashion themselves. . . . We find the Lord in our encounters with others, especially the poor, marginated, and exploited ones. An act of love towards them is an act of love towards God. (114–15)

Gutierrez is aware of the dangers of this formulation. He explicitly rejects the view that I later examine in regard to Augustine's reading of Matthew 25; namely, the charge that the neighbor becomes "an occasion, an instrument, for becoming closer to God" (116). According to Gutierrez, "that my action towards another is at the same time an action towards God does not detract from its truth and concreteness, but rather gives it even greater meaning and import" (116). In fact, as one recent interpreter helpfully characterizes it, "the actualization of faith in love—which is understood in terms of liberative praxis—provides [Gutierrez's] most explicit account of human action."[96] On this view, actions are more than the *application* of fundamental theological claims about God and the world. Actions reveal and make manifest beliefs and internal dispositions through social practices. The revelation of love makes this notion of action possible. It is sin that gets in the way of obedient action oriented toward this revelation. The importance of my appeal to Gutierrez lies in the example of this reading of the double love commands for political ethics.

Gutierrez makes the critical turn from love as a dimension of interpersonal relation to political analysis. He writes:

> It is also necessary to avoid the pitfalls of an individualistic charity. As it has been insisted in recent years, the neighbor is not only a person viewed individually. The term refers also to a person considered in the fabric of social relationships, to a person situated in economic, social, cultural, and racial coordinates. It likewise refers to the exploited social class, the dominated people, the marginated. The masses are also our neighbor. . . . This point of view leads us far beyond the individualistic language of the I-Thou relationship. Charity is today a "political charity," according to the phrase of Pius XII. . . . It means the transformation of a society structured to benefit a few who appropriate to themselves the value of the work of others. This transformation ought to be directed toward a radical change in the foundation of society, that is, the private ownership of the means of production. . . . This is what Christ reveals to us by identifying himself with the poor in the text of Matthew. A theology of the neighbor, which has yet to be worked out, would have to be structured on this basis. (116)

I am not here endorsing Gutierrez as a model for Augustinian or feminist political ethics. I only wish to point out the richness of his exploration of

96. Thomas A. Lewis, "Actions As the Ties that Bind: Love, Praxis, and Community in the Thought of Gustavo Gutierrez," *Journal of Religious Ethics* 33, no. 3 (2005): 539–67, at 541. Lewis valuably associates Gutierrez's conception of action with Charles Taylor's expressivist theory of action. He also argues, *against* both Milbank and conservative critics of liberation theology, that Gutierrez is not committed (in principle) to Marxist social theory. Lewis's appeal to Taylor implicitly offers a suggestive response to Milbank's invocation of Blondel's phenomenology ("the completed thought *is* the completed action," *TST,* 213) over against Gutierrez's supposed foundationalism.

love and a theology of the neighbor for political ethics. Regardless of one's evaluation of Gutierrez and his own political program, he helpfully identifies important theological issues for Christian social ethics through his exploration of love. His proposal of a non-univocal identification of the love of God and love of neighbor stands as a powerful recognition of the possibilities of the love commands for political ethics and social theory.

King's self-critical commitment to the (as yet unfulfilled) promise of American liberalism distinguishes him from Gutierrez's liberation theology in the context of Latin American revolutions. Both theologians claim a living God is at work in their communities, springing forth dynamically and agapeically into history. These communities stand in need of refreshment through active practices of love that find God as the transformative center of moral and political life. Indeed, both saw political activity as part of a "theological drama" where "everyday people gathered in fellowship in the free space of divine love."[97] As with liberation theology, King's politics, eschatology, and anthropology can hardly be contained within dominant forms of contemporary liberal theory. He also resists placement in the camps of Niebuhrian realism, Social Gospel liberalism, or antiliberal Augustinianism. His reading of Niebuhr made him "aware of the complexity of human motives and the reality of sin on every level of man's existence."[98] The Fall reached deep into human reason and our social practices. Nevertheless, like Ramsey, King did not revel in paradox, dialectics, and the hiddenness of the neo-orthodox God. He criticized Walter Rauschenbush for coming "perilously close to identifying the kingdom of God with a particular social and economic system," but he also praised him for giving "American Protestantism a sense of social responsibility that it should never lose."[99] King's sense of responsibility to the needs of his neighbor allowed him (perhaps surprisingly) to sound an Augustinian trope about loving the sinner, hating the sin: "The attack is directed against forces of evil rather than against persons who are caught in those forces."[100] King's nonviolent direct action sought to enable and sustain liberal justice. It is important to note that his particular commitment to nonviolent *agape* still advocated coercive measures of fed-

---

97. Marsh, "Civil Rights Movement," 235 and 239.
98. King, "Pilgrimage to Nonviolence," in *A Testament of Hope*, 36.
99. Ibid, 37.
100. King, "Nonviolence and Racial Justice," in *A Testament of Hope*, 8.

eral government action. This advocacy moved beyond dissent and endorsed regulating and sanctioning behavior in order to combat persistent racism in American law and politics. Civil rights legislation, and King's calls for regulatory reform of housing markets, transportation systems, and public education, are good examples of liberal perfectionism with an egalitarian strain. Indeed, rather than focus on a liberal ideal of noninterference, King claimed "the law itself is a form of education."[101] King's attention to grassroots activism and local community decision-making, however, show that he did not simply advocate a top-down conception of democratic politics wary of the intensity of politics.

In a word, King's "beloved community" is not Rawls's "well-ordered society." He was not preoccupied with questions of justification and its strictures of stability without addressing the fate of those who do not fare well in a society governed by highly liberal theory. In addition to King's enduring claim that rights are "God-given," he worked for a liberal society that would ensure both positive and negative liberties. Indeed, in his last Sunday morning sermon, King preached that Dives "went to hell because he maximized the minimum and minimized the maximum."[102] His confident language of Christ, community, friendship, and personality was not embarrassed to admit that citizens are "tied together in a single garment of destiny, caught in an inescapable network of mutuality . . . for some strange reason I can not be what I ought to be until you are what you ought to be."[103] Segregation, for King, was spiritually corrosive and not simply unjust—something more than (but not less than) justice was necessary. King's account of love and justice is a striking example of a prophetic liberalism that might provide fertile soil for Augustinian and feminist political ethics.

101. King, *Stride Toward Freedom,* in *A Testament of Hope,* 473.

102. King, "Remaining Awake Through a Great Revolution," in *A Testament of Hope,* 274.

103. Ibid., 269. For King, "the Negro must love the white man, because the white man needs his love to remove his tensions, insecurities, and fears" ("An Experiment in Love," in *A Testament of Hope,* 19). King's personalism resonates with another African bishop besides Augustine: Bishop Desmond Tutu. Tutu's sermons consistently invokes the concept of *ubuntu,* a call "to be available for others, and to know that you are bound up with them in the bundle of life, for a person is only a person through other persons" (Desmond Tutu, *The Rainbow People of God* [New York: Doubleday, 1994], 117).

King was able to coordinate various streams in theology, prophetic biblical literature, and American democratic philosophy. He blended his lived theology of the black Baptist church and the Gandhian method of nonviolent social change with various features of liberal Protestantism and philosophical personalism. It is King, more than any other individual, who came to lead and symbolize the civil rights movement and the black church from which it emerged. Preston Williams argues that King fundamentally shares the Augustinian claim that a political society is "determined by its people's love, and that without love or loyalty the state would deteriorate and finally collapse."[104] Love, once again, is neither private virtue nor materially cut off from justice and equity. It is a commanding, listening, and empowering presence that is necessary for a just society that is not focused solely on justice as fairness. It is the vision of a "beloved community" that generates a host of duties and responsibilities. *Agape* transforms citizenship, placing strenuous demands on citizens. Like Ramsey, King used the parable of the Good Samaritan in order to call for structural transformations in American society. Drawing from Paul Tillich (the subject of King's doctoral dissertation), King understood love as the creative element implicit within justice. King believed that the "universe is under the control of a loving purpose and that in the struggle for righteousness man has cosmic companionship."[105] He was quick to reject suspicious readings of love by "the Nietzsches of the world" who could only see it as cowardly, sentimental, and weak emotionalism.[106] King refused any love mysticism that did not highlight the relationship of love and justice:

104. Williams, "Conception of Love," 18. Williams highlights King's anthropology and ontology of love, power, and justice. James Cone heuristically distinguishes three periods in King's thought: (1) an early period focusing on justice, (2) a middle period focusing on love, and (3) a late period focusing on hope ("The Theology of Martin Luther King, Jr.," *Union Seminary Quarterly Review* 40, no. 4 [1986]: 21–39).

105. King, "Pilgrimage to Nonviolence," in *A Testament of Hope*, 40. This loving purpose recalls Tillich's claim that "love is the drive towards the unity of the separated" (*LPJ*, 25). This love "preserves the individual who is both the subject and the object of love" (*LPJ*, 27). For Tillich, "justice is that side of love that affirms the independent right of object and subject within the love relation. Love does not destroy the freedom of the beloved and does not violate the structure of the beloved's individual and social existence. Love as the reunion of those who are separated does not destroy or distort in its union" (Tillich, *Systematic Theology*, 1:282).

106. King, "A Time to Break Silence," in *A Testament of Hope*, 242.

One of the greatest problems of history is that the concepts of love and power have usually been contrasted as opposites—polar opposites—so that love is identified with a resignation of power, and power with the denial of love. . . . What is needed is a realization that power without love is reckless and abusive, and love without power is sentimental and anemic. Power at its best is love implementing the demands of justice, and justice at its best is power correcting everything that stands against love.[107]

King's formulations, especially the criticisms of sentimental appeals to love, are consistent with the influence of Tillich on King. For Tillich, "nothing is more false to say to somebody: since I love you and you love me, I don't need to get justice from you or you from me, for love eliminates the need for justice" (*LPJ,* 82). In fact, he argued that this apparently noble rhetoric of a love transcending justice "is said by tyrannical rulers to their subjects and by tyrannical parents to their children" (*LPJ,* 82). King's "Letter from a Birmingham Jail" can be read as a dramatic historical enactment of this claim in the face of white Christian supremacists and the brutality of American racism.

James E. Gilman faults King for imposing a "Kantian" division between love and emotion that denies "love's affective power."[108] According to Gilman, King denies "love's emotional quality [in theory] while invoking love's emotional power [in practice]."[109] Gilman's charge is true at the rhetorical level. But I think he reads too much into these statements if he intends a strong alliance between Kantian rationalism and King's personalism. Like Augustine, King was a master rhetorician. Occasional denials of love's emotional quality need not imply a deep philosophical commitment. It can be a trope to avoid misunderstanding the appeal to love as confined to the simple possibilities of affections without relevance for structures of power. This reading, both King and Tillich fear, leads to confusion. Tillich emphasized the ethical and ontological dimensions of love in order to avoid wholesale contrasting of love, justice, and power. But he clearly admits that "there must be something at the basis of love as emotion which justifies both its ethical and ontological interpretation" (*LPJ,* 4–5).[110] King's claims about love's

---

107. King, "Where Do We Go From Here?," in *A Testament of Hope,* 247.
108. Gilman, *Fidelity of Heart,* 186n12.
109. Ibid.
110. For Tillich, love should not be "*reduced* to its emotional or ethical quality" (*LPJ,* 12, emphasis mine); love can not be "*basically* understood as emotion" (24, emphasis mine); and, most explicitly, "there is no love without the emotional element" (26).

relation to justice gave rise to practical expressions of the creative justice of reuniting love. In fact, as I have noted, King's religious ideals were effective and persuasive because of their attention to the legislative political process.

Major differences would emerge from a more detailed examination of these authors. Most obviously, important questions about violence and the nature of forgiveness have been left aside. My aim in this section has been to show the deep normative roots of efforts to bind love and justice with attention to personal need in modern Christian social ethics. I think they could provide neglected conversation partners for a feminist political ethics of care that does not idealistically imagine extensive ties of natural sentiment. These influential theologians, while critical of schizophrenic aspects of liberal theory and liberal society, did not abandon the achievements of liberalism. Unlike King, Ramsey, and Gutierrez, most Augustinian liberals rarely display more than the requisite gesture to love itself before turning to questions about the nature of self-love or the relation of neighbor-love to other more "politically relevant" themes of justice and freedom. This neglect of love parallels or, more cynically, imitates the conceptual fate of love in modern political theory. Augustinian civic liberalism can be traced back to these authors and the legacy they inspired. In order to make good on the promise of this connection, however, we need more closely to examine Augustinian arguments for a liberal concept of political love that does not cut itself off from an Augustinian understanding of sin. These arguments will be the focus on the remainder of this book. Hannah Arendt's reading of Augustine provides a useful route into this investigation.

4

Love as Political Vice
Hannah Arendt's Augustine

*Be careful what you love, Augustine warned.
And Arendt took him seriously.*

JOANNA VECCHIARELLI SCOTT,
"Secular Augustinianism"

*What madness not to understand how to love human
beings with awareness of the human condition?*

AUGUSTINE, *Confessions* 4.7.2

M y particular interest in Hannah Arendt stems from a reading of her
1929 Heidelberg dissertation on Augustine's idea of love and its
connections to her broader analysis of the dangerous relation of love to
liberal politics. Written under the influence of Martin Heidegger, Rudolph
Bultmann, and Karl Jaspers, Arendt's text has been neglected in both Augustine and Arendt studies.[1] Her criticisms of Augustine predate Anders
Nygren's more influential reading for modern Christian ethics and are no
less problematic for Augustinian civic liberalism. In fact, her challenge to
Augustinian politics is more relevant for my project than Nygren's challenge

---

1. The influence of Heidegger and Jaspers—her mentors in German *Existenzphi-
losophie* with its emphasis on "Being-with-others" and "limit situations"—is apparent
throughout the dissertation. During the 1920s, Heidegger had lectured extensively on
Paul, Augustine, Luther, Feuerbach, and Kierkegaard. Jaspers served as the director of
the dissertation.

to Augustinian theology. She challenges the political implications of both divine love and the goodness of love itself—finding in neither the capacity for action nor mutual respect. In the previous two chapters, I showed how some modern proponents of political Augustinianism have rejected Augustine's theology of love even as they have developed subtle accounts of love's relation to liberal justice and other political values. My turn to Arendt, then, is neither idiosyncratic nor simply a matter of historical interest. Her secularization of Augustinian themes, coupled with her representative account of love as a political vice, offer crucial challenges to my constructive proposal. And yet, Arendt's concerns about self-absorption and the demise of the public realm amidst a plurality of fleeting, fragile, and inauthentic human loves mirror Augustine's own concerns as developed in his moral psychology of love and sin. She offers a prism, then, through which I can more fully identify and address these central issues.

The recent publication of the first English annotated translation of Arendt's dissertation, *Der Liebesbegriff bei Augustin*, does signal emerging interest in what her translators call "the Augustinian root of Arendt's critique of modernity."[2] A strong case can be made that Arendt's reading of Augustine, and the categories that govern this reading, remain with Arendt through her career.[3] A complete study of the Augustinian influence

2. Arendt, *Love and Saint Augustine*, 115. Page references in the text refer to this translation.

3. In addition to the lengthy interpretive essay by Scott and Stark that defends these connections, see Julia Kristeva, *Hannah Arendt*, trans. Ross Guberman (New York: Columbia University Press, 2001), 30–48, and Gillian Rose, *The Broken Middle* (Oxford: Blackwell Publishers, 1992), 153–246. Some reviews of the new translation, however, push these connections too far and mistake influence for endorsement. See, for example, Peter Dennis Bathory, "Augustine Through a Modern Prism," *Society* 34, no. 4 (May/June 1997): 72–76, and Leah Bradshaw, "Communion with Others, Communion with Truth," *Review of Politics* 59, no. 2 (Spring 1997): 368–72. Other Augustine scholars are unclear about this distinction because they too quickly naturalize her reading of Augustine. For example, Lauren Swayne Barthold claims that Augustine's theology of love provides Arendt with her innovative "capacity to see beyond ourselves . . . freeing ourselves from becoming cogs in the 'predictable' wheel of history" (Barthold, "Toward an Ethics of Love," 17). Von Heyking holds that Augustine provides Arendt with a "healing concept of love on the will as the way to uniting thought and action. She learned from Augustine that no matter how miserable the world becomes, no matter how wearisome, it is always a place of new beginnings" (*Longing*, 10). These connections are suggestive for those outside the

in Arendt's thought—such as can be found in her concepts of worldliness, freedom, responsibility, ambiguity, natality, mortality, memory, gratitude, forgiveness, and the "banality of evil"—would take us beyond the specific interests of my project. However, the relation of her description of evil to her reading of Augustine (perhaps most surprisingly neglected in Arendt studies) is particularly relevant. Fortunately, it has received welcome attention in Christian ethics.

This attention has come by way of two Augustinians, Jean Bethke Elshtain and Charles Mathewes. Both authors focus on the category of evil for comparison of Augustine and Arendt. Augustine's experience of imperialism and Arendt's experience of totalitarianism invite the comparison itself. But both authors suggest a deeper philosophical connection. In particular, they focus on the structural similarities between Augustine's privative account of evil as nonbeing and Arendt's controversial analysis of Adolf Eichmann, the Nazi bureaucrat, as the banal embodiment of "sheer thoughtlessness."[4] Elshtain locates Arendt's effort to "deprive evil of its seductive power" (*LP*, 74) in terms of Augustine's anti-Manichean understanding of evil as the privation of good. Augustine's theological metaphysics serve the same purpose as Arendt's political ontology: "evil is denuded, stripped of its glory, depleted" (*LP*, 80). Recall that for the mature Augustine, evil cannot bear the same ontological weight as the good. Evil is a negation, a no-thing. It is "deficient." To seek the cause of evil in an efficient cause is like "wishing to see darkness or hear silence" (*CD* 12.7). For Mathewes, this view parallels Arendt's thesis about Eichmann. Mathewes puts it this way: "Eichmann's crimes were not

---

Christian tradition, but Richard Wolin is more correct in his judgment: "The argument for intellectual continuity proves difficult to sustain; for whereas the later Arendt is known primarily as a philosopher of 'worldliness,' such concerns are hard to reconcile with an orientation as manifestly other-worldly as Augustine's.... The notion of community that Arendt discovers in Augustine is rather morbid and oblique, drenched in a veil of theological tears" (Wolin, *Heidegger's Children*, 43). I disagree with Wolin's confident rejection of any Augustinian influence and his characterization of otherworldly Augustinianism. In the next chapter, for example, I will offer a very different interpretation of Augustine's tears. To see Augustine's tears as morbid and oblique is to obscure their moral salience for political participation. To only gesture a contrast here, consider Levinas's claim that there are "tears that a civil servant cannot see: the tears of the Other," in Emmanuel Levinas, "Transcendence and Height," in *Basic Philosophical Writings* (Bloomington: Indiana University Press, 1996), 11–32, at 23.

4. Arendt, *Eichmann in Jerusalem*, 287.

rooted in a wicked character: he had no character to be wicked."[5] Neither Arendt's banality thesis nor Augustine's privation theory should be read as fantastical philosophical efforts to trivialize or to dismiss evil as an illusion. Moreover, a privation theory should not reduce *persons* to nonbeing (as Mathewes's language mistakenly could be read). To the contrary, precisely because of their awareness of the monstrous consequences of evil, both Arendt and Augustine struggled to find practical ways to mitigate despairing fascination with evil's grip—seeking understanding without indulging in the vanities of mere metaphorical consolation.

Mathewes advances Elshtain's insights by placing them in a larger vision of Augustinianism as "a way of life offering a vibrant and world-affirming response to evil" (10).[6] He finds Arendt at her most Augustinian in the recognition that "Eichmann's shallowness was as deep as evil could go . . . evil gets its pseudo-profundity, and indeed its pseudo-reality, by being the absence of good" (168). Readings of Arendt that fault her for letting Eichmann off the hook ("he was just one of us") miss the point of her account of totalitarian evil as a perennial danger for a modern politics that denies the creativity of human freedom. Arendt's agonistic image of a participatory politics that resists injustice, Mathewes avers, is finally Augustinian in that it pictures constructive political engagement as a struggle not of good against evil but as "against the void" (170).

Mathewes claims, however, that Arendt's valorizing account of this perpetual struggle avoids Manicheanism only to perpetuate a Pelagian fiction that the will is capable of spontaneous agency, "unconditioned by any external factors at all—including intention or desire" (174). Indeed, the limits of Arendt's account of politics, like Reinhold Niebuhr's, can be traced to a modern notion of autonomy that fails to "understand our relations to the world as essentially relations of love" (8). In order to place this argument in the context of my project, I need to turn from these authors' treatments of Arendt's implicit debts to Augustine on evil and consider her more explicit statements about Augustine on love.[7]

---

5. Mathewes, *Augustinian Tradition,* 167. Parenthetical references in the next two paragraphs are to this work.

6. Drawing upon resurgent interest in philosophy's relation to tragedy, Mathewes believes the Augustinian tradition "offers not in essence a *theory*, but a *therapy*" (72).

7. At least one Arendt scholar does register some doubt for an Augustinian connection to Arendt's "banality of evil" thesis by suggesting the more immediate influence of

The chapter proceeds as follows. First, by referring to her larger corpus, I outline Arendt's rejection of love as a relevant political virtue under the heading of "the problem of passion." Here I place Arendt in the context of broader characteristics of modern liberalism on the relation of love to politics that were introduced in my previous discussion of feminist political theory. Second, and more systematically, I present Arendt's specific criticism of Augustine's theology of love under the heading of "the problem of God." This criticism focuses on the Augustinian structure of love as desire for eternal beatitude and the supposed dualism generated by the priority of love for God in ways that jeopardizes genuine love for neighbor. In the final two chapters, I will offer my own reading of Augustinian love that responds to these objections as they relate to Augustinian civic liberalism.

LOVE AND THE PROBLEM OF PASSION

The "liberalism" of Hannah Arendt has been the subject of intense debate that continues today in both scholarly and popular forums.[8] Like Augustine, Arendt has suffered from the caricatures of her interpreters and political opponents. Like Niebuhr, she rejected political labels: "The left think that I am conservative, and the conservatives sometimes think that I am left or I am a maverick or God knows what."[9] Standard views of Arendt place her as a deeply conservative thinker who—under the influence of ancient Greek and Roman political philosophy—tended toward political existentialism and antidemocratic elitism rather than liberal justice. Such caricatures

---

Socrates and Heidegger. On this view, Arendt concentrates her attention on the "connection between *thinking* and evil, whereas Augustine . . . had focused on the connection between *willing* and evil" (Vetlesen, "Hannah Arendt," 8). Vetlesen, however, does not reject the view that Arendt's account "is part of a heritage from Augustine" (14).

8. See, especially, Lisa Disch, *Hannah Arendt and the Limits of Philosophy* (Ithaca, N.Y.: Cornell University Press, 1994), 68–105; Richard Wolin, "The Illiberal Imagination," *The New Republic*, November 27, 2000; and the subsequent exchange with Jeffrey Isaac in *The New Republic*, January 1 and 8, 2001.

9. Cited in, "On Hannah Arendt," in *Hannah Arendt: The Recovery of the Public World*, ed. Melvyn Hill (New York: St. Martins, 1979), 334. Ronald Beiner calls for something similar in his praise of Michael Sandel's civic republicanism and Christopher Lasch's "left-wing conservatism" (Ronald S. Beiner, "The Quest for a Post-Liberal Public Philosophy," in *Debating Democracy's Discontent*, ed. Anita L. Allen and Milton C. Regan Jr [Oxford: Oxford University Press, 1998], 1–13).

emerge from her controversial stands on political issues, her rhetoric of civic republicanism, her contemptuous attacks on romantic individualism and bourgeois culture, her education in German high culture, and the multiple sources of her unconventional thinking that reject ideologies of any kind. As Jeffrey Isaac puts it:

> Arendt was a strange radical indeed, inspired by Nietzsche and Heidegger as well as Jefferson and Kant, a passionate critic of Marxism who nonetheless declared the revolutionary workers' movements represented the primary agencies of freedom in the modern world. . . . Her elusiveness is frustrating to the theorist and activist. But as we confront a world in which existing ideological commitments seem increasingly hollow, it is also a source of much richness and vitality.[10]

My own sympathies lie with those interpreters, like Beiner, Benhabib, and Isaac, who read Arendt as an unorthodox, critical friend of liberalism despite her powerful assaults on its failures in modern times. Her searing analysis of modern societies of "laborers and jobholders" does not give rise to lonely nostalgia. In these accounts, one can find Arendt in the service of egalitarian liberalism, agonistic liberalism, liberal cosmopolitanism, radical democracy, Habermasian liberalism, and even Rawlsian liberalism. More measured characterizations also appear. With a reserve that emphasizes Arendt's penchant for unmasking the delusions of liberalism and her attraction to a grander style of politics, George Kateb remarks that Arendt "reluctantly tolerates liberal politics *faute de mieux* while denying that it is the real thing. And she goes on to construct an image of true politics that often taunts us in its unavailability."[11]

Reluctant toleration and taunting unavailability? Interestingly, this reading of Arendt exactly parallels Rowan Williams's reading of Augustine in relation to Roman politics. Williams cites Arendt throughout his important essay, but he does not draw this particular connection. On Williams's view, Augustine offers a *"redefinition* of the public itself, designed to show that it is life outside the Christian community which fails to be truly public,

10. Isaac, *Democracy in Dark Times*, 60. Though he does not pursue the philosophical or religious dimensions of a chastened progressivism, Isaac's effort to read Arendt outside the terms set by Cold War orthodoxies is similar to my reading of Augustine.

11. Kateb, *Hannah Arendt*, 28. My reading of Arendt is particularly indebted to Kateb.

authentically political."[12] This parallel may explain some of Arendt's fascination with Augustine as her "old friend" and "the last to know what it once meant to be a citizen" (*HC*, 14).[13] But let me note one similarity and one contrast. Augustine shares Arendt's frustrated lament that the "the greatest forces of intimate life—the passions of the heart, the thoughts of the mind, the delights of the sense—lead an uncertain, shadowy kind of existence unless and until they are transformed, deprivatized and deindividualized, as it were, into a shape to fit them for public appearance" (50). Augustine wanted the world to become public, to know itself socially. Arendt's image of true politics, however, recalls a past ideal where "to be political, to live in a *polis*, meant that everything was decided through words and persuasion and not through force and violence" (26). The Greeks and the Romans, Arendt claims, were able to overcome the "futility of individual life" through a public realm where "being seen and being heard by others derive their significance from the fact that everybody sees and hears from a different position" (56–57). It is this public realm of politics that is "the proper place for human excellence" (49). Julia Kristeva has pointed to the Augustinian resonance of Arendt's protest against "a consumerism that swallows up human life, when that life has lost sight of what is lasting."[14] But Augustine would have none of this limited imagination for a radical publicity, let alone the historical folly that the *polis* (even as an ideal type) was not predicated on coercion. Indeed, Augustine looks to a heavenly city that is so public that there will be need neither for coercion nor for language itself. For in that place, Augustine writes, "the thoughts of each of us will then also be manifest to all" (*CD* 22.6). The truly public world is eschatological. Arendt wants to sustain love of the world without this exorbitant theology, a transcendence fit for "potential earthly immortality" (*HC*, 55).

Keeping Kateb's gloss in mind, the influence of the liberal tradition (Montesquieu, Tocqueville, and especially, Kant) can be found throughout Arendt's corpus. This liberal reading helps us understand her persistent attention to human freedom, the formal equality of citizens, and the impor-

12. Williams, "Politics and the Soul," 58. For Williams, the opposition of Augustine's two cities is "not between public and private, church and world, but between political virtue and political vice. At the end of the day, it is the secular order that will be shown to be 'atomistic' in its foundations" (58).

13. For the "old friend" reference, see Arendt, *Love and Saint Augustine*, 295n4.

14. Kristeva, *Hannah Arendt*, 7.

tance of principled political judgment in a tension-ridden liberal culture. Jeffrey Isaac likens Arendt's analysis of totalitarianism to the "hard liberalism" of Reinhold Niebuhr.[15] A number of Arendtian themes certainly resonate with core features of liberalism: her controversial effort to maintain sharp distinctions between the public and the private, her rejection of politics as natural, the recognition of the plurality of communities that make up the modern world, the interest in identifying and resisting the totalitarian tendencies of politics without denying the creative possibilities of democratic politics and civil society, the need for "representative" thinking, the priority of speech in political life, and the vigorous defense of human dignity through the rule of law and viable political institutions.

I do not intend to settle the question of Arendt and her "liberalism" simply by invoking this list. Arendt may not be a liberal theorist, particularly in the pre-shrunk terms of debates between liberals and communitarians in contemporary political theory. But, in terms of the relation of love and the politics, I take Arendt to be a representative of modern liberalism, which has displaced the role of love in an ethics of citizenship.

Her position represents an extreme version of this account, both in terms of the phenomenology of love and the ethos of respect as the primordial public virtue. For example, I cannot imagine John Rawls making the direct statements about the incompatibility of love and politics that Arendt is willing to make. Arendt, we might say, is a *passionate* liberal critic of love as a political virtue. Her concerns about love in relation to the political run deeper than Rawls's political liberalism. Whatever philosophical issues attend to Rawlsian liberalism and the relation of public life and private morality, Rawls's paradigmatic formula—"political, not metaphysical"—is motivated primarily by the facts of pluralism and the epistemic burdens of judgment. Arendt shares these concerns. But Arendt's robust commitment to separate goodness from the political is governed by her account of the nature of the political and its relation to morality as such.

Arendt's misamorism, and the image of the citizen that it promotes, is particularly acute because of her reaction to what she sees as the negative effects of sentimentalism on political action. Politics requires the freedom of appearance in speech and deed, not the apolitical interests of goodness. Arendt is more suspicious of love than Rawls, and here displays her mutual

---

15. Isaac, *Democracy in Dark Times,* 62.

debts to Nietzsche and Kant. Arendt's writings reflect some of the deep assumptions and anxieties about love as a political "passion" that motivates the modern separation of love from the core value of mutual respect.

At the heart of Arendt's philosophical and political project is a defense of the freedom of political action from both ancient and modern depoliticizing subordinations of the world. In a kind of inverted or secularized Augustinianism, the structure of Arendt's thought is helpfully illuminated by the theme of love for the world as the central virtue of active citizenship.[16] The "world," for Arendt, is not simply the material earth. That sense of the "world" is affirmed. The earth, she writes, "is the very quintessence of the human condition, and earthly nature, for all we know, may be unique in the universe in providing human beings with a habitat in which they can move and breathe without effort and without artifice" (*HC*, 2). But, this earthly nature is only the site for those cultural achievements that human beings call into existence through their creative speech and public action. It is this world of the *vita activa* that Arendt fears is eroding in the modern technological and bureaucratic world, just as it had under the influence of the "otherworldliness of Christianity" (74).

As a matter of the historical record, Arendt blames the individualism of Christian eschatological salvation for the loss of the "esteem and dignity of politics" (*HC*, 314). Christianity, she claims, substituted the transcendence of individual salvation for the earthly immortality of the "political life of the body politic" (315). I will return to this familiar characterization in my last chapter. It is enough to note that Arendt's own sense of transcendence is radically this-worldly, and her account of Christian transcendence is radically other-worldly. What matters for Arendt is the *world* itself, not the integrity of the moral self, because it is this visible world that provides the space for those principled actions that are significant. There is, so to speak, no upward turn for Arendt. And, for her, Augustinian Christianity is relentlessly dedicated to the upward turn toward God. George Kateb states bluntly that Arendt represents a "reversal of Plato" and a "reversal of Christianity."[17]

16. Arendt initially offered a different title for *The Human Condition*; in a letter to Karl Jaspers in 1965, she reports that she wanted to call the book, *Amor Mundi* (cited by Young-Bruehl, *Hannah Arendt*, 324).

17. Kateb, *Hannah Arendt*, 13. Seyla Benhabib, however, emphasizes Arendt's continuing reliance on Platonic models of the unity of the soul for her conception of morality (as opposed to politics). See Benhabib, *Situating the Self*, 138.

Ronald Beiner states with characteristic clarity:

> [Arendt] agrees with Augustine that we are not naturally at home in the
> world but contrary to Augustine, she believes that we can make ourselves at
> home in this world. . . . To be more precise: For Augustine, we are more "at
> home" in the world than we ought to be; for Arendt, we are more estranged
> from the world than we ought to be.[18]

There is something very right about Beiner's summary. Augustine holds that
our true home is in God, not in any worldly thing or set of worldly things.
But this portrayal of Augustine as lingering Manichee is problematic if it
does not recognize the extent to which Augustine also holds that we are
estranged from God's good creation (and our own creatureliness) as well.
Creation is itself a revelation of God's love. Arendt seems to operate with a
philosophical notion of eschatology without Christology, or at least without
a Christology that ensures love of God is correlative with love of neighbor
such that to love God is to love the whole of creation that exists in God. The
appearance of Jesus of Nazareth, as once for Augustine, could only be for
her "a profoundly paradoxical event" (HC, 74). For Arendt, we are reconciled
to the world by loving the world, not God or God in Christ. The "love" for
the world relevant to Arendt's vision of political citizenship is a particular
notion of love. It is a love drained of religious affectivity or moral passion so
as to be suitable for the responsibilities of the political world of action. This
love does not take "into account motives and intentions on the one hand
and aims and consequences on the other—action can be judged only by the
criterion of greatness" (205). As Shin Chiba observes, Arendt "attempts to
take the notion of love out its original religio-ethical context in order to
ground it in the discourse of political theory."[19] Arendt must reconfigure

---

18. Beiner, "Love and Worldliness," 281.

19. Chiba, "Hannah Arendt on Love and the Political," 509. For Chiba, modern liberals like Rawls, Dworkin, and Berlin recognize love as a political virtue in the form of
fraternity (513n17). My own reading suggests that liberal accounts of fraternity do not
capture an appropriate account of love. Even this attention to fraternity seems to have
dropped out of liberal theorizing of the ethics of citizenship and is now placed through
the cipher of "respect." Chiba admits that even Arendt's "notion of *political* forgiveness
does not seem to make sense, unless it presumes a certain quality, an attitude, or an ethos
of *agape*, such as contrition, repentance, kindness, altruism, a heedless or adventurous
spirit of self-denial, the willingness to live together with others, or the readiness to start

love so that it can be suitable for the constructed worlds of the political. It is a kind of love without sentiment so as not to contaminate the world of "public appearance" (*HC*, 50).

Focusing on Arendt's severing of politics from moral motivation, George Kateb offers a response that is directly relevant to the main themes of this book:

> Surely there must be something seriously mistaken in her approach if this is its upshot. Specifically, to purge true politics of love, goodness, compassion, and pity is to purge it of the largest part of moral inhibition. . . . She purges politics of too much.[20]

> That perhaps the most searching and original theorist of political horror in the twentieth century could, as if in self-forgetfulness, accuse compassion and pity as the sponsors of more cruelty than cruelty itself is bizarre, aberrant. . . . Although Arendt has much to teach on the bad tendencies of raw passions (including compassion) or self-induced emotions (including pity) in political life, the moral energy that these passions and emotions provide political actors seems indispensable. Without them, any ameliorative movement in human affairs could barely get started.[21]

To be sure, like other liberals, Arendt's effort to purge politics of love is not motivated by immoralism. On this point, Arendt has been particularly maligned. Rather, we might say that Arendt is herself motivated by a moral concern not to render politics impotent before the exhausting demands of a morality informed by the excessive virtue of love.[22]

---

anew. . . . What is problematic, however, is Arendt's assumption that forgiveness is possible even when it is dissociated from the ontological ground of *agape*" (526). For Chiba, "*agape* implies a corrective power which the Kantian concept of 'respect,' for example, does not possess" (529).

20. Kateb, *Hannah Arendt*, 28.

21. Ibid., 95. For Kateb, however, Arendt's diagnosis of love is simply a "miscalculation" that does not recognize the utilitarian power of religion. He writes: "The world cannot do without it in some 'demythologized,' 'revaluated,' attenuated condition. It cannot do without the politicized love of humanity" (96). This appeal is interesting given his recognition that Arendt refused to treat religion as "functionalist social scientists do" (158).

22. Kateb helpfully notes that Arendt's misamorism is not that of Nietzsche or Machiavelli. He writes: "To say that Arendt wants the ostensibly praiseworthy emotions and

Arendt's faith imagines a common political world that "gathers us together and yet prevents our falling over each other" (*HC*, 52). It is as if the temptations of goodness hasten a premature intimacy that pridefully obliterates the diversity of public appearances and so shatters the common world. My Augustinian civic liberalism, shaped by Augustine's moral psychology of love and sin, is deeply sympathetic to this concern and stresses a love appropriate to democratic citizenship. For Augustinians, it is God's act of creation (not the common political world) that gives creatures the "space" to be themselves in relation to one another. Like other modern liberals, however, Arendt misconstrues love by focusing on its political pathologies and construing love solely in terms of sentimental benevolence. In Augustinian terms, by focusing on the hubris of disordered love, she allows sin to overwhelm the possibilities of love. She fails to discern the legitimacy and, at times, the necessity of love for healthy politics.

Like much of the literature on love in the twentieth century, Arendt distinguishes various forms of love: *eros*, *philia*, *agape*, *cupiditas*, *caritas*, and *fraternitas*. These standard distinctions, however, are not as illuminating for my purposes as the further distinctions that Arendt helpfully draws between empathy, pity, compassion, solidarity, and respect. In these discussions, Arendt's representative liberal voice is dominant. Rather than identifying her preference for political principles of solidarity and respect *precisely as forms of love*, she persistently contrasts these principles with love of any kind. Rather than accounting for deficient loves that are misdirected or misplaced, Arendt simply banishes love from the political. Love is too demanding, too partial, too intimate, and ultimately too dangerous for Arendtian politics. It is here that her overarching rejection of love as dangerous moral sentiment is most at odds with Augustinian civic liberalism.

Arendt's rejection of love runs throughout her writing. In a particularly revealing passage from *The Human Condition*, she writes:

---

passions of love, goodness, conscience, compassion, and pity kept out of political life is not say that she wants hatred, evil, ruthlessness, coldness, or cruelty kept in. . . . The best in private life is not the measure for what is best in political life. . . . This is not Nietzsche's pathos of distance that Arendt preaches: There is nothing hierarchical in the distance she insists on. Love is great; it is rare; it is too easily mistaken for romance; but whatever it is, it is antipolitical. It leads to calamity when directly politicized" (*Hannah Arendt*, 26).

> Love, for reasons of its passion, destroys the in-between which relates us to and separates us from others.... Love by its very nature is unworldly, and it is for this reason rather than its rarity that it is not only apolitical but antipolitical, perhaps the most powerful of all antipolitical forces. (*HC*, 242)

Love, like pity, is an emotion that overwhelms and corrupts politics—which for Arendt, by its very freedom from the self-absorbed need for moral authenticity, is the only redemptive sphere of human striving. Politics must be rational, rising above the ethical life of feeling. In contrast to love, Arendt explains, genuine humanity "should be sober and cool rather than sentimental."[23] Genuine humanity "is exemplified not in fraternity but in friendship; that friendship is not intimately personal but makes political demands and preserves reference to the world."[24] As citizen, the human person must resist the desire to love.[25] The ethics of citizenship requires principled civic equality and the courage of mutual respect. This may resemble a kind of political friendship, but it is not governed by love, compassion, or fraternity.

In fact, love as political virtue is the font of cruelty itself. Jesus, according to Arendt, recognized the danger and the impossibility of the publicity of love. Citing Matthew 6:3, she notes that Jesus counseled his followers to "let not thy left hand know what thy right hand doeth" (*HC*, 74). George Kateb helpfully summarizes this section from *The Human Condition*: "In an amazing meditation on Jesus she tries to read his life as the story of one who knew that goodness could never show itself in public without destroying both itself and the public realm."[26] Love, for Arendt, is always a kind of mysterious force in the universe. She writes:

> Love, in distinction from friendship, is killed, or rather extinguished, the moment it is displayed in public. ("Never seek to tell thy love / Love that never told can be.") Because of its inherent worldlessness, love can only become false and perverted when it is used for political purposes. (*HC*, 51–52)

23. Arendt, *Men in Dark Times*, 25.
24. Ibid., 25.
25. Arendt, *On Revolution*, 38–39.
26. Kateb, *Hannah Arendt*, 26. Later Kateb glosses: "The goodness of Jesus destroys the world; the morality of love destroys the world . . . thus the very spirit of goodness shuns the world of human appearances.... One cannot be in love with goodness and have any remaining desire or energy for the worldly life of political action" (89–90).

Love is the moral virtue of the religious zealot, the sentimental soul, or the romantic embrace. It is because of this power that love becomes a political vice that must be domesticated or transformed.

Public love is the intense, violent destroyer of freedom. The archetypes of political love for Arendt are Robespierre, Saint-Just, and Melville's *Billy Budd*.[27] This is the love that needs to be kept in check, the love that always turns into a crime when it demands public appearance. "Respect" is to govern the sphere of politics. She writes:

> Yet what love is in its own, narrowly circumscribed sphere, respect is in the larger domain of human affairs. Respect, not unlike the Aristotelian *philia politike*, is a kind of "friendship" without intimacy and without closeness; it is a regard for the person from the distance which the space of the world puts between us, and this regard is independent of qualities which we may admire or of achievements which we may highly esteem. (*HC*, 243)

Again, one finds in this passage a characteristically restricted notion of love in modern liberalism—and, I might add, a notion that has no place for the politics of "righteous anger" that makes "private" suffering a "public" issue found throughout Hebrew and Christian scriptures. Rather than imagining respect and friendship as appropriate forms of love in politics, Arendt consistently characterizes love as a passionate sentiment appropriate only to a private, domesticated sphere.[28] Respect is seen as a counter value that offsets love (which is seen as intrinsically reckless) rather than an internal element of love itself.

This characterization of love recalls Immanuel Kant's controversial account of "pathological" love (arising from temperament or feeling) as being

27. Arendt, *On Revolution*, 77–80 and 107. As Kateb puts it, "Arendt sees Herman Melville's *Billy Budd* as one of the deepest examinations of the inner meanings of the French Revolution.... Confronted with motiveless evil, innocence (already reticent) becomes speechless and in its—[Billy's]—rage murders the evil one. She reads the story as a vindication of Captain Vere, the man who has the kind of virtue fit for the world. Unable to prevent the crime of absolute evil, he must, in his virtue, punish innocence, absolute goodness, when it acts" (*Hannah Arendt*, 27). Like Robespierre and Saint-Just, Billy Budd is not a "bloodthirsty madman" but simply "in thrall to Christian absolutism" (90).

28. Shin Chiba helpfully tries to rehabilitate Arendt's notion of political friendship through a kind of discourse ethics, but I am afraid Chiba does not finally alleviate what she herself calls "Arendt's Kantian bias concerning this Aristotelian notion" ("Hannah Arendt on Love and the Political," 520).

at odds with beneficent duties done out of the will's respect for the rationality of the moral law (*Groundwork*, 4:399).[29] In this famous discussion of the biblical love commands, Kant contrasts "pathological" love with "practical" love in terms of the latter's capacity to be commanded by the will and so experienced as duty rather than arising from sensible inclination. Practical love lies "in principles of action and not of melting sympathy" (*Groundwork*, 4:399). Arendt surprisingly does not refer to Kant's repeated opposition of love and respect, but her political views appear similar to the structure of Kant's moral theory. As Kant strikingly puts it, "The principle of **mutual love** admonishes [persons] constantly to *come closer* to one another; that of the **respect** they owe one another, to keep themselves *at a distance* from one another" (*Metaphysics of Morals*, 6:449). For Kant, the best kinds of friendships are "the union of two persons through equal mutual love and respect," continuing the suggestion that love and respect are countervailing weights (*Metaphysics of Morals*, 6:469). Kant may not reject love's relation to ethics, but it does seem that respect is *morally* more significant than love since it is universalizable as moral duty:

> Failure to fulfill mere duties of love is lack of virtue *(peccatum)*. But failure to fulfill duty arising from the respect owed to every human being as such is a vice *(vitium)*. For no one is wronged if duties of love are neglected; but a failure in the duty to respect infringes upon one's lawful claim. (*Metaphysics of Morals*, 6:464)

29. References to Kant's work cite the Akademie Ausgabe, and English translations from the *Cambridge Edition of the Works of Immanuel Kant*, general editors Paul Guyer and Allen Wood (Cambridge: Cambridge University Press, 1992–). Kant's mature account of love as motivation, as opposed to later Kantian tradition, is an important feature of revisionist Kant scholarship. On the contested nature of interpreting Kant's ethical position on the role of emotions and love (especially the distinctive role of *Menschenliebe*), see Wood, "Kant's Practical Philosophy," and Velleman, "Moral Emotion." Wood admits that the *Groundwork* clearly claims that "the properly moral motive for benefiting others apparently can have nothing to do with any sort of affective or emotional involvement with them or their needs" ("Kant's Practical Philosophy," 16). However, he argues that Kant's late theory of moral motivation presupposes "a certain kind of *felt* love for other human beings that is not of empirical origin but is an effect that the moral law has on the mind" (17–18). In the next chapter, I draw from Velleman's attempt to "juxtapose love and Kantian respect in a way that is illuminating to both" ("Moral Emotion," 344).

Kant recognizes a relation between love and respect. But, as Marcia Baron argues, he "exaggerates the contrast and opposition" in a way that "overestimates the degree to which keeping a distance from others is needed in order to respect others' freedom and self-direction, and to preserve self-respect."[30] Respect (or perhaps more precisely, the absence of disrespect)—universalized in the moral law and motivated by reverence for the ideal of the rational, self-governing will—places negative moral constraints on this positive desire for the intimacy of love. In the next chapter, I will argue that Kant and Augustine share many of the same intuitions about the potential dangers of the desire for intimacy and of emotions more generally. Kant, however, does not simply worry about the potential of love's failures in the face of the demand to respect persons. He seems to associate love with the affects and passions that are themselves to blame as causes of immorality because they uncontrollably (or, at least, unreflectively) get in the way of the self's moral activity of reason giving and commanding. He claims affects involve a "*lack of virtue*" and passions are "*properly* evil" (*Metaphysics*, 6:408).[31] Emotions are not condemned wholesale; in fact, Kant (much like Kierkegaard in *Works of Love*) argues that we have a moral duty to cultivate certain emotions which promote regard for others.[32] But love, at least at the level of motivation within the structure of his moral theory, is identified with the affects and passions that are thought to short circuit the rational capacity of respect central to his understanding of virtue. In fact, perhaps to overcome this possibility, Kant suggests that "any respect for a person is properly only respect for the law (of integrity and so forth) of which he gives us an example" (*Groundwork*, 4:401). This view reveals its Lutheran heritage of opposing love and justice. It privileges the representation of abstract justice against concrete love as the appropriate public virtue of the "enlarged mentality" of political judgment. As Henry S. Richardson writes, "love of humankind, which Kant champions, pulls upon us like the gravitational field of the stars in the heavens:

30. Baron, "Love and Respect in the *Doctrine of Virtue*," 396 and 406.

31. Frierson helpfully points out the distinction between affect and passion in Kant: "Passions are uncontrolled *inclinations*, related to the faculty of desire, while affects are uncontrolled *feelings*, related to the distinct faculty of pleasure and displeasure" (*Freedom and Anthropology*, 60). I return to a similar distinction in Augustine in the next chapter.

32. Baron distinguishes between "having" a feeling and "harboring, cultivating, or failing to cultivate certain desires or feelings" (Baron, *Kantian Ethics*, 199).

measurably but weakly and diffusely. In our relationships with strangers, it is instead the strict duties of justice, embodying respect alone, that principally control us."[33] "Love," Richardson counters, "motivates a risky attunement to embodied particulars, whereas a Kantian respect maintains a safe distance."[34] For Kantian respect of persons, however, only this detachment preserves the distance necessary for autonomy and a non-humiliating approach to the duties of morality.

Love, in the liberal Kantian view, is dangerously vulnerable and too particular. It exposes us and draws us to others. As such, it threatens either to make others' ends simply a function of my own project or to lead me to lose my autonomy in theirs. Even John Rawls, who initially linked his difference principle with the virtue of fraternity and Christian neighbor-love, becomes uncharacteristically lyrical when he sounds this Kantian note.[35] Arendt would affirm Rawls's statement:

> Those who love one another, or who acquire strong attachments to persons and to forms of life, at the same time become liable to ruin: their love makes them hostages to misfortune and the injustice of others. . . . Once we love we are vulnerable: there is no such thing as loving while being ready to consider whether to love, just like that. And the loves that hurt the least are not the best loves.[36]

33. Henry Richardson, "Nussbaum: Love and Respect," 254–55.

34. Ibid., 257.

35. Helmut Pape offers an interesting comparison between Rawls's treatment of fraternity and Charles Peirce's theory of love as "social sympathy." For Pape, Rawls tries to incorporate fraternity into his ethics of liberalism but fails because of his initial assumptions regarding rational egoism. Pape writes: "But to define the conditions for an equal gratification of egoism is not to give an account of the relation of sympathy for others, or *fraternite.* The confusion here occurs when balancing the egoistic interest of individuals is taken for sympathizing or loving for its own sake. The second may sometimes be the consequence of the first, but no account of how to balance egoisms will ever give us a positive notion of what social sympathy between humans consists in" ("Love's Power and the Causality of Mind," 81).

36. Rawls, *Theory of Justice*, 573. This passage resonates with Freud's claim that "we are never so defenceless against suffering as when we love, never so helplessly unhappy as when we have lost our loved object or its love" (Freud, *Civilization and its Discontents*, 30).

Love, for many modern liberals, is not only inadequate but a dangerous moral motivation for politics.

A famous passage from *On Revolution* helpfully conveys this aspect of Arendt's thought. She writes:

> Pity may be the perversion of compassion, but its alternative is solidarity. It is out of pity that men are "attracted toward *les hommes faibles*," but it is out of solidarity that they establish deliberately and, as it were, dispassionately a community of interest with the oppressed and exploited. The common interest would then be "the grandeur of man," or the dignity of man. For solidarity, because it partakes of reason, and hence of generality, is able to comprehend a multitude conceptually, not only the multitude of a class or a nation, but eventually all mankind. But this solidarity, though it may be aroused by suffering, is not guided by it, and it comprehends the strong and the rich no less than the weak and the poor; compared with the sentiment of pity, it may appear cold and abstract, for it remains committed to "ideas"—to greatness, or honour, or dignity—rather than to any "love" of men.[37]

This passage captures several Arendtian themes that are typical of liberal characterizations of love as antipolitical, or beneath the realm of the political.

Two interesting identifications can be noted in this passage. In these identifications, one hears the voice of modern liberalism that, as I have argued, has come under attack in feminist theory.[38] First, there is the claim that solidarity requires the "deliberate" and "dispassionate" establishment of a "community of interest." Second, there is the claim that solidarity is an appropriate political principle because "it partakes of reason, and hence of generality."

Unlike dispassionate reason that secures political judgment, love is an emotion not to be trusted. In *The Human Condition*, Arendt describes the failure of politics in the face of "the modern individual and his endless conflicts, his inability either to be at home in society or to live outside it altogether, his ever-changing moods and the radical subjectivism of his emotional life" (*HC*,

---

37. Arendt, *On Revolution*, 88–89.

38. In her commentary, Adrienne Rich concludes that Arendt "embodies the tragedy of a female mind nourished on male ideologies" (*On Lies, Secrets, and Silence* [New York: W. W. Norton, 1979], 212). For criticism of Arendt's statements on compassion and politics, see Elizabeth V. Spelman, *Fruits of Sorrow: Framing Our Attention to Suffering* (Boston: Beacon Press, 1997).

39).[39] For Arendt, love can only be particular and, as such, radically subjective and volatile. Love is vulnerable to prejudice, withdrawal, and collective ideology.[40] Indeed, she suggests that love is a luxury enjoyed only by those obsessed with self-reflexivity and "unburdened by care for the world."[41] As we will see, Augustine's moral psychology responds to precisely this pathology. However, Arendt's response to these concerns is itself one of withdrawal. As Margaret Canovan puts it, "[Arendt] insisted on the importance of a formal, artificial public realm in which what mattered was the people's actions rather than their sentiments . . . in which there was enough space between people for them to stand back and judge one another coolly and objectively."[42] Love, for Arendt, represents a moral sensitivity and emotional intimacy that destabilizes politics. In fact, politicized love expresses itself in terror and crime.

Arendt searches for an appropriate phenomenology of political consciousness that would provide the basis of citizenship in terms of public bonds of respect and solidarity. Politics requires the "enlarged mentality" of Kantian impartiality.[43] In *On Revolution*, she criticizes Rousseau, who "introduced compassion into political theory," and Robespierre, who "brought it to the market-place with the vehemence of his great revolutionary oratory" (81). Arendt writes:

> Even if Robespierre had been motivated by the passion of compassion, his compassion would have become pity when he brought it out into the open

39. Arendt's aversion to emotion and its tendency to blur the boundaries between public life and private intimacy is clearly expressed in one of her earliest works, *Rahel Varnhagen: The Life of a Jewish Woman* (New York: Harcourt Brace Jovanovich, 1974). Also, in her essay "On Humanity in Dark Times," Arendt claims that the search for intimacy is characteristic of excluded groups such as the Jews under Nazism. This intimacy is a form of worldlessness, which is a "form of barbarism" and represents "psychological substitutes . . . for the loss of a common, visible world" (*Men in Dark Times*, 13 and 16).

40. The relation of love's particularity and Arendt's "Jewishness" is a matter of intense debate in Arendt studies that I do not pursue. In general, Arendt's universalism caused suspicion among a number of Zionists. See, for example, the exchange with Gershom Scholem in Hannah Arendt, *The Jew as Pariah* (New York: Grove Press, 1978), 247, and the discussion in Richard Bernstein, *Hannah Arendt and the Jewish Question* (Cambridge, Mass.: MIT Press, 1996), 189.

41. Arendt, *Men in Dark Times*, 68.

42. Canovan, "Politics as Culture," 632.

43. Arendt, *Lectures on Kant's Political Philosophy*, 73.

where he could no longer direct it toward specific suffering and focus it on particular persons. What had perhaps been genuine passion turned into the boundlessness of an emotion that seemed to respond only too well to the boundless suffering of the multitude in their sheer overwhelming numbers. By the same token, he lost the capacity to establish and hold fast to rapports with persons in their singularity; the ocean of suffering around him and the turbulent sea of emotion within him . . . drowned all specific considerations, the considerations of friendship no less than considerations of statecraft and principle. (*On Revolution*, 85)

We note again the characterization of the "boundlessness of an emotion" and the "turbulent sea of emotion" in contrast to the steady principles of statecraft. Rawls also uses this imagery in his rejection of love as a political virtue: "Benevolence is at sea as long as its many loves are in opposition in the persons of its many objects."[44] In stark contrast to the feminist and Christian ethicists I discussed in the previous chapter, Rawls and Arendt both seem to think that love is rendered dumb when confronted with the challenges of principled political judgment.

In her celebrated work, *Love's Knowledge*, Martha Nussbaum has identified this tendency of Western philosophy since Descartes and Kant to view emotions either as "blind animal reactions, like or identical with bodily feelings, that are in their nature unmixed with thought, undiscriminating, and

---

44. Rawls, *Theory of Justice*, 190. Later, Rawls repeats this claim: "Benevolence is at a loss when the many objects of its love oppose one another. The principles of justice are needed to guide it. The difference between the sense of justice and the love of mankind is that the latter is supererogatory" (476). Here, however, Rawls provides a significant qualification: "Yet, clearly the objects of these two sentiments are closely related, being defined in large part by the same conception of justice" (476). This qualification resists a stark division between "love" and "justice" in Rawls, even though it still privileges justice and marginalizes love as a supererogation. But, as Seyla Benhabib points out, the Kantian presuppositions "are so weighty that the equivalence of all selves qua rational agents dominates and stifles any serious acknowledgement of difference, alterity and of the standpoint of the 'concrete other'" (*Situating the Self*, 167). Unlike many Christian critics, Benhabib distinguishes the false charge that Rawlsian theory is egoistical from a more accurate concern that it is "disembedded." If this is the case, then Rawlsians might benefit from a conception of benevolent love that is attentive to alterity in ways that strict justice principles of right are not. His justice might need love as much as benevolence needs universalist principles of justice. As Benhabib puts it, "obligations and relations of care are genuinely moral ones, belonging to the center and not at the margins of morality" (186).

impervious to reasoning" or "pieces of reasoning that are actually false."[45]
Arendt's attack on Rousseau and Robespierre, however, extends particularly
to her reading of Christian accounts of love.

For Arendt, unlike the worldly *eros* of the Greeks and the Renaissance
humanists or the Kantian notion of respect for others, true Christian love—
like the revolutionary compassion of a Rousseau or the strict conscience of
a Thoreau or Socrates—is worldless and can not withstand liberal politics
because it is wedded to what she calls the "activity of goodness" (*HC*, 74).[46]
Christian love, like the European revolutionary spirit, is too concerned with
the integrity of the self and compassionate responsibility for the neighbor.
In either case, to be motivated by moral concern for the self's authenticity or
the neighbor's good eclipses the public world of politics. Christian love leads
either to inwardness or intimacy, both of which are worldless.

This characterization is clearly revealed in another passage from *The Human
Condition*:

> Historically, we know of only one principle that was ever devised to keep a
> community of people together who had lost their interest in the common
> world and felt themselves no longer related and separated by it. To find a bond
> between people strong enough to replace the world was the main political task
> of early Christian philosophy, and it was Augustine who proposed to found not
> only the Christian "brotherhood" but all human relationships on charity. . . .
> The unpolitical, non-public character of the Christian community was early
> defined in the demand that is should form a corpus, a "body," whose members
> were to be related to each other like brothers of the same family. (*HC*, 53)

Love, rather than providing a founding principle for politics, turns out finally to prevent politics itself.

Thomas Breidenthal, in a rare theological review of Arendt, associates
Arendt's critique of the relation between ethics and politics in Christianity
in a way that recalls the work of Emmanuel Levinas. According to Breidenthal, on this understanding:

> The ethical, inasmuch as it denotes the infinite claim of the neighbor upon
> me in his need, runs at cross-purposes with the political, which depends on

45. Nussbaum, *Love's Knowledge*, 40–41 and 42.
46. For Thoreau and Socrates, see Hannah Arendt, *Crises of the Republic* (New York:
Harcourt, 1972), 60–62.

the mutual enjoyment of freedom that can only come when economic lack is held sufficiently at bay. . . . Absolute goodness is the enemy of the political, because it demands that the political be forsworn until the ethical can be fully satisfied—that is, the political be forsworn forever. . . . The absolute demands of ethics, which are impossible to fulfill, consume the surplus on which politics depends.[47]

Christian love for Arendt, like some interpretations of Emmanuel Levinas's infinite responsibility, dramatically condemns and subverts politics in the face of the priority of ethics. Arendt's attacks on concern for the ethical integrity of the self are primarily directed against Rousseau's emphasis on self-perfection and various streams of romanticism. But the relation to Christian discipleship and the hope for a fellowship in virtue is apparent. For Arendt, Christian love that tries to go public as an expression of its inner compassion is finally destructive of the more limited hopes of political action. In fact, as Kateb forcefully puts it, "the most consuming interest of the compassionate soul is that there be enough suffering in the world to keep itself torn and hence continuously fascinating to itself as internal spectacle."[48] As in Kant, politics requires an artificiality and distance that is foreign to Arendt's conceptualization of love, especially Christian love.[49] Love becomes self-consuming of politics, legitimates violence, and therefore cannot ground an ethics of liberal citizenship that respects the separateness of persons. As we see in the next section, this self-consumption mixed with self-absorption is only exacerbated if love seeks any relation to the divine.

LOVE AND THE PROBLEM OF GOD

In order to purse this claim more directly, I turn to Arendt's dissertation. In a 1965 letter to her friend Mary McCarthy, Arendt claims that she had not

47. Breidenthal, "Arendt, Augustine, and the Politics of Incarnation," 493.

48. Kateb, *Hannah Arendt*, 94. Kateb helpfully analyzes Arendt's skepticism about self-knowledge and the "world alienation" of efforts to cultivate the inner life (ibid., 6–7). He writes that for Arendt, "no one can know himself; no one can know others. . . . The desire to substitute the inner life for a worldly life is understandable, but for Arendt not forgivable. . . . In the modern age, the many consume or aspire to consumption, and the few withdraw into themselves. Both are prisoners" (6).

49. Oliver O'Donovan argues that Kant's discussion of ethics and politics in *Perpetual Peace* renders "political morality" untenable (*DN*, 6).

read her dissertation for nearly forty years.[50] Of course, there are numerous references to Augustine in her works, especially in those works composed during this period of revisiting her dissertation. Historians will have to judge the relevance of Arendt's choosing the path of many graduate students in putting aside her dissertation. Nonetheless, however one judges Arendt's mature relation to Augustine, her dissertation represents an important development in Augustine scholarship. Mixed reviews of Arendt's work from the period show that her reading was a dramatic departure from standard Augustine studies. As if anticipating criticism, Arendt persistently characterizes her approach as philosophical rather than theological. She defends her claims on the grounds that Augustine "never wholly lost the impulse of philosophical thinking" (6). This modern construction of a radical choice between philosophy and theology obscures dimensions of Augustine's thought and would at the very least be foreign to much of ancient philosophy. Despite its neglect in scholarly circles, however, Arendt's phenomenological method prefigures much of today's revived interest in Augustine's notions of "inwardness," "subjectivity," and "otherness." How Arendt's existentialist reading affects her already disputed relation to religious thought, feminism, and liberalism complicates my decision to focus on the dissertation as another avenue into a reading of love and political Augustinianism.[51] Arendt's

50. Hannah Arendt to Mary McCarthy (October 1965), in *Between Friends: The Correspondence of Hannah Arendt and Mary McCarthy 1949–1975*, ed. Carol Brightman (New York: Harcourt, Brace and Company, 1995), 189–91. Arendt writes: "I got myself into something absurd—Macmillan had asked me years ago for my dissertation on Augustine. I needed the money (not really, but could use it) and said yes. The translation arrived two years ago and now I ran out of excuses and have to go over it. It is kind of a traumatic experience. . . . It is probably not worth it and I should simply return the money—but by now I am strangely fascinated by this rencontre" (190).

51. On Arendt and religious thought, see William Paul Wanker, *Nous and Logos: Philosophical Foundations of Hannah Arendt's Political Theory* (New York: Garland Publishing, 1991); James W. Bernauer, S.J., ed., *Amor Mundi: Explorations in the Faith and Thought of Hannah Arendt* (Dordrecht: Martinus Nijhoff, 1987); and Philip Rieff, "The Theology of Politics: Reflections on Totalitarianism as the Burden of our Time," *Journal of Religion* 32 (April 1952): 119–26. On Arendt and feminism, see Seyla Benhabib, *The Reluctant Modernism of Hannah Arendt* (London: Sage Press, 1996), Bonnie Honig, ed., *Feminist Interpretations of Hannah Arendt* (University Park: Pennsylvania State University Press, 1995); Mary Dietz, "Hannah Arendt and Feminist Politics," *Feminist Interpretations and Political Theory*, ed. Mary Lyndon Shanley and Carol Pateman (University Park:

ascendancy in recent political theory has renewed the vigor and complexity of these already active debates.[52]

Throughout her dissertation, Arendt exploits what Søren Kierkegaard called the "frightful collisions" between the love of God and the love of neighbor.[53] The possibility of such a collision arises from the apparent priority that the biblical tradition assigns to the love of God and love for God. For Arendt, it is this particular theocentric and eudaimonistic structure of Augustine's account of love that is doubly problematic.

Many modern theorists share Arendt's political concern about the "otherworldliness" of Augustinian Christianity as a kind of Platonic idealism focused on eternity. She joins the familiar charges made by Machiavelli, Rousseau, Nietzsche, and those whom Schleiermacher called "the cultural despisers of religion." In this account, Christian religion devalues this world by positing another heavenly world that regulates (and so diminishes) sources of value in the temporal world. Politics is not simply a necessary evil as classically opposed to a school of virtue for the good life. Augustinian Christianity suspends politics altogether. Between the ages, in Arendt's view, Christians bide their time waiting for the arrival of the Kingdom. Of course, much of twentieth-century religious thought (particularly Christian social ethics) has responded to this charge.

As we saw in the previous chapters, many of these responses from theological friends of liberalism come from those who reject Augustine's theology of love and its supposedly world-denying and individualistic form of piety. In her dissertation, however, Arendt tries to pursue the Augustinian logic on its own terms. As Breidenthal puts it, "If Arendt stopped here, her critique would amount to little more than a reminder (if we needed one) that

---

Pennsylvania State University Press, 1991), 232–52; Joann Cutting-Gray, "Hannah Arendt, Feminism, and the Politics of Alterity," *Hypatia* 8, no. 1 (Winter 1993): 35–54; and Amy Allen, "Solidarity after Identity Politics: Hannah Arendt and the Power of Feminist Theory," *Philosophy & Social Criticism* 25, no. 1 (1999): 97–118. On Arendt and liberalism most generally, see *Hannah Arendt and the Meaning of Politics*, ed. Craig Calhoun and John McGowan (Minneapolis: University of Minnesota Press, 1997).

52. For criticism of Arendt's popularity in contemporary theorizing about citizenship, see Peter Berkowitz, "The Pearl Diver," *The New Republic*, June 14, 1999: 44–52.

53. Søren Kierkegaard, *Either/Or*, trans. Walter Lowrie (Princeton: Princeton University Press, 1987), 2:205.

Christians have often held the political life in contempt."[54] The real challenge is that Arendt "goes on to suggest that it is of the essence of Christianity to be anti-political, just as some have suggested that it is of the essence of Christianity to be anti-semitic."[55] What is interesting about Arendt's claims, Breidenthal shows, is the seriousness with which she actually pursues the internal logic of Augustinian Christianity.

In a sense, she tries to think with Augustine against Augustine in terms of a competitive relation of love of God and love of neighbor. As her editors put it, "Arendt wants to show how Augustine can reconcile the confessional discourse of the individual's journey to the Creator with the obligation to the neighbor in the human community" (124). This theological seriousness (characteristic of German existentialism), ironically, stands at odds with her claim that she purposely defends her study as one of "purely philosophical interest" (6). She was willing and able to think theologically in order to overcome what she took to be incoherent theology.

As we shall see in the next chapters, however, Arendt and others pay a high analytic price for abstracting Augustine's account of love from his mature theology and its own polemical contexts. Understanding the competing issues that motivate Augustine's particular rhetoric of love, and attending to the distinctively Trinitarian dimensions of his account of love and sin, corrects many of Arendt's caricatures of Augustine. Augustinian love, to return briefly to my argument, motivates and secures love for the neighbor even as it recognizes the limits of love in a fallen world constrained by sin. His philosophical and theological energies are devoted more to *how* one is to love in an actively ordering way rather than to an abstract metaphysical speculation on *what* one is to consider as appropriate objects of love. To love the neighbor in God, Augustine's mature formulation, aims to protect the neighbor from the self's prideful distortion that the neighbor exists only in terms of one's own ends, or that the self is the personal end of the neighbor. Moreover, the doctrine of the union of the two natures of Christ in the person of Jesus demonstrates the radical unity of the love of God and love of neighbor. Responding to Jesus, the word become flesh, is always responding to God and neighbor. God (whether as Father or Son) does not compete for the self's attention, as if God were simply the biggest object under

54. Breidenthal, "Arendt, Augustine, and the Politics of Incarnation," 490.
55. Ibid., 490–91.

consideration as an object of love. In the end, I believe Arendt's seductive misreading fundamentally distorts both our understanding of Augustine and political Augustinianism. Before turning to my response, however, it is important to outline Arendt's representative rejection of Augustinian love.

The essential argument of her dissertation relies on a familiar reading of the neo-Platonic structure of Augustine's thought in such a way that worldly loves are stripped of value. Particularly, Augustine's infamous oppositions of *cupiditas* and *caritas* and *usus* and *fruito* make, as she strikingly puts it, "a desert out of this world" (18). Arendt, however, is fascinated by Augustine's struggle to find a place for neighbor-love in the context of the overwhelming desire for God in the tensed living between time and eternity. The question that guides her inquiry, "how the person in God's presence, isolated from all things mundane, can be at all interested in his neighbor," expands throughout her interpretive scheme into a discussion of the grounds of moral and political action in a world with others (7). Despite her efforts to redeem Augustine against himself, love of neighbor in Augustinian theology is finally held to be a mockery of love. The concrete horizontal encounter with the neighbor is always only mediated, and finally deferred, to the vertical relation to God. In the end, Augustinian *caritas* collapses and so (in contradiction to its stated purpose) estranges love for neighbor through a monistic love for God. This love of God overwhelms that which is not God. The One does not tolerate the Many, the eternal shuns the temporal. The theocentric quality of Augustinian *caritas* deadens the vitality of worldly loves. As Shin Chiba puts it:

> Both the deindividualization of the other and the dehistoricization of his or her situation take place in exchange with standardized equality and uniformity in which everyone is treated. Thus, Arendt understands that the theological notion of neighborly love cannot ground the relevance of the others. Hence, it is incapable of grounding the public *vinculum* in social life. She thinks that there is such an acosmic and otherworldly tendency present in the theological notion of love.[56]

Indeed, even Augustine's Trinitarianism does not save him from what Gregory Vlastos controversially identified as problems of Platonic love in general: the loss of the individual and intrinsic concern for others in their

---

56. Chiba, "Hannah Arendt on Love and the Political," 527. Chiba notes the connection with Nietzsche's "The Antichrist" (528n62).

particularity because one is motivated by abstract concern for the Good. According to Vlastos, Plato's theory of love fails because "what we are to love in persons is the 'image' of the Idea in them."[57] While he disagrees with Nygren's restrictive reading of classical philosophy, Vlastos fundamentally agrees that the flaw of the Platonic scheme is its instrumentalization of persons. The Platonic lover either loves the individual as a means to the lover's happiness (egoism) or only in terms of their virtue rather than for their own sake (impartialism). One would think Augustine's Christian rejection of the Platonists might open space for Arendt's better Augustine. But, as we see, the Incarnation itself serves as a distraction from attending to the other in his or her alterity. Christ as the divine neighbor absorbs the integrity of all neighbor love.

Arendt divides her essay into three parts: (1) "Love as Craving: The Anticipated Future"; (2) "Creator and Creature: The Remembered Past"; and (3) "Social Life." The first two parts pursue parallel strands in Augustine that confirm her suspicions that Augustine's account renders the love of neighbor "incomprehensible in its true relevance" (98). Love for neighbor has no place in a desiring love either for God as the highest good of the absolute future or for the memory of God's love in the absolute past. In a much shorter third section, Arendt offers a possible theological way out for Augustine. In the end, however, even this possibility proves elusive.

In the first part, she puts forward the "pretheological" metaphysics of Augustine's classical eudaimonism and its subsequent phenomenology of love. To love, Augustine learned from the Greeks, is to experience a craving *(appetitus)*, a motion of desire.[58] Desire as craving, however, gives rise to a

---

57. Vlastos, "The Individual as Object of Love in Plato," 31. In a response to Vlastos, David Brink relies on Paul Ramsey's discussion of Nygren and endorses Ramsey's claim that "in caring about one's beloved, one cares about his virtue" (Brink, "Eudaimonism, Love and Friendship, and Political Community," 273). Catherine Osborne's attack on this "popular prejudice against" Plato also includes an appendix on Vlastos and Nygren (Osborne, *Eros Unveiled*, 222–26). She argues, against both Vlastos and Nygren, that Platonism "points out the importance of seeing the individual as a whole person, with appetites and emotions as well as intellect, and so far from denying a concern for individuals, it rather presupposes just such a concern" (223).

58. For discussion of the various terms Augustine uses in his account of desire, see Robert Innes, "Integrating the Self through the Desire of God," *Augustinian Studies* 28, no. 1 (1997): 67–109. Innes emphasizes that, for Augustine, "the Christian God is not only the end of the soul's journey but also supplies the way. We must therefore properly

menacing fear of losing the good against our will, a good that itself seems always beyond our desire and outside ourselves. Arendt writes:

> Happiness *(beatitudo)* consists in possession, in having and holding *(habere et tenere)* our good, and even more in being sure of not losing it.... The trouble with human happiness is that it is constantly beset by fear. It is not the lack of possessing but the safety of possession that is at stake. This enormous importance of security—that nothing subject to loss can ever become an object of possession—is due to the condition of man and the objects he desires. (10)

Love seeks the good, indeed the *summum bonum*, that casts out anxiety and fear. As such, it is the good that cannot be lost against your will (even in death) that is most to be desired for Augustine.

Citing Augustine's famous passage on mourning the death of a friend in the *Confessions*, Arendt asserts, "there can be no doubt that death, and not just fear of death, was the most crucial experience in Augustine's life" (13). As Augustine would later put it, "the whole duration of our life is nothing but a progression towards death" (*CD* 13.10). What Augustine yearns for is that life where "our existence will have no death, our knowledge no error, our love no obstacle."[59] It is in the face of death, Arendt claims, Augustine abandons the Stoic sense of self-sufficiency and *apatheia*. But this is a difficult turn. Augustine can make it only by becoming "an enigma to myself, and herein lies my sickness" (*Conf.* 10.33). The terror of death and the perpetual living in the "not yet" ultimately drives him from Stoic self-reliance to the Pauline assurances of resurrection. But, for Arendt, this is to get ahead of herself in framing Augustine's "pretheological" voice. Augustine's rhetoric of desire, for Arendt, is simply not Christian. It is part of his lingering philosophy. The answer to love's question, to the fear of losing what is good, can only be a philosophically conceived eternity.

This neo-Platonic inheritance, Arendt claims, pushes Augustine "to strip the world and all temporal things of their value and to make them relative"

---

speak not simply of desire for God but rather desire of God. God is both the object of our desire and he who places this desire for himself within us" (72).

59. The original German text of the dissertation contains a reference to this passage (*Love and Saint Augustine*, 10n6). Arendt also cites *DT* 13.8.11: "Since all men want to be happy, they want also to be immortal if they know what they want; for otherwise they could not be happy" (*Love and Saint Augustine*, 10–11), and *S.* 306.7: "The true life is one that is both everlasting and happy" (10).

(14). Drawing comparisons to Plotinus's projection of the good into eternity, she quotes Augustine:

> Who will hold [the heart], and fix it so that it may stand still for a little while and catch for a moment the splendor of eternity which stands still forever, and compare this with temporal moments that never stand still, and see that it is incomparable ... but that all this while in the eternal, nothing passes but the whole is present. (*Conf.* 11.11.13 [15])

The tragedy of the world quickly becomes apparent on this view of eternity. Lovers sacrifice the true good and become lovers of the world, enslaved by the multitude of its false and fleeting promises. Again, Arendt tries to capture the flow of Augustine's argument:

> In its flight from death, the craving for permanence clings to the very things sure to be lost in death. This love has the wrong object, one that continually disappoints its craving. ... Mortal man, who has been placed into the world ... and must leave it, instead clings to it and in the process turns the world itself into a vanishing one, that is, one due to vanish with death. (17)[60]

At this point in Arendt's exposition, she turns to the two kinds of love that famously emerge in Augustine's writings. Love that turns to the world, the

---

60. Arendt's implicit (and at times explicit) dialogue with Martin Heidegger is apparent throughout the dissertation, particularly in the relationship between Augustine's account of neighbor-love and conversion and Heidegger's notions of "care," "Being-with-others," "authentic resolve," and the attempt to unify the fragmented experience of time (in the flow of past, present, and future). As her editors point out, however, Arendt rejects the place of death in Heidegger's thought and (alongside the reversal of Augustinian Christianity) seeks "a reversal of the ontology of death" (181). Resources for this reversal, the editors note, ironically are found by Arendt's appropriation of Augustinian *caritas* as a 'miracle' despite death that grounds the possibility of "reconstituting relationships through friendship, forgiveness, and social bonding" (*Love and Saint Augustine*, 181). On the fragmentation of time, see Martin Heidegger, *Being and Time* (Oxford: Basil Blackwell, 1962), 236–37, 279–80. For a detailed treatment of Heidegger's seminars on Augustine, see Thomas Kisiel, *The Genesis of Heidegger's "Being and Time"* (Berkeley and Los Angeles: University of California Press, 1995), 192–219. For illuminating accounts of Heidegger's reading of Augustine, see Brian Elliot, "Existential Scepticism and Christian Life in Early Heidegger," *Heythrop Journal* 45 (2004): 273–89, and Peter J. Burnell, "Is the Augustinian Heaven Inhuman? The Arguments of Martin Heidegger and Hannah Arendt," *Augustinian Studies* 30, no. 2 (1999): 283–92.

wrong object, is *cupiditas*. In the end, it is slavery. Love that turns to eternity and "the absolute future," the right object, is *caritas*. In the end, it is freedom.[61] Here, Arendt claims, is the force of Augustine's warning, "Love, but be careful what you love."

All love, we are reminded by Arendt, remains a craving desire, a movement of the will from isolation to possession in happiness, from dispersion to recollection. Arendt recognizes that, for Augustine, human beings love of necessity, whether as *cupiditas* or *caritas*. Unlike the Stoics, he cannot advocate the suppression of desire itself (even if right desire is not to be fixed upon things of this world). In directing our dynamic love, we actually constitute ourselves and choose who we will be. Arendt here offers a significant gloss:

> Hence, in *cupiditas* or in *caritas*, we decide about our abode, whether we wish to belong to this world or to the world to come. . . . The question of who he is can only be resolved by the object of his desire. . . . Strictly speaking, he who does not love and desire at all is a nobody. . . . If [humanity] could be said to have an essential nature at all, it would be lack of self-sufficiency. Hence, he is driven to break out of his isolation by means of love—whether *cupiditas* turns him into a denizen of this world or *caritas* makes him live in the absolute future where he will be denizen of the world-to-come. Since only love can constitute either world as man's home, 'this world is for the faithful [who do not love the world] what the desert was for the people of Israel'—they live not in houses but in tents. Would it not be better to love the world in *cupiditas* and be at home? Why should we make a desert out of this world? The justification for this extraordinary enterprise can only lie in a deep dissatisfaction with what the world can give its lovers. (18)

While this passage hints at deeper troubles that await Augustine's efforts to find a place for neighbor-love, the problem for Augustine at this point is the very notion of love as desire. Arendt wonders whether Augustine can reconcile the "internal" motion of desire with an "external" object. How can this gap between lover and beloved be overcome? How can the highest good be both eternal and internal? This problem, according to Arendt, is exacerbated

---

61. See *Confessions* 13.7.8: "To whom can I expound, and with what words can I express, the weight of cupidity pulling us downwards into the precipitous abyss and the lifting up of love given by your Spirit who was 'borne above the waters'? . . . The impurity of our spirit flows downwards because of our love of anxieties, and the holiness which is yours draws us upwards in a love of freedom from anxiety."

for Augustine because the "external" object cannot be seen to have its origin in the self yet must resonate within the self.

Given that Augustine's anthropology is committed to the claim that self-discovery depends on being discovered by God, there must be a teleological connection between the desiring self and the highest good. Plotinus, who provided Augustine with such a compelling vision of "man's utter strangeness in the world he is born into," can no longer be his guide (22). The "noble serenity" of Plotinus's divinization of the soul cannot still the fears of the Christian Augustine. A different kind of love than *appetitus* must be conceived, a love that is truly divine in origin.

Arendt hints that Augustine tries to resolve the problem by imagining God's love as "circulating within us" (*S.* 163.1.1, Arendt 21). Perhaps eternity, briefly muses Arendt, functions differently for Augustine than for Plotinus. In the *Confessions*, Augustine makes it clear that God is his helper, the guide of right self-love and compassion. It is this God who brings unity to his multiplicity, allowing him to give "a coherent account of my disintegrated self, for when I turned away from you, the one God, and pursued a multitude of things, I went to pieces" (*Conf.* 2.1.1). Again, one might expect Arendt to discuss Augustine's perplexing claim that even here on earth God is "more intimately present to me than my innermost being [*interior intimo meo*]" (*Conf.* 3.6.11). But the self that is to be loved, Arendt quickly argues, is the true self projected into the future that stands in relation to God in eternity. It is this self, the inner invisible self of the future, that belongs to the invisible God. The human mode of existence, "which is mortality," must be transcended for the divine mode of existence, "which is eternity" (28).

Arendt discerns a danger in this attempt to make sense of a love that desires, of a self that extends itself but does not attain its good. This leads Augustine to a view of temporality that gets in the way of being, a mortal self in the way of an immortal self. There is "no manifestation of an original interconnectedness between man and God" (30). Augustine writes: "Hence so that you too may be, transcend time" (*IoEv.*, 38.10, Arendt 29). Again, Arendt's gloss here is telling because she claims that Augustine himself mischaracterizes the true nature of Christian love. Arendt writes: "It should be obvious that this kind of self-denial, even if it is called *caritas*, is actually pseudo-Christian. . . . By anticipating eternity (the absolute future) man desires his own future self and denies the I-myself he finds in earthly reality" (30). Echoing critics like Martha Nussbaum and Annette Baier, Arendt concurs "from this it follows that man should not love in this life, lest he lose in eternal life" (30). For Arendt, the structure of love conceived as desire can only be calmed by the Augustinian vision of eternity that now jeopardizes the meaningfulness of the worldly self through its denial. Arendt calls this self-hatred, "the last, desperate consequence" of Augustine's account of love that desires but never attains its own good (31).

Arendt interrupts her reading of Augustine at this point with a brief but revealing excursus of her own interpretation of Pauline Christianity. Augustine's self-alienation from the world is "much more radical than any-thing requested or even possible in orthodox Christianity" (41). She writes: "For Paul love is by no means a desire that stands in need of fulfillment. . . . The reason that *caritas* is greater than faith and hope is precisely because *caritas* contains its own reward and will remain what it is in this life and the next" (31). As such, like Timothy Jackson, Arendt finds that the "crucial im-portance that love of neighbor had for Paul as the possibility of 'perfection' even in this world is not shared by Augustine" (31).

For Arendt, love as desire lies at the root of Augustine's distinction between that which is to be enjoyed (*frui*) and loved for its own sake *(propter se ipsum)* and that which is to be used (*uti*) and loved for the sake of something else *(propter)*. According to Arendt, to conceive of love as desire always leads to the problematic alternatives of use or enjoyment. Arendt reasons: "If the object of desire is God, the world is related to God by using it. Since it is used, the world loses its independent meaningfulness and thus ceases to tempt man" (33). *Amor mundi*, so to speak, competes with *amor Dei* for attention and loses.

In this first Augustinian formulation of love, the world, Arendt writes with telling pathos, "loses its awesome character" (34). A provisional sense of the world as a means to the eternal end secures a certain kind of function for the world. But this function is again displaced by the priority of the absolute future in determining one's relation to the world. Arendt recognizes that the world for Augustine is not really a means to the end in this first formulation. The final end does structure how one is to love in the world:

> In the absolute future [humanity] has at the same time acquired a point of reference that lies, in principle, outside the world itself, and which therefore can now serve as regulator of all things inside the world as well as of the relationships by which they are interconnected. (37)

Returning from the absolute future, everything in the world, including the self, is now a thing among things that assumes a role in the governed reality that is ordered toward the "highest good." Things are to be loved proportionately, in right order and proper measure, and under a mode of living marked primarily by enduring hope and anticipation. This "order of love" (*CD* 15.22) comes from the absolute future and is not given by any immanent or prior relation between the world and God. This God, who stands only in the future, can not secure the worthiness of the world. Nygren claimed that Augustine's appeals to neighbor love seem "like an alien intrusion, present only because the Christian tradition requires it" (*AE*, 500). Similarly, for Arendt, the command to "love thy neighbor" in the Augustinian framework "appears here like a *deus ex machina*" (39). Augustine has been led astray by the account of love as desire and allows the absolute future to be the only horizon of experience.

In fact, the idea of love as desire appears to contradict itself, breaking under the weight of the opposition between *uti* and *frui*. It has yielded a love that is no longer "determined by any particular object but by the general order of everything that is" (39). This is the love that is "swept towards the same destination as that to which the whole flood of love is directed" (*DDC* 1.22.21). It takes account only of those things that are below or above and not that which is "beside and next to me, I-myself and my neighbor" (40). That which is *supra nos*, once again, not only relativizes but also obscures that which is *iuxta nos*. And, yet, Arendt recognizes that Augustine is driven by the biblical injunction to connect love of neighbor and life in the world with the happiness of the absolute future. Love as desire, when tied to his Stoic and neo-Platonic formulations of eternity, has brought Augustine to a conceptual dead-end and bypassed the true love of neighbor.

This dead end, Arendt concludes, is manifest in Augustine's tortured explanation of the command to "love thy enemies." For Augustine, Christians love even their enemies because they have no reason to "fear them, for they cannot take away from us what we love" (*DDC* 1.29.30). On this account, love of enemies is not really love at all, but a consequence of the fearless and abstract calm inspired by the objectivity of the "highest good." Augustine loves his neighbor and his enemy "in sublime indifference regardless of what or who he is," precisely because of "the notion of God as *summum bonum*"

(43, 43n24).[62] The neighbor is relevant not in concrete reality but only as a possible companion or, more likely, a mutual help in the enjoyment of God. This love, Arendt writes, is a degradation of love "which contradicts the central place love occupies in Augustine's thought" (43). Another source of love, "altogether different from appetites and desires" must be found (44). Love as desire oriented to the absolute future is inadequate.

In the second part of the essay, Arendt explores a different possibility for Augustine. In the first part, she focused on Augustine's orientation to the future as a function of love as desire. This focus, however, neglects Augustine's equal concern with the relationship between the past and desire, between happiness and that which is prior to worldly experience. The absolute future, Arendt claims, is "guaranteed by a kind of absolute past" (47). In order to desire "we must know what happiness is and that this knowledge of the desired object necessarily precedes the urge to possess it" (46). It is within this context of memory and desire that "knowledge appears as the 'referring back' to the self for whose sake man aims at whatever he desires" (46). Arendt's Augustine, for all of his orientation to the future, was also a philosopher of the past, of remembrance and recollection. He famously argues: "Just as we call memory the faculty of remembering things past, thus we may without absurdity also call memory what in the present enables the mind to be present to itself that it may understand by virtue of its own thought" (*DT* 11.7.12, Arendt 46). Memory preserves the past by bringing it to the present. Indeed, in making the past present, "memory transforms the past into a future possibility" (48). Desire exists between past and future, transcending the present even as the absolute future "turns out to be the ultimate past" (49). In this context, the question about our love as craving "does not turn about goals and *whither* I shall go, but about origins and *whence* I come, and not about the faculty of desire but the faculty of remembrance" (48).

---

62. I reserve my criticism of Arendt for the next chapter. But I should point out that Arendt here misses the force of Augustine's passage on the love of enemies by disrupting the flow of his argument which he later extends to the love of angels. The next line reads: "If they turned to [God], it is inevitable that they would love [God] as the goodness which is the source of all happiness and love us as joint participants in such goodness" (*DDC* 1.29.30). The accent falls not so much on the fear of losing the good but on the concern that others share in this good.

In remembering the absolute past, the self can be guided not so much by a love for God *(amor Dei)* as such but by a love of the love that God bestows in the past *(amor amoris Dei)*. To remember this love, this past, is to "confess" it. This confession changes the mode of Augustinian desire from craving to a different mode of creaturely dependence in recollection.[63] The self extends itself through memory, looking back to the origin and forward to the return.

Augustine's Creator is still outside of humanity, but now both in front and behind. God is the Supreme Being of the future *(summe esse)* and the Primal Being of the past *(primitus esse)*. "You, O Lord," Augustine confesses, "who live forever and in whom nothing dies, since before the beginning of the centuries and before anything can be called 'before,' you are" (*Conf.* 1.6.9, Arendt 49–50). To love rightly is, then, to move forward by returning. Love as desire for the future, which was determined by the fear of death, is now reconfigured by remembrance and a "gratitude for life" (52). The relationship to the Creator is no longer contingent on desire (as is the case for the volitional desire for the "highest good"). Importantly, this relatedness "as such does not depend upon what man does or fails to do in *caritas* or *cupiditas*; it is a constitutive element of human existence and indifferent to human conduct" (53). In turning to the past, however, the self still anticipates a future that will once again make the past available.

Memory allows Augustine to escape the conceptual dead-end of love as desire for the highest good in the absolute future, but it preserves the problem of loving in a world that is not representative of one's "true being" (57). Augustine remains a "question to himself" in such a way that he continues to "ask himself out of the world in his quest for 'true being'" (58). Temporality remains as important a problem for the self in strict relation to the past as the self in strict relation to the future. Both equally devalue mundane life and the concrete neighbor in the contemplation of eternity. Again, Arendt continues to identify Greek sources that compete for Augustine's Christian attention.

63. James Wetzel summarizes the centrality of this view for Augustine: "We appropriate grace in recollection, and through recollection we are able to effect the gradual convergence of virtue and self-determination" (*LV*, 125). Wetzel's account of memory and grace in terms of the "temporal extension of our identities" dislodges the centrality of debates about compatibilism and follows something more like Arendt's account (ibid., 138). Still, for Wetzel, Augustine's redemptive use of memory is more successful than Arendt allows.

Arendt's brief discussion of Augustine's appropriation of Platonic cosmology and theories of time, particularly in terms of the relation between the wholeness of Being and individual parts of the universe, need not detain us. What matters for this second reading of Augustine, even without love as desire, is the possibility that the world can be both God's creation and an entirely human world, "which constitutes itself by habitation and love [*diligere*]" (66). God's creation becomes "worldly" in those who love the world and seek to make it their home. Those dependent upon God, constantly referring back in memory to creation, can remain strangers in the world. But, just as the desire for the future yielded insecurity and love of the world, remembrance can become forgetfulness and yield the same insecurity and love of the world *as worldly*. It is this forgetfulness that can now constitute an immanent world, enclosed within the love of the world to the neglect of the true "divine fabric of the world" (74).

The worldly self neglects both the "before" and the "not yet." Arendt writes: "When man sets up the world anew by his love of the world, he simultaneously sets himself up as one who belongs to the world. . . . That is why pride is the perverse imitation of God's grandeur, because it lets man imagine himself a creator" (81). Creatures, then, can mistake "the before" as much as "the future" because of their *cupiditas*. The self covets the world, loves it for its own sake, and mistakes the creation for the Creator. Through habit more than passion per se, "covetousness constantly seeks to cover this real source by insisting that man is 'of the world,' thereby turning the world itself into the source. . . . Thus man's own nature lures him into the service of 'things made' instead of service of their Maker" (82).[64] The original relation of dependence persists, but *caritas* now requires a movement of God's grace to remind us of our chosen death. Divine grace must now call us out of this world of our self-making. More natural helps are given in God's providence. Through the law of conscience and the ever presence of physical death itself, the world can become strange and recall the self *coram Deo*. But, for Augustine, the self habituated to the world in its corruption needs further assistance. The law comes from afar and cannot bring the creature back to God. Grace must come nearer, and, here for the first time, Arendt introduces

---

64. Augustine writes: "Do not love to dwell in the building, but dwell in the Builder" (*EnPs.* 141, 15; Arendt, *Love and St. Augustine,* 82).

the significance of the Incarnation for Augustine as the notion of a God that becomes the neighbor. In Christ, God comes near again to the creation and makes possible the life of *caritas* through faith (90). This important move, however, is held off until the third part of her essay.

For now, in relation to the neighbor, serious problems remain. The turn to the past does not mitigate the problem of worldly self-denial in looking "beyond the world" (94). The self, even the self restored in Christ and called to the imitation of God, remains isolated from the neighbor because "for the lover who loves as God loves, the neighbor ceases to be anything but a creature of God. The lover meets a man defined by God's love simply as God's creation" (94). Arendt writes: "What we cannot understand is how, through this love by which we deny both ourselves and the world, another person can still be considered our neighbor, that is, as someone specifically connected to us" (95). The structure of the turn to the past has led to the same call for self-denial that obscured the relevance of the neighbor in the turn to the future. Arendt summarizes:

> Since man is both "from God" and "to God," he grasps his own being in God's presence. This return though recapturing his own being, and the isolation achieved in it, is the sole source of neighborly love. And just as I do not love the self I made in belonging to the world, I also do not love my neighbor in the concrete and worldly encounter with him.... I love something in him, that is, the very thing which, of himself, he is not: "For you love in him not what he is, but what you wish that he may be" (*IoEp.* 7.10). This denial corresponds to "willing that you may be" and "carrying off to God." I deny the other person so as to break through to his real being, just as in searching for myself I deny myself. (95–96)

Love of neighbor, for Augustine, can not mean a loving of the other in his or her mortality, "but to love what is eternal in him, his very own 'whence'" (96). In short, "*the lover reaches beyond the beloved to God in whom alone both his existence and his love have meaning*" (96, emphasis mine). Love of neighbor is merely an occasion to love God in the neighbor.

As we saw in her interpretation of love as desire oriented to the future, Christian love becomes an indifferent mockery of love. The Christian love of enemy again becomes a degraded love. Echoing Freud's critique of the universality of Christian love, Arendt writes: "The Christian can thus love all people because each one is only an occasion, and that occasion can be everyone. Love proves its strength precisely in considering even the enemy and even the sinner" (97).[65] In the end, "It is not really the neighbor who is loved in this love of neighbor—it is love itself. Thus the neighbor's relevance as neighbor . . . is overcome and the individual is left in isolation" (97). The Augustinian lover simply "must love love itself" because "in loving love, he is loving God" (*IoEp.* 9.10). Can Augustine escape these two trains of thought that have left the neighbor irrelevant? Arendt turns in the third part of her essay toward such a possibility.

The split that Arendt describes between time and eternity in Augustine's thought underlies his problematic accounts of the individualized self, standing between absolute past and absolute future. The self can "see his neighbor as well as himself only from an absolute distance" and so both the worldly self and the worldly neighbor are forgotten (98). And, yet, Arendt ponders, why does the love of neighbor "play so large a role even in these originally alien contexts of Augustine's work?" (98). There must be a different origin, or context, for the persistence of the theme of neighbor-love in Augustine. Arendt locates this different origin in the experience of the community of faith, grounded in two historical communities. It is these historical communities that are to be decisive for the self and the neighbor.

The experience of God in the absolute past or the absolute future had alienated the self from the world and the neighbor. The neighbor cannot appear in true relevance in either scheme. At this point, Arendt claims that the reality of the neighbor and the command to love the neighbor are secured by "a historically pre-existing reality, obliging as such even for redeeming death of Christ" (99). Faith, in this context, is not so much the restless self inquiring into its own being, but turning to "the factuality of history and to the past as such" (99). In this past:

> The redeeming death of Christ did not redeem an individual but the whole world *(mundus)*, understood as the man-made world. However faith may isolate the individual, the object of faith (redemption by Christ) has come into a given world and thus into a given community. (99)

This community, the community established in Christ, is the *civitas Dei.* Another community, the community established in the common descent of Adam, is the *civitas terrena.* It is in the relation between these two commu-

---

65. For Freud, "a love that does not discriminate seems to me forfeit a part of its own value, by doing an injustice to its object; and secondly, not all men are worthy of love" (*Civilization and its Discontents*, 57).

nities that Arendt's Augustine locates a twofold origin for the significance of the neighbor.

In order to understand the nature of the community established in Christ, however, Arendt first emphasizes the importance of the common descent from Adam. It is in Adam that Augustine sees a "foundation of a definite and obligatory equality among all people" (100). Augustine's God "chose to create the human race from one single man," a creation that united humanity "in fellowship by a natural likeness" and a "kingship in the unity of concord" (*CD* 14.1). This equality in Adam creates a kinship among humanity, not in terms of traits or talents but "of situation" (100). The self in Adam can not be a self alone but is a member of the fellowship *(societas)* of humanity. Adam himself was created "not, certainly, that he might be alone and bereft of human society, but that, by this means, the unity of society and the bond of concord might be commended to him more forcefully" (*CD* 12.22). Peter Brown emphasizes the importance of this common kinship in Adam as "the mould into which Augustine, in his middle age, will pour his continuing preoccupation with friendship, with true relations between human beings."[66] This friendly equality and this kinship, as Arendt points out, are both concealed and revealed by sin.

The self can only imagine this equality and kinship by imagining the other's similar situation before God as a sinner. All people stand before God as equally sinful, and this sinfulness "necessarily attaches to everyone" (102). The creature derives its being from the absolute "unworldly past," but the worldly equality of humanity stretches not back to an absolute past but to the "most distant historic past" (103). Arendt paradoxically writes: "The human race as such originates in Adam and not in the Creator. . . . The human community is thereby a society from and with the dead; in other words this community is historical" (103). Human society is, then, a curious mix of grace-filled creation and sinful history. It is this strange worldliness that is to be transformed by the heavenly city.

Arendt notes that Augustine's reading of Adam and Christ locates his account of neighbor-love in an entirely different context from the lonely philosophical meditations of the individual concerned with Being. In Adam, humanity understands itself "by generation and not by creation" (104). The world becomes "familiar and belongs to him" (104). Love of neighbor can now be understood as an authentic feature of mutuality and shared nature.

66. Brown, *Augustine of Hippo*, 220.

And, yet, this love is grounded not in shared dependence on the Creator but in common sinfulness and rebellion against the Creator. This equality "of situation" raises a problem for the believer. How can those given the grace of faith, those who know their dependence on a source out of the world, ground their love in "a past that is to be totally eradicated?" (104).

The answer, Arendt reasons, can only be found in a historical fact that parallels the common descent of Adam: "God's revelation in Christ" (105). In Christ, "all are redeemed together, just as all were found together in the same situation [in Adam]" (105). The universality of sin is taken up and transformed by the humility of the Incarnation. "While the kinship of all people prior to Christ was acquired from Adam by generation, all are now made equal by the revealed grace of God that manifests everyone's equally sinful past" (106). The historical past (the worldliness of Adam) is not "wiped out," but "is newly experienced and reinterpreted out of the new situation of man redeemed" (105). In this reinterpretation, however, the preexisting past continues independently, and the neighbor "is the constant reminder of one's own sin, which does not cease to be sin because divine grace has made it a thing of the past" (105). The neighbor, loved now as a fellow sinner, still remains "a sign of our own peril along with the reminder of our past" (106). The very intelligibility of the heavenly city of God (and the possibility of grace) is dependent upon the earthly city (and the reality of sin). Arendt writes: "It is against the world, not simply without it, that the message of salvation has come to all people" (106). The world is relevant, "not because the Christian still lives in it, to a certain extent by mistake, but on the ground of his constant tie to the past and thereby to original kinship" (107). The very structure of love is related to this existential sense of struggle and danger in the world. The neighbor remains a "constant reminder of one's own sin," a troubling source of equality and interdependence that nevertheless makes "human relations definite and explicit" (110). Redemption requires that "what was once necessary by generation has now become a danger involving a decision" (110). It is a decision for God and against death that now involves the neighbor. But it is a decision that must be made by the self in its isolation. According to Arendt, "the human race as such is not in danger, but every individual is" (111). The neighbor now "appears either as one in whom God has already worked his grace ... or he appears as one who is still entangled in sin" (106). This duality once again threatens the relevance of the neighbor *as neighbor*. For Arendt, Augustine is still unable to view the neighbor as he or she happens to be in the world. For the Christian, to love the neighbor is "to bring one's neighbor to this explicitness of his own being, to 'carry him off to God' [*rapere ad Deum*]" (108). Genuine neighbor-love consists in drawing the neighbor into the stream of God's love.

Philosophical solitude is no longer possible in this theological context (as it was in the context of love as desire in relation to the absolute past or the absolute future). The concreteness of the reality of grace in Christ "gives a new meaning to human togetherness—defense against the world" (108). It is this defensiveness that lays the foundation for a new social life that "is defined by mutual love [*diligere invicem*], which replaces mutual dependence" (108). In the faithful body of Christ, the neighbor can become explicit in his or her own being and a new moral community arises that unifies and stabilizes the will in the power of love. The neighbor is no longer a fellow sinner, but a member of the community of the redeemed—where the neighbor becomes "my brother" (108). *Caritas* grows only in the community of faith grounded in the body of Christ. It is a collective body that contains each member within itself, suffering with each other, united by a common love of the God of Jesus Christ. Arendt writes: "Mutual love becomes self-love since the being of one's own self is identified with the being of Christ, that is, with the being of the body in which it shares as a member" (109). Arendt recognizes that Augustine remains aware of the ambiguity of being human in the world, consistently expressed by the intermingling of the two cities in his writings (*CD* 11.1). The point to be stressed, Arendt maintains, is the way in which the "necessity of *caritas* is maintained against any tendency to isolate the believer altogether" (109). This love still remains contingent on the neighbor's own relation to God, but it enlarges the self's desire through the mutuality of the body of Christ.

Problems remain even on this third attempt at Augustine's doctrine of love. In loving the neighbor, what is at work is a love for God at work in the neighbor, rendering it relative to the activity of grace in the life of the neighbor. Rather than securing the relevance of the neighbor *qua* neighbor and assuring the relevance of the creation, even the coming of God in Christ finally transfers attention away from the neighbor to God. Arendt writes: "We are commanded to love our neighbor, to practice mutual love, only because in so doing we love Christ. . . . When Augustine frequently quotes Paul's words that love never fails, he means solely the love of God, or Christ, for which all human neighborly love can only provide the impetus" (111). In a passage that could have been written by Anders Nygren or Paul Ramsey, Arendt writes that for Augustine:

I never love my neighbor for his own sake, only for the sake of divine grace. This indirectness, which is unique to love of neighbor, puts an even more radical stop to the self-evident living together in the earthly city. This indirectness turns my relation to my neighbor into a mere passage for the direct relation of God himself. (111)

This indirectness allows the believer "to grasp the whole being which lies in God's presence" (111). The fellowship of saints, then, is a wandering collection of individuals—truly resident aliens—knit together by the love of God as a defense against the world. For Arendt, the individual self is invented by Augustine, and the neighbor comes to have relevance. But it is a discovery and a relevance that is determined wholly in relation to God and the newly founded community of Christ. We meet the other as a common member of the human race, but "it is only in the individual's isolation in God's presence that he becomes our neighbor" (112). The other as other, she claims, "does not come into this field of vision at all" (112).[67]

For Arendt, the twofold relation of the self to the other, as a given member of sinful humanity tied to the historical past and as a chosen member of the new community of faith in God, expresses the fundamental contradiction of Augustinian neighbor-love. Dean Hammer nicely summarizes this difference and its relevance for my larger project:

67. This claim resonates with postmodern critics of Augustine in contemporary political theory. For example, Romand Coles argues that the Augustinian Christian imagination is "profoundly blind to the possible being and value of radical alterity in people who live resolutely outside the Christian story. That which lies beyond or rejects the Christian tale is, in this beyondness or rejection, understood as tending toward nothingness and evil. This malignancy at the heart of the loving gift rears its head in *City of God*, when Augustine writes that to love my neighbor as myself is to try to give him or her what I myself most need and want, namely the will to love God. Hence, the generosity engendered by the Augustinian Christian narrative is one whose overarching aim is given entirely from within itself. The profoundest goals, meanings, and textures of the generous act do not emerge from a receptive encounter with the other that risks—through opening onto aspects of alien needs, perceptions, desires, pleasures, and understandings—transgressing the self-enclosures of one's own narratives in ways that might transfigure the movement of giving" (*Rethinking Generosity*, 3). I return to Coles in the next chapter, where I draw a connection between Coles's metaphor of a generosity that is separated from receptivity as a kind of *theft* and Augustine's own account of the false autonomous love that is a kind of theft.

There remains a critical difference here between a Kantian world citizen and an Augustinian kinship. A consciousness of ourselves as world citizens, for Kant, proceeds through the enlarged thought of an autonomous being who can uncorruptly take others into account. For Augustine, our inherent corruption always requires a transcendent third through which we recognize ourselves as sharing a fate with others. Arendt never lost sight of the importance of this mediation, but she never resolved its nature, either. Arendt could not seek recourse in an Augustinian God.[68]

According to Arendt, it is not simply Augustine's failure to overcome his Stoicized Platonic heritage. That charge of otherworldliness is common enough.[69] Rather, for Arendt, it is woven even into the triune rendering of Augustine's God. Thomas Breidenthal echoes Hammer's point:

> For Arendt, Christianity's anti-politicality is one with its belief in the incarnation of God in Jesus. If love of neighbor means not only regarding the neighbor as an end in himself, but also regarding interaction with any and all neighbors as an end in itself, then the Divine Word's appearance on the scene as neighbor can only mean that neighborlove is about to be made the instrument of its own demise. To state Arendt's view plainly: if God has become my neighbor, then love of God has outsmarted love of neighbor on its home turf. The claim of Jesus is greater than all other human claims . . . so to love him as neighbor is to be drawn away from all other human loves, except as they serve and repeat the love of Jesus. But since Jesus-my-neighbor is also God, the love of Jesus as neighbor effects the absorption of neighborlove into love of God.[70]

For Breidenthal, this reading turns the Incarnation on its head and misses the Augustinian claim that God comes in the kenotic form of the servant Jesus. It is this compassionate God, not an unknown or essentialist one, which shapes Augustine's theology—perhaps even to the point of an intra-Trinitarian *kenosis*.[71] By becoming our neighbor in salvation history, Jesus

---

68. Hammer, "Freedom and Fatefulness," 97.

69. On this particular point, see Kirk, *Vision of God*, 133–37.

70. Breidenthal, "Arendt, Augustine, and the Politics of Incarnation," 491.

71. In fact, based on a reading of *DT* 15, Peter Burnell argues that since "the interrelationship among the Persons of God is understood as a Trinity of charity, the Incarnation is logically prior to the Trinity" (*Augustinian Person*, 121). There is no change in God because "the relationships within the Trinity are precisely eternal in their reference to the

does not stand between neighbor and neighbor, but "engagement with the neighbor opens the door to engagement with Jesus" and "by implication, engagement with Jesus catapults one into further engagement with other neighbors."[72] Jesus is "the neighbor who is able to give us the means to address other neighbors out of abundance rather than out of lack."[73] Rather than either being morally paralyzed by the infinite claims of the neighbor or spiritually distracted by the infinite claims of God, the Augustinian self loves the neighbor in God who lovingly identifies with the neighbor as God's own. Breidenthal's resolution, which relies on the two natures in the person of Jesus, implies that love of God and love of neighbor can coincide in loving God by loving the neighbor. A response to Jesus, then, always involves a response to God and neighbor. They are not univocally the same response, but, because of the Incarnation, they are bound together. According to Breidenthal, "if there is a tension between the two loves, it is a tension only the saints can know since love of God and love of neighbor are both constrained and broken under the condition of sin: this side of the Fall, both loves are the gift of grace."[74]

In the next two chapters, I examine the plausibility that this view is Augustine's own, and more directly, assess its moral and political implications. It is one that sees moral motivations in terms of the "nonpossessive *eros*" mentioned in my introduction and one that distinguishes love for God and love for neighbor but insists the two loves are correlative. In so doing, I am able to overcome the two strongest challenges to my account of an Augustinian ethics of democratic citizenship.

Incarnation" (121). In Protestant dogmatics, Bruce McCormack has proposed a controversial reading of Karl Barth's doctrine of God that makes a similar move regarding God's eternal self-determination to be God with us. Or, more precisely, the pre-incarnate Son is always already the *logos incarnandus*, the Son who will become incarnate. According to McCormack, "the decision for the covenant of grace is the ground of God's triunity, and, therefore, of the eternal generation of the Son and of the eternal procession of the Holy Spirit from Father and Son" ("Grace and Being: The Role of God's Gracious Election in Karl Barth's Theological Ontology," in *The Cambridge Companion to Karl Barth*, ed. John Webster [Cambridge: Cambridge University Press, 2000], 92–110, at 103). On this view, Barth offers a correction to Calvin's Augustinian doctrine of double predestination because Barth holds that Jesus Christ is the "eternal, *ontic* ground of election" (92).

72. Breidenthal, "Arendt, Augustine, and the Politics of Incarnation," 497.

73. Ibid., 499.

74. Breidenthal, personal correspondence, May 30, 2002.

5

Love as Political Virtue
"Stoics" and the Problem of Passion

*We are on a road which is not a road from place
to place but a road of the affections.*

AUGUSTINE, *On Christian Doctrine* 1.17, Robertson

*To be sure, this power of sympathy derives from the stream
of friendship. But where does it flow to, whither is it bound?*

AUGUSTINE, *Confessions* 3.2.3

Hannah Arendt's provocative reading of Augustine issues strong challenges to a political ethic that moves beyond the formality of liberal reciprocity to recognize and affirm love as a political virtue. Her arguments threaten any such ethic, whether justified on secular or religious grounds. They crystallize the two primary concerns that repeatedly emerged in my discussions of a political morality that expands concern about epistemology and democratic justification by drawing attention to the motivational components of civic virtue. My final two chapters address these challenges in turn by looking more closely at Augustine's interrelated account of love and sin as a basic feature of his moral psychology. It is a moral psychology aptly described by Peter Brown as a "psychology of 'delight.'"[1] In this chapter, I consider the *problem of passion*, responding to Arendt's concerns that the capricious intimacy of love is not suitable for the political world of action and appearance. In the next chapter, I consider the *problem of God*, responding to

---

1. Brown, *Augustine of Hippo*, 148.

Arendt's concerns that Augustinian eudaimonism issues in a world-denying and individualistic form of apolitical piety. In both chapters, I suggest several points at which a political theology that prominently features ordinate loving coheres with Augustinian civic liberalism. These points have the further advantage of expanding the textual range of Augustinian liberalism.

Arendt herself saw the value of such readings, especially in her attention to *On Christian Doctrine* and the *Confessions*. Even in her dissertation, however, one can identify her attraction to a stream in the liberal tradition that devalues both love and emotion in order to protect the public realm of politics. Rhetorically positioned in terms of rationality and affirmation of the world, these efforts promise a clarity and rigor necessary for a more just politics that overcomes the heat of unstable emotions and religious desire. I have already contrasted this position with a number of feminist and Christian authors who highlight the need for a liberal civic virtue that recognizes the extent to which human beings are vulnerable and dependent and finds at least some emotional capacities as themselves politically salutary. These efforts typically affirm a call to solidarity and mutual recognition as necessary for the preservation of liberty and equality. They defend the compassion of love as a proper moral orientation for democratic citizens without commitment to excessively erotic or communitarian politics. They also do not aim at the paternalistic cure of souls in ways that liberals rightly fear will abandon justice.

In order to connect Augustinianism more fully with this alternative, I return to an important feature of Augustine that has been overshadowed and distorted by realist and Rawlsian interpretations. I have argued these interpretations marginalize love, by making it either merely eschatological or merely private. They tend to valorize sin by highlighting this aspect of Augustine's thought as the most significant contribution of Augustinianism for liberal politics. To be sure, Augustine's anthropology has been mined for purposes beyond the "tragic sense of life" or the "pessimism" that realist interpreters attach to his doctrine of original sin with the goal of deflating the pretensions of both politics and virtue. General interpretations of Augustine highlight areas of his anthropology that proved formative for Latin theology. These include the nature of the will, the interiority of the self, and the relation of the body and the soul. These issues remain prominent features of contemporary philosophy of religion.

Theologically minded interpreters offer suggestive ways in which Augustinianism might reject Cartesian assumptions about the self's agonistic relation to the world and the psychologism that emerges from this picture. They argue that Augustine's "anthropology allows us to accommodate the best of what modern concepts of autonomy offer without obliging us to believe our agency to be as unmoored as many moderns think."[2] Augustine's correlative emphases on the interiority of the subject and the objectivity of the external world are taken by most modern readers to imply troubling epistemological and metaphysical contradictions. But these contradictions, his defenders argue, emerge only when grafted onto a philosophical account that already pits interiority (self-determination) against objectivity (mind-independent reality). The intersubjective ontology that gives rise to this alternative account of autonomy and God-relatedness will be an important part of my next chapter. It is an ontology that "proceeds only by affirming that an irreducible otherness stands at the heart of subjectivity—the otherness of God."[3] To go deeply into oneself, for this Augustine, is already to be scattered into a plurality that recognizes (and loves) God and neighbor. Others are necessary, and not simply as conduits for self-awareness. Selves are constituted in compassionate relation: "A person is for Augustine the complete self-constitution of a rational nature by compassion toward other human beings."[4] These Augustinian proposals affirm Paul Ricoeur's claim that "the selfhood of oneself implies otherness to such an intimate degree that one cannot be thought of without the other."[5] Sin is fundamentally the prideful and self-defeating rejection of this relation. It stems from a desire to be a solitary god rather than a relational creature dependent on the good. Augustine describes this phenomenon in terms of a human who "thinks it has achieved something great if it can also dominate its peers, by which I mean other men. For it is the instinct of a corrupt mind to covet and claim as its due what is really due to God alone" (*DDC* 23.23). So, for Augustine, love of God entails love of neighbor and hatred of God generates hatred of neighbor. In this, John Rist argues, "Augustine expands on Plotinus: wishing to be one's own master is tied to wishing to master others" (*ATB*, 189). This intersubjective ontology,

2. Mathewes, "Augustinian Anthropology," 204.

3. Mathewes, "Augustinian Anthropology," 198. See also, Susan Mennel, "Augustine's 'I': The 'Knowing Subject' and the Self," *Journal of Early Christian Studies* 2 (1994): 291–324; and, Michael Hanby, "Desire: Augustine beyond Western Subjectivity," in *Radical Orthodoxy*, ed. John Milbank, Catherine Pickstock, and Graham Ward (New York: Routledge, 1999): 109–26.

4. Burnell, *Augustinian Person*, 123.

5. Ricoeur, *Oneself as Another*, 3.

and subsequent anthropology, is basic to Augustine's account of value and valuing. It is one that few liberal theorists today share.

Charles Mathewes, in fact, argues that liberalism fails to understand Augustinianism because it tends to have a very different "ontology that pictures the world as an archipelago of alterities, each negotiating its way around the others."[6] This reading implicitly challenges Romand Coles's assertion that Augustinianism is a "self-defeating generosity based on an ungenerous ontology that too heavily accents identity."[7] For Mathewes, an Augustinian ontology—one in which "mind is already in the world, always already related to 'other' realities, inner as well as outer"—would actually relieve much of the anxiety that now characterizes political concerns about autonomy, otherness, and pluralism.[8] In a sense, this view extends Charles Taylor's now familiar association of Augustinianism with modern subjectivity (the elevation of the will as the center of the self) in order to highlight the Augustinian character of Taylor's own emphases on the dialogical character of self-awareness.

Like Christology, explicit attention to ontology has not been at the forefront of either Augustinian liberalism or liberal political theory. This neglect may account for why it has proved possible for Augustinians to forge practical coalitions with many other liberals who do not share their ontological commitments but want to bracket ontology in order to achieve an overlapping consensus. It also may account for why the appeal of Augustinian liberalism, or even its self-understanding, has fallen on hard times

6. Mathewes, "Augustinian Anthropology," 214.

7. Coles, *Rethinking Generosity*, 3.

8. Mathewes, "Augustine's Anthropology," 213. While I share Mathewes's effort to provide a theologically and morally robust Augustinian liberalism, I fear that his readings of 'secularism' and 'modernity' too often perpetuate the sort of intellectualism that I have criticized in figures like Milbank, Santurri, and Jackson. Despite his differences with these authors, he is too focused on "modernity's anthropological dogma of individual autonomy" (Mathewes, "Pluralism, Otherness, and the Augustinian Tradition," 85) and too quickly claims that "what initially seems a contingent political question is revealed to be a deep and inescapable metaphysical issue" (86). Mathewes confuses the issue by referring to "first-order religious language" rather than something like "first-order liturgical confession" and "second-order theological language" (Mathewes, "Author Replies," 480). However, he backtracks from this kind of intellectualism when he emphasizes his more general 'therapeutic' approach that resists valorizing either metaphysics or theology (Mathewes, *Augustinian Tradition*, 72 and 203).

among theologians unsure about the Christian commitments of Augustinian liberals (especially when theological doctrines are "demythologized" in order to support particular policy agendas). Augustinian political ethics has flourished without sustained recourse to the theology that animates his social ontology. As we have seen, it focuses primarily on the limiting effects of sin at the phenomenological level of human overreaching and the element of hope that any eschatological vision might provide. This chapter does not deny the importance of sin or eschatology; indeed, they remain central to my version of Augustinian civic liberalism. Parallel to my previous account of love's relation to justice, sin is not replaced by love. Other binaries should also be resisted: reason is not replaced by emotion, and concern for concrete action or social consequences is not replaced by motivation. The invocation of "love" is not a panacea or consolation for the discontents of liberalism. No retrieval of Augustinianism could bear such idealism or sentimentalism. Moreover, to fashion prematurely a politics of *caritas* that allows the state to be the institution that purifies desire constitutes not simply hubris and naïveté but that form of idolatry and resistance to secularity discussed in chapter 1. By accenting the dialectical relation between sin and love in the moral and political experience of a fallen world, I want to stick close to my emphasis on the practical consequences of this moral psychology for a political society that is neither wholly good nor wholly evil. Augustine's rejection of Stoicism invites this possibility.

Theorizing sentiment and the political character of love need not travel down the road of political romanticism or illiberal paternalism. It is in his analysis of love that Augustine locates his suspicions of politics and virtue in this passing age of "miserable pilgrimage" (*CD* 17.13) and "hell on earth" (*CD* 22.22). No doubt, for Augustine, social life is surrounded by "darkness" (*CD* 19.6.). The temporal peace of this world provides "solace for our wretchedness rather than the joy of blessedness," and earthly righteousness consists in "the forgiveness of sins rather than in the perfection of virtues" (*CD* 19.27). Virtue stands against pretty tough odds. Augustinian liberals, however, should have more to say than just repeat these familiar claims like spectators to a human tragedy.

The limits of politics and virtue do not require abandoning the full range of human needs and values, including their relation to the divine. This chapter attempts to make good on my claim that understanding the ways in which love and sin constrain each other offers a better kind of Augustinian liberalism.

My account focuses on this possibility for Augustinians, but this model also suggests that *any* political ethic requires an account of their relation (or its secular analogues) in order to avoid the arrogant forms of perfectionism and essentially negative forms of liberalism outlined in my introduction.

There is a focal theological sense in which love *is* prior to sin. Augustinians hold that human beings are sinners because they are bad lovers; but it is incorrect to hold that they are lovers because they are sinners. This reversal would give rise to a Manichean struggle if there were a lexical priority of sin. Augustinianism, if anything, is a refusal of Manicheanism. Original sin should not be the opening gambit for an Augustinian political theology, even though the reality of sin is a persistent recognition that constrains notions of perfectibility in civic life. The first parts of this chapter make this case.

For the post-Manichean Augustine, sin is parasitic on love in the same way that evil is parasitic on the good. Sin is perverse because it is privative; it is a parody of the good. It presents itself, albeit mysteriously, as a form of the good (whether as knowledge in Eden or humility in Roman civic mythology and Platonic philosophy). Augustine's worry about pagan virtue and Pelagian Christianity, for example, draws its energy from his relentless suspicion of the close counterfeit that pridefully masquerades as the real thing: "in vice there lurks a counterfeit beauty" (*Conf.* 2.6.12). False lovers pollute and distort their love by seeking their own glory—their own praise or self-mastery—in the work of compassion. Pagan virtue can be simply another way for the pagan to experience and display her own self-possession. Augustine thinks this problem is built into conceptions of virtue that do not refer to God and conceptions of rationality that do not admit emotions. But, importantly, he also worries that Christians can exercise false virtue in this way as well. Church membership, proper belief, and even right action itself are good as far they go, but they are no guarantees of good loving. Good works can be motivated by pride or humility, both within and outside of the church.[9]

Yet even here there is a charitable end to an Augustinian hermeneutics of suspicion. Augustinian theology, as Milbank and Mathewes argue, is predicated on the priority of the grace of both creation and redemption. This turn focuses on Augustine's "positive, indeed ecstatic cosmology" that imagines

---

9. This Augustinian theme is picked up by Kierkegaard in his discussion of "forming a heart in the eternal sense" (*Works of Love*, 30).

a social world "organized around love."[10] Creation and temporality are not themselves problematic for these Augustinians. When viewed "wisely," Augustine himself maintains, even the "the wonders of the visible order of nature ... are greater than the least familiar and rarest of miracles" (*CD* 10.12). True virtue does require a proper orientation of the intellect and the will to God, but conversion to this God opens one up to the world, into creation. A fixation with evil, tragedy, sin, and hypocrisy would constitute a denial of this deeper claim and, to my mind, has truncated an Augustinian account of social life and political citizenship. I have noted that critics of Augustine often charge that his ethics is too preoccupied with goodness or too preoccupied with evil to be of use for liberal democratic politics. But for Augustinians, it is theologically appropriate to assign lexical priority to love, especially because of its neglect in contemporary thought.

An Augustinian civic virtue based in love requires re-reading some familiar texts about Augustine's own passions in ways that challenge their use by critics of Augustinian liberalism. Before turning to two important passages from Augustine's narrative about his own life, I want to establish more clearly the fundamental centrality of love. Anders Nygren focused on Augustine precisely because "ever since his time the meaning of Christian love has been expressed in categories he created, and even the emotional quality it bears is largely due to him" (*AE*, 450). It is hard to understate this centrality, a point that makes its neglect in political Augustinianism and its relevance for contemporary secular discussions even more striking. I place this account within the context of the significant development of Augustine's understanding of reason and emotion. At the end of the chapter, I return to more explicitly political issues and suggest how Augustine's criticism of the Stoics might be appropriated today.

LOVE IS ORDINARY BUT HARD

Augustine—immersed in both the scriptural culture of Christian faith and the philosophical culture of late antiquity—considers love not simply to be the aim of philosophy (the ascent of the love of wisdom through the wisdom of love) but constitutive of being human. Love is ineliminable. It is a deep fact about the world. One cannot *not* love. Augustine can simply announce

10. Mathewes, *Augustinian Tradition*, 64 and 18.

to his parishioners in Carthage that "there is no one of course who doesn't love."[11] Love is movement, and there are no idle souls (*EnPs.* 121.1). The question for his community becomes what kind of lovers will they be? "I am not saying that you should have no loves," Augustine preaches, "I simply want your loves to be properly ordered" (*S.* 335C, 59). Against those who hold that love is a particularly dangerous or fleeting passion (i.e., pathological feeling), Augustinians can find in this conception a way of recognizing love as basic for political anthropology and ethics.

We are lovers in all that we do, think, feel, know, and will. To invoke an analogy frequently repeated in Augustine's writings, our loves are like weights that guide us—or enchain us—through life.[12] Augustine declares, "my weight is my love, and wherever I am carried, it is this weight that carries me" (*Conf.* 13.9.10). This imagery of love as *pondus* has important implications. For an ethics of citizenship, it challenges the view that love is simply sentimental, supererogatory, and exclusively preferential. Augustinian *caritas* is not an emotional feeling that disrupts practical reason and political stability; neither is it only a disciplined virtue for spiritual elites. That human beings are lovers is an anthropological fact, and so ordinary to the human condition. Love is everywhere and ordinary. But the right practice of ordered love is hard.

The ordinariness of Augustine's claim that we are always already lovers has interesting connections to recent moral philosophy that highlights

---

11. Augustine, *Sermon* 34.2, in *The Works of Saint Augustine*, trans. Edmund Hill, part 3, vol. 2 (Hype Park, N.Y.: New City Press, 1990), 166.

12. The negative association of love as a weight is central to Augustine: "I was drawn toward you by your beauty but swiftly dragged away from you by my own weight, swept back headlong and groaning onto these things below myself; and this weight was carnal habit" (*Conf.* 7.17.23). However, Augustine also uses the image in a more neutral way: "A body gravitates to its proper place by its own weight. This weight does not necessarily drag it downward, but pulls it to the place proper to it: thus fire tends upward, a stone downward. Drawn by their weight, things seek their rightful places" (*Conf.* 13.9.10). And: "For the specific gravity of a body is, in a manner, its love, whether a body tends downwards by reason of its heaviness or strives upwards because of its lightness. A material body is borne along by its weight in a particular direction, as a soul is by its love" (*DDC* 11.28). Harrison notes several references to Augustine's use of *pondus* imagery (*Augustine*, 96n30). For the connection to Platonism, see Rist, *ATB*, 173–74, and Burnaby, *Amor Dei*, 94–96. Despite her criticisms of Augustine, Arendt refers positively to this love as weight imagery (Arendt, *Life of the Mind: Willing*, 104).

the significance of emotions for a life of virtue and for political societies themselves. Recall Linda Zagzebski's emphasis on the motivational components of intellectual and moral virtues. She offers an epistemological account of virtue where "cognitive activity cannot be sharply separated from feeling states and motivations."[13] Emotions are complex evaluative cognitions and energies that focus ethical attention and develop understanding and judgment. They are not just irrational impulses or sensations—"itches and throbs"—that need to be controlled and mastered by the will. They play an important role in motivating political action.[14] But to frame the issue simply in this way concedes too much to the traditional liberal picture that emotions get morality going just in time for rationality to step in and take charge. As embodied creatures, rationalized emotions allow for the very condition of the possibility of moral choices themselves. They motivate their own reasons for action. Love, on this model, admits a cognitive and volitional structure because it shapes how we experience and engage the world. They do not simply overwhelm us like an alien invasion. Martha Nussbaum, modifying classical Stoicism, argues for something like this view when she claims that "emotions are forms of evaluative judgment that ascribe to certain things and persons outside a person's own control great importance for the person's own flourishing" (*UT*, 22). Modern philosophy, critics like Nussbaum argue, goes wrong when it privileges reason against emotion. Liberal political philosophers too often take "emotions at their worst and most irrational and reason at its best, usually as a corrective to emotion."[15] Charles Taylor controversially argues that this attitude to emotions is a signature of the Cartesian self anticipated by Augustinian inwardness. This inwardness is now embedded within a mechanistic worldview rather than teleology tying the cosmos to a moral order. It is a defining hallmark of Taylor's diagnosis of modernity:

13. Zagzebski, *Virtues of the Mind*, xv.

14. See Michael Walzer, *Politics and Passion: Toward a More Egalitarian Liberalism* (New Haven: Yale University Press, 2006), and Jeff Goodwin, James Jasper, and Francesca Polletta, eds., *Passionate Politics: Emotion and Social Movements* (Chicago: University of Chicago Press, 2001).

15. Solomon, *Passion for Justice*, 44. Solomon contrasts Christian moral reflection with modern portrayals of the emotions as ineffable, noncognitive, and subjective (209). He argues that "justice is a passion to be cultivated, not an abstract set of principles to be formulated, mastered, and imposed upon society" (33).

Here for the first time we are in the modern framework, where what is relevant is the design. Our goal must be to subordinate the passions to their proper functions. But we come to understand what these are purely through disengaging reason. The lived experience of the passions teaches us nothing; it can only mislead. Our passions should in the end function only as cold disengaged understanding shows us they ought to.[16]

By contrast, according to Taylor, moral philosophy requires an account of moral sources, "the love of which empowers us to do and be good."[17] Whatever we make of Taylor's intellectual history, political theorists of various stripes have started to re-think what it means to take emotions and virtues seriously.[18] Neo-Aristotelians and feminists have led the way, but it is becoming clearer to mainstream liberal theorists as well. To cite one example, Brian Barry argues that "the most important and at the same time perhaps most elusive of circumstances of impartiality is a motivational one."[19] Motivating impartiality, of course, has a distinct valence in liberal philosophy. It is tied up with received Kantian or utilitarian assumptions that I have suggested feminist and Augustinian liberals rightly reject. These assumptions leave liberals in a state of "frustrated noncomprehension" when faced with "the intransigence of 'irrational' social ties of religion, ethnicity, patriotism, or tradition."[20]

16. Taylor, *Sources of the Self*, 283.

17. Ibid., 93.

18. Taylor has been justly criticized by Quentin Skinner for the disappointing conclusion to his important work because it remains rather inarticulate about the character of his theism and his appeal to *agape* as well as their consequences for political theory. See Quentin Skinner, "Modernity and Disenchantment: Some Reflections on Charles Taylor's Diagnosis," in *The Politics of Postmodernity*, ed. James Good and Irving Velody (Cambridge: Cambridge University Press, 1998), 49–60, and "Who are We? Ambiguities of the Modern Self," *Inquiry* 34 (1991): 133–53. Taylor's recent work on Catholicism and modernity suggests that he is correcting this vagueness with more explicit theological inquiry (though, of course, he could respond to Skinner that theism could never be *fully* articulated). For a nuanced account of Taylor's reading of Augustine (and its reception in Augustine studies), see Hanby, *Augustine and Modernity*, 8–11. For a qualified defense of Taylor in light of his Augustinian critics, see Wayne J. Hankey, "Between and Beyond Augustine and Descartes: More than a Source of the Self," *Augustinian Studies* 32:1 (2001): 65–88.

19. Barry, *Justice as Impartiality*, 100.

20. Wills, *Augustine*, 119. Wills claims that Augustine offers a better *description* of political societies, even though liberalism provides a better *prescription* "in situations where it can work" (119). I want to argue that Augustinianism has more to say about both prescription and description (if we can divide the two) than Wills suggests.

J. David Velleman points out that philosophical attention to love suffered under the influence of Freud, who "embedded love deep within the tissue of fantasy, thereby closing it off from the moral enterprise."[21] By contrast, Augustine's account of love offers a complex picture of human motivational structures that does not flatly oppose narrow self-interest or personal fantasy to a moral point of view that adopts a detached universal perspective on the needs and desires of others. Egoism or altruism, the apparent dilemma of modern ethics, offers an impoverished account of the moral life. Since Augustine's moral psychology highlights emotions and motivations, it seems fruitful to insert the Augustinian tradition into these debates.

Augustine can speak of ordered love as a motivation, a virtue, and a desire that organizes the disorders of love itself. Love is not a blind drive but a complex disposition that informs a way of being in the world. Unlike most analytic philosophies of love, Augustinian love is not simply about motivating beneficent actions in a way that focuses on maximizing desirable outcomes or fixed understandings of what might constitute a good outcome. Outcomes, of course, should matter for any eudaimonist who links morality to happiness and thinks there is more to morality than sets of obligation. John Milbank has argued that "charity indeed is *not* for Augustine a matter of mere generous intention: on the contrary, it involves that exact appropriateness of action necessary to produce a 'beautiful' order, and in this sense, charity is the very consummation of justice and prudence" (*TST*, 411). But, as Milbank recognizes, that consummation has not yet arrived. It has been delayed and distorted by sin. More proximate outcomes and perceived actions, however, provide helpful ways to test the quality of our earthbound loving motivations

---

21. Velleman, "Love as a Moral Emotion," 351. Velleman's article admirably connects love as a form of moral attention with the ethics of both Iris Murdoch and Kant. He writes: "If respect arrests our self-love, as Kant asserts, then what does love arrest? I suggest that it arrests our tendencies toward emotional self-protection from another person, tendencies to draw ourselves in and close ourselves off from being affected by him. This hypothesis would explain why love is an exercise in 'really looking,' as Murdoch claims" (361). Consistent with my argument that Augustinian love is neither reducible to beneficence nor irrational feeling, Vellemen argues that Kantian ethics and Rawlsian liberalism go wrong in thinking that love is "essentially a pro-attitude toward a result, to which the beloved is instrumental or in which he is involved. I venture to suggest that love is essentially an attitude toward the beloved himself but not toward any result at all" (354). See also Richard Rorty, "Freud, Morality, and Hermeneutics," *New Literary History* 12 (1980): 177–85.

("by their fruits you shall know them"). Augustine is famous for reducing morality to motivation. This reduction, critics claim, opens the door to the justification of immoral actions if they are done with a proper disposition. Augustine does claim that an agent's motivations (and role-specific duties) fundamentally differentiate apparently similar moral actions. Motivations distinguish both acts and persons.[22] I am less certain, however, that he provides a fully systematic ethical theory that hinges on agent-referring motivation in any load-bearing way. It would be odd for Augustine so thoroughly to insulate or "spiritualize" motivation that it loses its grip on the social realities of loving. If the interpreters I cited above are correct, Augustine does not offer a mentalist picture that sharply contrasts subjectivity and objectivity. In any case, Augustinian liberals should not.

It is important here to note that an Augustinian ordering of love is committed to a breaking away from the self's *disordered* approach to the world. In his letter to Marcellinus, Augustine discusses this disorder in terms of good or bad loving that is a matter of "the training of the heart within" (*Ep.* 138, 37). Fascination with the purity of one's own "inner" motivations—whatever the consequences may yield—can be a troubling sign of a disordered love that refuses to look beyond the self. In fact, given the powers of self-deception, outcomes can do more than "test" motivations. They can also reveal them. Augustine writes: "Do you want to discern the character of a person's love? Notice where it leads" (*EnPs.* 121.1). The need to order love is one aspect of the Augustinian way to address the intuitions that give rise to more standard Kantian principles of impartial respect and, to a certain extent, utilitarian concerns about consequences.

How might an Augustinian ethic accomplish these goals? I want to suggest that Augustinian love is neither manipulation nor alienation but a form of arresting attention that knows the dangers present within love for others.

---

22. Augustine writes: "Even when one human being kills another, it makes a great difference whether this is done out of passion to hurt someone, or in order to steal something unjustly say, by an enemy or robber; or within a system of retribution and obedience, as by a judge or executioner, or else, when it is necessary in order to escape or help someone else, as when a robber is killed by a traveler, or an enemy by a soldier" (*Ep.* 153, 81; see also *IoEp.* 7.7). For modern proposals that emphasize the importance of agent-intention for act-description, see G. E. M. Anscombe, *Intention* (Ithaca: Cornell University Press, 1958), and Edward Vacek, "Divine-Command, Natural-Law, and Mutual-Love Ethics," *Theological Studies* 57 (1996): 633–53.

Love attends to reality and emotionally wills good for another, but it does not grasp the neighbor with an agenda. At times, Augustine's own views are consistent with such claims: "We should not, indeed we cannot love men in the sense in which a glutton will say, I love partridges: the object of his love being the killing and eating of them. . . . Men are not to be loved as things to be consumed, but in the manner of friendship and goodwill, leading us to do things for the benefit of those we love" (*IoEp.* 8.5). Augustinians should see here something like a Kantian respect for persons. "The true Christian," Augustine claims, "will never set himself up over other men" (*IoEp.* 8.8). Oliver O'Donovan, in fact, argues that the most mature aspect of Augustine's notion of love blends rational love and benevolent love. Rational love "is neither 'appetite' nor 'movement' but estimation, appreciation, and approval," and benevolent love wills that "something which has its existence from God should fulfill its existence for God" (*PSL,* 29 and 33). This attention to the agent's needs and desires involves both reason and emotion. Love is engaged by reason in admiration of the good.[23] Augustine does have a notion of love as benevolence, in the sense of a standing disposition to promote another's welfare. This active "benevolent love" includes both material duties to aid and evangelical duties of spiritual witness.[24] But the structure of Augustinian love

23. Charles Mathewes, by a misleading reference, claims that "reason is, or truly ought to be, the slave of the passions" ("Augustinian Anthropology," 214). For Mathewes, this claim is true only because "passions" are not "fixed and unquestionable sources of motivation" (214n30). He argues that "our practical reasoning capacities may be guided by our passions and interests," but human beings are "not the slaves of passions" (214n30). Another typically nuanced interpreter of Augustine, Carol Harrison, appears to make a similar move but even more problematically without Mathewes's significant qualification: "Love, operating through the passions, therefore takes the place of reason in directing man's will towards God" (Harrison, *Augustine,* 95). Harrison may hold this opposition descriptively to be true after the Fall, when reason and will are divided. But my guess is that both interpreters are using rhetorical effect, bending the wood the other way to overcorrect a bad history of interpretation.

24. On interpretive debates about the relation between spiritual and material duties in Augustine, see Canning, *Unity of Love for God and Neighbor in St. Augustine,* 172–85. Canning shows an "impressive body of post-400 texts which present material giving to the poor as a highly significant dimension of love for neighbour" (179). John Rist notes that even *De moribus* is "a much less otherworldly work than its contemporaries, where love of neighbour includes love of his body, that is, corporal works of mercy, as well as concern for his soul" (*ATB,* 159).

(like Platonism) is couched primarily in terms of an arresting vision—the proper perception of the reality of the other and the obligations this reality commands. Iris Murdoch similarly employs the category of perception: "The best picture of serious contemplative thinking is serious contemplative perception; as when we attend to a human face, music, a flower, a visual work of art."[25] For Augustine, "love has eyes which give intelligence of him who is in need" (*IoEp.* 7.10). These eyes, recalling the language of affectivity, are the eyes of the heart and, as Charles Taylor rightly notes, "God is behind the eye, as well as the One whose Ideas the eye strives to discern clearly before it."[26] The emotional aspect of this attention is not a passion *(pertubationes)* that disrupts reason but is itself a kind of willing and judging, similarly to what Taylor also describes as "seeing which also helps effect what it sees."[27] Augustine agrees with the Stoics that the passions are rooted in the mind rather than the body: "Yet such is the force of love that when the mind has been thinking about things with love for such a long time and has got stuck to them with the glue of care, it drags them along with itself . . . it wraps up their images and clutches them to itself" (*DT* 10.2.7). Passions are the source of bad judgments, and bad judgments are the source of the passions. That is to say, there are volitional and cognitive dimensions of passion.

Against the Platonists (Augustine believes), passions are not a symptom of having a body (*CD* 14.3). They are expressions of a wrongly directed desire. The body is not the prison house of the soul. If anything, it is the other way around. The mind corrupts the goodness of all desire that is continuous with the healthy desire for God by stopping it short. Augustine is preoccupied with the New Testament's claim that evil comes "out of the heart of man" (Mark 7:21). His emphasis shifts from the passionate intellect of the mind *per se* to the entire self metaphorically expressed as the thoughtful "heart" in relation to God: "Our heart is His altar when we lift it up to Him" (*CD* 10.3). Augustine, according to James Wetzel, appreciates what most classical philosophers ignored: "the difficulties creatures of habits and passions . . . have in appropriating philosophical wisdom" (*LV*, 15). I think this appreciation opens a new form of social theorizing. John Milbank hints at this idea:

25. Murdoch, *Metaphysics as a Guide to Morals,* 424.
26. Taylor, *Sources of the Self,* 136.
27. Ibid., 449.

For antique thought, on the whole, desire was split between an inherently 'proper' desire under control of right reason, and the excessive desires of disordered passions. But Augustine introduces the novel thought that reason itself can be perversely subordinate to a willful desire for a less than truly desirable object. Hence there opens up a new perception of a possible radical perversity for both human beings and societies. (*TST*, 400–401)

As we have seen, many liberals fear the dangerous effect of "letting" emotions back into morality and politics, particularly when couched as a politics of the soul and the heart. This fear is expressed in critical responses to feminist ethics of care and, more recently, to postmodern accounts of radical solidarity with the other. Augustine's fundamental argument with the rationalism of pagan (or Pelagian) moral psychology is structurally similar to feminist critics of liberal rationalism: affections have "a *ratio* of their own; otherwise they would never move us" (*LV*, 101). Emotions involve the will; in fact, for Augustine, "they are nothing other than forms of will" (*CD* 14.6).[28] Thus, "a righteous will, then, is a good love; and a perverted will is an evil love" (*CD* 14.7). This break from accounts of rationality that see emotions only as threats should play a larger role in political Augustinianism.

Before proceeding to expand these themes, it is necessary to introduce another feature of Augustine's account of love. A fuller study might develop soteriological and ecclesiological implications of Augustine's account of love, but I choose to focus primarily on Christology. The Christological dimensions of Augustine's account of love are politically salient precisely because of their role in his criticisms of Stoicism and Platonism. Augustine's Christology, historically at least, has not been held to be very original, influential, or even important.[29] With the exception of Oliver O'Donovan and

---

28. I here adopt Wetzel's translation (following Babcock) that renders *voluntas* as "forms of will" rather than Bettenson's (and now Dyson's) "acts of will" because the latter "carries too much the suggestion that the affections are voluntarily controlled" (Wetzel, *LV*, 101n26). In either case, both translations distance *voluntas* from a faculty psychology.

29. The view that assumes from this that neither Christology nor Nicene trinitarianism are central to Augustine—a view popularized by Adolph von Harnack—has been strongly challenged in recent Augustine studies. See, for example, Lewis Ayres, "Augustine's Trinitarian Theology," in *Augustine and His Critics,* ed. R. Dodaro and G. Lawless (New York: Routledge, 2000), 51–76; Lewis Ayres, "The Christological Context of Augustine's *De Trinitate* XIII: Toward Relocating Books VIII-XV," *Augustinian Studies* 29, no. 1 (1998): 111–39; and Michael Cameron, "The Christological Substructure of

Robert Dodaro, it is rarely considered in modern political Augustinianism. Christology, however, determines Augustine's story about God and the love commands. Christ's Incarnation and Passion are central to his thought, especially in terms of the political implications of the central Book 10 of the *City of God*. Augustine's complex relation to his Stoic and Platonic sources cannot be understood without this theological context. This focus might seem to jeopardize the coalition between liberalism and Augustinianism that I want to advance. Augustinian liberals, of course, cannot expect liberals to "confess Christ is Lord" in order to become good lovers and good citizens. Augustinians also should resist the temptation to believe that they themselves hold a monopoly on God's grace or virtue.[30] But more importantly, for my purposes, I want to show how basic Augustinian commitments about the nature of love can ward off Arendt's challenges and affirm those aspects of liberal perfectionism discussed in the previous chapters. This account is aware of the dangers of a love that aims at more than liberal respect, but it develops a more complex relation between love and respect (or reason and emotion) than a strict opposition allows.

SELFHOOD, OTHERNESS, AND TRAINING IN LOVE

Remember the Augustinian story. Human beings are bundles of loves. The objects of their loves are various and in conflict, much like Freud's account of human desire. Natural loves need to be healed and restored by a form of the will dependent on recognition of others. Augustine imagines the process of sanctification as the "transference of weight" from bad loves to good loves. He distinguishes good emotions from bad passions as a conceptual parallel to the distinction between love as *caritas, amor,* or *dilectio* and love as *cupiditas, concupiscentia,* or *libido*. Different loves determine and differentiate human agency and action. Charity entails the humility of right

---

Augustine's Figurative Exegesis," in *Augustine and the Bible*, ed. Pamela Bright (Notre Dame, Ind.: University of Notre Dame Press, 1999), 74–103.

30. Timothy P. Jackson correctly notes that holding that "charity is not causally possible without the grace of God mediated by the Son and the Spirit" is distinct from insisting "that explicit belief in the Biblical God or the historical Christ is a necessary condition for the embodiment of charity" (*Love Disconsoled*, 25).

use and enjoyment, while cupidity entails the pride of wrong use and enjoyment.[31] True virtue, ultimately, is a matter of loving well and loving freely. True lovers freely enact the perfectly willed and perfectly rational acts of a social creature responsive to the charity of God. This is the goal that inspires Augustine's meditations, even as it is one that is only progressively received and always in danger of being corrupted by the pridefulness of self-possession.

Oliver O'Donovan counsels that in thinking about Augustine's understanding of love, "we do well to speak of 'aspects' of love rather than of 'kinds'" (*PSL,* 13).[32] All human beings love and live in a reality governed by love. There is a fundamental continuity between all loves and desires whether or not they are distinguished as "natural" or "supernatural." O'Donovan writes:

> When we find ourselves distinguishing different strands of thought about love-of-God and love-of-neighbor, then it is not that there are several different loves, immanently distinguished, but that the loving subject stands in a complex and variable relation to the reality which his love confronts. Pluriformity is imposed upon his love from outside by the pluriform structure of reality; or in Augustine's favorite phrase, his love is "ordered." (*PSL,* 13)

Indeed, much of Augustine's theory of value hinges on the type of loving that determines the self's relation to objects rather than any value or disvalue objects may hold in themselves. Virtues and values critically depend on the manner in which the self exercises virtue or responds to value. Augustine frequently relies on this sort of argument to counter Manichean assertions that threaten the goodness of creation. It is the *way* of loving that corrupts, not the object itself that is loved (*CD* 15.22). As such, there could never be a *complete* theory of virtue or value.

---

31. For an application of Augustine's appeal to humility that counters traditional readings of Augustinian voluntarism, see Gerald W. Schlabach, "Augustine's Hermeneutic of Humility: An Alternative to Moral Imperialism and Moral Relativism," *Journal of Religious Ethics* 22, no. 1 (Spring 1994): 299–327.

32. O'Donovan discerns four aspects of love in Augustine that avoids the traditional bifurcation of "ontological" and "psychological" love. In addition to rational and benevolent love, he identifies a *cosmic love* (the movement of the universe toward its ultimate end in God) and *positive* love (the self's pursuit of God as the ultimate end). O'Donovan notes that, for Augustine, benevolence is not reduced to acts of charity *(beneficentia)* but can refer to a general attitude *(benevolentia).*

Like most classical theorists, Augustine does defend a hierarchy of goods "which exist in the order of nature" (*CD* 11.16). God, in a heuristic sense, occupies the highest value in this hierarchy—thus securing a radical distinction between God and creation (*CD* 5.11). But Augustine's God is outside of the order of nature or any analogy of being (*CD* 8.6). There is an order to creation that adheres within goods themselves in terms of the extent to which they image the excellences of God. In fact, the differential relations of the entire order themselves image the excellences of God. Human beings have a distinctive status in God's creation because they are endowed with rational souls that bear the image and likeness of God—rational souls able to praise God with understanding rather than by instinct. This account of "order" and "being" often serves to confirm the suspicions of Augustine's critics. These critics associate hierarchy with a Platonic metaphysics fixed upon the highest good or a single *telos*.[33] Augustine does argue that "the precept by which we are to love God is distinct from love of neighbor because the divine essence is superior to and above our nature" (*DDC* 1.30.33). His rhetoric in describing the origins of evil and sin also betray this pattern. Two passages suggest this reasoning:

> How, therefore, can a good thing be the efficient cause of an evil will? How, I say, can good be the cause of evil? For when the will relinquishes that which is superior to itself and turns to that which is inferior, it becomes evil not because that towards which it turns is evil, but because the turning itself is evil. The inferior thing, then, did not make the will evil; rather, the will made itself evil by wickedly and inordinately desiring the inferior thing. (*CD* 12.6)

> Sin gains entrance through these and similar good things when we turn to them with immoderate desire, since they are the lowest kinds of goods and we thereby turn away from the better and higher: from you yourself, O Lord our God, and your truth and your law. These lowest goods hold delights for us indeed, but no such delights as does my God, who made all things; for in him the just man finds delight, and for upright souls he himself is joy. (*Conf.* 2.5.10; see also *DVR* 20.38)

---

33. For compelling challenges to the view that Augustine's concept of "order" is static rather than dynamic, see Vernon J. Bourke, *Augustine's View of Reality* (Villanova, Penn.: Villanova University Press, 1964), and Emilie Zum Brunn, *St. Augustine: Being and Nothingness* (New York: Paragon House, 1988).

I will return to the thorny issues that this supposed "scale of being" meta-physic tends to promote, especially in the next chapter where I discuss the ef-fect of imagining the highest good (God) as also the common good (Christ). For now, I note that Augustine's critics correctly identify this aspect of his thought but often fail to identify the theological work that it can do for an Augustinian.

In terms of love, Augustine's account does not devalue inferior goods as evil. Proximate (or, subsidiary) goods are capable of tempting the self. But "there are also various standards of value arising out of the use to which we put this thing or that" (*CD* 11.16). In fact, Augustine emphasizes, "a good will and a rightly ordered love have, as it were, such great weight that, even though angels rank above men in the natural order, good men are nonethe-less placed above the wicked angels" (*CD* 11.16). His focus is persistently on the quality of the loving itself and on the need to go deeper and deeper into participation in God's own love. James Wetzel captures this difference in his gloss on Augustine's account of sin:

> Sin accrues to those who evaluate goods without having incorporated in their judgments the eternal measure of goods. Instead they seek their standard for the good from within the world of time and change, and whatever measure they arrive at will unduly magnify for them the importance of possessing particular temporal advantages. (*LV*, 67)

Augustine emphasizes the contrast between the dispositions with which we encounter proximate goods and God, not the value of these goods. The value of creation is secure in Christ, "since apart from you there is nothing that could burst in and disrupt the order that you have imposed on it" (*Conf.* 7.13.19; see also *CD* 11.21). Indeed, it is perhaps because Augustine so strongly presupposed the objective order and diverse goodness of created reality that the accent of his ethical thought falls on the attitude or disposition with which one values goods rather than the order of goods themselves.[34]

This emphasis on the orientation of the will, while causing problems for his account of pagan virtue, is why Augustine's ontology leads to a focus on the agent's engagement with the world. Augustinian ethics often is said to be both teleological and deontological as a way to account for an Augustinian

---

34. For an elegant response to critics of Augustine's doctrine of creation, see Rowan Williams, "'Good for Nothing'? Augustine on Creation," *Augustinian Studies* 25 (1994): 9–24.

"voluntarism" that does not compete with moral realism. There is both *usus* and *res* in Augustine's understanding of the self's relation to the world, but the emphasis is on *usus* rather than *res*. This account resists both pure constructivism and Thomist theologies which can defend natural goods apart from the context of their use.

This view lies at the heart of Augustine's formative account of the two loves that form two cities. Love is not simply determinant of an individual's life. It is the key to understanding world history itself. Augustine famously writes: "Two cities, then, have been created by two loves: that is, the earthly city by love of self extending even to contempt of God, and the heavenly city by love of God extending to contempt of self" (*CD* 14.28). In commenting on this passage, Oliver O'Donovan highlights the significance of the subject's disposition rather than the intrinsic value of the objects that are loved. He points out the importance of the entire phrase—*usque ad contemptum Dei* and *usque ad contemptum sui*: "The force of the qualifications, missed by commentators who simply refer to *amor sui* and *amor Dei*, is to emphasize that the attitudes contrasted are comparative evaluation" (*PSL,* 64). This comparative (rather than competitive) aspect of Augustine's account of love highlights his awareness of the fragility of stable loving and the need to resist loves that aim only at selfish possession and domination. Securing stable love by fixing upon the highest good was an important lesson Augustine learned from the Greeks, but it was a lesson he soon developed in his own theological way.

Despite my criticisms of John Milbank, he and other "postmodern" Augustinians have rightly emphasized love as primordial. In particular, they have demonstrated the importance of love for a political theology that includes a radical sense of exteriority—the "otherness" of the neighbor and God. This construal of Augustine's anthropology rejects certain liberal accounts of autonomy, but it does not reject individuation and the separateness of persons. Unlike some versions of care that jeopardize the separateness of persons, Augustinianism wants only to resist a self-identity that is not other-directed. It is part of a human perfection to be in relation to others. Like other goods, love is an ambivalent but persistent reality of human life. It is the dangers of loving, however, that motivate Augustine's interest in training one's love. As Milbank has made clear, Augustinian love is a "learned practice" (*TST,* 236). Loving is inevitable, even when one loves in the wrong way, but it is not simply a passive fate that befalls us.

Love has multiple directions and is beset by many dangers and potentially pathological corruptions. In romantic relations, we experience this aspect of love intensely. This kind of love, as well as political love, can be immature, fragile, and fleeting. It can cause deep wounds in our psyche. But, despite our experience of nonideal kinds of romantic love, we develop in our capacity to both give and receive love. In fact, it is a mark of psychological dysfunction if one simply abandons the development of love. Timothy P. Jackson encourages us to "distinguish between the ideal of love itself and the various hypocrisies and cruelties that stem from a refusal to acknowledge that we fall short of it."[35] Augustine is aware of the difference between mature and immature love. The wrong love grasps at both divinity and the neighbor. This love steals identity. The right love "refers" loving to God. This love recognizes identity, an identity secured in God's love for humanity.

Individuation in relation, in fact, is the gift of God. Consider Augustine's description of the earliest generations of humanity:

> For affection was given its right importance so that men, for whom social harmony would be advantageous and honourable, should be bound together by ties of various relationships. The aim was that one man should not combine many relationships in his one self, but that those connections should be separated and spread among individuals, and that in this way they should help to bind social life more effectively in their plurality a plurality of persons. (*CD* 15.16, Bettenson; see also *CD* 12.22 and 14.1)

This "plurality of persons" is part of the goodness of creation. Augustine praises his God because he has given "mankind the capacity to understand oneself by analogy with others" (*Conf.* 1.6.10, Chadwick). Otherness reaches into self-love itself. Again, Augustinians should see here an important distinction between the affirmation of created finitude and the fragmentation of sin. It is also important to note Augustine's eschatological affirmation of this plurality. Plurality and separateness of identity are not simply providential aspects of creation or a mark of sin that will be overcome in the drawing together of the Eschaton—as if Pentecost was simply a negative undoing of Babel. In the heavenly city, there will be perfect freedom of will and perfect love. There will be no evil and "we shall be free to give ourselves up to the praise of God, Who will be all in all!" (*CD* 22.30). But the unity that partakes in the divine life will not be a conflation of identities. Like the triune life of God, Augustine imagines that "it will be one and the same freedom in all, indivisible in the

35. Jackson, *Love Disconsoled*, 146.

separate individuals" (*CD* 22.30, Bettenson). Sociality on earth is a different story. It is filled with so many objects of love that scatter our loves.

Love must be trained and ordered or, better yet, always training and ordering. One's loves form one's character, and the loves of a society form its character as well. We have seen the significance of this formulation for Augustinian social criticism attentive to the way in which economic and political structures artificially construct moral imagination. Less commented upon, however, is the significance of the way in which Augustine does not oppose love of self to love of God but highlights the quality of the loving ("to contempt of God") and not simply a bad choice of objects (loving self rather than loving God). What Augustine rejects is a love of self that becomes self-absorbed. The good lover needs to learn how to love well, or to use and enjoy things well. Using an analogy that recalls a number of Aristotelian discussions of virtue, Augustine can even liken good loving to good craftsmanship.[36] Augustine's account of right loving can sound very Aristotelian:

> The person who lives a just and holy life is one who is a sound judge of these things. He is also a person who has ordered his love, so that he does not love what is wrong to love, or fail to love what should be loved, or love too much what should be loved less (or love too little what should be loved more), or love two things if one of them should be loved either less or more than the other, or love things either more or less if they should be loved equally. (*DDC* 1.27,28)

> The judgment of the cleverer will be better than that of the slow witted; that of the skilled than that of the unskilled; that of the more experienced than that of the less experienced; and, as the same person, grows more proficient, so does his judgment become better than it was formerly. (*CD* 8.6)

36. Augustine offers this parable of God's love that Christians are to imitate in their love of enemies: "Imagine the trunk of a tree lying before you: a good carpenter may see such a piece of timber, unhewn, as it was cut in the forest. He loves it at sight, because he means to make something of it. The reason for his love is not that it may always remain as it is; as craftsman, he has looked at what it shall be, not as lover at what it is; and his love is set upon what he will make of it, not upon its present state. Even so has God loved us sinners. . . . Like trees from the wood, we have been looked on by the Carpenter, and his thought turns to the building he will make of us, not to the timber that we are. So may you look upon your enemy, standing against you with his angry passion, his biting words, his provoking insults, his unrelenting hate. But in all this you need only think that he is a *man*. . . . Therefore the perfection of love is the love of enemy, and this perfect love consists in brotherly love" (*IoEp.* 8.10).

Through a kind of *askesis*, the self must learn to love rightly, transferring those "weights" of bad loving to good loving.[37]

This moral psychology, grounded in rightly ordering love, highlights human *agency* that is directed toward human fulfillment. Augustinians do not ground ethics with an assertion of autonomy as the contingent power to choose. In relation to the good, Augustine is preoccupied with the "internal" problems of habit, affection, motivation, and perception. There is the *mala voluntas*. The integrity of loving well is not simply a matter of having a properly functioning autonomous faculty called a "will" that can be separated from Augustine's account of nonpossessive desire.[38] Volition and cognition are not split apart. Loving depends fundamentally on the whole desiring and knowing person relating rightly to the objects of love. For heuristic purposes, Augustine divides these objects into temporal goods, oneself, the neighbor, and God (*DDC* 1.23.22). Relating rightly to these objects requires the cultivation of a proper love—which, for Augustine, ultimately entails recognition of the prior initiative of God's gracious love in Christ. This aspect of Augustine is the usual site where his critics charge he devalues all that is not God, a challenge that fears the Augustinian emphasis on realizing one's selfhood in relation to God. I return to this fear in the next chapter, but it is first necessary to emphasize the Augustinian claim that loving is an ineliminable feature of being human.

The centrality of love is demonstrated by Augustine in his much discussed reformulation of the cardinal virtues as rooted in charity. The classical virtues are reinterpreted and integrated not in terms of practical reason or justice but aspects of love:

37. G. Scott Davis argues that Augustinian virtues differ from Aristotelian virtues precisely in the sense that the former are "not crafts, but disciplines" (Davis, "The Structure and Functions of the Virtues in the Moral Theology of St. Augustine," 15). However one judges the Stoic influence on Augustine's account of continence (or the general climate of fifth century asceticism), Augustine's willingness to employ this craft analogy might cast Davis's thesis in a different light. Of course, the entire problem would be recast if one allows for an Augustinian rejection of the very terms of "natural" and "supernatural."

38. John Milbank similarly argues: "'Act of will' does not therefore imply, as it would for Aquinas, a formal operation on a matter, or the direction of the emotion by reason-informed will, but instead a *dilectio* that is itself both an emotion and a will, and is right or wrong according to its own tendency to a goal, not in relation to an external ordering by reason.... For Augustine all apprehension occurs through appetition" (*TST*, 415).

If virtue leads us to the happy life, then I would not define virtue in any other way than as the perfect love of God. For in speaking of virtue as fourfold, one refers, as I understand it, to the various dispositions of love itself. Therefore four virtues—would that their efficacy were present in all souls as their names are on all lips—I would not hesitate to define as follows: temperance is love giving itself wholeheartedly to that which is loved, fortitude is love enduring all things willingly for the sake of that which is loved, justice is love serving alone that which is loved and thus ruling rightly, and prudence is love choosing wisely between that which helps it and that which hinders it. Now since this love, as I have said, is not love of things in general, but rather love of God, that is, of the supreme good, the supreme wisdom, and the supreme harmony, we can define virtues thus: temperance is love preserving itself whole and unblemished for God, fortitude is love enduring all things willingly for the sake of God, justice is love serving God alone, and therefore, ruling well those things subject to man, and prudence is love discriminating rightly between those things which aid it in reaching God and those things which might hinder it. (*Mor.* 1.15.25)

This passage reveals a number of important moves for Augustine's positive account of virtue language, including the theocentric context that qualifies the extent to which virtues are goods in themselves. On one level, the reformulation is problematic in that it appears effectively to collapse all the virtues into one. This reduction, a critic might claim, fails to attend to the complexity of the virtues. The richness of the virtues is not given its descriptive due if they are held to be numerically identical. Virtues are liable to be folded dangerously into the supreme virtue of love for God without remainder. To borrow from my Chalcedonian proposal for love and justice, it risks a kind of meta-ethical "docetism": justice appears to be justice but is really only love, prudence appears to be prudence but is really only love, courage appears to be courage but is really only love, and temperance appears to be temperance but is really only love.

In heaven, Augustine claims, "one virtue alone will exist there: both virtue and the reward of virtue. . . . It is the completion of our good to cling to this for ever" (*Ep.* 155, 96). This virtue (loving wisdom that clings to God) and its own reward (blessedness) constitute the life of the saints. But I have already noted that Augustine holds the somewhat odd view that justice also is immortal—even when the liberal "conditions of justice" disappear. He also clearly states the same view for courage, prudence, and moderation. The life of virtue will be transformed without the presence of vice, "where the one supreme God rules an obedient City according to His grace" (*CD* 19.23). We rightly wonder what does justice look like if there is no injustice? What is fortitude if obstacles to a life of virtue do not exist? Augustine is committed to the idea that virtues are in some sense permanent, even if they themselves are not the *summum bonum*. John Milbank puts this point well:

> In heaven, in a sense, only charity remains, because this concerns a gratu-
> itously received exchange, and not the necessary inhibition of something
> threatening. This is not to say that other virtues altogether disappear; it is just
> that they are no longer in any sense 'in addition' to charity. (*TST*, 411)

Even as the cardinal virtues are transformed into forms of love, Augustine is quite willing to maintain plural classification of virtues.[39] The parallelism of the virtues and the beatitudes in his *Commentary on the Sermon on the Mount* is perhaps our best example.[40] T. H. Irwin points out that Augustine approves the specific virtues of the pagan philosophers and even the noninstrumental value of virtue itself; what Augustine condemns is "the philosopher's views about what the virtues are like and how we can achieve them in this life."[41] Of course, there is a difference that Augustine picks up from the New

39. John Langan argues that Augustine maintains a version of the inseparability of the virtues but allows them to be distinguished in order to ward off the perfectionism of Stoic arguments that all sins are equal, a view inconsistent with the moral life understood as a progressive development of virtue (see "Augustine on the Unity and the Interconnection of the Virtues"). Robert Dodaro has argued that Augustine's theory of virtue also parallels Neoplatonist "explanations of the purification of the soul through a hierarchy of virtue" ("Political and Theological Virtues," 432). He points out that Augustine's nuanced account of grades of virtue means that interpreters are wrong to think that Augustine "denies the pagan ethical virtues or virtuous people exist" (463n125).

40. For general discussion of the significance of Augustine's commentary, see Servais Pinckaers, O.P., *The Sources of Christian Ethics* (Washington, D.C.: Catholic University Press of America, 1995), 140–63.

41. Irwin, "Splendid Vices?," 115. Irwin defends a moderate form of a revised Augustinian account of pagan virtue: "Some features of [pagan virtue] make them virtues and other features make them vices" (120). He thinks Aquinas expresses this view by distinguishing genuine (or "true") virtue from imperfect virtue, and perfect from imperfect happiness (Irwin cites *ST* 1–2q5a5 and *ST* 2–2q23a7). Against more traditional views that Irwin admits have textual warrants, he claims that Aquinas explicitly states what "Augustine implicitly recognizes, since Augustine also recognizes that pagan virtues

Testament's emphasis on love. Love suffuses the entire range of the virtues which, in the end, can only be shared in common. It is a virtue, but also the root of virtue: "It is also what makes virtue virtuous" (*TST*, 360).

Love does not absorb all other virtues. We might think of Augustine's *caritas* in the same way that Aristotle would speak of *phronesis*, a virtue "without which none of the virtues of character can be exercised."[42] Augustine claims that "because God is love the man who loves love certainly loves God; and the man who loves his brother must love love" (*DT* 8.5,12). Love is the source of virtue, the ground upon which all the virtues find their soil. But this is not to say that the fruits of virtue can be essentially considered as undifferentiated species of only this one virtue. Virtues and vices are too diverse to be captured by the word "love" within Augustine's taxonomy of the virtues or description of virtuous or vicious action—consider, for example the famous account of the theft of pears which, in a single passage, differentiates justice, prudence, love, generosity, humility, and simplicity from pride, ambition, curiosity, sloth, envy, avarice, and timidity (*Conf.* 2.6.12–13). After citing several virtues, Augustine elsewhere claims:

> But who is sufficient to name them all? There is as it were an army of an emperor seated within in thy mind. For as an emperor by his army does what he will, so the Lord Jesus Christ, once beginning to dwell in our inner man, (*i.e.*, in the mind through faith), uses these virtues as His ministers. (*IoEp.* 8.1, Browne and Myers)

Aquinas, more carefully than Augustine, would also affirm these distinctions and still maintain the Augustinian notion that "charity is the form of the virtues" (*ST* 2.2q23).[43] Aquinas would also distinguish moral and theological

---

identify some genuine elements of happiness" (121). For a contrasting position, see Davis, "Structure and Function of the Virtues," 12–13, and Bonnie Kent, *Virtues of the Will: The Transformation of Ethics in the Late Thirteenth Century* (Washington, D.C.: Catholic University Press of America, 1995), 27–33.

42. MacIntyre, *After Virtue*, 154.

43. For Aquinas, "Charity is called the form of the other virtues not as being their exemplar or their essential form, but rather by way of efficient cause, in so far as it sets the form on all" (*ST* 2–2q23a8). Aquinas relies heavily on Augustine's account of pagan virtue in his questions on charity (see also *ST* 1–2q63–65). In fact, despite his formal distinction between natural and theological virtues, Aquinas's views on charity (especially the relation of the love commands) are fundamentally Augustinian. If there is to be a contrast, I

virtues with painstaking clarity. What Augustine does hold is that just or prudent *persons* may appear to be perfectly just or prudent, but their justice or prudence is vitiated unless it is suffused with love (indeed, love for God and neighbor).

Augustine, for example, praises the virtue of Marcus Regulus: "Among all their praiseworthy and illustrious men of outstanding virtue, the Romans offer no one better than this man" (*CD* 1.24). He kept his oaths and loved his country. He "was so conscientious in his worship of the gods that he would neither remain in his own country nor go anywhere else, but did not in the least hesitate to return to his bitterest foes, because he had sworn an oath" (*CD* 1.15). He acknowledged his vulnerability and his dependence without desire for temporal success. He was one of the Romans who through "their own sort of integrity" show "how powerful are civic virtues even without true religion" (*Ep.* 138, 40–41). His "fidelity to his oath and his most cruel death" should "make the gods blush" (*CD* 3.18). Augustine even allows that Christians should "seek such true virtue" (*CD* 1.15). Regulus seems to be a model of what it might mean to be "on the way" to virtue, still learning to acknowledge dependency and vulnerability—a partial and flawed model for all of us who need to be "yet more vigilant" (*CD* 2.29). But, in the end, it seems Augustine could only admit that he was among the "good men according to the lights of the earthly city" (*CD* 5.19). He does display an "imperfect kind of virtue" (*CD* 5.19). Perhaps Augustine could have said that Regulus showed an incomplete virtue. Does he mean simply that Regulus is a worthy example of a virtue perfect of its kind on earth, but imperfect for a creature destined for the eternal?

---

think a difference lies in Aquinas's more detailed and developed attention to the analysis of a human action rather than Augustine's persistent focus on the character of persons. Aquinas, therefore, allows for descriptions of human acts that do not immediately entail an account of the entire moral character of the person acting (cf. *ST* 1–2q65a2 and *ST* 2–2q23a7). Thomas M. Osborne Jr puts the contrast well: "Unlike Augustine, Thomas carefully distinguishes between the goodness of an act, which comes from the act's object, and the end of an act. Thomas is much more concerned with the goodness or badness of an isolated act. Augustine is almost always concerned with the fundamental orientation of the agent towards God or towards his own self" ("Aquinas's Moral Theory," 298). Despite their fundamental theological agreements on grace and virtue, this emphasis makes Aquinas a more appealing interlocutor for contemporary jurisprudence than Augustine. We should not underestimate, however, the importance of Augustine's famous claim that an unjust law is no law at all (*De libero arbitrio* 1.5.11).

Augustine does not say, perhaps because to admit this possibility would open the door for defeat in his effort to undermine Roman mythology and its civic ideals. He does suggest the problem is not so much with Regulus but with the gods he worshipped (*CD* 2.29). But, much like the supposedly noble suicides of Lucretia and Cato, Regulus's death appears also to be a product of the vanity of self-regarding heroism. The real reason for even Regulus's imperfection, Augustine writes, was "his great avidity for praise and glory [that] induced him to impose upon the weary Carthaginians conditions harsher than they could bear" (*CD* 3.18). Without a more completely social conception of love, the practice of the virtues is deficient and, ultimately, sterile. Without love, the virtues are not completely virtuous. Acts performed without love for God and neighbors are thereby diminished and less than perfect.[44] Augustine's view entails problems of its own, but it is not here a problem in terms of the classification of the virtues themselves.[45]

Augustine's reformulation should be taken as a rhetorical expression of his moral psychology rather than as a conceptual statement of his ethical theory. John Rist has noted that Augustine here can be read as replacing the Stoic conception of "right reason" with a Christianized Platonic conception of "love" (*ATB*, 161). The Christian rhetoric of love marks, as I have argued, an intellectual and cultural watershed with important political consequences. I think it is not hyperbole to think that if Augustine had not begun this reevaluation of classical philosophy, we would live in a very different moral and political universe—he provides the soil for a deeply humanitarian ethic, a concern for the suffering of creatures who bear the image of God.[46] There

44. Rist suggests that Augustine seems "to wish to assert that, if a choice must be made, such acts must be classed as vices rather than virtues, but to recoil from condemning them outright as vicious" (*ATB*, 172).

45. John Langan notes that Augustine's focus on persons is problematic because it "converts our ascriptions of virtues to persons into total moral judgments on the persons involved" ("Augustine on the Unity and Interconnection of the Virtues," 88). This move puts pressure on Augustine's phenomenological account of the diversity of the virtues and "takes the agent's intention of and loving relation to the last end as fundamental" (94). Langan concludes Augustine's view "opens the way for the purely interior morality of intention developed by Abelard" and an exclusivist moral theory that is "troubling . . . for Christians who live in a world that characterized by both religious pluralism and secular unbelief" (95).

46. The complexities of Christian compassion and early modern politics are helpfully traced in Norman Fiering, "Irresistible Compassion: An Aspect of Eighteenth Century

are three original moves that now deserve mention: (1) virtue is a loving disposition that requires an openness of the soul to other realities, (2) virtue involves an overarching relation to God, and (3) virtue is a power which is fundamentally God's, not our own.[47] The centrality of God is as remarkable as the centrality of love in Augustine's account of virtue.

This radically theocentric account of love casts a spell. In the crucial book of the *City of God*, Augustine argues that "our good, concerning the nature of which there has been such great contention among the philosophers, is nothing other than to cling to Him, by Whose incorporeal presence alone the intellectual soul is, if one may so put it, filled up and impregnated with true virtues" (*CD* 10.3). But is the virtue of piety sufficient for our human good? Augustine notes an ambiguity in the term itself: "'Piety,' which the Greeks call *eusebia*, is usually understood in the strict sense to mean the worship of God; yet this word is also used to denote the duties which we owe to parents. Also, in common speech, the word frequently refers to works of mercy" (*CD* 10.1).[48] What is the reason for this ambiguity? Augustine holds that the worship of God cannot be separated from the "works of mercy" or "acts of compassion" because "God especially commands the performance of such works, and declares that He is pleased with them instead of, or in

---

Sympathy and Humanitarianism," *Journal of the History of Ideas* 37, no. 2 (1976): 195–218. Fiering refers to Augustinians (especially Nicolas Malebranche) and the importance of the passions for the patristic period, but he does not consider Augustine's account of emotions in relation to the early modern development of sympathy.

47. Oliver O'Donovan points out that Augustine's reformulation stands in sharp contrast to Plato's four cardinal virtues predicated on the tripartite soul (*Republic* 435a–441e): "The most striking difference is that Augustine has described both virtue as such and its differentiation into the cardinal virtues in terms of the relation of an undifferentiated soul to a differentiated external reality that it encounters in its history, to God, to adversity, to the lower creation. Plato's account, on the other hand, is given in terms of the self-contained organization and operation of a differentiated soul; and in so far as this account presupposes his doctrine of the transcendent good, the soul is ordered to an undifferentiated reality, encountered unhistorically by the mind alone" (O'Donovan, *Resurrection and Moral Order*, 223).

48. *Misericordia* can also be translated as "acts of compassion." Traditional corporal works of mercy include feeding the hungry, giving drink to the thirsty, clothing the naked, harboring the stranger, visiting the sick, ministering to the prisoner, and burying the dead; see Robert L. Wilken, *The Christians as the Romans Saw Them* (New Haven: Yale University Press, 1984).

preference to, sacrifices" (*CD* 10.1).[49] Commenting on this passage, John von Heyking argues:

> Augustine's attempt to isolate a term for the worship of God distinct from other forms of piety or reverence reflects his view that the love of God is expressed through various other kinds of love (for example, for neighbor or for the city,) and it reflects the difficulty of separating out the love of God that is exclusive from these other types of love.[50]

It is this vision of love—in piety, worship, and service—that characterizes Augustine's account of the formation of one's character and the true "end" of virtue.

This account serves as an important instance of Augustine's decisive innovation on classical philosophy even as it nurtures his polemical account of pagan virtue. Martha Nussbaum points out that Augustine was consumed with the task of "rewriting and correcting the pagan ascent of love."[51] This task is part of Augustine's larger project of defending the Christian narrative, particularly the Incarnation, against the best of pagan philosophy. Aside from the novel account of Trinitarianism in Book 8 of *On the Trinity* and the experimental language of use and enjoyment in Book 1 of *On Christian Doctrine*, however, there are few systematic discussions of love in Augustine. Rather, we might say that it is the overarching grammar of his entire thought. It is woven throughout his writings.

Dilige, et quod vis fac. "Love, and do what you will" (*IoEp.* 7.8). This notorious line is perhaps one of his most famous expressions of love, one that has been used for all sorts of purposes.[52] It has promoted the interioriza-

---

49. "I desire mercy, and not sacrifice" (Hosea 6.6). Augustine glosses this passage: "Mercy is the true sacrifice. . . . All the divine commandments, therefore, which we read concerning the many kinds of sacrifice offered in the ministry of the tabernacle or the temple, are to be interpreted symbolically, as referring to the love of God and neighbor" (*CD* 10.5). Augustine's Christology is in full force in this book: "The whole of the redeemed City—that is, the congregation and fellowship of the saints—is offered to God as a universal sacrifice for us through the great High Priest Who, in His Passion, offered even Himself for us in the form of a servant, so that we might be the body of so great a Head" (*CD* 10.6).

50. Von Heyking, *Augustine and Politics as Longing in the World*, 176.

51. Nussbaum, "Augustine and Dante," 63.

52. The context of Augustine's controversial precept is the brotherly correction discussed in 1 John 4:4–12, and is later formulated in *IoEp.* 10.7: "Love, and you cannot but do well" (*dilige, non potest fieri nisi bene facias*). The earliest version of this maxim is

tion of Christian ethics and fueled appeals to situation ethics. It has been offered as an excuse for moral laxity: love and do whatever you want! And, most importantly for my interests, it has been offered in justification of self-deceptive projects of aggrandizement and coercion. These abuses are said to betray a misunderstanding of Augustine's ideal in context—the perfectly ordered lover. Augustine, I think, knew the many conflicts that exist between loves that express a first order desire and a higher order preference.[53] But we should first hesitate and simply recognize how Augustine's maxim starkly highlights the primacy of love in his ethics and his anthropology. The formal structure of Augustine's thought, especially in his discussions of the will, is grounded in this appeal to love as the most general disposition of discipleship: "It is not he who knows what is good who is justly called a good man, but he who loves it" (*CD* 11.28). Or, even more forcefully, "when we ask whether somebody is a good person, we are not asking what he believes or hopes, but what he loves" (*Enchiridion* 31.177). More traditional readings of Augustine that sharply distinguish various faculties of reason, emotion, and the will tend to obscure the internal relation among these "faculties" in Augustine's treatment of love.[54] William Babcock notes:

> *Caritas* is distinctively intertwined with mind, with reason, and with knowing (just as *cupiditas* is distinctively intertwined with fear and apprehensiveness); and contemporary habit prefers to oppose reason and emotion rather than to join them together. . . . On this score too, then, we are ill-equipped with words to convey the passion of Augustine's *caritas*. The result is a reading of Augustine in which, as in Yeat's poem, the best lacks all conviction and the worst is full of passionate intensity.[55]

---

found in Augustine's *Commentary on Galatians* (394/395): "Love, and say what you like" (Plumer, *Augustine's Commentary on Galatians*, 57). Augustine here counsels "never undertake the task of rebuking another's sin without first examining our own conscience by inner questioning and then responding—unequivocally before God—that we are acting out of love. . . . You should not respond in any way until you are healed first, lest perhaps carnal emotions lead you to consent to doing harm." After such examination, Augustine encourages the reader to remember that love requires you to "liberate the person from the siege of vices" but love does not "proudly scorn the sins of others."

    53. I refer here to Harry Frankfurt's formulation in his classic article, "Freedom of the Will and the Concept of a Person," *Journal of Philosophy* 68 (January 1971): 5–20.

    54. See, for example, Dihle, *Theory of the Will*, 123–29.

    55. Babcock, "*Cupiditas* and *Caritas*," 32.

Debates about the primacy of the will or the primacy of the intellect need not detain us in identifying the priority of love for Augustinian anthropology and ethics. I invoke Augustine's dictum and his reformulation of virtue to show that love engages the will and the intellect in moral action.

While there is a moralistic tenor to modern receptions of this dictum, the larger corpus reveals that love is the "motion of the soul" toward God or away from God. As John Burnaby, for example, holds that "when Augustine speaks of love as the 'soul's movement' *(motus animi),* he is thinking not of an 'emotion' but of the directive energy of the will in its most general aspect."[56] The dynamism of the will in Augustine repeats the dynamism of love. Carol Harrison offers this picture of this feature of Augustine:

> For Augustine the will is synonymous with love; to will is not just to rationally deliberate and choose to act, rather it is to love something and to be moved to act on the basis of that love. It is at the root of everything man does, it informs every movement he makes . . . and thus constitutes his very being, making it what it is. A man whose love is directed to God and neighbour is therefore a man of good will.[57]

Harrison's claim confirms the central notion of this section: love is not merely an ideal virtue but is descriptive of all agency and action. For Augustine, the vision of a gracious loving God opens the space for a loving self that is open to others because it is beloved.[58] This is the confessed self who is no longer "panting with anxiety and seething with feverish, corruptive thoughts" (*Conf.* 6.6.9). Love transforms the intellect.[59] This vision is at

56. Burnaby, *Amor Dei,* 93–94.

57. Harrison, *Augustine,* 94–95.

58. Emphasizing the responsive character of Augustine's account of redemption, James Wetzel contrasts Augustine's account with Platonism: "[Augustine's] way out is not through knowledge but through love—God's responsive love for Augustine—and there marks Augustine's departure from Platonism. He responds in will to God's willing of his redemption. If Augustine were strictly a Platonist, he should have had need for only one conversion, that of his intellect" (*LV,* 4).

59. Iris Murdoch paints a similar picture of the self: "We are anxiety-ridden animals. Our minds are continually active, fabricating an anxious, usually self-preoccupied, often falsifying veil which partially conceals the world. Our states of consciousness differ in quality, our fantasies and reveries are not trivial and unimportant, they are profoundly connected with our energies and our ability to choose and act. And if quality of consciousness matters, then anything which alters consciousness in the direction of unselfishness, objectivity, and realism is to be connected with virtue" (*Metaphysics as a Guide to Morals,* 84).

the core of his descriptions of persons and political communities in terms of their loves.

Augustine's rich picturing of the self—the self imagined as *cor inquietum*—emerges from this attention to love and the affective dimensions of existence. This movement seeks its rest in God: "You arouse us so that praising you may bring us joy, because you have made us and drawn us to yourself, and our heart is unquiet until it rests in you" (*Conf.* 1.1.1). Whatever else may be true about human beings, Augustine conceives all human beings as lovers because at the heart of existence is a fundamental spiritual relation to God. It is God's love for us that is the source of our love for this God. Love gathers the scattered self and restores the "ruins" of the "house of the soul" (*Conf.* 1.5.6).

Burnaby's response to Nygren does not shrink from recognizing this central thrust of Augustine's thought:

> Augustine's Platonism is manifested in the centrality for his religion of *amor Dei*—the love of God which appears in men as the pursuit of eternal values and the delight in whatsoever things are lovely. His Platonism is Christian because he finds the Supreme Value and the most compelling loveliness in the love which is God's own being; and because he believes that *amor Dei* is God's gift of Himself to His children—a gift which, offered in the divine humility of Christ's Incarnation and Death, and sealed by the continuing presence of the Spirit of Holiness, brings God and man, without confusion into a most intimate and most real unity.[60]

This desire for intimacy and unity with God governs Augustine's thought. But the nature of the desire is itself transformed by the mode in which it is fulfilled. Augustine tells his listeners "our whole business in this life is to heal the heart's eye by which God is seen."[61] The language of the "heart's eye" poetically conveys Augustine's affective account of existence, suggesting that the good can only be seen when it is approached in the right manner. Salvation lies on the "road of the affections" (*DDC* 1.17.16). Human beings are lovers, but their loves are in need of correction—which is to say organization. They are prone to disorder and error. They make the self vulnerable to the pathologies of love by their own possessiveness. Our loves are scattered and scattering (*Conf.* 2.1.1; 10.29.40).

60. Burnaby, *Amor Dei*, vi.
61. Augustine, Sermon 88.5, cited by Burnaby, *Amor Dei*, 70.

The constant need for affective organization is an important part of the Christian *padeia* and *askesis*, of an education in loving rightly (*DDC* 1.25.26). Jean Bethke Elshtain observes that Augustine's account of love "is not a sentimental tale. . . . It is a discipline that creates a self" (*LP*, 90). Moral education involves the whole person in relation to God. It is a kind of intellectual, emotional, and spiritual therapy that gathers together the dispersed affections in order to release them without damaging the soul and its others. Freedom is the gathering together of the affective and cognitive. This reintegration is linked to Augustine's overall eschatological vision. As Oliver O'Donovan puts it, "the eschatological 'wisdom' toward which . . . redeemed humanity moves is no less a matter of ordered emotions than of rational perspectives" (*PSL, 60*). It is this Augustinian emphasis on the need for training in affectivity that has similarities with feminist theory.

Augustine's famous testimony that "our heart is restless until it rests in you [God]" is a signal theme of both the *Confessions* and the Augustinian tradition itself. Love is a kind of unsatisfied longing. But, if my interpretation is right, the longing itself is ambiguous: it can fuel love and sin, depending on whether it is received as gift or taken as possession. The *Confessions* secured Augustine's reputation as a subtle analyst of the human heart, and it is this Augustine that continues to elicit the fascination of his modern readers. His explorations of the heart, with all of its fears and ambitions, are found throughout his commentaries and sermons. Before considering how this account fits into Augustinian civic liberalism, we need a better sense of how this famous critic of his passions arrives at this position. How did Augustine arrive at this view of reason and emotion in the first place?

REASON AND EMOTION IN AUGUSTINE

The mature Augustine holds that affections are necessary for the life of virtue. He came to praise not bury emotion. How does this famous critic of his passions arrive at this position? How is it that his Christianity becomes "notably 'emotional'"?[62]

As mentioned at the outset, this study aims more at conceptual analysis than historical and exegetical study. But recognizing the development of Augustine's characterization of love is an important part in the larger normative argument for the centrality of love for political Augustinianism. Like

---

62. O'Donnell, *Augustine: Confessions, Latin Text with English Commentary*, 3:185.

other developments in Augustine, it follows his effort to transform Greek philosophy into Christian idiom. This evolution, however, is not a simple progression. Augustine's education in classical philosophy and the resurgent Stoicized Platonism of his youth left impressions that would be impossible simply to abandon. He credits Neoplatonism, in particular, for helping to deliver him from the rational certainties of the Manichees and the radical skepticism of the Academics. Reading Augustine requires recognizing the extent to which his refutation of both "heretics" and "pagans" is an internal struggle within himself, but also part of an emergent Christian orthodoxy that was keen on defining itself in relation to other schools. Given that Augustine assumes various roles in his writing and teaching, charting the development of his thought is extremely difficult.[63]

A standard contrast points to an early Augustine who privileges the role of "reason" and "order" under the influence of Greek and Roman philosophy and a later Augustine who reveals a pronounced emphasis on "sin" and "grace." This development is thought to reflect the impact of his re-reading of Saint Paul in the 390s. The important works of the late 390s, *Confessions* and *On Christian Doctrine*, begin to show the effect of these changes. Whatever one makes of this broad structural contrast, there are clearly significant changes in tone and rhetoric.[64] The experience of reading the early philosophical treatises and dialogues, for example, is different from reading the later homilies and commentaries.

There is a typically intellectualist and ascetic bent to Augustine's early writings that trade on conventional tropes of Stoicism and Neoplatonism.[65]

63. For a subtle historical and philosophical account, see Menn, *Descartes and Augustine*, 194–206. For Augustine's classical education, see Harrison, *Augustine*, 1–78.

64. For a challenge to the traditional view, see Carol Harrison, *Rethinking Augustine's Early Theology: An Argument for Continuity* (Oxford: Oxford University Press, 2006).

65. The influence of Stoicism in Cassiciacum is stressed by Wetzel, *LV*, 55–76. Others, like TeSelle, stress a mixture of Ciceronian and Neoplatonic influences. For an interesting thesis that illumines both theses by highlighting Augustine's rhetorical purposes, see Asiedu, "The Wise Man and the Limits of Virtue in *De Beata Vita*." Asiedu claims that Augustine, by endorsing the pious voice of Monica, is subtly and comically criticizing the follies of ancient philosophy (a rhetorical device that is accentuated in later works). O'Donnell also points out the remarkable status of Monica in the *Confessions* and the early dialogues: "Plato's Diotima in the *Symposium* may be the only truly comparable example" (O'Donnell, *New Biography*, 56).

In his early philosophical writings of the mid-380s, Augustine adopted the hope that virtue and self-sufficient happiness could be found in philosophical continence through a kind of second-hand Stoicized Platonism. The dialogues composed at Cassiciacum, for example, stress the deceptions of the sensible world and the corrosive influence of the bodily passions on the mature life of reason and virtue. Abandoning Skepticism and Manichaeism, he thinks that the "voyage to the port of philosophy—from which, indeed, one enters the hinterland of the happy life—must be charted only by rational choice" (*DBV* 1.1). He delights in this contemplative time as a happy life removed from the "fever of inordinate desires, keeping the mind free from every bodily taint and devoting ourselves to reason" (*CA* 1.4.11). He personifies reason as the "soul's vision" and defines virtue as "right and perfect reason" (*Solil.* 1.6,13). These writings show his debts to classical moral philosophy, particularly the inner retreat from the world of conflict and attending to the rational order of the eternal. While Neoplatonic accounts of the immutable good influence his ethics, he is especially taken by the Stoic emphasis on mental tranquility and adherence to the life of reason and virtue. This life of *apatheia*, moderated by the autonomous will, does not invest emotionally (either in anger or grief) in external goods, including the disturbances of other's people suffering. Very shortly, however, Augustine's formulations of virtue and happiness make a significant shift and come to turn on the central category of love.[66]

66. There are exegetical and historical issues that I do not intend to address. Most scholars agree that Augustine's early work is distinctively Christian even if not preoccupied or shaped by Christian concerns (Harrison, *Augustine*, 15 and 84). Wetzel, however, argues that the Christian content of the turn to love in the works after Cassiciacum is "overdramatized" because the "actual description of the consummation of virtuous love is coolly intellectual" (*LV,* 72; see also 56n15). For example, Wetzel argues that "the mere invocation of love [in *Mor.*] does not compromise Stoic autarky with divine initiative" (*LV,* 72). The more standard view that Augustine breaks from Stoic thought is found in Colish, *The Stoic Tradition from Antiquity to the Early Middle Ages*, 216, and Byers, "Augustine and the Cognitive Cause of Stoic 'Preliminary Passions' *(Propatheiai)*." Wetzel's concern primarily hinges on Augustine's development of doctrine regarding divine agency rather than the nature of love. It may be true, as he argues against Colish, that "it is hard to imagine that love of God in *De moribus* sets the fuse for the explosion of affections in the *Confessiones*. . . . Several years after his conversion, Augustine continues to worship the God of Abraham at that altar of the philosophers" (Wetzel, *LV,* 73). Wetzel may overstate his case. As Asiedu points out, love is invoked even in *DBV* (4.35), ("Wise Man," 220). As an overarching category, however, I think Wetzel is right that a fully Christian concept

While concern with moral virtue conceived as admiration and preservation of one's own virtue continues, Augustine's theological narrative and his "narrative emotions" reflect a break from Neoplatonic and Stoic philosophy.[67] Wetzel nuances this sort of claim by suggesting that Augustine "never gives up the ideal, common to much of late antique philosophy, of bringing together virtues, autonomy, and human flourishing. What changes in his philosophy is not the nature of the ideal but the manner of its appropriation" (*LV*, 16). Given the radical change in appropriation, however, I think it does not overstate the case to claim that he would see in the classical theories a theory of beatitude that was deeply immoral, or at any rate untenable for a human being. Augustine's Christian "philosophy" catapults the movement of love to the forefront. Love, and its relation to willing and desiring, comes to play a much more prominent role in the works after Cassiciacum. For example, as we have seen, the eudaimonistic context of Augustine's appeal to the language of love is clearly set out in a work like *De moribus*. Here, as Arendt points out, Augustine introduces the contrasting rhetoric of *caritas* as a love for eternal things and *cupiditas* as a love of lower, temporal things (*Mor.* 12.21). *Cupiditas* carries a normative evaluation, referring to the inordinate love of lower things. Throughout the text, the reader is encouraged "to love Virtue, to love Wisdom, to love Truth, to love with all your heart, and with all your soul, and with all your mind" (25.47). Indeed, perhaps recalling Augustine's formative reading of Cicero's *Hortensius*, love is personified in the quest for happiness and wisdom: "It is love which asks, love which seeks, love which knocks, love which finds, love which dwells in what is found" (17.31). And yet, the transition to the language of love is theologically determinate. Oliver O'Donovan points out how this feature of Augustine's use of love "innovates on the [classical eudaimonist] tradition" by substituting the verb *love* for its more standard verbs of *pursuit* and *desire* (*PSL,* 24).[68] Love

---

of love waits for the mature works when "[Augustine's] diagnosis of the corrupting influence of affections on virtue marks his break with pagan philosophy and begins to give content to his own conception of the will and its connection to conceptions of virtue and autonomy" (*LV*, 15).

67. I borrow the term, "narrative emotions," from Nussbaum, *Love's Knowledge*, 286–313.

68. O'Donovan notes that "*De moribus ecclesiae* marks Augustine's determination to convert the Christianized Neoplatonism of the Cassiciacan dialogues into theology, and to speak in terms of the love of God, as the Bible does. It is from this point that the

278 ‡ CHAPTER FIVE

is now central to the life of virtue. While some Stoic elements remain (for example, the invulnerability of the wise sage in 1.27.53), they are beginning to fade and will soon disappear. Raymond Canning argues that by the time of the *Tractates on the First Epistle of John* (406), "there is a wholehearted appeal to help the needy 'out of a deep feeling of mercy.'"[69] This transformation regarding the possibility of virtuous affections and other-regard is singularly significant for political ethics. How did this de-Stoicizing move that connects loving, understanding, and willing happen?

We are by now familiar with an Augustine who rejects his human passions for the sake of true love for God. Augustine can depict the capricious and unstable character of the experience of the emotion of love with the best of modern liberals and ancient stoics. They seem to involve risks not worth taking. Augustine remembers his student days at Carthage, where "the din of scandalous love affairs raged cauldron-like around me" (*Conf.* 3.1.1). Augustine can paint a dim picture of the "irrational passions of the soul" that toss a person "like a stormy sea" (*CD* 9.4). Augustine's account of willing, however, distinguishes rational "emotions" from irrational "passions." Passions alienate us from ourselves through our own prideful self-possession. In Augustine's careful terminology, passions (experienced as disturbances, *perturbationes*) are always bad, but emotion (usually *motus* or *affectus*) like loving, can be good or bad. As John Cavadini has argued, passions should be thought of as "pathologized" versions of emotions.[70] The bad passions, and

---

verb 'to love' begins to dominate his teleological thought, an innovation on the classical tradition that has not been accorded sufficient notice" (*"Usus* and *Fruitio,"* 375). Babcock also notes Augustine's conversion of the classical language of "wanting" to Christian vocabulary of "loving" (Babcock, "*Cupiditas* and *Caritas*," 8–9).

69. Canning, *Unity of Love for God and Neighbor*, 183.

70. Cavadini, "Feeling Right," 199. Charting Augustine's use of these terms, Cavadini argues that "Augustine is suspicious not only of lust in the sexual sense but of all of the passions, and not only of the passions themselves but of the very idea of 'passion' as though it offered a complete description of the range of human emotions, or as though 'emotion' were equivalent to 'passion'" (198). This chapter, in many ways, is an extension of Cavadini's reading of Augustinian sexual desire for Augustinian political ethics. Augustine's account of passions as morally bad emotions is also found in Byers, "Augustine and the Cognitive Cause." Byers suggests Augustine adopts the distinction from Stoic sources but adds a Christian twist by placing the incomplete distinction in the context of false judgments about temporal goods as eternal goods. Anastasia Scrutton also highlights the linguistic range of Augustine's account of emotions and passions

even potentially salutary emotions such as grief, remorse, and fear, belong only to this earthly life of sin. They are part of "the infirmity of our human condition" (*CD* 14.9), emotions and passions that properly speaking have no reason. They are lusts and disorders that cause us to yield against even our own will when "the vigilance of a man's mind is almost entirely over-whelmed" (*CD* 14.16). He describes the earthly city itself as "convulsed by those emotions as if by diseases and upheavals" (*CD* 14.9). Augustine's ascetic descriptions of the dangerous world of finite loves and emotion are the Augustine that his feminist theological critics usually cite (and, ironically, may lend support to the Kantian conclusions they often oppose). This is the Augustine who seeks in the changeless God a kind of "rest and tranquil life" where "he will fear nothing" (*Conf.* 2.10.18).[71]

The two most famous examples of Augustine's supposed attraction both to Stoic invulnerability and the Neoplatonic ascent of love that undermines finite loves and the affirmation of emotion are found in the *Confessions*: his regret at weeping over the death of Dido and his analysis of his grief after the death of his unnamed friend from Thagaste. A close reading of these examples as they relate to Augustine's theology is not possible here. But I would like to suggest that their common use in criticism of Augustinian love is misguided, given their dramatic and theological function. At the very least, the examples do not admit the reading that Augustine condemns both emotion and finite loves as distractions from the purity of love for God through mental contemplation. To the contrary, the logic of Augustine's appeal to these examples suggests the opposite conclusion. Burnell argues, for example, that Augustine suggests that "the whole mind is rightly character-ized as emotional."[72] Augustine desires authentic emotion and authentic love for the finite by temporal creatures. The problem, he discovers, is that his emotions and loves were illusions and phantoms—enchantments of a lover

---

(see Scrutton, "Emotion in Augustine"). Wetzel also notes that *pertubatio* best represents Augustine's interest in "the way in which emotions can disorder the rational operations of the human mind" (*LV,* 51n13).

71. It is noteworthy that Augustine's conception of rest is not a static end to desire. Boulding's translation captures the vision well: "I want to gaze with eyes that see purely and find satiety in never being sated" (*Conf.* 2.10.18). The eschatological vision fits with his description of his self in his memory: "What am I, then, O my God? What is my nature? It is teeming life of every conceivable kind, and exceedingly vast" (*Conf.* 10.17.26).

72. Burnell, *Augustinian Person*, 62.

refusing to love. On my reading, these episodes of regret are motivated by a moral concern with self-enclosure rather than a spirituality of otherworldly escapism. These episodes are not about getting stuck on the Platonic ladder but about prideful possession as a tempting psychology of desire. In fact, Augustine shares C. S. Lewis's insight that "it is dangerous to press upon a man the duty of getting beyond earthly love when his real difficulty lies in getting this far."[73] It is only when he sees the compassion of God, the God who would become human and so identifies and commands the love of neighbor, that Augustine would break from classical philosophy.

DEATH AND SOLIDARITY: DIDO AND THE UNNAMED FRIEND

Augustine's regret at weeping over the death of Dido and his analysis of his grief after the death of his unnamed friend is both shocking and moving. I appeal to them because a common reading of these stories cites them as signs of his excessive Platonic spirituality. The setting for the weeping over Dido is not primarily a consideration of the value of emotion or even the value of finite goods. Rather, Augustine places emphasis on his attraction to the "legendary" world of literature and theater to the neglect of the real world of his own soul.[74] The contrast he draws throughout Book 1 is between illusion and reality—a contrast between the need to attend to reality and his own "love for play and the absurd anxiety with which I craved to gawk at worthless shows and imitate what I watched" (*Conf.* 1.19.30). In Book 2, he characterizes this adolescent preference for the imagined as a "shadowy jungle of erotic adventures" (*Conf.* 2.1.1, Bettenson). Augustine, as Marilynn Desmond has argued, may be conflating female sexuality and pagan reading

---

73. Lewis, *Four Loves*, 165. Lewis, however, thinks he must reject Augustine's regret. They are "less a part of St. Augustine's Christendom than a hang-over from the high-minded Pagan philosophies in which he grew up. It is closer to Stoic 'apathy' or neo-Platonic mysticism than to charity" (168). Lewis mistakenly refers to Augustine's unnamed friend as Nebridius.

74. Iris Murdoch also emphasizes that the "chief enemy of excellence in morality (and also in art) is personal fantasy: the tissue of self-aggrandizing and consoling wishes and dreams which prevents one from seeing what is there outside one" (Murdoch, *Metaphysics as a Guide to Morals*, 59). Murdoch links goodness with the "acceptance of real death" (103).

in this retrospective description of his "early captivation with Virgil's Dido as fornication *(fornicatio)*."[75] The passage is certainly related to "Augustine's concern to discipline desires, both sexual and readerly."[76] I do not wish to defend Augustine's complicated attitude toward sexuality. Desmond's overly sexualized reading, however, fits too neatly into a view of Augustine that I here reject. Desmond contrasts this early Augustine (the one who can still weep for Dido) with a later Christianized Augustine who "relies on reason, not emotion."[77] Nancy A. Jones, in an illuminating article on the role of tears in Augustine's *Confessions*, argues that Augustine's narrative draws upon a "deeply rooted cultural opposition between female emotionality and male knowledge and control."[78] This view is one that I want to make problematic given Augustine's late discussion of the Stoics.

The seduction that Augustine describes in relation to his remembrance of Dido may be both gendered and sexually coded, but this seduction should be set against the larger background of a primarily cultural and educational re-imagining that occurs in the *Confessions* and, more extensively, in Book 2 of the *City of God*.[79] Augustine's regret is regret about the possessiveness of

75. Desmond, *Reading Dido*, 77. According to Desmond, Dido represents the *libido* in a way that connects both sex and reading as seducers linked to the experience of death.

76. Ibid., 79. Desmond links discipline to repression, a move Augustinians would not share.

77. Ibid., 78. Desmond interestingly points out that "Augustine's vision of Christian history in *De civitate Dei*, a text that purposefully revises Virgil's historical vision concerning the City of Rome, does not include Dido. Unlike the pagan Augustine who wept when he read Dido, the elderly Christian Augustine manages to form an interpretive structure that might subsume Virgil's text yet simultaneously erase Dido" (78). The erasure of Dido, like other named and unnamed women in Augustine's corpus, is significant. But its significance can not be described in turns of a triumph of reason over emotion. On naming and not naming in Augustine's texts, see Conybeare, *Irrational Augustine*, 64–69.

78. Jones, "Woman's Tears Redeemed," 33. Jones, however, focuses on the role of Monica's tears in representing "conversion as a primarily male experience," not Augustine's tears for Dido (17).

79. For an interesting discussion of the relation of sexual and cultural seduction in early Christian and Rabbinic literature, see Joshua Levinson, "An-Other Woman: Joseph and Potiphar's Wife. Staging the Body Politic," *The Jewish Quarterly Review* 87, nos. 3–4 (January–April 1997): 269–301. Levinson, drawing on Peter Brown's account of the body as a site of social mediation in classical antiquity, argues that sexual struggle in the

self-deception and self-enclosure: how could he be diverted so as to be struck by the theatricality of Dido's death (a characteristic theatricality he ascribes to pagan literature) when he did not even realize his own real death? He writes:

> What is more pitiable than a wretch without pity for himself who weeps over the death of Dido dying for love of Aeneas, but not weeping over himself dying for his lack of love for you, my God, light of my heart, bread of my inner mouth of my soul, the power which begets life in my mind and in the innermost recesses of my thinking. (*Conf.* 1.13.21, Chadwick)

Augustine's concern is with escapism and spectatorial curiosity, a projection or retreat into simulacra that is actually more a failure of emotion and love than an instance of their affirmation. A modern analogy, with apologies to Virgil, might be crying over reality TV or the infotainment packaging of death for media consumption just before we go off to "bowl alone" in Robert Putnam's America. They allow you to enjoy weeping without demanding compassion. To love in this passive, aesthetic, and consumerist way, ironically, is yet another way to take possession, to consume the other as only part of one's own imaginative world. In Book 3, Augustine continues his lament over his captivity by theatrical shows as a critique of ancient ethics itself.[80] He argues that this world of "fictitious and theatrical inventions" does not elicit

---

Genesis story becomes a "trope for cultural continence, and the battle for cultural identity is intertwined with the conflict of sexual identity. For Joseph, to be seduced by Potiphar's wife, to give in to his own desires, is to lose not only the defining characteristic of maleness itself, but also his cultural identity" (294). Levinson makes explicit references to the negative attitudes of the Church Fathers to theatricality, including an association of the theater with the synagogue. I thank John Gager for this reference.

80. Chadwick points out that Augustine's discussion of the theater is similar to Plato, *Republic* 10.606–7 and *Philebus* 48ab. Augustine's rejection of the theater is not simply because of its evil content but "also because of the fictional character of the plays, fiction being, to his mind, a form of mendacity" (*Confessions*, 36n3). James K. A. Smith argues that Augustine's affirmation of the Incarnation "undoes his (largely Platonic) critique of drama" and opens "the space for an affirmative Augustinian account of theatre as part of a broader Christian aesthetic" (Smith, "Staging the Incarnation," 123). For a discussion of the problematic relation between humane literature and compassion, see George Steiner, *Language and Silence* (New York: Atheneum, 1967). For a reading of the *Aeneid* as itself social critique, see Steven Farron, "The Aeneas-Dido Episode as an Attack on Aeneas' Mission and Rome," *Greece & Rome* 27, no.1 (April 1980): 34–47.

concern for others but allows the audience to enjoy the spectacle of watching others suffer. Or, to add to the diversion, we enjoy an imaginary self-pity that deflects real pain, both of our own and of others. Augustine asks, "but how real is the mercy evoked by fictional dramas? The listener is not moved to offer help, but merely invited to feel sorrow?" (*Conf.* 3.2.2). John Milbank notes that "this theatrical drug is for [Augustine] no true medicine, since it achieves no catharsis, but rather induces addiction" (*BR*, 31). It is a fake, passive compassion cut off from the real world of suffering. All compassion, we have seen, is dangerous. But it is clear in this passage that Augustine's view is "it is sometimes right to entertain compassionate feelings" (*Conf.* 3.3). His regret is not that he experienced "female" emotion as a disruption of his "masculine" pursuit of tranquil happiness. The problem is not even literature itself. The problem is that he preferred imaginary suffering rather than attending to the real life of suffering. Iris Murdoch, arguing against the extremes of existential voluntarism, vividly expresses the Augustinian picture I am trying to paint:

> The freedom which is a proper human goal is freedom from fantasy, that is the realism of compassion. What I have called fantasy, the proliferation of blinding self-centered aims and images, is itself a powerful system of energy, and most of what is often called 'will' or 'willing' belongs to this system.[81]

Love that sees real others breaks open this fantasy world, a fantasy consumed with our own feelings. As Augustine puts it elsewhere in the *Confessions*, the emptiness of these illusions reveals "the superficial appearance of a virtue that was but feigned and fake" (*Conf.* 6.7.12). Moral attention, by contrast, requires "respect for the real."[82]

Augustine's preoccupation with illusion and vanity helps us understand one of his darkest moments—his grief over the death of a schoolboy friend who he had turned away from God at the start of his teaching career. Augustine, whom Garry Wills calls "the antirhetorician rhetorician," begins Book 4 highlighting the dangers of rhetoric and eloquence in ways that parallel his

---

81. Murdoch, *Metaphysics as a Guide to Morals*, 67.

82. Murdoch, *Sovereignty of Good*, 91. For Murdoch, "attention is our daily bread" (44) that requires a "just and loving gaze directed upon an individual reality" (34). For a perceptive comparison of Iris Murdoch with Simone Weil and Martha Nussbaum, see Peta Bowden, "Ethical Attention: Accumulating Understandings," *European Journal of Philosophy* 6, no. 1 (1998): 49–77.

account of the theater.[83] This educational concern is the backdrop to his story. Arendt took Augustine's lament that he allowed himself to be "chained by friendship with mortal things" and his appeal to God to cleanse him of the "uncleanness of such affections" as further evidence of his rejection of the world (*Conf.* 4.6.11).[84] Augustine does not help his case by his description of his devotion to his friends as a kind of adulterous fornication, or, as he puts it, "a substitute for you [God]; and this was a vast myth and a long lie" (*Conf.* 4.8.13, Chadwick). Arendt seems to think that the world itself is for Augustine a lie—a cheap temptation to forget about the really good thing, God. Her Augustine could not say yes to the worldliness of time.[85] He needs to make a "desert" out of the world in order to protect his love for God. But is this all that Augustine's tears could mean and all that Augustinianism has to offer?

Gerald Schlabach offers a more positive reading: Augustine's grief consists in the revelation that he had valued the ideal of friendship more than the friend itself. His lament is not over his grief, or over the love of the finite, but expresses his recognition of the poverty of the sort of love he had for his friend. The problem is not the distraction of his friend (or whatever finite good); the problem is his incontinent self. For Schlabach, "continence is

83. Wills, *Augustine*, 144.

84. Critics often link this rejection of misery with his rejection of delight in church music, watching rabbits in the countryside, and his account of the death of Monica (Werpehowski, "Weeping at the Death of Dido"; Wolterstorff, "Suffering Love"; Sorabji, *Peace of Mind*, 390–406; and Nussbaum, *UT*, 529). I agree with Werpehowski that "ethics should be concerned with the feelings or affections that a human person of good character ought to have" ("Weeping," 175). For Werpehowski, however, "Augustine's ambivalence toward his tears, and toward the temporal relation to which they are a response, suggests that perhaps another and better sort of valuation of worldly bonds is to be commended; such a valuation is a condition of sorrowing well, lest affections that seemingly arise from patience display an unfitting distance from goods that are lost" (187). While my reading moves away from this preoccupation with Augustine's subordination of temporal goods, Werpehowski's essay draws interesting connections between Dido and Monica and also points to passages on friendship in *City of God* 19.8 that may redeem Augustine even from this negative reading (189n11).

85. Ronald Beiner argues that Arendt's fundamental political question is this: "Under what conditions can we say yes to time? As posed either by Augustine or by Nietzsche, the problem—which haunts all of Arendt's philosophical work—is how to subdue temporality, how to consolidate and stabilize a mortal existence, rendering it less fleeting, ontologically less insecure.... A public space of judgment is needed to render the world of appearances more durable" ("Interpretive Essay," 155).

the operative mode of Augustinian *caritas*."[86] This reading actually supports the claim that Augustine recognizes the dangers of loving love in a way that eclipses the particularism of love. Augustine recognizes the immaturity of his love that was more concerned with his own fragmented world of false desires than the "more real and more lovable" person that he had lost (*Conf.* 4.4.9). This seems right to me. I want to add a friendly amendment to Schlabach's reading and suggest that there is more at work in this passage than Augustine's grief over an unnamed friend.[87]

Augustine draws an analogy between the "phantom" love he had for this friend and the "phantom" God that he was worshipping. His grief over the loss of his friend is intense, and it suggestively parallels his description of his life without God. He writes:

> Feverishly I thrashed about, sighed, wept and was troubled, and there was no repose for me, nor any counsel. Within me I was carrying a tattered, bleeding soul that did not want me to carry it, yet I could find no place to lay it down. Not in the pleasant countryside did it find rest, nor in shows and songs, nor in sweet-scented gardens, nor in elaborate feasts, nor in the pleasures of couch or bed, nor even in books and incantations. All things loured at me, even daylight itself, and everything that was not what he was seemed to me offensive and hateful, except for mourning and tears, in which alone I found some slight relief. (*Conf.* 4.7.12)

This restlessness recalls the restless self before God. Indeed, the parallel suggests that Augustine is using the story as an allegorical opportunity to

---

86. Schlabach, *For the Joy Set Before Us*, 58. I agree with Schlabach that continence and humility are fundamental to *caritas*, but I prefer to accent ordering rather than continence as its operative mode because it does not carry the implication that love needs to be restrained as such, rather than properly ordered.

87. I thank James Wetzel for discussion of these passages. My reading also differs from O'Donovan, who sees in this passage "an element of pretence in that bitter grief, a self-deception which hid the plain truth about himself and his friend, that they were both men and not gods" (*PSL*, 31). In addition to Schlabach and Wetzel, the closest reading to my own is found in Romand Coles. Unlike many Christian readers, Coles recognizes that Augustine's "highly developed sense of the miseries that are a part of human experience" is actually a function of his high view of the world as a "polyphonic *sign* of the God who created it" (*Self/Power/Other*, 42n17). Augustine worries when the self replaces God as "the origin and ground of things," but this "is a problem of the self, not of the world" (42n17).

confess and to mourn his forgetfulness of God.[88] He claims that he had a false materialist image of God: "For what I thought of was not you at all; an empty fantasy and my error were my god" (*Conf.* 4.7.12). Just as there can be no substitute for his lost friend, so too he cannot substitute God with the phantoms of his own imagination. That is the pain that he confesses: not that he loved too much, but that he did not really love (either the world or God) at all. It was not that he loved his friend, a mortal creature, or even that he loved him intensely. It was that he loved him "as though he would never die" (*Conf.* 4.6.11). To love in this way was to take possession of his friend (and, so, of his private image of God) as his own—as belonging to him rather than to God. What is the "vast myth and long lie" of Book 4? Later in the *Confessions*, Augustine makes it clear. The sin that corrupts love is the lie that God and God's creation exist for one's own private possession (*Conf.* 12.25.34; see also *GL* 11.14.19). Instead of loving the neighbor with attention, or any part of the created world, the self "wants to claim them for itself" (*DT* 10.2.7) and "slides away from the whole which is common to all into the part which is its own private property" (*DT* 12.3.14). This is the self that "wraps up their images and clutches them to itself, images made in itself out of itself" (*DT* 10.2.7). Augustine's problematic is not loving what you can not lose, but loving what you can lose as if it were yours not to lose.

In Book 7 of the *Confessions*, Augustine returns to this imagery of loving "some figment of imagination" in place of God (*Conf.* 7.17.23). Loving created things for oneself and apart from the light of God is the fiction for Augustine. The arrival of Lady Continence in Book 8 and the testimony to the God known in Christ, the mystery of the Word made flesh, invites him to let go of his clutching anxiety in order to share God's world. Accepting this shared gift of divine love—a love that secures the self as a beloved—transforms Augustine's account of the love for God and God's good creation. As he later puts it in Book 10 of the *City of God*: "We are His temple, each of us and every one of us together, since He deigns to dwell both in the whole harmonious body and in each of us singly" (*CD* 10.3). The emphasis on active receptivity to grace, and the vulnerability this entails, are keys to his Christological reshap-

88. The absence of a name for his friend may borrow from biblical narratives where the appearance of an unnamed individual suggestively alludes to the hidden God (for example, the story of Jacob's wrestling at Jabbok in Gen. 32:24–32, or even the "least of these" in Matt. 25:45). Augustine discusses a number of other examples in *DT* 3.10.20.

ing of *eros*. But even here in Book 4 of the *Confessions*, Augustine introduces the wisdom that heals the distortions of his will and the habit-formed passions that had made him blind to God and to loving humanly. It is God's love for us that would humble itself that grounds the affective life of virtue. This love is to shape our own love for others; that is not to grasp after neighbors like he had for his boyhood friend. Grasping was a way of death, but Christ showed Augustine a way of loving that ascends to life. Augustine writes in what I take to be the central passage of the *Confessions*:

> He who is our very life came down and took our death upon himself. He slew our death by his abundant life and summoned us in a voice of thunder to return to him in his hidden place, that place from which he set out to come to us when first he entered the Virgin's womb. There a human creature, mortal flesh, was wedded to him that it might not remain mortal for ever; and from there he came forth like a bridegroom from his nuptial chamber, leaping with joy like a giant to run his course. Impatient of delay he ran, shouting by his words, his deeds, his death and his life, his descent into hell and his ascension into heaven, shouting his demand that we return to him. Then he withdrew from our sight, so that we might return to our own hearts and find him there. He withdrew, yet look, here he is. (*Conf.* 4.12.19)

As in Book 10 of the *City of God*, Augustine's Christology is fundamental for his theology of love and clarifies the otherwise obscure relation between the love commands. Christ is the eternal Word who satisfies our restlessness, the *res* and the *signum* that Augustine earlier identifies in *On Christian Doctrine*. Christ, the God who is fully human, is not only the mediator between God and the self. Christ also mediates between God and neighbor in the self's vision (*CD* 9.17 and *Conf.* 7.9). As I show more fully in the next chapter, it is this Incarnationalism that distinguishes Augustinianism from Platonism.

STOICISM AND PASSION

But what about the Stoics like Seneca? Augustine's Christianity is also significant for his account of the passions in *City of God* books 9 and 14. These books explicitly challenge his Stoic background and figure prominently in his mature attitude toward the place of love in the moral life. They offer insights for an Augustinian ethic of citizenship through their reevaluation of his early indebtedness to Stoic ideas of self-sufficiency and *apatheia*.[89] The contents of these books challenge both Arendt's reading of Augustine and her account of the passions.

Augustine comes to think that the Stoic hardness does not imply rectitude; in fact, the Stoics are seen as defacing their humanity and more interested in "words rather than in realities" (*CD* 14.9). After recounting a number of biblical passages that portray emotions in a positive light, Augustine claims:

> If these emotions and affections, which come from the love of the good and from holy charity, are to be called vices, then let us allow that real vices should be called virtues. But since, when they are exhibited in the proper circumstances, these affections are the consequences of right reason, who would then dare to say that they are unwholesome and vicious passions? (*CD* 14.9)

Augustine links the experience of emotion to a person's character and the need to experience and properly cultivate emotions. He enlists the examples of Paul and Peter, but it is primarily Christ himself that authorizes moral emotions. His tears always have a "reason." In the humility of the Incarnation, God experiences emotions and invites us to share in solidarity with these emotions. Augustine writes:

> Hence, when the Lord Himself deigned to live a human life in the form of a servant, though having no sin, He displayed these emotions in circumstances where He judged that they ought to be displayed. For human emotion was not feigned in Him Who truly had the body of a man and the mind of a man. (*CD* 14.9)[90]

89. For a schematic presentation of the use of the term *apatheia* in Greek and Latin theological traditions, see Augustine Michael Casiday, "*Apatheia* and Sexuality in the Thought of Augustine and Cassian," *St. Vladimir's Theological Quarterly* 45, no. 4 (2001): 359–94. Andrew Louth makes a case that *apatheia* plays an important role in Eastern asceticism, though it was replaced in the West by the "less alarming-sounding *puritas cordis*" ("Love and the Trinity," 1–16). Louth presents an interesting challenge to Augustine's claim that love characterizes the inner reality of God as much as God's love for humanity: "We run the risk of reducing the mystery of the Godhead to human categories" (14). But, in terms of the passions rather than apophatic approaches to the Trinity, Augustine's criticism of Stoic *apatheia* would not apply to Louth's presentation of *apatheia* in Clement or Maximos. In fact, they strike me as remarkably similar.

90. Augustine's criticism parallels Calvin's later criticism of Stoicism as "iron philosophy": "Among the Christians there are also new Stoics, who count it depraved not only to groan and weep but also to be sad and care ridden" (Calvin, *Institutes* 1:3.8). Ironically,

Virtue could not demand the overcoming of affect. In fact, the illusory strategy of insulating reason from emotional attachment paves the way to vice. It promises safety, but it never delivers on this promise of salvation by way of a emotionless will. In Book 9, after telling Gellius's story of a sea voyage with a well-known Stoic, Augustine informs his pagan readers that the Christian Scriptures counsel that emotions "should be turned to righteous use":

> Within our discipline, then, we do not so much ask whether a pious soul is angry, as why he is angry; not whether he is sad, but whence comes his sadness; not whether he is afraid, but what he fears. . . . The Stoics, indeed, are wont to reproach even compassion. But how much more honourable it would have been if the Stoic in Aulus Gellius's story had been disturbed by compassion for a fellow man, in order to comfort him, rather than by fear of being shipwrecked! (*CD* 9.5)

Compassion is not always a threat to action. It is a "kind of fellow feeling in our hearts for the misery of another which compels us to help him if we can . . . [but] the Stoics are not ashamed to number it among the vices" (*CD* 9.5). He repeats these arguments in Book 14: "If *apatheia* is to be defined as the condition such that the mind cannot be touched by any emotion whatsoever, who would not judge such insensitivity to be the worst of all vices?" (*CD* 14.9). Heroic self-reliance might temper the worst excesses of a lust for power, but Augustine could not seek refuge in this refusal of emotional investment in the happiness of others. The self should not divest itself of these attachments: "A righteous life will exhibit all these emotions righteously, whereas a perverse life exhibits them perversely" (*CD* 14.9). Importantly, love entails solidarity with others not exclusively in terms of their spiritual welfare. Augustine's loving also makes him "anxious lest they be afflicted by famine, war, pestilence, or captivity, fearing that in slavery they may suffer evils beyond what we can conceive" (*CD* 19.8). This anxiety is a sign not of a troubled soul but of a properly engaged lover. This is a true transvaluation of ancient values. Carol Harrison finds:

> Far from relegating the passions to the irrational soul he makes them a part of the rational soul, as forms in which the will works, and which are capable

---

Augustine and Calvin often are taken to be rationalistic theologians. See, for example, Ralph Hancock, *Calvin and the Foundations of Modern Politics* (Ithaca: Cornell University Press, 1989).

of both positive and negative applications. . . . The passions are not only possible, but necessary. The Stoic ideal of passionlessness (Gk. *apatheia*, Lt. *impassibilitas*), however it is understood—as the absence of disordered passion or the complete absence of any emotion whatsoever—is neither desirable or attainable in this life, or even in the life to come.[91]

Unlike Harrison's interpretation, Richard Sorabji finds that Augustine still relied on "a Platonic view of the soul, which, in contrast to the Stoic view, holds that emotion is the product of irrational forces in the soul and does not have to await the assent of reason, as the Stoics suppose."[92] Augustine counts this Stoic belief as one more sign of pride and vanity.[93] In fact, contrary to Arendt's account of Augustine's passion for invulnerability and tranquility in love, Augustine makes the case *for the moral dangers of evading emotion.*

In his recent Gifford Lectures, Sorabji has carefully traced Augustine's decided rejection of "the Stoic ideal of freedom from emotion as being neither practical nor desirable."[94] He tells a fascinating story of Augustine's misreading of Stoicism (failing to distinguish between "first movements" and "emotions") and argues that this misreading led to a pernicious notion of a divided will that has bedeviled attitudes toward sexuality and throughout Western culture more generally. Sorabji offers his own kind of intellectually viable form of therapy in dealing with emotions for a post-Christian era. Whether or not Augustine (or Sorabji) is right about Stoic views of the emotions, Augustine's argument against what he understands the Stoics to believe is crucial to his own development and consistent with broader themes in his understanding of love that I have identified.[95]

The negative aspects of passions, however, are only half the story for Augustine. Augustine's strategy in redeeming emotion is similar to what I claimed earlier about loving more generally. Love expresses itself in both positive and negative ways, according to the proper ordering of love. This

91. Harrison, *Augustine*, 93–94.

92. Sorabji, *Emotion and Peace of Mind*, 10.

93. Peter Dennis Bathory more strongly writes: "He abhorred *apatheia* and feared that the solitude that accompanied that Stoic disposition could too easily lead people away from the confrontation with the *saeculum* that he saw as each person's obligation" ("Augustine through a Modern Prism," *Society* 34, no. 4 [May/June 1997]: 72–76, at 72). See also O'Daly, *Augustine's City of God: A Reader's Guide*, 156.

94. Sorabji, *Emotion and Peace of Mind*, 10.

95. For a lucid account of Stoic moral psychology, see John Cooper, *Reason and Emotion: Essays on Ancient Moral Psychology* (Princeton: Princeton University Press, 1998).

position is extended to the emotions (now contrasted with passions). As such, Augustine writes, "if the will is perverse, the emotions will be perverse; if the will is right, the emotions will be not only blameless, but praiseworthy" (*CD* 14.6). Put another way, "good and evil men alike feel desire, fear, and joy. But the good feel these emotions in a good way, and the bad feel them in a bad way, just as the will of men may be righteous or perverse" (*CD* 14.8).[96] Even in heaven, where Augustine believes humanity will participate in the divine *apatheia* that properly orders all loves, the healed will "will exhibit a love and gladness" (*CD* 14.9). This kind of dynamic tranquility is not the refusal of emotion or feeling. It is the blessed state when emotions are freely ordered *(imperturbabilitas)*. We might generally summarize by way of this formulation: Aristotelians teach the moderation of emotion. Stoics counsel strategies for passing through them. Kantians worry about emotion but maintain it is indifferent to moral value, thereby keeping respect at a safe distance from love. Augustinian Christianity places the emotions squarely in the context of morality itself. Augustine's image of persons as lovers is not reducible to moralistic notions of beneficence or rationalistic depictions of love as uncontrollable feeling.

ADVICE TO LOVING LIBERAL CITIZENS

Arendtian worries about political love, no doubt, still remain. Are there any other sources to comfort worries about compassion for a political ethic? Does Augustine offer anything beyond my previous endorsement of Joan Tronto's frank recognition that there is no theoretical recourse that will ensure that care will not be exercised badly when it goes public? I here suggest three further caveats that follow from this discussion before finally turning to the most problematic aspect of Augustine's loving. They are three ways that Augustine himself imagines we might direct our love given the conditions of sin. They are not guarantees, but the life of virtue does not offer guarantees. Given Augustine's pastoral duties, I think they can be assimilated into the genre that Brian Walker describes as "cultivational advice giving as a way of encouraging the habits and dispositions entailed in human

---

96. While some emotions can become passions, Augustine persistently characterizes "lust" negatively as a passion because it is never directed by an integrated will (see *CD* 14.6 and 14.19; *Conf.* 8.5 and 8.9–10). For Augustine, there was no lust before the Fall (though, in principle, there could have been sexual activity).

democratization."[97] They are not knock-down arguments or theoretical resolutions, but they are ways of imagining what good citizenship might look like.

First, like Kant, Augustine cautions against allowing excessive compassion to interfere with prudence and judgment. Identification with another's suffering has limits. He offers the following example:

> And therefore, in respect to such states of mind, you must take on somewhat the very affliction from which you want the other person to be freed through your efforts, and you must take it on in this way for the purpose of being able to give help, not achieve the same degree of misery. Analogously, a man bends over and extends his hand to someone lying down, for he does not cast himself down so that they are both lying, but he only bends down to raise up the one lying down. (*DeDiv.* 83.71.2; see also *DVR* 49.91)

Augustine is not devaluing emotions but taking them seriously in his account of the moral life. He is, at least implicitly, recognizing that other-regard requires an autonomy of its own—an autonomy of both the lover and the beloved. Responsibility and compassion are not antithetical to autonomy, as Arendt would lead us to believe, but are correlated notions. Augustine wants a certain kind of compassion.

Interestingly, Kant offers a similar example. His interpretation mirrors Augustine's. In *Lectures on Anthropology*, Kant considers someone who sees a child fall into water and is "so shocked that one thereby cannot do anything" (25:592).[98] Kant's example serves to highlight his concern that affects are bad for morality because they empirically get in the way of the rational

97. Walker, "Thoreau on Democratic Cultivation," 155.

98. Cited and discussed by Frierson, *Freedom and Anthropology in Kant's Moral Philosophy*, 60. Frierson notes that Kant offers several practical remedies for preventing the power of affect to overwhelm one's moral decision-making, including the avoidance of "romances and maudlin plays" (61). Kant claims that "when another suffers and, although I cannot help him, I let myself be infected by his pain (through my imagination), the two of us suffer, though the trouble really (in nature) affects only *one*. But there cannot possibly be a duty to increase the ills in the world and so to do good *from compassion*" (*Metaphysics of Morals*, 6:457). Kant, however, also claims that there is a "duty not to avoid the places where the poor who lack the most basic necessities are to be found but rather to seek them out, and not to shun sickrooms or debtors' prisons and so forth in order to avoid sharing painful feelings one may not be able to resist. For this is still one of the impulses that nature has implanted in us to do what the representation of duty alone might not accomplish" (457).

judgments that a good will makes when faced with such a situation. Augustine shares this empirical concern, but he does not separate affect and compassion in the way Kant does. For Kant, affects do not involve the will. For Augustine, they do. As with Aristotle, virtue is about learning to act and to feel well. Augustine's church is where this sentimental education and moral cultivation takes place. He likens the church to "sacred lecture halls for the peoples of the world" (*Ep.* 91, 3). But, with Kant, Augustine does not want feelings to overwhelm and render charity useless. Kant's deeper worry, however, seems to be that compassion provokes a "holier than thou" attitude that demeans the dignity of persons and reduces them to an object. Augustine again shares this concern that might corrupt our service to others:

> Once you have bestowed gifts on the unfortunate, you may easily yield to the temptation to exalt yourself over him, to assume superiority over the object of your benefaction. He fell into need, and you supplied him: you feel yourself as the giver to be a bigger man than the receiver of the gift. You should want him to be your equal, that both may be subject to the one on whom no favour can be bestowed. (*IoEp.* 8.5)

Nietzsche would echo Augustine's suspicions, but in the service of exposing Christian morality as pretence: "You crowd around your neighbor and have fine words for it. But I say unto you: your love of the neighbor is your bad love of yourselves. You flee to the neighbor from yourselves and would like to make a virtue out of that: but I see through your 'selflessnes.'"[99] Augustine does not allow this psychological suspicion to get in the way of his recognition that circumstances arise in human life that can overwhelm individuals. To reject the possibility of responsiveness to suffering as simply disguised self-interest would carry a doctrine of sin too far. Compassion does not require stripping the neighbor of her dignity in order rescue a helpless victim. Against classical Stoicism, Martha Nussbaum supports the view that a political society must take account of the noncontradictory fact that "people are dignified agents, but they are also, frequently, victims" (*UT*, 406). Augustine's moral psychology, with its recognition of the many features of social life that render us vulnerable and dependent, supports this stance. He tries to find a way to ensure that autonomy, human dignity, and caring service are correlated rather than antithetical notions. He knew the moral and psychological

99. Nietzsche, *Zarathustra*, 60–61.

dangers of making others objects of compassion. Augustinian liberalism has not paid sufficient attention to the political implications of this aspect of Augustine's own thought. Arendt claimed that public compassion inevitably becomes a degrading and selfish form of "pity." My reading of Augustine's tears suggests he also knew this danger. Augustinian liberals, however, should refuse Arendt's effort to shield public life from compassion. That would cut short the sort of activity of compassion that Augustine wanted to motivate. But how might an Augustinian discriminate among the many victims? Here we see a second possible way to relieve Arendt's worries.

With the Donatists in the back of his mind, Augustine exhorted his parishioners: "If you would love Christ, stretch out your charity over all the world: for Christ's members are spread the world over" (*IoEp.* 10.8). Charity should not be confined to Africa. But Augustine also claims that while Christian love is unconditional and universal, it begins "at home" but extends "outward." The compassionate citizen need not be overwhelmed by cosmopolitan demands:

> All people should be loved equally. But you cannot do good to all people equally, so you should take particular thought for those who, as if by lot, happen to be particularly close to you in terms of place, time, or any other circumstances. Suppose that you had plenty of something which had to be given to someone in need of it but could not be given to two people, and you met two people, neither of whom had a greater need or a closer relationship to you than the other: you could do nothing more just than to choose by lot the person to whom you should give what could not be given to both. Analogously, since you cannot take thought for all men, you must settle (rather than by lot) in favour of the one who happens to be more closely associated with you in temporal matters. (*DDC* 1.28.29)[100]

"As if by lot." "One who happens to be more closely associated." Those are strikingly egalitarian and universal formulations. Arendt also admitted that

---

100. Edmund Hill notes that Augustine's "rather casual way of leaving the order of charity to chance will not satisfy the scholastic mind, certainly not that of Saint Thomas. He devotes thirteen articles to the subject in his *Summa Theologiae*, IIa IIae, q.26 . . . going into great detail. He decides, for instance, that love of parents takes precedence over love of one's children and love of one's father over love of one's mother—other things, of course, such as their goodness and holiness, being equal. . . . Augustine, I suggest, is to be congratulated on not being so meticulous in the matter" (*DDC* 127n28, Hill).

Augustine's doctrine of love, however problematically, provides a strong doctrine of equality. This equality is expressed in the Christian tradition by the parable of the Good Samaritan (Luke 10:29–37) and formulations of the Golden Rule (Luke 6:31 and Matt. 7.12).[101] Augustine suggests that a good lover will not love *every* neighbor as much as she will love *any* neighbor who happens across her way. He does endorse special relations ("closer connection"), but this endorsement does not lead to a kind of partial preference that would deny the claims of strangers. Augustine's evolving view of providence, however, appears to include a particularized notion by which one's friends and immediate community can be seen as providential gifts of God.[102] No doubt, Augustine found it difficult to reconcile his affirmation of special relations on the basis of his commitment to universal neighbor-love and his conviction that partiality was something to be overcome eschatologically.[103] The love characteristic of civic virtue, however, does not demand or rely upon the special depth of emotional attachment that is characteristic of friendship or familial relations. Our embodied natures place constraints on our capacity to love others in need; but, importantly, they also place constraints on our capacity to harm others. Even tyrants, Augustine thinks, cannot overcome the mysteries of the human heart and the frustrations of language (*DDC* 2). These frustrations place constraints on the full extent to which charity can degenerate into collective egoism. How these universal and particular obligations are to be organized in the complex sets of relations that characterize global interdependence today remains a live issue for Augustinians. There is no strict moral calculus that might determine them, though Augustine's formulation based on finitude suggests something like Gene Outka's account of

101. Augustine, like most patristic authors, generally interpreted the Good Samaritan parable as a "spiritual" allegory about Christ and the church. The "moral" interpretation, however, is not rejected. For a compelling effort to refuse this modern distinction, see Roland Teske, "The Good Samaritan (Lk 10:29–37) in Augustine's Exegesis," in *Augustine: Biblical Exegete*, ed. Frederick van Fleteren and Joseph C. Schnaubelt, O.S.A. (New York: Peter Lang, 2001), 347–67.

102. Anne-Isabelle Bouton-Touboulic, *L'ordre Caché: La notion d'ordre chez saint Augustin*, (Paris: Institut d'Études Augustiniennes, 2004).

103. The turn toward the particularity of love in someone like Martha Nussbaum usually is contrasted with the universalism of Christian love. For example, Richardson points out that Nussbaum places love "in harness for morality—not, indeed, by being converted into the chaste *agape* of the Christians, but by being made a powerful engine of particularistic concern for others" ("Nussbaum: Love and Respect," 258).

"equal consideration but not identical treatment."[104] Augustine does admit at least one further criteria: "Love, like a nurse nurturing her children, puts the weaker before the stronger—in the order of helping them rather than loving them.... She wants the weak to become strong; the strong she passes over for the time being, not out of contempt for them, but out of confidence in them" (*Ep.* 139, 69). This might guide practical deliberations in agenda-setting for scarce resources. Here I simply point out that Augustine does not allow his elevation of neighbor-love to deny either special relations or the spontaneity of compassion that might arise by attention to any neighbor—a spontaneity seen in the notably extensive range of Christian service throughout the world beyond its own religious borders and beyond any simple notion of ethical duty.

Third, it is significant that Augustine's most succinct summary of neighbor-love begins with counsel against harm: "Now God, our master teaches two chief precepts . . . and the order of this concord is, first, that a man should harm no one, and, second, that he should do good to all, so far as he can" (*CD* 19.14; see Rom. 13:10).[105] Augustine's ordering reflects a profound awareness of the sorts of harms that human beings inflict on one another. He knew the dangers of loving wrongly, especially the ways in which we deceive ourselves into thinking that our loves are ordered to another person's good. Bonnie Kent writes: "For all his praise of love, Augustine never forgets the power of human love to warp the priorities that one ought to have.... As the human craving for companionship has its advantages, so it also has its dangers."[106] Augustine was preoccupied with the various ways in which human beings are "seduced and seducers," capable of being "deceived ourselves and deceivers of others amid a welter of desires" (*Conf.* 4.1.1). This awareness should caution against efforts to make others our moral projects rather than fellow participants in God's. It is also suggests something like the liberal asymmetry between avoiding evil (negative duty) and promoting good (positive duty). Augustinians should not "crush the bruised reed" in their efforts of loving. However, as indicated by Augustine's appeals, the asymmetry must avoid a too easy opposition. Rather, Augustine affirms the propriety of both

104. Outka, *Agape*, 269.

105. For a contemporary discussion of this formula, see Schweiker, *Responsibility*, 123–24.

106. Kent, "Augustine's Ethics," 216.

avoiding harm and promoting good: "There are two ways in which a man may sin against another, one by doing him harm, and the second by refusing to help him when one is able" (*Mor.* 1.26.50).

Misdirected loves issue in dramatic social pathologies when neighbor-love is subjected only to the false autonomy of the self's egoism. This recognition accounts for why Augustine is hesitant to entrust the neighbor with unmediated status as an object of love for its own sake—not because he devalues the neighbor, but because he fears what the self might do to the neighbor. Consistent with my earlier claim about training in love, Augustine laments how difficult it is to learn to love others rightly:

> Would that it were as easy to do something for one's neighbor's good or to avoid injuring him as it is for the kind-hearted and well-instructed individual to love him. But here *good will alone does not suffice, for it is a work demanding great understanding and prudence.* (*Mor.* 1.26.51, emphasis mine)

Such thoughtfulness and prudence requires loving neighbors in the same way that you should love yourself: as a creature of equal dignity, a fellow human being bearing the image of God, deserving of justice. In a passage that can easily issue into something like Kantian respect for persons that does not treat others merely as means to an end, Augustine reasons:

> If a man were to love another not as himself but as a beast of burden, or as the baths, or as a gaudy or garrulous bird, that is for some temporal pleasure or advantage he hoped to derive, he must serve not a man but, what is much worse, a foul and detestable vice, in that he does not love man as he ought to be loved. When that vice is dominant it leads to the lowest form of life or rather to death. (*DVR* 46.87)

Augustine was aware of humiliation, of not being loved as he would wish. In addition to his own experiences as an outsider in Italy and North Africa, he also remembers how in his school days "my stripes were laughed at by my elders and even my parents" (*Conf.* 1.9.14). With the pain of someone who has experienced rumor and gossip, he prays that those who correct him will "let it be a brotherly mind which when it approves of me will rejoice over me, and when it disapproves will be saddened on my account, because whether it approves or disapproves it still loves me" (*Conf.* 10.4.5). Hurt feelings, of course, are not the same thing as the cruelty of deliberate humiliation wrought by Christian disciplines. The looming problem is the Donatist controversy. It is one that has haunted this discussion so far without mention. Augustine gave into a prideful paternalism—one that showed the practical psychological possibilities of rationalizing coercion under the guise of love. If we can undermine Augustine's willingness to employ physical harm to achieve spiritual ends, however, we can better secure a morally robust Augustinian civic liberalism. The possibility of religious coercion needs to be surgically removed from an Augustinian account of love. It can partially be done using scalpels fashioned from Augustine's own writings. The final section addresses this issue by offering a concrete example of how love can be "operationalized" as a political virtue, even given the sordid legacy of Augustinian coercion.

LOVING AND HARMING: COERCION, VIOLENCE, AND WAR

I have suggested three practical ways for Augustinians to alleviate some of their own liberal anxieties about political solidarity. We might also add to them Augustine's persistent call for prayerful self-examination of conscience when embarking on works of love (evident throughout his many discussions of pastoral rebuke or "fraternal correction"). Augustine admonished Christians to remember their own sins when loving others. Human beings, he believes, are "eager to pry into the lives of others, but tardy when it comes to correcting their own" (*Conf.* 10.3.3). Political acts of judgment made for the sake of others and their good are to be made with the fear and trembling characteristic of humility: "When earth judges earth it ought to fear God who is in heaven . . . judging its own equal, a human judging a human, a mortal judging a mortal, a sinner judging a sinner" (*S.* 13, 122; see also *Ep.* 153, 53). Reinhold Niebuhr was right to emphasize that God's judgment casts a certain reserve over our own judging tendencies even if it should not paralyze us.[107] Modern cynics might dismiss these points as self-serving or too easily manipulated. Augustine and Augustinians rightly take them with utter seriousness. Pride may not be the dominant vice of all (as feminist theologians have taught us), but the prideful expressions of love should be appropriately restrained in all politics. Efforts to discipline love, rather than dismiss it as dysfunctional or narcissistic, play a significant role

107. For discussion of these themes in biblical literatures, see Wayne Meeks, "Apocalyptic Discourse and Strategies of Goodness," *Journal of Religion* (2000): 461–75.

in my reconstruction. Augustinians are not consumed by either the abstract promotion of a fixed *summum bonum* or a singular focus on one's own life project of virtue. The dangers of a love that seeks to promote the good of another, however, should not be taken as the whole story.

The risks of political solidarity are not unique. The desire for justice as a response to wrongdoing has pathologies as well. A strict observance of nonmaleficence as the only way to respect another person risks its own kind of moral failure, both to others and ourselves. Problems, however, remain for the Augustinian lover. They are particularly acute given Augustine's theory of political education that tempts him to secure spiritual health by inflicting physical harm, coercing the body to free the soul. The history of Augustinian political ethics—dating back to Augustine's own reluctant disciplinary "loving" persecution of the Donatists—makes this danger a pressing problem for an Augustinianism that also considers itself a kind of liberalism.

It is a short step (though still a step) from Augustine's account of compassion to the Inquisition. As Mennonite scholar Gerald Schlabach argues, "Augustine's Donatist policy . . . struck a fissure in his doctrine of love, so that to appropriate his thought at all we must do so selectively, reading Augustine against himself."[108] Schlabach offers important emphases on the importance of continence and the priority of persuasion to coercion for Augustinianism. Augustinian liberals, I think, have effectively performed part of this selective appropriation by distinguishing the civic identity of the church from that of other political communities. This is not to deny the renewed possibility of really evangelical "wars of religion." Given the history of twentieth century, however, it is not the most apparent possible abuse of Augustinian loving. The real conceptual danger for Augustinian liberalism is not so much state-sponsored coercion on behalf of theological orthodoxy but the analogous forms of moral paternalism and the self-righteous production of "moral heresy" that liberals also rightly fear. This relation between Augustinianism and moral hereticization is a marked feature of the revival of interest in Augustine in postmodern political theory. William Connolly, for example, argues that Augustinianism is governed by "the quest to uncover an intrinsic moral

108. Schlabach, *For the Joy Set Before Us*, 56. For Schlabach, "the paternalism deep within the structure of Augustine's conception of *caritas* was like a fuel tank hidden within a vehicle—potent and necessary, but explosive enough to destroy the whole construct" (127).

order" that can be represented authoritatively through political imperatives that rely on hegemonic moralization and scapegoating.[109] Romand Coles can see an Augustine who disrupts the prideful autonomy of egoism that imagines oneself as a "self-originating being."[110] He admires an "Augustine who views the world to be the infinitely rich incarnation of God's Word."[111] But he also sees an Augustine who abandons this "allegorical Church" and "launches a new form of power intent on extirpating all that does not accord with the voice of the 'one true God.'"[112] It has been my claim that an Augustinian civic liberalism that prominently features love can be sensitive to the conditions of pluralism and the great political values of justice, equality, and respect. Augustinians, in fact, hold that love itself heightens these sensitivities because these exclusionary persecutions of moral egoism and moral purity are themselves failures of loving. But what does my emphasis on affectivity and love add to this feature of Augustinian liberalism that affirms typically liberal emphases on the limits of politics and respect for individual persons as they pursue their life projects?

Love's relation to coercion *per se* is a larger question than the distinctive issue of religious coercion. Augustine does equate love for others with the wish that they "should live justly by cleaving to the truth" (*DT* 8.5.10). His interest in willing, rather than simply knowing, and its relation to appropriately loving the good (which involves desiring the good in a new way) problematizes a liberal reconstruction. Loving the good requires a radical reorientation of the will that in part consists in calling others to love the good. "Calling" the neighbor to her good is an intentionally weak version of Augustine's more violent rhetoric of "seizing," "grasping," or "compelling" the neighbor to join the Catholic Church: "Let them be loved in him, and carry off to God as many of them as possible with you" (*Conf.* 4.12.18). Augustine frequently appeals to the parable of the great banquet, "compel them to come in" (Luke 14), as scriptural warrant for compulsion of schismatics (*Ep.* 93, *Ep.* 173, and *Ep.* 408). The recalcitrance of fallen humanity, for Augustine, demands the "bitter draughts of salutary discipline to recall us from the venomous pleasure which led us away from [God]" (*Conf.* 1.14.23).

109. Connolly, *Augustinian Imperative*, 88.
110. Coles, *Self/Power/Other*, 17.
111. Ibid., 52.
112. Ibid., 10.

Peter Brown notes that Augustine's "view of the Fall determined his attitude to society."[113] It is divine providence that "coercion checks the free play of curiosity" (*Conf.* 1.14.23).[114] Of course, few people, especially parents, hold that moral character is self-generating. Virtues are inculcated in some fashion, even if many liberals resist the idea that all earthly politics is a form of coercion. The "violence" of Augustine's rhetoric—a *per molestas eruditio*—is a disturbing but central element of his erotic account of spiritual *askesis* (the violence of the heart, not the flesh) that restores the will's capacity to see the good. It is dangerous rhetoric for ecclesiastical discipline. It is even more dangerous for liberal politics.

Recent studies suggest that Augustine's authoritarian tone mirrors the violent rhetorical practices of Roman law.[115] John von Heyking, in fact, has argued that Augustine's justification of coercion (only of schismatics not pagans, heretics, or Jews) did not rely upon demands for religious conformity or orthodoxy. Augustine sought the legal preservation of civic peace in "an emergency situation, where it appears that a group's beliefs will lead inexorably to violence."[116] Apart from its obvious connection to today's global security concerns, this argument provides a nice resolution to the apparent contradiction between Augustine's theology of the *saeculum* and his defense of imperial coercion. This contradiction has left most Augustinian liberals simply at a loss to explain this "unresolved tension" (Markus, *SAE*, 146). Von Heyking admits that Augustine was torn between concern for the integrity

113. Brown, *Augustine of Hippo*, 232. Brown continues: "The persecution of the Donatists was another 'controlled catastrophe' imposed by God, mediated, on this occasion, by the laws of the Christian emperors; in Augustine's mind, it was no more than a special instance of the relationship of the human race as a whole, to its stern Father, who would 'whip the son He receives'" (232).

114. There is another Augustine. He remembers, for example, learning Latin "by paying attention, without any fear or pain at all, amid the cuddles of my nurses, and teasing, and playful, happy laughter. . . . I learned then without the painful pressure of people pestering me" (*Conf.* 1.14.23). This is the Augustine who learned "not from teachers but from speakers," an Augustine who could claim that "the free play of curiosity is a more powerful spur to learning these things than is fear-ridden coercion" (*Conf.* 1.14.23). It is rare for Augustine to praise curiosity as a virtue rather than a vice. It may be that Augustine intends an allegory in this memory of his infancy. Might this be Augustinian "education" in Paradise?

115. See Brown, *Authority and the Sacred*, 44–46, and von Heyking, *Longing*, 222–57.

116. Von Heyking, *Longing*, 219.

of the political community under the rule of law (threatened by the violence of the Donatists) and the need to restrain the excessive use of force characteristic of Roman authorities. Augustine appealed to Donatus that he would "be happier if the church in Africa were not so troubled as to need the help of any earthly authority" (*Ep.* 100, 134). But the Donatists forced the issue:

> If you don't like us because you are being forced into unity by the imperial decrees, well, you brought this about yourselves. Whenever we were happy simply to preach the truth and let each person listen to it in security and choose of his own free will, you have always prevented us from doing this by your violence and terrorism. (*Ep.* 105, 163–64)

Stability and the need to protect innocents, according to von Heyking, trumped Augustine's concerns. This move provides a helpful distinction that fits well with a liberal reconstruction of the "two cities" theology. It resists a utopian view that human beings are responsible for the salvation of the others or the world, but it also allows for the necessary and authorized response of government to curb evil. It divests political authorities of any claim they might make to adjudicate theological confessions, save perhaps the religious character of this admission itself. This should encourage a political restraint—not simply a lamentable fact of earthly existence—but as a positive recognition of the goods enjoyed by a free conscience inwardly willing them as one's own good. This restraint does not require that Augustinians simply mourn and gnash their teeth at moral incommensurability and religious difference. I am afraid, however, that von Heyking's solution does not work for Augustine.

It is an anachronistic reading that grants Augustine the distinction between political security and religious conformity. To be sure, Augustine did not equate being Roman with being Christian. He was neither an Orosius nor a Eusebius, even though the Donatists wondered why he was so willing to cozy up to the empire for support. Augustine did think that Christians should "tolerate those who want the commonwealth to remain with its vices unpunished" (*Ep.* 138, 40). The "civil laws" cannot make people good users of earthly gifts, but rather are intended "to make them less oppressive in misusing them" (*Ep.* 153, 87). He counseled gentleness in the treatment of schismatics to uphold their oaths, and he tells his fellow bishops not to rely too much on the corrupt Roman lawyers. One can detect something like the distinction between legality and morality which will play an important role for many Christian jurists who laid the groundwork for constitutional democracy. Legal coercion can do more harm than good.[117] Augustine's anthropology would not expect moral sanctity in the activities of either church or state. But this is cruel comfort for those who rightly abhor his "loving" pastoral logic of coercion.

Augustine was committed to the idea that citizens of the heavenly city, as much as possible, work for a civil authority that does not "impede the religion by which we are taught that the one supreme and true God is to be worshiped" (*CD* 19.18). Indeed, Christian citizens are "to become a burden to those who think differently" (*CD* 19.18). That is why Augustine would hope that "those who are gifted with true godliness and live good lives also know the art of governing peoples" (*CD* 5.19). Church schism was an evil that the political authority was competent to judge. After citing Romans 13, Augustine argues that "the entire issue, then, amounts to this: is a schism nothing evil?" (*Ep.* 87, 141). That is why he could endorse not only the compulsion of the Donatists but also a variety of imperial practices that suppressed non-Christian religious practices—practices that he took to be more harmful to the soul than pagan philosophy itself. That is why he does not bemoan the legal privileges of the "established" church or the Christian ruler, even though he was more attentive to the moral qualities of citizens and their rulers rather than questions of institutional design.

My interest is in the pastoral logic of coercion that Augustine adopts in his parental and medicinal analogies for political rule. Whatever actual justifications might retrospectively be made about the violence of the Donatists, it is this "tough love" rhetoric that has been pressed into service by contemporary antiliberals. It is a fundamental part of Augustine's anti-Donatist writings:

> Whatever we do in our dealings with you, though we may do it contrary to
> your inclinations, yet we do it from our love for you, that you may voluntarily

117. Von Heyking points out that Augustine held that "human law must not attempt to remove all vices, such as prostitution, because removing them only makes vices find other and more unsettling ways of expressing themselves" (*Longing*, 98). Rist points out, however, that Augustine thinks that "although no one can be morally bettered by legislative severity, if he is restrained from vice he thereby profits from the enforced opportunity, perhaps otherwise unavailable, to take a few hesitant moral steps" (Rist, *ATB*, 226).

correct yourselves, and live an amended life. For no one lives against his will; and yet a boy, in order to learn this lesson of his own free will, is beaten contrary to his inclination, and that often by the very man that is most dear to him. (*Contra Litteras Petialini* 2.95.217)

Augustine claims to want to avoid the appeal to secular power to coerce schismatics; it is a matter of spiritual authority. In the end, he has a change of heart: "Such coercion displeased me because I had not yet learned either how much evil their impunity would dare or to what extent the application of discipline could bring about their improvement" (*Retr.* 2.31). It is a line of reasoning that remains with him throughout his career. James O'Donnell has argued for the strange neglect of the Donatists in the *Confessions* and *City of God*.[118] They are not there (for O'Donnell), but they always seem to be implicitly in the background. We might imagine Augustine thinking of them when he writes:

If anyone in the household is an enemy to domestic peace because of his disobedience, he is corrected by a word, or by a blow, or by whatever other kind of punishment is just and lawful, to the extent permitted by human society; but this is for the benefit of the person corrected, so that he may be readmitted to the peace from which he has sundered himself. For just as it is not an act of kindness to help someone if he thereby loses a greater good, so it is not a blameless act to spare someone if he thereby falls into a graver sin. If we are to be blameless, therefore, our duty includes not only doing no harm to anyone, but also restraining him from sin or punishing his sin, so that either he who is chastised may be corrected by his experience, or others may be warned by his example. (*CD* 19.16)

118. O'Donnell, following the work of Brent Shaw, also revises traditional theological and sociological interpretations of the Donatist controversy. He argues against the view that "catholicism" was the urban norm and "donatism" was divergent rural minority (*New Biography*, 211). The debate still hinges on the status of purity in the church, but O'Donnell couches the debate in terms of Augustine's effort to enforce a geographical "catholicity" through state coercion against an anti-imperial Donatist "catholicity" that meant "having the totality of faith—that is, possession of the whole of Christian doctrine in a given local community" (218). According to O'Donnell, with admitted rhetorical excess, Augustine "succeeded in destroying the morale and organization of the native African Christian church, the so-called Donatists, and left it prey to the combined forces of Arians and Vandals who arrived in Africa just as he was dying" (81).

Augustine's sermons contain some of the most alarming accounts of a 'kindly harshness' politicized as compassionate beneficence. For example, Augustine tells his listeners:

> If there be any of you, my brothers, that would get charity and keep it, you must above all avoid thinking of it as a poor, inactive thing, wanting no more than a sort of gentle mildness for its keeping, or even a careless indifference.... You are not to suppose that you love your servant when you do not beat him, or love your son when you relax your discipline over him, or love your neighbour when you never find fault with him. That is not charity, but weakness. Let charity be zealous to set right, to correct faults, to delight in good behaviour, but to correct and improve what is bad. Love the man, not his errors; for God made the man, his errors are his own doing. (*IoEp.* 7.11)

It is difficult to read Augustine's letters without eliciting the memory of their political (and ecclesial) abuse. His words haunt Western politics and theology: "When doctors see some gangrene that needs cutting and cauterization, they often show mercy by shutting their ears to the patient's copious flood of tears" (*Ep.* 104, 15); "surely it is far more appropriate to drag you away from your disastrous errors, which make you your own enemy, and lead you to recognise and choose the truth" (*Ep.* 173, 153); "if an evil must always be allowed its own freedom, then why does sacred scripture advise a father faced with an obdurate son not just to rebuke him with words, but also to beat him" (*Ep.* 173, 154); and "it is God himself who does this through us, whether by entreaty or threat or censure; by fines or by hard work; whether through secret warnings and visitings, or through the laws of the temporal powers" (*Ep.* 105, 169). In fact, Augustine suggests the more severe the punishment, the greater the love. Augustinian liberals condemn the political abuse of these passages. Nonetheless, even though I disagree with his interpretation, von Heyking's suggestion is interesting because it puts Augustine back into a moral world of intelligibility for a liberal society. Von Heyking's Augustine is not simply condemned as another intolerant religious zealot or an unenlightened premodern thinker. My rejection of von Heyking's solution does not mean that I wish to abandon this possibility of intelligibility, especially given the continued relevance of thinking about the coercive practices of liberal politics. Augustine does not yield the stirring defense of universal human rights and freedom of conscience that is now official Roman Catholic teaching. Augustine, however, may shape modern liberal thinking about coercion more than his many critics allow.

John Bowlin, for example, argues that the most remarkable feature of Augustine's understanding of coercion is his very effort to justify (and constrain) it. Bowlin notes: "It is this reason-giving enterprise, this attempt to make sense of a practice that most of his contemporaries consider morally unproblematic, that distinguishes Augustine, not his participation in this or that persecution."[119] The need to give moral reasons may have begun the slow process of coercion being stripped of its normalizing splendor: its capacity to make acceptance of any act of coercion as a natural fact of politics. The justification of state coercion—of whatever kind (i.e., taxation, seatbelt laws, fair housing laws, gambling regulation)—remains a contestable feature of liberal practice that continually tries to fend off its libertarian critics. Liberals offer various reasons that try to justify the monopoly of state coercion in a wide array of practices.[120] For example, they distinguish coercion from violence and consent to power from subjugation. They also distinguish between different types of liberties and different types of coercion (i.e., religious coercion from economic coercion). These discussions tend to invoke some version of Mill's harm principle as prelude to a registry of liberal rights. Liberal perfectionists affirm these rights alongside the belief that political societies should "enable citizens to search for the good life" (Nussbaum, *UT*, 404). These latter arguments, to my mind, make better sense of many state activities that seem to sacrifice negative liberties for the sake of positive liberties that otherwise would be unavailable without state intervention (i.e., legislation against sexual commodification and certain classes of drugs, restrictive immigration laws, government funding of the arts and scientific research, more expansive regulation of financial markets that entrench class divisions and of various public goods like environment, health care, and compulsory education). Any kind of liberalism, given its commitment to individual liberty, is perpetually trying to justify the rationality of this coercive public order. If Bowlin is right, Augustine is interesting because he does not simply abandon coercion to necessity for fear of exacerbating or legitimating its abuse. He submits it to unrelenting moral analysis. That is why Bowlin takes Augustine's account of coercion seriously. Bowlin's Augustine, however, offers more than an early exercise in justifying coercion with candor. He argues that Augustine

---

119. Bowlin, "Augustine on Justifying Coercion," 53.

120. For a critical survey of these strategies that puts them in conversation with the thought of Thomas Aquinas, see E. A. Goerner and Walter J. Thompson, "Politics and Coercion," *Political Theory* 24, no. 4 (November 1996): 620–51.

shares something like the liberal worry that resort to coercion violates human freedom—even the *liberum arbitrium* that allows a person to believe false-hood and participate in evil goods.[121]

Augustinian civic liberals should support this argument. True virtue, for Augustine, requires an integrated willing, knowing, and loving subject. Like many ancient authors, he also accepts the view that "having a virtue is having one's character developed in such a way that one not only grasps what the right thing to do is but takes pleasure in doing it."[122] The aspiration follows a difficult path that can be threatened by imprudent concessions to an authoritarian coercion or certain kinds of action that should never be undertaken even when the consequences appear very good. Fear and compulsion are paradigmatic experiences of sin's consequence for a thinker who values volitional integrity in the way Augustine does. Bowlin writes: "Because he believes that negative liberty is a genuine good he refuses to conclude that every negative liberty lost can be justified by this or that positive liberty gained."[123] Augustine does affirm the troubling belief for many political liberals that "when *x* loves *y*, *x* wishes the best for *y* and acts, as far as he or she is able, to pursue the good for *y*."[124] This benevolent love implies a commitment to the good of the beloved that tries to promote rather than diminish their agency. It should not always be redescribed as a manipulative expression of self-love, though it can be that as well. Loving relations are not always raw assertions of power in a setting of rivalry. Indeed, to see only ideology *everywhere* is itself a failure

121. Patrick Riley claims that "without that strong Augustine-forged link between consent and will, the social contract tradition—of which Kant is (in part) a part—would be unthinkable, since it defines consent in terms of will, in terms of Lockean 'voluntary agreement'" (Patrick Riley, "The 'Elements' of Kant's Practical Philosophy: The *Ground-work* after 200 Years (1785–1985)," *Political Theory* 14, no. 4 [November 1986]: 552–83, at 556). Riley's claim may be historically excessive, but he maps interesting connections between Augustinianism and Kantianism.

122. Annas, *Morality of Happiness*, 55.

123. Bowlin, "Augustine on Justifying Coercion," 66. Bowlin here refers to the Isaiah Berlin's concepts of negative liberty (liberty "from") and positive liberty (liberty "for").

124. Soble, "Union, Autonomy, and Concern," 65. Soble identifies various types of love in light of liberal concerns about autonomy and paternalism. I disagree with his conclusion that love is not a feature of general moral concern and his characterization of Christian love as egocentric. In the same volume, Keith Lehrer makes a better case for integrating the values of autonomy and love without trying to offer a "fixed scheme" (Lehrer, "Love and Autonomy," 107–21).

to imagine social relations in terms other than self-interest and manipulation. Stanley Hauerwas is right to claim that "insofar as we are people who care about anything at all, we necessarily impinge on the 'freedom' of others."[125] At the same time, Augustine would perhaps be more suspicious than some Augustinian liberals about the inevitable forms of coercion that surround all forms of socialization (including the modern emphases on being a productive consumer or a loyal patriot).[126] But can "good" love ever justify "good" coercion in this fallen world? Augustine thinks it can. As we saw in the work of Paul Ramsey, Augustinian liberals latch on to Augustine's claim that "even wars will be waged in the spirit of benevolence" (*Ep.* 138, 38).

This Augustinian application of the spirit of benevolence is not governed simply by moral analysis of motives. The justification of coercion relies on a set of criteria that Bowlin discerns in Augustine's famous letter to Boniface (*Ep.* 185): (1) "coercion must be confined to certain role-specific relationships"; (2) "coercion must track the truth, its methods must be deployed for the sake of genuine human goods"; and (3) "coercion must be tempered with charity, with care for the coerced, and with worry about the negative freedom lost."[127] For Bowlin, these arguments are not so different from the moral intuitions that ordinary people adopt every day: parents have role-specific relationships in their disciplining of children, initiation into the art of playing baseball is different from initiation into the art of stealing, and those who initiate people into worthy practices should not love the practice more than the person. Of course, state action is a different sphere of activity than these examples suggest—though Augustine's moral condemnation of torture, lying, and the

125. Hauerwas, *Peaceable Kingdom*, 9. Hauerwas argues: "I do not mean to suggest that there has ever been a time or social order from which manipulation was absent. What is new about our present situation is that our best moral wisdom can conceive of no alternative. We seem able to only suggest ways to make the game more fair" (9).

126. William T. Cavanaugh argues that Augustine's effort to distinguish good coercion from bad coercion helps us see forms of coercion that often go unnoticed in liberal political theory because they are so pervasive: the homogeneity and conformity of the selves produced by consumer capitalism. According to Cavanaugh, "the ability to feel coerced is perhaps the beginning of resistance" (Cavanaugh, "Augustine and Disney," 290). I note, however, that Augustinians should remember that consumer desire predated Disney; it was in Eden as the possessive desire, grasping at what was meant as gift, only to be disappointed by the actual possession. All action, capitalist or not, can become a variation of consumption.

127. Bowlin, "Justifying Coercion," 66–67.

death penalty is significant if not exculpatory. Bowlin admits Augustine's assumptions about the relations between church and state and between spiritual and physical integrity are very different from those of a liberal society. Nevertheless, he also challenges the stereotype that Augustine is so vastly distant from our moral world and even our political practices.

Augustine's fledgling criteria, for example, can be seen as the kernel of ideas and moral practices that lie behind the development of an evolving just war tradition that has come to be very significant in liberal politics. Bowlin's reconstruction supports the view that Augustine is a prominent source of just war thinking. For many, it represents the most compelling development of Christian neighbor-love for liberal politics. I have argued that Ramsey's Christian just war thinking might be extended to various political practices consistent with Joan Tronto's discussion of care and Martha Nussbaum's discussion of capabilities. That is, love as a civic virtue motivates a concern for the vulnerable and afflicted that subsequently justifies (potentially extensive but not unlimited) state coercion on their behalf. When the state acts, it acts on behalf of the vulnerable and for the sake of justice. This love is against that which is not love, "but not [against] him who is the bearer of that which is against love" (Tillich, *LPJ,* 114). This appeal to love involves the exercise of communal power to meet the needs of others and protect the best possible conditions for human flourishing. Augustine is more confident than most Augustinian liberals that we can identify a broad range of such goods. However, in a passage that sounds strikingly similar to Nussbaum's liberal perfectionism, Augustine holds:

> There is indeed such a unanimity within the same living and reason-using nature, that while to be sure it is hidden from one man what another man wants, there are some wishes that all have which are known to every single individual. While each man is ignorant of what another man wants, in some matters he can know what all men want. (*DT* 13.2.6)

Augustine does not assume that we can enter deeply in the minds and hearts of others in order to discover their needs and desires (*CD* 19.5). Indeed, he had a hard enough time discovering his own needs and desires! But the shared goods of political life do not require a mystical insight into a fellow citizen's mind.[128] Liberal society should debate the policies that try to address

128. See, for example, Philip Pettit, *The Common Mind* (Oxford: Oxford University Press, 1993). For a theological rejection of "seeing" into each other's minds, see Phillip

these wants and needs (for example, poverty relief and provision for health care and education). An Augustinian emphasis on divine grace will resist political efforts at a full-fledged paternalist reorientation of desire according to a fixed, univocal conception of the human good secured by legal sanction. Some goods are too vulnerable and rich to be the focus of the state's direct concern. Prudence suggests that too many dangers await when the state explicitly aims to shape the desires of its citizens, particularly when it is deceived by attempts to "hate the fault but love the man" (*CD* 14.6; see also *CFaust* 19.24 and *S.* 13, 124). This famous Augustinian formulation implicitly recognizes the distinction between evaluation of acts and evaluation of agents. At the level of moral theory and political practice, it is a formulation worth embracing despite its potential for abuse in practice.[129] Citizens should engage in robust deliberation about what constitutes human goods, and this will inevitably shape the sort of policies that political communities adopt in facilitating the effective freedom to pursue these goods—both in terms of the legality of particular acts as well as determining the activities of public welfare more broadly. As Robert M. Adams argues, "taking one's own conception of another person's good as one's guide in choosing what assistance to offer is quite different from taking it as grounds for coercing the other person, and the former does not entail the latter."[130] This deliberation and assistance is itself motivated by love. Good citizens can be motivated by love even if the state can not make citizens loving. Fear of paternalism does not warrant a thin public discourse any more than it justifies a limited state; this would be a morally incoherent type of liberalism.

More traditional Augustinian liberalism reconstructs a separation of the "two cities" that conceptually denies evangelical civil religion. The structure of the "two cities" removes theological rationale for investing in war a significance of the sort that would identify any political cause with the economy of God's salvation. It also denies the pacifist claim that Christians cannot

---

Cary, "Believing the Word: A Proposal about Knowing Other Persons," *Faith & Philosophy* 13, no. 1 (1996): 78–90.

129. Velleman offers a nice rejoinder to its critics: "While I agree that we want to be loved warts and all, as the saying goes, I don't think that we want to be loved for our warts. Who wants to be the object of someone's wart love? What we want is to be loved by someone who sees and isn't put off by our warts, but who appreciates our true value well enough to recognize that they don't contribute to it" (Velleman, "Moral Emotion," 370).

130. Adams, *Finite and Infinite Goods*, 344.

resort to force to protect innocents and enact the rule of law. This distinctive feature of the Augustinian tradition should not be underestimated.[131] It is complemented here by more explicit attention to an Augustinian conception of love and motivation.

The ambiguous status of Augustine as the source of the flowering of just war thinking in the late medieval period is now well documented.[132] For some, these later developments represent a case of canonists and jurists invoking his authority without adopting his actual positions. For others, it is enough to point out that Augustine's experience of "war" was actually more akin to "police actions" than contemporary international relations. But some scholars now go further than these contextualizing moves.

They question Augustine's contribution for thinking about justice and war altogether. Or, more to the point, they suggest his contribution is wholly pernicious. Robert L. Holmes, for example, argues that Augustine's views actually "put him closer to the tradition of Hobbes and recent political realists than to either the pacifists of the early church or subsequent just war theorists."[133] Far from issuing constraints on war in the service of justice and neighbor-love, Augustine's thought was "to reorient Christianity to the path of militarism."[134] On the face of it, this challenge is surprising. No doubt later just war thinkers developed the tradition in ways that were unimagined by Augustine. But does this reading present a case of philosophers and historians missing the forest for the trees, imposing one distinction too many? Generations of students have been taught that Augustine's portrayal of war as a "stern necessity" waged for the sake of peace is an extension of his more general attitude to politics. They have been taught that Augustine crucially

131. Early in his career, Augustine was tempted by holy war ideology, particularly in his exegesis of the Hebrew Bible (*CFaust* 22.71). On the polemical context of this work, see Robert A. Markus, "Saint Augustine's Views on the 'Just War,'" in *The Church and War: Papers Read at the Twenty First Summer and Twenty Second Winter Meeting of the Ecclesiastical History Society,* ed. W. J. Shiels (Oxford, 1983), 1–13.

132. Russell, *Just War*, 26. Modern interpreters challenge Paul Ramsey's claim that Augustine justifies war as beneficent love for innocents. See, for example, James Turner Johnson, "Historical Roots and Sources of the Just War Tradition in Western Culture," in *Just War and Jihad,* ed. John Kelsay and James Turner Johnson (New York: Greenwood Press, 1991), and Richard Miller, *Interpretations of Conflict: Ethics, Pacifism and the Just-War Tradition* (Chicago: University of Chicago Press, 1991).

133. Holmes, "St. Augustine and the Just War Theory," 324.

134. Ibid., 325.

distinguishes the wrongness of private lethal self-defense from the moral permissibility of public defense of innocent others.[135] But, for Holmes, these misreadings do not adequately address what has been a dominant theme of this chapter: "his emphasis upon subjective inner states."[136] This emphasis, Holmes argues, allows for a radical distinction between inner disposition and outward conduct—reducing Augustinian ethics to a disturbing form of subjectivism. In the name of love, Holmes's Augustine promotes injustice and fuels "the organized, deliberate, and systematic infliction of death and destruction."[137]

How might an Augustinian civic liberal respond? There are general issues that call into question Holmes's story about just war thinking. As Oliver O'Donovan has argued, "this tradition is in fact neither a 'theory,' nor about 'just wars,' but a *proposal for doing justice in the theatre of war*."[138] Contrary to Holmes's stated purpose, his criticism of Augustine might really be a restatement of just war orthodoxy: there are no just wars. But I want to focus on the status of motivation and the arts of political judgment. In the next chapter, I return to the supposed "otherworldliness" of Augustine's theology that feeds Holmes's account of the "inner-outer dualism of his interiority" and the "radical dualism of Augustine's metaphysics."[139] For my purposes here, Holmes's criticisms neglect the possibilities of Augustine's discussion of war in terms of an ethic of virtue. Holmes's misgivings about Augustinian interiority appear related to this attention to virtue rather than to deontological rules and norms. But, as John Langan has argued, "it is reasonable to think that care to develop a regard for certain moral virtues and values among soldiers would contribute in an important and perhaps decisive way to the preservation of many values which the rule of *jus in bello* are designed to

---

135. For a recent endorsement of this reading that relies heavily on Ramsey, see Jackson, *PL*, 108n44. The position was adopted by a number of scholars who signed the petition, "What We're Fighting For: A Letter from America" (Elshtain, *Just War Against Terror*, appendix, 182–207). This 2002 statement advocated just war reasoning for the American response to 9/11 and global terrorism. It invoked Augustine in defense of the claim that "the moral principle of love of neighbor calls us to the use of force" (189).

136. Holmes, "Just War Theory," 325.

137. Ibid., 337.

138. O'Donovan, *Just War Revisited*, vii; see also *Ways*, 224–27.

139. Holmes, "Just War Theory," 330 and 331.

protect."[140] Langan is right to see this connection. In 2003, for example, the much discussed contrast between the way British soldiers humanely treated Iraqi citizens in Basra and approaches used by American soldiers might offer a modern example of this phenomenon.[141] The codification of the rule of law and military conduct rather than the sheer power of brute force is a historical development to be celebrated by Augustinians. The cultivation of virtue need not be blind to consequences of action. An ethics of virtue, however, need be redeemed only in this subsidiary way.

Augustine does not deduce moral action from a catalogue of rules or principles. His emphasis on motivation is bound up with his conception of morality as formation in the creativity of charity, not slavish obedience to rules or the maximization of good outcomes. This does not mean, however, that the loving person in this life does not care about consistency in appeals to justice or the norms that govern social practices. Considerations about justice and utility may give shape to the experience of love without grounding morality in either of these values as a sole justification. The moral "empires" of deontology and consequentialism, we might say, have their place even if they ultimately have only the "fragile splendour of glass" (*CD* 4.3). The truly loving person acts well because the character of her loves place her in just relations with others; that is, love is ordered. These loves, for Augustine, are ordered precisely because they participate in the rational order of God's justice and beauty: "the lawful use of the law for the purpose envisaged by his commandment, pure charity" (*Conf.* 12.30.41). Plumbing the moral depths of this law, enacting its love as a way of life, and tirelessly reproaching oneself and one's societies for failing to fulfill this command is precisely the sort of perfectionism that Augustine encourages. His fondness for musical and poetic analogies illustrate his concern that the practice of virtue could never inspire an anarchic aversion to law (i.e., *Conf.* 3.7.14). There is, so to speak, an unending normativity to his account of freedom and love as the power to act in accordance with infinite goodness.

Whatever his failures as a bishop, Augustine knew that practical judgment involves attending to the complex elements of a moral situation. Contemporary advocates of agent-based virtue ethics argue that the priority of

---

140. Langan, "St. Augustine's Just War Theory," 32.
141. See, for example, Allen, *Talking to Strangers*, 148–52.

motives does not defeat concern for right action or good consequences.[142] Christian approaches that highlight the centrality of love also offer suggestive ways to join "aretology, deontology, and consequentialism into a higher unity."[143] By contrast, Holmes pushes Augustine's "purity of heart" into a radical subjectivism, unresponsive to and closed off from external reality. It masquerades as love but promotes injustice. It is a self-referential love that abandons others. I have stressed the normative relation between other-regard and attention to the qualities which inhere in an agent as a way of bringing together agent-evaluation and act-evaluation. Holmes reconstructs a positivistic Augustine who severs the rationality of moral judgment from the rightness of actions, prudent consideration of consequences, and communal deliberation on the meaning of the moral law. He takes what Augustine has to say about good motivations (as necessary for true virtue) and then forces it do all the work in what Augustinians have to say about justice and moral action. Augustine, for the sake of argument, might have understood someone saying "I am regrettably going to destroy this village in the spirit of love," or "I am regrettably going to torture you in the spirit of love." He might even allow these claims to differentiate assessment of the moral agent in a fallen world (i.e., the repentant judge from the vicious terrorist). He might also note the felt need to offer some form of moral justification. But he certainly could not endorse the acts themselves as morally right: "Nothing appalling, nothing inhuman, should be done" (*Ep.* 153, 83).

Is the Augustine I have presented in this chapter tone deaf to the temptations of invoking love as justification of immoral and politically imprudent action? Too many thickets would entangle us if I now tried to present Augustine's account of virtue and its relation to the rightness of external action. Despite my reservations about his reading of the Donatist controversy, John von Heyking has made a persuasive case for something like Augustinian casuistry, though not of the sort found in later Catholic manualist tradition. In particular, he makes clear that Augustine "never permits the performance of an evil act so that good may come of it."[144]

142. Michael Slote, "Agent-Based Virtue Ethics," *Midwest Studies in Philosophy* 20 (1995): 83–101.

143. Jackson, *Love Disconsoled*, 214.

144. Von Heyking, *Longing*, 137.

There is something revealing in Holmes's aversion to Augustine's moral analysis of war. Contrary to those who cite Augustine as a decisive break with early Christian pacifism, Augustine's scattered remarks reveal the inheritance of the already non-pacifist writings of Eusebius, Athanasius, Clement of Alexandria, and Ambrose. Augustine repeatedly cites their familiar appeals to classic New Testament proof texts such as Jesus' praise of the faithful centurion in Matthew 8 and John the Baptist's response to the soldiers in Luke 3. But it was Augustine's theology that came to impress its stamp. He is more systematic than his predecessors, even if a more extensive treatment of act-evaluation can be found in thinkers like Aquinas. Against Holmes, I think one can detect the beginnings of *jus ad bellum* and *jus in bello* criteria. In his ironic defense of war as a "stern necessity" in the service of justice, one certainly detects the refusal of war as a nursery for heroic virtue (*CD* 4.15). His letters reveal many examples of just war reasoning. He claims that "the might of the emperor, the judge's power of the sword, the executioner's hooks, the soldier's weapons" have their "limits, causes, explanations, and uses" (*Ep.* 153, 80). This force "puts a check on the bad, so that the good may live peacefully among the bad" (*Ep.* 153, 80). While he does not develop a systematic analysis of these limits and uses, he offers practical judgments against reducing an enemy to extreme poverty or rash adventures in war motivated by revenge or glory. Holmes is right to note that Augustine's discussions of war do not include extended discussions of just cause, proper authority, or proportionality. I also grant that Ramsey innovates on Augustine's account of benevolent love in making beneficence (not the preservation of relative justice through lawful retribution) the justificatory ground of coercion.[145] Holmes also correctly identifies Augustine's failure to distinguish intention and motivation. This distinction between the various motives of an agent and the specific intention revealed by an action plays an important role in contemporary just war thinking. I am less certain that these developments are radically *inconsistent* with an Augustinian ethics of love. Augustine, the virtue thinker, certainly is concerned with the quality of inward dispositions. But, if this chapter is persuasive, these dispositions need not be frozen "inside" the mind of the agent. They are intrinsically related to right intentions and real outcomes. It

145. For the contemporary implications of this correction, see J. Warren Smith, "Augustine and the Limits of Preemptive and Preventive War," *Journal of Religious Ethics* 35, no. 1 (2007): 141–62.

is this Augustinian moral psychology that needs to be recovered not only in contemporary just war discussions but political morality as such.

Augustinian liberalism can rely upon intention understood as something other than a Cartesian form of introspection. Intentions are revealed by acts and not necessarily by stated motivations. Augustine knew that "we love by work and truth, not by words and tongue only" (*IoEp.* 6.3). His preoccupation with motivation can issue in rather unappealing moral conclusions. Consider this rhetorically disturbing and often cited passage:

> What is the evil in war? Is it the death of some who will soon die in any case, that others may live in peaceful subjection? This is mere cowardly dislike, not any religious feeling. The real evils in war are love of violence, revengeful cruelty, fierce and implacable enmity, wild resistance, and the lust of power and such like; and it is generally to punish these things, when force is required to inflict the punishment, that, in obedience to God or some lawful authority, good men undertake wars, when they find themselves in such a position as regards the conduct of human affairs, that right conduct requires them to act, or to make others act in this way. (*CFaust* 22.74)

This strange passage fuels the criticism that Augustine spiritualizes the ethics of coercion. John Langan observes that Augustine's "approach to the whole problem of war sees it in primarily spiritual and attitudinal terms rather than as a threat to human interests and survival or as the doing of actions which are evil."[146] Langan's remarks on this passage are true enough in the context of Augustine's emphasis on the pedagogy of retributive justice. But given the context of Augustine's anti-Manichean polemic, it would be odd to foist upon Augustine a spiritualizing interpretation of a New Testament call for "purity of heart" that would deny the materiality of human existence.

Augustine orders the health of the body to the health of the soul because he thinks humanity tends to rest sinfully in its concern for the body (*Mor.* 1.28.56; see Eph. 5:29). The healthy soul, however, is open both to God and bodily creation—just as God became open to a body and human bodies will be resurrected. Modern Augustinians can augment concern for bodily integrity as part and parcel of spiritual integrity. They also might augment the distance between Augustine's own asymmetrical account of the negative and positive duties of charity. Augustinians also should allow concern for love of neighbor

---

146. Langan, "St. Augustine's Just War Theory," 22.

to include concern for institutional structures in ways that Augustine could not imagine. But Augustine might also challenge modern assumptions. He stands in the center of the Christian tradition in his denial that physical death is the worst of all evils: "Do not fear those who kill the body but cannot kill the soul; rather fear him who can destroy both soul and body in hell" (Matt. 10.28). Augustine's mature position need not denigrate the body for the sake of the soul. As John Rist puts it, "'escaping the body' would be not only a metaphysical mistake, but a desertion of the love for the body which God has intended" (*ATB*, 110). In the disturbing passage above, Augustine does not say that there are *no other evils* in war. He is not indifferent to material harms, the real suffering of the flesh in historical time. Augustine rhetorically offers a comparative remark to highlight the importance of rightly ordered desire for healthy politics, a standing reminder that what we do to others matters for who we are and who we are matters for what we do to others. Moreover, while he may distinguish motivation from action (*benevolentia* from *beneficentia*), Augustine consistently binds motivation "toward concrete love of neighbor rather than mystical contemplation or metaphysical speculation."[147] The danger of paternalism arises precisely because Augustine refuses to separate love of God from love of neighbor. Augustine's emphasis on interiority enlarges political ethics by attending more concretely to the effects of our actions on ourselves without neglecting their impact on others.

It is ironic that Augustine's postmodern critics worry that he provides a perverse appeal to an intrinsic moral order (intellectually apprehended), and his pacifist critics worry that he provides a perverse appeal to inward dispositions as subjective affect (emotionally apprehended). Both worries reflect a rejection of one pole of my integrated Augustinian account of motivation that is both "spiritual" and "material," and "rational" and "emotional." Augustine's psychological eudaimonism (with its emphasis on the self's dispositions) is consistent with his teleological ontology (with its emphasis on order and the revelation of love in Christ).[148] To understand this consistency requires not only a richer Augustinian imagination for both the relation

147. Schlabach, *For the Joy Set Before Us*, 125. Augustine distinguishes benevolence and beneficence but he does not oppose them (*DVR* 47.91; *CD* 8.26 and 18.51).

148. Recall Paul Tillich's argument that "there must be something at the basis of love as emotion which justifies both its ethical and ontological interpretation. And it may well be that the ethical nature of love is dependent on its ontological nature, and that the ontological nature of love gets its qualifications by its ethical character" (*LPJ*, 4–5).

between the body and the soul, or God and the world, but an account of the sociality of virtue itself. Rowan Williams argues that in reading the *City of God* we should "look less for a systematic account of 'church' and 'world' (let alone church and state)" and "more for a scheme reflecting the nature of social virtue."[149] This is the subject of my final chapter.

In this chapter, I moved from a general discussion of the centrality of love for an Augustinian political ethic to some specific remarks about political practice. The basic claim has been that love need not be abandoned by liberal civic virtue. Liberals fear the dangerous effect of emotions in morality and politics, particularly when couched as a politics of the soul and the heart. With modern and ancient "Stoics," Augustinian civic liberals know the moral and political dangers of passions (even passions for justice and love). But Augustinians should follow Augustine and feminist theory in not pitting the "public" reasons of justice against the "private" emotions of love. A psychologically viable liberal account of civic virtue involves attention to the cultivation of certain kinds of emotions. A healthy liberal society requires a citizenry with developed habits and dispositions to care for others, not just formal subscription to liberal principles and procedures. It may be true in this life that "virtues without principles are blind, as principles without virtues are impotent."[150] Some liberals may still think cultivation of virtues like love is too dangerous. Better to subdue them. They prefer the chastity of civic apathy to the fanaticism of excessive civic responsibility. Augustinian civic liberalism offers one way to avoid this unappealing choice. Augustine's texts encourage a eudaimonistic loving that is other-regarding without domination. Augustine's love is not merely an affect of the agent but an intersubjective movement of self and others. Love is operative throughout the whole encounter between the self and a reality governed by the movement of love as divine compassion. We have reached the point in my discussion were we can investigate this claim through another set of Augustine's most contested texts.

149. Williams, "Politics and the Soul," 57.
150. Frankena, "Ethics of Love," 32.

6

Love as Political Virtue
"Platonists" and the Problem of God

*For no one ought to live a life of leisure in such a way
that he takes no thought in that leisure for the
welfare of his neighbour; nor ought he to be so active as
to feel no need for the contemplation of God.*

AUGUSTINE, *City of God*, 19.19

*Would the gods, then, be contaminated if they
were to mingle with men, even if, in helping them,
it were necessary to touch them?*

AUGUSTINE, *City of God*, 9.16

There is an important difference between conceptions of love and the concept of love.[1] A central claim of this book is that the concept of love has been unduly neglected in both liberal and Augustinian discussions of civic virtue. A secondary claim, however, has been that Augustine's particular conception of love offers a more positive political resource than its critics allow. This final chapter responds to the second of Arendt's representative challenges by refuting the claim that Augustine's "otherworldly" love for God either eclipses or instrumentalizes love for neighbor in ways that render Augustinianism inconsistent with liberal politics. My argument turns this

---

1. I here adapt Rawls's distinction between conceptions of justice and the concept of justice (Rawls, *Theory of Justice*, 5). Rawls follows H. L. A. Hart, *Concept of Law* (Oxford: Clarendon Press, 1961), 155–59.

criticism on its head: where Arendt and others find antiliberal otherworldliness, I find a profound resource for an ethics of democratic citizenship. In the previous chapter, I argued that the recognition of sin places constraints on Augustinian loving. This loving recognizes a certain kind of autonomy that is itself part of the good of the beloved. In this chapter, I argue that Augustinian liberals can resist (even combat) paternalism not only by recognizing the limits of politics in relation to the life of virtue but by reflecting on the conceptual role of love for God within the Augustinian ethics of love itself.

Augustine's critics, like Arendt and Nygren, admit that he was preoccupied with love for neighbor. Neighbor-love pervades his writings. He repeatedly enjoins the love commandments as summaries of Christian discipleship. This repetition occurs throughout his discussions of what moderns conventionally distinguish as piety and morality. Two passages from Oliver O'Donovan put it well:

> Augustine was aware (what theologian ever more so?) that the Bible sums up the Christian ethic in two love-commands with two objects of love, God and neighbor. To these he is constantly alluding; they are the very heart of the meaning of Scripture, they are the two wings on which we must mount, they are the two feet on which we approach God, the two pence paid by the Samaritan at the inn, and even the twin lambs borne by all the flock in the Song of Songs. (*PSL*, 22–23)

> The "second great command," "You shall love your neighbor as yourself," dominated Augustine's moral thinking. In one or another of its biblical contexts, or indifferently, it is quoted or referred to on more than a hundred and twenty occasions. (*PSL*, 112)

The concern that Augustine's critics identify is not that he neglected love for neighbor but that his theology finds no secure place for it. His constant appeals compensate for this insecurity rather than demonstrate an adequate commitment to the love of neighbor. In a curious way, Augustine places the dual love commandments at the center of Christian moral reflection only because of his failure to provide a satisfying account of their relation. I do not agree with this position.

The complex relation of the love commands was a vexed one for Augustine. As I have suggested, his greatest question may not be his celebrated claim that he "had become a great enigma to myself, and I questioned my soul" (*Conf.* 4.4.9). The logic of Augustinian love is to be found in the *magna quaestio* that he asks in *On Christian Doctrine*: "whether man is to be loved by man for his own sake, or for the sake of something else" (*DDC* 1.22.20). This is his topic of "great difficulty" (*Mor.* 1.26.51).[2] This difficulty pervades his eudaimonistic theology, and it should be central for any political ethics that attends to the Augustinian tradition. This question of selfhood before God would powerfully come to involve the pervasive question of otherness, the presence of fellow creatures in his journey.

This chapter argues that Augustine's initial and much maligned "use" and "enjoyment" distinction is not as philosophically or theologically problematic as its many critics claim. There are stronger and weaker versions of this Augustinian distinction. I will argue for a weak version that does not involve the active and conscious referral to God of each instance of love.[3] Dogmatic emphasis on explicit reference to God can be a prideful rejection of the limits of our self-interpretations. Augustinians, after all, believe that God can do more with our loves than we can. It is enough that loves are referable to God, even if they are not referred to God in each instance. Love for God can be implied by love for neighbor; in fact, for the mature Augustine, any act of proper love involves love for God. God is love and, in the final analysis for Augustine, love is God (*DT* 8.8.12 and *DT* 13.10.13).[4] But even to frame

2. Augustine writes: "But I do not know whether these two loves rise up together to fullness and perfection, or whether, while love for God begins first, love for neighbor is first to be accomplished. For perhaps divine love draws us more quickly to itself at the outset, but we accomplish smaller things more easily. However that may be, the main point to be held is this, that no one should think that while he despises his neighbor he will come to beatitude and to the God whom he loves" (*Mor.* 1.26.51). Apart from the emphasis on love for neighbor in the passage, I cite it in order to highlight Augustine's recognition of the problem and the tentativeness in his writing.

3. Iris Murdoch makes a similar move in her claim that "we are not always responding to the magnetic pull of the idea of perfection" (Murdoch, *Sovereignty of Good*, 43). For Murdoch, "the task of attention goes on all the time and at apparently empty and everyday moments we are 'looking,' making those little peering efforts of imagination which have such important cumulative results" (43).

4. Van Bavel marshals several texts in support of Augustine's "daring" inversion of the phrase "God is love" (*Deus dilectio est*) into "Love is God" (van Bavel, "Double Face of Love in St. Augustine," 172). He argues that Augustine effectively reduces love for God to love for neighbor, and associates this reduction with Karl Rahner's theory of "anonymous Christians" (177). Van Bavel is careful to distinguish the identity of the love commands from the identification of the creature and God: "I wish to stress that in Augustine's view human love does not dislodge God . . . identification supposes non-identity" (179). I am not sure how van Bavel understands the relationship of identification (which maintains

the question in this way (a linguistic move prevented in biblical Greek) risks misunderstanding by imagining love either as a univocal predicate of God's goodness or a scarce commodity that should be distributed with caution. Augustine's mature understanding of love resists these calculations: "We need not let the question worry us about how much love we should expend on our brother, how much on God" (*DT* 8.5.12). The two loves are interdependent, but not in a zero-sum fashion. Augustine's formulations of "contemplation" and "activity" suggest that the two loves are not completely substitutable for one another (at least in this life). God and creation, to be sure, are radically distinct for Augustine and Augustinians. Creatures are to be loved according to their status as creatures, and God is to be loved according to God's status as God: "With one and the same charity we love God and neighbour; but God on God's account, ourselves and neighbour also on God's account" (*DT* 8.5.12). There can be no love of God apart from the love of neighbor, but this is not to say that explicit love of God involves nothing more than love of neighbor. In fact, as Gene Outka explains, "love of God may involve discrete attitudes and actions whose very intelligibility . . . depends on their not being reducible to neighbor-love."[5] The two loves cannot share the same formal object for Augustine, if only because God is not an object of simple comparison for that which is within the world. The

---

distinction) and reduction (which implies conflation), but my reading of the correlativity of the love commands resists reducing either love for God to neighbor-love or neighbor-love to love for God. To speak Christologically, a response to Jesus Christ involves responsiveness both to God (the Second Person of the Trinity) and neighbor (the Word made flesh). Karl Barth would reiterate this theme in modern theology: "The neighbour's humanity reminds me of the humanity of the Son of God" (*Church Dogmatics* 1.2, 425) and "the structure of this humanity of Jesus Himself is revealed in this two-fold command" (*Church Dogmatics*, 3.2, 216). Peter Burnell argues that when "K. Barth says that because of the Incarnation humanity is eternally enclosed in the Godhead, at the core of divine compassion, he is in effect affirming what Augustine has already implied" (Burnell, *Augustinian Person*, 189). Barth, however, would read Augustine as a Pelagian and Platonist (Karl Barth, *The Holy Spirit and the Christian Life* [Louisville: Westminster/John Knox, 1993)], 4, 51n57, and 60–61). For discussion of Barth on *agape*, see Outka, *Agape*, 207–56, and David Clough, "*Eros* and *Agape* in Karl Barth's *Church Dogmatics*," *International Journal of Systematic Theology* 2, no. 2 (July 2000): 189–203.

5. Outka, *Agape*, 52. Some interpreters attribute this position to Rahner as well. Breyer maintains that Rahner "posits a radical unity, rather than identity of the two loves" (Breyer, "Karl Rahner on the Radical Unity of the Love of God and Neighbour," 264).

Creator-creature distinction supplies the logic for his distinction between use and enjoyment: creation is to be loved in relation to the Creator so that our loves "will no longer be covetousness but charity" (*DT* 9.2.13).

I have tried to shift the "use" and "enjoyment" distinction away from its usual dualistic metaphysical settings. Such metaphysical settings generate interpretive strategies that focus on the relative value of finite and infinite goods. But Augustine's main concern is with the psychology of valuing itself: "using things badly and enjoying them badly" (*DT* 10.13). In this sense, the categories of use and enjoyment need not be at odds with one another when both use and enjoyment occur in God. The ontology of Augustinian eudaimonism remains important, but it is radically transformed by a Christology which resists the competitive tournament of loves that critics imagine is inspired by a Platonic theory of the *summum bonum*. If God is in solidarity with humanity through the Incarnation, then creatures can enjoy the gifts of God even as they are perennially tempted to enjoy them in the wrong way. There is, then, an ethical and ontological relation between God and the world.

Augustine abandons the precise formulation of the distinction that most irritates his critics. But the spirit of *"uti et frui"* can be found throughout his writings. They provide "the analytic factors for understanding the role of love *(caritas)* in the ethics of Augustine."[6] A political Augustinianism that draws from Augustine's theology of love need not abandon the distinction in its ontological, ethical, or psychological dimensions. If it does abandon the distinction, even for the sake of loving the world, it does not remain Augustinian. The possibilities of referral of love to this God are not defeated by moralistic criticisms of a jealous devotion to a detached and immutable God. Augustine's God is a worldly God—"more intimately present to me than my innermost being, and higher than the highest peak of my spirit" (*Conf.* 3.6.11). Augustine's God is to be recognized in the intersubjectivity accomplished through the revelation of Christ as the divine neighbor.[7] To love God is to love the whole of creation existing in God. The love for God is expressed in an ordered love that loves God *in loving* God's world, a world that bears "His footprints" (*CD* 11.28). To speak anachronistically, Augustine suggests something like the "this-worldly" supernaturalism that Paul Ramsey denies

6. Bourke, *Joy in Augustine's Ethics,* 30.

7. On the relation between interiority and intersubjectivity in Augustine's doctrine of God, see Canning, *Unity of Love for God and Neighbor in St. Augustine,* 314–30.

to Augustine (*BCE*, 132) and the "supernaturalizing of the natural" that John Milbank identifies with Augustinianism (*TST*, 223).

There are several strategies that defenders of Augustine employ in order to avoid the most objectionable features of his "love monism" and "dualist otherworldliness." I argue that the spirit of Augustine's early and exploratory distinction coincides with dispositions and moral motivations that flow from his mature understanding of rightly ordered loving. Augustine orients "all loves according to a single gestalt, a single theocentric vision of love-as-a-whole-in-coordination-with-its-parts."[8] While this account may remain philosophically objectionable to many secular liberals because all loving remains oriented within "God," it is not in principle at odds with the goods of liberal politics or an ethics of democratic citizenship.

As we saw in the last chapter, Augustine was acutely aware of the human tendency to justify prideful domination in the name of love. Humility, then, is the preeminent virtue that attaches to proper love: "The more we are cured of the tumor of pride, the fuller we are of love" (*DT* 8.5.12). Pride may not be the dominant vice of all (as feminist theologians have pointed out against Augustine), but the prideful expressions of love are appropriately restrained in an Augustinian civic liberalism. An ethics of political Augustinianism should highlight these moments in Augustine as a way to provide appropriate parameters for love, especially in the political arena. In order to make room for an alliance between Augustinian love and civic liberalism, I have employed Augustinian psychology that undermines the paternalist temptations of love which mark Augustine's own political appeals to neighbor-love. In this chapter, I turn to the political implications of Augustine's theology in order to show how they cohere with my readings of his moral psychology. I show how Augustine's ontology is bound up with his ethical account of relationality in the world. Rather than trap the self in a religious quest, it is these relationships that are meant to overcome alienation in a private world.

CHANGING THE SUBJECT:
FROM SELF-LOVE TO NEIGHBOR-LOVE

Since the publication of Anders Nygren's *Agape and Eros*, the controlling interest in Augustine on love has been whether or not his doctrine of love

8. Schlabach, *For the Joy Set Before Us*, 38.

implies a self-seeking acquisitive love at odds with basic Christian affirmations. Most scholarly discussions of Augustine on love focus on this relation of *love of God* and *love of self* in the context of the influence of Neoplatonism on his eudaimonism.

Unlike much of political Augustinianism, Nygren recognizes that "love is unquestionably central in Augustinian Christianity" (*AE*, 464). But Nygren continues, "it is not easy to say what kind of love it is, whether its features are mainly those of Eros or those of Agape" (*AE*, 464). Nygren claims that the "great and fatal contradiction" in Augustine's view of love is the attempt to "maintain Eros and Agape at once" (*AE*, 470). The erotic self—what Nygren took to be the Platonic adversary of a truly Christian anthropology—remains the basic category of the Augustinian schema. Augustinian *caritas* remains acquisitive and egocentric as it tries to bootstrap itself up to God: "Not even the ideas 'Uti' and 'Frui' were able to deliver Augustine from the prevalent Hellenistic Eros theory" (*AE*, 512; see also 98, 549, and 550). Even if Augustine allows the *agape* found in Christ to be the answer to the human condition, it is the *appetitus* of the desiring self that grounds his very questions. God simply becomes "the means for the satisfaction of human desire" (*AE*, 500). Nygren, following Luther, identified this desiring self with the curse of the law. The speculative "object" of Augustine's love is God. To turn God into an "object" is to preserve the "nature" of a selfish love deeply at odds with the Christian narrative (*AE*, 546).[9]

We have seen many readers, even those sympathetic to Augustine, persuaded by this sort of account. Apart from the connections that I already identified with Arendt and Nussbaum, it also attracts those who otherwise endorse a kind of Augustinian liberalism. Nygren's reading of Augustine furnishes what Timothy P. Jackson calls Augustine's "aim-enhanced *eros*" and what Paul Ramsey calls the "Neo-Platonic view reducing love for neighbor to love for God" (*BCE*, 117).[10] For them, the *caritas* synthesis of transcendent eudaimonism (marked by the language of ordered loves) cannot deliver Augustine from the reduction of *agape* to erotic self-love. Augustine's valiant efforts to baptize *eros* ultimately fail for Nygren, Jackson, Niebuhr, and Ramsey because of the intrusion of natural self-love into every aspect of Augustinian

9. The young John Rawls, also under the influence of Nygren, adopted the same view. See Gregory, "Before the Original Position," 185–90.

10. Jackson, *Love Disconsoled*, 56.

ethics. This failure ramifies throughout Augustinianism and undermines the Christian content of its ethics. All loving supposedly remains derivative of self-love or reducible to love for God. This reading of Augustinianism has provoked intense theological discussions that typically lead to broader soteriological concerns about the relation of nature and grace.[11] Theological discomfort with eudaimonism illuminates fundamentally different conceptions of God and salvation in various Christian traditions.

On my understanding, Augustine's eudaimonism should not be reduced to the self's erotic quest for happiness. There is no doubt that Augustinian *caritas* involves desire for union with God as the source of happiness. But Augustine's account of this union and this happiness—as John Burnaby, Oliver O'Donovan, and Raymond Canning have argued—is governed by Christian confession rather than the inherited eudaimonism of Neoplatonic and Plotinian categories that run into modern ethical criticism.[12] Among Nygren's critics, O'Donovan most helpfully shows that Christian debates over *eros* finally involve ontology as well as ethics. Recalling my early discussion of pure nature, he argues that the most fundamental issue at stake in the moral charge of egocentricity is actually the underlying question of God's relation to Creation as both Creator and Redeemer. O'Donovan finds that Augustine's "picture of the universe shows us one who is the source and goal of being, value, and activity, himself in the center of the universe and at rest; and it shows us the remainder of the universe in constant movement, which, while it may tend toward or away from the center, is yet held in relation to it" (*PSL*, 157). Creation relates to God in reciprocity—these "moving galaxies of souls" respond to a force "immanent to them, a kind of dynamic nostalgia rather than transcendent summons from the center" (157).[13] Both Nygren and Augustine require an eschatological summons beyond our "natural" capacities to experience this relation of mutual loving. Both emphasize it is

11. For sketches of these debates, see Outka, *Agape*, 49–50, and Vacek, *Love, Divine and Human*, 141–46.

12. O'Donovan argues that Augustine's discussions of self-love do not immediately involve the search for happiness. In fact, of the 150 references to self-love in Augustine, "in only two texts are self-love and the desire for happiness mentioned together in a way that suggests their synonymity" (*PSL*, 57).

13. O'Donovan claims that "in the last resort what is at issue is whether all movement in the universe is from the center to the circumference or whether there is also this responsive movement" (157).

the work of God's love in a theology of the cross. For Augustine, "all the surer is our love for the face of Christ which we long to see, the more clearly we recognize in his back how much Christ first loved us" (*DT* 2.6.28). This is the love that Augustine identifies with grace itself. Nygren, however, implicitly rejects Augustine's picture of immanent teleology in order to protect a particular understanding of Creation as it relates to the gratuity of God's grace. Making space for Creation is an important element in my own defense of secular politics. However, in the end, O'Donovan strikingly argues that Nygren's effort to defend Creation against Augustinian *caritas* ends up leaving no room "for anything other than the doctrine of Creation, since every movement from the divine center has to be presuppositionless" (*PSL,* 158). This criticism speaks not only to the status of Creation but Augustine's Christology itself.

Augustine's teleology is immanent because it is Christological. It is governed by a God who becomes the neighbor of humanity and—to cite one of Augustine's favorite texts—brings it about that "God may be all in all" (1 Cor. 15:28). Augustine's Trinitarian and Christological emphases are not simply cover for his Platonism that really wants to love only God.[14] They help to make sense of his account of the second great commandment, even in *On Christian Doctrine*. Augustine emphasizes that the radical interruption of the Incarnation precedes the liberal arts (*DDC* 1.11.11). This incarnate Word of the Second Person is God's own sign—God's rhetoric that is "both doctor and medicine" (*DDC* 1.14.13). Christ is both the "native country" and the "the Way to that country" (*DDC* 1.11.11, Robertson). Christ is the sign that signifies itself but also anticipates a fuller disclosure.[15] To follow the personal narrative

---

14. According to Walter Hannam, "it is precisely because God the Trinity is the Creator *in quo omnia* that the *usus-fruitio* distinction in regard to neighbour holds together as a Christian framework for love of other" ("*Ad illud ubi permanendum est,*" 171n11). I agree with Hannam's general framework, but I emphasize Augustine's Christology because I do not see a strong role for the Spirit in the works of the 390s. Following Rist, I think Augustine's pneumatology awaits until later works for its full development (Rist, *ATB,* 156n13).

15. For Incarnational rather than "Platonic" readings of Augustine's developed Christology, see M. D. Jordan, "Words and Word: Incarnation and Signification in Augustine's *De doctrina christiana,*" *Augustinian Studies* 11 (1970): 177–96; James K. A. Smith, "Between Predication and Silence: Augustine on How (Not) to Speak of God," *Heythrop Journal* (2000): 66–86; and Michael Cameron, "The Christological Substructure of Augustine's

of this capacious sign could never mean an escape from history, the time of the flesh. Christology places Augustine's doctrine of love in an altogether different context than a "Platonic" theory of appetitive love: "Love is no longer the appetitive power that defines our moral struggle, but, reconceived through the incarnation, it has now become identified with God himself."[16] Against Arendt, we might say that God's Word in Christ is also God's word in the command to love the neighbor. In one of his catechisms, Augustine writes:

> Thus, before all else, Christ came so that people might learn how much God loves them, and might learn this so that they would catch fire with love for him who first loved them, and so that they would also love their neighbor as he commanded and showed by his example—he who made himself their neighbor by loving them when they were not close to him but were wandering far from him. (*De catechizandis rudibus* 4.8)

It is Augustine's collectivist Christology *(totus Christus)* that refigures both what the desire for God entails and the sort of God that constitutes this desire.[17] For Augustine, because the Word became flesh, "there can be no separation of love" (*IoEp.* 10.3, the *locus classicus* of Augustine's high Christology and his ecclesiology). Indeed, because of Christ's saving work (*DT* 2.6), human beings become "partakers of his divinity" (*DT* 4.1.4). This collectivism, however, is not a metaphysical unity of essence but an affective unity of love. Like the Stoic elements of his account of the happy life, the Platonic language of ascent as a kind of stepping up metaphysical platforms fades throughout Augustine's career. It yields to a Christological conception of divinity, revealed in salvation history through the Spirit as the bond of love between Father and Son. O'Donovan argues:

> But the unified soul is no longer an immanent fact about the cosmos but an eschatological achievement, the accomplished work of the Holy Spirit in the church of Christ. . . . It is no nostalgia for lost unity but an imperious summons from above which effected this attachment, both horizontal and verti-

---

Figurative Exegesis," in *Augustine and the Bible,* ed. Pamela Bright (Notre Dame, Ind.: University of Notre Dame Press, 1999), 74–103.

16. Davies, *Theology of Compassion,* 81.

17. Though it carries implication for a politics of solidarity, "collectivist" Christology is not to be confused with collectivism in political theory. It is a technical theological term for Christologies that emphasize the participation of Christians in the body of Christ.

cal. By this double movement of reunification, the love-of-neighbor acting as cradle for the love-of-God, the Spirit whose name is *Dilectio* completes his redemptive work. (*PSL,* 135–36)[18]

Recall that God for Augustine is not simply another object that might fulfill the desires of the individual self in her subjective interiority. To picture Augustine's God in this way renders an antithetical caricature of his sweeping vision of what it means to worship and serve God as the *Bonum Commune*.[19] This all too familiar reading subverts the precise character of his theological innovation.

True love of self is now itself taken into the intersubjective triune love of God. It is this participatory love that frees the self from its own needy self-enclosure. Augustine's self (and his needs) finds its rest in God (who, strictly speaking, has no need *in se* but shares love in community as the expression of Godself). The self that is ordered toward God is released to love rather than grasp or possess the neighbor. This love is not a communion of lovers that "share this love as a kind of third object, like two people share a bench in the park . . . rather, they share this love as something that constitutes each."[20] It is a love "poured abroad in our hearts by the Holy Spirit who is given to us" (*Conf.* 4.4.7).[21] The true good of this self participates in God's good—a good that has a decidedly social aspect in Augustine's Trinitarian theology. Raymond Canning observes:

> The good that accrues to the self loving God is not a prize which the subject earns through having orientated his instinctual love for self appropriately to his best advantage. It is rather the gift which flows from the subject's

18. For O'Donovan, "The teleological thrust of love was always toward exact mutuality of subject and object, a state that must obtain when 'God shall be all in all'" (*PSL,* 130).

19. John Burnaby writes: "If the *Summum Bonum* is by its very nature the *bonum commune*, a good which can be possessed only by being shared, then the desire and pursuit of it can never be the desire and pursuit of a *bonum privatum*" (Burnaby, *Amor Dei,* 127). Milbank argues that when Augustine arrives at this vision of love "where 'fruition' evidently includes a social dimension, it is much clearer that nothing is merely used, but, being used rightly, is also, enjoyed" (*TST,* 421).

20. Von Heyking, *Augustine and Politics as Longing in the World,* 199.

21. Romans 5:5 is one of Augustine's favorite verses, which he cites over two hundred times. For Augustine, the Holy Spirit acts as "the glue of the universe" which is "simply the love of the Godhead in his *operationes ad extra*" (O'Donovan, *PSL,* 135).

preferring to be God's rather than his own, that gift which, unsolicited, embraces his total gift of self in response to the commandment.[22]

Edward Vacek is wrong, then, to claim that "when we pray, 'Thy kingdom come, Thy will be done' we are not just praying, as Augustine would have it, for our own good."[23] Vacek's rejection of an Augustinian conception of salvation as a personal reward—something we also saw in Jackson's reading of Augustine—is a chimera. Salvation could only be social for Augustine because human beings cannot remain in themselves. Augustine writes:

> [Christ] wants his disciples to be one in him, because they cannot be one in themselves, split as they are from each other by clashing wills and desires, and the uncleanness of their sins; so they are cleansed by the mediator that they may be one in him, not only by virtue of the same nature whereby all of them from the ranks of mortal men are made equal to angels, but even more by virtue of one and the same wholly harmonious will reaching out in concert to the same ultimate happiness, and fused somehow into one spirit in the furnace of charity. (*DT* 4.2.12)

This love of God is revealed in the biblical story of Christ's identity as the Word become flesh that decenters any privileging of the self's relation to God. In fact, for Augustine, a failure to love the neighbor constitutes a denial of the Incarnation itself: "Whoever has not charity, denies Christ's coming in the flesh" (*IoEp.* 6.13). The Incarnation issues a challenge to any form of deistic or Neoplatonic ontology that perpetuates a competitive tournament of loves between God and the world. Augustine's account of love is not, *pace* Nygren and his followers, a Platonic story about the exclusive aspiration for the Good or a program of scales of ascending perfection in a great chain of being.

Proper self-love remains a guide for neighbor-love ("as yourself"), but the dominant movement in Augustine's theology of love is explosively outward and communal. The self's happiness for Augustine does not compete with the neighbor's happiness precisely because all loving remains Christocentric rather than egocentric. Consider, for example, Augustine's distinctive prefer-

---

22. Canning, *Unity of Love for God and Neighbor in St. Augustine*, 150.
23. Vacek, *Love, Human and Divine*, 96.

ence for the Psalms rather than the Songs of Songs in his language about the union of souls to God. Apart from the significant example of the Song of Songs 2:4 *(ordinat in me charitatem)*, Augustine's surprisingly infrequent appeals to the erotic imagery of this familiar text may have less to do with an anxiety about sexuality and more to do with a worry that "conjugal love remains fundamentally exclusionary, whereas the love of God is to be shared with others."[24] God's agapic goodness means there is no need for a fearful grasp of a lover or God in order to satisfy desire. Love, as Augustine's more mature formulations insist, is always *in Deo* and *propter Deum*. The well-being of the self is not jealous of the well-being of the neighbor; in fact, the self is constituted in the very love of neighbor that participates in the love of God without fear of loss. Augustine writes:

> A man's possession of goodness is in no way lessened by the advent or con-
> tinued presence of a sharer in it. On the contrary, goodness is a possession
> which is enjoyed more fully in proportion to the concord that exists between
> partners united in charity. He who refuses to enjoy this possession in part-
> nership will not enjoy it at all; and a man will find that he possess it more
> abundantly in proportion to the fullness with which he loves his partner in
> it. (*CD* 15.5)

The relation of *eros* and *agape* is not the specific interest of this book, but the above formulation is emblematic of Augustine's mature position on love and goodness. Arendt and Nygren (and those who follow their reading of Augustine on this point) link the structure of motivated *eros* to a subsequent insecure standing of love of neighbor in Augustine. However, I want to change the subject of Augustinian inquiry.

My focus is not so much on the relation of *self-love* to love for God and neighbor, but on the latter relation itself. Critics argue that Augustine pays tribute to love for neighbor because of the biblical witness but that he provides no conceptual place for it in his system. How might the Augustinian tradition reconcile *love for neighbor* with the *love for God?* The problems of "otherworldliness" and "instrumentalism" are in many ways parasitic on larger charges about selfhood in Augustine's Neoplatonic eudaimonism. A more basic question for political Augustinianism is whether or not love for

---

24. Asiedu, "The Song of Songs," 316.

God can express itself in other-regarding love for that which is not immutable and perfect.

This theological problem is of central concern for Augustinian conceptions of love apart from the specific context of the ethics of democratic citizenship. But it is in this context that the theological difficulties become conceptually acute. Arendt's dissertation introduced the problem: namely, the eclipse of political concern for the neighbor in the overarching commitment to the love for God.

I think there are alternative interpretations of Augustine that can help relieve political Augustinianism of these concerns about the joining a vision of God with a teleological structure of virtue and motivation. The aim of this chapter, again, is not to justify Augustinian beliefs about God or even *eros* and eudaimonism. Rather, by responding to Augustine's critics, I want show how Augustine's account of the relation of love of God and neighbor can find a coherent place within an Augustinian ethics of democratic citizenship. Theorizing virtues for citizens in a liberal society does not *necessarily* require this teleological structure. But, for Christians, something like this teleological structure is both warranted and compatible with liberal self-understandings.

Arendt's criticisms resonate with a number of theological and philosophical critics of Augustinian ethics more generally. As we have seen, many of these critics are theists who might share much in common with Augustinian civic liberalism but who reject an Augustinian account of the relation of the love commands. The particular problem has been crystallized most recently by Robert M. Adams in his important book, *Finite and Infinite Goods*.[25]

Despite my defense of the *uti et frui* distinction, I am deeply sympathetic with the framework Adams develops—both in terms of its moral theory and its commitment to political liberalism. Against the dominant concern with the right in contemporary Anglo-American philosophy, Adams's work emphasizes the centrality of the good. In fact, he stresses a *"transcendence of the infinite Good"* (4). Like my proposal, he argues for a conception of "human love for the good as a fragmentary and imperfect participation in an inclusive and perfect divine love" (8). In fact, he similarly proposes an erotic love of an overflowing good that "escapes the dichotomy of benevolence and self-interest" (137). His effort to incorporate the virtue of *hesed* into a liberal ethics of citizenship also parallels my effort to incorporate a notion of love

25. References in this section of the text refer to this book.

that likewise "should obtain between members of different groups in the society whether or not their relations are close" (172). In putting forth his theses regarding excellence as the central type of goodness, Adams argues that "a variety of religious concepts may enrich the texture of ethical thought" (4). I do not intend to defend or criticize Adams's larger project. I offer it as yet another example of Augustine's misfortune. Given that Adams's framework for ethics is broadly Platonic and theistic, his presentation shows the extent to which Augustinian love has been rejected even on its home turf.

Adams wants to preserve the important sense in which all love bears upon interest in its relation to God. He presents "a human motivational ideal of devotion to the Good as organizing one's whole motivational system" (8). Since he believes the Good is God and we are to love that which resembles or images God, Adams identifies a particular problem as basic to theistic commitment. He writes:

> The really hard question is whether the sort of maximal devotion to God demanded by theism is compatible with love for anything finite at all. If we are to love God with all our heart and soul and strength, will any room be left in our hearts for the love of anything else (such as our neighbor)? An integrative ideal of theistic devotion will seek room for love of finite good within love for God rather than in competition with it; but how? (186)

Adams's "really hard question" recalls Augustine's *magna quaestio* of *On Christian Doctrine* and the "great difficulty" of *De Moribus*. Before outlining his own resolution that distinguishes but also integrates love for God and love for that which is not God, Adams contrasts his position to Augustine's failed attempt. Adams reports to his readers:

> One of the more influential approaches to this problem in Western religious history—perhaps the most influential—was proposed by St. Augustine of Hippo, and has often provided a rationale for asceticism in concrete programs of religious devotion. It turns on the subordination of means to end. Augustine distinguishes between *enjoying* something and *using* it.... Augustine introduces this distinction in order to make the point that God is to be enjoyed but other things, God's finite creatures, ought only to be used. (186)

Echoing Arendt and Nygren, Adams thinks this resolution does not provide for anything "that really deserves the name of *love* of one's neighbor, or of any other finite thing" (186). Augustine's teleological subordination of love for those goods other than God (including most especially the neighbor) only values these finite goods as a means to an ulterior (usually future) end. This end is the enjoyment and rest found in the mystical vision of God.

In a telling footnote, Adams suggests that "there are passages in Augustine's works that suggest a more attractive conception of the relation between neighbor-love and devotion to God; but what I present in the text is, so far as I know, the most clearly articulated and the most influential on this subject" (186n20). As in most other treatments of Augustine on neighbor-love, Adams presents the *uti et frui* distinction found in the first book of *On Christian Doctrine* as a foil for a more adequate account of the relation of the love commands. For Adams, this particular teleological structure "infects" the "content of the attitudes" that governs neighbor-love by mediating and deferring such love to the controlling love of God (188). The neighbor is not loved for her own sake, because (in Kantian terms) that which is not God is conceived as mere means to an end.

Adams's own resolution relies on the validity of loving God *in* loving neighbors for their own sake. He proposes an ideal of religious piety "in which love for God is an organizing principle into which one integrates genuine love for other goods that one is to prize for their own sake, as God does" (275). He thinks the Augustinian tradition cannot support this position because of its emphasis on explicit love of God rather than more implicit ways of loving God by loving that which is not God.[26] Adams does not wish to deny other ways of loving God more directly. But he takes the Augustinian tradition to be inadequate in its failure to allow a love for the neighbor for her own sake. This love—modeled by God's love

26. Adams writes: "The loves and concerns of nontheists as well as theists may be inspired by their attention to goods that in my view are images of God. And theists as well as nontheists may be moved by manifestations of the glory of God much more often than they think of them in consciously theological terms. So we can think of a sort of implicit alliance with God as helping to constitute an implicit love for God. Doubtless alliance with God can be more fully developed if it is theologically explicit, but theological explicitness does not guarantee the authenticity of such alliance" (Adams, *Finite and Infinite Goods*, 198). I agree with this final claim about authenticity, but I side more with Edward Vacek in his belief that conscious motivation of love for God can constitute a different kind of moral action (see Vacek, *Love, Human and Divine*, 141–46). Adams's argument resonates with, but does not require, Rahner's belief that the love of neighbor is the primary act of love of God (see Rahner, "Reflections on the Unity of the Love of Neighbour and the Love of God").

for the neighbor for her own sake—is an "important part of loving God" (197). Adams recognizes that traditional efforts to distinguish the love commands rest upon theological suspicions of idolatry and the persistent need to distinguish Creator and creature. Against Augustine, however, Adams thinks his way of integrating the love commands better guards against idolatry because it does not demand an explicit thematization of the love of God (210).

This strong reading of a *subordinationist* teleology (one that subordinates proximate goods as means to an ultimate good) dominates most understandings of Augustine. Even a sympathetic interpreter such as Oliver O'Donovan claims that Augustine's "mistake was to see the ordering of the two loves in terms of an imposed subordination of means to an end" (*PSL*, 24). As we saw in the previous chapter, this problem threatens the equal dignity of human beings and motivates liberal fears of paternalism because it assumes a love that aims exclusively to promote the neighbor's good in light of the self's understanding of the good. Liberal anxieties are exacerbated when the neighbor's good is thought of in terms of not only her moral virtue but her eternal well-being in God. Are there other ways to read Augustine and Augustine's God? Is this the only word that can be spoken of Augustine's account of love for God and love for neighbor?

Recent Augustine scholarship suggests that there are at least three basic strategies for relieving Augustine and the Augustinian tradition of the objectionable features of the *uti et frui* distinction.[27] Underlying each of these strategies is an effort to locate Augustine's distinction in its intellectual context, including its pastoral and rhetorical function as well as its general relation to his theological imagination. In the next sections, I examine these strategies before putting forth a theological proposal that is particularly relevant to the political dimensions of Arendt's second challenge to Augustinian loving.

RE-READING *UTI ET FRUI*

Exploratory and Abandoned ‡ The first strategy claims that, after *On Christian Doctrine*, Augustine himself abandoned the "use" and "enjoyment" formu-

---

27. For a general survey of this massive literature, see A. Dupont, "Using or Enjoying Humans: *Uti* and *frui* in Augustine," *Augustiniana* 54 (2004): 475–506.

lation. His rhetoric betrays an early exploration of this fundamental Christian *aporia*. It was a heady exploration at a time when Augustine was just beginning to come to terms with the transformation of Greek philosophy focused on desire for the Supreme Good into a theological idiom responsive to the Incarnation and the dual command to love God and neighbor. As such, the popularity of *uti et frui* obscures "the experimental and finally inconclusive character of its solution to the problem of the order of love" (O'Donovan, *PSL*, 26).

The *uti et frui* distinction makes its first appearance in *Eighty-Three Different Questions*. Augustine takes the distinction from the Stoic distinction between *honesta* (ends) and *utilia* (means). Augustine writes:

> There is the same difference between the terms *honorable* [*honestum*] and *useful* [*utile*] as between the terms *enjoyable* [*fruendum*] and *useful* [*utendum*]. For although it can be maintained (though requiring some subtlety) that everything honorable is useful and everything useful is honorable, nevertheless, since the term *honorable* more appropriately and usually means "that which is sought for its own sake," and the term *useful*, "that which is directed to something else," we now speak in terms of this distinction, while safeguarding, of course, the fact that the word *honorable* and the word *useful* are in no way opposed to one another. For these two terms are sometimes thought to be mutually exclusive, but this is an uninformed opinion of the crowd. Therefore we are said to enjoy that from which we derive pleasure. We use that which we order toward something else from which we expect to derive pleasure. Consequently every human perversion (also called vice) consists in the desire to use what ought to be enjoyed and to enjoy what ought to be used. In turn, good order (also called virtue) consists in the desire to enjoy what ought to be enjoyed and to use what ought to be used. Now honorable things are to be enjoyed, but useful things are to be used. All useful things, however, ought to be used according as there is need for each of them. . . . Accordingly those who do not use things well are usually and more correctly called *abusers*. . . . Therefore he does not use anything who uses it badly. (*DeDiv.* q30)

This early passage resonates with the two more famous expositions of *uti* and *frui* that most critics of Augustine cite. In *On Christian Doctrine* Augustine writes:

> There are some things which are to be enjoyed, some which are to be used, and *some whose function is both to enjoy and use* [*aliae quae fruuntur et utuntur*]. Those which are to be enjoyed make us happy; those which are to be used as-

sist us and give us a boost, so to speak, as we press on towards our happiness, so that we may reach and hold fast to the things which make us happy. And we, placed as we are among things of both kinds, both enjoy and use them; but if we choose to enjoy things that are to be used, our advance is impeded and sometimes even diverted, and we are held back, or even put off, from attaining things which are to be enjoyed, because we are hamstrung by our love of lower things. To enjoy something is to hold fast to it in love for its own sake. To use something is to apply whatever it may be to the purpose of obtaining what you love—if indeed it is something that ought to be loved. (The improper use of something should be termed abused.) (*DDC* 1.3.3, emphasis mine)

It is therefore an important question whether humans should enjoy one another or use one another, or both. We have been commanded to love one another [John 13:34; 15:12, 17], but the question is whether one person should be loved by another on his own account or for some other reason. If on his own account, we enjoy him; if for some other reason, we use him. In my opinion, he should be loved for another reason. For if something is to be loved on its own account, it is made to constitute the happy life, even if it is not as yet the reality but the hope of it which consoles us at this time. (*DDC* 1.22.20)

These passages prick the modern reader's "Kantian" ears, especially if Robertson's 1958 translation error is followed (as is often the case).[28] They suggest an exploitation and manipulation that cast a purely "instrumentalist" role for the neighbor. Given Augustine's frequent pilgrimage imagery of the journey to our true homeland, the sense that the neighbor is merely a temporal vehicle for the individual's journey to eternal beatitude is particularly acute. The common interpretation of Augustine's early appeal "treats

28. In the first passage from *On Christian Doctrine*, I highlight Green's translation rather than Robertson's incorrect translation of the italicized clause: "and there are others to be enjoyed and used" (*DDC* 1.3.3, Robertson). Robertson's misleading translation neglects the fact that *uti* and *frui* are deponent verbs—passive in form but active in meaning. Green's rendering lends further evidence to my claim that Augustine's account of use and enjoyment accents the quality of the loving (and the lover) rather than simply the metaphysical status of the objects loved. The problem of neighbor-love, however, is not resolved. But there is a very important conceptual distance between these translations. I thank Oliver O'Donovan, Timothy P. Jackson, and Philip Reynolds for discussion of this translation issue.

the order of means and end as an *instrumental order within the project of the loving subject.*"[29] However, to hang all of Augustine's thinking on these few early passages does not recognize the extent to which the book itself is "an exploratory study, in which he is still feeling his way towards a satisfactory conception of *ordo amoris*" (363). Augustine's efforts to bring together his emerging blend of Neoplatonism, Ciceronian concerns about loving friends for the sake of something else, and Christian eschatological language about life as a pilgrimage to our eternal destiny, put too much pressure on this early work. O'Donovan concludes, "there is simply too much going on" (383).

Augustine himself appears unsatisfied with the formula even within *On Christian Doctrine*. By the end of the work, "the neighbor does not belong simply among the things of this world; he belongs at the 'end' and 'fulfilment' of the command, beyond the limits of the temporal dispensation" (390). O'Donovan claims that Augustine never again refers to love of neighbor as "use."[30] Augustine continues to speak of loving things for God's sake, but he comes to prefer the formulation that one loves the neighbor *in God* rather than in terms of any "*project of our need*" (389). For example, Augustine argues that the peace of the Heavenly City consists in "the enjoyment of God, and of one another in God" (*CD* 19.13). He commends his readers to "enjoy both ourselves and our brothers in the Lord" (*DT* 9.13).[31] O'Donovan elsewhere claims that the spirit of the distinction remains: "Inappropriate as the use-enjoyment contrast may be to express it, the point is simply that our neigh-

---

29. O'Donovan, "*Usus* and *Fruitio*," 361. Page references in this section of the text refer to this article.

30. O'Donovan ends his influential article: "It would appear that a defence of the classification proposed in *De doctr. Christ.* was more than even Augustine himself was prepared to undertake" (397). Augustine's later discussions (*DT* 8.6–10 and *CD* 8.8 and 10.3) focus on love of neighbor as *fruitio* rather than *usus*. But he remains willing to speak about the good making "use of this world in order to enjoy God" (*CD* 15.7). Rist points out that Augustine here implies that is "it is ambiguous institutions, not people, which are to be treated as means to an end" (*ATB*, 166).

31. These formulations are prefigured in *On Christian Doctrine*, where Augustine speaks of the *societate dilectionis Dei*: "The greatest reward is that we enjoy Him and that all of us who enjoy Him may enjoy one another in Him" (1.32.35); moreover, "enjoyment is very like use with delight [*cum delectatione uti*]" (1.33.37).

bor is an ontologically dependent being" (*PSL*, 114).[32] This recognition of dependency does not overwhelm genuine love for the neighbor: "When we care for our neighbour's welfare, it is because we are delighted by our neighbour: by the sheer facticity of this other human that God has made; by the fact that God has given, and vindicated, a determination of our neighbour to health, rationality, and relationship" (O'Donovan, *DN*, 183). Nevertheless, O'Donovan concedes to Augustine's critics that this early "daring and contentious" appeal to "using" the neighbor is confusing and "scandalous."[33] It is best to regard the formulation from *On Christian Doctrine* as a "false step," not Augustine's "final thoughts on teleology" (*PSL*, 28–29). O'Donovan realizes that the question of teleology does not go away.

Expanding the Sense of "Use" ‡ Some interpreters, however, find this resolution too easy. Rather than focus on the extent to which Augustine transforms classical eudaimonism, they have challenged the Kantian reading of *uti* and *frui*. They do not claim that Augustine abandons the formulation. They contextualize Augustine's use of *use* and the rhetorical purposes it serves. This strategy more directly disrupts the modern subordinationist reading of *uti* and *frui* as a relation between means and end.

Many interpreters have pointed out that *uti* is a standard Latin locution, "found also in earlier English, e.g. 'He used him well'—indicating how people are to be 'treated'; the notion of exploitation is not to be read into it" (Rist, *ATB*, 163–64). Latin authors sometimes appeal to "use" in the same way that modern English allows "use" to suggest a sense of necessity. We often say, "I could really use a cup of coffee."[34] John von Heyking argues that the meaning of *usus* in Augustine "is closer to the old English notion of 'usage' or 'practice.'"[35] For example, Augustine claims that "fruit is what one enjoys, a practice is something of which one makes use. . . . Nonetheless, in speech as it is customarily used, we both use fruits and enjoy practices" (*CD* 11.25).

---

32. O'Donovan argues that "we seriously misunderstand our author unless we appreciate that the *regula* confers the highest possible status upon the obligation to love the neighbor. Love-of-neighbor-as self is never, for Augustine, a second best to love-of-neighbor-more than self" (*PSL*, 117).

33. O'Donovan, "*Usus* and *Fruitio*," 386.

34. I owe this example to Peter Brown in conversation.

35. Von Heyking, *Longing*, 201.

Edmund Hill points out that *usus* can mean a combination of intimacy and enjoyment, even a euphemism for sexual intercourse (*DT* 215n16). Vernon J. Bourke contrasts Kant's meaning of "use" as "scheming manipulation" with Augustine's designation of "use" to "any willed application of one's energies."[36] Each of these arguments serves to dislodge the anti-Kantian tone of the appeal to use. In fact, Augustine's language assumes that "only a living being possessed of reason can use anything" (*DeDiv.* q30). We "use" simply as reasoning creatures who engage the world with thinking and feeling. Rhetorical dislodging, however, also serves philosophical purposes.

Helmut David Baer draws on these rhetorical moves but expands them beyond the philological. According to Baer:

> *Uti* and *frui* are . . . not closed and rigid terms. We will understand Augustine's meaning better if we bear in mind that he is a rhetorician. His form of argument is not that of a systematic philosophical presentation and investigation; rather, it is a looser form of discussion in which ideas are more fully developed as the discussion progresses. Augustine does not define the concepts *uti* and *frui* rigidly at the outset and then systematically apply them to problems of Christian love; rather, he works with the terms, creating new meanings as the conversation progresses. Drawing an analogy with music, we might say that the structure of Augustine's argument has less in common with the well-organized sonata-allegro form of a Mozart sonata, and more in common with the free flowing rhapsody of modern jazz.[37]

The musical imagery is fitting for Augustine's own description of love, which makes reference to the musicality of a life governed by the double commandment of love. Augustine writes:

> Indeed the Decalogue pertains to the two precepts, that is, those of love for God and neighbor. Three strings belong to the first precept because God is Trinity. While to the other precept, that is, love for the neighbor, there are seven strings: how one should live with other human beings. . . . For two tablets of the law were given. . . . The three commandments on one tablet pertain to God, the seven on the other pertain to the neighbor. . . . Let us

36. Bourke, *Joy in Augustine's Ethics,* 95.

37. Baer, "The Fruit of Charity," 49. Baer's analogy borrows from O'Donnell, *Commentary,* 1:xlix–l, n. 99.

join these seven to those three pertaining to love for God, if we wish to sing a new song on the ten-stringed lute.[38]

Baer goes on to exploit the semantic range of *uti* in ways that undermine the merely instrumentalist interpretation. He tries to show that Augustine describes many relationships as kinds of use that do not warrant the negative modern interpretation. He points to the function of Christ in Augustine's writing as an example of persons "using" Christ to find "their blessedness in God, or to speak more properly, God makes himself 'useful' to humanity through Christ."[39] Christ, however, is not simply a means to an end. Christ is active in securing salvation such that "through his salvific activity Christ makes himself useful to us, so that he can be 'used.'"[40] In imitating Christ, the Christian is called to imitate this sense of use as "an act of charity and self-giving . . . a *usus* that seeks to be useful to the beloved."[41]

William Riordan O'Connor adopts a similar strategy in expanding the Augustinian sense of "use." Like O'Donovan, O'Connor concedes that Augustine's early efforts to "make room for the love of neighbor within the context of the desire for vision . . . meet with little success."[42] But, like Baer,

38. *Sermo* 9.7 (as cited by Canning, *Unity*, 14). Canning notes the connection between this musical imagery with Bonhoeffer's musical analogies on the relation between love for neighbor and love for God in Dietrich Bonhoeffer, *Letters and Papers from Prison* (New York: Macmillan, 1997), 303. In a letter to Eberhard Bethge, Bonhoeffer writes: "What I mean is that God wants us to love him eternally with our whole hearts not in such a way as to injure or weaken our earthly love, but to provide a kind of *cantus firmus* to which other melodies of life provide the counterpoint. . . . Only a polyphony of this kind can give life a wholeness and at the same time assure us that nothing calamitous can happen as long as the *cantus firmus is* kept going." See also Catherine Pickstock, "Music: Soul, City and Cosmos after Augustine," in *Radical Orthodoxy*, 243–77.

39. Baer, "Fruit of Charity," 53 (see *DDC* 1.14.13 and 1.17.16). I think this is what C. S. Lewis implies by his claim that "God is a 'host' who deliberately creates His own parasites; causes us to be that we may exploit and 'take advantage of' Him" (*Four Loves*, 176).

40. Baer, "Fruit," 55.

41. Ibid., 57. A number of structural problems arise, however, for Baer's account. At the very least, his own rhetoric remains open to the charges of instrumentalism and egocentrism. For example, Baer speaks of love as "seeking to bring even the enemy into its stream" (58) and of "lifting the sinner up to the object of his 'enjoyment'" (59); and "in drawing others to God, they themselves draw closer to God" (61).

42. O'Connor, "The *Uti/Frui* Distinction in Augustine's Ethics," 50. References in this section refer to this article.

O'Connor tries to free Augustine from his post-Kantian interpreters of "use." Rather than focusing primarily on Christology (like Baer), he points to Augustine's use of "use" in describing the relations of the Trinity.

Discussions of using and enjoying can be found throughout Augustine's late work on the Trinity. Consider this example:

> To use something is to put it at the will's disposal; to enjoy it is to use it with an actual, not merely anticipated joy. Hence everyone who enjoys, uses; for he puts something at the disposal of the will for purposes of enjoyment. But not everyone who uses, enjoys, not if he wants what he puts at the disposal of the will for the sake of something else and not for its own. (*DT* 10.4.17)

O'Connor offers a helpful gloss for this important passage:

> We would do well here to recall that according to Augustine's own definition to use merely means to take up something into the power of the will, i.e., to apply the will to something, consciously to allow the will to become engaged with it. This in itself does *not* dictate an instrumental attitude. (57)[43]

Indeed, the passage repeats Augustine's suggestion in *On Christian Doctrine* that enjoyment is itself a type of use with appropriate delight rather than a term that is held in stark contrast to use (*DDC* 1.33.37). O'Connor points out that Augustine even is willing to use the term "use" in discussing Hilary's formulation of the internal personal relations of the Trinity as a joyful unity of "use in the gift" (*DT* 6.2.11). As such, if "there is no question of an exploitative relationship existing within the Trinity" *and* the Trinity is the model of all intersubjective relations, then Augustine's appeal to *uti* and *frui* is delivered from a primarily instrumental sense (58).

O'Connor's article introduces another aspect of Augustine's use of "use" that plays a significant role in the final strategy we discuss below. Rather than justifying Augustine in terms of his development or appealing to the semantic range of *usus*, he makes a philosophical or theological argument about the nature of benevolence. O'Connor is willing to endorse the con-

---

43. Bourke points out that Thomas Aquinas adopts the language of "use" in describing the eschatological exercise of spiritual gifts and the virtue of charity (*Joy in Augustine's Ethics*, 77).

tested Augustinian notion that "the Christian loves his neighbors as he loves himself because he wants them to attain the same vision of God that he hopes to enjoy himself" (50). But he provides two helpful caveats about this notion and its impact on how one conceives of benevolence.

First, he distinguishes between two types of "instrumental" actions: those that "include the other in their ends in the sense of having the other enjoy the benefits produced by such actions," and those that "exclude the other from their ends" (50). This distinction allows O'Connor to turn arguments against Augustine's supposed instrumentalism on their head. "Inclusive" instrumentality, so to speak, does not treat the neighbor merely as a means because the neighbor's own end is respected in this sense of rightly "using" the neighbor. "Exclusive" instrumentality, the perverse form of love, manipulates the neighbor for the self's own ends and rejects the proper ordering of love. In an illuminating paragraph that reflects a number of Augustinian themes raised in the previous chapter, O'Connor writes:

> In the course of this earthly life . . . true intersubjectivity is impossible to achieve. This is an important point for Augustine, the major stumbling block for personal, temporal relations. *The neighbor in this life is always in some sense an object for us, whatever degree of intimacy we have with him.* A kind of instrumental attitude, then, is present in all temporal relationships. In charity, however, we treat the neighbor with a regard for his eternal destiny and include him in the desired end, while in cupidity he is excluded from the desired end. It is in cupidity, in the final analysis, that we discover a purely instrumental, exploitative attitude toward other persons. But we do not find it in Augustinian charity. (59, emphasis mine)

The second caveat trades on the first. Augustine's mature conception of love entails a social vision of using and enjoying one another in God just as the persons of the Trinity use and enjoy one another in community of mutual love. O'Connor concludes: "Augustine's eudaemonism is ultimately an intersubjective eudaemonism" (60). What does this mean? For this, we turn to our final strategy.

ORDERED LOVE IN CHRISTOLOGICAL CONTEXT

The most sustained scholarly attempt to come to terms with Augustine's understanding of the two love commands is the meticulous study of Raymond

Canning, *The Unity of Love for God and Neighbour in St. Augustine.*[44] Canning offers a compelling account of Augustine's eudaimonism that is compatible with authentic love of the other rather than the selfish egoism of the mystical ascent. Canning's reading argues that "for Augustine, it is not as if God and the neighbor are in competition for the subject's affections" (12–13). Rather, Augustinian love aims to release the creative generosity and receptivity that allows for genuine community.

Canning confronts Augustine's critics with clarity and exegetical skill. Early in his book, he concedes some ground to the sorts of modern readers I have challenged (such as Nygren, Arendt, Nussbaum, Niebuhr, Ramsey, Jackson, and Adams). Canning admits that "at times it can seem that the neighbor comes out a poor loser in the face of God's greatness" (11). Augustine's rhetoric and metaphors, usually shaped in polemical contexts, do encourage the misreadings of *uti* and *frui* that concern most ethicists and liberal political theorists. However, Canning argues that even in the first book of *On Christian Doctrine*, a careful reader "will fail to discover any statement to the effect that the human subject is to use his neighbors with a view to attaining his own individual happiness in the enjoyment of God" (103). How does Canning support this reading?

First, he emphasizes a number of the points already found in the other strategies. Canning notes the "cautious, exploratory language" of Augustine's early formulations (3). In fact, like O'Donovan, he locates many of Augustine's earliest discussions of love for neighbor in terms of "the spiritual headstrongness of the new convert" that later "gives way to a more balanced vision" (175). He notes the positive sense of *uti* in Ciceronian Latin that is at odds with the Kantian sense of "making use of things for the accomplishment of one's own ends" (89). In particular, he emphasizes the point that the expression *propter aliud*, as the qualifier of *uti*-love, does not treat the neighbor as means but expresses the appropriate orientation of the subject's loving. Augustine's account of *propter aliud* or *propter Deum* (rather than *propter se*) reflects the other-regarding impulse of Augustine's love. Even so, Canning admits that Augustine's early rhetoric leads in another direction.

Canning, however, adds to our understanding of why Augustine chooses certain formulations in certain periods. Augustine's mature attitude insists that the two love commands have different objects but intimately contain

44. Page references in this section of the text refer to this book.

one another. There can be no separation. These unifying features of love are captured in a sermon where Augustine tells his parishioners:

> The love which loves the neighbor is no other than that which loves God. It is not therefore a matter of two loves. With the same love we give the neighbor we love God too. But since God and the neighbor are not the same, while they are loved with the one love, those who are loved are not one and the same. Therefore, the great love for God is first to be commended, love for neighbor is second. But we have to begin from the second in order to arrive at the first, "for if you do not love your brother whom you see, how can you love God whom you do not see?" (1 John 4:20)[45]

As such, neither commandment can be fulfilled without the other. At times, Augustine emphasizes love for God as the only way to ensure the capacity to love the neighbor. For example, he claims that "when the mind loves God, and consequently as has been said remembers and understands him, it can rightly be commanded to love its neighbour as itself. . . . Now it loves with a straight, not a twisted love, now that it loves God" (*DT* 14.4.18). Gerald Schlabach notes: "When we love friends or neighbors rightly, the value they lose is their value as a tool of our own egocentric self-interest."[46] At other times, however, Augustine suggests a priority of love for neighbor as the concrete and given opportunity for loving. In fact, in Augustine's anti-Pelagian and anti-Donatist homiletic contexts, love for the neighbor in this life can be the test of and the preparation for true love for God.[47] Augustine even claims that the two love commandments can be summed up in the command to love the neighbor (*IoEp.* 10.3). Like Christ's love for sinners, this love for neighbor is both extensive (a universalist point Augustine makes against Donatism) and intensive (an affective point that Augustine makes in exhorting members of his congregation).

In this light, the stress Augustine places on the love for neighbor as a cradle or step to love for God (usually found in homiletic contexts) owes more to his anti-Pelagian and anti-Manichean context than any Neoplatonic metaphysics that fuels the Kantian means/end reading. Canning shows

---

45. *Sermo* 265.8.9 (cited by Canning, *Unity*, 26).

46. Schlabach, *Joy Set Before Us*, 37.

47. Canning, *Unity*, 19–31. On neighbor-love as a test of love for God, see Outka, *Agape*, 44–45.

that Augustine does not view love for neighbor as a transitory stage to love for God, "a mere flexing of the muscles for the love of God by which the subject hopes to acquire restful contemplation of wisdom" (69). Rather, Augustine is warning his readers about the impossibility of perfect love for God in this life. His pastoral setting is exhortative, admonishing his listeners to love their neighbor with the hope of the joy that awaits. Augustine comments: "We have not yet reached the Lord, but we do have the neighbor with us" (*IoEv.* 17.9).[48] According to Canning, these metaphors "are concerned not with a deliverance from other human beings, but with a liberating detachment from the shackles of 'mortal affections,' from both presumption and despair" (65).

On the other hand, the radical emphasis on love for God can also protect prideful human beings from failing to recognize their dependence on others in loving their neighbor. As we saw in the last chapter, Augustinian liberalism knows the dangers of making others the object of our moral projects, and of trying to be like God in saving others.[49] Far from understanding the neighbor as a spiritual distraction for the self, Canning argues that Augustine "hesitates to commit the neighbour to the love of other human beings for fear that the neighbor might be diminished by the encounter" (155).[50] To

---

48. Cited by Canning, *Unity*, 20. According to Canning, Augustine assigns priority to the love for God at the level of "precept" but assigns priority to the love of neighbor at the level of "practice" (30 and 250). Van Bavel also notes that "though love of God comes first in the order of commanding *(ordo praecipiendi)* love of neighbor has to come first in the order of execution *(ordo faciendi)*" ("Double Face," 170). Schlabach also distinguishes between an Augustinian love for God that is "ontologically" and "authoritatively" prior to love for neighbor, but not necessarily "chronologically" prior in practice (*Joy Set Before Us*, 37).

49. On this theme, see Gene Outka, "Following at a Distance: Ethics and the Identity of Jesus," in *Scriptural Authority and Narrative Interpretation*, ed. Garrett Green (Philadelphia: Fortress Press, 1987), 144–60.

50. Canning argues that the accent of Augustine's account of neighbor-love emphasizes the equality of the neighbor with the self rather than an interest in the self's own happiness or the neighbor's secondary position to the self. He writes: "The love of self which is to be the pattern of love for neighbour cannot possibly be understood as arbitrariness or self-will, nor as the individualistic desire for private joy sought in one's love for God. . . . One's equality with the neighbour summons one to reject the desire to conduct one's own life as if no one else existed; it calls one to acknowledge and to take the neighbour into account even in one's love of self. It is as if, then, a precept of self-love could be formulated as follows: love yourself in relation to your neighbour to whom you have been created equal" (162).

love the neighbor "in God" is the best way to check one's selfish tendencies. It provides a norm against the abuse that can arise in a love for neighbor full stop. This check attests to the only certainty about the neighbor: she equally shares in your own status as a creature of God.[51] Consistent with my account of the relevance of the love for God in democratic citizenship, Canning argues that Augustine's insistence of equality between the self and the other aims to protect the equal interests of the neighbor (119).[52] In fact, "attachment to God shores up the foundations of love for neighbour by giving the lover new strength and light, beauty, and joy" (134).

Canning's third chapter rehearses the main interpretations of *uti* and *frui*. He concludes that Augustine's account leads to a conclusion opposite to that of his modern critics: "When the human subject's *uti* and *frui* are rightly focused, the outcome will be a loving concern for others *(caritate consulendi)*, which is presented as the very opposite of every kind of dominating 'use' of others *(dominandi cupiditate)*" (114). While this third chapter provides tremendous support for my own argument, the most original aspects of Canning's reading of Augustine become clearer in the second half of his book.

Here, Canning moves from an analytic perspective that primarily reviews the secondary literature and offers a synthetic theological account of how Augustinian love for God entails love for neighbor. Canning highlights the changes in Augustine's treatment of love after the 390s by focusing on the development of Augustine's *una caritas* formula and its relation to more general issues in systematic theology. He pursues a number of Augustinian theological themes that support his thesis about the unity of love for God and neighbor: God's command to love the neighbor, Christ's becoming the neighbor, the frequent replacement of one command for the other, and the ecclesial context of love. However, because of these themes' relation to contemporary liberation theology, I end this section by highlighting Canning's

---

51. Oliver O'Donovan writes: "That is why Augustine seems so often to represent benevolent love-of-neighbor as consisting exclusively in the attempt to bring him to God. It is not that he rejects other goals which may be adopted from time to time but that this one is fundamental, for it is the only purpose that the subject can conceive for the object which he can be absolutely sure is not willful imposition" (*PSL*, 35).

52. Canning suggests that Luther's understanding of the *ordo amoris* tradition was misguided by Augustine's interpreters and translators, especially Nicholas of Lyra (*Unity*, 119n8).

own elevation of the significance of Augustine's favorite scriptural text: Matthew 25:31–46.[53]

Canning begins his chapter on this text with the claim that "an important, but hitherto largely untapped, source for Augustine's thought on the relationship between love for God and love for neighbour is his use and interpretation of the Matthean last judgment pericope, 25:31–46, especially verses 35–40 and 42–25" (331).[54] The particular verse that Canning identifies is an influential verse in liberationist ethics: "When you did it to one of the least of these brothers of mine, you did it to me" (v. 40).[55] Canning argues that Augustine's explicit use of this verse is most concentrated both at Hippo and at Carthage in his preaching during the years 410–13, a time "when refugees are flooding into Africa after the fall of Rome" (342n33). Consider, for example, the following sermon passage:

> Now, thanks to God's good favour, winter is here. Think of the poor, think how you can clothe the naked Christ. . . . Sisters and brothers, repeat it aloud, so that you might realize that you are not deprived of Christ's presence. Listen to what the judge will say: "When you did to one of the least of mine, you did

53. According to Canning, there are more than 275 references to this pericope in Augustine's writings (342).

54. Canning contrasts this pericope with the Good Samaritan parable (which is preceded by the classic formulation of the love commands) in order to highlight the pericope as a neglected resource in Augustine studies.

55. Canning himself does not emphasize this connection. He interacts more with the theology of Karl Rahner than with Gustavo Gutierrez or other liberation theologians. This attention, I think, is related to his speculative theological interest in Augustine's "bold" inversion of 1 John 4:8 ("God is Love") (309) and in his account of the "hidden neighbours" of the Christian community (191) rather than in the traditional concerns of political theology or in political engagement as such. For Canning, "turning to the neighbour forms such an integral part of human turning to God that the latter may be defined by it" (420). He argues that this inversion does not promote a "love monism/mysticism" because, for Augustine, "love indeed loves itself, but, unless it loves itself loving something, it does not love itself with love" (*DT* 8.8.12). The "love of love" and the "vision of the interior God" do not exclude the neighbor but entail a redirection of the self to the other (322). Before turning to Augustine, Canning rehearses a number of controversial exegetical issues in contemporary biblical scholarship: Are "the least of these brothers" specifically Christians in need? Is God's identification with "the least of these brothers" thinkable within the framework of the Jewish tradition? Is this verse a Hellenizing redaction?

it to me." Each of you expects to receive Christ seated in heaven. Turn your attention to him lying under the covered-walk; direct your attention to Christ who is hungry and suffering from the cold, Christ in need and a stranger.[56]

This identification of Christ with the "least of these" can fuel the concern that Augustine's account of love (even in acts of mercy) remains essentially a concern for one's salvation.[57] However, Canning argues that Augustine's theological and ethical focus is Christological rather than merely soteriological (particularly in terms of an anachronistic notion of forensic justification). For Augustine, "Christ's continuing presence with humankind in all-embracing love and in need of love is the surprising message of Matt. 25" (401).[58] While Canning at times suggests a univocal identification between Christ and the neighbor, the thrust of his larger argument suggests that this identification is not univocal. It remains analogical. The neighbor is a sacramental presence (a repetition of the first sacrament of the Christ), a real subject of love that still points beyond herself. Augustine's *magna quaestio*, and the rich ambiguities of his account of the love commands, suggests openness to the neighbor that also always is open to the transcendent God. But, it seems, the universal can only be loved in the particular. In the end, as Augustine's own early tentativeness suggests, the relation of the love commands may resist a satisfactory theoretical resolution. It is always an unfinished task to relate the love of God and the love of neighbor.[59] To use Barthian rather than Rahnerian terms, I think Augustine himself suggests

56. *Sermo* 25 (cited by Canning, *Unity*, 369).

57. Canning notes that even a defender like Burnaby admits that Augustine's appeals to Matthew 25 are egocentric (see Burnaby, *Amor Dei*, 133n2).

58. Other critics have argued that Augustine's collectivist Christology threatens to blur his own consistent distinction between the Creator and the creature. See W. Shrage, "Theologie und Christologie bei Paulus und Jesus auf dem Hintergrund der modernen Gottesfrage," *Evangelische Theologie* 36 (1976): 121–54.

59. I have been influenced here by Charles Mathewes's discussion of the relation between *technological* knowledge and contemplation in the Augustinian tradition. For Mathewes, "following a long line of hermeneutical thinkers such as Heidegger, Gadamer, and Ricouer, I think that any account of questioning that reduces it to the hunger for essentially technological knowledge is dangerous because it obscures the root openness in ourselves to which the phenomenon of questioning attests" ("Liberation of Questioning in Augustine's *Confessions*," 545).

that the neighbor both hides and reveals the hidden and revealing God.[60] As Rowan Williams eloquently puts it:

> To 'use' the love of neighbour or the love we have of our bodies (a favourite example of Augustine's) is simply to allow the capacity for gratuitous or self-forgetful *dilectio* opened up in these and other such loves to be opened still further. The language of *uti* is designed against an attitude towards any finite person or object that terminates their meaning in their capacity to satisfy my desire, that treats them as the end of desire, conceiving my meaning in terms of them and theirs in terms of me.[61]

FRIENDSHIP AND CITIZENSHIP

Each of these three strategies helps mitigate the strong claims that love for God is simply a philosophically eudaimonist context which leaves an insecure place of neighbor-love. In order to draw these strands together in relation to political Augustinianism, I end this chapter with a discussion introduced earlier in my critical remarks about Gilbert Meilaender. It is a topic more familiar to classical thought than modern political theory—friendship and political citizenship.

Friendship preoccupies Augustine's mind, but like love it is a neglected theme in Augustinian liberalism. This neglect, in part, is a product of the modern Augustinian preoccupation with a minimalist concept of the nation-state that is hostile to claims of political solidarity. Given the influence of Aristotle's discussion of friendship, most interpreters still look to Aquinas rather than Augustine for a Christian conception of civic friendship (or, indeed, of salvation as becoming friends with God). Even critics of Augustine, however, have recognized that the "most notable attempt to define civic friendship after Aristotle is St. Augustine's."[62] Augustine, no less than Aquinas, always encourages the view of "others" as potential friends rather than

---

60. For comparison of Barth and Rahner on love of God and love of neighbor, see Paul D. Molnar, "Love of God and Love of Neighbor in the Theology of Karl Rahner and Karl Barth," *Modern Theology* 20, no. 4 (October 2004): 567–99.

61. Williams, "Language, Reality and Desire in Augustine's *De Doctrina*," 140.

62. Swanson, *Public and Private in Aristotle's Political Philosophy*, 180.

as threats to one's self or private community.[63] By highlighting Augustine's account of love, I am suggesting that there are resources for Augustinian civic friendship.

I have always found the familiar criticisms of a Platonic theory of love at odds with the rich particularity of characters in the Platonic dialogues. This unease with standard representations of "Platonism" is consistent with recent efforts to expand our appreciation for the dialogical character of Platonic political philosophy. Interestingly, feminist interpretations of Platonism have also challenged traditional scholarship.[64] I have already pointed out similarities between Gregory Vlastos's seminal criticism of Plato and the theological critics of Augustine.[65] Vlastos himself did not extend his criticism of Platonism to Christianity: "Jesus wept for Jerusalem. Socrates warns Athens, scolds it, exhorts it, condemns it. But he has not tears for it."[66] Augustine, as we saw in the previous chapter, also emphasizes the tears of Jesus as a way of indicting a Stoic philosophical project of virtue. But this book has not been about Plato's understanding of love. I have tried to show how interpreters argue that Augustine's conception of love evades analogous charges about the status of the world that often are brought against Neoplatonism. I have emphasized that Augustine's Christology forced him consistently to reevaluate his own Christian Platonism.

Traditionally, critics argue that the universalism of Augustinian *caritas* came to displace or oppose the intimacy of classical accounts of *amicitia*.[67]

---

63. This theme in the writings of Aquinas, and its political implications, are discussed in Paul J. Waddell, *Friendship and the Moral Life* (Notre Dame, Ind.: University of Notre Dame Press, 1989).

64. See, for example, Irigaray, *Ethics of Sexual Difference*, 20–33.

65. See chapter 4, footnote 57. A helpful comparison of these debates (consistent with my argument) is provided in Kevin Corrigan, "Love of God, Love of Self, and Love of Neighbor: Augustine's Critical Dialogue with Platonism," *Augustinian Studies* 34, no. 1 (March 2003): 97–106.

66. Vlastos, "The Paradox of Socrates," in *The Philosophy of Socrates* (Garden City: Doubleday, 1971), 6, cited by Outka, "On Harming Others," 392–93n28. Elsewhere, Vlastos offers a strong defense of the connection between love and social justice: "Justice and Equality," in *Social Justice*, ed. Richard B. Brandt (Englewood: Prentice Hall, 1962), 31–72.

67. See Marie Aquinas McNamara, O.P., *Friends and Friendship for Saint Augustine* (New York: Alba House, 1964), and David Konstan, "Problems in the History of Christian Friendship," *Journal of Early Christian Studies* 4, no. 1 (1996): 87–113.

But Augustine's ambivalent descriptions of friendship as "a tender bond" contradict the image that critics often paint (*Conf.* 2.5.10). Peter Brown notes the sense in which "having read the life of this extremely inward-looking man, we suddenly realize, to our surprise, that he has hardly ever been alone."[68] It is hard to imagine an Augustine without Alypius, Possidius, Nebridius, Evodius, Severus, or Monica. Augustine's letters can be as particularistic and moving as the most intense tributes to the pleasures of friendship (i.e., *Ep.* 73, *Ep.* 130, *Ep.* 189). Friendship is where together we find comfort in the sadness of life's fragile journey, relief from its pain and poverty. In the *Confessions*, he paints an even more lighthearted picture:

> There were other joys to be found in their company which still more power-fully captivated my mind—the charms of talking and laughing together and kindly giving way to each other's wishes, reading elegantly written books together, sharing jokes and delighting to honor one another, disagreeing occasionally but without rancor, as a person might disagree with himself, and lending piquancy by that rare disagreement to our much more frequent accord. We would teach and learn from each other, sadly missing any who were absent and blithely welcoming them when they returned. Such signs of friendship sprang from the hearts of friends who loved and knew their love returned, signs to be read in smiles, words, glances and a thousand gracious gestures. So were sparks kindled and our minds were fused inseparably, out of many becoming one. (*Conf.* 4.8.13)

The shared goods of friendship—including the recognition of difference in one another—should not to be denied by Augustinians: "The divine life

---

68. Brown, *Augustine of Hippo*, 174. For Brown, "when Augustine describes his friends, we feel we know them, in those few strokes, far better than many more famous ancient men" (167). O'Donnell, however, points out how little we actually know about Augustine's friends, especially Alypius. In fact, O'Donnell's reading challenges Brown: "Aloof and alone. In all the books and sermons and letters we have of Augustine's, a consistent pattern emerges. The fundamental human relationship is the solitary individual's relationship with his god. Every other human relationship in Augustine's life that we know of gets rewritten in his books to be a story about him and his god. Over and over, the small and large distances that separate people from one another persist and usually grow larger for Augustine as he intensifies the divine connection, until he ends there, alone with his god, alone" (O'Donnell, *A New Biography*, 317). For discussion of the importance of (particularly male) friendships in Augustine, see Brown, *Body and Society*, 389–90.

is not bare unity but community, and that love can have no other purpose, as it can have no other sources, but the mutual 'inherence' of persons, life in one another."[69] To be sure, Augustine is aware that friendship (or, better, the illusion of a true friendship) can be seductive and dangerous. It was in friendship that Adam sinned in Eden and in friendship that Augustine sinned in his own vineyard: "Sin gains entrance through these and similar good things" (*Conf.* 2.5.10). Sin, like love, is bound up with sociality—even though Augustine refuses to blame others for his sin. Sin is essentially relational, but also self-wrought. Personal identity is not that vulnerable even if existence is constituted in relation to others. Referring love to God is Augustine's basic strategy for avoiding this danger. O'Donnell is suspicious that Augustine never had friends (apart perhaps from Alypius), only disciples and potential disciples.[70] But Augustinian love of any kind always has friendship in view. It may not be governed by reciprocity, but it is not indifferent to it either. Friends are loved in God as a particular gift of providence. That move allows for the critical distance necessary for the sake of ourselves and our neighbors. But Augustine's efforts to democratize love in the name of the equality of humanity offer a second strategy. This move raises again the problem of particularism that I mentioned in my account of Augustinian advice to loving citizens.

The emphasis on the equality of humanity, through *both* our common origin and common destiny, pushes in the direction of a more universalistic account of love that is thought to be at odds with more preferential kinds of love. As O'Donovan puts it, "it is plain that if Augustine errs, he errs toward inappropriate universality rather than to inappropriate particularity" (*PSL*, 123). For Augustine, the exclusiveness and damaging intensity of special relationships in the ancient world often conceals the pride *(superbia)* and domination *(libido dominandi)* of this world. Rowan Williams suggestively reconstructs this attitude. According to Williams, Augustine's "condemnation of 'public' life in the classical world is, consistently, that it is not public enough, that is incapable of grounding a stable sense of commonalty because of its pervasive implicit elitism, its divisiveness, its lack of a common human *project*."[71] In fact, in his earliest writings, Augustine flirts with the possibility that the special relations of the biological family as well as the civic

69. Burnaby, *Amor Dei*, 306.
70. O'Donnell, *New Biography*, 103.
71. Williams, "Politics and the Soul," 68.

commonwealth are a result of human fallenness, another example of the pridefulness of private enclosure (*DVR* 46.88). Christians are to love even their children as they belong to God, as human creatures and fellow neighbors. Every human being is simply a neighbor of everyone else. Modern Protestant thinkers have radicalized this aspect of Augustinianism, worrying about the dangers of natural loves as simply (to borrow from Kierkegaard) the "I intoxicated in the other-I."[72] However, perhaps also like Kierkegaard, Augustine will substantively give back what he rhetorically takes away. In fact, he *abandons* this early view in favor of a more nuanced mediation between the universal and the particular. Even in Paradise, he comes to think, "there would have been relatives and kindred even if no one had sinned" (*Retr.* 1.12). To use current vocabulary, Augustine provides an early discussion on the proper relationship between cosmopolitanism and particularism as it relates to citizenship. Providence and finitude affirm special relations, even if love continually expands the circle of neighborly concern.

Augustine's discussion of friendship owes much to the classical world, particularly Cicero.[73] However, his Christian theological imagination puts pressure on this account of friendship by extending love for neighbor beyond the particularity of one's given social or natural relationships. As Williams suggests, Augustine distinguished the Christian vision of friendship from that of the classical world by extending the possibilities of virtue beyond a philosophical elite. James Schall explains:

> Where Augustine differed from the classics was in their estimate of the possibility of virtue for everyone, even for those who were not philosophers. The classical writers argued that only a few could be expected to be philosophers or eminently virtuous. The Christian thinkers, on the other hand, argued that there were means, nonphilosophical means, that could supply what the classics did not know about how, in practice, to be virtuous.[74]

72. Kierkegaard, *Works of Love*, 68.

73. Augustine praises Cicero's definition of friendship as "a friendly and affectionate agreement on human things and on divine" (*Answer to the Skeptics* 3.6.13). For discussion of Augustine and Cicero, see Eoin Cassidy, "The Recovery of the Classical Ideal of Friendship in Augustine's Portrayal of Caritas," in *The Relationship Between Neoplatonism and Christianity*, ed. Thomas Finan and Vincent Twomey (Dublin: Four Courts Press, 1992), 127–40. Cassidy also points out the connection between Augustine's eschatological imagery of the Body of Christ and Stoic motif of the corporate body (138).

74. Schall, "Friendship and Political Philosophy," 132–33.

Because it is grounded in the gratuitous love of God, friendship is open to all. Indeed, Gilbert Meilaender positively describes Augustine's account of friendship in terms of a "divine lottery."[75] This metaphor may strike us as disturbing. We may not choose our parents, but the pleasure of friendship in part consists in its chosen quality. We like to think our friends love us for who we are, not because they happened to run into us one day on the street. Augustine, however, puts pressure on this notion without stripping friendship of its distinctive qualities. To see these gifts in the light of divine providence does not lead to "grudging concessions made to the constraints of time, space, and particular bonds of affection rather than glad affirmation of these as essential for human existence."[76] In fact, I think the metaphor provides a healthy complement to accounts of preferential love rooted in the "ordering work of creation."[77] In this sense, Augustine both *democratizes* and *publicizes* love through a theological (and so political) populism.[78]

Arendt recognized that for Augustine every neighbor signifies the presence of Christ, and so every neighbor is to be loved equally. At the same time, however, Augustine recognized that preference and particularity are necessary features of creaturely finitude. His ethic of love places universalist and impartialist demands upon the Christian believer, but the nature of love (given the temporal and geographic limits of human condition) implies a

75. Meilaender, *Friendship*, 19. Meilaender argues that Augustine's "divine lottery" combines the universalism of "Platonic" *eros* and the "particularism" of Aristotelian friendship.

76. Ibid., 28.

77. William Werpehowski, "'Agape' and Special Relations," in *The Love Commandments: Essays in Christian Ethics and Moral Philosophy*, ed. Edmund N. Santurri and William Werpehowski (Washington, D.C.: Georgetown University Press), 138–56 at 140.

78. Bonnie Kent puts it this way: "The strangely democratic aspect of Augustine's ethics, often unnoticed, is that neither native intelligence, nor wealth, nor sound 'parenting,' nor a well-ordered political community, nor any combination of these makes any great difference to whether we shall eventually become virtuous and attain happiness. Without God's grace, the most brilliant, aristocratic philosophers and the most illiterate, penurious peasants are all in the same boat; and those with God's grace have no reason to feel proud" ("Augustine's Ethics," 229; see also Mathewes, *Augustinian Tradition*, 197). Many recent interpreters have emphasized the populist implications of Augustine's theology. See, for example, Conrad Leyser, *Authority and Asceticism from Augustine to Gregory the Great* (Oxford: Clarendon Press, 2000); Peter Brown, "*Gloriosus Obitus*"; and Markus, *The End of Ancient Christianity*, 45–62.

kind of "build up" or "build on" strategy that relies on a multilayered discussion of the universal and the particular.[79] How is the believer to adjudicate these demands in the plurality of their relations?

In the previous chapter I argued that Augustine holds that love begins "at home" and extends "outward." It is a fire that spreads. Apart from the passage I cited from *On Christian Doctrine*, there is evidence from his preaching as well. He tells his parishioners:

> Friendship therefore begins with one's spouse and children, and goes on to include strangers. But if we reflect that *we have one father and one mother*, who will be a stranger to us? All people are neighbours to one another. Ask nature. Is a person unknown to you? He is a human being. Is he an enemy? He is a human being. Is he a foe? He is a human being. If he is a friend, may he remain a friend. If he is an enemy, may he become a friend.[80]

This view holds throughout his writings, despite the other developments in his doctrine of love that I have noted. Book 19 of the *City of God* repeats the idea that human relations are like sets of expanding concentric circles, to the point of expanding and intensifying even Varro's claims that "a man's fellow citizens are also his friends" (*CD* 19.3). As Emerson would point out, Augustinian circles do not have a circumference.[81] Much like the cosmopolitan Stoic, Augustine wants to be friends with the angels of the "universe itself" (*CD* 19.3). But he argues that the person wishing to follow the way of love must first "care for his own household; for the order of nature and of human society itself give him readier access to them, and greater opportunity of caring for them" (*CD* 19.14). Particular friendships are the school of virtue

---

79. I here borrow from Gilbert Meilaender's typology of relating Christian love and special relations (see Meilaender, *Friendship,* 40–41). Meilaender considers three types: "build down" from *agape* to friendship, "build up" from friendship to *agape,* and "build around" friendship by using agapic side-constraints. For a contemporary theological discussion of how particularism and universalism can be integrated in Christian ethics, see Stephen Pope, "'Equal Regard' versus 'Special Relations'? Reaffirming the Inclusiveness of Agape," *Journal of Religion* 77 (July 1997): 353–79, and Julia E. Judish, "Balancing Special Relations with the Ideal of Agape," *Journal of Religious Ethics* 26, no. 1 (Spring 1998): 14–76.

80. Augustine, *Sermo Denis* 16.1 (cited by Canning, *Unity,* 188).

81. Ralph Waldo Emerson, "Circles" (1841), in *Essays and Lectures* (New York: Library of America, 1983), 401–14.

for Augustine—the place where compassion and social trust are first learned. There is a "double movement" in Augustine's account of friendship: "*Philia* is transcended in *caritas* but not destroyed, for the intensely personal sharing which friendship involves is added to charity as its internal fruition."[82] Time and opportunity place limits on the realization of universal love that Augustine thinks must await the consummation of love. But it is human sin that prevents this achievement in time, "no matter how much we may wish to" (*CD* 19.4). Augustine's concerns seem to be that both private relations and the politics of empire are themselves prone to the instrumentality that critics often attribute to his account of "use" and "enjoyment." Augustine does not condemn earthly life to the experience of the master-slave dialectic. Preferential friendship can be a site that resists these political dynamics. But even the most special and intimate of Christian relationships await (and only proleptically anticipate) the full consummation of eschatological love: "Who is secure even in such friendship as this, when such grievous ills have so often arisen even from the secret treachery of people within the same family?" (*CD* 19.5). The breadth of the empire, or even the catholicity of the church, might fool a lover into believing this kind of unity has already arrived. This eschatological dimension of Augustine's account of love and friendship has important effects on political Augustinianism.

Augustine argues that a network of smaller kingdoms would have been preferable to the violent extension of Roman imperial rule: "There would be as many kingdoms among the nations of the world as there are now houses of the citizens of a city" (*CD* 4.15). In terms of political structures, John von Heyking suggests that this view supports political arrangements typically favored by classical republicans. Von Heyking writes: "Smaller civic units bound in loose and fluid federations might constitute an alternative that cultivates political friendships."[83] While it undergoes dramatic reformulation in the context of his own theological vision, this view also resonates with John Milbank's advocacy of "complex, gothic space."[84] Federalism and localism

---

82. Meilaender, *Friendship*, 17–18.

83. Von Heyking, *Longing*, 221. Von Heyking's speculation is consistent with his effort to read Augustine in more Aristotelian terms. There also seems to be a connection with Leo Strauss, *The City and Man* (Chicago: University of Chicago Press, 1964). Interestingly, this view also is consistent with Romand Coles's vision of "empowered local democratic institutions" (Coles, *Self/Power/Other*, 168; see also Coles, *Rethinking Generosity*, 180–219).

84. Milbank, "On Complex Space," 293.

may be implied in Augustine's social ontology, but what is the phenomeno-logical connection between friendship and citizenship?

Despite her many criticisms of his "otherworldliness," Hannah Arendt surprisingly claims that "Augustine seems to have been the last to know at least what it once meant to be a citizen" (*HC*, 14). The salient feature of Augustine's discussion of friendship focuses on what friends share in common. For Augustine, the best friendships share a love for wisdom, funded by a mutual love for God. Liberal political citizenship does not have the same intimacy or closeness as personal friendship or Christian fraternity. It does not seek to share all of the same things in common. What makes for a good friend is not the same as what makes for a good liberal citizen.

However, the experience of citizenship does suggest that the basic phe-nomenology is similar to friendship. Civic friendship is a species of friendship that highlights the ethical relation as fundamental for political community even given the affirmation of finitude and the radical possibilities of sin. It relies on the same Augustinian anthropology of desire and love that I have outlined. Consider, for example, Robert Nozick's account of why we read newspapers:

> People seek to engage in sharing beyond the domain of personal friendship also. One important reason we read newspapers, I think, is not the importance or intrinsic interest of the news; we rarely take action whose direction depends upon what we read there, and if somehow we were shipwrecked for ten years on an isolated island, when we returned we would not choose to peruse the back newspapers of the previous ten years. Rather, we read newspapers be-cause we want to share information with our fellows, we want to have a range of information in common with them, a common stock of mental contents. We already share with them a geography and a language, and also a common fate in the face of large-scale events. That we also desire to share the daily flow of information shows how very intense our desire to share is.[85]

My account of feminist theory and Augustinian civic liberalism argues that much of liberal theorizing fails to give an account of this desire. But Au-gustinians affirm this social desire and its implied connection to a more expansive understanding of politics. Unlike much of modern political theory that either denies this desire by narrowing the definition of politics and

---

85. Nozick, "Love's Bond," 429.

lowering the standards of virtue, Augustine affirms the desire but qualifies its possibilities for fulfillment in this life. Like Aristotle, Augustine pushes in the direction of "declaring that the good man will conduct himself towards other persons in a spirit, not merely of rectitude (mere justice) but actually of friendship."[86] Reading newspapers can be mundane and trivial. They can be another experience of self-absorption in a commuter lifestyle, Hegel's morning prayers on the cheap or Augustine's own delight in the drama of Dido's death. It is not the fullest indication of human love or sociality, but the experience of political citizenship in the modern world can also be mundane and not very glamorous. Given that so many encounters with our modern neighbors pass through relations of citizenship, political Augustinianism should elevate love as the proper virtue of a democratic ethics of citizenship. Citizenship and discipleship enjoy a more dialectical relationship than that allowed by many contemporary formulations that pit them against each other in the name of either Christian fidelity (discipleship) or worldly responsibility (citizenship). To romantically privilege an ethics of personal encounter or an institutional politics of structural analysis repeats this error of false opposition. Paul Ricoeur offers a more compelling alternative that is consistent with my reading of Augustinianism:

> The theme of the neighbor therefore effects the permanent critique of the social bond: in comparison to love of neighbor, the social bond is never as profound or as comprehensive. It is never as profound because social mediations will never become the equivalent of encounter or immediate presence. It is never as comprehensive because the group only asserts itself against another group and shuts itself off from others. The neighbor fulfills the twofold requirement of nearness and distance. Such was the Samaritan: near because he approached, distant because he remained the non-Judean who one day picked up an injured stranger along the highway. We must never lose sight, however, of the fact that personal relationships are also the victim of passions, perhaps the most fierce, dissimulated, and perfidious of all passions. After all, what have three centuries of bourgeois civilization made of the concept of charity? Charity may be nothing more than an alibi

---

86. Cooper, "Aristotle on Friendship," 303. Cooper refers to several passages that show the centrality of emotional bonds for Aristotle in "characterizing ordinary social intercourse" (335n9).

for justice. And so the protest of the "private" against the "social" is never entirely innocent.[87]

In fact, Ricoeur concludes, "its seems to me that the eschatological Judgment means that we 'shall be judged on what we have done' to persons, even without knowing it, by acting through the media of the most abstract institutions."[88] These passages capture a central theme of this book: the loving citizen imagines and embodies a different world from the "just" citizen who abandons love. To connect with themes from the previous chapter, the political imagination of a citizen shaped by Augustinian love goes beyond that shaped merely by liberal respect or principles of justice. In this light, despite my criticisms of his work, I share in Stanley Hauerwas's proposal that the first task of Christian ethics is not announcement of rules, but "to help us rightly envision the world."[89]

The Augustinian citizen does not expect this desire and this love to be exhaustively satisfied through political participation. We do see through a glass darkly. Augustine's *comparatively* somber vision of political life (predicated on his own utopian sense of a common good that extends to the entire universe) rightly chastens those who expect this kind of satisfaction. He also rightly chastens those who imagine a progressive realization of love and justice in history. Sin does distort everything. But it would be a mistake to allow this description to normatively shape an Augustinian ethics of citizenship. Citizenship cannot be simply an ideological temptation, leading Christians only to a politics of witness and resistance. Like the realist readers I identified in chapter 2, Oliver

87. Ricoeur, "The *Socius* and the Neighbor," 109. According to Ricoeur, "what the final judgment implies, it seems to me, is that we will be judged by what we did in very abstract institutional settings and structures to make them serve neighbor-love, often without being personally conscious of how our actions in these social structures actually impacted on the lives of the individual human beings touch by them."

88. Ibid., 109. For a helpful discussion of Ricoeur's theology of charity as it relates to politics, see John Coleman, "The Two Pedagogies: Discipleship and Citizenship," in *Education for Citizenship and Discipleship*, ed. Mary Boys (New York: Pilgrim Press, 1988), 35–75.

89. Hauerwas, *Peaceable Kingdom*, 29. For Hauerwas, "the Christian life is more a recognition and training of our senses and passions than a matter of choices and decisions" (149). I would not oppose attention and decision in this way, but more importantly, what I think Hauerwas fails to see is the analogy between the temporal political life outside the church and the sort of loving and seeing that he imagines.

O'Donovan argues that Augustine anticipated aspects of modern political thought because he "severed the connection between society and virtue."[90] But unlike those moderns who base political society on passion or those realists who abandon language of the virtues, Augustine "re-formulates something like the traditional virtue-based concept of society, but in new terms which will give due recognition both to the reality of the moral order which makes social existence possible and to its fundamentally flawed character."[91] O'Donovan, I think, captures the moral earnestness of Augustine's ironic yet scathing tone that characterizes his unmasking of the ancient political world.

Augustine's relative praise of the Romans paints a picture of political vice as a perversion of virtue that opens the door for a relation between politics and virtue. O'Donovan, recalling the theme I pointed out in Rowan Williams and Hannah Arendt, argues that Augustine's critique of earthly politics is fundamentally a form of disenchantment. Like any human relationships, political relationships are susceptible to the problems of sin. However, the disenchantment is neither total nor final. There is no comprehensive ironic stance or infinite resignation. The disenchantment fosters recognition of the limits of mortal life but at the same time does not counsel withdrawal from social life. Can there be this kind of idealist disenchantment without political disengagement? In fact, O'Donovan helpfully draws together the various types of political Augustinianism under a single common thread: "a disinterest, we may say, in the worldly political surface . . . but a warning against an idealistic spirit of withdrawal."[92] Augustine warned against the false piety of those who believed that "because the pagans dedicated temples to Justice and Virtue and adored in stones what should be performed in the heart, we should therefore avoid justice and virtue" (*DDC* 2.28.28). This kind of disenchantment with civic virtue is based on an eschatology that is foreign to modern liberalism, which distinguishes between public and private in ways that relieve politics of the hopeful pressures that Augustine is willing to place on all politics. Thus Augustine wants (but does not expect) more from politics than most liberals. In the end, Augustine finds earthly political com-

90. O'Donovan, "*City of God* 19," 63.
91. Ibid.
92. O'Donovan, "Augustine of Hippo," 104 and 109. In this short essay, O'Donovan repeats his claim that Augustine acknowledges "derivative, shadowy reflections of true order in the actual political societies of history" (110).

munities wanting because they do "not overcome the privacy of the human heart and its resistance to mutual knowledge."[93] The temporal hiddenness of the human heart (both to itself and to other hearts) is the real crisis that Augustine thinks earthly politics cannot escape. He consistently laments, "we mortals do not know the hearts of other mortals" (*Ench.* 32.121; see also *EnPs.* 41.13 and 55.9). It is this sociality that Augustine desires: for others to know "the word which we utter in the heart" (*DT* 15.3.19). Unlike those who cannot abide this tension, the Augustinian civic liberal does not try to relieve the human heart through earthly politics or ecclesial comfort. Augustine believes it is these "corporately felt commitments and unarticulated common impulses that really determine the character of communities."[94] It is this feature of Augustine's political anthropology that joins my Augustinian civic liberalism with the Augustinian realists.

Rather than identifying this realism with Augustine's doctrine of sin, however, I have couched it in terms of his doctrine of love.[95] The categories of "use" and "enjoyment" are properly understood not in terms of Platonic metaphysics but as eschatologically shaped ways of disciplining and ordering love that take their cue from the radical determination of a good God. "Use" and "enjoyment" do proceed from an ontological framework for Augustinian political ethics that relieves the pressure citizens place upon each other and politics. Augustine's God creates, or to use further theological language, justifies the space for the vulnerable encounters with others that is characteristic of liberal politics. Those beloved of God are set free, to a certain extent in this life, to love others. At the same time, these categories serve as psychological reminders of the dangers (to the self and the other) of a love that prematurely rests in the neighbor, in institutional purity, or the anxieties of our own moral confidence. It is this premature rest that denies the ceaseless dynamic of loving which is fundamental to Augustine's vision of God.

93. O'Donovan, "*City of God* 19," 72.

94. O'Donovan, "Augustine of Hippo," 112. O'Donovan writes: "These make the rational plans and conscientious judgments of their leaders look like waves on the surface of the ocean. Augustine's last and greatest word is a warning not to ignore the currents of the depths" (112).

95. There are interesting parallels between the phenomenology of sinning and loving in the Christian tradition. As with loving, sinning against God *(coram Deo)* is differentiated from sinning against one's neighbor *(coram homnibus)*. A comparison of the logic of these different relations, however, is beyond the capacity of this project.

Remembering Augustine
The Exhausted Politics of Pessimism, Skepticism, and Nostalgia

*When days grow dark and nights grow dreary, we can be
thankful that our God combines in his nature a creative synthesis of
love and justice which will lead us through life's dark valleys
and into sunlit pathways of hope and fulfillment.*

MARTIN LUTHER KING JR,
"A Tough Mind and a Tender Heart"

*It is not an easy task to do justice to the distinctions of
good and evil in history and to the possibilities and obligations of
realizing the good in history; and also to subordinate all these
relative judgments and achievements to the final truth about life
and history which is proclaimed in the Gospel.*

REINHOLD NIEBUHR,
The Nature and Destiny of Man

*Nonetheless, if any man uses this life in such a way that he directs it
towards that end which he so ardently loves and for which he
so faithfully hopes, he may without absurdity be called happy even
now, though rather by future hope than in present reality.*

AUGUSTINE, *City of God*, 19.20

✢

Liberals are supposed to be wary of demanding too much of politics. Some allow this fear to generate an entire philosophical anthropology, either by carving out a distinct space where "religion" can safely happen or by adopting a religious devotion to liberalism itself. Some celebrate this austerity as the welcome separation of spirituality from politics that is liberating for both. Others fear that by (ostensibly) abandoning religious horizons, liberalism has cut itself off from roots that inspire, motivate, and make sense of its strenuous demands. Still others are attracted to even grander visions of individuals in communities liberated from consuming ambition and competitive praise that values things more than persons. They tolerate and sustain liberal practices because of concerns about misplaced passion regarding the sacred, often a disenchanted *Christian* passion "to sanctify in advance all forms of secular life."[1] There is something deeply Augustinian in this regard: restless caution of where and how our affections find their rest—a salutary disposition that counters the romantic sentimentalities of communitarian thought and the idolatries of totalitarian practice.

The liberal tradition is in some sense about accepting people as they happen to be. Liberal perfectionists, however, seek to transform political society to the extent possible in a world where we tend to fall over, crash into, and dominate one another. Arendt never abandoned this possibility in her commitments against injustice and political inequality. American thinkers like Thoreau, Emerson, Whitman, Ellison, and King express similar commitments and longings. I have tried to claim a space for a more dynamic Augustinian civic liberalism that avoids theocracy and status quo defeatism. It puts political existence under religious and moral pressure, but it does not expect salvation from liberal democracy. As Augustinians are prone to point out, there could be worse forms of secular politics and worse forms of idolatry (especially those that pretend to be the most "religious"). We should be grateful for the best of liberalism even as we endeavor to make it better.

This is an ambitious task. So much has been said about Augustine's politics. Augustine and his retrospective interpreters cast a long shadow over modernity, that enigma which Oliver O'Donovan describes as "a great carcass around which a shoal of shark-toothed narratives forever wheels and

---

1. Leszek Kolakowski, "The Revenge of the Sacred in Secular Culture," in *Modernity on Endless Trial* (Chicago: University of Chicago Press, 1990), 63–74, at 69.

hovers."[2] Any effort to think with Augustine about love, sin, desire, God, feminist theory, emotion, virtue, and liberal democracy invites skepticism and risks incoherence. I have narrowed its ambitions by bracketing many questions about Augustinianism and many debates about "secularization" or "desecularization." My focus on the reception of Augustine in modern political thought does not mean to imply that these issues are not important. In fact, I believe my focus on love and sin can be a helpful route into these issues as well, especially in light of the atomistic consumption of religion in advanced liberal democracies. This consumption is ripe for criticism, and it has been the subject of severe interrogation by Radical Orthodoxy in its resistance to capitalism. Augustinians, however, should remember that Augustine was a seeker-sensitive consumer of so many religions himself. The nice thing about desire, even consumer desire, is it keeps going and leaves open the potential for redemption. Unlike the fallen angels, those pure intellects without bodies that fall completely, we embodied souls, are always on the move, especially in commercial society.

I also have not pursued some of the large issues raised by the current renaissance of political theology and the return of religion and empire in both the academy and global politics. In the academy, this renaissance, promoted by religious and secular theorists alike, implicitly invokes my themes in its "new" political dialogue with figures like Paul, Luther, Hegel, Kierkegaard, Benjamin, Freud, Barth, Rosenzweig, and Levinas.[3] Some post-secularists explicitly propose the double love commands as "the *mysterium sanctum* underlying political theology,"[4] while others identify a "need to recuperate the public and political conception of love common to premodern tradition."[5] These latter calls reflect a desire to reconnect spiritual traditions with prophetic politics. My reconstruction of a particular aspect of Augustinian theology has focused on the sensibilities and the virtues that should characterize an ethic of democratic citizenship. I have not offered a *solution* to the multifaceted debates about modern liberalism. I hope to have given some language that might liberate Augustinianism from the caricatures of our big

---

2. O'Donovan, *Ways of Judgment*, 298.

3. See, for example, Creston Davis, John Milbank, and Slavoj Žižek, eds., *Theology and the Political: The New Debate* (Durham: Duke University Press, 2005).

4. Reinhard, "Toward a Political Theology of the Neighbor," 12.

5. Hardt and Negri, *Multitude*, 351.

intellectual histories—the sorts of histories that Augustine himself promoted. At the same time, I tried to provide vocabularies that might relieve the conceptual power of some unhelpful dichotomies, i.e., love vs. justice, realism vs. idealism, egotism vs. altruism, and transcendence (God) vs. immanence (neighbor). These dualisms can have heuristic value, but they also get in the way of thinking seriously about both Augustinianism and liberalism. In short, I have tried to make good on my stated effort to expand the Augustinian imagination for liberal democracy and the liberal democratic imagination for Augustinianism.

In the introduction, I confessed that my interest in retrieving and extending an Augustinian account of politics grounded in the virtue of love has its own motivations. In addition to adjudicating relevant issues in Augustine studies and extending discussions of political Augustinianism, my interest stems from a belief that the myths, symbols, and practices that govern liberal society are either dangerously anemic or excessively prideful. This may be the fate of a political culture that paradoxically displays, at the same time, apathetic resignation and polarizing mobilization of group interests. We have seen that received versions of Augustinianism can contribute to both of these two tendencies. In light of our political situation, unlike many Augustinians, I applaud Richard Rorty's effort to join solidarity and liberal democracy.[6] I especially admire his effort to overcome the "principled, theorized, philosophical hopelessness" of the contemporary left.[7] Rorty interestingly contrasts Dewey and Whitman by noting "the difference between talking mostly about love and talking mostly about citizenship."[8] Augustinian civic liberalism, I have argued, talks mostly about both. It does not abandon theological aspiration, as Rorty might counsel in his Deweyan call to forget about eternity. I do not, however, subscribe to Rorty's vague proposal that Whitman and Dewey "gave us all the romance, and all the spiritual uplift, we Americans need to go about our public business."[9] More dominant liberal

---

6. I do share Eugene McCarraher's worry that "what marks Rorty's overtly 'secular' project as a desperate form of state fetishism and soteriology is his curious need to sacralize the democratic state" (McCarraher, "The Enchanted City of Man," 277).

7. Rorty, *Achieving Our Country*, 37.

8. Ibid., 25.

9. Ibid., 97. Rorty makes passing mention of "admirers of Saint Augustine such as Reinhold Niebuhr and Jean Bethke Elshtain" (ibid., 33). But they are cast merely as those who "take the notion of sin seriously" (33) in order to criticize Deweyan agency. My

theories contribute to this weakness because they sacrifice love on the altar of a restricted conception of justice in order to fend off pathological expressions of love. Augustinian liberals should share Joan Tronto's concern that "care's absence from our core social and political values reflects many choices our society has made about what to honor."[10] The confession Augustinians believe is necessary for progress in true righteousness is not the same thing as the charitable civility that is demanded by a pluralist society. *Caritas* has its different expressions (both personally and institutionally), but awareness of the reality of others is fundamental to a political morality that aims neither too high nor to low.[11] To "refer" virtue to God, within the Christ-centered logic of Augustinian loving, is perpetually to release self-righteous possession of moral goodness in ways that counsel against both the *prideful* possession of virtue by oneself and the *prideful* promotion of virtue in others. Augustinian liberalism has tradition-dependent resources to reject a coercive paternalism predicated on appeal to a loving politics that is not also constrained by the recognition of sin. It resists those political perfectionisms that threaten human dignity by blurring appropriate distinctions between moral and political life, between discipleship and citizenship.

In chapter 1, I alluded to the fact that liberals recognize that a liberal society cannot contain all possible social worlds, even those worlds that do not contradict the basic aims of liberalism. Augustinian dispositions support liberal admissions (both theoretical and sociological) about the incommensurability of certain goods in this life. The virtue of love as part of an ethics of citizenship, however, can and should be affirmed as an appropriate virtue for citizens. For Augustinians, love is a good that can not be abandoned in

---

project tries to upset thinking about Augustinians simply as pessimistic spectators. For a project that tries to upset thinking about Deweyans simply as optimistic technocrats, see Eddie S. Glaude, *In a Shade of Blue: Pragmatism and the Politics of Black America* (Chicago: University of Chicago Press, 2007).

10. Tronto, *Moral Boundaries*, 179.

11. I am intrigued by the connections between this reading and Mark Cladis's understanding of Rousseau and Durkheim as communitarian liberals. He also reads Rousseau's religion and politics as a "middle way" between Augustinian pessimism and Enlightenment traditions. See Mark S. Cladis, *Public Vision, Private Lives: Rousseau, Religion, and 21st-Century Democracy* (New York: Columbia University Press, 2003). I am trying to get more out of Augustinianism than just the pessimist side of the contribution.

order to achieve other goods.[12] Neither justice nor realism demand this much chastity about love. However one judges the practical constraints of citizenship, incommensurability should not be built into the possibilities of liberal theorizing. Theorizing the virtues of liberalism should operate under less rigid constraints than civic practices in political societies might themselves allow, especially when even the communitarian challenge essentially "has been turned around so that it functions as a rationale for greater complacency with our own historically evolved liberal way of life."[13]

The possibility of imagining love's normative relation to both justice and respect is part of my more ambitious Augustinian liberalism. Words and concepts have histories. I have not made a historical claim as to when political theorists and political theologians stopped talking about love, or at least stopped talking about love in the way that is relevant for the ethics of liberalism and Augustinianism. Certain figures, dates, and texts suggest themselves. They include the familiar list of late medievals and early moderns who today preoccupy the minds of critics of modernity and liberalism. As we saw in writings of Hannah Arendt and John Rawls, contemporary liberal theory has not completely abandoned discussion of love. But their attention to love has primarily served a strategy of exclusion—a strategy that privatizes loves and renders them beyond the pale of liberal reciprocity. This exclusion is particularly stringent with regard to any love that is connected with religious desires. By not finding a secure place for love within its account of politics, liberalism mistakenly alienates those citizens who are unwilling to sacrifice the norm of love as their basic moral orientation in political life. Feminist writers have sought to restore something like an ethic of love back into the discursive regime of liberal political theory. My refigured Augustinian Christianity provides another, different voice. It uses Augustine's grammar of love and sin to open up more conceptual space within liberal politics.

---

12. I remain open to the possibility of tragic dilemmas internal to a Christian ethics of love. However, wholesale rejection of the virtue of love in order to achieve liberal justice is not one of them. For a poignant account of Christian love, tragedy, and providence, see Philip Quinn, "Tragic Dilemmas, Suffering Love, and Christian Life," *Journal of Religious Ethics* 17, no. 1 (Spring 1989): 151–83.

13. See Ronald Beiner, *Philosophy in a Time of Lost Spirit* (Toronto: University of Toronto Press, 1997), 16. Beiner rightly challenges us not to "bore ourselves to death by reducing the grand tradition of Western theory to ridiculously modest proportions—that is, by merely tinkering with the economic and political details of the liberal order" (17).

While not driven by sociological analysis, my interest in this topic stems from the increasing self-absorption displayed in a rights-governed and consumer-oriented liberal culture. This preoccupation with the self has been exacerbated in Christian social ethics by certain trajectories in recent theology that reject political liberalism in the name of authentic piety. I have Augustinian suspicions about the religious sources of these laments about liberal democracies. I also have Augustinian suspicions about the enthusiasm of democratic optimism. No generation has a monopoly on either virtue or vice. I am sympathetic with Jean Bethke Elsthain's assessment of contemporary liberal society:

> By any standard of objective evidence, those who point to the growth of corrosive forms of isolation, boredom, and despair; to declining levels of involvement in politics; to the overall weakening of that world known as democratic civil society, have the better case. . . . This bodes ill, for any ongoing way of life requires robust yet resilient institutions that embody and reflect, mediate and shape, our passions and our interests. As these overlapping associations of social life disappear or are stripped of legitimacy, a political and ethical wilderness spreads. (*LP*, 2)

Augustinians might think the wilderness always spreads. But Augustinian ambivalence demands a more balanced assessment. To imagine liberal societies merely in terms of aestheticism, boredom, and corrupt individualism is the mirror image of a reading that imagines Augustinianism merely in terms of dogmatism, religious coercion, and ascetic otherworldliness. It is helpful here to cite Milbank against his more popular image as theological critic of modernity: "Finding the right perspective on the infinite is a matter (to adapt Augustine) of being open to the risks of new and unexpected beauty" (*TST*, 431). This dialectical perspective generates a "*dramatic* sense of history as ceaseless loss and gain: the Enlightenment has gained for us the formal principles of individual liberty and equality, which sometimes guard against the very *worst* tyrannies, but at the same time we have lost certain practices of free association for common purposes."[14] I would extend Milbank's argument by not only recognizing that the shared goods that liberalism secures

---

14. Milbank, "On Complex Space," 279. I do not know how Milbank can also write that there is "small practical difference between naked totalitarianism and a liberalism that is, nonetheless, in essence totalitarian" (*TST*, 319). The context of this sentence is Milbank's description of *nouveaux philosophes*, but he appears to endorse the claim.

are good, but that liberal theory is itself a moral resource for those Augustinian pilgrims still on the way. The practice of moral criticism that emerges within democratic faith—a critical discourse itself grounded in social movements, virtuous practices, and institutions—can not be read as simply another kind of nihilism beholden to the hegemonic empire of capitalism. The experience of democratic liberalism offers its own moral wisdom. And, while I have not explicitly pursued this claim, it harbors its own theological significance. Sometimes, there really are treasures in earthen vessels.

Liberal democracy is not the defeat of Christian witness. To the contrary, the achievements of the liberal tradition can be cast as triumphs of a long history of Christian social and political theory. These achievements not only include an emphasis on freedom of conscience and speech, local communities, and natural equality but the very notion of a responsible and legitimate state humbled by the merciful rule of law guided by constitutional principles (especially in the aspirations of positive international law). This rendering, which turns much of the antiliberal rhetoric of contemporary political theology on its head, relies on Oliver O'Donovan's patient contextualism. To think of other liberalisms is not a concession to fate, a celebration of the end of history, an accommodation of the revolutionary gospel to reformist secular discourse, or a rejection of the need for solidarity with those marginalized by the etiquette of liberal culture and theory. It is to recognize that social forms, like religions, are historically contingent, morally ambivalent, and socially resilient. Just as no one today can really be a "medieval knight" or even a "Marxist," it is also hard to imagine a political way of life that does not at the very least perpetuate aspects of a liberal society.[15] This is not to deny the need for Christians to continually imagine some other social world, to prophetically put the current one in question, and to subversively hope for the unpredictable arrival (à la Macintyre) of some new Benedict or Athenian Stranger. But it is to refuse the luxury of simply condemning liberal democracy. I think the

---

15. Aladsair MacIntyre has noted that "the contemporary debates within modern political systems are almost exclusively between conservative liberals, liberal liberals, and radical liberals. There is little place in such political systems for the criticism of the system itself, that is, for putting liberalism in question" (*Whose Justice? Which Rationality?*, 392). I take the examples of the medieval knight and the Marxist from Macintyre as well. In the concluding paragraphs of *After Virtue*, he admits "he sees no tolerable alternative set of political and economic structures which could be brought into place to replace the structures of advanced capitalism" (262). Marxism is "exhausted as a *political* tradition" (262).

task for Christian social ethics today is to critically engage this reality with something like the Augustinian humanism of an Erasmus rather than a new Augustinianism assailing the "pagans." Christian humanism need not always compete with general humanism.

My project has been a rational reconstruction. I have not argued for what Augustine would say, or claimed to have discovered something new about Augustine. I have tried to lift up a neglected strand of the Augustinian tradition that gets buried in conventional invocations outside of specialist academic books. But I do wonder what Augustine would make of our world and its self-images. He might find Francis Fukuyama's enthusiastic thesis about liberal democracy as the final form of politics in light of the unexpected changes in the global order all too similar to Eusebius' wonder at the coronation of Constantine that marked the inauguration of Christendom.[16] Such triumphalism about the progressive march of freedom was ripe for Augustinian polemics well before 9/11. All human political arrangements display the "fragile brilliance of glass" (*CD* 4.3).[17] How might Augustine read more cautious interpretations of the fragile moral ecology and political sociology of democratic liberalization? There are a number of signs that even consolidated liberal political societies and the intellectual environments that sustain them are in "dark times."[18] A post-9/11 world dramatizes these longstanding threats and developments. Arrogance and apathy are equal temptations in light of the pluralities of historical possibility and the insecurities wrought by historical change. Neither fundamentalism nor secularism is a viable choice for Augustinians. I have avoided the speculative thought experiment of what Augustine would say to us now. But for Augustine, I think, this darkness would require going beyond questions of technical procedure in order to revisit the moral and religious sources of liberal commitments. It was within such broader horizons that liberal societies were born—Augustine the genealogist would claim—and it is within these now perhaps alien environments

16. Francis Fukuyama, *The End of History and the Last Man* (New York: Free Press, 1992).

17. For a response to Fukuyama that resonates with a number of Augustinian themes, see Samuel P. Huntington, "No Exit: The Errors of Endism," *National Interest* 17 (Fall 1989): 3–11. Other responses are found in Arthur Melzer et al., eds., *History and the Idea of Progress* (Ithaca: Cornell University Press, 1995).

18. Isaac, *Democracy in Dark Times.* Isaac's title and book borrows heavily from Hannah Arendt and offers a number of implicitly Augustinian claims.

that creative and constructive response might be made. He would see our world of ethnic conflict, religious strife, disempowering mass politics, and alienating forms of economic relations, and he would try to articulate a richer moral vocabulary attentive to goods that attract us as human beings, but one that also maintains the eschatological vision which makes "secularity" a coherent and necessary Christian concept.

Interpretative debates about the reception of the intellectual legacy of seminal figures should not blind us to the fundamental questions that such figures were willing to ask. Our task is to develop traditions of thought that draw from, and respond to, their answers and their questions. This task is all the more pressing if it is true that "fundamental assumptions that he made about humankind, assumptions that undergird everything he wrote even before his religious conversion, are on the brink of a historical challenge."[19] The problem of love and justice, like the problem of evil, is not a mere intellectual conundrum for ethicists and psychologists. It is a lived problem for ordinary political life shared by Christians and non-Christians alike. It is one reason that Augustine has inspired so many readers, even among those who reject his theology and its influential legacy. Indeed, in rejecting Augustine, we pay tribute to the power of his religious ideas, which often make him appear as an unexpected contemporary. The existentialized Augustine is famous for his explorations of the inner life and the journey to selfhood. He is credited (and blamed) by some for inventing this intimate way of imagining what it means to be human. But we do well also to consider Augustine's insight that how a political society thinks about the directions of its desires and loves has important consequences for the sort of life such a society might lead. A liberal political climate so practiced in the arts of suspicion, disenchantment, and irony is in danger of becoming wary of moral and religious dispositions themselves. The antiliberalism of many religious communities fuels this climate. Anders Nygren launched a thousand ships of criticism with his claim that Augustine instrumentally pictures the world and the neighbor as "given to us to be used as a means and vehicle for our return to God" (*AE*, 505). I have sought to undermine this reading. Liberal societies need both prudence and political friendships across religious divides in order to sustain practices that maintain the humanism and self-critical vision that inspired its origins. A welcome feature of recent political Augustinianism is its willingness to

19. O'Donnell, *A New Biography*, 316.

enter "into conversation with Augustine" as a means to "reawaken ourselves to the possibilities of our aspirations and find the true meaning of wisdom and friendship with those who seek it with us."[20] If Christian thought is like a language, then political Augustinianism should employ the full range of its vocabulary and speak more explicitly about love's relation to politics.

Because my main focus has been an exploration of the grammar of love within Augustinian civic liberalism, I have not continually focused on the general relation of Christian to non-Christian virtue. These relations are implicit within my account of love and the ethics of citizenship. For Augustinian Christians, virtue is understood in Christological terms. Could it be otherwise? As A. H. Armstrong argues, "the essential uniqueness of Christianity lies, not in any theory about love or anything else, but in the fact of Christ."[21] But Augustine's incarnate Christ, humble in descent, is the revelation of goodness that resists claims of possession:

> O Lord, for your Truth is not mine, nor his, nor hers, but belongs to all of us whom you call to share it in communion with him, at the same time giving us the terrible warning not to arrogate truth to ourselves as private property, lest we find ourselves deprived of it. For anyone who appropriates what you provide for all to enjoy, and claims as his own what belongs to all, is cast out from this commonwealth, cast out to what is truly his own, which is to say from the truth to a lie; for anyone who lies is speaking from what is his own. (*Conf.* 12.25.34)

For Augustinians, Christ is no one's *proprium* but the *omnium bonum*—the highest good that is also the common good, both the way and the end. Augustine theologically criticizes the Donatists for denying this fact. He thought they seek, like Cain, in order to possess: "now Cain, which means 'possession,' is the founder of the earthly city" (*CD* 15.17). This possession denies the radical transcendence of Augustine's God become flesh. In Christ, Augustinians claim, all loves are bound together—God's love for humanity and humanity's love for God and neighbor. But Christ is not the possession of Christianity, the church, or Augustinianism. To borrow from a prominent critic of liberalism, Christ is a "good in common that we cannot know alone."[22] The

---

20. Von Heyking, *Augustine and Politics as Longing in the World*, xii.

21. Armstrong, "Platonic *Eros* and Christian *Agape*," 120.

22. Sandel, *Liberalism and the Limits of Justice*, 183.

scope of this spectacular goodness is why John Milbank rightly insists that "only that which is in common is truly good at all, or can be truly possessed, though only in the mode of reception of a gift, which must be relinquished and passed on" (*BR*, 178). For Milbank, this common good is "always enjoyed (Augustine again) from different perspectives as something absolutely individual and unique. . . . In other words, collectivity is seen to arise through the uttermost individualism, just as the transcendent universal is only available through local and specific refraction" (178). This view of a common good, I think, entails a theological commitment to a plurality of sites for the practice of Christian virtue (especially during life under grace). Augustinian social ethics, because of these commitments, encourages political and moral attention to the shared loves of human society. It also encourages a radically fallibilist epistemology in one's understanding of the purposes of God in Christ for the human community. Openness to the risk and frustration of moral and political dialogue is central to both liberalism and Augustinianism. Confidence in the goodness of God (but not in our knowledge of this goodness) secures such openness without guaranteeing political harmony or an ontology immune from vulnerability.

Examining these basic commitments would be significant for a dialogue with those liberal theorists who otherwise are sympathetic to Augustinian unmasking of certain anthropological presuppositions of liberal theory. Romand Coles thinks that the possibilities of such an engagement with Augustine himself remain bleak:

> For all of Augustine's profound insights into depth, remembering, willing, and unifying the scattered self in confession, the edge where he faces the non-Christian—even within himself—is still a battlefield, not a region where fertile intermingling might be possible.[23]

Augustine, it seems, is still too safe. He is a *possible* radical, but too afraid of the wild possibilities of becoming. I should note that most moderns are not

---

23. Coles, *Self/Power/Other*, 11. Coles links this erasure with Augustine's "inward-seeking, hermeneutical deep self" that has a "distinctly monological quality" (170 and 172). According to Coles, "the death of at least a *sovereign* God and subjectivity constitutes a desirable space" for "articulating, soliciting, and (to a much lesser extent) practicing an 'ethic of receptive generosity'" (*Rethinking Generosity*, 23). Elsewhere, Coles imagines the possibility of "giving and receiving between Christians and their others" ("Storied Others and the Possibilities of *Caritas*," 350).

used to thinking of Augustine as a radical *anything*. But, as William Connolly says to Augustine, "you peer more deeply into the abyss than anyone before and most after."[24] Yet, for Connolly and Coles, Augustine is unwilling to leave the enclosure and security of boundary maintenance. More strongly, he finally refuses dialogue because of his many monologues with himself. These monologues allow him to stabilize his unstable self only by stabilizing others, including his God. Confession becomes simply another route into vanity, pride, glory, and domination. James O'Donnell sees (at least) both Augustines: one who fearfully "insists that his way and his way alone shall prevail" and another who imagined a God "too big to grasp."[25] The latter, for O'Donnell, Connolly, and Coles, gives way to the former. Signs become fixed in an effort to hunt down idolatry and heresy. In this, perhaps, Augustine betrays himself and the God who continues to summon. I hope my Augustinian liberalism might alter Coles's pessimism about Augustinian liberals at least (without losing the infinite richness of Augustine's God that Coles admires). It might also contribute to Connolly's call to "cultivate those fugitive spaces of enchantment lodged between theistic faith and secular abstinence."[26] These possibilities of enchantment, of course, do occasion Christian anxieties. It is not only cultural conservatives who worry that fugitive spaces and sublime enchantment tend to their own kinds of sin, their own Foucauldian "regimes of power."[27] Piety without god and playful creation without Creation is not always benign. Augustine may have been wrong to see only the semblance of virtue in his non-Christian enemies, but we might

24. Connolly, *Identity/Difference*, 126.

25. O'Donnell, *New Biography*, 4 and 7.

26. Connolly, *Why I Am Not a Secularist*, 15. Connolly admits "moments when the Augustinian love of divinity makes contact with critical responsiveness to difference" (151).

27. I am sympathetic to J. Joyce Schuld's criticisms of Connolly and Coles that their attention to the confessing self blurs the distinction between "Augustine's descriptions of the spiritual life of those in the church with a totalizing expectation of political regeneration" (*Augustine and Foucault*, 215–16). But I fear she says too much in response. There is a contradiction between her criticisms of these authors and her own effort to describe "the political import of the wisdom of sorrow" (218) for a non-arrogant and non-despairing politics. She undermines their fundamentally Augustinian (and Foucauldian) point: theological discourse migrates or secretes beyond its own circumscribed borders. For an insightful reading of post-Nietzschean political theory in conversation with Augustinianism, see Kristen Deede Johnson, *Theology, Political Theory, and Pluralism: Beyond Tolerance and Difference* (Oxford: Oxford University Press, 2007).

learn again from him that there are such things as semblances of virtue. Despite resistance to the singularity of an event of revelation (especially the public event of the Incarnation), many theorists troubled by the moral complacency of liberal theory have re-opened an interdisciplinary conversation between political theory and religious thought (even of a naturalistic kind). I have noted that the imagination for the "religious" in some of Augustine's most profound critics—Arendt, Coles, and Connolly—is extraordinary in the literal sense. It certainly is welcome in light of the restricted accounts of "religion and politics" in contemporary political science. This diagnostic awareness of structural analogy between theology and political theory may serve historicist purposes, but it also suggests a revived interest in theology and its influence on political culture.

These developments suggest an even more ambitious mode of political theology beyond evaluation of shared concepts toward religious ways of thinking. These authors are interested in political theology precisely for the sake of the secular. For example, Jacques Derrida's criticisms of the liberal "knights of good conscience" and his effort to move beyond the predictable liberal economy of "melancholy to triumph and triumph to melancholy," are promising notes for an Augustinianism that wants to be more than a rationalized politics of necessity.[28] The post-Christian writings of Slavoj Žižek are another promising site for engagement, especially in light of his argument against what he calls the "ethical 'gentrification' of the neighbor."[29] Recent work on Hegel that emphasizes the relation of institutions to social practices for freedom, love, and community offers still more relatively uncharted dialogical waters.[30] And still another promise, perhaps the most pressing and the most fraught, is implicated in each of these possibilities: the contemporary renaissance of Jewish political thought.[31]

28. Derrida, *Gift of Death*, 67 and 22.

29. Žižek, "Neighbors and Other Monsters," 163.

30. See, for example, Thomas A. Lewis, *Freedom and Tradition in Hegel: Reconsidering Anthropology, Ethics, and Religion* (Notre Dame, Ind.: University of Notre Dame Press, 2005).

31. See, for example, David Novak, *The Jewish Social Contract: An Essay In Political Theology* (Princeton: Princeton University Press, 2005), and Leora Batnitzky, *Leo Strauss and Emmanuel Levinas: Philosophy and the Politics of Revelation* (Cambridge: Cambridge University Press, 2006).

From a very different perspective, I have tried to show why the analytic philosophy of Robert M. Adams and Nicholas Wolterstorff deserves more serious attention within political Augustinianism. I also have appealed to the work of Timothy P. Jackson and Oliver O'Donovan as Christian social ethicists attempting mediation, despite all the political and theological dangers, between normative Christian thought and liberalism. For Jackson, this mediation functions as an archaeological act of remembrance:

> The resources of Christianity have proven more versatile than most.... Christian teachings have repeatedly been employed to subordinate and tyrannize the "unorthodox," including indigenous peoples, but the practical means to criticize such abuse are internal to the teachings themselves. Humility before common ignorance and sin, appreciation of the value of uncoerced conscience, promotion of the equal worth of lives bearing the *Imago Dei*, and thankfulness for the mercy of God were all ingredient in the emergence of Western civilization, however forgetful of these virtues that civilization may now be.[32]

Such remembrance, however, is only one aspect of my theorizing of Augustinian liberalism. Remembrance can be dangerous. I have tried to restore the primacy of love as crucial to remembering Augustine but also as a way of relating the Augustinian tradition to the interests of contemporary liberalism. This primacy of love has been eclipsed by the immediate political and philosophical concerns of twentieth-century political Augustinianism. Political Augustinianism has learned to speak with only a limited vocabulary. It is rapidly becoming an obsolete vocabulary that confirms the prejudices of the status quo. Both O'Donovan and Jackson speak of liberal modernity as a prodigal son. Niebuhr also used such imagery, but he was quick to remind Christians not to play the role of elder brother either. In fact, for Niebuhr, "the younger son might well have been prompted to leave his father's house because of the insufferable self-righteousness of the elder brother."[33] Augustinian civic liberals should remember that we are all prodigal.

In practice, the arts and disciplines of loving have remained central to Christian communities. Milbank and Hauerwas are right to argue that it is these liturgical, homiletic, and catechetical practices that render symbols meaningful. They actually produce Christian dispositions that are otherwise

---

32. Jackson, "Naturalism, Formalism, and Supernaturalism," 503.
33. Niebuhr, "The Christian Church in a Secular Age," in *The Essential Niebuhr*, 87.

shaped by alternative social, political, and economic practices. These Christian practices continue to influence the secular practices of liberal society. I have not pursued a close examination of these secular analogues of neighbor-love.[34] If love is to assume flesh, it should not be ideas all the way down. However, as with love and justice, a strict dichotomy between theory (as doctrine) and practice (as cult) seriously misleads any moral endeavor. If willing and knowing are aspects of loving, Augustinians especially are committed to the idea that theory is part of our practice. If my larger argument has been persuasive, theorists should engage particular religious discourses and practices rather than general discussions of religion and politics. Different conceptual schemes and ways of articulating virtue in the world should expand the liberal imagination for citizenship.[35] But I agree with Robert Adams's claim that "doubtless alliance with God can be more fully developed if it is theologically explicit, but theological explicitness does not guarantee the authenticity of such alliance."[36] My recovery and reorientation of the conceptual legacy of the Augustinian tradition is but one example of trying to be more theologically explicit.

The significance of theological ideas, however, should not be overwhelmed by attention to practices. The opening line of Paul Ramsey's *Basic Christian Ethics* reads: "The first thing to be said concerning Christian ethics is that it cannot be separated from its religious foundation" (*BCE*, 1). For Ramsey, the human relation to God is "of vital importance, not simply *for* ethics, but *within* ethical theory itself" (*BCE*, 1). Ramsey did not operate with a universal definition of religion. In fact, he claimed that his approach to ethics stands "in decisive relation to Jesus Christ" and is "less merely theocentric"

34. Several contemporary sociologists and ethnographers investigate cultural practices of relevance to theorists of love and the influence of religious motivation. For example, see Robert Wuthnow, *Acts of Compassion: Caring for Others and Helping Ourselves* (Princeton: Princeton University Press, 1991); Robert Wuthnow, *Learning to Care: Elementary Kindness in an Age of Indifference* (Oxford: Oxford University Press, 1995); and Christian Smith, ed., *Disruptive Religion: The Force of Faith in Social Movement Activism* (New York: Routledge, 1996).

35. Martha Nussbaum encourages this empirical approach in "Non-Relative Virtues," 35. I am sympathetic with Nussbaum's larger project about "human capacity" that involves providing a framework for richer moral dialogue about political matters. However, Nussbaum's empiricism is limited by her exclusion of those stories that involve an appeal to transcendence. For criticism of Nussbaum on this point, see Jones, *Transformed Judgment*, 14–15.

36. Adams, *Finite and Infinite Goods*, 198.

in its religious and ethical outlook "than was Jesus himself" (*BCE*, 23). One upshot of my book is that *Christology and neighbor-love* rather than *theism and self-love* are the central conceptual terms for any Augustinian liberalism that wants to be theological. Loving the neighbor involves the virtues of active receptivity and vulnerable responsibility that I have suggested are central to an Augustinian ethic of *caritas* and moral psychology of enjoyment. But Christology can not simply provide another metaphysical placeholder, another transcendental signified. While historical theologians often claim that Augustine's Christology is neither original nor significant for the development of doctrine, I have argued that Augustinians should make it central for their understanding the relation between the love commands and Augustinian citizenship. Christology shapes a way of seeing the world that offers insights for political citizenship. Within the symbolic world of Augustinian theology, the humble dispossession necessary to be good takes its cue from an event of dispossession that animates Augustine's theological semiotics. Thus Christology is both the form and substance of Augustinian theology. To put it bluntly, Book 10 of the *City of God* is the basic text for Augustinian politics: the heart of Augustine's account of the true worship of the crucified God and the charitable service of neighbor in collective *caritas*. Augustine's God, however, tends to be absent from political Augustinianism. A thicker vision of politics and citizenship that is Augustinian is necessarily tied to the kind of God and the kind of desire disclosed in Jesus Christ. Christology should be *political* for Augustinians—a recognition that would also invite more explicit dialogue between political Augustinians and followers of Karl Barth.

This book promotes political Augustinianism by highlighting the theological dimensions of Augustinian love. It affirms a secularizing of politics (in the Augustinian sense), but it rejects the modern separation of politics from the aspirations of virtue that should characterize all citizens. Of the many important contributions of Alasdair Macintyre's renewal of philosophical attention to the nature of tradition is his claim that "traditions, when vital, embody continuities of conflict."[37] These "continuities of conflict" are emblematic of "those internal, interpretative debates through which the meaning and rationale of the fundamental agreements come to be expressed."[38] The three types of Augustinian liberalism that I describe all fit this description. Despite their significant overlaps, they encourage different dispositions and

---

37. MacIntyre, *After Virtue*, 222.
38. MacIntyre, *Whose Justice? Which Rationality?*, 4.

moral orientations for liberal citizens. My construction of an Augustinian civic liberalism is at odds with the dominant constructions of both those who reject and those who celebrate political Augustinianism. It is a nontraditional defense of the tradition. But my criticism is not wholesale. Each of the types identifies important agreements between Augustinianism and liberalism.

Like Augustine's treatment of Stoicism and Platonism, my reconstruction affirms and criticizes by changing the subject of investigation. In terms of the ethics of political Augustinianism, I have tried to shift political Augustinianism away from an account of sin abstracted from theology to an account of love that provides the context for understanding this account of sin. Within this account, I have tried to shift attention away from the problem of self-love *per se* to the problem of neighbor-love. And, for both liberals and Augustinians, I have shifted attention within the ethics of citizenship away from epistemology to the phenomenology of motivation and the virtue of love. I have affirmed the value of justice and respect, but also suggested their limits. And I have likened Augustine's account to liberal feminist moves that emphasize care as a complex emotional and practical virtue relevant for democratic politics.

In order to place these moves under a larger Augustinian rubric, I have challenged traditional readings of the categories of "use and enjoyment" in order to show the creative moral and political possibilities of an Augustinian approach. I have shown how different strategies ameliorate concerns that Augustinians can not value the dignity of neighbors and the world. In terms of Augustinian political ethics, these categories register not only an ontological account of the self's relation to the world and God, but also a practical disposition of the self toward itself. To *use* rather than *enjoy* is a way of protecting neighbors (and the political community) from the self, even as it may also reign in the self's tendency to idolatry. Idolatry is dangerous for both the self and the other. This reading is consistent with Rowan Williams's Augustinian portrait of the Christian life:

> The Christian life . . . is in constant danger of premature closure, the supposition that the end of desire has been reached and the ambiguities of history and language put behind us: and thus the difficulty of Scripture is itself a kind of parable of our condition. We cannot properly enjoy what we swiftly and definitively possess: such possession results in inaction and ultimately contempt for the object.[39]

39. Williams, "Language, Desire, and Reality," 142.

Rather than invest the neighbor with desires she cannot fulfill, Augustinians "use" their neighbor for their neighbor's sake. Rather than invest politics with desires it cannot fulfill, Augustinians "use" politics—grateful for its accomplishments and committed to its purposes—but not as a final site of human wholeness. This practice recognizes the dangers of a love that is enclosed, but it also affirms love's necessity and beneficial possibilities. Augustinian citizens engage their wills, which is to say their loves, in the political community. But the political exercise of their loves is conditioned by (and flows from) their love for God which is always already part of God's own love for them. In this sense, we might say that Augustinians "use" liberal politics as an expression of their loves, but they do not "enjoy" it. This is part of the freedom of Augustinian Christianity: to make "use of the world as if not using" (*CD* 1.10). It may not sound terribly counter-cultural in this age of critique to admonish us not to enjoy liberal politics. But, in the precise Augustinian sense, the logic of modern culture does insist on perpetual enjoyment, even of liberal democracy. Augustinians should use liberal politics along the way to enjoying the politics of an infinite God. This theological kind of utopianism need not denigrate liberal politics and inspire spiritual aloofness. It does not reject all that is human in its more demanding hope beyond earthly happiness "when there is no more need for the regime of symbols" (*DT* 1.3.16). It does not perpetuate "Platonism" because it dares to speak of God's sacramental love as binding the temporal and the eternal. Whether liberal societies can imagine such an incredibly social happiness like Augustine wanted—the perfect peace and wholeness of the Heavenly City—is a difficult question. In that peace, "the beauty of the entire temporal universe, with its individual parts each appropriate to its time, will flow like a great song by some indescribably great composer" (*Ep.* 138, 32).

Augustine himself found it hard to imagine "how great that felicity will be" (*CD* 22.30), but he encouraged his readers to long for this strange and beautiful happiness with patience and forbearance. Indeed, "the whole life of the good Christian is a holy longing. . . . Through longing [God] makes the soul extend, by extending it [God] makes room in it" (*IoEp.* 4.6). Why, then, must we endure this present unhappiness? What could justify misery and tragic suffering? How can the fulfillment of the ideal compensate for the actual? What happens to Abel's blood even within the eschatological praise? Is history pathetic as well as tragic? To ask these questions about divine justice is, of course, to raise the most difficult challenge to an Augustinian (or, for that matter, any theist). It raises not so much my major problematic of loving the neighbor in the sensible world but instead the question how one could love anything in heaven itself given the suffering of the world. This is the case regardless if one appeals to universal salvation—the theological analogy of a world without Rawlsian "social loss." Augustine, of course, did not rely on this speculative possibility (*CD* 21.17). He does suggest that human beings (unlike angels) participate in the heroic compassion of God for us and for others only through this wonderful fleshly redemption of history. This redemption brings each of us to completion through faith in the healing grace of both Creation and Incarnation: "so that we can live the life of the Gospel by dying the death of the Gospel" (*Ep.* 95, 23). Love (literally) takes time, an experience of time that makes nonpossessive love possible. There is something important to our striving to make progress through such a journey, some kind of fitting relation between reconciliation and the birth of enjoying a different way of desiring in God through Christ—without lack or domination. The confessions of a vulnerable creation on the way are the means to the end of this redemption. He writes: "It is as if the force which dwells in human beings is to rise above that of other animals all the higher, in proportion as its release has been delayed, just as, the further back the bow is bent, the higher the arrow flies" (*CD* 13.3). Recognition of sin (rather than sin itself) gives birth to maturity. This is a *felix culpa* trying hard not to turn Christian sin into Stoic virtue: "By the greater and more wondrous grace of the Saviour, even the punishment of sin has been turned to the service of righteousness" (*CD* 13.4). I signal this response (if it is one) neither to affirm Augustine's answer nor offer one of my own.[40]

Because of my discrete concerns with modern political Augustinianism, I have not entered into every thicket of Augustine's theology of freedom and grace. Most notably, I have not examined in detail his doctrine of reprobation as it appears in his anti-Pelagian texts. This doctrine of eternal damnation for what appears to be the majority of human beings is distinct from a doctrine of election or predestination. It may be one of the most "illiberal" themes in Augustine—however one understands freedom (i.e., as alternative possibil-

---

40. Peter Burnell concludes that although Augustine has "prompted us to expect heaven to make sense of such moral absurdities, his speculative description of heaven, near the end of his work, holds in prospect the mere termination of wrongs, not a comprehensible resolution of their absurdity. . . . He entirely ignores the most poignant evil evoked in Book 19, the failure of human life in this world to make adequate moral sense" (*Augustinian Person*, 202).

ity or participation in goodness). Readers, hoping for a book I did not write, might think it would threaten my defense of the traditional liberal values of liberty and equality by encouraging a fatalistic elitism. It might well be that receptions of this view promoted political inequalities and suppression of liberty, though the political history of Calvinism as its theological heir does not bear this out. Augustinian notions of creatures as bearers of the image of God and a *corpus permixtum* that hides knowledge of the elect and the damned could (and did) encourage tolerance and equality within such political communities. In any case, I do not find this challenge as difficult a living political problem as the more general one I have directly addressed throughout: the complex relation of love and sin in political moralities.

For my purposes, the main point with regard to salvation is to register the eschatological (and so Christological) tapestry that weaves together the Augustinian notions of use and enjoyment. Eschatological eudaimonism does not trap Christian love up in heaven. It is precisely the end that perpetually calls forth not simply longing but also a new ethical beginning in the "secular" time of Incarnation: "Let us consider this process of cleansing as a trek, or a voyage, to our homeland; though progress towards the one who is ever present is not made through space, but through integrity of purpose and character" (*DDC* 1.10). Augustine exclaims: "Look, he is here even now, and he was here, and he is always here; and he never departs, he departs nowhere" (*IoEv.* 2.8.2). To enjoy liberal politics, in the end, turns on an unhealthy desire to enjoy only ourselves. That is the real danger: not individuality as such, but the tendency to become comfortable in the black hole of one's own privacy. If I am right about Augustinianism, however, dangers lie less in the nature of desire itself and more in the practice of all desire. The future of Augustinian liberalism—and so much more—may turn on whether or not we human beings can learn to desire more than ourselves without killing each other or simply forgetting about the shared goods of political life in pursuit of private perfection, aesthetic delight, entertaining distractions, economic security, and even spiritual freedom.

Some Christians today tell a somber narrative about modernity as a fall from grace—from an age when something called the Judeo-Christian ethic made sense. The villains in this story of disintegration are varied—the Enlightenment, the French Revolution, the 1960s, atomistic individualism, Nietzsche, and now John Rawls come to mind. But one common theme is the idea that we live in the liberal ruins of inherited moralities whose authority is gone, if not lost. There are both academic and popular expressions of this story. A second reaction to the difficulty in achieving agreement is a retreat into skepticism about religion and public life itself. This skepticism is also familiar in both academic and popular contexts. It comes in different shapes and sizes, but I am thinking of those deep skeptics who imagine religion as only and everywhere a code word for ideology. A third assessment is nostalgia—evident in both liberal and conservative laments over the absence of another Reinhold Niebuhr, Abraham Joshua Heschel, or Martin Luther King Jr. I think each of these assessments is wrong or at least unhelpful. All three are self-referentially defeating. If the world is such a mess, how could we or someone like us know it was that bad? And the problem with deep skepticism is its tendency to assert itself with great certitude. Nostalgia has its own dangers, both religious and practical, because it freezes the past in memory and blinds us to present possibility. Ironically, all three dispositions rely on an idealized notion of the extent of previous consensus and today's moral differences. They underestimate the actual agreements that societies like ours exhibit, as in the historically remarkable agreements about human rights and practical commitment to their extension in the past fifty years. We disagree about the language and meaning of rights, but we are disagreeing about shared concerns nonetheless. For me, modernity, if there is such a thing, is a mixed bag. Augustinian liberals recognize that earthly politics cannot fulfill the deepest longings of a human person or community. Rights, respect, and democracy are good things, even if they are not the fulfillment of love. Unsatisfied longings for genuine peace and righteousness are sources of love's grief in this world. Ambivalence is a good Augustinian disposition, though it should not trump works of love and justice. Even those members of Augustine's heavenly city "have a life in this age which is not in the least to be regretted: a life which is the school of eternity, in which they make use of earthly goods like pilgrims, without grasping after them" (CD 1. 29). To love without grasping remains a work in progress, like our selves, our traditions, and our politics. This is true even for those who still hope that someday the work in progress becomes unending perfection.

BIBLIOGRAPHY
✢

Adams, Robert M. *Finite and Infinite Goods: A Framework for Ethics*. Oxford: Oxford University Press, 1999.

———. "Religious Ethics in a Pluralist Society." In *Prospects for a Common Morality*, edited by Gene Outka and John P. Reeder, 93–113. Princeton: Princeton University Press, 1993.

Allen, Danielle S. *Talking to Strangers: Anxieties of Citizenship since Brown v. Board of Education*. Chicago: University of Chicago Press, 2004.

Andolsen, Barbara Hilkert. "Agape in Feminist Ethics." *Journal of Religious Ethics* 9, no. 1 (Spring 1981): 69–83.

Annas, Julia. *The Morality of Happiness*. Oxford: Oxford University Press, 1993.

Aquinas, Thomas. *Summa Theologica*. Translated by Fathers of the English Dominican Province. New York: Benziger Brothers, 1948.

Arendt, Hannah. *Eichmann in Jerusalem: A Report on the Banality of Evil*. New York: Viking Press, 1965.

———. *The Human Condition*. Chicago: University of Chicago Press, 1958.

———. *Lectures on Kant's Political Philosophy*. Edited by Ronald Beiner. Chicago: University of Chicago Press, 1982.

———. *The Life of the Mind: Willing*. New York: Harcourt Brace Jovanovich, 1978.

———. *Love and Saint Augustine*. Edited and translated by Joanna Vecchiarelli Scott and Judith Chelius Stark. Chicago: University of Chicago Press, 1996.

———. *Men in Dark Times*. New York: Harcourt, Brace, and World, 1968.

———. *On Revolution*. New York: Viking Press, 1963.

Aristotle. *Nichomachean Ethics*. Translated by David Ross. Oxford: Oxford University Press, 1998.

———. *The Politics*. Translated by Carnes Lord. Chicago: University of Chicago Press, 1984.

Armstrong, A. H. "Platonic *Eros* and Christian *Agape*." *Downside Review* 79 (1961): 105–21.

Asiedu, Felix. "The Song of Songs and the Ascent of the Soul: Ambrose, Augustine, and the Language of Mysticism." *Vigilae Christianae* 55 (2001): 299–317.

———. "The Wise Man and the Limits of Virtue in *De Beata Vita*: Stoic Self-Sufficiency and Augustinian Irony?" *Augustiniana* 49, no. 3–4 (1999): 215–34.

Audi, Robert, and Nicholas Wolterstorff. *Religion in the Public Square: The Place of Religious Convictions in Political Debate*. Lanham, Md.: Rowman & Littlefield, 1997.

Augustine. *Augustine: Political Writings*. Edited by E. M. Atkins and R. J. Dodaro. Cambridge: Cambridge University Press, 2001.

———. *The Catholic and Manichaen Ways of Life*. In *The Fathers of the Church: A New Translation*, vol. 56. Translated by Donald A. Gallagher and Idella J. Gallagher. Washington, D.C.: The Catholic University Press of America, 1966.

———. *City of God*. Translated by R. W. Dyson. Cambridge: Cambridge University Press, 1998.

———. *City of God*. Translated by Henry Bettenson. New York: Penguin Books, 1984.

———. *Confessions*. Translated by Henry Chadwick. Oxford: Oxford University Press, 1991.

———. *Confessions*. Translated by Maria Boulding. New York: Vintage Books, 1998.

———. *Contra academicos: Answer to Skeptics*. In *The Fathers of the Church: A New Translation*, 1:103–225. Translated by Translated by Dennis J. Kavanagh. New York: Cima Publishers, 1948.

———. *Contra Faustum*. In *Nicene and Post-Nicene Fathers*, 4:155–345. Translated by R Strothert. Peabody, Mass.: Hendrickson Publishers, 1994.

———. *Contra litteras Petiliani*. In *Nicene and Post-Nicene Fathers*, 4: 519–628. Translated by J. R. King. Peabody, Mass.: Hendrickson Publishers, 1994.

———. *De beata vita*. In *The Fathers of the Church: A New Translation*, 1:43–84. Translated by Ludwig Schopp. New York: Cima Publishers, 1948.

———. *De catechizandis rudibus*. Translated by Raymond Canning. Hyde Park, N.Y.: New City Press, 2006.

———. *Eighty-Three Different Questions*. In *The Fathers of the Church: A New Translation*, vol. 70. Translated by David L. Mosher. Washington, D.C.: The Catholic University Press of America.

———. *The Enchiridion on Faith, Hope, and Love*. Translated by Bruce Harbert. Hyde Park, N.Y.: New City Press, 1999.

———. *Expositions of the Psalms, 121–150*. In *The Works of Saint Augustine: A Translation for the 21st Century*, part 3, vol. 20. Translated by Maria Boulding. Hyde Park, N.Y.: New City Press, 2004.

———. *Homilies on 1 John*. In *Augustine: Later Works*, 259–348. Translated by John Burnaby. Philadelphia: The Westminster Press, 1955.

———. *Of True Religion.* In *Augustine: Earlier Works,* 225–83. Translated by John H. S. Burleigh. Philadelphia: The Westminster Press, 1953.

———. *On Christian Doctrine.* Translated by D. W. Robertson Jr. Upper Saddle River, N.J.: Prentice-Hall, 1958.

———. *On Christian Teaching.* Translated by R. P. H. Green. Oxford: Oxford University Press, 1997.

———. *The Retractions.* In *The Fathers of the Church: A New Translation,* vol. 60. Translated by Sister Mary Inez Bogan. Washington, D.C.: The Catholic University Press of America, 1968.

———. *The Spirit and the Letter.* In *Augustine: Later Works,* 193–250. Translated by John Burnaby. Philadelphia: The Westminster Press, 1980.

———. *Soliloquies.* Translated by Kim Paffenroth. Hyde Park, N.Y.: New City Press and Augustinian Heritage Institute, 2000.

———. *Teaching Christianity.* Translated by Edmund Hill. Hyde Park, N.Y.: New City Press, 1996.

———. *Tractates on the Gospel of John 1–10.* In *The Fathers of the Church: A New Translation,* vol. 78. Translated by John W. Rettig. Washington, D.C.: The Catholic University Press of America, 1988.

———. *The Trinity.* Translated by Edmund Hill. Hyde Park, N.Y.: New City Press, 1991.

Babcock, William. "*Cupiditas* and *Caritas*: The Early Augustine on Love and Fulfilment." In *Augustine Today,* edited by Richard John Neuhaus, 1–34. Grand Rapids, Mich.: Eerdmans, 1993.

Badhwar, Neera Kapu. "Love, Politics, and Autonomy." *Reason Papers* 9 (Winter 1983): 21–28.

Baer, Helmut David. "The Fruit of Charity: Using the Neighbor in *De doctrina Christiana.*" *Journal of Religious Ethics* 24, no. 1 (Spring 1996): 47–64.

Baier, Annette C. *Moral Prejudices: Essays on Ethics.* Cambridge, Mass.: Harvard University Press, 1994.

Baron, Marcia. *Kantian Ethics (Almost) Without Apology.* Ithaca, N.Y.: Cornell University Press, 1995.

———. "Love and Respect in the *Doctrine of Virtue.*" In *Kant's Metaphysics of Morals: Interpretative Essays,* edited by Mark Timmons, 391–407. Oxford: Oxford University Press, 2002.

Barthold, Lauren Swayne. "Toward an Ethics of Love: Arendt on the Will and St. Augustine." *Philosophy & Social Criticism* 26, no. 6 (2000): 1–20.

Batnitzky, Leora. "Dependency and Vulnerability: Jewish and Feminist Existentialist Constructions of the Human." In *Women and Gender in Jewish Philosophy,* edited by Hava Tirosh-Samuelson, 127–52. Bloomington: Indiana University Press, 2004.

Beinart, Peter. *The Good Fight: Why Liberals—And Only Liberals—Can Win the War on Terror and Make America Great Again.* New York: HarperCollins, 2006.

Beiner, Ronald. "Interpretive Essay." In Hannah Arendt, *Lectures on Kant's Political Philosophy*, edited by Ronald Beiner, 89–156. Chicago: University of Chicago Press, 1982.

———. "Love and Worldliness: Hannah Arendt's Reading of Saint Augustine." In *Hannah Arendt: Twenty Years Later*, edited by Larry May and Jerome Kohn, 269–84. Cambridge, Mass.: MIT Press, 1996.

Benhabib, Seyla. *Situating the Self: Gender, Community, and Postmodernism in Contemporary Ethics.* Cambridge: Polity Press, 1992.

Borresen, Kari Elisabeth. "In Defence of Augustine: How *Femina* is *Homo.*" In *Collecteana Augustiniana*, edited by B. Bruning, M. Lamberigts, and J. van Houtem, 411–28. Leuven: Leuven University Press, 1990.

Bossuet, Jacques-Benigne. *Politics Drawn From the Very Words of Holy Scripture.* Edited by Patrick Riley. Cambridge: Cambridge University Press, 1990.

Bourke, Vernon. *Joy in Augustine's Ethics.* Villanova, Penn.: Villanova University Press, 1979.

Bowlin, John. "Augustine on Justifying Coercion." *Annual of the Society of Christian Ethics* 17 (1997): 49–70.

Brandom, Robert. *Tales of the Mighty Dead: Historical Essays in the Metaphysics of Intentionality.* Cambridge, Mass.: Harvard University Press, 2002.

Breidenthal, Thomas. "Jesus Is My Neighbor: Arendt, Augustine, and the Politics of Incarnation." *Modern Theology* 14, no. 4 (October 1998): 489–504.

Breyer, Gerald J. "Karl Rahner on the Radical Unity of the Love of God and Neighbour." *Irish Theological Quarterly* 68 (2003): 251–80.

Brink, David. "Eudaimonism, Love and Friendship, and Political Community." In *Human Flourishing*, edited by Ellen Frankel, 252–89. Cambridge: Cambridge University Press, 1999.

Brooks, David. "A Man on a Gray Horse." *The Atlantic Monthly*, September 2002: 24–25.

Brown, Peter. *Augustine of Hippo: A Biography.* 2d ed. Berkeley and Los Angeles: University of California Press, 2000. First ed. 1967.

———. *Authority and the Sacred: Aspects of Christianisation of the Roman World.* Cambridge: Cambridge University Press, 1995.

———. *Body and Society: Men, Women, and Sexual Renunciation in Early Christianity.* New York: Columbia University Press, 1988.

———. "Introducing Robert Markus." *Augustinian Studies* 32, no. 2 (2001): 181–87.

———. "*Gloriosus Obitus*: The End of the Ancient Other World." In *The Limits of Ancient Christianity: Essays on Late Antique Thought in Honor of R. A. Markus,* edited by William E. Klingshirn and Mark Vessey, 289–314. Ann Arbor: University of Michigan Press, 1999.

———. *Power and Persuasion in Late Antiquity: Toward a Christian Empire.* Madison: University of Wisconsin Press, 1992.

———. *Religion and Society in the Age of Saint Augustine.* New York: Harper & Row, 1972.

Burnaby, John. *Amor Dei: A Study of the Religion of St. Augustine.* London: Hodder & Stoughton, 1938.

———. "*Amor* in St. Augustine." In *The Philosophy and Theology of Anders Nygren*, edited by Charles Kegley, 174–86. Carbondale: Southern Illinois University Press, 1970.

Burnell, Peter. *The Augustinian Person.* Washington, D.C.: The Catholic University Press of America, 2005.

Byers, Sarah. "Augustine and the Cognitive Cause of Stoic 'Preliminary Passions' *(Propatheiai)*." *Journal of the History of Philosophy* 41, no. 4 (2003): 433–48.

Calvin, John. *Institutes of the Christian Religion*, vol. 1. Translated by Ford Lewis Battles. Philadelphia: The Westminster Press, 1960.

Canning, Raymond. *The Unity of Love for God and Neighbor in St. Augustine.* Heverlee, Belgium: Augustinian Historical Institute, 1993.

Canovan, Margaret. *Hannah Arendt: A Reinterpretation of her Political Thought.* Cambridge: Cambridge University Press, 1992.

———. "Politics as Culture: Hannah Arendt and the Public Realm." *History of Political Thought* 6, no. 3 (Winter 1985): 632–52.

Cary, Phillip. *Augustine's Invention of the Inner Self: The Legacy of a Christian Platonist.* Oxford: Oxford University Press, 2000.

Cavadini, John. "Feeling Right: Augustine on the Passions and Sexual Desire." *Augustinian Studies* 36, no. 1 (2005): 195–217.

———. "Simplifying Augustine." In *Educating the People: Exploring the History of Jewish and Christian Communities*, edited by John van Engen, 63–84. Grand Rapids: Eerdmans, 2004.

Cavanaugh, William. "Coercion in Augustine and Disney." *New Blackfriars* 80, no. 940 (June 1999): 283–90.

Chiba, Shin. "Hannah Arendt on Love and the Political: Love, Friendship, and Citizenship." *The Review of Politics* 57, no. 3 (Summer 1995): 505–35.

Cochrane, C. N. *Christianity and Classical Culture.* Oxford: Oxford University Press, 1940.

Coles, Romand. *Rethinking Generosity: Critical Theory and the Politics of Caritas.* Ithaca: Cornell University Press, 1997.

———. *Self/Power/Other: Political Theory and Dialogical Ethics.* Ithaca: Cornell University Press, 1992.

———. "Storied Others and the Possibilities of *Caritas*: Milbank and Neo-Nietzschean Ethics." *Modern Theology* 8, no. 4 (October 1992): 331–51.

Colish, Marcia. *The Stoic Tradition from Antiquity to the Early Middle Ages,* vol. 2. Leiden: Brill, 1985.

Connolly, William E. *The Augustinian Imperative: A Reflection on the Politics of Morality.* Newbury Park, Calif.: Sage Publications, 1993.

———. *Identity/Difference: Democratic Negotiations of Political Paradox.* Ithaca: Cornell University Press, 1991.

———. "Response: Realizing Agonistic Respect." *Journal of the American Academy of Religion* 72, no. 2 (June 2004): 507–11.

———. *Why I am Not a Secularist.* Minneapolis: University of Minneapolis Press, 1999.

Conybeare, Catherine. *The Irrational Augustine.* Oxford: Oxford University Press, 2006.

Cooper, John. "Aristotle on Friendship." In *Essays on Aristotle's Ethics,* edited by Amelie Oksenberg Rorty, 301–40. Berkeley and Los Angeles: University of California Press, 1980.

Davies, Oliver. *A Theology of Compassion: Metaphysics of Difference and the Renewal of Tradition.* Grand Rapids, Mich.: Eerdmans, 2001.

Davis, G. Scott. "'*Et Quod Vis Fac*': Paul Ramsey and Augustinian Ethics." *Journal of Religious Ethics* 19, no. 2 (Fall 1991): 31–69.

———. "The Structure and Function of the Virtues in the Moral Theology of St. Augustine." *Acts of the International Congress of Augustine Studies,* vol. 3 (Rome, 1987): 9–18.

De Lubac, Henri. *Augustinianism and Modern Theology.* Translated by Lancelot Sheppard and introduced by Louis Dupre. New York: Herder & Herder, 2000.

Deane, Herbert. *The Social and Political Ideas of St. Augustine.* New York: Columbia University Press, 1963.

Derrida, Jacques. *The Gift of Death.* Translated by David Wills. Chicago: University of Chicago Press, 1995.

Desmond, Marilynn. *Reading Dido: Gender, Textuality, and the Medieval Aeneid.* Minneapolis: University of Minnesota Press, 1994.

Dihle, Albrecht. *The Theory of the Will in Classical Antiquity.* Berkeley and Los Angeles: University of California Press, 1982.

Dionne, E. J. "Faith Full." *The New Republic* 232, no. 7 (February 28, 2005): 12–15.

Dodaro, Robert. "Augustine's Secular City." In *Augustine and His Critics: Essays in Honour of Gerald Bonner,* edited by Robert Dodaro and George Lawless, 231–59. New York: Routledge, 2000.

———. "Between the Two Cities: Political Action in Augustine of Hippo." In *Augustine and Politics*, edited by John Doody, Kevin L. Hughes, and Kim Paffenroth, 99–115. New York: Lexington Books, 2005.

———. *Christ and the Just Society in the Thought of Augustine*. Cambridge: Cambridge University Press, 2004.

———. "Eloquent Lies, Just Wars and the Politics of Persuasion: Reading Augustine's *City of God* in a 'Postmodern World.'" *Augustinian Studies* 25 (1994): 77–138.

———. "Political and Theological Virtues in Augustine, Letter 155 to Macedonius." *Augustiniana* 54 (2004): 431–74.

Eberle, Christopher J. *Religious Convictions in Liberal Politics*. Cambridge: Cambridge University Press, 1992.

Elshtain, Jean Bethke. "Augustine and Diversity." In *A Catholic Modernity?*, edited by James L. Heft, 95–103. Oxford: Oxford University Press, 1999.

———. *Augustine and the Limits of Politics*. Notre Dame, Ind.: University of Notre Dame Press, 1995.

———. *Just War against Terror: The Burden of American Power in a Violent World*. New York: Basic, 2003.

———. *Public Man, Private Woman: Woman in Social and Political Thought*. 2d ed. Princeton: Princeton University Press, 1993.

———. "An Unbridgeable Chasm." *Journal for Peace and Justice Studies* 8, no. 2 (1997): 45–47.

Emerson, Ralph Waldo. "Circles." In *Essays and Lectures*, 401–14. New York: Library of America, 1983.

Farley, Margaret. *Compassionate Respect: A Feminist Approach to Medical Ethics and Other Questions*. Mahwah, N.J.: Paulist Press, 2003.

Fern, Richard. "Religious Belief in a Rawlsian Society." *Journal of Religious Ethics* 15, no. 1 (Spring 1987): 33–58.

Finnis, John. *Aquinas: Moral, Political, and Legal Theory*. Oxford: Oxford University Press, 1998.

Fitzgerald, Alan, ed. *Augustine Through the Ages: An Encyclopedia*. Grand Rapids, Mich.: Eerdmans, 1999.

Flescher, Andrew. "Love and Justice in Reinhold Niebuhr's Prophetic Christian Realism and Emmanuel Levinas's Ethic of Responsibility: Treading Between Pacifism and Just-War Theory." *Journal of Religion* 80, no. 1 (2000): 61–82.

Fortin, Ernest. "Augustine and the Hermeneutics of Love." In *Augustine Today*, edited by Richard John Neuhaus, 35–59. Grand Rapids, Mich.: Eerdmans, 1993.

Fox, Richard Wightman. *Reinhold Niebuhr: A Biography*. New York: Pantheon Books, 1985.

Frankena, William. "The Ethics of Love Conceived as an Ethics of Virtue." *Journal of Religious Ethics* 1, no. 1 (Spring 1973): 21–36.

Frankfurt, Harry. *The Reasons of Love.* Princeton: Princeton University Press, 2004.

Freud, Sigmund. *Civilization and Its Discontents.* Translated and edited by James Strachey. New York: Norton & Company, 1961.

Friedman, Marilyn. "Beyond Caring: The De-Moralization of Gender." *Canadian Journal of Philosophy* 13 (1987): 87–110.

Frierson, Patrick R. *Freedom and Anthropology in Kant's Moral Philosophy.* Cambridge: Cambridge University Press, 2003.

Fukuyama, Francis. *The End of History and the Last Man.* New York: Free Press, 1992.

Geertz, Clifford. *The Interpretation of Cultures.* New York: Basic, 1973.

Gilligan, Carol. *In a Different Voice: Psychological Theory and Women's Development.* 2d ed. Cambridge, Mass.: Harvard University Press, 1993.

Gilman, James. *Fidelity of Heart: An Ethics of Christian Virtue.* Oxford: Oxford University Press, 2001.

Grant, Colin. *Altruism and Christian Ethics.* Cambridge: Cambridge University Press, 2001.

Gregory, Eric. "Before the Original Position: The Neo-Orthodox Theology of the Young John Rawls," *Journal of Religious Ethics* 35, no. 2 (June 2007): 179–206.

Greer, Rowan. *Broken Lights and Mended Lives: Theology and Common Life in the Early Church.* University Park: The Pennsylvania State University Press, 1986.

Groenhout, Ruth E. *Connected Lives: Human Nature and an Ethics of Care.* Lanham, Md.: Rowman & Littlefield, 2004.

———. "Theological Echoes in an Ethic of Care." Occasional Papers of the Erasmus Institute, University of Notre Dame, 2003.

Gunton, Colin. *The One, The Three, The Many: God, Creation, and the Culture of Modernity.* Cambridge: Cambridge University Press, 1993.

Gutierrez, Gustavo. *A Theology of Liberation.* 2d ed. Maryknoll, N.Y.: Orbis Books, 1988.

Gutting, Gary. *Pragmatic Liberalism and the Critique of Modernity.* Cambridge: Cambridge University Press, 1999.

Hadot, Pierre. *Philosophy as a Way of Life: Spiritual Exercises from Socrates to Foucault.* Edited by Arnold I. Davidson and translated by Michael Chase. Oxford: Blackwell, 1995.

Hammer, Dean. "Freedom and Fatefulness: Augustine, Arendt, and the Journey of Memory." *Theory, Culture & Society* 17, no. 2 (2000): 83–104.

Hanby, Michael. *Augustine and Modernity.* New York: Routledge, 2003.

Hannam, Walter A. "*Ad illud ubi permanendum est*: The Metaphysics of St Augustine's *usus-fruitio* Distinction in Relation to Love of Neighbour, *De doctrina christiana,* I." *Studia Patristica* 38 (2001): 169–73.

Harrison, Carol. *Augustine: Christian Truth and Fractured Humanity*. Oxford: Oxford University Press, 2000.

Hardt, Michael, and Antonio Negri. *Multitude: War and Democracy in the Age of Empire*. New York: Penguin Press, 2004.

Hauerwas, Stanley. *After Christendom? How the Church is to Behave if Freedom, Justice and a Christian Nation are Bad Ideas*. Nashville: Abingdon Press, 1991.

———. *Against the Nations*. New York: Seabury Press, 1985.

———. *Dispatches from the Front: Theological Engagements with the Secular*. Durham: Duke University Press, 1994.

———. "On Being 'Placed' by Milbank: A Response." In *Christ, Ethics, Tragedy*, edited by Kenneth Surin, 197–201. Cambridge: Cambridge University Press, 1989.

———. *The Peaceable Kingdom: A Primer in Christian Ethics*. Notre Dame, Ind.: University of Notre Dame Press, 1983.

———. *Performing the Faith: Bonhoeffer and the Practice of Nonviolence*. Grand Rapids, Mich.: Brazos Press, 2004.

———. *Truthfulness and Tragedy: Further Investigations in Christian Ethics*. Notre Dame, Ind.: University of Dame Press, 1977.

———. *With the Grain of the Universe: The Church's Witness and Natural Theology*. Grand Rapids, Mich.: Brazos Press, 2001.

Holmes, Robert F. "St. Augustine and the Just War Theory." In *The Augustinian Tradition*, edited by Gareth B. Matthewes, 323–44. Berkeley and Los Angeles: University of California Press, 1999.

Holmes, Stephen. *Passions and Constraint: On the Theory of Liberal Democracy*. Chicago: University of Chicago Press, 1995.

Horton, Michael S. *Lord and Servant: A Covenantal Christology*. Louisville, Ky.: Westminster John Knox, 2005.

Hunsinger, George. *Disruptive Grace: Studies in the Theology of Karl Barth*. Grand Rapids, Mich.: Eerdmans, 2000.

Huntington, Samuel P. "No Exit: The Errors of Endism." *National Interest* 17 (Fall 1989): 3–11.

Irigaray, Luce. *An Ethics of Sexual Difference*. Translated by Carolyn Burke and Gillian C. Gill. Ithaca: Cornell University Press, 1993.

Irwin, T. H. "Splendid Vices? Augustine For and Against Pagan Virtues." *Medieval Philosophy and Theology* 8 (1999): 105–27.

Isaac, Jeffrey. *Democracy in Dark Times*. Ithaca: Cornell University Press, 1998.

Jackson, Timothy P. "Christian Love and Political Violence." In *The Love Commandments: Essays in Christian Ethics and Moral Philosophy*, edited by Edmund Santurri and William Werpehowski, 182–220. Washington, D.C.: Georgetown University Press, 1992.

———. "The Disconsolation of Theology: Irony, Cruelty, and Putting Charity First." *Journal of Religious Ethics* 20, no. 1 (Spring 1992): 1–35.

———. "Is God Just?" *Faith & Philosophy* 12, no. 3 (July 1996): 386–99.

———. "Love in a Liberal Society: A Response to Paul J. Weithman." *Journal of Religious Ethics* 22, no. 1 (Spring 1994): 28–38.

———. *Love Disconsoled: Meditations on Christian Charity.* Cambridge: Cambridge University Press, 1999.

———. "Naturalism, Formalism, and Supernaturalism: Moral Epistemology and Comparative Ethics." *Journal of Religious Ethics* 27, no. 3 (Fall 1999): 477–506.

———. "*Prima Caritas, Inde Jus*: Why Augustinians Shouldn't Baptize John Rawls." *Journal for Peace and Justice Studies* 8, no. 2 (1997): 49–62.

———. *The Priority of Love: Christian Charity and Social Justice.* Princeton: Princeton University Press, 2003.

———. "The Return of the Prodigal? Liberal Theory and Religious Pluralism." In *Religion and Contemporary Liberalism*, edited by Paul Weithman, 182–217. Notre Dame, Ind.: University of Notre Dame Press, 1997.

———. "To Bedlam and Part Way Back: John Rawls and Christian Justice." *Faith & Philosophy* 8, no. 4 (October 1991): 423–47.

Joas, Hans. "Social Theory and the Sacred: A Response to John Milbank." *Ethical Perspectives* 7, no. 4 (December 2000): 233–43.

Jones, L. Gregory. *Transformed Judgment.* Notre Dame, Ind.: University of Notre Dame Press, 1990.

Jones, Nancy A. "By Woman's Tears Redeemed: Female Lament in St. Augustine's Confessions and the Correspondence of Abelard and Heloise." In *Sex and Gender in Medieval and Renaissance Texts*, edited by Barbara K. Gold, Paul Allen Miller, and Charles Platter, 15–31. Albany: State University of New York Press, 1997.

Kateb, George. *Hannah Arendt: Politics, Conscience, Evil.* Totowa, N.J.: Rowman & Allanheld, 1983.

Kant, Immanuel. *Groundwork for the Metaphysics of Morals* (1785). Translated by Mary J. Gregor. In *Practical Philosophy*, 37–108. Cambridge: Cambridge University Press, 1996.

———. *The Metaphysics of Morals* (1797). Translated by Mary J. Gregor. In *Practical Philosophy*, 353–605. Cambridge: Cambridge University Press, 1996.

Kavka, Martin. "Judaism and Theology in Martha Nussbaum's Ethics." *Journal of Religious Ethics* 31, no. 2 (Summer 2003): 343–59.

Kent, Bonnie. "Augustine's Ethics." In *The Cambridge Companion to Augustine*, edited by Elanor Stump and Norman Kretzmann, 205–33. Cambridge: Cambridge University Press, 2001.

King, Jr., Martin Luther. *A Testament of Hope: The Essential Writings of Martin Luther King, Jr..* Edited by James Washington. San Francisco: HarperSanFrancisco, 1991.

Kierkegaard, Søren. *Either/Or.* Translated by Walter Lowrie. Princeton: Princeton University Press, 1987.

———. *Works of Love.* Translated by Howard and Edna Hong. New York: Harper & Row, 1962.

Kirk, Kenneth. *The Vision of God, the Christian Doctrine of the Summum Bonum.* New York: Longmans, Green & Company, 1931.

Kittay, Eva Feder. *Love's Labor: Essays on Women, Equality, and Dependency.* New York: Routledge, 1999.

Kraynak, Robert F. *Christian Faith and Modern Democracy: God and Politics in a Fallen World.* Notre Dame, Ind.: University of Notre Dame Press, 2001.

Kristeva, Julia. *Hannah Arendt: Life is a Narrative.* Toronto: University of Toronto Press, 2001.

———. *Strangers to Ourselves.* Translated by Leon S. Roudiez. New York: Columbia University Press, 1991.

Kroeker, P. Travis. *Christian Ethics and Political Economy in North America.* Montreal: McGill-Queen's University Press, 1995.

Kymlicka, Will. *Liberalism, Community, and Culture.* Oxford: Oxford University Press, 1989.

Lamb, Roger, ed. *Love Analyzed.* Boulder: Westview Press, 1997.

Lamberigts, Mathijs. "A Critical Evaluation of Critiques of Augustine's Views of Sexuality." In *Augustine and His Critics*, edited by Robert Dodaro and George Lawless, 176–97. New York: Routledge, 2000.

Langan, John. "Augustine on the Unity and the Interconnection of the Virtues." *Harvard Theological Review* 72 (1979): 81–95.

———. "The Elements of St. Augustine's Just War Theory." *Journal of Religious Ethics* 12, no. 1 (Spring 1984): 19–38.

Lehrer, Keith. "Love and Autonomy." In *Love Analyzed*, edited by Roger Lamb, 107–27. Boulder: Westview Press, 1997.

Lewis, C. S. *The Four Loves.* New York: Harcourt Brace Jovanovich, 1960.

Lindbeck, George. *The Nature of Doctrine: Religion and Theology in a Postliberal Age.* Philadelphia: The Westminster Press, 1984.

Louth, Andrew. "Love and the Trinity: Saint Augustine and the Greek Fathers." *Augustinian Studies* 33, no. 1 (2002): 1–16.

Lovin, Robin. *Reinhold Niebuhr and Christian Realism.* Cambridge: Cambridge University Press, 1995.

MacIntyre, Alasdair. *After Virtue: A Study in Moral Theory.* London: Duckworth Press; Notre Dame, Ind., University of Notre Dame Press, 1985.

———. *Against the Self-Images of the Age*. London: Duckworth Press, 1971.

———. *Dependent Rational Animals*. Chicago: Open Court Publishers, 1999.

———. *Whose Justice? Which Rationality?* Notre Dame, Ind.: University of Notre Dame Press, 1988.

Margalit, Avishai. *The Decent Society*. Translated by Naomi Goldblum. Cambridge, Mass.: Harvard University Press, 1998.

Markus, Robert. *Christianity and the Secular*. Notre Dame, Ind.: University of Notre Dame Press, 2006.

———. "*De Ciutate Dei*: Pride and the Common Good." *Collectanea Augustiniana* 1 (1990): 245–59.

———. *The End of Ancient Christianity*. Cambridge: Cambridge University Press, 1990.

———. "Evolving Disciplinary Contexts for the Study of Augustine, 1950–2000: Some Personal Reflections." *Augustinian Studies* 32, no. 2 (2001): 189–200.

———. *Saeculum: History and Society in the Theology of Saint Augustine.* Cambridge: Cambridge University Press, 1970.

———. *Signs and Meanings: World and Text in Ancient Christianity*. Liverpool: Liverpool University Press, 1996.

Marsh, Charles. "The Civil Rights Movement as Theological Drama—Interpretation and Application." *Modern Theology* 18, no. 2 (April 2002): 231–50.

Mathewes, Charles. "Agency, Nature, Transcendence, and Moralism: A Review of Recent Work in Moral Psychology." *Journal of Religious Ethics* 28, no. 2 (June 2000): 297–328.

———. "Augustinian Anthropology: *Interior intimo meo*." *Journal of Religious Ethics* 27, no. 2 (Summer 1999): 195–221.

———. "The Author Replies." *Journal of Religious Ethics* 28, no. 3 (2000): 478–81.

———. *Evil and the Augustinian Tradition*. Cambridge: Cambridge University Press, 2001.

———. "The Liberation of Questioning in Augustine's *Confessions*." *Journal of the American Academy of Religion* 70, no. 3 (September 2002): 539–60.

———. "Pluralism, Otherness, and the Augustinian Tradition." *Modern Theology* 14, no. 1 (January 1998): 83–112.

McCabe, David. "Knowing about the Good: A Problem with Antiperfectionism." *Ethics* 110 (January 2000): 311–38.

McCann, Dennis. *Christian Realism and Liberation Theology*. Maryknoll, N.Y.: Orbis, 1981.

McCarraher, Eugene. "The Enchanted City of Man: The State and the Market in Augustinian Perspective." In *Augustine and Politics*, edited by John Doody, Kevin L. Hughes, and Kim Paffenroth, 261–95. New York: Lexington Books, 2005.

McWilliams, Wilson Cary. *The Idea of Fraternity in America*. Berkeley and Los Angeles: University of California Press, 1973.

———. "Reinhold Niebuhr: New Orthodoxy for Old Liberalism." *The American Political Science Review* 56, no. 4 (December 1962): 874–85.

Meilaender, Gilbert. *The Way that Leads There: Augustinian Reflections on the Christian Life*. Grand Rapids, Mich.: Eerdmans, 2006.

———. *Friendship: A Study in Theological Ethics*. Notre Dame, Ind.: University of Notre Dame Press, 1981.

———. *The Limits of Love: Some Theological Explorations*. University Park: The Pennsylvania State University Press, 1987.

Mendus, Susan. "The Importance of Love in Rawls's Theory of Justice." *British Journal of Political Science* 29 (1999): 57–75.

Menn, Stephen. *Descartes and Augustine*. Cambridge: Cambridge University Press, 1998.

Milbank, John. *Being Reconciled: Ontology and Pardon*. New York: Routledge, 2003.

———. "Enclaves, or Where is the Church?" *New Blackfriars* 73, no. 861 (June 1992): 341–52.

———. "The End of Dialogue." In *Christian Uniqueness Reconsidered: The Myth of a Pluralistic Theory of Religions*, edited by Gavin D'Costa, 174–91. Maryknoll, N.Y.: Orbis, 1990.

———. "An Essay Against Secular Order." *Journal of Religious Ethics* 15, no. 2 (1987): 199–224.

———. "The Gift of Ruling: Secularization and Political Authority." *New Blackfriars* 85, no. 996 (March 2004): 212–38.

———. "The Invocation of Clio: A Response." *Journal of Religious Ethics* 33, no. 1 (Spring 2005): 3–44.

———. "The Name of Jesus." In *The Word Made Strange: Theology, Language, and Culture*, 145–68. Cambridge, Mass.: Blackwell, 1997.

———. "On Complex Space." In *The Word Made Strange: Theology, Language, and Culture*, 268–292. Cambridge, Mass.: Blackwell, 1997.

———. " 'Postmodern Critical Augustinianism': A Short Summa in Forty Two Responses to Unasked Questions." *Modern Theology* 7, no. 3 (April 1991): 225–37.

———. "The Poverty of Niebuhrianism." In *The Word Made Strange: Theology, Language, and Culture*, 233–54. Cambridge, Mass.: Blackwell, 1997.

———. "Sacred Triads: Augustine and the Indo-European Soul." *Modern Theology* 13 (1997): 452–74.

———. *Theology and Social Theory: Beyond Secular Reason*. Oxford: Blackwell Publishers, 1990.

Murdoch, Iris. *Metaphysics as a Guide to Morals*. New York: Penguin Books, 1994.

———. *The Sovereignty of Good.* London: Routledge & Kegan Paul, 1970.

Nicholls, David. *Deity and Domination: Images of God and the State in the 19th and 20th Centuries.* New York: Routledge, 1989.

Niebuhr, H. Richard. *Christ & Culture.* New York: Harper & Row, 1951. Reprinted with preface by James M. Gustafson and foreword by Martin E. Marty. New York: HarperCollins, 2001. References are to the 2001 edition.

Niebuhr, Reinhold. "Augustine's Political Realism." In *Christian Realism and Political Problems*, 119–46. New York: Charles Scribner's Sons, 1953.

———. *The Children of Light and the Children of Darkness.* New York: Charles Scribner's Sons, 1944.

———. "The Concept of 'Order of Creation' in Emil Brunner's Social Ethic." In *The Theology of Emil Brunner*, edited by Charles W. Kegley, 265–71. New York: Macmillan, 1962.

———. *An Interpretation of Christian Ethics.* New York: Meridian, 1956.

———. *Man's Nature and His Communities.* New York: Charles Scribner's Sons, 1965.

———. *Moral Man and Immoral Society.* New York: Charles Scribner's Sons, 1932.

———. *The Nature and Destiny of Man*, vol. 1: *Human Nature.* New York: Charles Scribner's Sons, 1941.

———. *The Nature and Destiny of Man*, vol. 2: *Human Destiny.* New York: Charles Scribner's Sons, 1943.

———. "The Providence of God." In *The Essential Niebuhr*, edited by Robert McCaffee Brown, 33–40. New Haven: Yale University Press, 1985.

———. *Reflections on the End of an Era.* New York: Charles Scribner's, 1934.

Nietzsche, Friedrich. *On the Genealogy of Morals.* Translated by Walter Kauffman. New York: Random House, 1967.

———. *Thus Spoke Zarathustra.* Translated by Walter Kauffman. New York: Penguin Books, 1966.

Noddings, Nel. *Caring: A Feminine Approach to Ethics and Moral Education.* Berkeley and Los Angeles: University of California Press, 1984.

———. *Starting at Home: Caring and Social Policy.* Berkeley and Los Angeles: University of California Press, 2002.

Noonan, John T. *Persons and Masks of the Law.* New York: Farrar, Straus & Giroux, 1983.

Nozick, Robert. "Love's Bond." In *The Philosophy of (Erotic) Love*, edited by Robert Solomon, 417–32. Lawrence: University of Kansas Press, 1991.

Nussbaum, Martha. "Augustine and Dante on the Ascent of Love." In *The Augustinian Tradition*, edited by Gareth Matthews, 61–90. Berkeley and Los Angeles: University of California Press, 1999.

———. *Love's Knowledge.* Oxford: Oxford University Press, 1990.

———. "Non-Relative Virtues: An Aristotelian Approach." *Midwest Studies in Philosophy* 13 (1988): 32–53.

———. *Upheavals of Thought: The Intelligence of Emotions.* Cambridge: Cambridge University Press, 2001.

Nygren, Anders. *Agape and Eros.* Translated by Philip Watson. Philadelphia: The Westminster Press, 1953.

O'Connor, William Riordan. "The *Uti/Frui* Distinction in Augustine's Ethics." *Augustinian Studies* 14 (1983): 45–62.

O'Daly, Gerard. *Augustine's City of God: A Reader's Guide.* Oxford: Oxford University Press, 1999.

O'Donnell, James. *Augustine: A New Biography.* New York: HarperCollins, 2005.

———. *Augustine: Confessions, Latin Text with English Commentary.* 3 vols. Oxford: Oxford University Press, 1992.

———. "The Authority of Augustine." *Augustinian Studies* 22 (1991): 7–35.

———. "The Next Life of Augustine." In *The Limits of Ancient Christianity: Essays on Late Antique Thought and Culture in Honor of R. A. Markus,* edited by William Klingshirn and Mark Vessey, 215–31. Ann Arbor: University of Michigan Press, 1999.

———. "The Strangeness of Augustine." *Augustinian Studies* 32, no. 2 (2001): 201–206.

O'Donovan, Oliver. "Augustine of Hippo." In *From Irenaeus to Grotius: A Sourcebook in Christian Political Thought,* edited by Oliver O'Donovan and Joan Lockwood O'Donovan, 104–13. Grand Rapids, Mich.: Eerdmans, 1999.

———. *The Desire of the Nations: Rediscovering the Roots of Political Theology.* Cambridge: Cambridge University Press, 1996.

———. *The Just War Revisited.* Cambridge: Cambridge University Press, 2003.

———. *Resurrection and Moral Order: An Outline for Evangelical Ethics.* Grand Rapids, Mich.: Eerdmans, 1986.

———. "The Political Thought of *City of God* 19." In *Bonds of Imperfection: Christian Politics, Past and Present,* edited by Oliver O'Donovan and Joan Lockwood O'Donovan, 48–72. Grand Rapids, Mich.: Eerdmans, 2004.

———. *The Problem of Self-Love in St. Augustine.* New Haven: Yale University Press, 1980.

———. "*Usus* and *Fruitio* in Augustine, *De Doctrina Christiana* I." *Journal of Theological Studies* 33, no. 2 (October 1982): 361–97.

———. *Ways of Judgment.* Grand Rapids, Mich.: Eerdmans, 2005.

Okin, Susan Miller. *Justice, Gender, and the Family.* New York: Basic Books, 1989.

———. "Reason and Feeling in Thinking about Justice." *Ethics* 99 (January 1989): 229–49.

Osborne, Catherine. *Eros Unveiled: Plato and the God of Love.* Oxford: Clarendon Press, 1994.

Outka, Gene. *Agape: An Ethical Analysis*. New Haven: Yale University Press, 1972.

———. "Universal Love and Impartiality." In *The Love Commandments: Essays in Christian Ethics and Moral Philosophy*, edited by Edmund N. Santurri and William Werpehowski, 1–103. Washington, D.C.: Georgetown University Press, 1992.

Pagels, Elaine. *Adam, Eve, and the Serpent*. New York: Vintage Books, 1989.

Pape, Helmut. "Love's Power and the Causality of Mind: C. S. Peirce on the Place of Mind and Culture in Evolution." *Transactions of the C. S. Peirce Society* 33, no. 1 (Winter 1997): 59–90.

Pecknold, C. C. *Transforming Postliberal Theology: George Lindbeck, Pragmatism and Scripture*. New York: T & T Clark, 2005.

Peretz, Martin. "Losing our Delusions: Not Much Left." *The New Republic* 232, no. 7 (February 28, 2005): 17–19.

Pickstock, Catherine. "Music: Soul, City and Cosmos after Augustine." In *Radical Orthodoxy*, edited by John Milbank, Catherine Pickstock, and Graham Ward, 243–77. New York: Routledge, 1999.

———. "Radical Orthodoxy and the Mediations of Time." In *Radical Orthodoxy? A Catholic Inquiry*, edited by Laurence Paul Hemming, 63–75. (Burlington, Vt.: Ashgate, 2000).

Plumer, Eric. *Augustine's Commentary on Galatians*. Oxford: Oxford University Press, 2003.

Pope, Stephen. " 'Equal Regard' versus 'Special Relations'? Reaffirming the Inclusiveness of Agape." *Journal of Religion* 77 (July 1997): 353–79.

Rahner, Karl. *The Love of Jesus and the Love of Neighbor*. New York: Crossroad Publishers, 1983.

———. "Reflections on the Unity of the Love of Neighbour and the Love of God." In *Theological Investigations*, translated by Cornelius Ernest, 6:246–47. Baltimore: Helicon Press, 1969.

Ramsey, Paul. *Basic Christian Ethics*. New York: Charles Scribner's Sons, 1950.

———. *Deeds and Rules in Christian Ethics*. New York: Charles Scribner's Sons, 1967.

———. *The Just War: Force and Political Responsibility*. New York: Charles Scribner's Sons, 1968.

———. *Nine Modern Moralists*. Englewood Cliffs, N.J.: Prentice Hall, 1962.

———. "The Theory of Democracy: Idealistic or Christian?" *Ethics* 56, no. 4 (July 1946): 251–66.

———. *War and the Christian Conscience: How Shall Modern War Be Conducted Justly?* Durham, N.C.: Duke University Press, 1961.

Rawls, John. "The Idea of Public Reason Revisited." In *John Rawls: Collected Papers*, edited by Samuel Freeman, 573–615. Cambridge, Mass.: Harvard University Press, 1999.

———. *The Law of Peoples.* Cambridge, Mass.: Harvard University Press, 1999.

———. *Political Liberalism.* New York: Columbia University Press, 1996.

———. *A Theory of Justice.* Cambridge, Mass.: Harvard University Press, 1971.

Reeder, John P. "Analogues to Justice." In *The Love Commandments: Essays in Christian Ethics and Moral Philosophy,* edited by Edmund N. Santurri and William Werpehowski, 281–307. Washington, D.C.: Georgetown University Press, 1992.

Reinhard, Kenneth. "Toward a Political Theology of the Neighbor." in Slavoj Žižek, Eric L. Santner, and Kenneth Reinhard, *The Neighbor: Three Inquiries in Political Theology,* 11–75. Chicago: University of Chicago Press, 2005.

Reno, R. R. "The Radical Orthodoxy Project." *First Things* 100 (February 2000): 37–44.

Richardson, Henry S. "Nussbaum: Love and Respect." *Metaphilosophy* 29 (1998): 254–62.

Ricoeur, Paul. *Oneself as Another.* Chicago: University of Chicago Press, 1992.

———. "The *Socius* and the Neighbor." In *History and Truth,* translated by Charles A Kelbley, 98–109. Evanston: Northwestern University Press, 1965.

Rist, John. *Augustine: Ancient Thought Baptized.* Cambridge: Cambridge University Press, 1997.

Rorty, Richard. *Achieving Our Country: Leftist Thought in Twentieth Century America.* Cambridge, Mass.: Harvard University Press, 1998.

———. "The Historiography of Philosophy: Four Genres." In *Philosophy in History,* edited Richard Rorty, J. B. Schneewind, and Quentin Skinner, 49–75. Cambridge: Cambridge University Press, 1984.

Ruether, Rosemary Radford. "Augustine and Christian Political Theology." *Interpretation* 25 (July 1975): 252–65.

Russell, F. H. *The Just War in the Middle Ages.* Cambridge: Cambridge University Press, 1975.

Sandel, Michael. *Liberalism and the Limits of Justice.* Cambridge: Cambridge University Press, 1982.

Santurri, Edmund. "Rawlsian Liberalism, Moral Truth, and Augustinian Politics." *Journal of Peace and Justice Studies* 8, no. 2 (1997): 1–36.

Schall, James. "Friendship and Political Philosophy." *The Review of Metaphysics* 50 (September 1996): 121–41.

Schlabach, Gerald. "Augustine's Hermeneutic of Humility: An Alternative to Moral Imperialism and Moral Relativism." *Journal of Religious Ethics* 22, no. 1 (Spring 1994): 299–327.

———. *For the Joy Set Before Us: Augustine and Self-Denying Love.* Notre Dame, Ind.: University of Notre Dame Press, 2001.

Scobey, David. "The Specter of Citizenship." *Citizenship Studies* 5, no. 1 (2001): 11–26.

Scott, Joanna Vecchiarelli. "Hannah Arendt's Secular Augustinianism." *Augustinian Studies* 30, no. 2 (1999): 293–310.

Shklar, Judith N. "The Liberalism of Fear." In *Liberalism and the Moral Life*, edited by Nancy Rosenblum, 22–38. Cambridge, Mass.: Harvard University Press, 1989.

———. *Ordinary Vices.* Cambridge, Mass.: Harvard University Press, 1984.

Schuld, J. Joyce. *Foucault and Augustine: Reconsidering Power and Love.* Notre Dame, Ind.: University of Notre Dame Press, 2004.

Schwarzenbach, Sibyl. "On Civic Friendship." *Ethics* 107 (October 1996): 97–128.

Schweiker, William. *Responsibility and Christian Ethics.* Cambridge: Cambridge University Press, 1995.

Scrutton, Anastasia. "Emotion in Augustine of Hippo and Thomas Aquinas: A Way Forward for the Im/possibility Debate?" *International Journal of Systematic Theology* 7, no. 2 (April 2005): 169–77.

Slote, Michael. "Love and Justice." In *The Philosophy of the Emotions*, Midwest Studies in Philosophy 22 (1998): 146–61.

Smith, James K. "Staging the Incarnation: Revisioning Augustine's Critique of Theatre." *Literature & Theology* 15, no. 2 (June 2001): 123–39.

Soble, Alan. "Union, Autonomy, and Concern." In *Love Analyzed*, edited by Roger Lamb, 65–92. Boulder: Westview Press, 1997.

Solomon, Robert. *A Passion for Justice: Emotions and the Origins of the Social Contract.* New York: Addison Wesley Publishing Company, 1990.

Solomon, Robert, ed. *The Philosophy of (Erotic) Love.* Lawrence: University of Kansas Press, 1991.

Song, Robert. *Christianity and Liberal Society.* Oxford: Oxford University Press, 1997.

Sorabji, Richard. *Emotion and Peace of Mind: From Stoic Agitation to Christian Temptation.* Oxford: Oxford University Press, 2000.

Spragens, Thomas. *Civic Liberalism: Reflections on Our Democratic Ideals.* Lanham, Md.: Rowman & Littlefield, 1999.

Stock, Brian. *Augustine the Reader: Meditation, Self-Knowledge, and the Ethics of Interpretation.* Cambridge, Mass.: Harvard University Press, 1996.

Stout, Jeffrey. *Democracy and Tradition.* Princeton: Princeton University Press, 2003.

———. *Ethics after Babel: The Language of Morals and Their Discontents.* 2d ed. Princeton: Princeton University Press, 2001. First ed., Beacon Press, 1988.

Sverdlik, Steven. "Motive and Rightness." *Ethics* 106 (January 1996): 327–49.

Swanson, Judith. *The Public and the Private in Aristotle's Political Philosophy.* Ithaca: Cornell University Press, 1992.

Tanner, Kathryn. "The Care that Does Justice: Recent Writings on Feminist Ethics and Theology." *Journal of Religious Ethics* 24, no. 1 (Spring 1996): 171–91.

————. *Jesus, Humanity, and the Trinity: A Brief Systematic Theology.* Minneapolis: Fortress Press, 2001.

————. *The Politics of God: Christian Theologies and Social Justice.* Minneapolis: Fortress Press, 1992.

Taylor, Charles. *A Catholic Modernity? Charles Taylor's Marianist Award Lecture.* Edited by James L. Heft. Oxford: Oxford University Press, 1999.

————. *Sources of the Self: The Making of Modern Identity.* Cambridge: Cambridge University Press, 1989.

TeSelle, Eugene. "Toward an Augustinian Politics." *Journal of Religious Ethics* 16, no. 1 (Spring 1988): 87–108.

Tillich, Paul. *Love, Justice, and Power: Ontological Analyses and Ethical Applications.* Oxford: Oxford University Press, 1954.

Tinder, Glenn. *Against Fate: An Essay on Personal Dignity.* Notre Dame, Ind.: University of Notre Dame Press, 1981.

Tronto, Joan C. "Beyond Gender Difference to a Theory of Care." *Signs: Journal of Woman in Culture and Society* 12, no. 4 (1987): 644–63.

————. *Moral Boundaries: A Political Argument for an Ethic of Care.* New York: Routledge Press, 1993.

Turner, Denys. *The Darkness of God: Negativity in Christian Mysticism.* Cambridge: Cambridge University Press, 1995.

Vacek, Edward. *Love, Human and Divine: The Heart of Christian Ethics.* Washington, D.C.: Georgetown University Press, 1994.

Van Bavel, Tarsicius J., O.S.A. "The Double Face of Love in St. Augustine." *Augustinian Studies* 17 (1986): 169–81.

Velleman, J. David. "Love as a Moral Emotion." *Ethics* 109 (January 1999): 338–74.

Vlastos, Gregory. "The Individual as Object of Love in Plato." In *Platonic Studies,* 3–42. 2d ed. Princeton: Princeton University Press, 1981.

————. *The Philosophy of Socrates.* New York: Doubleday, 1971.

Vetlesen, Arne Johan. "Hannah Arendt on Conscience and Evil." *Philosophy & Social Criticism* 27, no. 5 (2001): 1–33.

Von Heyking, John. *Augustine and Politics as Longing in the World.* Columbia: University of Missouri Press, 2001.

Von Rautenfeld, Hans. "Charitable Interpretations: Emerson, Rawls, and Cavell on the Use of Public Reason." *Political Theory* 32, no. 1 (February 2004): 61–84.

Walker, Brian. "Thoreau on Democratic Cultivation." *Political Theory* 29, no. 2 (April 2001): 155–89.

Walker, Graham. "Virtue and the Constitution: Augustinian Theology and the Frame of American Common Sense." In *Vital Remnants: America's Founding and the Western Tradition,* edited by Gary L. Gregg II, 99–149. Wilmington, Del.: ISI Books, 1999.

Walsh, David. *The Growth of the Liberal Soul.* Columbia: University of Missouri Press, 1997.

Wannenwetsch, Bern. "The Political Worship of the Church: A Critical and Empowering Practice." *Modern Theology* 12, no. 3 (July 1996): 269–99.

———. *Political Worship: Ethics for Christian Citizens.* Oxford: Oxford University Press, 2004.

Weithman, Paul J. "Augustine and Aquinas on Original Sin and the Function of Political Authority." *Journal of the History of Philosophy* 30, no. 3 (July 1992): 353–76.

———. "Augustine's Political Philosophy." In *The Cambridge Companion to Augustine*, edited by Eleonore Stump and Norman Kretzmann, 234–52. Cambridge: Cambridge University Press, 2001.

———. *Religion and the Obligations of Citizenship.* Cambridge: Cambridge University Press, 2002.

———. "Toward an Augustinian Liberalism." In *The Augustinian Tradition*, edited by Gareth Matthews, 304–22. Berkeley and Los Angeles: University of California Press, 1999.

Werpehowski, William. *American Protestant Ethics and the Legacy of H. Richard Niebuhr.* Washington, D.C.: Georgetown University Press, 2002.

———. "Anders Nygren's *Agape and Eros*." In *The Oxford Handbook of Theological Ethics*, edited by Gilbert Meilaender and William Werpehowski, 433–48. Oxford: Oxford University Press, 2005.

———. "Weeping at the Death of Dido: Sorrow, Virtue, and Augustine's Confession." *Journal of Religious Ethics* 19, no. 1 (Spring 1991): 175–91.

West, Cornel. *The American Evasion of Philosophy: A Genealogy of Pragmatism.* Madison: University of Wisconsin Press, 1989.

Wetzel, James. *Augustine and the Limits of Virtue.* Cambridge: Cambridge University Press, 1992.

———. "Snares of Truth: Augustine on Free Will and Predestination." In *Augustine and His Critics*, edited by Robert Dodaro and George Lawless, 124–41. New York: Routledge, 2000.

———. "Splendid Vices and Secular Virtues: Variations on Milbank's Augustine." *Journal of Religious Ethics* 32, no. 2 (Summer 2004): 271–300.

Whitman, Alden, "Reinhold Niebuhr is Dead; Protestant Theologian, 78." *The New York Times,* June 2, 1971, A1.

Williams, Preston. "An Analysis of the Conception of Love and Its Influence on Justice in the Thought of Martin Luther King Jr." *Journal of Religious Ethics* 18, no. 2 (Fall 1990): 15–31.

Williams, Rowan. "Language, Reality and Desire in Augustine's *De Doctrina*." *Literature & Theology* 3, no. 2 (July 1989): 138–50.

————. "Politics and the Soul: A Reading of the City of God." *Milltown Studies* 19/20 (1987): 55–72.

Wills, Garry. *Saint Augustine*. New York: Viking, 1999.

Wolin, Richard. *Heidegger's Children: Hannah Arendt, Karl Lowith, Hans Jonas, and Herbert Marcuse*. Princeton: Princeton University Press, 2001.

————. "The Illiberal Imagination." *The New Republic* 223, no. 22 (November 27, 2000): 27–35.

Wolterstorff, Nicholas. *Divine Discourse: Philosophical Reflection on the Claim that God Speaks*. Cambridge: Cambridge University Press, 1995.

————. "Suffering Love." In *Philosophy and Christian Faith*, ed. Thomas Morris, 196–237. Notre Dame, Ind.: University of Notre Dame Press, 1988.

Wood, Allen. "The Final Form of Kant's Practical Philosophy." In *Kant's Metaphysics of Morals: Interpretative Essays*, edited by Mark Timmons, 1–21. Oxford: Oxford University Press, 2002.

Yack, Bernard. *The Problems of a Political Animal: Community, Justice, and Conflict in Aristotetlian Political Thought*. Berkeley and Los Angeles: University of California Press, 1993.

Young-Bruehl, Elisabeth. *Hannah Arendt: For Love of the World*. New Haven: Yale University Press, 1982.

Zagzebski, Linda. *Virtues of the Mind: An Inquiry into the Nature of Virtue and the Ethical Foundations of Knowledge*. Cambridge: Cambridge University Press, 1996.

Žižek, Slavoj. "Neighbors and Other Monsters: A Plea for Ethical Violence." In Slavoj Žižek, Eric L. Santner, and Kenneth Reinhard, *The Neighbor: Three Inquiries in Political Theology*, 134–90. Chicago: University of Chicago Press, 2005.

INDEX

61938814R00260

Made in the USA
Lexington, KY
24 March 2017